HANNIBAL

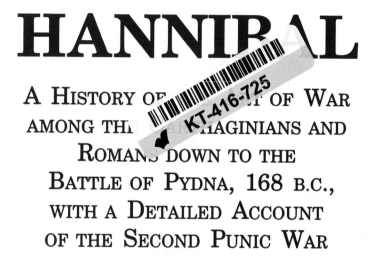

A History of the Art of War
among the Carthaginians and
Romans down to the
Battle of Pydna, 168 B.C.,
with a Detailed Account
of the Second Punic War

Theodore Ayrault Dodge

DA CAPO PRESS • NEW YORK

Library of Congress Cataloging in Publication Data

Dodge, Theodore Ayrault, 1842-1909.
    Hannibal: a history of the art of war among the Carthaginians
and Romans down to the battle of Pydna, 168 B.C., with a detailed account of the second Punic war / Theodore Ayrault Dodge.
        p.   cm.
    Originally published: Boston: Houghton-Mifflin, 1891.
    Includes index.
    ISBN 0-306-80654-1 (alk. paper)
    1. Hannibal, 247-182 B.C.—Military leadership. 2. Punic War,
2nd, 218-201 B.C. 3. Military art and science—History. I. Title.
DG249.D63 1995
937′.04′092—dc20   95-21078
                                                         CIP

First Da Capo Press edition 1995

This Da Capo Press paperback edition of *Hannibal*
is an unabridged republication of the edition first published
in Boston in 1891.

Published by Da Capo Press, Inc.
A Subsidiary of Plenum Publishing Corporation
233 Spring Street, New York, N.Y. 10013

To
THE AMERICAN SOLDIER

Who, not bred to arms, but nurtured by
independence, has achieved the proudest
rank among the veterans of history

THIS VOLUME IS DEDICATED

"*Faites la guerre offensive comme Alexandre, Annibal, César,
Gustave Adolphe, Turenne, le prince Eugène et Frédéric; lisez, reli-
lisez l'histoire de leur quatre-vingt-huit campagnes; modélez-vous sur
eux, — c'est le seul moyen de devenir grand capitaine et de surprendre
le sécret de l'art; votre génie, ainsi éclairé, vous fera rejeter des max-
imes opposées à celles de ces grands hommes.*" — NAPOLEON.

"*La tactique, les évolutions, la science de l'officier de génie, de
l'officier d'artillerie peuvent s'apprendre dans les traités; — mais la
connaissance de la grande tactique ne s'acquiert que par l'expérience
et par l'étude de l'histoire des campagnes de tous les grands capitaines.*"
— NAPOLEON.

PREFACE.

In the study of the campaigns of Alexander, original research has been limited to a few travelers and geographers, or to military men conducting explorations under the auspices of some government and provided with facilities denied to most of us. In the case of Hannibal it is different. Spain and Italy are accessible, as Persia and Afghanistan are not, and the topography of the theatre of the Second Punic War can be readily examined and ascertained. No historian of Hannibal appears, however, to have studied his campaigns on the ground. Almost all accounts of his extraordinary marches, manœuvres and battles borrow their topography, if they give any, from some predecessor equally limited in his facilities, or from very insufficient maps. Many errors have thus been propagated.

The author has been fortunate enough repeatedly to visit the scenes of the Punic captain's achievements. With Polybius and Livy in the hand, he has followed Hannibal from Cartagena across the Pyrenees, the Rhone and the Alps, crossing every pass in the latter range by which the Carthaginian army could possibly have made its way; he has visited every section of Italy and has compared the facts given by the ancient writers with the existing topography; he has been able to consult the best authorities as to the geological changes which the centuries may have wrought: and what he has herein described is from diligent study of the authorities on the ground. This course has enabled him to correct some errors which naturally.enough have crept into history, and to harmonize some of the statements of the old authors which have been deemed irreconcilable. In the case of Cannæ, for instance, all historians have found it necessary to discard one or more of the positive statements of Polybius and Livy. But a study of the battlefield has made it possible to explain the positions and manœuvres so as to coincide with every statement of these, our two most important authorities, as well as to accord with the probabilities. No modern historian of the Second Punic War has mapped out Hannibal's wonderful marches in Italy. Most histories are very inexplicit as to the exact locations and routes. The charts in the text of this volume will be found to show every essential topographical feature of Hannibal's movements over the length and breadth of the peninsula.

Much of what was said in the preface to the volume on Alexander applies to this. The best chroniclers of the war against Hannibal are Polybius and Livy, whose relations are full and explicit. The former exists in its entirety only down to the battle of Cannæ; the latter covers the whole period. Cornelius Nepos, Appian, and Plutarch in his lives of Fabius and Marcellus, give us many facts. The little which remains of Dion Cassius is useful. Florus and Orosius are meagre. Stray facts may be gleaned from references in Velleius Paterculus, Sallust, Justinus, Pausanias, Eutropius, Josephus and the Maccabees. To the opinions of the great modern historians and critics due heed has been given. Practically, however, Polybius and Livy are the source from which we draw all our information.

In a few instances the author has been compelled to treat historical matter controversially. As in the case of the passage of the Alps, upon which subject he has found some three hundred and fifty treatises, mostly devoted to the establishment of some pet theory, it has been sometimes impossible to state facts without controverting the opinions of others, if for no other reason than to show that they have not failed of due consideration. The first men who wrote exhaustively on the Little St. Bernard route were Wickham and Cramer. Their views have been stoutly combated, but most of them remain sound. In the case of the battles of the Ticinus, the Trebia, Lake Trasimene and Cannæ, the author has been led by the topography of the several fields to disagree with many of the most highly considered historians and critics; but he has in all cases given his reasons for so doing.

The author desires once more to disclaim the writing of a military text-book. Apart from the peculiar qualifications requisite for such work, it is doubtful whether history can be written on lines suitable for a treatise of the kind. History is a consecutive narrative of facts accompanied by suitable comment; a text-book should enunciate certain principles and select historical facts as illustrations. So far as history, pure and simple, is valuable to the military student, — and it has always been pronounced by great leaders and critics to be the most fruitful of studies, — so far will these volumes reach. But they aim rather, for the benefit of the general reader, to enlarge upon those military facts to which the histories devote small space, and thus narrate the origin and growth of the art of war, than to spread before the young military student those principles which lie at the basis of the profession he proposes to embrace.

In a few places the author has undertaken to show that Livy's statements are inexact. In such cases he has construed Livy by Livy, and has always taken the distinguished historian as a whole. No doubt has been cast on any particular fact, unless Livy himself, taking every passage relating to the subject into consideration, shows that such a fact is inconsistent with his own statements elsewhere.

It is perhaps impossible for a soldier to write about Hannibal — or of the other great captains — without exhibiting some traces of hero worship. That the author is subject to the sentiment it is not attempted to conceal; but he trusts that it is subordinated to the truth. There is not a fact connected with the history of Hannibal, nor a slur upon his character, which has not been duly weighed in writing this history. Nor is there any material fact, either making for or against him, which has not found its place in these pages. The sum of all which the ancient authors tell us describes a man and a captain on whom hero worship is not wasted.

If, in its perusal, the reader will frequently refer to the table of dates, as well as the large map at the end of this volume, so as to keep the skeleton of the entire Italian war in mind, the author believes that he will conceive a clear impression of the gigantic whole of Hannibal's unequaled campaigns. He can rely upon the legend at the head of each chapter as a fair summary of such portions as he desires to skip.

TABLE OF CONTENTS.

LIST OF ILLUSTRATIONS.

HANNIBAL.

I.

CARTHAGE. 900–200 B. C.

IN the third century B. C. Rome and Carthage divided the power of the Mediterranean world. Rome was first on land, Carthage first at sea. Intolerant of powerful neighbors, Rome quarreled with Carthage, and in the First Punic War brought her to her knees. The Carthaginians were of Phœnician origin, one of the early settlements of Tyre. By their energy and intelligence they succeeded in acquiring the hegemony of all the Phœnician colonies on the Mediterranean, as Tyre had done at home. The government was an aristocracy of capitalists, controlled by a senate. This "London of antiquity " gradually extended her conquests all around the western Mediterranean. The city was strongly walled and beautifully built; and in addition possessed vast commercial works, harbors and arsenals. Agriculture was as highly esteemed and practiced as commerce, and the land was worked by rich planters. The prosperity of the city was equally indebted to either art. Carthage was really the capital of a great North African empire, as Rome was of the Italian peninsula.

Two generations after the death of Alexander, Carthage and Rome divided the power of the Mediterranean world between them. Carthage was the most powerful colony planted by Tyre, and inherited all the enterprise, intelligence and courage which the mother city showed in her extended commerce and many wars, and notably against the great Macedonian. Carthage was first at sea; Rome on land. Rome, always intolerant of powerful neighbors, of necessity fell to quarreling with her great rival, unwilling to content herself with less than the supremacy on both elements. The first conflict between these cities was over the island of Sicily, situated midway between them. Rome, as usual, won, and at the end of the twenty-three years, during which lasted the First Punic War, imposed severe terms on her conquered adversary. This was in B. C. 241.

The Phœnicians had originally been nomads inhabiting the plains which extend from the Mediterranean to the Tigris, but, pushed by the Egyptians and Jews into the narrow

Rome and Carthage.

region between Mt. Libanus and the seashore, they ended by making the sea their home. Libanus furnished them the best of shipbuilding material, and such was their native enterprise that they soon commanded the entire commerce of the Mediterranean, as well as became its most active pirates. Of all the towns the chief in activity and size, Tyre eventually grew to the hegemony of the land. The Phœnicians were in antiquity celebrated, among other products, for their wines, salted fish and mineral resources, as well as for distributing the products of the world; and learning, the arts, mechanics and architecture grew to a great height among this enterprising people.

Occasional overgrowth, or discontent of some part of the

population, lay at the root of emigration from Tyre. Gades (Cadiz) was founded a dozen centuries before Christ; Utica soon after; and from 1000 to 600 B. C. Tyre founded many colonies — all naturally to the westward and upon the Mediterranean coast.

Herodotus, who visited Tyre about 450 B. C., gave the then age of the city as twenty-three hundred years. This is mere tradition. In the time of Joshua (1250 B. C.) Tyre was certainly a town of respectable size. Originally a republic, in the years immediately preceding David and Solomon Tyre appears to have been brought under the sway of a line of kings. The struggles between aristocrats and rich burghers were at all times fierce, but the strength of the city none the less grew apace. She resisted many sieges, notably those of the Scythians and Nebuchadnezzar, eventually to perish before the conquering hand of Alexander. The proud history of Tyre shows what it was that animated the Carthaginians in their vigorous growth, as well as their vigorous opposition to Rome; for it is thought by some authorities to have been to an emigration of Tyrian aristocrats, and not mere traders, that the great metropolis owed her origin. And though we know little about the great city except from her enemies, it is certain that a high degree of intelligence, culture and courage must have gone to raise her to her high estate.

According to other writers Carthage (Karthada, or new town) was founded in the ninth century B. C., as a mere trading colony by the Tyrians, who were joined in the venture by some other Phœnician cities. The new colony carried on her affairs with considerable vigor and intelligence, and soon won the supremacy of all the cities of the African coast, as Tyre had done before her in Phœnicia. Her population was steadily increased by immigration from the mother country. Her form of government grew to be an aristocracy of capital-

ists with a limited popular suffrage, controlled by a senate
of one hundred and four members, — " a democracy inclining
towards an oligarchy," says Aristotle, who has told us much

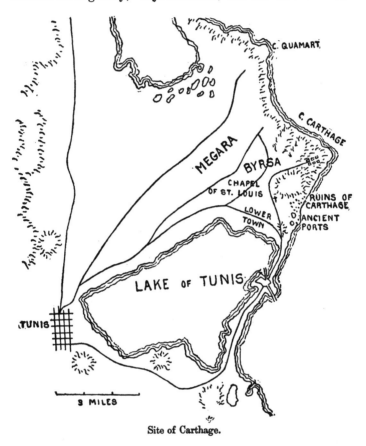

Site of Carthage.

about Carthage. The executive officers were two magistrates,
who have been likened to the Spartan kings, and who were
annually elected by the citizens. But there was a council of
twenty-eight elders, elected at the same time, who really possessed the power. During her period of prosperity, Carthage
must have had a good government, however constituted.

Carthage was constantly at war, for commercial rather than international reasons, and in the sixth century B. C. Mago I. is said to have laid the foundation of her solid military organization. This ruler was the progenitor of a remarkable line of generals, who made Carthage celebrated for one hundred and fifty years. The growth of this financially splendid city — "the London of antiquity" — warranted her in seeking constant accessions among the islands of the Mediterranean, and her commercial navy soon grew into a military arm of the most powerful description. From the beginning of the fifth to the middle of the third century B. C. Carthage was at the height of her power.

The plateau of Byrsa, now the hill of St. Louis, on and at the foot of which Carthage was built, stands up nearly two hundred feet above the sea level, and commands a magnificent view of the whole surrounding country. The situation of Carthage could not be improved for a city or for commerce, situated as it was at the narrows of the Mediterranean. Appian gives us very interesting details of Carthage, but from them we can reconstruct the city only in part. The extent of the entire capital as it was when destroyed in 146 B. C. has been hidden by the ages. Excavations have so far been limited; but in the Middle Ages, Carthage, like other perished cities, became a quarry for the world. The Cathedral of Pisa, among many other vast structures, was built from blocks of marble dug from the ruins.

That the works about Carthage were enormous is shown by the fact that the artificial harbors covered an area of some fifty acres, a much larger amount than those of any other ancient city. That the architecture of the city was splendid we know, and that there was a Phœnician style is shown by the fact that Tyrian architects were hired to build the temple of Solomon. Circular and semicircular and horseshoe-shaped

edifices seemed to be the rule, and stone work was fitted like
carpentry in male and female joints, as well as held together
by the famous cement which so long resisted Alexander's
rams at Tyre. The arms of Carthage displayed a horse resting under a palm-tree. The first emigrants to land on the
heights of Byrsa are said to have dug up the skull of a horse
at the foot of a tree, at the spot which commands the entire
landscape, and to have adopted the emblem for the city
they proposed to build. But, however splendid, Carthage
was essentially of the earth, earthy. She was wrapped up in
money-making ; there was a sad lack of higher motives and
intelligence in her statecraft, though her social life was unquestionably of a high order. Albeit her commercial activity
made her prosperous, Carthage was able only to propagate ;
she could not create.

Carthage had not been the first, but she was the most prom-

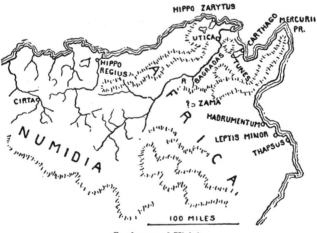

Carthage and Vicinity.

inent settlement of the Phœnicians in the west. A rich
corn-growing district, peopled by splendid agriculturists, on
the greatest roadstead of Northern Africa, could not fail to

prosper. In expatiating upon the extended commerce of the Carthaginians, we must not forget that they were in the highest degree remarkable as an agricultural people. The Carthaginian territory was exceptionally rich by nature and by art, and extensive agricultural products not only assured a certainty of exportation, but kept the indigenous population prosperous and busy. Not only this, but their flocks and herds were of the best. Polybius calls Africa a land marvelous for grain and fruits and animals ; Scylax especially vaunts it. After Zama, it was agriculture to which the Carthaginians turned under the leadership of Hannibal, and it helped them to rise again as nothing else could. Irrigation was practiced in its best methods, and to-day the plains of Tunis are covered with the ruins of numberless towns and villages, which only the most exceptional fertility could have sustained. Mago's treatise on agriculture was the best known of antiquity. It was used even by the Romans and is highly praised by Cato and Pliny.

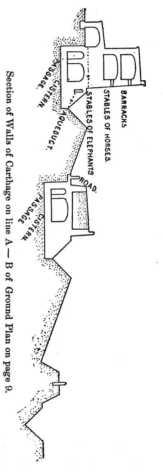

Section of Walls of Carthage on line A — B of Ground Plan on page 9.

Carthage, like Tyre, was practically free, though she paid occasional tribute to the Great King. The Greek colonies and migrations struggled long with those emanating from Phœnicia, but finally bounds were set to further Grecian

progress about 500 B. C. The towns of Hippo, Hadrumetum, Thapsus, Leptis and others on the coast of Africa
were made colonies of Carthage and paid her tribute. Utica
was an earlier settlement than Carthage, had been her patron,
and remained free. Carthage was really the capital of a
great North African empire, extending from the desert of
Tripoli to the Atlantic, and protected inland by a chain of
fortified posts. Gades, though earlier colonized by Tyre, fell
under the hegemony of Carthage, as did all subsequent western colonies of Phœnicia.

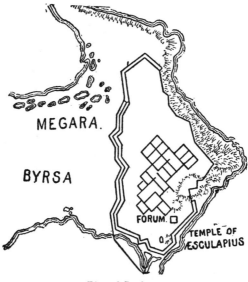

Plan of Carthage.

About 500 B. C. Carthage appears to have been at war
with the Greek colony of Massilia (Marseille), and to have
got a foothold on Sardinia, on the west and northwest coast
of Sicily and on the adjacent islands. Finally, after much
friction, the Greeks and Carthaginians agreed to tolerate
each other, and by 300 B. C. Carthage controlled almost all

Sicily and fully monopolized the trade of the western Mediterranean. She had become the richest city in the world, says
Polybius, and is by some authorities reckoned to have had
a population of seven hundred thousand souls.

It was indeed fortunate for Carthage that Alexander did
not advance so far along the African coast after he had conquered Egypt. The dis-
tance from the then centre
of the world — Babylon
— had in like manner
saved her from Cyrus.
Carthage is said, however,
to have sent a deputation
to congratulate Alexander
on his return to Babylon.

The city of Carthage
was about twenty miles in
circumference, including
the citadel on the Byrsa,
whose walls were two miles
in extent. We know from
Appian how these walls
were made. That the en-
gineers who could plan so
good a profile would also
make an admirable line
of walls may be assumed;
and reëntering and salient
angles, curtains and tow-
ers, arranged to give good
cross-fire, were part of the
mural scheme. Facing
the sea, the citadel stood

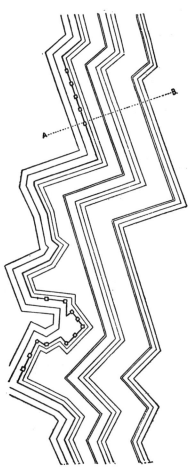

Ground Plan of Walls of Carthage as restored by Daüx.

on an almost perpendicular line of rocks, where the walls need be less strong. On the west and northwest there were triple walls, for here the lay of the land demanded strength. On the north and south were double walls, on the east but a single one. The citadel had accommodation for fifty thousand souls. The temple, used as a redoubt, could hold one thousand men.

The walls were built of huge blocks of tufa, protected from the elements by bitumen, jointed and cemented. They were over thirty feet thick and nearly fifty feet high. The three lines had each the same profile. Three hundred elephants, four thousand horses and twenty thousand foot could be housed in them. In these walls were double vaulted passages, used both for storage and barracks, and intended as well to break the vibration of the blows of rams. The towers were usually of four stories. Along the wall was a terrace thirty feet wide. The thickness of wall slopes and ditch was nearly six hundred feet. Recent excavations prove the accuracy of the description of Appian. The construction of these walls goes to show great military skill among the Carthaginian engineers, as well as great ability in the builders.

Silver Tetradrachma, with supposed head of Hannibal; probably not authentic.

II.

THE PUNIC ARMY AND NAVY. 500–200 B. C.

CARTHAGE depended for both army and navy on mercenaries, which she got from all her dependencies and the barbarian nations with which she traded. Her harbors were the largest of antiquity and the size of her fleet was enormous, consisting principally of triremes, but with many quinquiremes and still more transports. Few Carthaginian citizens served, except in the Sacred Band. The Liby-Phœnicians, Iberians and Gauls made up the bulk of the army, supplemented by light troops from all quarters. In peace, the *cadres* were kept afoot and the arsenals were full of war-material. This mercenary system was weak, in absolute contrast to the inherent strength of the Roman system of personal service; for the mercenary had neither fealty nor a sense of honor; nor was he to be quickly obtained in serious emergencies. The generals were under control of the war-council, which interfered with their freedom of action, to the great detriment of military operations. The Carthaginian army was organized on the Greek method, though foreign mercenaries were wont to retain their own habits. The heavy foot was phalangial, the light foot irregular. The heavy cavalry was good, the light, especially the Numidians, exceptionally valuable. The arms, equipment and discipline were inferior to the Roman. Chariots and elephants were in use. The train consisted of pack animals and was moderate in size. The army was able to march well, but was subject to epidemics, on account of the number of foreigners unused to caring for their health. In fortification the Carthaginians excelled, but they did not intrench a daily camp until they came in contact with the Romans. In the time of the Barcas, the Carthaginian power was on the wane, but the remarkable ability of the Barca family gave it an impetus which all but carried it to success, and, under Hamilcar in Spain and Hannibal during the first few years in Italy, the Carthaginian army was of the highest order of material and discipline.

CARTHAGE preferred mercenary troops to a system of personal military service. Her citizens being mostly traders or rich planters, whose time was too valuable to the state, or whose social position was too high, to allow them to spend their years in the ranks, it was natural that a standing army should grow up by permitting substitution. Moreover the hiring, for such an army, of soldiers and sailors among the numerous semi-civilized tribes with which Carthage traded, kept up her pleasant relations with these tribes and enabled her gradually to extend her influence over their neighbors. Commerce with the barbarians was highly remunerative. The same rule applied to the navy, which was in like fashion manned by bought and hired crews.

The harbor, dockyards and arsenal of Carthage were well fortified, and were the largest and finest of the times. They afforded an abundant refuge for their fleets, which were more numerous and efficient than any then afloat. The Lake of Tunis also afforded unlimited accommodation to any number of bottoms.

Down to the Punic wars the warships of the Carthaginians were mostly triremes, — in number reaching in the third century over three hundred and fifty, — and were rowed by slaves and manned by land troops. The number of small vessels was enormous. In the treaty with Xerxes, 480 B. C., Carthage agreed to put afloat and at Xerxes' disposition two thousand war-vessels and three thousand transports. Even at the close of the Second Punic War she gave up five hundred vessels to the Romans.

The rowers were as a rule about three fourths of the crew, and were a standing force purchased by the government for this purpose. The vessels were commanded by naval officers who were only under the control of generals when associated with an army. Both land and sea forces were under the direct orders of the senate. The fleet was of necessity the more important arm. We shall have, however, in narrating the Second Punic War, to deal almost exclusively with the land forces, though these were, as an element in the growth of Carthage, by far of less importance.

That the navy of Carthage was much larger and more important than the army was natural enough. The competition for power with Syracuse, the other Greek colonies in Sicily and with Rome, obliged Carthage to keep her marine, despite often great losses and depletion, on the highest footing. We find in Diodorus, Polybius, Appian and Aristotle much more detail regarding the navy than the army of Carthage. The splendid harbors and fleets and organization are fully

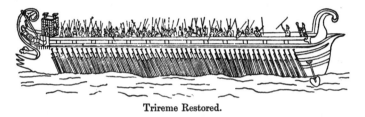

Trireme Restored.

set forth. As a rule the " long " or war ships were triremes, carrying some three hundred rowers and one hundred and twenty soldiers; but the use by Alexander of larger ships, and especially their increase in size by Demetrius Poliorcetes, gave an impetus to naval architecture everywhere, and we find quinquiremes and even a septireme in the war against Pyrrhus, and in the First Punic War. Quinquiremes were thenceforward common in the Carthaginian navy. The increase in rowers in these latter brought greater speed and ability to manœuvre and made them much more dangerous in battle. On the whole, the Carthaginian ships were ahead of any others, and the size of their fleets was remarkable. In the battle against Regulus, as we are told by Polybius, no less than three hundred and fifty Carthaginian ships were engaged, containing one hundred and fifty thousand rowers and soldiers, while Regulus had three hundred and thirty galleys, with one hundred and forty thousand men aboard. Fifty Carthaginian galleys are said to have been sunk and thirty thousand men lost. This is hard to believe, and yet Polybius is our most credible authority. The width of a vessel of the first class in Carthage was, we happen to know, about seventeen feet. This, judging from the old delineations of warships, might give her a length of one hundred to one hundred and twenty feet. This is, however, a mere estimate.

Appian tells us that the arsenals of Carthage held two hundred thousand complete suits of armor, an immense number of darts and javelins and two thousand catapults, and Strabo repeats the fact, making the number of engines three thousand. Trained artificers in these arsenals were able to turn out each day one hundred to one hundred and twenty shields or bucklers, three hundred swords, one thousand catapult-missiles, five hundred lances and a number of engines.

The Carthaginian citizen was found only to a limited numerical extent in the army. But in the cavalry, where wealth was required and honor sought, and especially in a *corps d'élite* called the Sacred Band, — the body-guard of the commander-in-chief and a sort of training-school for officers like the Macedonian Pages, — and in the higher official berths, he was fairly well represented. The Sacred Band, which consisted of fifteen hundred infantry, was sumptuously clad and equipped, and was noted for its courage and discipline. The cavalry, one thousand strong, came next in order of importance, and appears to have formed an appendage to the Sacred Band. Thus but twenty-five hundred of those who were fortunate enough to hold Carthaginian citizenship served in an army then numbering seventy thousand men. Though not commonly in the ranks, the citizen was in times of public danger held to service, and the city alone could put on foot an army of forty thousand hoplites and one thousand horse.

The next grade of land troops came from the Liby-Phœnicians, peoples lying near by and tributary to Carthage, and the outcome of an admixture of the colonial and native blood. These tribes furnished a much higher number than Carthage herself. The foreign mercenaries were the bulk of the army. These last troops were recruited among all nations in Africa and Europe with which Carthage had commercial relations, with the idea, says Polybius, of avoiding conspiracies and mutiny by having no common political aspirations among the several divisions of the army. Indeed, the different bodies did not generally understand each other's language. They were apt to be devoted only to their immediate chief. These troops were got in bodies of hundreds and thousands by bargain and sale from the governments of their respective countries. As a rule, some senator was sent as ambassador to such nations as it was desired to reach, and a given number of troops arranged for on given terms of payment.

The best of these mercenary troops were the Iberians from the Spanish peninsula. Among the most recklessly brave were the half-naked Gauls, who at a very early period served for pay in the Carthaginian ranks. The most numerous were the nomad soldiers collected from every part of the African coast, from Egypt to the Pillars of Hercules.

The general plan of recruitment was not dissimilar to the Persian. The Great King assembled under his banners all the peoples of the East; Carthage all the nations of the West. The numbers under arms have probably been vastly overestimated by the ancient Greek and Roman historians. Still, no doubt Carthage could, with little effort, put under the colors a force of over one hundred thousand men. The wars in Sicily probably called out the largest force Carthage ever had in the field; and at times she had numbers on foot much exceeding this estimate, though the sum of three hundred thousand men which has been given can scarcely be accepted as a reliable estimate of forces assembled at any one time for one campaign.

In seasons of peace, the nucleus of the army was kept intact, with plenty of weapons in the arsenals, and horses and beasts of burden. The citadel was not only the centre of military defense, but the headquarters of the army as well. Here were the barracks for the troops ; and here the commander of the citadel and of the troops in garrison was in sole authority.

It is unnecessary to point out how vastly such a mercenary organization as has been described must in the long run be inferior to the system of personal service, to the theory which makes every man's breast a bulwark for the honor and safety of the fatherland. It had its advantages. Mercenaries are apt to be of low stock, and with more animal than moral or intellectual qualities. But they enlist because they have more to gain than to lose, and are often of great reliability so long as they can clearly see their object. As above remarked, the hiring of mercenaries kept Carthage on a very friendly footing with all the nations which it thus subsidized ; and so long as the state coffers were full, it mattered not what gaps were rent in the armies ; they could be quickly patched with gold ; for the supply of men happy to serve for pay and plunder was unfailing among the barbarians. Moreover, this system left the native Carthaginian free to pursue his lucrative commercial and agricultural schemes. On the other hand, the troops were without ties either to the state or among themselves. There could be no feeling of loyalty ; the better virtues, which are quite essential to make a permanently effective army, were absent. The various detachments were ready at any time to turn their arms against Carthage on the slightest pretext for dissatisfaction ; the offer of a higher rate of pay would quickly deprive the city of their services, perhaps at a time of gravest danger. The dependence on hiring mercenaries might leave the state helpless against a sudden invasion or insurrection, for it consumed time to bring together any considerable force of purchased soldiers. It may be said that the Carthaginian government was at the mercy of the men it paid. No nation can ever build a permanent structure, unless the individuals who govern are and remain themselves the defenders of the country. But such an army was in strict keeping with the commercial and political aims and tendencies of Carthage, and after a fashion did very well, except in times of serious danger. If a foreign enemy suddenly landed on its shores, Carthage could not always oppose him with a sufficiently large and well-disciplined army; and in case of internal dissensions, all was uncertainty and confusion. The government was apt to be the victim of surprises. We shall see notable instances of this.

The generals were chosen from the citizens by the people. The political system of Carthage from the earliest times was rotten, and money could buy anything. Capacity was by no means the primal reason for appointment. Popular fancy or the power of gold could procure military position, though it could not purchase the soldier's skill or fame. Jealousies and fear lest a successful captain might turn his arms against the state made the senate an uncertain master, and the senate was all-powerful. This fact was fraught with constant danger, for changes in command were by no means unusual, even in the midst of a campaign; or the general had his hands tied by the withholding of supplies or reinforcements. Worse still, at the side of the general in command stood a deputy of the senate, who not only watched his proceedings, but to a certain extent might direct them. In the fifth century there had been an attempt by an army-commander named Malchus to seize the reins of government, and there was at once constituted the above-named *gerousia* or Elders'

War Council of one hundred and four senators, who thereafter were the supreme commanders, and who directed and controlled all military operations, however distant, drew up the plans of campaign, required strict compliance with their demands, and rewarded or punished the successful or unsuccessful captains as they chose. Even a reasonable or necessary variation from their plan was sometimes mercilessly chastised.

The War Council's plan could rarely accord with the existing facts; generals dared assume no responsibility; their conduct was apt to be indecisive or weak; and if a campaign was successful, it was in spite of the system. Over half-civilized or quite barbarous nations victory could be easily won. But when the Carthaginians met even smaller armies of well-disciplined troops under good generals whose hands were free, they were apt to fail. The defeats they suffered at the hands of Gelon, the elder Dionysius and Timoleon abundantly prove this fact.

Sacred Band Footman.

In view of this thoroughly wrong-headed policy, it is a wonder that Carthage rose at all. But her growth was not a military growth like that of Rome. It was due strictly to successful commerce and rich agriculture, and to the fact that she stood in a location which kept her from contact with the stronger nations. Her military prosperity was due to the mere weight of gold and men, excepting always the few brilliant accidents, among them the star, Hannibal, which have shed eternal radiance upon the Carthaginian arms, as well as thrown into relief the selfishness, ingratitude and lack of patriotism and virtue of the Carthaginians as a race.

The Carthaginian foot and horse were each divided into heavy and light, regular and irregular. The weapons, equip-

ment and manner of fight-
ing were almost as various
as the nationalities. Each
petty detachment came to
swell the host of irregulars
with its own peculiar arms
and habits.

The Sacred Band was a
body of heavy-armed in-
fantry, composed, says Diodorus, only of leading Carthaginian citizens. Plainer
citizens served in the phalanx when on duty. The

Sacred Band Cavalryman.

infantry of the Sacred Band carried a large circular shield
over three feet in diameter, a short sword and probably also

a pike or lance ; were clad in a red tunic and wore
sandals. Though not mentioned in the authorities,
they no doubt wore armor. Others among the richer
of the Carthaginians who entered service were appointed to the heavy cavalry, a position which entailed great expense to maintain at a proper level.
These cavalrymen were distinguished by wearing
golden rings, one for each campaign served by them,
and their weapons were a buckler, a longer and a
shorter lance and a wide, short sword. They were
clad in mail and wore a helmet and greaves. That
there were so few of these leading Carthaginian citizens in a large army shows the system up in its

Spanish
Sword.

weakest aspect. The Liby-Phœnicians fought mainly as
heavy foot and horse. All these infantry troops carried a

Spaniard.

heavy and long spear as their chief weapon, much like the Greek hoplite, on whom indeed they were at this time patterned, so far as race peculiarities permitted.

The Spanish infantry and horse were also classed as heavy, but their chief weapon was a powerful cut-and-thrust sword for close quarters, in the use of which they were wonderfully expert. They wore white woolen tunics, with red edges, and carried a buckler made of bull's hide. The Spaniards were then, and have always been, under good generals, the making of excellent soldiers. The Gauls were of light complexion, and were fond of dyeing their hair red.

They wore it long, hanging over the shoulders or tied in a knot at the top of the head. The men wore full beards, the officers only a mustache. Up to the time of the wars with Rome, the Gauls fought on foot, almost naked, with a sword good only for cutting, of no use except at swinging distance and apt to be dulled or bent by the first blow upon a good helmet or shield. The Roman soldier, who with gladius and scutum closed sharply

Gaul.

with his man, had the Gaul at an utter disadvantage. The Gauls were noted for genial qualities and courage, but equally for inconstancy, wildness and brutality. When not in battle, they were clad in a shirt, loose tunic and cloak. Their helmets, not always worn, were decked with horns or feathers, and were made of considerable height to give to the soldier a taller look and thus increase the terror of his aspect. They wore many bracelets, necklaces and rings. For additional arms they had slings, a lance with fire-sharpened point, a pike or halberd with curved blade and a club. They were most dan-

Slingers.

gerous as swordsmen, and Hannibal replaced all their other weapons with their one peculiar arm, manufacturing these in Cartagena, so as to give them the advantage of the best of material. They later adopted armor and a shield, which in early days they had despised.

The next most valuable arm was the corps of two thousand Balacrean slingers, then peculiar to Carthage. They carried two slings, one for long, one for short distance firing. The distance and accuracy of their aim with pebble-stones and leaden bullets are so well vouched for that we are fain to believe the feats narrated of them, and can fully understand their military value. We know that the Jewish left-handed slingers could cut a hair set up as a target; and on the Retreat of the Ten Thousand, Xenophon was not satisfied with his light troops until he had organized a band of slingers, for these seemed best able to keep the enemy at a distance when protecting the column.   Their fire was more severe than that of the best archers of the day.

The ordinary light footman had lance and javelins and a small round shield of hide-covered wood.   He was a fine marcher, and some of the men could keep pace with a galloping horse.   They and the Gauls were wont to indulge in fearful outcries in battle.   They were very clever in casting darts, and were not apt to miss their aim at any fair distance.

Light Footman.

The Africans were straight-featured, strong and hardy.   They shaved their heads and left but a small fringe of beard. They tattooed extensively.   They wore a red hood, a white woolen shirt hanging to the knees and belted at the waist. A bournous, or cloak, or the skin of a goat or some wild beast, covered their shoulders. Their legs were bare.   A long lance, bow and arrows, a buckler of elephant's or bull's hide, sometimes a long sword, were their weapons.   Some had special arms, such as flails, and harpoons held by a cord.   Later, Hannibal armed these men with the Roman weapons picked up on the battle-fields of the Trebia and Trasimene and Cannæ.   The Africans were peculiarly tough, faithful and uncomplaining.   They

African.

were hideously cruel to their prisoners, and hard to restrain from massacre; but they were the best of material from which to make a devoted army.

Spanish Cavalryman.

The ordinary heavy cavalry was African, Spanish and Gallic. The Spaniards had good horses, used to a hilly country, and these habitually carried two warriors, one to fight on foot and one on horseback. The Gallic horse was better even than the foot. The African was, however, the best, and was exceedingly well mounted and equipped.

Numidian.

The Numidian cavalry, under which name came the irregular light horse of scores of tribes, was the most numerous and perhaps the most useful of the Carthaginian soldiery. Their appearance, say Strabo and Appian, belied their value. Almost naked, covered with but a leopard or tiger skin, which, hung over the left arm, served also as a shield with those who carried none, and armed with lance, casting darts and sword; mounted on the small mean-looking runt of the steppes or desert, which, innocent of saddle or bridle, was guided solely by the voice or a slender rod, they were yet warlike, plucky, tireless, satisfied with little, and made up a wonderful body for partisan warfare. Useless if separated from their horses, so long as they were with them they were of distinct and unequivocal value. In attack they charged with fiery élan, but at once turned on meeting opposition ; not, however, to fly, for they charged again and again, riding up into the very teeth of the foe, but never remaining to fight hand to hand with heavier troops. As a curtain for the army in which they served, and as an element to unsettle the morale of the enemy, they ranked among the best of light horse. They were equally useful on level or broken terrain, and were peculiarly clever in taking advantage of the accidents of the ground for ambush or temporary defense. In pursuit they never tired, and here they were the most dangerous of opponents. Like our own broncos or the Cossack horses, their little nags were wonderful for endurance and

Chariot.

activity, and throve on food which would kill a civilized horse. On the other hand, they were cruel, reckless and noted for plundering and rapacity.

In early times the Carthaginians employed chariots ; and after the war with Pyrrhus, elephants. It is not known whether they brought the habit of using chariots with them from Phœnicia, or found it in Africa. The employment of elephants they learned probably from the Epirot king, and made good use of it, as they could find an abundant supply of these animals in Africa.

The elephants of the Carthaginian army were an uncertain feature. If they acted successfully they were, in conflict with nations which knew little about them, of untold moral value. If they lost their heads and turned, they might be still more dangerous to their own friends. For this reason, during the Second Punic War, their drivers carried mallet and spike to kill them in case they should grow unmanageable or treacherous.

A Carthaginian army presented a singular aspect. In the centre the heavy Carthaginian or Liby-Phœnician, Spanish or Gallic foot; in front the Balacrean slingers, light troops and perhaps chariots; on the flanks some heavy and swarms of Numidian cavalry. The method in early days was not unlike that of the mobs of the Orient, but grew better by imi-

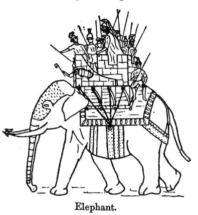

Elephant.

tating Greek models. Still it was patched up of such diverse elements that it is a wonder that even a good general could make it available.

The train consisted generally of beasts of burden, mules, horses and beeves. In Italy, however, carts were often employed. The management of the trains in the days of Hannibal was extremely efficient, and at all times the trains were of moderate extent.

The Carthaginian army was quickly moved because not loaded down with baggage, nor consisting of much heavy material. It could march long distances, and its light troops preserved it from surprises. But these light troops at the same time devastated the country, making subsistence difficult and retreat impossible; and were often hard to control.

There was little organization, and under the every-day general little discipline. Owing to the vast numbers of cavalry-horses, and generally the presence of elephants, it could not be readily transported across sea ; and, like all armies full of unintelligent material, it was subject to severe epidemics of sickness.

It must not be understood that such was the complexion of the army of Hamilcar or Hannibal. These partook peculiarly of the genius of their leaders, as armies always do. The above description applies to the Carthaginian army as a whole, and in most points not to those bodies which did such wonderful work in Spain and Italy.

It is probable that the Carthaginians made use in fortification and siege-proceedings of what was within the common knowledge of all civilized nations at that day. Castrametation was certainly practiced. Troops, we know, were camped behind temporary fortifications when awaiting shipment or after disembarking. This is shown by the first commercial treaty with Rome in 509 B. C. But they did not fortify the daily camp.

So far as minor tactics, arms, organization, and marches and battles are concerned, we do not know as much about those of the Carthaginians as about those of other nations. It is generally understood that, during the First Punic and down to the beginning of the Second Punic War, the heavy and regular foot and horse approximated largely to the Macedonian type. Xanthippus, during the First Punic War, joined the Carthaginian army with a body of Greek mercenaries. These of course retained the phalangial habit, and as they were the best troops in the army, and Xanthippus was placed in command of all the Carthaginian forces, the Greeks no doubt gave a phalangial training to the Carthaginians, whose foot was already set up somewhat after this fashion ;

for intercourse with Greece as well as the traditions of Tyre would no doubt accomplish so much ; and the knowledge of Alexander's wonderful successes would lead the Carthaginians to imitate his method, so far as they could learn it. The light and mercenary troops retained their own methods of combat, regulated by such masters as Hamilcar or Hannibal to suit the occasions which might arise. We shall see the latter introducing a number of Roman methods.

The Carthaginian phalanx, then, like the Greek, was a mass designed to give one heavy shock. The details of the

Phalanx.

phalangial organization have been given in describing the army of Philip and Alexander. The tetrarchia of sixty-four hoplites in four files sixteen deep, or the syntagma which contained four of these companies, that is, two hundred and fifty-six men in a body sixteen square, was the fighting unit. The smaller phalanx had sixteen syntagmas, or a total of four thousand and ninety-six hoplites or heavy infantrymen. In open or parade order the hoplites occupied six feet each way ; in close or battle order (the usual one), three feet ; in very close order to receive a charge, one and one-half feet, in which formation the whole was called a synapism.

The hoplite had a shield and a pike from twelve to sixteen feet long, which the first three to five ranks held horizontally and the others vertically or slanted forward. The pike of even the fourth rank man projected beyond the first rank. That the Carthaginian soldier used the twenty-one foot Macedonian sarissa is improbable. The Greeks never employed it. It required too much drill to use the sarissa to advantage.

Whether the phalanx had, in addition to the hoplite, a somewhat less heavily armed soldier, like the Greek peltast, is not known. The peltast, midway between the hoplite and the light-armed footman, had sword, shield and lighter pike, and armor adapted to quicker movements. But it is highly probable that the peltast, or some equivalent of the peltast, was found in the Carthaginian phalanx, and it unquestionably had its light troops disposed like the Greek psiloi, to the extent of about half the hoplites in number, to fight as skirmishers on front and flanks.

There were practically no intervals in the phalanx. It was not a good body for hilly countries, lacking entirely the mobility of the Roman legion. Its advantages and disadvantages have been already discussed in the period of Alexander, and will be elsewhere in this.

The cavalry, if organized on a Greek basis, was light and heavy, the former being mostly used in outpost duty. The heavy fought in a unit of sixteen ranks, four men deep, called an ilē. How the Numidian and other light cavalry was organized is not known, but the Carthaginian army decidedly lacked homogeneity.

The phalanx of this era had, in Greece, and probably in Carthage : —

Heavy infantry	4,096	
Light infantry	2,048	6,144
Heavy cavalry	512	6,656

Of light cavalry there was an indefinite number. Several of these phalanxes acting together in one line were known as a grand phalanx. That the Carthaginian army adopted exactly this formation is not known, but its organization was unquestionably phalangial.

From the time of the First Punic War, the military power of Carthage was markedly on the wane. It was only the wonderful military capacity of Hamilcar Barca and his family which made the light to brighten — as it did indeed in a manner seen but a few times in the world's history — before it finally flickered and went out. According to Aristotle it was the corruption of the political atmosphere which led to this condition, the bald fact that everything had become purchasable, and that the same individual could hold more than one office. This circumstance, coupled to one other, that the government was, as it were, a shuttlecock between the two families headed by Hamilcar Barca, representing the patriotic aristocrats, and by Hanno, who marshaled the democratic peace-party, could terminate in but one way.

It cannot be gainsaid that the successes of Hamilcar in Spain, brilliant as they were, contributed to the political decline of Carthage. The Iberian silver mines furnished means of purchasing what could not be otherwise got at home, and accelerated the growth of political dishonesty. Added to these causes was the fact that the Carthaginian fleet had suffered a fatal blow at the close of the First Punic War, from which it never rallied. All the efforts of the Carthaginians were unable to replace it on the proud plane it had occupied for generations. The power of Carthage had resided in its splendid fleet; it now went over to its army, and this lay in Spain in the hands of the Barcas. Nothing so fully demonstrates the lack of vessels and the increased value of the army as the march of Hamilcar from Carthage to the Pillars of Hercules, and his crossing to Gades by transport. Two generations before, a Carthaginian army would have been transported by sea from the harbor of Carthage itself.

But it must be noted, though the military power of Carthage was about to expire, that, owing to the extraordinary military talent of the Barcas, Carthage never possessed an army so hardened by campaigns, so inured to discipline and so devoted to its chief as the one which Hannibal commanded when he left Spain on his way to Italy. This was in spite of the decadence of Carthage, and purely the individual work of this remarkable family. Military capacity is infrequently transmitted to posterity. The few exceptions to this rule shine with all the more radiance from their rarity. It is a curious fact that out of the six greatest captains of history, three, Alexander, Hannibal and Frederick, owe their armies to their fathers' skill as organizers, and the two former came honestly by their military genius.

Gladius.

III.

CARTHAGINIAN WARS. 480–277 B. C.

By 480 B. C. Carthage had acquired abundant territory in Africa, Spain, Sicily, the islands of the Western Mediterranean, and beyond the Pillars of Hercules. Her main energies for over two centuries were devoted to the conquest of Sicily, in which scheme she was vigorously opposed by Syracuse. Through good and ill, Carthage ended by owning the western half of the island; and during all this period she had repeated commercial treaties with Rome. It was her hold on Sicily which finally brought on the Punic wars, the result of Roman jealousy of her controlling influence so near the Italian peninsula.

BEFORE the beginning of the Sicilian wars, 480 B. C., Carthage had won for herself a very substantial footing. She

Sicily.

had a large territory in Northern Africa ; possessed Sardinia, the Balearic Islands and some of the other smaller ones, a part of Sicily, probably Corsica, Madeira and the Canaries; and had colonies on the coast of Spain and beyond the Straits of Gibraltar. Her naval accomplishments were extraordinary. A fleet under Hanno had sailed down the coast of Africa, it is thought as far as the equator, and his brother Imilco had at the same time sailed north to the shores of Great Britain, exploring the coast of Spain and France on the way. Her position Carthage is stated to have owed largely to the skill of Mago I., though its growth was probably gradual. From this time to the First Punic War — the period of the greatest prosperity of Carthage — almost her entire energies were bent upon the sole ownership of Sicily. In this she was opposed by the city of Syracuse, whose purpose was the same; and while Carthage nearly attained her object, she was eventually thwarted, and suffered meanwhile many bloody defeats.

The first attempt of Carthage was made under orders of, or at least in connection with, Xerxes, whom she still acknowledged as Great King, and to whom, as above stated, she had occasionally paid tribute. This was in 480 B. C. While Xerxes was to attack Greece from the east, Carthage would attack Sicily and prevent the Greeks of Sicily and southern Italy from aiding their countrymen at home. But the invasion of Sicily by Carthage was repelled by Gelon, king of Syracuse, with a loss to the Carthaginians, according to Herodotus and Diodorus, of three hundred thousand men, — not a soul of this vast force returning to Carthage. This is not improbably an exaggeration.

Sundry descents were thereafter made by Carthage on the island, with forces variously stated at from one hundred thousand to three hundred thousand men, and a not inconsiderable part of it was conquered or laid under contribution. Even Syracuse was besieged. But in 396 B. C. Dionysius, tyrant of Syracuse, defeated the Carthaginians with a loss of one hundred and fifty thousand men, as we are informed by Diodorus and Plutarch.

Not discouraged, the Carthaginians of the next generation renewed their attempts, and in B. C. 343 got possession of the town but not the citadel of Syracuse. Still this success was not lasting, and two years later the Carthaginians were all but driven from Sicily. Other invasions were made in 340 and 339 B. C., but had no better results. The Carthaginians were beaten back by Timoleon and finally begged for peace.

This peace lasted nearly a generation. War then broke out again between Carthage and Syracuse, of which city Agathocles was tyrant. A Carthaginian army again besieged the town of Syracuse, and Agathocles replied by transporting his army to Africa and attacking Carthage. This resulted in relieving Syracuse, and brought Carthage to the verge of ruin (311–306 B. C.). This carrying of the war into Africa is interesting as a prototype of the later invasions of the Romans. In 278–276 B. C. the Carthaginians were again on foot and again besieged Syracuse. This city called to its aid Pyrrhus, king of Epirus, then in Italy. At first in a large measure successful, Pyrrhus was eventually compelled to leave Sicily. Carthage, however, retained much of her hold on the island, keeping her most important western city, Agrigentum, and more than half its superficial area. Her next opponent in Sicily was Rome.

In the wars thus summarized there is little of military interest. They are merely given to show with what equipment and experience in arms Carthage entered into her great struggle with Rome.

The two great western cities had long had some connection, brought about naturally enough by commercial matters.

The mariners of one nation were apt to be driven by storms
into the waters of the other, and as piracy and commerce
largely went hand in hand in those days, were not infrequently subjected to grievous hardships.   To prevent or to
rectify these, the first treaty between Rome and Carthage
was made in 509 B. C., followed by a second in 347 B. C.   A
synopsis of both is on record.   They show that Carthage held
a much stronger hand than Rome.   A third, of which we have
no details, was made in 306 B. C.; but it was manifest that
jealousy and friction between the rival cities was on the increase.   This was for the moment suspended by a fourth

Possessions of Carthage at the Beginning of the First Punic War.

treaty, in 277 B. C., of an offensive and defensive nature
against Pyrrhus, and Carthage offered to aid Rome with one
hundred and thirty ships.   It was not long after this that the
first serious breach occurred, — a breach resulting in wars
which for generations bathed the territories of both in blood.

IV.

THE EARLY ARMY OF ROME. 500–350 B. C.

FROM the most remote times the Romans were peculiarly patriotic and subject to discipline. It was this which lay at the root of their strong military system. The earliest Roman organization was derived from the Greeks in southern Italy, and was practically the old Dorian phalanx. Servius Tullius divided the population into tribes, according to wealth, and every able-bodied citizen was bound to serve (or rather he alone had the privilege of serving), from seventeen to forty-five years of age. When the monarchy gave way to a republic, the consuls became the army-leaders instead of the kings. The youth of Rome was scrupulously trained to arms, and underwent a rigorous gymnastic drill. Both the Greeks and Romans began with the phalangial idea, which is rather a defensive than an offensive one. But the Romans had a peculiar way of taking the initiative in war, and out of the phalanx they developed the germ of the legion, some time prior to 500 B. C. The heavy foot was set up in three lines, with intervals between centuries or companies, and the first and second lines checkerwise, the horse on the flanks, and the light troops in front or rear, as needed. This enabled the second or third line to advance through the intervals to sustain the first and renew a failing combat. The number of men in the century and the legion was changed from time to time. Not till the Second Punic War was the legion the settled body which is commonly described, and even after this date it was materially altered. The Romans were good distance marchers, but careless in camp and outpost duty. In fortification and sieges they were behind the Greeks. But the one thing in which they excelled was in making every detail of their organization bend to the offensive idea, and in carrying this out with vigor and consistency. Their one rule was always to attack.

THERE has never been a people better adapted for war by nature and training than the Roman. At the root of this national aptitude lay two characteristics, intense love of Rome and unremitting zeal in subordinating all individual aspirations to the necessities of the state. These two virtues, patriotism and discipline, were infused into the Roman blood as early as the traditional time of the first kings. To trace the details of the growth of the organization of the Roman army from the earliest era is an engrossing study, but it must here be done in brief space. The legion as it existed at the time of the war against Hannibal will be more fully treated.

Rome under its earliest conditions was apparently little more than a den of robbers, a fortified asylum for adventurers, the rendezvous of all manner of roughs and outcasts. The heroes of remote antiquity were most of them of this stripe. The interesting traditions of the imperial city are inventions of later days. But this turbulent crowd showed one marked virtue. It had the good sense to perceive that by organization alone and the strictest of discipline could it hold its own in the midst of its warlike neighbors. This motley company of brigands by no means lacked leaders or intelligence, nor indeed high ambitions and admirable purpose, and out of their efforts to fit themselves to struggle against surrounding danger grew the most splendid military organization the world has ever seen. Whatever the early leaders may have been, or however named, they laid the foundation of an enduring people.

The earliest Græco-Italian military organization, from which Rome derived its own, was probably a Homeric collection of the stoutest warriors on horseback. By the time of the kings this had, from the demands for greater numbers, changed to the Dorian phalanx of hoplites, with the horsemen on the flanks, and no doubt a few irregular skirmishers in front or flank.

The entire population was early divided by the magnates of Rome into three tribes, each of which was held to furnish on call one thousand fully armed footmen, and one hundred horsemen, who should serve at their own cost and furnish arms and rations. This body of one thousand infantry was divided into ten centuries of one hundred men each, and the

horse, generally made up of the richest citizens, into ten
decuries of ten men each. The three thousand foot and
three hundred horse thus provided for made up the legion
which was the successor of the Dorian phalanx. There ap-

Early Legion.

pears to have been a body-guard for the king or leader, consisting of three hundred specially selected mounted men,
called *celeres*, who were paid and kept constantly on foot.
These were the first standing force of Rome. Each thousand
men were under a tribune, or colonel, each one hundred
under a centurion or captain. Such was the bare skeleton
upon which later changes were grafted. But what gave this
body life was a singular spirit of discipline, subordination
and patriotism, — an *esprit de corps*, — rarely equaled in
the world's history. Gymnastic training and warlike exercises were of later growth. The early Roman was by his
vagabond life already a vigorous soldier.

To Servius Tullius (? 578–534 B. C.) is ascribed by tradition the division of the population into classes according to
wealth. The distinction between patricians and plebeians was
already marked. There were raised from these classes, and
armed according to the ability of each, one hundred and
sixty-eight centuries of foot, or sixteen thousand eight hundred men, in four legions of forty-two hundred men each,
two of juniors, seventeen to forty-five years old, and two
of seniors, forty-six to sixty. There were also centuries of
pioneers and musicians, and the total cavalry was twenty-
four hundred strong. Every citizen must serve sixteen, or in
case of need twenty, campaigns of six months each, if in the

foot, ten if in the horse; no one might look for state employment on less than ten years' service in the foot or five years in
the horse, unless sooner disabled by honorable wounds.

Service laid burdens upon the citizens, but brought honor
and power in the state. None but citizens in good standing
were permitted to bear arms. The Servian classes were cen-
sus-tribes for both service and taxation. Political and military rights and duties ran side by side. The first class contained those who had farms of twenty jugera or more, or
money to the amount of one hundred thousand asses or over.
The value of the as (originally a pound's weight of copper or
copper alloy) was very variable, being often reduced according
to the necessities of the public treasury, — during the First
Punic War to two, during the Second to one ounce, as Pliny
tells us. Before the reduction, one hundred asses are stated
to have been equal to nearly two dollars, which was the price
of an ox. But this is quite unsatisfactory as a measure of
value. The jugerum was about two thirds of an acre. The
second class comprised those who had three fourths as much
land or seventy-five thousand asses; the third class, one half
as much land or fifty thousand asses; the fourth, one fourth
as much land or twenty-five thousand asses; the fifth, one
eighth as much land or twelve thousand five hundred asses.
Those belonging to the sixth class, who had less than this,
were reckoned as supernumeraries. There were also classes
of artificers and musicians. At the close of the Second Punic
War, the sixth class was diminished by only exempting those
who had but six thousand asses. The small area of the farms
must have demanded considerable skill in cultivation; judging from the money qualification, even the fourth class was
what we should call well-to-do. The arms of the first class
were a helmet, breastplate or coat of mail, greaves, shield,
sword and long lance; the second class had no greaves, the

third neither greaves nor breastplate, the fourth no metal helmet, and the fifth was, like the Greek psilos, armed alone with darts or bows.

Under the kings, Rome had no soldiers who were not citizens; but in the fifth century B. C. they began to make treaties with neighboring states, and these furnished legions to serve in connection with the Roman troops. These allies (socii or civitates federatæ) kept their own laws and customs, but were bound to furnish each its quota of men, in legions assimilated to those of Rome.

An army thus composed of soldiers called out in the spring, discharged in the fall, serving at their own cost and armed each according to his own fancy, was naturally subject to many inconveniences. It could not march far from home, could make no lengthy or distant campaigns, could not garrison captured cities. This weakness grew so marked that before the end of the siege of Veii, 405 B. C., the senate was forced to begin to pay, feed and equip the men. It is believed by Niebuhr that the men were paid at a much earlier period. The pay was at first three and one third asses silver a day — one hundred asses a month — for a footman, twice as much for minor officers and cavalrymen, and thrice as much for a cavalryman who furnished his own horse. If the statement be true that one hundred asses would purchase an ox, this was a very high rate of pay; but arms, equipments and rations may have been deducted from the pay. The rations consisted of corn, which the men ground themselves in handmills and made into porridge or a sort of pancake. And there were probably occasional meat rations as well. This step was the first towards the creation of a standing army in Rome; for so long as the soldier was fed, he was not restless if constrained to remain in the ranks, when he saw there was distinct need for his services. Longer campaigns could now be undertaken, and the leader of an army was less hampered in his manœuvres.

The change from kingdom to republic in no wise altered the military scheme of Rome. The commanders of the army were the two consuls instead of the kings. These, outside of Rome, had almost unlimited power. If there was but one army, the consuls drew lots for command. If two, each commanded one. If these two armies served together, each consul commanded on alternate days. This absurd habit continued for centuries, and, despite its absurdity, worked fairly well. On occasions of grave public danger, a dictator was chosen to take the entire military power in hand. This officer was then given full authority over army and state, peace and war, for the term of the war, but not usually for a period longer than six months. Associated with him was a master of the horse (magister equitum) whom he appointed, and who commanded the cavalry, as the dictator did specifically the foot.

To serve in the Roman army was looked upon rather in the light of a privilege than a duty, and was confined only to the worthy and to the free-born. The right to serve in the army was the exact complement to the duty to so serve ; to be a citizen meant to be a soldier. Stated shortly, the *jus militiæ* called all men into service between seventeen and forty-five years of age, with certain stated exceptions.

No citizen under seventeen or over forty-five could be obliged to serve on active duty, though he might elect to do so and be perhaps accepted. After forty-five still remained service in the city - garrison (legiones urbanæ), or home guard-duty, which was confined to manning the defenses of the city or town in case of war. Men who reënlisted (emeriti or veterani) enjoyed especial honor and privileges.

A citizen who had served twenty campaigns of six months

each in the foot, or ten in the horse, was exempted. And as above stated, only he who had served half this number could aspire to any political office. Gallant service in war was the only stepping-stone to civic honors.

Those physically wanting — generally not many among this plain and hearty people — were exempt. Small stature was not a grave objection. The burly Gauls laughed at the little Romans until they got to close quarters with them. The height was usually from five feet to five feet three inches. Men exceeding this height were not considered strong. Men under five feet were sooner accepted. Any disablement of hand or foot which rendered the man unable to wield his weapons, any weakness of sight or hearing, or any clear physical defect exempted. The following was the man wanted, according to Vegetius, and a pretty good man he was, though the description belongs to a later period. "The recruit must have sharp eyes, a head carried erect, broad breast, stout shoulders, big fists, long hands, not a big belly, of well proportioned growth, feet and soles less fleshy than muscular. If he has all this, no stress need be laid on the height, for it is far more important that the soldier should be strongly built than tall." The man must also be of good moral character, as, in this era of simple life and national virtues, was apt to be the rule.

Citizens in the public service were exempt, but might volunteer. Priests and augurs were not expected to serve, unless in Gallic invasions, when they must guard the treasury in the Capitol. In recognition of extraordinary services to the republic, citizens were sometimes exempted for a term of years, as were also at times towns or entire districts.

No freedman or slave was allowed to serve, the latter being considered on a level with the beasts of burden. But there were occasions in a later epoch when slaves were armed, served with distinguished credit and thereby earned their freedom. The bitterest punishment for a Roman citizen was to be declared unworthy to serve. Whole provinces were thus punished on more than one occasion, as Bruttium, Lucania, Picenum and many cities, for joining Hannibal after Cannæ.

The youths of Rome were early trained to war. Under seventeen years of age, all boys were called tirones or recruits, and were systematically put through certain exercises by experienced drill-masters to fit them for their duty as soldiers, namely, setting-up, marching, running, jumping, climbing heights, swimming, the use of arms and bearing heavy weights. These exercises were constant and uninterrupted. The grown men kept up this training almost throughout life.

From all this, of which the above is the baldest sketch, we can readily see why the Roman army grew to what it was. Not even the Spartans in their palmiest days had a system in which physique and personal devotion, added to broad intelligence, were thus united.

Speaking in general terms, the arms and equipment of the Roman soldier were much like those of the Greek. No doubt they came originally from the Greek colonists in Italy. No doubt, too, the original legion more nearly approached the phalanx than it did the legion of the later years of Rome. The three tribes were set up, each in ten centuries, without intervals, and the several classes of heavy troops stood close behind each other in two or three lines, while the light troops skirmished around the flanks and front, much as with the phalanx. The cavalry was uniformly on the flanks. Each levy-district furnished, by a regular system, an equal part of each century and each legion, so that the entire body and its several parts were homogeneous; and the best men, that is, the non-commissioned officers, were in the front rank, so as to make the steel edge to the legion, as it had existed for centuries in the phalanx.

The early Roman army was set up in eight to twelve ranks, and in a legion of three thousand men there were from two hundred and fifty to three hundred and seventy-five files, covering a front of something less than a quarter of a mile. It was practically a phalanx. But starting from this common point there was a divergence between Greek and Roman methods. The Greeks stuck to their one-shock idea, and used the light troops for duty requiring an open order. The Romans conceived the idea of a formation which would give each man more individual scope, and which would provide for renewing a failing battle by bringing in fresh troops as occasion demanded. Out of this grew their later formation. The fourth and fifth class men were used as skirmishers, and the three first classes were set up as three lines, the best in the rear, the least good in front, and with the centuries at such intervals that the rear lines could advance through the leading ones to the attack, to relieve the others if overmatched, or to close up the line in one compact mass. This was an outgrowth of what originally was a phalangial order, and seems to have been already in use about 500 B. C. It was phalanx or legion, at will. It was reached by a process of individualizing. The Hellenic phalanx was a close order, and nothing else ; the Roman legion was an open order, which could be made close by the simple advance into the intervals of the rear lines. The pilum and gladius were the weapons representing both distant and hand-to-hand fighting, and the use of the fortified camp allowed the offensive and defensive to be waged at will.

This order was again improved, about the time of the siege of Veii, by making the intervals equal to the front of the centuries, thus forming a checkerwise line (quincuncialis) of great

mobility. At the same time the arms of the men underwent
a change from similar causes. The long pike of the Greek
hoplite was shortened down to the hasta, to which was added
a casting lance or pilum. Both could be used equally at
long distance or hand to hand. Darts replaced bows and
slings, except in special corps of light troops. All these
changes tended towards closer quarters, and finally grew into
making the sword the chief weapon of the heavy-armed for
the final struggle; and the sword was the terror of all who
met the Roman legion.

Many of these changes are ascribed to the Dictator Furius
Camillus. At the time of the second invasion of the Gauls
(366 B. C.) he is said to have given to the Roman soldier
steel helmets to resist the cut of the heavy Gallic sword, iron-
rimmed shields and better lances, and to have drilled them in
their use.

About the middle of the fourth century B. C. the lines of
the legion had got changed. The third class was now in the
middle line, and the men were called hastati, from their long
lance ; the second class, esteemed better, was in front, and
hence called principes. This order gave the first blow with
seasoned troops. The first or best class was in the third line,
and hence called triarii. These three made up the heavy
foot of the phalanx — or legion — which was still about three
thousand strong, of which six hundred were triarii and twelve
hundred each principes and hastati, more or less according to
circumstances. The fourth and fifth classes were rorarii,
young soldiers, and accensi, supernumeraries, who furnished
the light troops. They varied from one thousand to sixteen
hundred in number. In line they stood in the rear; in
battle they had no special place, but were used wherever
needed.

At a period not well established, each line was divided into

fifteen centuries, but these had ceased to number one hundred
men. Each century of principes and hastati had two centurions, sixty men in ten files six deep, a trumpeter and an
ensign-bearer, sixty-four men in all. The centuries of the
triarii had the same depth, but half the front and thus half the
number. Intervals equaled century-fronts of the first two
lines, and there were thirty to sixty paces between lines. The
principes and hastati still stood checkerwise. After this the
centuries were not again recruited up to one hundred.

There were three hundred cavalry and three hundred slingers and archers attached to each legion. The cavalry, when
in line, stood on the flanks; in battle it was dispatched wherever it could be best employed. It sometimes fought dismounted to good effect. The archers and slingers had no
specific place.

Thus the legion had grown to consist of about forty-six
hundred men, according to the numbers of the several bodies.
The checkerwise formation, with the mobility it gave the
several lines, must be considered a great advance in tactical
formations, due to Roman ingenuity and the spirit which
prompted them to come to hand-to-hand work. In detail the
formation was later much changed, but not in principle.

In line of battle the Roman army thus had two lines and a
reserve with the cavalry on the flanks. Often a reserve of
supernumeraries was put between the lines, or the triarii were
left to protect the camp. The cavalry was not infrequently
placed in rear of flanks or centre, or indeed between the
lines. The armies leaned their flanks on obstacles, woods,
rivers or hills, but fought only in parallel order. They were
not unapt to try to surround the enemy's flank, or to send
out detachments to fall on his rear, by a circuit or from ambush. An attack in mass on the centre to separate the
enemy's wings was occasionally seen, but an oblique attack as

practiced by Epaminondas and Alexander was not known to the Romans. Their tactics was simple.

What is peculiarly marked in the tactics of the Romans, and worthy of repetition, is the fact that they always took the initiative; they always attacked, never awaited attack. It was the defensive idea which bred the phalanx; it was the offensive idea which out of the phalanx evolved the legion. The arrangement for renewing the fight with the fresh lines in the rear savored distinctly of the offensive.

In camp, in early times, the Romans were careless. Their campaigns were undertaken only in summer, and they had not even tents. These they later made of sheepskin; but in their stead they were apt to build huts of twigs and straw in permanent camps. There was at this early day no particular order of camping, nor any outpost-service deserving the name.

Marches the Romans could, in all eras, make long and fast. They were used to their arms and carried their rations with them. But the extent of Roman territory was not great, nor the distance the armies had to move.

Fortification and the art of sieges had not yet grown to any degree of perfection, though the Romans had got the general principle of the art from the Greeks. Though it was an ancient custom to do so, up to the time of the war with Pyrrhus (beginning of the third century) the daily camp was not fortified with any system or regularity, says Livy. Cities were better fortified, in the manner usual with the ancients. Rome, from early times, was well protected by good walls. The old walls of Roma Quadrata on the Palatine had probably no great strength; but some king, Tarquinius Priscus it is said (? 616–578), surrounded the city with stone walls and towers, and began the construction of the Capitol or citadel. Under Servius Tullius the city counted its seven hills within a strong and massive wall. The kings of Rome spent a large part of the public treasure and booty in this way.

Towns as a rule were taken by sudden attacks, by assault
or ruse. In assaults, both ladders and tortoises were employed in the early times, but
gradually more skillful means
came into use, no doubt learned
from the Greeks. Undermin-
ing walls and the use of man-
telets and covers for the men
date back to the fifth and
sixth centuries. But the first
real growth of which we have
any record was at the siege of
Veii, which lasted nine years,
thus showing great inexpert-
ness in management. Here
the Romans first used walls of

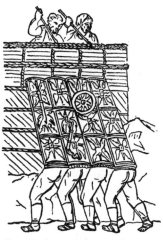

Testudo (from Column of Trajan).

circumvallation around the town and contravallation against
outside attack, as well as a mound, all of which the Greeks
had used at Platæa, thirty years before. Finally the town
was taken (395 B. C.) by digging a subterranean passage
which led to the citadel. From this time on larger progress
was made. Catapults were soon introduced, having been
adopted from Sicily, according to Diodorus. Rams came later.
These siege devices have been fully described in connection
with Alexander's army.

On the whole the Romans had, from their adaptability and
the necessity for being always ready for war, developed a
system which promised far greater eventual results than the
system of the Greeks.

Such, briefly, was the growth of the art of war and its
status among the Romans down to the siege of Veii and somewhat later. At the time of the Punic wars there remained
in principle the same system, but the details had been changed
in many particulars.

V.

THE ROMAN ARMY OF THE THIRD CENTURY.

THE legions were raised by a rapid and careful system, which made the maniples of even strength and material. The recruits took an oath, were armed, and only then had the eagles delivered to their charge. The consul, powerless in Rome, was all-powerful in camp. Arrived at rendezvous, the organization was completed. The arms and equipment were helmet, shield, breastplate for the heavy foot, greaves, sword, pike and lance, all excellent of their kind. The special Roman weapon was the gladius. The cavalry was not as good as the foot, but during the Second Punic War it was much improved. The number of men in the legion varied in certain epochs from three thousand to six thousand men. The usual number was forty-two hundred foot and three hundred horse. The term *legion* meant one Roman and one allied legion, all told not far from ten thousand men, when full. The consular army was two *legions*, that is, from eighteen thousand to twenty-five thousand men. The early unit of service was the century, but each two centuries were later ployed together into a maniple ; and each set of maniples of principes, hastati and triarii, with its share of velites and horse, was a cohort. The cohort then became the unit. Intervals between maniples equaled their front, and the maniples of hastati and principes stood checkerwise. With cavalry on the flanks, a legion of ten thousand men covered a front of three quarters of a mile, and had a depth of about nine hundred feet. In line of battle, the Roman legions were in the centre, the allied on the flanks. The consular army covered a front of one and one half miles. The Romans were fast but careless marchers, and subject to surprises, until Hannibal taught them caution. They still invariably attacked. Battle was opened by the velites, followed up by the first line and decided by the second and third, the cavalry meanwhile fighting on the flanks. What lent the legion mobility was also a source of weakness, — the intervals. When they met an enemy who was apt to penetrate into these, they advanced the second line into or close up to the intervals of the first. The youth were still trained as soldiers from their earliest years, and drilled not only in the "Tactics," but in mock combat and camp-fortification as well. Labor was unremitting. The evolutions of the Romans at drill were much the same as to-day, and commands were given by the trumpets. The eagle of the legion was the rallying-point, as sacred as the "colors" of a regiment of modern days.

In the epoch to which this volume is devoted, the Roman army had not undergone material alteration, but it had been much improved in its details. The *jus militiæ* was still unchanged. Only citizens, with the exceptions already existing, were allowed or compelled to serve. By constant use in war the organization had become better settled.

Polybius tells us how the armies were recruited. When the consuls had been elected the war-tribunes were chosen, twenty-four in all, fourteen from those who had served five years and ten from those who had served ten. On the day set for the levy the citizens fit for military duty were assembled on the Capitoline hill, by means of a flag hoisted on the Capitol and public announcement by heralds. Later on, the field of Mars was the rendezvous. The arrivals grouped themselves in their tribes, at this time thirty-five in number. To raise the usual four legions, two for each consular army, the war-tribunes were first distributed by a sort of rote to the legions, six to each. The tribunes of each legion then by lot called up each tribe in turn and selected four men, as much alike in qualifications as was possible. One of these was assigned to each legion. This method proceeded by turn among the tribes until the required number had been chosen, and each legion was thus served as nearly alike as possible.

The recruits then took the oath, one of their number speaking for all: "I swear that I will obey my superiors, and use all my strength to carry out that which they order," and the rest, coming close to him, one by one, repeated "I also." This oath varied at different epochs.

No consul, by law, might exercise command within the boundary of the city of Rome. The chosen recruits were therefore assembled on a given day in their respective legions, unarmed, at the most convenient locality outside the city limits, were assigned to whatever part of the legion was legal or expedient, and armed and equipped according to assignment. The quæstors then delivered to their keeping the eagles, which had been kept for safety in the treasury in the Capitol. The consul, before joining the army, paid certain rites at the Temple of Mars, shook the shield and lance of the

statue of the war-god, and not until then assumed the appropriate garb of his office. He then joined the army. Before marching, the army cleansed itself by appropriate sacrifices (lustratio).

War, as with the Greeks, was declared by heralds, who first formally demanded satisfaction for injury done, and in case of refusal cast a bloodstained spear upon the territory of the opponent. Battles were preceded by sacrifices and religious ceremonies, and after a victory sacrifices were renewed.

Such were the formal proceedings. But these were often shortened by the requirements of haste, or were simplified when large bodies were raised. The four consular legions, in-

Consul with War Cloak.

cluding the cavalry, could be set on foot within twenty-four hours. L. Quintius Cincinnatus, dictator in 457 B. C., raised, armed and equipped the legions, and set forth on his march between sunrise and sunset of one day. One entire campaign in 445 B. C., beginning with the calling in of the tribes and including their armament, one day for the march out, the defeat of the enemy five miles beyond the boundary of Roman territory, and one day for the march home, was comprised in the space of four days.

In the cavalry only those knights (equites) could serve who were rated as own-ing fifty thousand asses. There was a general lack of horses and a decided preference for foot duty among the Romans, largely owing to the expense of cavalry service. In early days the Roman cavalry was very lightly armed, — much like ve-lites, in fact, — and was

Roman Cavalryman (from Column of Trajan).

correspondingly ineffective; later they were given helmet, breastplate, greaves, a shield, sword and stout lance, but none of these were as heavy as those of the infantry. The horsemen received their horses from the state. A gold ring

Velite.

was their badge. They stood (counting Romans and allies) in the ratio of about one to ten of the infantry, the same proportion as the three hundred cavalry to the old legion of three thousand men. They took the same oath.

The raising of legions among the allies was undertaken at the call of the consuls in the same manner and at the same time, but by somewhat simpler means. They then marched to the rendezvous and joined the Roman legions.

Arrived at rendezvous, the recruits were usually assigned

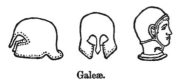

Galeæ.

by the tribunes: those from seventeen to twenty-five years old to the light foot, now all called velites; those from twenty-five to thirty to the hastati; those from thirty to forty to the principes; those from forty to forty-five to the triarii. Exceptions were, however, made in recognition of ability or service.

The arms and equipment were then issued to all. To each of the velites were given a leathern helmet (galea) lined with sponge and leather, a small round wooden shield (parma) three feet in diameter and a good protection against arrows or sling-stones, a

Ocrea.

sword and seven darts. These darts were usually thirty inches long and about the thickness of the finger, but their form varied materially. Their tips were long and slender, and after they had struck an object were generally so bent as to be useless to the enemy until repaired.

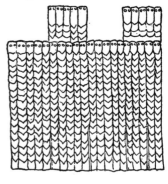

Darts.

To the legionaries, hastati and principes, were given as armor a leather helmet covered or strengthened with

Lorica.

iron, and ornamented with red and black plumes (cassis);

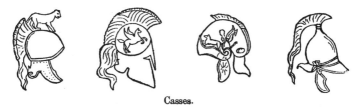

Casses.

a breastplate made of metal scales sewed upon stout leather, which covered shoulder, breast and abdomen (lorica);

greaves for the legs (ocrea), much like the Greek, but particularly stout for the right leg — for the Roman legionary soldier calculated to go at the enemy with his sword more than any other weapon — and a large square, curved shield (scutum), semi-cylindrical on a radius of about nine inches, made of stout, well-fitted wood, leather-covered and iron-edged, and often having in the middle a knob with

Scutum (Trajan Column).

which the legionary was expert in pushing and striking his enemy. His weapons were the terrible gladius, a two-edged sword of Spanish origin, with twenty-inch blade two inches wide, used both to cut and thrust, and vastly better than

Pilum.

the Greek sword, which was a mere knife; a heavy lance (pilum) of cornel wood, whose dimensions are variously given, but probably two inches square, with rounded corners, at one time five and a half feet long in the shaft, with nine-inch iron, at another with three feet shaft and two and one half feet iron, of Italian invention ; and a lighter lance (hasta) of equal length. The head of the lances was apt to be made with hooks or fins, so that they could catch an enemy's shield and pull it off his arm. The Romans had first used square shields ; they then adopted from an Hellenic source a round shield ; and lastly took up, not from the Samnites as tradition says, but probably from the Greeks, the cylindrical scutum.

The triarii, sometimes called pilani (and hence the hastati and principes antepilani), were the " Old Guard," to be called in to decide a victory or forestall defeat. They had, in lieu of the heavy lance, a pike which at times varied from ten to fourteen feet, and sometimes carried several darts in the left hand within the shield.

Gladius.

Gladius (from Pompeii).

This whole equipment, which, however, was changed from epoch to epoch, so that it is difficult to define it at any one time, was excellent. Defensively, while protecting the soldier, it allowed him the free use of body and limbs. The weapons were of thorough workmanship, and

Hasta.

the sword, in the hands of the practiced soldier, could penetrate any armor, as could the lance, well thrown. In the wars with Greece, Livy relates that the Romans inflicted

blows with the gladius which cut off arms and legs, and even
severed the head from the body of an oppo-
nent. It was the favorite weapon. The soldiers were trained to serve in any capacity,
and the heavy legionaries could act as skirmishers, the velites could charge in close order and the horse fight on foot.

The cavalry was by no means as good.
This arm had never been a favorite with
the Romans. It was considered as a mere
auxiliary to the foot. The horsemen's equipment was not as thoroughly made, nor were
their weapons as well fashioned, as those of
the foot. Even at the beginning of the Punic
wars the horsemen had no armor, only leather

Hastæ.

shields which the rain weakened, poor swords, and lances

Princeps.

Hastatus.

far from stout enough. They preferred to fight on
foot rather than
mounted. More-
over, the Roman
was not as natu-
rally a horseman as
were the wild tribes
from which Hanni-
bal drew his cav-
alry. It was, in-
deed, in this that
Hannibal saw and
used his great ad-
vantage. But the
Romans learned

the lesson, and before the end of the Second Punic War

had placed their cavalry on an excellent footing, giving it
helmets and armor, greaves and boots, darts, twelve-
foot lances, sharp at both ends, and a curved sword.
The cavalryman had neither saddle, which was introduced in the fourth century A. D., nor stirrups, which
date from the sixth. He rode on two blankets, the

inner one felt or leather, held in place
and fastened together by surcingle, breast-
strap and crupper. These were often
ornamented to a high degree. A bridle
completed the harness. In his left hand
the cavalryman carried his shield and bridle, and kept his right free for sword or
lance. No wonder, one might say, that
the Roman cavalryman, thus burdened,
was not effective. And yet Alexander's

Triarius.　　Companions, the most splendid body of
cavalry of antiquity, were armed in like manner. Rather
wonder that the ancient cavalryman ever was good.

Roman Cavalryman (from the Arch of Constantine).

Exactly how much space the cavalryman took up in the

ranks we do not know, but it is most credibly stated at five feet front by ten feet depth. Scipio Africanus later became the father of the Roman horseman, and made the arm effective and reliable. The description of the arms of the Roman soldier is carefully made by the old authors; the pictorial delineation, such as the procession on the column of Trajan, varies much from the histories. This is to be referred to the different eras of which the books and monuments treat. The variation is not material.

The number of men in the legion varied considerably at different times. In the third century B. C. there were still supposed to be twelve hundred velites, twelve hundred principes, twelve hundred hastati and six hundred triarii, besides three hundred horse, or in allied legions six hundred horse. The number of the triarii and horse was apt to remain the same, but the others varied so much at times that the legion was all the way from four thousand two hundred to six thousand men. After Cannæ there was five thousand foot in the legions; Scipio in Africa had fifty-two hundred; Æmillius Paullus in Macedon six thousand. Two hundred of the horse of the allied legions, added to eight hundred and forty of the foot, made up a special body called extraordinarii, who, with those of the other legions, were a sort of reserve body under immediate command of the general. Of this body, one fifth — the best of the men (ablecti) — formed his body-guard. These were hostages for the fidelity of their respective cities.

Other subject nations, not allies, were not figured in with the Roman legions, but their forces kept their own organization, being used as auxiliaries merely, and having no set place in line.

The term " legion " was apt to mean one Roman and one allied legion, nearly ten thousand men. Thus the usual consular army of two legions was really two Roman and two allied legions, eighteen to twenty thousand men, of which eighteen hundred were horsemen. If the two consuls were together, they had, during the Second Punic War, not far from forty thousand men.

In combat, the swaying to and fro of the lines often isolated the unit of service, separated as it was by intervals from its neighbors, and the Romans had gradually found that the century unit was somewhat too small to combat successfully on open ground with troops in more compact order. Though it had done abundantly well against the nations with some-

Maniple.

what similar organization which it had had to meet, it had found difficulty in resisting the masses of the Gauls and the phalanxes of Pyrrhus, and before the Punic wars they had combined each two neighboring centuries into one body, making a maniple. This added strength without loss of flexibility and ease of manœuvring. The light troops and the cavalry remained as they were. The three lines were also changed so as again to put the hastati in the lead, then the principes, then the triarii. This gave the first shock in action with the youngest and presumably most fiery troops, and followed it up with the older and steadier. Each of the two first lines, not counting officers, was thus in ten maniples of one hundred and twenty men each, in twelve files ten deep, and each was still divisible into two centuries or twelve decuries. The maniples of the triarii were but sixty strong, in six files ten deep. The velites, though numbered with the hastati and

the principes, sixty to each maniple, had no special place in
line. If the legion was nu-
merically strengthened, it
was done by adding more
men to each maniple of hastati and principes. Thus,
after Cannæ, the legion,
made up to over five thou-

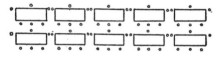

Turma of Cavalry.

sand footmen, had sixteen hundred hastati, sixteen hundred
principes, six hundred triarii, all in files ten deep, and from

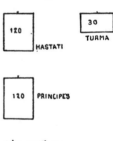

Ala of Cavalry.

twelve hundred to sixteen hundred velites. The horse remained the same.

The space allowed to each man is also variously stated.

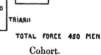

It seems to have been the ground he
stood on, plus three feet between him
and his neighbor, thus being about
five feet front by four feet and a half
deep. This gave him ample room to
use his weapons. It was nearly twice
the space allowed the phalangite in
battle order. He was drilled, however,
to close this distance down to three
or even one and a half feet to resist
cavalry or to form a tortoise. The
maniples still stood checkerwise in line
of battle, and two hundred and fifty feet or more were between the lines, as had been the case with the century formation.

The cavalry of each legion was divided into ten turmæ of thirty horsemen, and each turma into three decuriæ of ten horsemen. The turmæ stood in ten files three deep. The ten turmæ in line were called a wing (ala).

The maniples and turmæ were all numbered, and a maniple of hastati, one of principes and one of triarii, from front to rear, with the velites who belonged to them and one turma, were termed a cohort. From the right, the first maniple each of hastati, principes and triarii, their velites

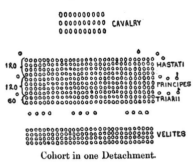

Cohort in one Detachment.

and the first turma, made up the first cohort of the legion. There were thus ten cohorts in each legion, each cohort having troops of all arms and numbering four hundred and fifty men, namely, one hundred and twenty velites, one hundred and twenty hastati, one hundred and twenty principes, sixty triarii and thirty cavalry, or up to five hundred and

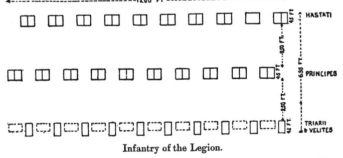

Infantry of the Legion.

seventy men, namely, one hundred and sixty each of velites, hastati and principes, sixty triarii and thirty cavalry. In this fashion, either a maniple or a cohort could be treated as the tactical unit, according to the duty required. The cohort was our battalion. Later its organization was materially changed.

The front space occupied by a legion, that is, one Roman and one allied legion of forty-two hundred men each, plus three hundred Roman and six hundred allied horse, total nine thousand three hundred men, may, in round numbers, be thus figured out: —

Infantry, each maniple with 12 files, each of 5 feet
front, making 60 feet front, or for 20 maniples, 10 in the Roman and 10 in the allied
legion. . . . . 1,200 feet
To this add 20 intervals between the 10 mani-
ples of 60 feet each, or . . . . 1,200 feet 2,400 feet
Cavalry, 900 men in 3 ranks or 300 files, each file
of 5 feet . . . . 1,500 feet
Intervals between cavalry and infantry, say . . 100 feet
Total . . . . 4,000 feet

The velites took up no front space. The legion thus covered about three quarters of a mile of front.

This gave eight thousand four hundred infantry to a frontage of twenty-four hundred feet or seven hundred and forty metres. There were thus but eleven men to each metre front as against twenty-eight men in the phalanx, and six or seven men, including reserves, in modern armies.

The depth of the legion may be thus reckoned: —

The hastati, file of 10 men at 4½ feet = 45 feet,
and the interval at its rear = 250 feet, say 295 feet
The principes, do. . . . . 295 feet
The triarii, do. 45   635 feet
The velites when out in front may have taken up . . . . . 265 feet
Making the depth of the legion . . . . 900 feet

The cavalry on the wings, if in one line, was less than forty feet deep. Thus the legion was a body of four thousand

feet front largely made up of intervals, by some nine hundred
feet depth, reckoned from the skirmishing line backward.

In the line of battle of the consular army
the Roman legions occupied the centre, the
allied were on their right and left. The entire cavalry was on the flanks of the army,
or in front or in rear as needed. At times,
placed between the lines, it broke out through
the intervals with good effect. The allied
extraordinarii and ablecti made up a special
reserve, whose place was determined by the
leader, and was often between the flank of
the infantry and the cavalry. The consular
army with its two Roman and two allied legions and intervals between them thus occupied a front space of a mile and a half or
over, with a depth of nine hundred feet.
The intervals between cavalry turmæ, and
between foot and horse are uncertain. The
exact frontage cannot be determined.

Such was the formation of the legion during the Punic wars. Later, the principes
were put back into the first line, the hastati
in second, and the velites, if not in front, in
a third line, while the triarii were held in a
sort of reserve still farther back or left to
guard the camp or baggage. This change
was made from the experience of the Second
Punic War, which showed that fiery assault
alone was not enough. It must be stanch
and lasting as well as gallant.

Some modern authorities read the ancient authors to give
the Roman soldier a total space of only three feet. Were this

so, the legion would occupy a correspondingly smaller front. The legion of Vegetius differs materially from those of Polybius and Livy, and the details are not reconcilable.

The Romans, up to the battle of Lake Trasimene, were careless about their order of march. The armies moved from one camp to the next in any convenient manner and without precautions, and were liable to surprises and ambuscades. Fabius Cunctator did much to obliterate this evil, and there was introduced a regular method of march (agmen) in one or more columns, by cohorts, or variously by the flank. In front, as a van, went the extraordinarii and part of the velites; then, if the army was marching by the right flank, the first allied legion, with its impedimenta; then the first Roman legion, the second Roman legion, the second allied legion, each with its train. Following was a rear-guard of the ablecti and the rest of the velites. By the left flank the order was reversed. The cavalry usually rode with the baggage train. In the front and on the flanks

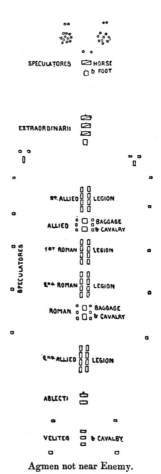

Agmen not near Enemy.

were thrown out a large number of scouts or flankers (speculatores) to give notice of the presence of the enemy. In retreat the extraordinarii and part of the velites were the

rear-guard. In passing a defile the column had to be ployed
into smaller space. The above order of march was suited
to the open country of a great part of Italy. But, except
the presence of artillery, all the difficulties of marching an
army to-day existed in greater measure in the time of the
Punic wars. The order was changed from day to day, to
make it easier for the troops and equalize the foraging.

In open country, in the presence of the enemy, the march

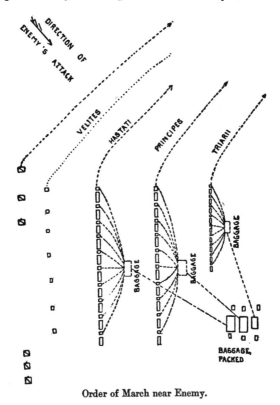

Order of March near Enemy.

was conducted by the flank in three columns, hastati, principes, triarii, the baggage of each maniple preceding it, so
that there would be no long train for the enemy to attack.

The baggage could readily turn out of the ranks and park, and the legions quickly form front to right, left or forward. The presence of the enemy on the right or left would dictate whether the march should be left or right in front. The velites and cavalry shielded the front and exposed flank.

As from earliest times, the Romans still always attacked. No nation ever grasped the idea of the initiative so firmly. Nothing but their dread of Hannibal ever altered this habit. The sign for battle having been given, the troops, duly prepared and often spurred on by a battle speech (allocutio) from the general, moved out of camp and drew up in line not far therefrom. They looked upon the intrenched camp as a fortress, and fought near by it if possible. All the baggage and heavy burden of the soldiers remained in camp under a specially detailed guard, — in time of great danger the triarii.

Polybius and Vegetius tell us that the Romans had seven orders of battle. But these were the development of the books rather than the field. In the period to which we refer the orders were confined to the parallel and some variations running towards the oblique, as we shall see. As a rule, only the parallel was used, and the cavalry operated round the enemy's flanks. A wedge was sometimes formed to pierce the enemy's centre, and turning movements by detachments or by one wing were common. The oblique order, as taught by Epaminondas and Alexander, was not known.

Battle was opened by the signal of the trumpets. At this, the army gave its battle-cry, from the sound of which the general could often foretell success or failure, or at least gauge the moral tone of the men. At the second signal the army advanced, at the quick-step. A third signal was sometimes given at the proper distance for the line to take the double-quick, which it did with loud shouts, the clashing of lance on shield and the sounding of all the horns and bugles,

— the better to encourage the men and demoralize the enemy.

The velites advanced in open order in front of the legionaries, hurled their darts and attacked in small companies, to tire the enemy and bring him into disorder. When the legion advanced, the velites retired through the intervals, part falling back behind the triarii, and the rest sustaining the hastati and principes, furnishing them with darts and spears, and carrying the wounded to the rear. For the latter service there was also a special corps of *deportates*.

The hastati now attacked the enemy, — or the principes, when these were in first line. At a distance of eight to ten paces from the enemy they hurled their spears, the javelins first and then the pike. The first ranks are described as bending slightly, to allow those in the rear to fire over their heads, though there was space enough between the men for this purpose. They then fell to with the sword. This attack might last a few minutes, or it might last for hours. If the first line was beaten back, it retired rapidly through the intervals of the second, or rather the second line advanced into or through its intervals, to sustain it or take its place. A tired line could be thus reinforced or entirely rested. The second line, or the first and second together, now attacked in like manner. If driven back, the triarii advanced to the attack.

These veterans had been waiting their turn. They are portrayed as having one knee on the ground, and holding their shields aloft to ward off the enemy's long-range missiles, though at their distance in the rear this would seem to be unnecessary. They now stood ready to make the third and final attack, either alone or in connection with the defeated lines, which may have formed in their intervals or in their rear, while the extraordinarii still remained for a last effort. The cavalry, during this time, had made its charges upon the enemy's horse, and, if successful, followed it up or turned upon the flanks and rear of the enemy's line. The use of ambush on the enemy's flank or flanks was common.

If the enemy was defeated, the cavalry followed him up with the velites, and the extraordinarii were in support. The legion followed after in three lines as before. In case of retreat, the cavalry, velites, extraordinarii and triarii covered the movement.

Of course all this was only the prescribed rule. As in all battles there was the usual wavering of the lines, the success of one group and the failure of its neighbors, the uncertainty and risk, the gallantry of some cohorts and the demoralization of others, the difficulty of managing a line perhaps two miles in length, and all the attendant features of armed conflict. The rule was what should be done; circumstances dictated what was done.

Such was the technical battle-method. But the Romans more than any other people, even the Greeks, excepting always Alexander and his lieutenants, paid heed to the ground on which they fought or the position of the enemy, and altered their dispositions accordingly. Their battles have a general similarity of character, but all vary much in detail.

One decided weakness of the legion was the very thing which lent it mobility, — its intervals. In its conflict with the Gauls and Spaniards, whose preponderance of force was great and whose individual bravery was marked, it was several times compromised by the enemy making his way in groups between the intervals and taking the maniples in flank and rear. This danger the Romans learned to overcome by moving the second line up into the intervals of the first, or by reducing the distance between the lines so as to cover these intervals effectually. We shall see quite another form of cohort used by Marius and by Cæsar in his Gallic wars. But at this era, whatever the exceptional changes, the formation prescribed by the " Tactics " was with the intervals mentioned.

To refer again to the groundwork of the Roman plan of military organization, — the training of youth. In this they varied wholly from the Greeks. They did not teach the young citizen the theory of war, but gave him a practical drilling in what he would have to do when at seventeen years of age he would be drafted into the ranks. They had no schools or teachers of science; they considered such learning unnecessary — certainly less excellent than the habit of obedience, coupled with strength and the expert use of arms. Thus they laid the foundation of exemplary discipline and a practical knowledge of what war was among the rank and file. The higher military education was left to the richer and more noble families to give by private instruction to their sons. But these sons, in common with all the rest, must report at given times on the field of Mars for drill. No exceptions were made. Here, under experienced drill-masters and headed by old soldiers, they were practiced in the soldier's setting-up, marching in correct time and style, the run, climbing heights and walls, singly and in squads, with and without arms and baggage, jumping ditches and obstacles, vaulting and swimming. They were taught the use of all the weapons they would be called on to handle, for which purpose heavy posts were set up at which the youths shot with bows, cast darts and spears, and on which they made sham attacks with the sword; and they were instructed how to use their shields so as to protect the body in every position. In these exercises all weapons were much heavier, Polybius says twice the weight of the actual ones, to inure the youth to his work. In addition to the above, heavy loads were carried, intrenchments dug, camps fortified and such works attacked and defended.

Once in service, the soldier had yet harder work to do. He was steadily drilled in the field, in camp and in garrison. But for proficiency here, handsome rewards were given. Constant occupation was believed to be the best means of keeping up the soldier's morale, — a truism which is not always acted on to-day. Hence practice-marches with full equipment and baggage, manœuvres, fortification so far as it was essential for the camp, were common; and the men were not infrequently put on public works. The vast amphitheatres, aqueducts and roads of Rome were largely the creation of the Roman soldier.

Such preparation of youth and soldier enabled Rome speedily to raise large armies of men fully ready for their task, fit for immediate duty and able to undergo great fatigues and perform exceptional work in every weather and under all conditions. Moreover, the Romans seemed unusually free from sickness and camp epidemics, — the very reverse of the Carthaginians.

All this must be borne in mind when we come to the question of what troops Hannibal had to encounter. Historians are wont to refer to Hannibal's men as veterans and to the Romans as raw recruits. At the outset such were the conditions, but they did not long obtain. The Roman raw levies needed but one or two short campaigns and a slight degree of success to be superior as soldiers to all but a few of the best Punic troops.

The tactical manœuvres of the Romans did not vary much from those of the Greeks, from whom they were unquestionably derived. But in its drill the legion was much more elastic and quick in motion than the average phalanx, though it might be hard to draw a comparison between it and the phalanx of Philip and Alexander. It was wont to move forward and to the rear, and by either flank; to open and

close order, ploy and deploy, double ranks and wheel; in
short, perform all the operations known to modern minor-tactics. The ancient minor-tactics were very cleverly devised,
and executed with the skill which comes of constant practice. The infantry common-time step was one hundred and
twenty to the minute, the quick one hundred and forty-five,
the double-quick and run according to circumstances.

The cavalry-drill was in this period much simpler than the
infantry. Not till after the Second Punic War did this arm
attain much suppleness in manœuvres. Scipio Africanus
was the first to introduce good cavalry tactics, which he did
in Spain. Polybius gives us interesting details of these.
The individual was well drilled, alone and in squads, and

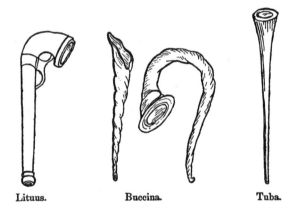

Lituus.　　　　　Buccina.　　　　　Tuba.

the turma was practiced in wheeling to right, left and rear;
in forming column to the right or left or forward from the
centre; in forming line with intervals or without; in ploying into column of more or less files, and in marching to the
front or by the rear rank, with many other exercises. All
these evolutions were practiced at every speed.

The usual musical instruments employed by the Romans
were four; the lituus, which was a horn made of leather-

covered wood curved at the end, was chiefly used by the cavalry; the tuba, made of copper, two and a half feet long, straight, was the infantry bugle; the buccina, a shell-shaped trumpet, and the cornu, also a curved trumpet, lighter in shape, were in general use.

The difference in tone of these several horns, and the variety of notes and calls which could be blown

Cornu.

on them, made them very useful. They were employed in camp, on the march, in battle, to indicate various evolutions, call the men to certain duties or meals, or change guards, apparently much more than bugle-calls are used to-day. The leader had a special call, classicum, which he alone might use. Drills were performed by the sound of the trumpet. Com-

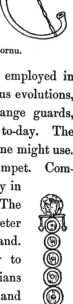

mands for all the manœuvres necessary in battle could be and were so given. The signal blown by the general-trumpeter was repeated throughout the command. There were no firearms or artillery to drown the trumpet-blast. The musicians belonged to the centuries, maniples, and cohorts, some generally to the legion, and each leader of a detachment had his special buglers.

Flags, like ours, were used only to call troops together. The standard was originally a simple affair, such as a bundle of hay tied on a lance; later it was a carved human fist on a lance, — hence *manipulus*, a handful or squad. The "colors" of the legion were an eagle of silver or gold mounted on a staff,

Cohort Standard.

Maniple Standard.

Vexillum (from Arch of Constantine).

with the number of the organization affixed to it on
a bit of stuff. The eagle
of the legion was carried
by the first centurion of
the first maniple of the
triarii. This man, called
primipilus, was held in
especial honor, and often
commanded the legion un-
der the tribunes. The
eagle was more sacred than
even the colors are to us.
The principes and hastati were called antesignani. The cavalry colors (vexillum) were scarlet.

Legionary Eagle.

VI.

RANK AND DISCIPLINE. — EQUIPMENT AND RATIONS.

RANK in the legion was: commander, who was consul or prætor; legate, or general of division; tribune, in turn battalion or brigade commander; centurion or captain; sub-centurion or lieutenant; signifer, ensign; decurion, corporal. The staff comprised quæstors, who were paymasters, quartermasters, commissaries and ordnance officers; contubernales or aides-de-camp; officers who were topographical engineers and scouts; augurs and priests. The clothing was tunic, at times short trowsers, cloaks, sandals, the cost of all of which was deducted from the soldier's pay, as were also lost arms and horses. The cavalryman was held to a higher grade of character and vigor than the footman. Unground wheat and beef issues made up the ration, which the men cooked themselves. They eat morning and evening. The Roman soldier carried, in addition to the burden of the modern footman, two or more stakes for the wall of the daily camp. His load was fully half as much again as that of the modern soldier. Armed, equipped and loaded as he was, he had but to lay down his baggage and put on his helmet and he was ready for battle. The baggage-train consisted of pack-horses and occasionally carts, and the doctors, servants and artificers accompanied it. Women were excluded from camp. Discipline was rigid. Rewards were generous, punishments immediate and cruel. The man's honor was strongly appealed to. He could gain much by good service; he was sure to suffer by neglect or crime. The Romans were careless though rapid marchers, until Hannibal taught them logistics; and their battle-method not only grew in art under the same great master, but he first showed them what strategy could do. The successful general was saluted as Imperator and allowed a triumph. Booty was divided by a strict rule. The main structure of the legion did not change for centuries; its details were frequently altered. At no one period can its every detail be given with certainty.

RANK in the legion, from the lesser up, was as follows: —

Decurions, set over the ten men of each file, — non-commissioned officers, — were the front men in the files, and made up the front rank of the maniple. Each maniple also had a standard-bearer (signifer), a chosen man who carried the maniple-flag (signum), and was distinguished by a helmet covered with a lion's or bear's head, and a trumpeter.

Sub-centurions, commanders of half a century, — subalterns, — appointed by the war-tribunes at the suggestion of the centurions, and acting as file-closers in rear of the maniples, to see that the rear ranks did their duty.

Centurions, originally set over the century of one hundred men, — captains, — appointed by the general, upon choice of the war - tribunes. Each maniple had two, a senior and a junior, whose places were on the right and left of the decurions in the front rank. The centurion who was the eagle - bearer had singular privileges. He was a knight, and could attend councils of war. The above-named officers were selected for courage, experience and good sense, and all wore badges of rank on

Signifer.

Centurion.

Eagle-bearer.

helmet and armor, and bore stout sticks of vine with which to inflict summary chastisement for minor offenses. In the cavalry, each turma was commanded by a decurio, having as lieutenant a sub-decurio. There was at times a third decurio as well as three file-closers. The senior decurio commanded the whole body of horse in a legion.

War-tribunes. Of these there were at first four to a legion — one senior and one of the juniors to each line; later six, or two to each line; still later ten, one for each cohort. They were nominated by the burgesses, and were in some respects like our staff-officers. The seniors sat in councils of war. The war-tribunes commanded the legion in turn, unless there was a legate in command.

Legates. These were at first civil envoys of the senate, who should advise with the leader and his council, and replace the leader in case of his death or disablement; later they were chosen by the general from among the war-tribunes. They were like our general-officers, and were placed in command of detachments or legions.

Thus the ranks, from the highest down, ran: consul, prætor or quæstor who was army-leader or general; legates, generals of division; tribunes, who in turn acted as brigadiers or as colonels, or when there was one for each cohort, as battalion-chiefs or majors; centurions or captains, sub-centurions or lieutenants; signifers, ensigns or color-sergeants; decurions or corporals. The rank was not as extended as in the Macedonian phalanx. The system of rotation in command obliged the higher officers to serve in subordinate capacity the most part of the time. This appears to have worked well among the Romans, though usually a bad plan.

Curiously, the army-leader, according to Plutarch, must legally serve on foot, or at least must ask permission of the senate to serve mounted. He was thus held to give an example of subordination to the legions. If two consuls were present with the army, each as formerly commanded in turn for twenty-four hours. On occasions of grave necessity there was the dictator, and his magister equitum, or cavalry commander. In three hundred and sixty-four years (497 to 133 B. C.) there were eighty-two dictators, showing their frequent election. Præfects commanded the allied legions and cohorts. The other officers of the allied legions were the same. In later days, when the Romans had many armies in the field, the command of these was given, in each province, to pro-consuls, pro-prætors and pro-quæstors, men who had occupied and retired from the dignity of consul, prætor and quæstor. These were held to a strict accountability; but the Roman senate wisely abstained from public investigation and punishment of mere misfortune in command, lest the gravity of the situation should alarm the

Army-leader in Mantle.   Lictor.

legions, or the punishment should weaken the standing of their representative. In this they were more discreet than the Greeks or Carthaginians.

The army-leader wore as a distinguishing mark a purple mantle, rode a horse very richly caparisoned, and was accompanied by lictors, who varied in number, according to a fixed rule, from two to twelve. These were a sort of non-commissioned staff, or provost-marshals, and had especially punishments under their control. They had as badge an axe tied in a bundle of rods, and came almost invariably from the lower classes, especially freedmen.

The general staff consisted of quæstors, of equal rank with legates, who transacted the business of our paymasters, quartermasters, commissaries, and ordnance officers, and who, their number being limited, were not always with an army, and were then replaced by a legate; of contubernales, tent-mates, who were our volunteer aides-de-camp; of officers whose peculiar duty was to make and break camp, (mensores and censores); of those corresponding to our topographical engineers (ante-mensores and ante-censores); of exploratores and sulcatores, that is, scouts; of assistants to the quæstors, or quartermaster and commissary sergeants; and finally of the augurs and priests, who always accompanied an army, and who foretold success or failure from the flight of birds, the feeding of hens, the entrails of sacrificial victims and other common occurrences. Nothing was undertaken without their advice and the customary divinations; but the able leader frequently managed to make their opinions and divinations coincide with his own ideas.

In early days, as above stated, the Roman soldiers had served without pay; from 405 B. C. — or perhaps earlier — the pay of the soldier was three and one third asses a day for the foot, ten asses for the cavalry, when the man furnished his own horse, six and two thirds asses for sub-officers of infantry and other cavalrymen. This was raised during the Second Punic War, on account of a much greater reduction in value of the as, to five and a half, sixteen and a half and eleven respectively, and so remained till Cæsar's day. This scale only shows relative compensation, for the actual purchasing value of the as at various times is quite indefinite. From this pay was deducted a given amount for arms, rations, horses, forage and other issues.

The clothing was the woolen tunic, close fitting next the body to the waist, with long plaited skirt to the knee, and with a broad leather belt, to which, on the right side, hung the sword ; a field cloak, first square, later round, reaching to the knee, brownish-red for the men, white for officers, held by lacing or buttons at the shoulder or in front; and for wet or cold weather hooded capes of wool, of several weights, according to the season. For foot gear, sandals. During the Empire the Roman soldier wore a species of short trowsers (braccæ) to just below the knee. In earlier times his legs were bare. Braccæ are shown in the monuments decorated with Roman military subjects, as these are mostly of the imperial era. The soldier cut his hair short and shaved.

While the value of his clothing and rations were deducted from the man's pay, this was no hardship, for one or two days' pay was equivalent to a month's rations. The capture of much booty often resulted in these deductions being merely nominal. Lost arms or equipments the soldier was held to replace. The cavalryman was similarly dressed, but had a long white purple-edged cloak for occasions of ceremony.

The arms have already been described. These were made by armorers especially employed, and later in arsenals duly equipped. To provide these was part of the quæstor's duty, and the manufacture appears to have been excellently organized. They remained the same for centuries.

The government furnished the cavalry horses. The citizens serving in the cavalry were held to a high grade of physical and moral ability. A yearly inspection in midsummer was made, and rigid requirements were enforced. Any testimony showing lack of courage, or indolent or weakly habits, inexorably excluded a knight from this service. The horses were individually inspected, and if an animal appeared to have been badly cared for he was rejected, and the knight lost his chance for honorable employment. After lapse of his ten years (or ten campaigns) the horse was returned by the knight to the government through the quæstors. The animal seems to have been hardy and serviceable.

Unground wheat was issued as ration, once in eight to thirty days, at the rate of four Roman measures, not far from one to one and a half bushels a month for the foot-soldier. This was between one and a half and two pounds of wheat a day, — what we should call a very scanty ration, if this was the whole of it. But beef cattle were also used, and no doubt generously issued, and the foragers or countrymen brought into camp fresh fruits and vegetables whenever the season warranted. The cavalryman received thrice as much, for self and two servants, beside forage for three horses. The allies received somewhat less. This corn the men carried, ground in hand-mills, and made into the usual cakes or porridge. They eat morning and evening only, — the common custom, — a slight breakfast taken standing, and a heartier supper, at which the men reclined; the latter was eaten in the first watch, six to nine P. M. Before an intended battle a more liberal breakfast was usual.

The purchase of rations in bulk was the affair of the quæstors. In the enemy's country rations were collected by forced contributions. Victual was stored in suitable magazines.

The burden carried by the Roman soldier is scarcely credible, though from youth up he was trained to bearing heavy loads at drill. The foot-soldier carried all through the campaign, on the right shoulder, two or more posts or palisades for the stockade of the nightly camp. These were quite long and two or three inches thick. Slung to the end of these was his bag of corn, calculated to last him at least two weeks. His shield, lance and as many as seven darts he carried on his left arm. The helmet, if not worn, hung by its strap upon

the breast. At times he must also carry axe, saw, spade, scythe, a rope, a basket and a pot to cook his rations in. His cloak was rolled up and slung on his back. About extra clothing or sandals we do not hear. All this, with the armor, made up a weight which had to be borne under the sun, dust and sand of Italy or Africa, through the heavy mud of spring and fall, through the everlasting snows of the mountains.

Legionary on the March.

The weight carried in modern days by the soldiers of various countries, including clothing worn, runs from fifty-six to sixty-four pounds. It is made up roughly of the following items: Clothing, say 18 pounds; rifle and cartridges, 20 pounds; knapsack, packed, 13 pounds; haversack, packed, 5 pounds; intrenching tools, 4 pounds; belts, etc., 2 pounds; canteen, filled, 2 pounds. Total, 64 pounds. Including his clothing, the Roman soldier, with the load above given, must have carried something over eighty-five pounds, much more than half his own average weight.

The Romans justly named the train-baggage impedimenta, and their constant effort was to increase the weight the soldier could bear and decrease what followed the army on wagons and beasts of burden.

In case of sudden attack, the footman thus accoutred had

but to lay down his posts and baggage and put on his helmet, and he was ready for the fray. The palisades and baggage were often tempora-
rily stuck up as breastworks against cavalry.

Sumpter-animals, horses, mules or ass-es, generally carried the tents and camp and garrison - equi-page, intrenching tools and necessary utensils. One pack

Army Cart (from Trajan Column).

animal per century is said to have been the ordinary allow-ance, though this seems very small. Everything was cal-culated to give the Romans a capacity to march quick and far, which was all but unequaled by any nation of anti-quity. But it took all the strength derived from constant work, as well as discipline rigidly enforced, to do it.

Among the non-combatants were doctors, the servants and slaves of the knights and offi-cers, and about two hundred artificers per legion. Women were absolutely forbidden to be seen in camp. This was a vast improvement on the habit of Alexander's army.

Pack Horse (from Trajan Column).

Obedience was more strictly enforced and persisted in among the Romans than among any nation of any age. The wisdom and skill of the found-ers of the Roman republic is in nothing more pointedly

shown than the placing upon the shoulders of a raw, obstinate and fiery population the yoke of such military discipline.
The groundwork of it rested on a judicious compounding of
rewards and punishments.   A review of the victories and
defeats of the Romans will show that so long as subordination was maintained at its proper standard, so long was
success assured.   While some Greek nations at times approached Rome in their army discipline, no nation ever possessed it combined with so much common sense and intelligence, or kept it through so many centuries.

His name and the number of each man's century — later
cohort — was painted on his shield, all shields of the same
century or cohort being of the same color, so that he was
easily identified.   No soldier might be used for private purposes, but all fatigue-duties were performed by the troops.
One mile beyond the limits of the city, the Roman general
had absolute power of life and death over every man and
officer in his army, — himself alone the judge, though indeed
it was usual for him to call a Council of War in important
cases.   Punishments were immediate and severe.   Stripes
were cruel; the Roman soldier was beaten with rods, the
allied with sticks.   Death was inflicted by beheading, hanging and flogging; the fustuarium was a species of running
the gauntlet of his fellow soldiers, who stoned or beat the
criminal, whom, if he escaped with his life, no one, not even
his family, thereafter dared harbor.   By the law of the
Twelve Tables (449 B. C.), he was condemned to death who
instigated war on Rome, betrayed a citizen to the enemy,
fought in battle without keeping his proper order, left his century or post, failed in his duty, deserted his post or his colors,
threw away his weapons or mutinied.   A body of men who
fled in battle was decimated, that is, each tenth, eighth or
even fifth man was executed; the troops were not allowed to

camp thereafter with the others, and in lieu of wheat received barley as rations. Misappropriation of booty was visited with banishment, sometimes death; deserters were beaten and sold into slavery; going over to the enemy — which any soldier was held to do who wandered beyond sound of trumpet — was punished with crucifixion in a Roman citizen, decapitation in an ally. Open disobedience was death. Sleeping on post or infraction of any rules of field or garrison-duty, stealing, false witness and minor neglects met with stripes, or even fustuarium. False claiming of an act of prowess in war was deemed stealing. Petty infractions were fined. From dishonorable dismissal, exposure in the stocks, the wearing of torn clothes as a badge of misconduct, equally with the severer penalties, no rank or influence could save any officer or soldier. Nor were these mere written statutes. They were carried out, and in such a manner that no nation of antiquity ever rivaled the Roman army in its perfect subordination and devotion to duty. It must, however, be observed that, in the early periods, the Roman citizen was of so simple a habit, so warm in his love of country, so earnest in his daily labors, so honorable and upright, that military crimes were rare and punishments infrequently ordered. The law was preventive rather than punitive. It did not always remain so.

Rewards were equally pronounced, and designed to heighten military aspirations. They consisted of promotion in rank or to a higher arm, increase of pay, presents of money, fine armor, silver and gold wreaths, necklaces, bracelets, deeds of land, freedom from taxes, pensions and shortening of service-years. Whole bodies were often thus rewarded, as well as had their standards peculiarly decorated. For freeing a body surrounded by the enemy or saving the life of a citizen, a wreath of grass or oak leaves, often ornamented with gold, was

awarded ; for first mounting a breach, a wreath of beech-
leaves wrought in gold ; for first entering the enemy's camp,
a golden crown in the form of palisades ; for any extraordinary deed of valor, a golden crown inscribed with its recital.
Whoso wounded an enemy in single combat received a spear
or lance ; whoso thus killed one a necklace, arms of honor, or,
if a knight, costly horse-equipments ; and there were many
others, often selected by the commander. All such distinc-
tions were publicly conferred, and gave the recipients peculiar honor at all times. Aged and crippled soldiers were
supported by the state or given land or positions in Roman
colonies.

Until taught by bitter experience in their defeats by Hannibal, the Romans practiced logistics little. They moved from
camp to camp without any particular order or precaution, and
were quite open to surprises. Outpost-duty was not well
done, but the Romans at all periods were rapid and untiring
marchers. After Trasimene, Fabius Cunctator saw the necessity of precaution, and the Roman marches were thereafter
more carefully conducted, with a proper van and rear-guard,
and flankers.

In consequence of the salutary lessons given the Romans
by Hannibal, battle-tactics became more scientific. But
though lacking science, the Romans, as no one else did, knew
the value of and practiced the offensive in battle. The notice to get ready for battle was the hanging of the general's
purple mantle in front of his tent. The troops prepared
their armor and weapons, ate and then moved into line in
front of the camp. The baggage was left in camp under a
special guard ; the soldier went out with only his arms. The
course of a battle has already been described. It remained
the same until, at a later day, the cohort formation was
changed. The camp enabled the Roman army to accept or
refuse battle at will.

The successful general was sometimes saluted by his troops as Imperator, and was allowed by the senate a triumph, greater or lesser (triumphus or ovatio). The former was a crowned entry into Rome and a march up to the Capitol, clad in purple and riding in a chariot, preceded by captives and spoil and followed by his army; the latter was a simpler entry on horseback, accompanied only by the plaudits of the people.

Booty, on the capture of a city, was collected and taken in charge by regular details and deposited in one place. Here it was sold by the quæstors and divided by strict rule, a set part being kept for the obsequies of the slain and other purposes, a third part going to the state and a third part to the leader. All received their share, those on detail and the sick as well as the combatants. When the custom grew of rewarding soldiers in land, all booty was placed at the disposal of the leader or in the state treasury. Part of it was employed for public games, monuments and other general uses.

It goes without saying that all the above mentioned rules were altered by circumstances. The Romans were quick to apprehend the desirability of change and to make it, while holding fast to the excellent structure of their military body. The above is but a synopsis of what is treated of at great length by the old authors. Like all manuals, the Roman "Tactics" was largely made up of exceptions. There is a vast deal of disagreement as to details in all the ancient writers, each one being apt to speak about a period with which he was most familiar. Vegetius, Onosander, Polybius and Livy are utterly at variance on many points. A life's work could not reconcile all their differences; nor is it worth while. One can come very close to the truth, and this is all that is called for. One finds at times in modern books the formation of the legion set down with dogmatic accuracy. We must remember that the legion was a slow growth, and that in the course of five or six centuries a great many changes were sure to be made. Its minute details cannot be given with absolute reliability for any one period, except perhaps Cæsar's. But the germ of the legion remained unaltered until the time of Marius; the variation in minutiæ in no wise affected its general features.

Roman Mounted Officer (from Statue in Naples).

VII.

FORTIFICATION. — CAMP DUTY. — WAR.

CAMPS and towns had always been fortified by the Romans. Of the camp-intrenchments we have full particulars. The daily camp, during war, was invariably fortified. It was square, always of the same shape and details, and every man knew just what his part of the work was. It had a ditch, and a wall surmounted by the palisades carried by the legionaries. Its interior arrangements were convenient. There was a regular guard, outside and inside ; and everything went by clock-work. The cities of Italy were fortified much like the Greek. Siege operations were about the same, but did not rise to as much perfection as under Alexander. The fighting force on which Rome could call, in case of emergency, at the beginning of the Second Punic War, was over three quarters of a million men. One fifth of the whole population could bear arms in some way. The Romans were active in studying out the problems of any war they proposed to undertake. They stood defeat and adversity bravely, and learned from each its appropriate lesson. Their army was usually only the consular one of four legions, but in the Gallic wars it rose to twenty-two legions. The Romans differed from the Greeks in their practical good sense. Less learned in war, they did better what they knew, and the army was constantly in superior condition. They always took the initiative, and came to battle as soon as possible. When the Greeks and Romans clashed, all the Greek science could not save them from the Roman hard knocks.

THE Romans were wont from comparatively early days to fortify both their towns and camps; and probably long before the time of the Punic wars a system had grown up which we must presume to have reached a high grade of perfection. Pyrrhus was much surprised at the art displayed in the Roman camp-intrenchments. Polybius and Hyginus — the latter himself a specialist, a topographical engineer in fact — have given us a good deal of detail on this subject, in which the Romans were easily ahead of all ancient nations. Polybius gives the most satisfactory description of the Roman

camp; but Hyginus enters into detail from which we can
give the profile of the breastworks and similar facts. Just
how far advanced the art was in the period of the Second
Punic War we must estimate. It is probable that the camp
was then about as carefully fortified as at any time prior to
Marius' day.

At the end of a day's march, in time of war, the Romans
invariably fortified their camp. They calculated to finish
their distance in season to prepare the camp with all due care.
The position chosen was preferably quite open ground, near

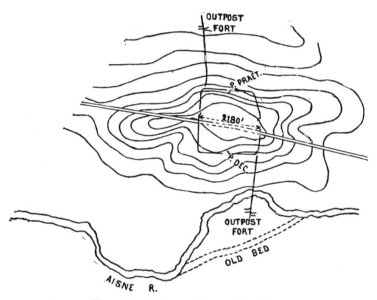

Excavation of Roman Camp on River Aisne.

forage, wood and water, and if possible on a slope, the front
of the camp facing downhill; such a location that the enemy
would have no place to plant an ambush near by. If ground
of this kind was not available, they camped wherever they
must, but in their dispositions paid close heed to the surround-

ing conditions. A tribune with some centurions, or the ante-mensores and mensores, went ahead of the army under suitable guard to choose the camp, locating with a flag and in a prominent place the prætorium or headquarters, and staking out the corners with flags of different colors. As the camp of a given body was always of the same size, shape and kind, every man knew exactly what he had to do so soon as he reached the ground, and all had from youth up been trained to do it.

The palisades carried by the infantry were at once put to use. A ditch was dug and a wall of earth was quickly thrown up and strengthened by these palisades, pointed sometimes upward, sometimes outward, and held together by the flexible branches, which the men had been careful not to cut off.

These were much better than the shorter, thicker palisades of the Greeks, and held so much more firmly in the earth that the enemy could not readily pull them out in assaulting the camp. In the presence of the enemy a portion of the troops was moved out to the front, as a protection to the camping - party. In case no enemy was near, the several bodies of the army at once repaired, each to its well-known place, and set to work. First, the outer intrenchment was completed; then the interior of the camp was put in order.

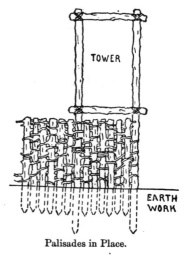

Palisades in Place.

The camp was square, — for a consular army of four legions (two Roman and two allied) something over two

thousand one hundred feet on each side, covering an area
of not far from one hundred acres. This was increased or
diminished according to the strength of the legions or army.
If the two consuls camped together, two similar camps were
made, sometimes back to back with each other. The camp

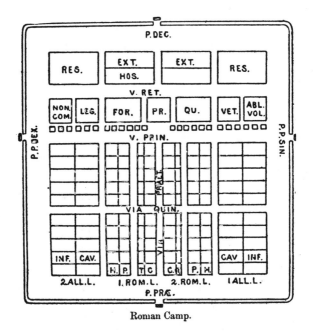

Roman Camp.

was divided by a street one hundred feet wide (via principalis) into a large part (prætentura) in front, which the men
occupied, and a smaller one (retentura) in rear, where were
headquarters (prætorium), the reserve, baggage, and sometimes a small place of arms. Headquarters, with all its be-
longings, was on a space two hundred feet square, if convenient in the highest part of the camp. In front of this were
the tents of the tribunes and præfects, in a space fifty feet
wide, all opposite their respective troops. To its left were
the quæstors, one hundred feet distant, with the quæstorium,

where rations were issued, the men paid and other similar
business transacted ; to its right the legates, non-combatants
and camp-followers, and the forum or market. On the flanks
of forum or quæstorium were the ablecti, voluntares and
veterani. In their rear was another street, one hundred feet
wide, the via retentura, behind which was the reserve-horse,
the reserve (extraordinarii) and the hospitals. When horse
and foot camped with each other, the foot faced the wall
for the purposes of quicker defense. The Roman legions
camped in the centre, the allied on the flanks, in regular
streets by cohorts, just so many feet to each. A street fifty
feet wide (via prætoriana) ran from the prætorium down to
the front of the camp, and the several bodies were separated
by regular camp-streets.

Each tent was allowed a space ten feet square, but for
how many men it sufficed is not stated. To each maniple
and each turma was allotted one hundred feet square, counting space for baggage and picketing horses. The triarii
maniples occupied but half as large a space.

On either side of the via prætoriana, the Roman horse
camped, and back to back with these the triarii. Facing the
triarii across a fifty-foot street came the principes, backed by
the hastati. Then across another fifty-foot street the allies.
The whole space of the prætentura was cut in halves by a
street parallel to the via principalis and called the via quin-
tana, because it had blocks of five maniples on each side.
The tents of the centurions came in the front line. A space
two hundred feet wide was left between the rows of tents
and wall for kitchens, sinks and other conveniences, and for
assembly for defense. In this space the velites camped,
somewhat more crowded. Polybius likens the whole camp
to a walled city with its streets and houses.

Each camp had four gates, the prætoriana in front, through

which the troops issued for battle or the march ; the decu-
mana in rear, for use mainly as a business exit, for fatigue
parties, etc. ; the principalis dextra and the principalis sinis-
tra on either side, also as debouches for the troops.   Additional smaller gates were usual, which were protected each by
its own little ditch and wall, and with heavy gates of logs.

Camps were for one or several nights (castra) or for a long
period (castra stativa).   For the former a ditch three feet
deep and five wide was usually dug and a corresponding
sodded wall made with palisades on the crest ; for the latter

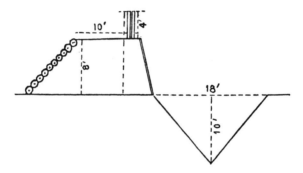

Profile of Camp Intrenchments.

a ditch twelve feet wide and nine deep, and the wall, which
was ten feet high and ten wide, was strengthened by logs,
hurdles and fascines.   These measurements varied at times.
The above profile is that of the camp on the Aisne.   At
the corners and on the faces of the wall, towers were sometimes erected to get a cross-fire on the ditch.   Bowmen,
slingers and engines were placed in these towers.   At this
period few except daily camps occur.   To each century and
maniple a particular part of the wall and ditch belonged, and
it was their duty to build and keep it in repair.   This part
was usually that lying nearest them.   Thus the front and
rear belonged to the Roman legions, the sides to the allied.

On the oldest centurion of each maniple lay the duty of inspecting the wall belonging to it.

The camp finished, an oath was taken to deliver all booty found or captured to the tribune of the day, two maniples per legion were selected to pitch tents for headquarters and officers, and details were made for fatigue-duty, to get wood and water, and to forage and water the animals, much as in modern times; the rest pitched the tents of the men, and a general guard-detail was ordered. The velites furnished the guard for the outside and the wall, the legionaries for the interior posts. The day and night, from six to six, were divided into four watches of three hours each, the first watch six to nine o'clock; the second, nine to twelve o'clock; the third, twelve to three; the fourth, three to six. A full watch-guard was composed of a decurion and eight men. Sentinels stood three hours, that is, through a watch.

Each morning the legates, tribunes and præfects of the allies came to headquarters for orders and the password. These were written on small wooden tablets and passed from maniple to maniple for the centurions to see, and then back to the tribunes. Each noon occurred a sort of guard-mounting parade at which the decurions received their orders. There were regular rounds in each watch, made to all posts on the walls by a cavalry-detail in regular rotation by turmæ, and a tribune of the day received their reports.

Camp was broken by three signals. At the first, tents were struck; at the second, they and all baggage were loaded on the pack-animals; at the third, the men fell in ready for the march.

The early Romans were deficient in their ideas of fortification, excepting that of the daily camp; they made their most marked advance in the art of permanent fortification during the period covering the Punic wars, or later. Much was borrowed from the Greek Italians, as indeed nearly all the Romans knew of the art of war had been; but a practical flavor was given to all the Romans borrowed and it was markedly improved.

The walls of the Italian cities were usually of stone and up to fifty feet high, with towers standing above and out from them at the corners or salients and along the faces at bow-shot intervals (say five or six hundred feet), so as to give a chance for cross-fire. The walls were broad, had roads upon them and a crenelated parapet. The ditch was a wet one when possible. A citadel within the town was uniformly present and strongly walled in like manner. All this was similar to the fortifications of other nations, Greek and Eastern. But the art of fortification did not rise to its fullest development with the Romans for two hundred years from this period. Nor did the walls of cities ever grow to the stupendous proportions of those of Nineveh and Babylon.

Siege-operations were the same as those in use by other nations, as they have been fully described in the volume on Alexander. They were not apt to rise to a high degree of art, except under distinguished generals, until later. But some of the sieges in the Punic wars, Lilybæum, Syracuse, Carthage, and later Numantia, are among the most celebrated in the annals of Rome. Field-works especially were well constructed. At Numantia, Scipio built walls of circum- and contravallation over eight miles long, ten feet high and eight thick, with heavy palisades, a battlemented parapet, and bastions at suitable intervals, mounted with missile-throwers (tormenta). In some low, swampy ground on the line, earthworks were thrown up, and the river Durius (Douro) was held by floating forts flanked by forts on the shore.

Ballistas and catapults were only used in regular sieges. The latter they had as long back as the siege of Veii; they now began to employ ballistas. The Romans at this time had no field artillery like that designed and used by Alexander, nor was the use of artillery in the line of battle, as employed by Alexander's successors, known to the Romans of this day. Rams underwent the same process of evolution as with the Greeks, being moved first solely by hand, then swung in a framework, then mounted on tracks, and finally covered in by buildings or mounted in towers. Terraces, machines for breaking down walls, mining operations and movable towers were generally in use. A large part of the art of the Macedonians had been lost, and did not reappear until Cæsar's day in a perfect form in general use. In capturing cities during the Second Punic War, the Romans rather relied upon a blockade by walls of circum- and contravallation very cleverly designed, than upon the energetic methods used with such astonishing success by Alexander in breaking down or surrounding the walls of cities.

The numerical force which Rome with its allies and colonies was capable of raising is thus given by Polybius. The time is between the First and Second Punic Wars. The figures are sustained by Diodorus and Pliny : —

In active service under the consuls (Romans and allies)	54,000	men, horse and foot
Sabines and Tyrrhenians	54,000	
Tribes of the Apennines	40,000	
Reserves in and near Rome (Romans and allies)	53,500	201,500 men
In addition to this, according to the lists handed in by the allies (Latins, Samnites, Messapians, Lucanians, Marsians, Frentinians and Vestinians), there could be furnished in case of need		294,000 men
Two legions in Sicily		8,800 men
General drafts in Rome and Campania could raise in case of need		273,000 men
Giving an enormous total of		777,300 men

of whom about 70,000 were mounted.   This was the fighting
body which Hannibal had to encounter.

This force came from a population stated at about three
and a quarter million free, and about an equal number of
slaves.   Thus every fourth individual in the entire free population was able to render military service in some capacity.
This means that every male capable of labor was capable of
bearing arms.

Rome was essentially a fighting nation, and, as the above
table shows, was at this time abundantly able to fight.   Her
organization, political and military, was well calculated to
this end.   She had as a nation the same hunger for territory,
the same jealousy of rival power in any of her neighbors,
which as an individual Alexander may be said to have had.
Her annual consuls saw conquest to be the safest road to
fame and standing for themselves, and were apt to be in
search of war.   Rome and all her officials were constantly
on the outlook for opportunities for conquest; she always
stuck her fingers into every pie, and never ceased to breed
quarrels in order herself to benefit by eventual interference.
She took sides with the weaker in order to weaken the
stronger, and eventually to subdue both.   Everything was
justifiable which led to its end.   Her political proceedings
with foreign tribes were far from having the same upright-
ness which was shown in the national home character.   In
other words, a Roman was held to be honest only towards
a Roman.   Her cry of "Punic Faith" against Hannibal has
its laughable aspect, as we shall see.

Rome could be patient under adversity, and bide her time;
but once at war, she carried on war with all her might; once
victorious, her opponent was ground into the dust.   It has
been observed that the statecraft of heathen Rome, from the
founding of the city till the fourth century A. D., and of

Christian Rome, from the sixth century A. D. till the present day, has always been the same, — a jesuitical statecraft, and a wonderfully able one.

The Romans were untiring in seeking information with regard to the peoples which it desired or might desire to attack. Their cities, armies, generals, the character and sentiment of their population, and all other conditions, were carefully studied. Meanwhile, every appearance of friendliness was maintained, and magazines of provisions, arsenals, and depots were established in suitable places.

So soon as preparations were completed, the Roman senate found no difficulty in picking a quarrel, and declared war through the festiales, or priests. These demanded, in the name of the senate and people of Rome, reparation for injuries claimed to have been done, and often imaginary enough. If the harsh terms thus imposed were declined, they threw a bloody lance upon the enemy's territory, — the ancient challenge to arms. Later this ceremony was gone through in the agger hostilis, near Rome, and the Roman army took the field. Then the doors of the temple of Janus were opened, and not closed until the war was ended.

As a rule, the Romans, relying on the discipline and courage of the troops, put only the consular army of four legions in the field; but at times several such armies were afoot. Against the Gauls (226 to 220 B. C.) there were five armies and two extra legions, — twenty-two legions in all, — not counting auxiliary troops. As the Roman conquests grew in extent and spread beyond seas, so the army grew. In such cases the Roman troops were left in the conquered provinces as reserve, and the provincial troops sent to the front.

The art of war with the Romans was much what it was among the Greeks; but so far in the history of Rome the wars had not generally been waged on a very extensive scale.

The conduct of war had been simple rather than scientific, but the simplicity had been supplemented by the wonderful capacity and character of the troops. The stanchness of the army rather than the ability of the generals had made Roman wars successful; and the rule in war was the same as in battle, — always to seize the initiative, at once to assume the offensive, and bring on a battle with the enemy as soon as possible. It was the old Donnybrook Fair rule: " Wherever you see a head, hit it." And the small baggage-trains, the capacity for marching fast and far, and the habit always to fortify the camp, even for a single night, and, if possible, always to fight near it, as at the gates of a fortress, gave the Roman army a distinct advantage over nations which did not practice this method. It was an advantage which even the Greeks did not possess. The Roman camp was in fact a movable fortress, always accompanying their marches, to which they could retire in case of disaster, and await help from their base, which was never very far. In a certain measure, in the light of the lack of military art by other nations, this camp enabled the Romans to dispense with a regular base and line of operations. They lived on the country they traversed, having no wars where breadstuffs were not grown and flocks and herds in plenty. They chose their own time for fighting.

Battle was the one thing needful. Tactics, therefore, was to the Romans of much more importance than strategy. The latter branch of the art of war first began to dawn upon the Roman mind after two years of victory by Hannibal. Prior to that time it had been exemplified only in the campaigns of the abler generals, and in a small degree; and the average Roman, the necessity being over, soon forgot to practice it. But battle-tactics, in their understanding of it, and as adapted to the conditions of the period, the Romans brought to a high state of perfection.

For centuries the Romans kept up an even, steady progress in practical war. What they lacked they were ready to learn from any source, and what they learned they put to good uses. The success of Rome lay in its homogeneity, its single purpose, its cohesion as a people and its persistency, and in the remarkable skill with which it moulded its military organization into the shape best suited to its purpose. All that Rome lacked — a knowledge of what the greater operations of war are, of what the genius of war teaches, the divine half of the art, as Napoleon calls it — she was now about to gain in the lessons of adversity she received at the hands of the greatest soldier the world had yet produced, excepting Alexander, and this was an experience which made her able thereafter to cope with any kind of foe, and to accomplish what Alexander had aimed at, the permanent conquest of the world.

The Greeks were more expert in the theory of war, which, indeed, they had created, or at least put into a form which was capable of perpetuation. The lessons of the great captains antedating the Greeks, however useful, have been swallowed up by the ages. The Greeks studied war in a learned way. They were in this sense head and shoulders above any other nation. The Romans did not do this, but they practiced war with heed to its minutest details, satisfied with waging simple war perfectly, rather than scientific war in an indifferent way, and the excellence of their discipline and its constancy gave them the upper hand. The Greeks, with all their cleverness, by refusing to learn from others, to alter their organization to suit changing times and conditions, and to conform to new ideas, remained at a standstill.

The Romans, vastly less cultured and able, had a marked advantage in their practical good sense, their common purpose, and their spirit of order and discipline. The Greeks had developed an art which they could not use. Without material, the art was of no avail, and their armies sooner or later degenerated. The Romans had no such art, but they had an army, sound and able to the last man, and that army remained so. When the clash came, not all the scientific ability of the Greeks could enable their rotten system to stand the blow of the less intellectual but sturdier opponent. While it cannot be denied that, up to this era, the Greeks and Macedonians had carried the art of war in its intellectual phases far beyond the Romans, and that Philip had created an army in all its details the equal if not the superior of the Roman army, it remains true that among the Greeks there was lacking that persistence which bore the Romans through so many centuries of war without decrease of purpose or slackening of discipline. For a period of six hundred years, from the foundation of Rome to the civil wars (754 to 133 B. C.), the Roman discipline, the fighting ability of its army, were steadily on the increase; and for half this period the army was at the apex of effectiveness.

Josephus says: " When we consider to what degree the Romans studied the art of war, we must acknowledge that the height of power to which they attained was not a gift of luck, but a reward of wisdom. They did not wait for war to make the use of weapons a business; they did not, sleeping in the lap of peace, then first begin to move their hands when necessity drove them to it; they never interrupted their warlike exercises, as if they were born with weapons in their hands, and as if weapons were a part of their bodily structure; and these warlike exercises are but a well-considered study of battle forms. Each day every warrior shows proof of his strength and courage, and therefore real battles bring him nothing new or difficult; habituated to close their ranks in fight, the Roman soldiers know no demoralization. nor dis-

order; never is their sight or understanding clouded by surprise or fear; never is their strength subject to weariness.
They are sure of victory, for they know well that they have
to do with enemies who are not their equals, and they cannot,
as we must allow, deceive themselves; for their exercises are
battles without bloodshed, and their battles bloody exercises."

Legionary Soldier (from Column of Trajan).

VIII.

EARLY ROMAN WARS. 400–272 B. C.

THE early wars of Rome had the character of raids. The two interesting facts in them are that Rome always took the offensive ; and that she always gained in strength by her wars, rather than lost. Even her defeats and disgraces were profitable in their lessons. After the siege of Veii war became somewhat more methodical, and the Samnite wars showed up Rome in the quality of conqueror. No less than ninety thousand men were on foot at one time, and her self-reliance grew apace with the extension of her sway. The most interesting operations of Rome, prior to the First Punic War, were in the war against Pyrrhus. This Epirot king, one of the most notable military adventurers of history, came to southern Italy at the invitation of Tarentum. He had been trained under Antigonus, and represented the art of war as waged by Alexander. He was a skillful soldier, but not always wise in his policy. He failed in his mission because his own allies were uncertain and because he met on its own soil a nation able and courageous to the last degree. Pyrrhus' army was set up in phalangial order, and at Heraclea he first met the Roman legion. The elephants and Pyrrhus' tactical ability really won this battle, not the phalanx. The same was the result of the second battle, at Asculum. The legion and phalanx were not evenly matched. In the third battle, at Beneventum, the elephants caused Pyrrhus' defeat by turning on their own line. Though these three battles were the first in which legion encountered phalanx, they cannot be said to prove the superiority of either. Pyrrhus won nothing by his victories ; the Romans gained strength and knowledge by their defeats. Not till later was the contest between the two formations decided. In fact, the legion and the phalanx never met under equal conditions and commanders. During the war with Pyrrhus, Rome and Carthage had joined in a treaty, offensive and defensive, but this soon gave way to arms. The extension of Roman policy could not allow Carthage to hold Sicily.

THERE is little which is interesting or which repays study in the early wars of Rome. But as the rise of the art of war in Greece has been fully sketched in a previous volume, it may be profitable to devote a few pages to the status from

which Rome rose to the full comprehension of what war
should be. The final polish to her education was given her
by Hannibal, and later by Cæsar. Let us see what she had
learned before she came under Hannibal's tutelage.

The character of the early wars of Rome was that of plundering raids, made both in quest of booty and for extension
of territory. One fact, which lifts itself into such prominence
out of these conflicts that one is fain to repeat it, is that the
Romans were always the attacking party. Even in repelling
invasion they assumed the initiative. Upon this feature of
the Roman method we cannot too strongly insist. The wars
of the Greek states among themselves were apt to partake of
a defensive character, against which the decided offensive
character of the Romans in their Italian wars stands out in
marked relief. The Romans always sought battle as the outcome of their campaigns. But there is nothing noteworthy
in the conduct of these early wars, except the persistency and
consistency of the Romans in the pursuit of their object.

The fact that the Romans almost uniformly came out of
their many wars as victors not only did not weaken them, but
gave them the strength of discipline and experience. They
gained by the one and in no wise relaxed the other. In this
they stand again in marked contrast to the Greeks, whose
wars among themselves were exhausting to the last degree.
The early Roman wars, in being those of a people ignorant
of war as a science, resemble the early Greek wars, but differ
from them in that the Romans showed by far the greater
vigor and cohesiveness.

The Roman programme was usually the same. A neighbor was selected for attack, and a quarrel foisted on him on
any pretense, good or bad ; troops were raised, the festiales
declared war, and one, or perhaps two, armies of from six
to twenty thousand men, under a king, or later a consul,

marched into the enemy's territory, and sought battle or besieged the capital. In the earliest days plunder was the main object of the campaigns; in later years plundering became only a means of coercion; accession of territory or increase in the list of subject allies was the purpose of the war.

The first noteworthy operation of the Romans was the siege of Veii, which occupied nearly ten years (404 to 395 B. C.), and like Troy, the city was finally captured by a ruse, namely, the digging of an underground passage from the Roman lines to the citadel, in which stood the temple of Juno. Through this tunnel a select party made its way, fell on the Veiians in the rear, and opened the gates, while the inhabitants were kept busy with a simultaneous attack at many points. Furius Camillus was the hero of this siege. The Romans here first employed lines of circum- and contravallation, which the Greeks had already used at the siege of Platæa, a generation before.

With the larger scope of operations succeeding the siege of Veii, the foray character of the Roman wars began to disappear; but for fifty years after the capture of Veii, the struggle between patricians and plebeians, coupled with the Gallic invasions and the Italian wars, narrowed the operations of Rome to something resembling defensive warfare. Then began her career of conquest.

The two invasions of the Gauls in 389 and 366 B. C. have no peculiar interest, except to show that even Roman discipline and good sense, unless the army was led by a man equal to the occasion, were powerless to meet the unexpected or overwhelming.

The Samnite wars (343 to 290 B. C.), which were the first real wars of conquest by the Romans, took place during the era of Philip of Macedon, and of Alexander and his successors. Rome was just beginning to build up an empire in Italy when Macedon had conquered the whole world. Neither Rome nor Carthage was at that time of any consequence in the Grecian economy. Livy doubts whether contemporary Romans had even heard of Alexander, and while Alexander had learned of Carthage through Tyre, if he had heard of

Theatre of Samnite Wars.

Rome, it was only through the dim mist of the stories of Greek tradesmen who sailed the western Mediterranean. Yet Rome and Carthage were preparing to fight for the supremacy of the world, while the vast possessions of Alexander were crumbling into dust.

The Samnite wars, more than any other, laid the foundation of the greatness of Rome, solidified the army organization, taught the men to fight in mountains as well as on the level, and to contend with the various difficulties, uncertainties and surprises incident to meeting a succession of new

Samnite Footman (from a Vase).

opponents. The forces put on foot by Rome during this period reached as high as ninety thousand men at one time, which, in view of its limited population and resources, is a wonderful exhibit.

The so-called Samnite wars were really wars of Rome with Samnium, the unconquered parts of Latium, Campania, Etruria, and Umbria, — with all her central Italy neighbors, in fact, — but all had the same characteristics and object. The countries surrounding Rome were rich, populous, able, and in many respects

superior to Rome, whose rugged patriotism and courage were almost her only strength. The Etruscans and Latins were, indeed, in no wise wanting in the courage, skill and ability in war which distinguished the Romans, and if they and the others had joined hands, Rome must have gone down. But happily for her, and largely by good management on her part, Rome was able to fight these enemies singly until towards the close of the war.

By admirably skillful policy and singleness of purpose, Rome did not lose heart or strength during the war. She bravely stood her

Etruscan Warrior (from a Bronze Statuette).

defeats and disgraces, **of**

which she had not a few, learned from each its proper lesson, and rose out of them stronger and more able, with her power to make war greater, her self-reliance ever on the increase. Weighing the difficulties, the trials, the failures and the losses of Rome, the Samnite wars showed what stuff there was in her.

Samnite Signifer (from a Vase).

The most interesting war, in a military sense, in which Rome was engaged previous to the Second Punic War was the war against Pyrrhus (281 to 272 B. C.). This was the first occasion on which legion and phalanx came into conflict; it was the link which bound together the art of war as practiced by the brilliant Greeks and the less scientific, but within its scope more perfect, art which had been developed from the same origin by the sturdy Romans.

Campanian Horseman (from a Bronze Statuette).

Pyrrhus, king of Epirus, was a military adventurer, but an interesting and an able one, — a species of Charles XII. His splendid personal gallantry, no less than his bold career, command our admiration and our sympathy. He had been trained to war under Antigonus, who himself had learned his trade under Alexander. Pyrrhus had lost his throne through Macedonian machinations, but, brought to Alexandria as a hostage after the battle of Ipsus in 301

B. C., he won the friendship of Ptolemy, and regained his kingdom five years later. In 287 B. C. he was called to the throne of Macedon, but shortly resigned it, unwilling to encounter the intrigues of his subjects, who were restless under any monarch not a Macedonian. Pyrrhus was ambitious to a degree of the glory which comes of conquest; and there soon arose an opportunity which promised the possibility of carving out an empire in the West, as his great sampler, Alexander, had hewn his from the East.

In the towns of southern or Grecian Italy the aristocrats universally leaned towards Rome, and sought her protection; the democrats opposed her. A multitude of towns were under her protection. Among these the allied town of Thurii, on the gulf of Tarentum, had been at war with and was hard pressed by the Lucanians and Bruttians. Rome sent a small fleet to

Theatre of War against Pyrrhus.

her assistance in 282 B. C. This was literally an infraction of an old treaty with Tarentum; but more recent conventions and the general state of amity existing between the towns had practically nullified this treaty. The fleet passed the promontory of Lacinium and anchored in the harbor of Tarentum. It was here unjustifiably attacked by a Tarentine mob, four triremes were sunk and one captured, with its crew. The Thurian democrats now rose, drove out the aristocratic party and placed the city under Tarentine rule. A Roman embassy, sent to demand reparation from Tarentum, was treated with contumely. Rome immediately declared war, and dispatched a consular army against the city.

The Tarentines called to their aid Pyrrhus, who was in many respects the most noted soldier of the day, and well known in Tarentum from her Greek affiliations. It is not likely that the king of Epirus was well informed about Rome or its power, much as Rome had known nothing of Alexander. He had perhaps heard of its conquests, but these the Tarentines would naturally underrate in telling him about their enemy, and he no doubt looked on Rome as a semi-barbarous nation which had won successes because it had never yet met the phalanx of the Greeks. This self-confidence was a thoroughly Grecian trait, by which Pyrrhus came honestly enough in his training under Antigonus.

The Roman army sent against these new foes accomplished nothing in the first year, and contented itself with ravaging the Tarentine territory. It then withdrew to Lucania and took up winter-quarters. Next spring Pyrrhus appeared on the scene with a force variously stated at from ten thousand men and fifty elephants to twenty-five thousand men and twenty elephants. His infantry consisted of Epirots, Greeks and Macedonians. His van of three thousand men, under Milon, had preceded him. He at once took matters in hand, arrogated to himself vastly more power than the Tarentines had dreamed of giving him, and placed the whole population under arms, despite protests and marked dissatisfaction. The Tarentines had called in a servant; they found a master, and

a harsh one.   Pyrrhus soon had — whether brought with him
or since recruited — an army of almost twenty thousand heavy
infantry, two thousand archers, five hundred slingers and
three thousand cavalry.   To these were added a number of
elephants.   The coming contest was to be not only one between phalanx and legion, but one between the regular militia
system of Rome and the method of hiring mercenaries to
which Greece had now succumbed.

While his colleague, Tiberius Coruncanius, was engaged in
Etruria, the consul Publius Lævinus had in the spring of
280 B. C. again invaded Lucania with the usual consular
army of about twenty thousand men, and devastated it.
Pyrrhus advanced to meet him.   On the rolling plain between
Heraclea and Pandosia, on the Siris, the Roman legion first
measured its strength against the Grecian phalanx.   Pyrrhus
had a slightly superior force.

When the king came in sight of the Roman camp, and
from across the Siris observed its orderliness and the soldierly
bearing and strong, hearty appearance of the men, he could
not conceal his surprise.   He saw that he had not barbarians
but a disciplined army to fight, one, indeed, whose organization was superior to his own.   Nor was his surprise quickly
lessened; for no sooner did the Romans perceive the approach
of the enemy than they filed from their camp with their
usual promptness and perfect order, pushed some light troops
sustained by a column of horse through the river-ford, smartly
attacked the van of Pyrrhus' army, which was holding the
ford, and drove it in on the main body.   Startled at this au-
dacious advance and his sudden check, Pyrrhus galloped to
the front with his three thousand cavalry, and though thrown
from his horse, at which his army was for a moment somewhat abashed, soon reëstablished the matter along his own
front.   The Roman van held the fords and enabled the legions to cross, when they deployed into line.

We have, unfortunately, few details of this battle. The thirteenth book of Livy, which contained them, has been lost. But we have the statements of Plutarch and Dionysius and Hieronymus, and the tenacity of the fighting is vouched for. If set up, as is probable, in strict phalangial order, the king's infantry covered a front much less than the consular foot. But its weight was as much greater. The phalanx had more than twice the number of infantry per metre of front that there was in the legion.

The two lines of heavy foot met; the ponderous phalanx struck its fearful blow, but failed to pierce the legion; it met

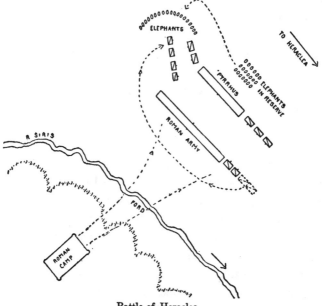

Battle of Heraclea.

such a foe as it had never yet encountered. In vain did the sarissas of the Epirots force back the Roman line; as often did the legionaries arrest its onset with their own fierce charge and greater front. The fall, in the fray, of Megacles, one of Pyrrhus' general officers, with whom the king is stated by Plutarch to have exchanged armor, — for what purpose is not clear, — for the second time threatened the destruction of the phalanx from sheer demoralization at the supposed death of its leader, while the Romans were correspondingly cheered, and Lævinus felt sure of victory ; but Pyrrhus, with bared face, rode through the ranks, and to see him revived their courage. The phalanx recovered and once more moved to the attack. The lines clashed again and again. Seven times the Roman charge broke on the phalangial masses, seven times the vaunted phalanx essayed vainly to crush the elastic structure of the legion. It was metal against rubber. The one could not break the other, nor could this tear its foe asunder.

Finally Pyrrhus, unable to make headway, brought to the front his elephants, until now held in reserve. The Roman horse was at the time seriously, and as Lævinus imagined successfully, threatening Pyrrhus' flank. Appalled at the aspect of these huge creatures, which none had yet beheld, and which now suddenly appeared in line from behind a roll in the ground, and severely handled, moreover, by the flights of arrows from the towers the elephants bore, the horse at once fell back in confusion and broke through the line of the legion in its panic. Pyrrhus launched his Thessalian cavalry upon the cohorts, which completed the defeat. The Roman forces fled across the river, but managed here to hold the fords against the king's pursuit. According to Dionysius fifteen thousand Roman legionaries lay dead or wounded upon the field ; Hieronymus says seven thousand ; two thousand were captured. Pyrrhus had suffered equally. Dionysius gives thirteen thousand as his casualties; Hieronymus only four thousand killed. But the smaller figure was a terrible loss, — nearly sixteen per cent. in killed

alone. Pyrrhus visited the field thus won. He saw that all
the dead Romans lay with faces to the foe. " One more such
victory and I am lost!" quoth he, according to the Roman
legend. He may indeed have thought so ; but he was too
good a soldier to speak it openly.

The elephants, debouching as from ambush, had decided
the day, or, as some had it, Lævinus was at fault. The table
of contents of Livy's lost books, still preserved, assigns the
cause of the defeat to the elephants. It was a moot question
yet between legion and phalanx. It is very doubtful whether
the discipline of Pyrrhus' phalanx, made up as it was from
many different sources, was in any sense equal to that of the
legion. But Pyrrhus had won a clear and important victory.
He proposed to the Roman prisoners to take service under
him, as was the habit of the Greeks, but was met by a stern
refusal. Not one wavered in his allegiance. Pyrrhus found
that he was not fighting mercenaries.

Lævinus retired to Apulia, whither two new legions had
been sent him. Pyrrhus moved by forced marches on Rome,
an act which we admire and commend for its boldness, but
which lacked the discretion and balance displayed by Hannibal after Cannæ. The Lucanians, Bruttians, Samnites and
some other tribes of southern and middle Italy made treaties
with him, but the confederates broke not faith. Reaching
Campania, Pyrrhus took Fregellæ and laid siege to Præneste,
thirty odd miles from Rome. His whole army had advanced
as far as Anagnia.

Rome was never for a moment in danger of capture.
Lævinus found his ranks again filled. Thousands flocked to
enlist. He held Campania against the king and followed
him up, while the other consul, Coruncanius, having quieted
Etruria, quickly moved towards the scene. The king deemed
it wise to withdraw, not wishing to be caught between two

Roman armies. He had tasted the quality of Roman valor and found it unsafe to run too great a risk. His march on Rome had manifestly been an error. Negotiations ensued, the senate listened, but Rome held firm for war.

Pyrrhus' next encounter was near Asculum (Ascoli) in Apulia, on the river now called Torrente Carapella, with the armies of the consuls Decius and Sulpicius. The king was aiming to cross the mountains by way of Beneventum, when the consuls headed him off. Each side had some seventy thousand men, of which in the Roman army twenty thousand were Roman citizens and eight thousand cavalry; in the king's army sixteen thousand were Greeks and Epirots and eight thousand cavalry. The balance was made up of allies. The Epirot and Greek infantry was in the centre of Pyrrhus' line, in a solid phalanx; his allies he set up, in imitation of the Romans, in manipular order, so as to extend his front, which, at Heraclea, had been dangerously outflanked. It must be remembered that the phalangial formation took up per thousand men a front much less than half that of the legionary.

The Romans had apparently again established their camp on the farther side of the river, intending to cross it to attack the king, and to use it as a ditch to their camp. The river flows through a narrow alluvial valley, with hills of five to seven hundred feet on either bank, and rising on the south to the dignity of mountains. Asculum lay on a plateau some thirteen hundred feet above the sea. The ground along the river was swampy, treacherous and much cut up by woods. The Romans crossed the stream and attacked the king on the rolling ground to the east.

The swampy condition of part of the ground delayed Pyrrhus in getting his elephants into line, while the wooded and cut-up nature of the country was unsuited to the operations of his cavalry. The first day's battle was ended only by night. Pyrrhus' forces slept on their arms; the Roman army, better provided, crossed to its camp. It had not been victorious.

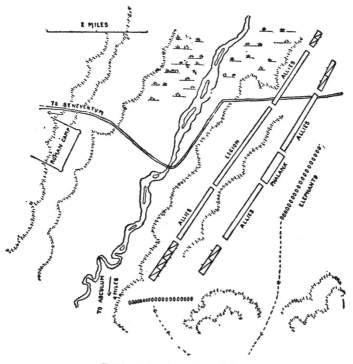

Battle of Asculum. Second Day.

Next day Pyrrhus early occupied the swampy land with some light troops, and managed to take possession of advanced ground where he could put his elephants into line, as well as confine the legion to a surface on which it could not so readily advance and retreat, in the swaying to and fro of the lines closing in battle. The Romans had prepared some chariots with long projecting spiked poles, to meet the onset of the elephants; but they proved unavailing on the rough ground.

The conflict of the second day was long and bitter. The legionaries fought among the spears of the phalanx, reckless of their own persons, determined to break through the bristling array; but time and again they were thrown back by the heroic personal efforts of Pyrrhus. Finally Roman pertinacity carried the day; the king's allies could no longer resist the better discipline of the Roman cohorts, and, the wings weakened, the legionaries began slowly to force the wavering phalanx back. Pyrrhus, foreseeing the gravity of his situation, sent his elephants by a circuit to attack the Roman horse, which stood all ready to fall on the phalanx when it should dissolve its ranks. The mighty creatures charged down in line with thundering tread upon the knights, and as at Heraclea, the frightened horse gave way. Even Alexander's Companions had been unable to face these monsters in a charge. Aided by this diversion, Pyrrhus rallied the phalanx and the allies, and with one advance all along the line forced back the startled legionaries. The Romans were driven beyond the river. Pyrrhus held the field.

Again the elephants had saved the phalanx, had worsted the Roman soldiers. The losses were enormous; fifteen thousand fell on both sides, says Dionysius; but Hieronymus gives the Roman loss at six thousand killed, while Pyrrhus' own accounts state his losses at three thousand five hundred and fifty killed. No doubt the Roman losses were the larger. The king himself was badly wounded. The Romans safely reached their camp, which Pyrrhus was in no condition to attack, and disabled by his wound he retired to Tarentum. The battle was a tactical victory for the Greeks, but the Romans were sizing up the phalanx.

Pyrrhus was losing ground. Nothing but constant successes could save him. The bulk of his Epirot infantry had perished; he could get more with difficulty; his allies saw that he was not holding his own and accordingly declined in their allegiance and aid. Still Pyrrhus must fight. No other course would serve his purpose or enable him to hold his ground. Next spring, 278 B. C., he again advanced to meet the consuls C. Fabricius and Q. Æmilius, who were on the boundary of the Tarentine territory. It was for the purposes of parley, however. The victor of Heraclea and Asculum desired peace. But the Romans knew not how to yield. Nothing but negotiations without result came of the movement, and having been invited to Sicily by the Syracusans, Pyrrhus set sail for that island. Here by his unsound policy he managed to accomplish no good end. It was not the soldier but the statesman who was at fault. The Romans, meanwhile, took possession of all southern Italy except the territory controlled by Tarentum and Rhegium. Pyrrhus returned to Italy in 276 B. C. with twenty thousand infantry, three thousand horse and a few remaining elephants. His veterans had disappeared. The Romans, despite their defeats, had recovered ground. Their constancy and hopefulness under adversity deserved the success they won.

In 275 B. C. Pyrrhus set out to aid the Samnites, who were being harassed by one of the consular armies. The other consul was in Lucania. On the way, the king detached a small force to hold head against the latter, who would thus be prevented from joining his colleague except by the roundabout way of Campania. He then pushed on to Beneventum. The consul Manius decided to avoid battle and sought to retire towards Campania, to enable his colleague to come up. But Pyrrhus pushed him home and forced him to battle on open ground near the city. The details of this, as of other battles of the Epirot king, are difficult to decipher from the old records. It can only be done by a study of the locality,

which will sometimes elucidate passages otherwise impossible
to understand.

Pyrrhus endeavored by a circuit to make a night attack
on his opponent, taking with him his best troops and elephants; but during the march he was obliged to make

Pyrrhus' March on Beneventum.

through a thickly wooded country, the torches of the guides
gave out, and the column lost its way. In consequence of
this bad hap, it was broad day when he reached the vicinity
of the Roman camp. The consul Manius came out to meet
him, and, attacking his van as it debouched from the hills,
threw it into confusion and cut out a number of prisoners
and elephants. But Pyrrhus withdrew, made his way into
the plain, deployed into line and confronted Manius. The
contest was obstinate. Manius appears to have had the better of the phalanx; but the elephants again came into play
and by a well-timed advance forced the legion back to the
trenches of the camp. Here, however, Manius ordered out
the entire reserve left within the walls, which, charging fresh
and unexpectedly upon the elephants, drove them back.

These, as so often happened in olden warfare, turned from their foes upon their friends, completing a destruction already begun. Pyrrhus was defeated with an enormous loss in killed, thirteen hundred prisoners and eight elephants captured. He fled to Tarentum, whence he soon sailed for Epirus, leaving Milon in command. This lieutenant managed to hold on till Pyrrhus died in 272 B. C., when he surrendered with promise of free exit.

Such were the first contests of legion against phalanx. The difficulty of gauging the comparative discipline and soldierly qualities of the two contestants make it impossible to

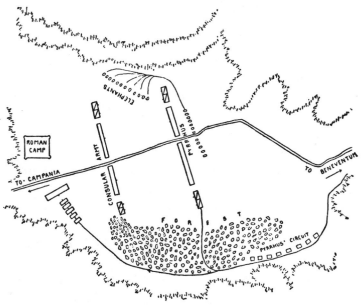

Battle of Beneventum.

award the wreath to either one or the other. The Romans were clearly both of better stuff and under better discipline; and they were fighting on their own soil against invasion. The relative value of Roman and Greek formation was not yet settled. The duel was fought out later. But even then the terms were never even. The best phalanx never met the best legion under equal commanders. While the legion was in many respects the better body, it was Roman grit and not its order of battle which eventually prevailed.

Pyrrhus cannot be counted among the great soldiers of history. He was brilliant, lacked not ability, had dash and many of the intellectual qualities which go to make up the great captain. But he was deficient in solidity. His intellectual grasp was not comprehensive. In his policy with the cities of Italy and Sicily he failed; in some of his military schemes he was bold rather than long-headed. His splendid career arrests our attention and commands our sympathy; but his claim to our study rests on his having commanded the phalanx in its initial struggle with the legion.

Rome now easily conquered all southern Italy and punished those towns which, after once accepting her protection, had joined their forces with Pyrrhus. Her hold on all Italy, won in the Samnite wars and this, enabled her to turn her attention to Sicily, where Carthage held main sway. During the troubles with Pyrrhus, Rome and Carthage had had a treaty for the common interest of expelling outside interference. This treaty now gave way to arms.

The conquered towns of Italy were classified in threefold manner: —

1. Municipal cities (municipia), which had Roman citizenship with all its burdens but no suffrage or claim to office in Rome. Some were allowed to keep their own city government; some were not.

2. Colonies (coloniæ), which were only captured cities turned into Roman fortresses, whose land was often divided among needy Roman citizens, who then became the ruling

class. Both municipal cities and colonies were governed by a Roman præfect.

3. Allies (socii, civitates federatæ), whose relations to Rome were regulated by treaty. They generally kept their own government, and in lieu of service in the Roman legion furnished auxiliary legions or ships.

Legionary Soldiers (from Column of Trajan).

IX.

THE FIRST PUNIC WAR. — THE ROMAN NAVY. — HAMIL-CAR BARCA. 264-218 B. C.

THE cause of the First Punic War was the jealousy of Rome at the holding of Carthage in Sicily. Rome had no navy. She saw that to succeed she must command the sea; and so intelligent and energetic were her efforts that not only did she create a fleet equal in size to the Carthaginian, but in the fifth and the eighth years of the war she defeated Carthage on her own element, by clever devices and good naval tactics. Despite tremendous losses — seven hundred ships in five years — Rome kept up her navy from this time on, though it ground her seacoast allies into the dust. The construction and management of her marine was on a Greek model. After the naval victory of Ecnomus, the consul Regulus landed in Africa and essayed to impose heavy terms on Carthage. This city resisted, and procuring the services of Xanthippus, a Spartan, with some Greek mercenaries, defeated Regulus in the battle of Tunes, mainly by the latter's unwise alteration of the manipular form of his legions. So far legion against phalanx had not done well. Towards the close of the First Punic War, Hamilcar Barca, father of Hannibal, came to the front, but, though his ability was marked, too late to redeem the Carthaginian cause. The naval battle of Ægusa finished the war. Carthage was heavily mulcted in money and territory, and evacuated Sicily, parts of which she had held for centuries. Succeeding this came a rebellion of the unpaid Carthaginian mercenaries, in which Carthage was sore pressed. Hamilcar, by very able measures, tactics and manœuvring, put down the rebellion. His work well shows whence Hannibal drew his own inspiration.

SHORTLY after the war with Pyrrhus came the First Punic War, which lasted from 264 to 241 B. C. The real origin of the wars against Carthage lay in the jealousy of Rome for the power at sea of the Carthaginians, and her fear lest the possession of Sicily by Carthage should become a threat to her own dominion in Italy. With increasing territory her ideas were broadening, and during this war, whose course it is not within the purpose of this volume to trace, the Romans steadily grew in warlike capacity, in the organization and discipline of their armies, and in all the minutiæ of war. No great soldier appeared on the side of the Romans in the First Punic War; on the Carthaginian side only Hamilcar Barca, the father of Hannibal, and he at a stage in the struggle when it was too late to rehabilitate a cause already lost. By their courage, steadfastness and patriotism, the Romans proved that no task was too great for them to accomplish.

For fifty years Rome had been making sundry efforts to create a fleet. She had needed none so long as she was only in conflict with the nations of Italy. But when the events of the First Punic War showed her the necessity of conquering Sicily if she would not continue to suffer a thorn in her flesh by the Carthaginian occupation of a large part of the island, a fleet became essential. Nothing exhibits the extraordinary energy of the Romans better than the fact that in the fifth year of the war (260 B. C.) the consul Duilius won a naval victory over the experienced Carthaginians, and in the eighth year (257 B. C.) the consul Regulus won a second, with a fleet of three hundred and fifty triremes carrying one hundred and forty thousand rowers and soldiers. This was a gigantic piece of work splendidly carried through. From this time on, Rome always had a fleet, though at times, after great naval losses, it sank to a low ebb, with the discouragement of the Roman people and the poverty of the public treasury.

No sooner had the Romans determined to make themselves strong at sea than they set heartily to work. The burden was put on the seacoast allies and colonies, the Etruscans and the Greek settlers of southern Italy, and these peoples were thereafter fairly ground into the dust by the constant demands made upon them. Polybius states that a captured

Carthaginian trireme served them as first model; but this is doubtful, for the coasts of Italy were full of good seamen, and the Greek knowledge of naval war had been brought to the Italian peninsula long before, though naval architecture had not been developed by any serious demand. No doubt ideas were borrowed, but there were ships and shipwrights in abundance. All the senate had to do was to order ships to be built, and the allies and colonies produced them.

The creation of a fleet so rapidly was wonderful enough, but that Roman generals, unused to the sea, should so soon have become clever admirals is marvelous. It was largely due to the fact that the ancient naval warfare was less of a

Corvus (from Folard's sketch).

distinct art than it is to-day; and that the Roman practical good sense came quickly into play. C. Duilius won his victory by means of a new device, of his own invention some allege, though probably ancient, — a huge crow, or hook (corvus), and a bridge, mounted on the prow of the war-ships, and fixed so as to be dropped either to front or either side, which, grappling on the Carthaginian ships, enabled the Roman soldiers to board and carry them. This device, used at the battle of Mylæ, west of Messana, in 260 B. C., was a complete surprise to the Carthaginians, who expected only to manœuvre their ships in the usual manner until they

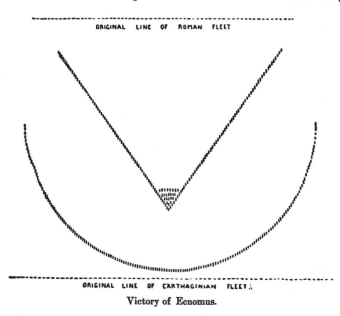

Victory of Ecnomus.

could run down the Roman galleys. The uniform tactics of the ancient men-of-war was to fight bows on, so as to run their spur into the enemy's sides, or break off the oars. As we hear little more of this corvus, likely enough the Carthaginians soon found a way to avoid its danger.

When in 256 B. C. it was determined by the Romans to carry the war to Africa, they were again enabled by good management to break through the Carthaginian fleet of three hundred and thirty triremes, opposing them off Mt.

Ecnomus in Sicily. This latter was extended in a huge concave line, intended to envelop the Roman fleet. But the consuls, M. Atilius Regulus and L. Manlius Vulso, formed their own fleet — with the almost incredible complement of ships and men above given on the authority of Polybius — in a wedge or triangle, lashed the triremes which formed the apex together in a body, and by forestalling the Carthaginians in their intention to manœuvre and come to individual combat of the galleys, broke through and landed on the African coast.

In 255 B. C. the Roman fleet was destroyed in a storm on the coast of Sicily, but the senate at once ordered the seacoast allies to build a new one, increasing the number of allies on whom was laid the duty of building, manning and equipping the new fleet, and in consideration of their so doing relieved them from all land-duty. The tremendous efforts of the senate are well shown by the fact that in five years (257 to 253 B. C.) no less than seven hundred triremes were lost, and yet Rome kept a navy afloat. The seacoast cities were ruined and could, they alleged, furnish no more ships. But the senate would not give up its determination to control sea as well as land, and in 250 B. C. another fleet was raised for the siege of Lilybæum. Then immediately followed the loss by the consul Appius Claudius Pulcher of one hundred and seventeen ships and twenty thousand men. The colonies being quite unable to build more vessels, the aristocrats did so at their own cost, and with these, near Lilybæum, at the Ægusa Islands, the consul Lutatius Catulus defeated the Carthaginians and put an end to the First Punic War in 241 B. C.

A fleet now became part and parcel of the military equipment of Rome. We shall see her planting her foot on Sardinia and other islands, and reaching out to Spain, Illyria, Macedonia, Greece, and the East. This growth of the naval power of Rome was even more astonishing than that of her army. Still it is the land-forces of Rome which lend peculiar interest to her military history.

In building, equipping and manning her fleets, Rome, as above said, followed the then accepted model of the Greeks, which had reached Italy by way of the Greek colonies. But upon this they imprinted their own practical good sense. The number of rowers was twice or more that of marines in a trireme. The command of the fleet was, as a rule, given to the leader of the military forces.

As with the Greeks, the Romans made but short passages of the sea. Usually they kept along the coast, landing every night, pulling the ships up on the beach and building an intrenched camp around them. Provisions followed on trans-

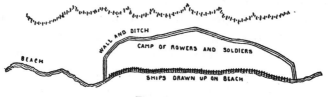

Fleet Camp.

ports, or "round" ships. In battle the Romans preferred boarding and hand-to-hand work. But despite success at sea, whenever it was possible they held it better to do their work on land.

One or two of the battles in the First Punic War are noteworthy as illustrating the conflict between the Grecian and Roman systems. Carthage had practically the phalangial idea, though the numerous bodies of frequently changed mercenary troops of divers nationalities made it impracticable for her to introduce perfect tactics.

After varying fortunes by land and sea, when the Roman fleet had won its great victory of Ecnomus in 256 B. C., had pushed aside the Carthaginian fleet and landed on African soil, the consul Regulus, having won an initial success, was unwise enough, in the common Roman fashion, to try to impose terms too harsh upon the Carthaginians, and was met by crisp refusal. Regulus was unable to enforce his terms on the instant. The Carthaginians sent to Greece for mercenaries, and the Spartan general Xanthippus entered their service. At this time the art of war was better preserved in Sparta than elsewhere in Greece. Xanthippus was an able leader. He saw that the situation to which Carthage had been brought was more due to blundering policy than lack of material strength. His knowledge and skill infused confidence into government and people alike, and he was given the supreme command of the army. Regulus, meanwhile, had subdued the surrounding country, — which, as all the cities had been deprived of their walls by Carthage, in her system of preserving her own preëminence, was no great task, — and was steadily approaching the capital. Xanthippus, having organized and drilled the Carthaginian foot in Lacedæmonian fashion, and raised their *esprit de corps* to a high pitch, marched out of Carthage with twelve thousand foot, four thousand horse, and one hundred elephants, purposing to seek the Romans on the plains, where cavalry and elephants could have free play.

Regulus was somewhat surprised at this new phase of Carthaginian affairs, but, nothing loath, he took up the challenge and advanced to meet Xanthippus. The armies came together near Tunes, in 255 B. C. The Carthaginians were in high spirits, of which fact Xanthippus took advantage, and drew up in line with perfect confidence. His heavy Carthaginian foot, eight to nine thousand strong, was in a sixteen-deep phalanx in the centre, in one mora divided into four lochoi, Lacedæmonian fashion, and under officers selected by

himself. The rest of his foot, three to four thousand mercenaries, was partly heavy, partly light. The heavy mercenaries Xanthippus placed on the right of the phalanx. In
front of this line of foot, well advanced, he put the elephants
in one line, close together, so as to cover exactly the front of

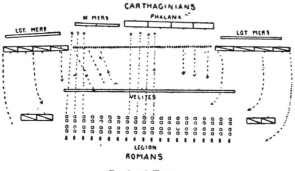

Battle of Tunes.

the foot. The cavalry, on which he mainly depended, he stationed on the flanks of the line of elephants, and in their
rear he placed the light mercenaries. The duty of the cavalry, sustained by the light mercenaries, was to brush aside
the Roman velites, defeat the Roman cavalry, and then fall
on the flanks of the Roman legion.

Regulus had the usual consular army of two Roman and
two allied legions, some sixteen thousand foot. His velites
he ranged in one line in front of the legions, and his horse, of
which he had but little, as he had come from beyond sea, in
their usual place on the flanks. The legions he drew up in
the common three lines, — hastati, principes, triarii, — but,
instead of forming the maniples checkerwise, he doubled his
maniples, ploying each two into a column, as it were. This
doubled the intervals, making his formation a line of columns
placed much too far apart. Such a formation might, perhaps, be useful against a charge of elephants, by giving them

wide lanes through which they could be driven to the rear, but was highly dangerous against Xanthippus' larger force of cavalry, which could readily make its way into the open spaces. Regulus apparently intended to gain both frontage and depth; but he was losing other and greater advantages, and his men were unaccustomed to this new formation. His dispositions were as mistaken as Xanthippus' were well considered.

Contrary to Roman habit and good judgment, Regulus allowed Xanthippus to attack. This the Spartan did with a will, first projecting his own horse against the Roman. From the line of elephants, pushed forward at the same time, the Roman velites quickly retired, falling back through the intervals of the legion, which meanwhile advanced to counter the impending blow. The elephants on the Carthaginian right, in their forward movement, had edged in towards the centre, and left a gap between their right and the Carthaginian cavalry. Through this the three legionary columns of the Roman left pushed their way, and threw back the heavy mercenaries in confusion; but the other columns, striking the line of elephants, made no headway, and by much wavering lost the crispness of their alignment. The Carthaginian horse, having by its superior numbers quickly dispersed the Roman cavalry, now fell upon the legions in flank. The centre legionary columns fought their way through the elephants and stoutly attacked the phalanx, where all fell with faces to the front; but the Carthaginian cavalry prevented the others from following in their lead. They were placed on the defensive: they formed a sort of square to protect themselves, but were surrounded and cut to pieces. Regulus and five hundred men were captured. Only the three legionary columns of the left escaped, some two thousand strong.

So much came of Regulus' alteration of the usual legionary

formation. Tactical changes immediately before battle are
dangerous, unless advisedly made, and such that they exactly
fit the conditions, and are thoroughly understood by the men.
Here the phalanx had beaten the legion; but still not on even
terms.

The employment of elephants was with the Carthaginians
a new thing, which they had learned in the war with Pyrrhus; but they had made good use of the new device, and,
in this battle and later in Sicily, the Romans found the huge
creatures hard to neutralize. The cavalry, as in Alexander's
battle at the Hydaspes, could not be got to face them, and
even the legionaries were nervous in their presence. But in
251 B. C. the proconsul Cæcilius Metellus won a decisive victory over Hasdrubal at Panormus, despite the great number
of elephants in the Carthaginian line, and captured one hundred and twenty of these animals. After this the Romans
ceased to dread this arm.

The rest of the war was a mixture of victory and defeat,
but the Romans, on the whole, gained ground and finally
confined the Carthaginians to the western end of Sicily.

It was not till 247 B. C. that Hamilcar, surnamed Barca
(or lightning), was placed in command of the Carthaginian
army. His ability and enterprise gave a decided promise
of success, and for six years he held his own against the
Roman armies in the mountains of the west coast of Sicily,
as well as inflicted heavy losses on them by privateers. Any
other man would have been driven from his position time
and again.

Rome had repeatedly lost her fleet. But she raised another and another, and, each time regaining the control at
sea, finally won a decisive victory over the Carthaginian fleet
under Hanno at Ægusa. Peace was forced on Carthage.
Even Hamilcar advised peace, having other projects in mind

for revenge at a future time. The Carthaginians gave up
Sicily and paid three thousand two hundred talents (four
million dollars) indemnity in ten years. Hamilcar, "the unconquered general of a vanquished nation, descended from the
mountains which he had defended so long and delivered to the
new masters of the island the fortresses which the Phœnicians had held in their uninterrupted possession for at least
four hundred years." The plan of Carthage to monopolize
the trade of the western Mediterranean was wrecked.

During the First Punic
War the Romans were as
much distinguished for
their persistent following
up of their one ob-
ject as the Cartha-
ginians were for a
poor use of their
natural advantages.
It redounded great-
ly to the glory of
Rome that she had defeat-
ed Carthage on her own
element, and one unknown
to herself, — the sea.

Revictualing Lilybæum.

It is well worth while
to cite two or three in-
stances, taken at random,
of the originality of Hamilcar Barca, to whom
Hannibal owed not only
his army but a large part of his ability, by birth as well as
by education.

Lilybæum had, in 245 B. C., been closely blockaded by the

Romans, and was all but reduced by famine. Hamilcar had undertaken to revictual the place. With his entire fleet he made a feint of trying to force an entrance into the harbor, meanwhile hiding in an adjoining bay thirty big transports laden to the water's edge with food. The Romans fell with their usual determination and singleness of purpose on the Carthaginian fleet, which, designedly retiring, induced the Romans to follow it out into the open. While thus engaged at a distance from the town, the thirty transports quietly made their way into the port. This simple stratagem of war was one of the acts of "Punic Faith" over which the Romans made so much ado, because it was a clever device of which they had never thought. It was no more than a common feint, novel at that time, and well executed in its details.

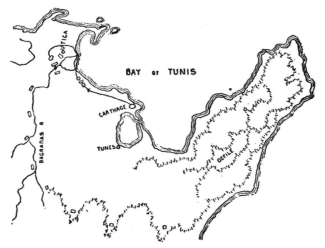

Theatre of Mercenary Insurrection.

The First Punic War was followed in 238 B. C. by a fearful insurrection among the unpaid African mercenaries of Carthage, and the city itself was besieged by a leader named Matho, at the head of a large force of the old soldiers.

Hamilcar had gone into retirement, but he was sought out and entreated to resume the conduct of affairs. Matho was zealously guarding the outlets of the mountain chain which closes in the isthmus of Carthage; had occupied in force all the fords of the Bagradas River on its west, and especially held the only bridge, three miles above Utica, by a bridge-head. Carthage was cut off from the mainland and in a desperate strait. Hamilcar alone saw a remedy. He had personally observed that a west-northwest wind always blew the water from the bar at the mouth of the Bagradas to such an extent as to make the bar fairly practicable for both foot and horse,— a fact lost on every one else. Acting on this knowledge he assembled the only forces Carthage could raise, organized them as carefully as time would allow, and one night, when the bar was available, he marched out of Carthage and across the bar, wading deep in water. Before dawn his little army of ten thousand men and seventy elephants had taken the enemy at the fords and the bridgehead, and the besiegers of Utica, in reverse; and the moral effect of his ingenious scheme — which recalls Alexander at the Pamphylian Ladders — relieved the blockade of Carthage. A march here had accomplished more than a battle. This was a novelty in the then art of war, and one which, excepting Hannibal, no one put into practice till Cæsar dawned upon the world; and from his day no general until Gustavus.

But the rebels nevertheless stood and fought, and Hamilcar had an opportunity to show them that he was a tactician as well as a marcher. To his paltry ten thousand men — raw, at that — the rebels opposed twenty-five thousand seasoned troops, without depleting their defenses. Hamilcar moved towards his enemy on a line parallel to their front, in three columns. He was about to "form front to a flank," but under the conditions was better justified in so doing than

Frederick later at the battle of Kolin. At all events he succeeded, — as indeed the Last of the Kings came close to doing too.

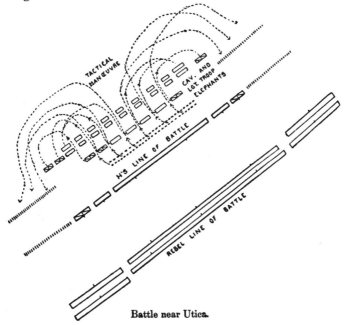

Battle near Utica.

The left column, nearest the rebels, was composed of the seventy elephants; the centre column of the cavalry and light infantry; the third, which was the column of direction, of the heavy foot. Hamilcar had drilled his men in the manœuvre he intended them to make. At the proper place, when he reached a position opposite the enemy, the two left columns filed to the right " by sections to the rear," and moved rapidly towards and through the heavy foot, which opened intervals to allow them to pass. As Hamilcar expected, the rebels assumed that this was a movement in retreat, and at once made ready to follow it up, which they did in careless order. The heavy foot, meanwhile, closed its intervals, and the two columns which had filed through to the rear, by a change of direction, right and left, marched to either flank and came to a front on the wings of the main line, when the whole body moved forward in perfect order. The rebels were seized with confusion at the unexpected resistance of a perfect line of battle when they had looked for a panic, and were defeated with great slaughter.

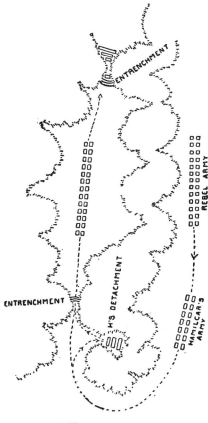

Hamilcar's Defile.

Still, a large body escaped to Tunes, and these had to be obliterated. Hamilcar closely followed the rebels, and by cleverly manœuvring for some weeks, without coming to a battle, he so wrought up the Libyan hot blood to the pitch of frenzied desire to fight that the rebels followed him about from day to day, wherever he chose to turn. Acting on this fact, Hamilcar managed to lure them to a defile on the cape which incloses the bay of Tunes on the east, which defile he had previously reconnoitred with care. So soon as the enemy, to the number of forty thousand men, had entered the defile, Hamilcar closed its rear exit with a body of men hidden for the purpose, which quickly threw up works at a chosen narrow spot, — while he, with the main body, turned on the rebels at the other exit, which was rugged enough to hold without much effort. This too he fortified, and here, in an immense trap, he had his enemy at his mercy. Here too he ended the war, — with a terrible massacre, to be sure, but one not then unusual, and perhaps well earned by the rebels. This manœuvre leads one to think that his great son in later years, at Trasimene, had his father in mind when he laid his stratagem to trap the Roman consul.

The interval between the First and Second Punic Wars (241 to 218 B. C.) was fully occupied by the Romans in contests with the Gauls, Ligurians and Illyrians. The war with

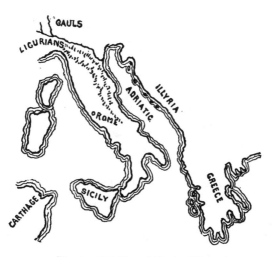

Theatre of Gallic and Illyrian Wars.

the latter originated in the piratical expeditions of this people, which kept the Adriatic in a constant ferment. They were thoroughly subdued, and during this war — noteworthy

for this, if for nothing else — Rome first got acquainted with
Greece. It was not long before her avaricious grasp was extended thither. The war with the Gauls included both the
cis- and transpadane Gauls, and Rome, during this struggle,
put two hundred thousand men on foot, showing a vast increase in military ability, — despite the abnormal exertions
of the First Punic War. The allied Gauls concentrated on

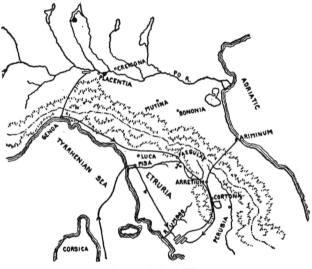

Theatre of Gallic Wars.

the Po and advanced through Etruria, plundering and devastating, and winning a battle at Fæsulæ against the prætor in
command of the province. Learning of the disaster, Æmilius Papus set out from Ariminum to relieve his colleague.
The Gauls intended to retire with their booty along the
Tyrrhenian coast. Meanwhile, Caius Atilius Regulus had
landed from Sardinia at Pisa, and with thirty-seven thousand
men advanced upon them, thus cutting off their retreat,
which must be across the Apennines, not far from the Gulf

of Genoa. They had no choice, for at this point there was
no other way open. The seventy thousand Gauls were shut
in between the eighty thousand men of Papus and the army,
half as large, of Regulus.

At Telamon, near the sea, and south of the Umbro, a battle occurred, which is interesting from its double lines. The

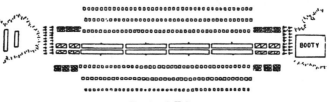

Battle of Telamon.

Gauls made ready to fight for their booty and for retreat,
and took up a position between coast and hills. Their foot,
as usual, was in deep masses and now in two lines, back
to back. Facing Papus were the Gæsatæ and Insubrians;
facing Regulus, the Boians and Tauriscans. Their cavalry
was on the flanks of the infantry, facing in similar manner,
and the flanks of the cavalry they protected with chariots,
headed outward. Their train laden with booty they placed
on a height to the east, under strong guard. Here was a
good formation in which to fight for life, but as bad an one
to get beaten in as could well be devised.

Regulus drew up on the northerly front of the Gauls, and
seeing a small height on their western flank, he occupied it
with a strong body of cavalry, sustained by foot. This body
the Gauls tried repeatedly to dislodge, but every assault on
the hill was driven back. From this hill Regulus could see
the army of Papus and signal to it, and both consuls prepared
to act in concert. Papus began the battle by sending some
cavalry to fall on the western flank of the Gauls, who were
assaulting the hill held by Regulus. Here occurred some

stout fighting, in which Regulus was killed.   Meanwhile, the line of battle advanced on the southerly front of the Gauls, where, despite the terrible aspect of the naked barbarians, — for the Gauls always stripped for battle, wearing solely their leggings, and ornamented with their golden bracelets and necklaces, — and the hideous din of trumpets and battle song, the legion made a serious impression upon it.   The velites acted well, and drove the van of the Gauls back on the main line, thus producing some confusion in the enemy's ranks at the moment when the legions were advancing to the charge. Papus sent a body from his right to seize the train-camp on the hill.   The Gauls made a splendid resistance; but the Roman cavalry hemmed in and defeated the Gallic horse, and then turned and fell upon the flanks of the footmen. This soon broke their formation and power of resistance; they were huddled together so as to lose their capacity to fight, and were cut to pieces.   It is said that forty thousand were killed or took their own lives, and that ten thousand were captured.

This battle is interesting as showing the difference between the ancient and modern art.   One can scarcely expect the Gauls to develop a science of war, but had they first moved sharply on Regulus, whom they outnumbered two to one, they might well have beaten him, and would then have been ready to turn on Papus with the consciousness of victory and equal forces, and with their line of retreat open and booty safe, of itself no mean provocative of courage.   Or, indeed, with a skillful rear-guard, after defeating Regulus, they might have made good their retreat with all their booty.   For the road afforded numberless positions suitable for defense.

The battle of Telamon was the beginning of a series of victories by which the Romans not only gained control of all northern Italy to the confines of the mountains, but learned to cope with a foe whom they were to meet under Hannibal. In order to hold the line of the Po they planted military colonies at Cremona, Placentia, Mutina and a number of other places. These came into play, as we shall see, when Hannibal, a few years later, debouched upon the Padane valley from the Alps.

By 220 B. C. Rome had placed her hand on the entire Italian peninsula, and held the seas on its either side, with Sicily, Corsica, Sardinia and other contiguous islands. This century had wrought great changes in her standing. But Rome was to be called on again to fight for her holding, and this time as never before. Had it not been for her sensible institutions and sound body-politic, she must have succumbed before the Carthaginian captain.

Rome was liberal to her colonies, all of whom in consequence desired her success; Carthage ground hers down with heavy tribute, so that they would really be benefited by her fall. Carthage destroyed the walls of her colonies because she feared them; Rome kept those of her colonies, and as a result possessed a rampart of fortified posts. An enemy landing on Roman soil had just begun his task; an enemy landing in Africa had all but completed his. In Carthage the land was owned by planters and tilled by slaves; in Rome the citizen himself tilled the soil. In Rome the landed interest was the highest; in Carthage the moneyed interest controlled everything. Rome was governed by men who fairly represented the people; the small farmer was a distinct power in the land; Carthage was governed by rich merchants or planters, whose money gave them influence, and who cared for nothing else. The Roman was simple; the Carthaginian luxurious. The Carthaginian citizen was averse to military duty; it was the pride of the Roman. The Roman senate and its generals worked in unison; the Carthaginian senate

and its officers were invariably at odds. Rome was sound;
Carthage was rotten. The revenues of Rome were but a
tithe of those of Carthage, but the Carthaginian system of
war was by far the more expensive. We shall see which
system worked the better.

Legionary (Column of Septimius Severus).

X.

THE LION'S BROOD. 241–220 B. C.

Two factions controlled Carthage, the Barcine or war-faction, and the Hanno or peace party. Hamilcar, the head of the former, planned to conquer Spain in order to replace Sicily, and in 236 B. C. led an expedition thither. In the succeeding eight years, Hamilcar, basing on Gades, subdued a considerable part of western Iberia. He was succeeded by Hasdrubal, his son-in-law, who continued his wise and energetic policy, and largely increased the Carthaginian holding. Hannibal was Hasdrubal's cavalry-commander, and in 221 B. C., on Hasdrubal's death, became head of the Iberian army. Saguntum, chief of the Greek colonies on the eastern coast, fearing the extension of Carthaginian power, applied to Rome for protection. This Rome gave her, and notified Carthage that her forces must not cross the Ebro, to which ultimatum Carthage was fain to agree. Hannibal had inherited from his father, not only an army, but the purpose to use it for an invasion of Italy overland. He was not strong enough at once to undertake this, and his first two years in Spain were spent in consolidating his conquests there. In this he showed wisdom, energy and intelligence; and in one of his campaigns when the barbarians, relying on his youth, had rebelled and cut him off from Cartagena, he showed the qualities of an Alexander in dealing with such enemies, and defeated them on the Tagus with great slaughter. Titus Livius, his bitterest enemy, has left us a pen-picture of the young commander, which testifies to his splendid attributes.

THERE were, as stated in a former chapter, two factions in Carthage. The one was headed by Hamilcar Barca, the leader of the liberal or aristocratic or patriotic party, so to speak, which was wedded to a war policy or policy of resistance, despite the late defeat and the serious condition of Carthage. The other was led by Hanno, the head of the democrats or conservatives, who represented conciliation and peace, or in other words the acceptance of the situation, and was suspected of playing into the hands of the Romans. The usual rôles of aristocrats and democrats seem to have been reversed. Hamilcar well knew that peace with Rome meant oppression by Rome and the extinction of all national growth and pride; and his life-work was a constant, unremitting effort to prepare the nation for war and then to make war upon this one arch-enemy of his country. The hatred he bore the great Italian city became a family instinct as well as a family purpose, rendered only the more keen by internal opposition; and the destiny of the Barca family was to express its hatred in war and to bury itself in its last great struggle with Rome. And, though eventually a failure, this policy was clearly shown by more than one unworthy and oppressive act of Rome to have been the true one for Carthage to pursue. It failed because of the half-heartedness of its support.

With this end in view, Hamilcar, still a young man, little over thirty, developed a plan to make good to Carthage its losses in Sicily by the conquest of Spain. This plan was at once undertaken, with the most statesmanlike method.

Iberia had long been not only a recruiting ground of Carthage, but from time immemorial had lured the Phœnicians to its fertile shores. Gades was the earliest of the Tyrian ventures; and Hamilcar was merely carrying out, with a vigor no one else had shown, a part of the old national policy, at a time when such a man and such energy in the proper direction were essential to save Carthage from dying out.

Iberia was a country of great natural resources. Abundant forests, large navigable rivers and inexhaustible mines were both a prize worth contending for, and a means by which, in addition to its mountainous territory, the strong warlike native population could indefinitely resist invasion. But Hamilcar felt in himself the strength to overcome these obstacles for the sake of the prize, and he foresaw that the peninsula might some day furnish him a base from which, with the aid of the brave Iberians, as well as the Rome-hating Gauls, both of which peoples had figured largely in the list of Carthaginian mercenaries, he might carry the war into Italy and attack his hereditary foe at his own hearth. The plan and the man were each worthy the other. And, despite the opposition of the Hanno faction, aided largely by the sentiment of the populace and by money, which was the

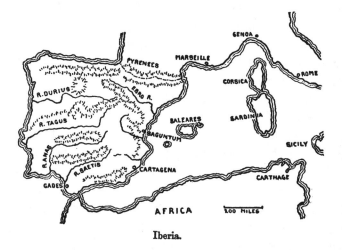

Iberia.

common means of control in Carthage and which he and his· family possessed in superabundance, Hamilcar gained from the Carthaginian senate permission to undertake the expedition; or at least his enterprise, if not authorized, was not forbidden.

Carthage had not been able to rebuild a fleet since the destruction of its last one in the First Punic War. The city, in its present condition of weakness, dared not undertake openly to build a navy, lest the jealousy of Rome should be again provoked to attack her before she was prepared. There was no means of shipping an army to Spain. But

Hamilcar, nothing daunted, found it possible, by careful and systematic measures, to undertake a march along the northern shore of Africa to the Pillars of Hercules, accompanied by such few transports as he could command to carry bread; for, though there were many colonies along the coast, there were stretches which could not be safely crossed without rations always at hand. From the Pillars, Hamilcar was able to cross to Gades in B. C. 236. This bold and intelligent undertaking showed how well Hannibal came by his own daring genius for dealing with the impossible.

Once on Iberian soil, Hamilcar conducted a series of campaigns, basing on Gades and moving eastward, and in these doughty blows were so admirably seasoned with generous conduct and far-sighted diplomacy that in nine years he had conquered the greater part of the southern extremity of the peninsula, and placed the power of Carthage on a firm foundation. Cato, a generation later, exclaimed that no king was worthy to be named beside Hamilcar Barca. And when we read the history of the wars which have been carried on in Spain from Hamilcar's era to Napoleon's, and look at the difficult nature of the country, and the bold resistance always offered by its people, this praise seems no whit too high.

In B. C. 228 Hamilcar was killed in a campaign against tribes somewhere between the Tagus and the Durius (Douro); but so strongly had the Carthaginians impressed themselves upon their Spanish allies that the chief command of all the troops, Carthaginian and Iberian, was at once, by unanimous consent, conferred on his son-in-law, Hasdrubal. The position was an important one, for the joint forces amounted to sixty thousand foot, eight thousand horse and two hundred elephants.

Hasdrubal — a common Carthaginian name, there being in Carthaginian history no less than eight generals thus

named, and this one was dubbed Hasdrubal the Handsome —
went on with the policy of Hamilcar in a thoroughly work-
manlike manner. He was noted for great personal strength
and beauty, justice, courtesy and intelligence. His administration increased the Carthaginian authority and territory.
It was he who founded Cartagena (New or Spanish Carthage), and he so firmly established the Carthaginian influence in the peninsula that most towns as far north as the
Iberus (Ebro) paid tribute to his native city. This was by
no means brought about without the usual bitter antagonism
of the conservatives at home ; but success, military and financial, in Spain reconciled the Carthaginians to Hasdrubal's
doings, and forbade the opposition party under Hanno to
interfere.

There were many rich and thriving Greek colonies along
the east coast, of which Saguntum, in the centre, was the
most flourishing. These colonists had grown rich in their
dealings with the Spaniards, and viewed with alarm the
threatening growth of Carthaginian influence. In the fear
that they might all eventually fall under the dominion of the
new power, and the mother country being unequal to the task
of helping them, the inhabitants of Saguntum unwisely
turned to Rome for protection.

Rome was only too happy to embrace this opportunity of
again weakening her ancient foe, whose growth in the Spanish peninsula she had long been suspiciously watching. She
took Saguntum under her protection, sent a garrison to the
city, and gave notice to Hasdrubal that the Iberus must be
the boundary of his advance. Rome clearly had no idea
then of an overland invasion being contemplated ; but Saguntum was an excellent base for her own operations in Spain,
should the successes of Carthage there make such a proceeding desirable. For Hasdrubal meant war when Carthage

should be strong enough, and Rome foresaw war. But Rome did not go at the matter on so broad and intelligent a scale, and the Gallic problem on the Po was difficult enough to rivet attention to northern Italy. "The policy of the Romans was always more remarkable for tenacity, cunning and consistency, than for grandeur of conception or power of rapid organization," says Mommsen.

Hasdrubal, not deeming Carthage strong enough to precipitate a war with the great city, was fain to agree to the terms so haughtily formulated.

Shortly after this treaty, in B. C. 221, Hasdrubal was assassinated, and again the Iberians showed their confidence in the Carthaginian policy, and in its leading family, by electing Hannibal, eldest son of Hamilcar Barca, then twenty-eight years old, to the command in chief; and, despite the vote of Hanno's party, the home government confirmed the election.

The army still consisted of the same elements, namely, Carthaginians, Liby-Phœnicians, Spaniards and Gauls, together with heavy and Numidian cavalry. But the army was in every sense an army, reflecting its noble leaders in all its characteristics. The power of Carthage had been transferred from its fleet to its land forces, and all there was of these which had a marked value lay in Spain, and under the command of the Barcas.

Hannibal ("Favorite of Baal," the chief Phœnician deity) was born B. C. 249. He had been a mere stripling when he first accompanied his father to Spain in 236 B. C. He had always shown clear-cut powers of intellect, and had received the best of educations, under the careful scrutiny of Hamilcar, who was equally fond of the lad and proud of his evident capacity. Hannibal and his brothers, Hasdrubal, Mago, and Hanno, — the lion's brood, — were all born and trained

to arms, and all nobly fulfilled their mission. Three died
on the field; the greatest lived to aid his country in her dire
extremity.

We do not know much about the character of Hannibal's
education. We do not even know what the Punic language
was, except that it was allied to the Egyptian and Hebrew.
That it had a literature of its own we are told by the Roman
historians; and Mago's book on agriculture, an exhaustive
treatise in twenty-eight volumes, and the only work of which
we are informed, was translated into Latin, and was the chief
text-book in Italy. We cannot fail to recognize the ability of
the Carthaginians; we know that they came of the stock to
which we owe our letters; but Carthage was so utterly destroyed that not a vestige remains to tell us the literary status
of the "London of Antiquity." Prophetic, indeed, had been
the exclamation of Cato, "Delenda est Carthago!"

We know that Carthage had borrowed much of the
Greeks, and no doubt this was true in a literary as it had
been in a military sense, though indeed the Greeks and Carthaginians were jealous of one another in a commercial way.
Dion Cassius states that Hannibal had studied all that the
Greeks could teach; and while the Carthaginians as a nation
were chiefly distinguished for their ability to turn all they
handled to gold, the Barca family had aspirations far above
mere filthy lucre. There can be no question whatever, from
the uniform leaning of the little testimony we have upon the
subject, that Hannibal's vast intellect was supplemented by a
mind stored with all that was then known to the world as
great and beautiful. And "his character has descended to
us throughout the ages, pure beyond the power of his enemies
to stain."

Love of his native land and intense hatred of Rome had
been Hannibal's hourly lesson since he could first speak, and

while his education was of the most liberal character, it was chiefly directed to the department of war. Hannibal remained in his father's camp nine years. During this period he was constantly in the field, and was near his father when he fell in battle. He was then sent back to Carthage, some say at an earlier date, the better to continue his education. At all events, he went home upon his father's death. But he returned to Spain in B. C. 224, at the age of twenty-five, called thither by Hasdrubal, and in the next three years received his maturer military training in the field, as commandant of Hasdrubal's cavalry.

Titus Livius, who harbored a solid Roman hatred of Hannibal, and has in the same breath abundant ill to say of him, gives us this photograph of the young chief: "No sooner had he arrived, than Hannibal drew the whole army towards him. The old soldiers fancied they saw Hamilcar in his youth given back to them; the same bright look, the same fire in his eye, the same trick of countenance and features. But soon he proved that to be his father's son was not his highest recommendation. Never was one and the same spirit more skillful to meet opposition, to obey or to command. It was hard to decide whether he was more dear to the chief or to the army. Neither did Hasdrubal more readily place any one at the head when courage or activity were required, nor were the soldiers under any other leader so full of confidence and daring. He entered danger with the greatest mettle, he comported himself in danger with the greatest unconcern. By no difficulties could his body be tired, his ardor damped. Heat and cold he suffered with equal endurance; the amount of his food and drink was gauged by natural needs and not by pleasure. The time of waking and sleeping depended not on the distinction of day and night. What time was left from business he devoted to rest, and this was not brought on by either a soft couch or by quiet. Many have often seen him, covered by a short field cloak, lying on the ground betwixt the outposts and sentinels of the soldiers. His clothing in no wise distinguished him from his fellows; his weapons and horses attracted every one's eye. He was by long odds the best rider, the best marcher. He went into battle the first, he came out of it the last. . . . He served three years under Hasdrubal's supreme command, and left nothing unobserved which he who desires to become a great captain ought to see and to do."

Thus equipped, it was by no means strange that Hannibal should succeed to the command. The manner in which he used his power forms one of the greatest pages in history.

Hannibal early declared that he would complete the conquest of all Spain, and it was a family secret that such a conquest was but the first step towards carrying the war into Italy. But he was wise enough to keep his own counsel on the latter point, and to follow up the excellent plans of his father and Hasdrubal towards making his position on the peninsula impregnable. The plan which this young chieftain carried in his head was no doubt the original conception of Hamilcar, and had by him been impressed upon his son-in-law and son. But the crude conception had long been seething in the soul of Hannibal, and it was his brain which truly gave the project birth, as it was his hand which carried it through to the close. The colossal nature of the plan, its magnificent daring, its boundless self-confidence, its contempt of danger, no less than the extraordinary manner of its execution in the succeeding years, are equaled only by Alexander's setting forth — also but a youth — to conquer the illimitable possessions of the Great King.

But Hannibal was far from being a mere dreamer. He well knew that he could not invade Italy without exceptional material resources in addition to the motive power furnished by his well-equipped head and self-reliant heart. He recognized that he had the Pyrenees and the Alps to cross, in addition to many mighty rivers, and that these, difficult indeed for small bodies of troops going from one friendly land to another, even at an auspicious season, might be all but insurmountable for an army of invasion, — particularly his, which must be accompanied by long and heavy trains as well as a number of elephants. Nor were these natural obstacles any worse than the possible opposition of the warlike Gauls, through whose land he must pass upon his way. He was wise enough to contemplate no actual movement until all his preparations were made, his army perfectly equipped, his base reliable, and his projected advance reconnoitred.

Hannibal, owing to the political combinations, could not rely on help from Carthage. The peace party was again in the ascendant and would not allow him to declare war. He was a mere servant of the senate, with his hands tied, and liable at any moment to be recalled, though the wealth and influence of the Barcas, and the results accomplished, had long left them in control of Spain. All his force in men and means must come from the peninsula. The mother-country was still weak from her struggle with Rome, and looked to him for aid rather than was able or willing to yield it. Without the revenues of the Iberian mines, in fact, the Barcine hold on command would have probably long before been severed. But Carthage needed the money which came from them and favored the generals who made war remunerative instead of costly. Hannibal did not conceal from himself the fact that the peace party in Carthage would oppose his scheme in every manner. What he did was done with his eyes wide open and with a full calculation of means and consequences. But the main factor in the proposition was that burning genius which made his heart bold to undertake any difficulty to avenge the wrongs of his down-trodden country, that lambent flame of the divine which—among soldiers—few indeed have ever shown in such effulgence.

In no wise blinded to the herculean·nature of his task, Hannibal spent the first two years of his command (B. C. 221–220) in consolidating his Spanish possessions, which the death of Hasdrubal had again in some parts threatened to

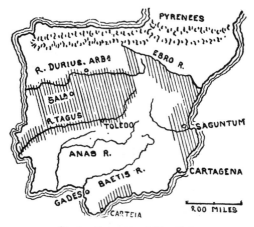

Iberian Conquests of Hannibal.

compromise. He reduced the town of Carteia, near the Pillars of Hercules, by a vigorous siege, overcame the tribes along the Tagus and made them tributary to his scheme, and then retired to Cartagena to winter. The next year he added the tribes of the Durius region to his standard, capturing both Arbocala, or Albucella, and Salmantica (Salamanca). His liberality to his soldiers, both from the public purse and still more from his private fortune, was a means of keeping them devoted to his person no less than that pride which, of all subordinates, the soldier most truly feels for his successful chief. He was sure of his army wherever he went, and his generous policy to the tribes he overcame promised to avoid trouble when his back should be turned, and he distant from the scene.

These conquests on the Tagus and the Durius were not made without many a hard struggle. One may well be instanced. While Hannibal was besieging Arbocala, certain

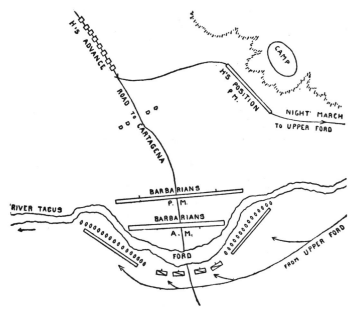

Battle of the Tagus.

of the tribes between the two rivers joined forces to the number of one hundred thousand men, and on his return stood awaiting him near modern Toledo, hoping to fall on his rear when he should cross the river, incumbered as he was with immense trains of booty. They undervalued the capacity of the young chieftain. The bed of the Tagus is difficult to ford, and the conditions offered the barbarians a fine opportunity of revenge. They occupied the right bank at one of the main fords.

Hannibal was suddenly called upon to show his qualities as a general; and he himself took advantage of the difficulties of the country on which the enemy chiefly relied. Declining to cross the Tagus with so large a force in his vicinity, he contented himself, when attacked, with holding his own, and at nightfall took up a strong position on the right bank of the river, fortifying it in such a manner as to lead the enemy to believe that he intended to act on the defensive in that position. Meanwhile, he sent out scouts to reconnoitre the river, who found up the stream, and not far off, a practicable ford. While the barbarians were debating how best to deliver an attack on the morrow, Hannibal, shortly after the fall of night, keeping his camp-fires bright and leaving a rear-guard to simulate the presence of the army, stole a march upon them, crossed the Tagus and took up a new and similar position on the left or farther bank, opposite the ford held by the barbarians, purposing to punish their temerity, as he must not fail to do if he was to quiet the land.

He had escaped the chief danger by acting on a common theory of barbarians, that no army will undertake an important march at night, of which Alexander so often, and he himself later in the Alps so ably, took advantage. He could now direct events himself.

Like all barbarians, these tribes ascribed Hannibal's retirement to fear. Early in the morning they followed him up and began fording the river in detached parties, expecting to make him an easy prey. Anticipating exactly this, Hannibal had made his plans. The main ford lay at a bend in the river, of which the convexity was nearest Hannibal's new position. Along the banks he had distributed his elephants as a curtain to his infantry. In the centre, opposite the ford, he placed his cavalry. No sooner had the enemy begun to throng the ford than the Carthaginian horse advanced and met them in midstream, where, riding them down by mere weight, the force of the current swept them off their feet and towards the banks. Here the elephants crushed them or the infantry cut them down. Foot had no chance whatever in the torrent against mounted men. Meanwhile, the light troops from between the elephants showered arrows and darts upon the barbarians in the water or entering the fords. Though without artillery, or long-range arms, Hannibal showed a clear idea of the value of the bend in the river which indented his own position.

New masses constantly appeared on the other bank, crowding out of all organization to gain the front. Hannibal saw that the day was his. He recalled his horse. This, retiring, unmasked the heavy infantry, which Hannibal called in from either flank and sent with a vigorous élan in close column across the ford against the ill-arrayed barbarians, followed by the cavalry, which had formed again in its rear. Nothing could resist the charge. The barbarian masses melted into a demoralized mob. A bitter defeat and merciless slaughter of these tribes taught the whole of Spain not to undervalue the new commander for his youth.

The entire operation reads like one of Alexander's battles in Asia; and shows that in dealing with similar enemies Hannibal possessed the same tremendous force. It was when pitted against the three quarters of a million of men which Rome could muster that Hannibal was called on to exercise caution and self-control, — virtues Alexander never possessed.

By this last victory Hannibal was enabled to make his conquests secure. Having, by the addition of the territory he had subdued, the whole peninsula south of the Iberus under control, he again returned to Cartagena for the winter.

XI.

SAGUNTUM. SPRING TO FALL, 219 B. C.

HANNIBAL was ready for his expedition against Rome. He controlled all Spain as far as the Ebro, save only the city of Saguntum. This he now attacked. The Romans, who had promised Saguntum their protection, did nothing but send an embassy to protest against the act. Saguntum lay on a high and naked rock, affording a besieger no facilities for the erection of works. The inhabitants were brave and skillful, and for eight months, during a part of which time he was called away to put down a rebellion on the Tagus, bid defiance to all Hannibal's efforts. Finally the city was taken; but the brave Saguntines buried themselves and their treasures in one vast conflagration. Nothing was left of the city but a heap of stones. Rome sent a second embassy to demand Hannibal's surrender. On the refusal of the demand, the senate declared war.

IN B. C. 219 Hannibal considered himself able to undertake his great expedition against Rome. Except Catalonia and the single city of Saguntum on the east coast, all Iberia was his. His army was of the best, and devoted to his cause; the chiefs of Spain promised men and means. His route he had already reconnoitred by envoys to the Gauls living on both slopes of the Alps, which envoys had returned with Gallic chiefs bearing many promises of good-will and assistance. He was ready and eager to provoke a quarrel with the great republic. Saguntum, still under Roman protection, was yet without much defense. Under a pretense that the Saguntines were attacking the Torboletes, subjects of Carthage, Hannibal advanced against the city and laid siege to it, — while the Roman senate, instead of flying to the assistance of its ward, contented itself, as it had done the year before, with sending protesting embassies both to Hannibal and to

Carthage. Hoping to force a declaration of war out of
Rome, Hannibal treated the ambassadors, when they reached
him, with marked discourtesy.

The siege of Saguntum, in 219 B. C., was no child's play.
This city was then situated about a mile from the sea. It is

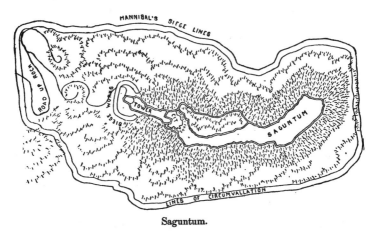

Saguntum.

now nearer three. On a long and naked rock, three hundred
to four hundred feet above the plain, commanding the entire
country, it was scarcely to be approached. On the west the
slope of the rock was least steep. Its defenses were thoroughly constructed, and it had a large population of courageous and well prepared inhabitants, plenty of stores and
the prospect of the help of its Roman allies. Hannibal
planted his main body at the western end, for though here
the walls were thickest and a great tower faced the assailant,
here also the more moderate slope of the ground alone afforded him a possible chance to work. He had an abundance
of men, stated by Livy at one hundred and fifty thousand,
and by Eutropius at one hundred and seventy thousand men,
but probably much less than either figure. The garrison was
not large, — "insufficient," says Livy. But it was not a

question of numbers. Only so many men could be put to work on the walls. The rest were mere blockaders. Hannibal hoped for a prompt surrender, but he was doomed to disappointment. He set to work to besiege the place, throwing up the usual lines of circumvallation, surrounded by numerous towers.

For a number of weeks he could make no impression whatever upon the city. Owing to the entire lack of earth upon the rock of Saguntum, the usual works could not be thrown up, and the common siege devices were unsuited to the ground. Resort had to be had to a novel kind of movable towers and engines. The besieged showed the greatest determination, and met Hannibal's siege arrangements with many daring sorties, in which both parties appear to have equally suffered. On one of these occasions Hannibal, exposing himself at the head of his troops, was so seriously wounded in the thigh that for some time he could not personally superintend the siege, which for lack of the master's hand degenerated into simple blockade. On his recovery he set to work with renewed vigor. He had as good siege material as was then known. We remember how expert the Tyrians were in their defense against Alexander a hundred years before; their daughter, Carthage, was presumably not behind her in inventiveness. But sieges were by no means Hannibal's strong point. His excellence lay in broader conceptions and more cunning manœuvres than are called out by the details of a siege.

No whit disheartened by the stubborn nature of his task, Hannibal advanced his vineæ or covered ways, erected towers with battering-rams of great size, and was finally successful in throwing down a portion of the wall and three of the towers of the town. He now ordered an assault, but though the breach was wide and the fighting was forced in heavy

columns, so that the Carthaginians were able to penetrate
even beyond the ruins of the wall, the besieged met him
with such bitter determination that, coupled with the novel
use of the falerica, — a sort of burning lance or dart, —
they drove him back with great loss, and speedily repaired
the walls; and this, though Hannibal headed the assault in
person. In the mêlée he was all but crushed by a heavy
stone. It is a curious fact that the entire experience of Hannibal in this siege was repeated in 1811 by the French.

Annoyed beyond measure at this unexpected resistance,
Hannibal now erected a wooden terrace and a huge movable
tower, armed with a goodly force of men and missile-throwers on every story, moved it up to the ditch, drove the besieged away from the wall and undermined it. This latter
was a work which could be done with pickaxes, because the
stones were not laid in cement, but clay. Thus a further
breach was opened. A fresh assault met with no greater result, for the troops found a demi-lune built behind the breach.
But Hannibal held what he had got, and though constantly
opposed by newly erected walls behind each breach he managed to operate, he made a slow but certain progress; for
with each point gained he had a proportionately better chance
for the next assault, lacking not men.

Meanwhile, the siege was interrupted by an uprising of
the Tagus barbarians, which was of so dangerous a nature
that Hannibal deemed it essential to go to the scene of action
in person. He left Maharbal, son of Himilco, in command.
This officer made some progress upon the defenses during
his chieftain's absence, while hunger and sickness had begun
to produce sad havoc within the walls. A new breach was
soon assaulted, and on this occasion the Saguntines were
driven into the citadel. Hannibal, when he had returned,
offered terms to the brave city, — hard, to be sure, but still

terms. But the inhabitants, with true Grecian pluck, refused any terms whatever. Death was to be preferred to what to them was slavery. The entire public treasure and all private wealth were collected in a huge pile, set on fire, and the most noble of the inhabitants destroyed themselves in the flames. At the same time the great tower of the burg, which had been gradually undermined, fell to the earth. Into the breach poured the Carthaginians, furious at the long defense, and spared no living soul. In the general horror of the sack, most of the inhabitants set fire to their houses and perished in the universal conflagration. There was but a pile of stones left of the once splendid city.

This siege does equal honor to the bravery and skill of both attack and defense, but little indeed to the Romans, who thus, for a period of eight months, allowed the city which they had taken under their protection to be besieged, and finally to suffer an appalling fate. Hannibal sent back to Carthage a vast amount of booty for distribution, which, being accepted, committed even the peace party to the war.

This siege shows Hannibal to have been familiar with, and able to use to good advantage, all the arts then known for besieging strong places. A fuller description of these arts is to be found in the volume on Alexander. It has been often said that the Carthaginian was not good at a siege, and he was certainly not the equal of Alexander and Cæsar in this respect. He was greater in other branches of the art. But we must not forget that in Spain he took Carteia, Arbocala and Salmantica, in addition to Saguntum; and that in Italy he captured Turin in two days, and a number of other cities as well, though unprovided with siege devices. Still Tyre and Alesia rank far beyond Saguntum.

Hannibal returned to Cartagena for the winter of 219–218 B. C., and furloughed all his Spanish troops till spring.

Rome contented herself with alleging a violation of the treaty made with her by Hasdrubal, and sent messengers, first to Hannibal and then to Carthage, the latter to demand the surrender of Hannibal and his principal officers. This demand being treated with the contempt it deserved, war was immediately declared. This war is known as the Second Punic War, or the War with Hannibal. It is in many respects the most wonderful struggle the world has ever seen.

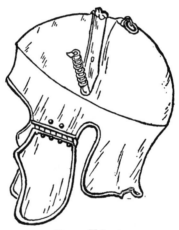

Roman Helmet.

XII.

HANNIBAL STARTS FOR ITALY. MAY, 218 B. C.

HANNIBAL undertook his expedition against Rome with his eyes wide open. He carefully made his preparations for the security of Carthage and Spain and for the equipment of the Army of Italy. He had sent embassies to the Gauls on both sides of the Alps, and from them received assurances of alliance and aid in the passage of the Alps and when he should debouch upon the valley of the Po. This secured him a base. Having no fleet to hold head against the Roman supremacy at sea, he could not operate directly from either Spain or Carthage. Southern Italy was, for this very reason, unavailable, as a single naval disaster would ruin his scheme, and the cities of lower Italy could not be relied upon to join him. Once on the Po, he would have allies, a base, and hope of aid from Macedon, with which country Rome had quarreled. The plan of an overland march to Italy was Hamilcar's; its details were all Hannibal's. It is intellectually the most gigantic plan of campaign known in military annals. Rome, unconscious of her danger, put seventy thousand men into the field, namely, twenty-six thousand under Sempronius in Sicily, for an expedition against Carthage; twenty-four thousand under Scipio for one to Spain; twenty thousand in Gaul. She was too slow to cope with Hannibal. She should have sooner sent out both her expeditions; but before either Sempronius or Scipio had got ready, Hannibal was well upon his road, and Sicily was kept busy by some naval raids cleverly pushed by the small Carthaginian fleet. With three quarters of a million men to call upon, Rome was opposing but forty-six thousand to the Army of Italy, which numbered ninety thousand.

HANNIBAL had not acted blindly in forcing a contest with Rome. He knew that sooner or later war must come, and he was prepared to carry it to her very gates. In this extraordinary undertaking Hannibal was perhaps justified, when a weaker man would have been to blame. A bold attack is always the surest defense; and aware that war must be mainly waged on land, — for Carthage had no fleet to cope with Rome, — Hannibal saw that to carry it into

Italy would do much to keep it away from Carthage, as well as put the waste of maintaining the struggle on the enemy's soil. Nothing exalts higher both this great man's military judgment and self-reliance than this step, taken, as it was, not blindly, but with all the facts considered. For there is more evidence of careful preparation by Hannibal for his invasion of Italy than by Alexander for the campaign in Asia. But it was a step which required no less a captain than Hannibal to dare and carry through.

Hannibal was anxious to make his descent on Italy before the Romans had got through with the Gallic and Illyrian wars. He had made many preparations to this end, not only in men and material, but in reconnoitring the to him unknown route. He had, as above stated, made friends of the tribes of Gaul so far as he was able to do with repeated embassies, and had, early in 220 B. C., sent across the Alps to offer to the Padane Gauls money and his coöperation against Rome. By thus securing their friendship he aimed to have an available base of operations when he should debouch from the mountain barrier of the Alps. He received flattering answers from many of these tribes, especially the Insubres on the upper Po, and the Boii farther down; but at the same time he heard from his envoys, among whom were perhaps some of his topographical engineers, by no means reassuring accounts of the difficulties to be encountered in crossing the Alps. These reports in no wise daunted Hannibal. He felt confidence in his ability to deal with the peoples through whose territories he should have to pass; he knew how to arouse their hatred of Rome as well as their love of adventure and plunder; and he believed that he could with equal readiness surmount any natural obstacles, however great.

It was evident to Hannibal that he must have a base nearer Rome than either Spain or Carthage. To operate solely from Spain or Carthage was mere hazard, — for Rome had too strong a fleet to rely on communications kept up alone by sea, and he could not protect so long a line by land. In fact, Hannibal could have, properly speaking, no communications such as Alexander had with Macedonia, or such as are essential to-day; reinforcements from Spain or Carthage must come to him in armies rather than in detachments; if in small bodies, always at the risk of capture. He practically cut himself off from any base, except such as he himself should make. Lower Italy was not available. The Roman allies in the south of the peninsula were too much committed to Rome to be relied on at the outset. Pyrrhus had found no permanent aid from them; how could he? No base presented itself which was in any respect as promising as cisalpine Gaul, in other words, the line of the Po. The insurrectionary tribes of the Gauls had but just been conquered, and their feelings were supremely bitter; many of their cousins, the Spanish Celts, were in Hannibal's ranks; the Insubres and the Boii had promised their own immediate aid on his arrival, had assured him reliable guides across the Alps, the aid of the transalpine tribes in the passage, and abundant supplies on his arrival. Thus the Po would be an effective base among allies who would look on him as their deliverer from the yoke of hated Rome. Macedon and Rome had come to a rupture, and perhaps aid might be persuaded to come through Illyria — though it was a long circuit — to meet him on the Po. With a good base on that river, with a supply of troops coming from Spain on his right, and with an allied army from Macedon to sustain him on his left, he would be firmly planted for a decisive struggle with his enemy. This was the hopeful side.

The plan was not altogether new; it had been canvassed again and again in the Barca family. The ground had, in fact, been already reconnoitred by Hamilcar; the Romans found a party of Carthaginians in Liguria in 230 B. C. But the scheme was none the less Hannibal's.

If Carthage had been mistress of the seas, southern Italy would have afforded a markedly better base than the Po. For Macedon might then readily have sustained the Carthaginian right, and reinforcements could come from home or Spain with much less time and risk. But southern Italy was full of fortified cities committed to the Roman cause; a foothold was not so easy to acquire there; and Carthage had no fleet which could compete with Rome.

Next came the question whether Hannibal should seek to reach the Po by land or by sea. Though the sea was commanded by the Roman fleet, a descent at Genoa was possible. But a single naval disaster would ruin the Carthaginian cause beyond redemption; by the overland route conflict would be avoided until the Gallic allies had been reached. Hannibal's knowledge of the topography of northern Italy was as yet meagre. He knew that from Genoa there was still a mountain range to cross to reach the Po; how much less an one than the Alps he was not advised. The Alps had already been crossed by many roving bands of large size; indeed, Gallic armies had accomplished the feat; why might not as much be done by a Carthaginian army? Moreover, in the plan to cross the Alps, there was the element of doing that which your enemy least expects, and Hannibal understood and had weighed this well.

Hannibal, says Polybius, " conducted his enterprise with consummate judgment; for he had accurately ascertained the excellent nature of the country in which he was to arrive, and the hostile disposition of its inhabitants towards the Romans; and he had for guides and conductors through the difficult passes which lay in the way natives of the country,

men who were to partake of the same hopes with himself."

Rome had acted in a vacillating manner in sustaining her
allies and in declaring war. She now committed other equal
mistakes in preparing for war. Nothing was farther from
her thoughts than that an attack could come overland from
Spain. She would have scouted the idea of the possibility
of such a thing.

The armies put into the field by Rome in B. C. 218 were as
follows: Tiberius Sempronius Longus, the consul destined
for Sicily, had two Roman legions, each of four thousand
foot and three hundred horse; sixteen thousand allied foot
and eighteen hundred horse: total twenty-six thousand four
hundred men, and one hundred and sixty quinquiremes and
twelve galleys. With this force Sempronius was to go to
Sicily, *en route* to Africa, on which he was to make a descent
like Agathocles and Regulus. The other consul, Publius
Cornelius Scipio, was to go to Spain with two Roman legions,
eight thousand foot and six hundred horse, and fourteen
thousand allied foot and sixteen hundred horse: total twenty-
four thousand two hundred men, and sixty quinquiremes.
The prætor Lucius Manlius was to march to Padane Gaul
with eighteen thousand foot and sixteen hundred horse, partly
with a view to plant colonies, partly as a military measure.

According to the table of Polybius above given, Rome was
capable at this time of putting on foot something like three
quarters of a million men. The senate must indeed have despised its adversary to send but a tenth of this force against
the Carthaginians, and to have divided this force into three
parts at that. Their eyes were opened when Hannibal
placed foot upon the soil of Italy.

The Romans had long been acting in a penny-wise, pound-
foolish manner. They had given Carthage twenty years to

recover her strength, when at any time a descent on Africa might have crushed her. They could not see the danger of a Punic occupation of Iberia. They could not believe that the Phœnicians would again wage an offensive war. They had unnecessarily quarreled with Macedonia. They had failed to finish the work of conquering the Celts and seizing the avenues of the Alps. They had delayed any systematic action on the mere notion that the next Punic war must be waged in Africa, until the enemy himself had decided on the theatre of war. The manifest Roman plan was to land in Africa while holding the Carthaginians in Spain by a stout diversion there. This they had failed to do with energy or speed. If they had been half as active as Hannibal, they could, with their fleet, have easily placed an army on the Ebro before Hannibal could reach it. As it was, Hannibal found none but natives on the Ebro; the consul Scipio had been detained on the Po by a threatened insurrection, which Hannibal's emissaries had been the means of raising. Had the Romans made a stout contest for Spain, Hannibal could not have left it. The fortunes of Carthage were too much bound up in the peninsula, as Hannibal later found to his sorrow. Had the Romans even delayed his advance a month more, snow would have closed the Alps, and they could have fallen on Africa unopposed. But Rome could scarcely conceive boldness such as Hannibal's. Time seemed ample to do things in her own way.

Hannibal was thirty-one years old when at the end of May, B. C. 218, he left New Carthage on his great expedition. The Spanish army was distributed in a very sensible fashion to meet the wants of Carthage, Spain and the " Army of Italy." It was altogether a fine body of men. It had no mercenaries, except a few Ligurians. The bulk of the forces were Carthaginian subjects, Libyans and Spaniards. Two thirds of the army were Africans, and all were hardened troops, committed to their chief by both discipline and affection.

Following was the distribution, as given by Polybius from Hannibal's copper tablet at Lacinium. The Army of Italy had eighty-two thousand infantry and twelve thousand cavalry, in addition to thirty-seven elephants, — the latter more for effect on the Gauls than for use against the Romans. Hannibal was too able a soldier to rely to too great an extent on these creatures, though he knew their value in their place. He had sent to West Africa about fourteen thousand troops from Spain, among them some deserters and disaffected men who would do well enough out of Spain, but could scarcely be relied on in the peninsula during his absence; and for the protection of Carthage had transferred four thousand West African troops to the capital. He had brought some African troops to Spain for a similar reason. He had left his brother Hasdrubal in command in the Spanish colonies with twelve thousand six hundred and fifty foot and two thousand five hundred and fifty horse, largely East Africans, twenty - one elephants and fifty-seven men - of - war, mostly quinquiremes, of which thirty-seven were equipped. The communications between Spain and Carthage were secured with as much care as the smallness of the fleet would allow, and, as a diversion, twenty quinquiremes, with one thousand soldiers aboard, were sent out to pillage the west coast of Italy; while twenty-five were dispatched to Lilybæum to essay its capture out of hand. More than this the fleet could not venture to do.

The plan was well devised and executed in all its details, and the main feature in it was, that while the Romans were sending their smallest army to cisalpine Gaul, Hannibal was ready to invade Italy through that province with a force more than twice their own.

Recent news from Carthage inspired Hannibal with more confidence in the support of his fellow-citizens than he had lately had. His army was wedded to him, as every army is to the man who exhibits the qualities of the great soldier. Hannibal laid his plans before them, told them the demand of the Romans, that he and all the principal officers of the army should be delivered up, explained the fertility of Italy to them, and the hearty allies they would there meet, and found the warmest support from one and all.

As a last act of self-denial, Hannibal sent his Spanish bride, Imilcea, and their infant son to Carthage. He did not dare expose them to the dangers he was himself about to encounter. He must do his work alone. Sixteen long years elapsed before he again embraced them. Surely no man ever undertook a great work to his own sorrow, from more purely patriotic instincts, than this same Carthaginian.

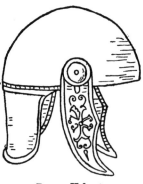

Roman Helmet.

XIII.

CATALONIA. JULY AND AUGUST, 218 B. C.

THE Army of Italy left Cartagena about the end of May. In July it crossed the Iberus in three columns, which, traversing Catalonia from south to north, by clever mountain tactics, heavy fighting and set purpose, succeeded in subduing the land. The several columns then crossed the Pyrenees and reunited at Illiberis, near modern Perpignan. The loss had been thirteen thousand men. Here Hannibal left Hanno with eleven thousand men; and here too he discharged an equal number of disaffected soldiers. He crossed the Pyrenees with less than sixty thousand men.

FROM Cartagena, where the army wintered after the capture of Saguntum, to the Ebro was twenty-six hundred stadia, three hundred and twenty-five Roman miles. Hannibal is thought to have left Cartagena about the end of May. He reached the Ebro the middle of July, having, no doubt, many things to do upon the way. This river lies in front of the Pyrenees, like a huge ditch, is the most prominent river in Iberia, and originally gave its name to the peninsula.

After crossing the Ebro, Hannibal was in Catalonia, a territory over which Rome pretended to exercise sway, — one which, at all events, had as yet been beyond Carthaginian assaults. In order to leave no danger in his rear, and to rob his enemy of a base for an invasion of the Spanish colonies of Carthage, Hannibal must first of all conquer and garrison the land. Catalonia is bounded by the eastern Pyrenees, the sea, the Ebro and the Sicoris. It is a mass of mountains, valleys, passes, precipices. It has, in history, the reputation of resisting invasion with the greatest desperation and success. Through this difficult country Hannibal made

a sharp, quick and costly campaign, of which unfortunately
there are sparse records, as there always are of Alexander's
mountain campaigns. The one thing which the old authorities invariably skip is mountain-campaigning.

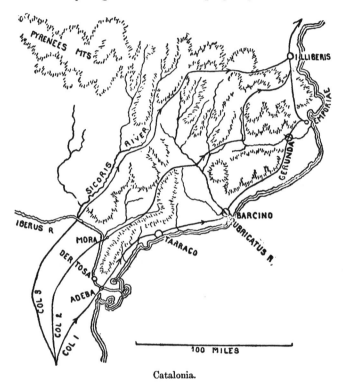

Catalonia.

Hannibal divided his army into three columns of not far
from thirty thousand men each. The right column, to judge
by the topography and the operations of later generals, and
probably with baggage and impedimenta, crossed at Adeba
(Amposta), and, aided by the fleet which skirted the coast,
overran Lower Catalonia. The second passed at modern
Mora, pushed up the valleys of the mountain range, and attacked the country at the heart. The third crossed near the

mouth of the Sicoris (Segre) and marched up the valley of that river.

The duty of the first column must have been to take possession of the coast cities, then as now many and thriving, as far as Emporiæ; that of the left column would be to follow the line of the Sicoris as far as its source in the main range of the Pyrenees. The centre would move by way of the valleys of the central range of Catalonia. Along the Rubricatus (Llobregat) was a road by which the columns could at need reunite midway, or assist each other in their operations.

Hannibal, no doubt, was with the right column, which had with it both treasure-chest and cavalry, and may be called the column of direction. Owing to the uncertainty of the Roman movements, he did not dare absent himself from the coast. The campaign covered two months and was very costly. The losses of the three columns footed up some thirteen thousand men. The Catalonians have always resisted invasion nobly. That the country could be subdued in so short a space speaks highly for Hannibal's lieutenants and the training they had received.

Having reduced Catalonia, he placed this territory under command of Hanno, and left with him ten thousand foot and one thousand horse, with headquarters probably at Barcino (Barcelona). Here too some of the Iberian regiments are said to have shown signs of disaffection, and three thousand to have deserted. But this is doubtful. At all events, Hannibal deemed it wise to state that he had given them leave to go, and also to let off eight thousand more. This act added to the devotion of the rest. He did not lose his moral power over his army. He is alleged to have had the additional motive of thus showing his confidence to accomplish what he had set out to do with limited numbers, and those only of such as were willing to cast in their lot with him for good or ill. He had so far set forth his object to his army as to inspire it with confidence, and his explanation to the Carthaginians of the alternative they had of victory or slavery raised the ambition of all to the pitch of following their venturesome young leader to the very end.

Catalonia thus reduced the Army of Italy by more than a third. It was with only fifty thousand foot and nine thousand horse that Hannibal crossed the Pyrenees.

Hannibal had waited at Emporiæ for the other columns to be ready to cross the mountain-range, and then, himself probably making his way by the pass nearest the sea, the centre and the left columns crossed at points farther west. The whole army reunited at Illiberis (Elne, near Perpignan), about the middle of September.

We know that Hannibal crossed the Iberus in three columns, and it is to be supposed that these were intended each to subdue a given part of Catalonia. The route of the columns is to a certain extent prescribed by the topographical features of the country. We know that Catalonia was subdued, and remained so until the Romans later came to its rescue. We assume, then, that the several columns traversed the country as indicated; but all we are told is of the points of departure and rendezvous, and of the result.

Hannibal had been the first man who ever frayed a passage for a regular army through the Pyrenees.

What Hannibal now had left were the best of his troops. They had been hardened by nearly twenty years of campaigning against warlike tribes in a difficult country, had been uniformly victorious, had captured many cities, including the strong fortress of Saguntum, and were well aware of their ability, hearty and self-confident. Hannibal was soldier enough to know that numbers are of less importance

than homogeneity, and was willing to carry with him no soldier whose fidelity was not unquestioned. And yet it is
probable that nothing less than the wonderful personal influence of this young general — an influence shown but seldom
in history — would have been able to weld these diverse elements into a mass capable of such unity of action as the
Army of Italy showed.

Tuba Player.

XIV.

FROM THE RHONE TO THE ALPS. FALL, 218 B. C.

FROM the Pyrenees to the Rhone, Hannibal's route was inland, on a line towards Roquemaure. Scipio, meanwhile, at Genoa, had embarked his legions for Spain, and when Hannibal reached the Rhone was at Massilia. Hearing with surprise of the presence of the Carthaginians on the Rhone, Scipio sent a scouting party up the river to discover their whereabouts. He should have marched his entire army upstream to prevent a crossing, or at least to bring Hannibal to battle before he could reach the Alps. Hannibal forced a passage at Roquemaure, and at once advanced up the river. Scipio, on receiving a report from his scouting-party, marched up to meet him; but he reached Roquemaure three days after the Carthaginian rear had left. He had lost a week's time. He then returned to Massilia, sent the bulk of his army into Spain, under his brother Cnæus, to attack the Carthaginians at their base, — a wise and long-headed policy, — and personally returned to Italy, to hold head against Hannibal when he should debouch from the Alps, with the army of the prætors, which was still upon the Po. His general scheme was good. It was weak in underrating his foe. Hannibal was cheered upon his way by an embassy from the Padane Gauls, which met him at the Rhone.

FROM the Pyrenees to the Rhone, Hannibal's progress was easy. Much interesting discussion has been made over the probable details of the route. These are more significant to the French, over whose territory it lay, than to us. The point of crossing the Rhone is more important. The populations along the road were, some friendly, some antagonistic, but Hannibal's sensible policy was an open sesame. He had a way of propitiating the native tribes which made his march safe and expeditious. Where honeyed words had no effect, gold was used. The Roman road later made, probably along the route Hannibal took (for Roman roads were not unapt to follow ancient paths, which themselves were dic-

tated by the topographical requirements), crossed the Pyrenees at Bellegarde, and went by way of Elne, Perpignan,
Narbonne, Beziers, somewhat to the north of Montpellier,
Pont d'Ambroise, Nîmes. From here Hannibal steered direct for Roquemaure, on the Rhone. It was the end of September. He reached the vicinity of this river, which flowed

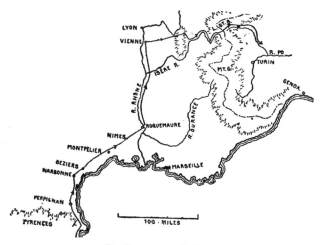

The Pyrenees to the Po.

in a mighty stream athwart his path, without opposition.
But, arrived at the Rhone, he reached the influence of the
Roman colony of Massilia (Marseille), which stood not only
herself ready to oppose his passage, but had successfully used
her power with all the tribes on the left shore, to turn them
against the Carthaginians.

Massilia was the natural ally of Rome, and Hannibal
showed a deal of political wisdom in making no effort to
pass her way, or even to conciliate her. The consul Publius
Scipio, who was to have command of the expedition against
Spain, having, after his enforced delay on the Po, made haste
to assemble his new legions, had set sail from Ostia, and

touched at Massilia to get news from Hannibal, whom he supposed to be still in Catalonia. On hearing, to his utter surprise, that Hannibal had crossed the Pyrenees, Scipio went into camp near Massilia, somewhat to the east of the mouth of the Rhone, expecting to arrest Hannibal's further progress at this wide and rapid river. He had a force of twenty-two thousand foot and two thousand horse.

Scipio was not aware of the exact time of Hannibal's arrival at the Rhone, as the latter had purposely marched some four days' distance inland. He had by no means expected such an event. It is possible that Scipio calculated that if Hannibal moved towards Italy at all, he would hug the shore of the Mediterranean until he reached the Rhone, and that he would essay an entrance to Italy by way of the Maritime Alps. Polybius says Scipio believed that Hannibal would not attempt a passage of the Alps at all; he may have looked on the Carthaginian march as a mere diversion to keep him away from Spain. But he was rudely undeceived. He at once threw over his expedition to Spain, unloaded his vessels, and sent a column of three hundred cavalry up the left bank to beat the country and to bring him notice of the approach of the rash invaders. He had no idea they were so near at hand.

Scipio must be held to blame for not sending out more numerous scouting parties to ascertain definitely Hannibal's whereabouts. He might have learned, long before Hannibal neared the Rhone, that he was not far away. He should then have taken up a central position farther from the coast, and reconnoitred the river up and down by small parties, holding himself in readiness to dispute the enemy's passage. He could not, of course, hold all the available places where the river could be crossed. This would have dispersed his troops too much and rendered them liable to be taken in the rear by a force which should manage a crossing, and thus to be beaten in detail. The central position was the best from which to move rapidly to any threatened point, while Hannibal was building boats or otherwise getting ready. In case Hannibal had still succeeded in forcing or stealing a passage, Scipio could have retired his parties concentrically to some prearranged position, and have forced Hannibal to battle before he could reach the Alps, and with the river in his rear; or else could have fallen on him in flank or rear in case he moved away. Scipio's evident duty was to bring Hannibal to battle as far from Italy as possible, even at great risk to his own army. For any pitched battle must weaken Hannibal and might ruin his attempt on Italy. But it was just this part of the art of war — strategy — of which the Romans were as yet ignorant, and of which Hannibal was so consummate a master. Scipio was no wiser than his times. It was strategy the Romans were to learn from Hannibal by so much bitter experience. As tacticians they had already made considerable strides.

It can be determined with reasonable accuracy where Hannibal crossed the Rhone. It was nearly midway between the coast and the Isère. There is a common agreement to identify the place as a little north of modern Avignon, near Roquemaure. Here Hannibal's smooth tongue came well in play. He not only gained the ear, but the active help of the inhabitants of the right bank. There were many boats on the Rhone capable of making trips at sea, and numberless canoes. These he purchased at a good price from the Gauls, and by getting their assistance, and timber for building others, — mainly common " dug-outs," — he was equipped in two days for crossing, " each one striving to stand in no need of his neighbor, but to put in himself all hope of effecting a passage," as says Polybius. This sentence well shows how

Hannibal had trained his men to self-reliance and helpful-
ness, just as Alexander had trained his Macedonians. They
could turn their hands to anything.

But on the other side of the Rhone was a tribe of Gauls
— the Cavares — who, if not imbued with Roman ideas,
were well alive to their own independence and stood ready
to oppose his passage.

Hannibal was not only fertile in resources, but he undoubtedly knew of Alexander's passage of the Hydaspes. Anticipating such opposition, he sent, on the third night, a detach-

Crossing the Rhone.

ment under Hanno, son of Bomilcar, one of his ablest
lieutenants, with local guides, some two hundred stadia
(twenty-five miles) up the river, where, near modern Pont

St. Esprit, they found an island dividing the stream; and by constructing some boats and rafts from material at hand, lashing the logs with cords which they had brought with them, they were enabled to pass to the eastern side, and at once moved downstream. Hannibal had allowed this detachment three days to accomplish its mission, and had, in the early morning of the fourth day after their leaving, all the troops of his leading division ready embarked and awaiting the signal — the smoke of a huge bonfire — which this flanking party was to give him. The Cavares were so much occupied with Hannibal's ostensible preparations to cross, about which he was particularly active for this very reason, ·and with their own schemes for opposing the passage, that they paid little heed to anything up or down the river and knew naught of Hanno's march.

Having reached a position not far upstream from the barbarian army, the flanking party hid behind an affluent of the Rhone and gave its signal. No sooner was this seen than Hannibal ordered the boats to start across. The Rhone was swollen and rapid, and it necessitated heavy work to pull through the turgid current. The flankers, who were now closing in upon the Cavares from up the river, as soon as they perceived the boats get under way, prepared to charge in upon the enemy's flank and rear. Their activity was taken advantage of by Hannibal. The heavy horsemen were in the larger boats, the infantry in the canoes. The former put across farthest upstream, so that the lighter and more frail craft could be rowed in their lee. The horses were mostly swum across, some at the side and some in the stern of each boat; but a few, ready saddled for immediate use, were aboard.

The barbarians had left their intrenchments and came down to the bank " in a scattered and tumultuous manner."

The passage began; "those who were in the larger boats vying with each other in loud cries and struggling against the rapidity of the stream, and both armies standing on each bank of the river; the Carthaginians anxious for and exhorting their men with their shouts, and the barbarians opposite raising their war-cry and daring them to come on; the scene was such as would be likely to create no small dread and anxiety in the minds of the spectators." (Polybius.) At this moment the flanking detachment debouched from hiding and took the barbarians utterly by surprise. A part of the force set the camp on fire, but the bulk fell on those who were guarding the passage. Some of the barbarians rushed to the defense of the camp; most of them remained on the shore; all were demoralized. Hannibal, who was in one of the first boats, headed his men as they landed, sharply attacked, and, without many casualties, dispersed the Gauls, who had lost their head in the surprise of Hanno, and who confusedly retired from the river to a place of safety. The work was vigorously pushed. By successive crossings before night, Hannibal's whole army, except the elephants, got put over. These latter were in the succeeding three days ferried across on huge earth-covered rafts, after much difficulty had been experienced in persuading them aboard. Here we may let Polybius tell his own story, upon which nothing can improve : —

"The elephants were brought over in the following manner : Having made a great number of rafts, they joined two of them together strongly and made them fast to the land on the bank; the breadth of the two thus united being about fifty feet. They then fastened two more to the extremity of these, which advanced out into the river; they secured also that side which was on the stream by cables from the land, fastened to some trees which grew on the bank, in order that they might not be forced away by the strength of the current. Having made this raft in the form of a bridge about two hundred feet in length, they added to the end of it two other larger floats very firmly joined together, but fastened to the rest in such a manner that the cable by which they were held might easily be cut asunder. They fixed also many ropes to these, by means of which the boats that were to tow them across might keep them from being carried down the stream; and thus resisting the current, convey the elephants on them to the other side. They next spread a great quantity of earth upon the rafts, laying it on until they had rendered them level, and similar in color with the road on the land that led to the passage. The elephants being accustomed to obey the Indians did so till they approached the water, but never daring to venture in, they first led forward two female elephants along the rafts, when the rest presently followed. Upon reaching the extreme rafts, the cables which fastened them to the rest were cut, and they were instantly towed by the boats towards the other side. At this, the elephants being thrown into great disorder, turned every way, and rushed to every part of the raft. But being surrounded on all sides by water, their fears subsided, and they were constrained to remain where they stood. In this manner were the greater part of the elephants brought over, two rafts being thus continually fitted to the rest. Some, however, through fear, threw themselves into the stream in the midst of the passage. The Indians who conducted these all perished, but the beasts themselves escaped; for owing to the strength and size of their trunks they were able to raise these above the water, and breathe through them; and thus discharging the water as it entered their mouth, they held out, and walked across the most part of the river."

Hannibal, hearing that the Roman fleet had neared the

mouth of the Rhone, at once sent a small party of five hundred Numidian cavalry down the east bank to ascertain the whereabouts of Scipio, of whose landing he had also heard rumors. He then called a meeting of the army. We are not told of what such an assembly consisted, as we are about the army-conclaves of Alexander. Probably, all officers, including syntagma — or battalion — commanders, were included. He introduced to them Magilus, and some petty chiefs of the Padane Gauls, who had come to meet the Carthaginian army. These chiefs assured the army of a march through a region affording plenty of supplies, of the fertility of Italy and the zeal of the Gauls in their behalf. Their presence had an excellent effect; and Hannibal's further exhortations put the army into first-rate cheer.

The Numidian scouting-party had very soon run into the three hundred Roman horse sent out by Scipio for the same purpose. A sharp conflict had ensued, in which the Numidians were defeated, with a loss of two hundred men to the Roman one hundred and forty, and pursued back to the Carthaginian camp-intrenchments. Here the Romans, ascertaining the fact of Hannibal's crossing, and seeing his elephants on the other side, at once turned and hurriedly made their way back to Scipio with the news. It was too late. Scipio broke camp at once, put his heavy baggage on board his ships and advanced up the river, but he reached Hannibal's camp three days after the Carthaginians had left it. His lost opportunity must have been sensibly felt.

Here is a chance to read between the lines of Polybius and of Livy, who copies him. The commander of the Roman cavalry, it is said, had penetrated to the edge of the Carthaginian camp. What easier for Hannibal than to drive him away? But Hannibal may have wanted him to see, and for this reason probably his Numidians had received orders to lure him on from wherever they found him to this spot, which orders they had courageously and admirably carried out by allowing themselves to be beaten with heavy loss and pursued. The Numidians were vastly better cavalry than the Romans, especially good on such service, and the defeat of five hundred of their number by three hundred Roman horse, with such casualties, would be incredible, were it not explained in some such way.

What Hannibal wished Scipio to believe was that he had not yet crossed the Rhone, and that it might yet be an affair of many days with him. Of this he proposed to convince Scipio's scouting-party. For if he could induce him to believe this, Scipio would probably move up the river, and thereby lose much time, which was exactly what Hannibal wanted him to do, as it would keep him the longer from Italy, Hannibal's goal. The elephants were still on the other side, with some few troops, and Hannibal made as much of a show of these latter as possible, and as little of the force on the left bank. This neat little stratagem succeeded admirably, for when the scouting-party returned to Scipio, its commander evidently gave him such information as to induce Scipio to waste nearly a week marching up the Rhone and back again. It was this week which prevented Scipio from reaching the Po in season to push on towards the passes of the Alps, to meet Hannibal there, or at least from demoralizing his Gallic allies by an attack before the Carthaginian army could reach them. All this is a mere assumption, but it is not a violent one.

When Scipio reached Roquemaure, he was much too late to make it worth while to follow up the invader, who was already far up the Rhone. The Gauls, except those under the influence of Massilia, would, from their excessive hatred of the Romans, be certain to take sides with Hannibal, and thus imperil and retard his pursuit. So he adopted the more rational policy of going back to Italy and preparing to meet Hannibal as he debouched, if he ever did so, from his harassing passage of the Alps into cisalpine Gaul.

He could reach Genoa in seven days, and would, he thought, have abundant time to prepare a warm reception for Hannibal on the Po. It has been said by some critics that he should have returned to Italy with his entire force; but, in the first place, Scipio did not fully gauge the danger Rome was running; and, in the second place, he may have thought that a descent on Spain would tend to handicap his opponent's plan. This was a sensible line of argument, and he followed it up by sending the bulk of his army by sea into Spain, under his brother, Cnæus Scipio, to carry out the original orders of the senate; while with a much smaller part he retired to northern Italy, where he could take command of the army of twenty-five thousand men which lay on the river Po, under the prætors Manlius and Atilius.

This course of Scipio's can scarcely have been a blind one. He had reason to believe that he could gather troops enough in Italy; and that he could best hamper Hannibal by attacking him at his base of supplies in Spain, and thus prevent his receiving further reinforcements, was by no means a shortsighted theory. Scipio should be commended for this reasoning, which looked beyond the immediate present. It shows that he could take a broad view of the military situation. A narrow mind may make a tactician. It never can make a strategist.

Napoleon observes: " La première qualité d'un général en chef, c'est d'avoir un esprit calme qui ne reçoive des objets qu'une impression exacte. Il ne lui est pas permis de se laisser éblouir par les bonnes nouvelles ni abattre par les mauvaises. Les sensations qu'il perçoit successivement ou simultanément dans le cours de la journée doivent se classer dans sa mémoire de manière à n'y occuper chacune que la place qui lui est dévolue ; car le raisonnement et l'appréciation des faits sont le résultat de l'exacte comparaison des différentes impressions qu'ils produisent. Il y a des hommes qui se font une singulière peinture des événements d'après leurs condi- tions morales et physiques ; aussi, malgré leurs connaissances, leur habilité, leur courage et toutes les autres qualités qu'ils possèdent, la nature ne les a pas appelés au commande- ment des armées, ni à la direction des grandes opérations militaires." Scipio showed the breadth of view Napoleon speaks of.

But Scipio, with true Roman self-reliance, underrated his adversary, and he was not yet informed of the defeat of the prætors by the Gauls, which had recently taken place. He believed that the twenty-five thousand men he expected to command in northern Italy would easily hold head against Hannibal. This proved to be an error, following on his care- lessness in allowing Hannibal to cross the Rhone without a battle, and distance him towards the Alps. Scipio's general plan was excellent ; the details were weak because he did not properly gauge the danger.

Hannibal had made haste to move up towards the moun- tains, as Livy says, fearing that Scipio would be upon his heels ; but more probably to get to the Alps before the sea- son grew too late. His infantry had been started the day after the assembly, followed by the trains. His cavalry was drawn up " towards the sea," to curtain his march, and it and the elephants formed his rear-guard under his own command, to fend off a Roman pursuit. He was forced to speed from more than one reason. He must cross the Alps before the heavy snows. Though he had allies on the Po, he was not certain of the populations through which he was to march.

Even eliminating the chances of an attack by Scipio, which, though not probable, might yet occur, his advance might excite hostility, and raise up enemies in front and flank and rear, all of which would consume time, and he had little time left. The difficulties before him were appalling; but he had burned his ships; there was but one course for him to pursue even if we assume that Hannibal was capable of turning back; he must push for Italy. And this he at once set about doing with characteristic vigor.

He was cheered on his way by the chiefs from cisalpine Gaul, whom he had met at the Rhone, and the knowledge that they and their allies had risen against the Romans. This was another fact urging him to speed in joining them. These chiefs promised him plenty of rations and reinforcements, so soon as he should reach the Po, and they hoped to conciliate their cousins along his line of march, though some of these, as will be seen, they failed to influence to peace.

Roman Helmet.

XV.

THE FOOTHILLS OF THE ALPS. OCTOBER, 218 B. C.

POLYBIUS and Livy are the two authors who have treated at length of Hannibal's passage of the Alps. The former wrote but a generation after the event, and had himself been over the ground and consulted those who lived through these times; the latter wrote in his study during the reign of Augustus. Polybius is universally accepted as the most reliable of the ancient historians; and as he and Livy are not to be reconciled, Polybius is the safer to follow. This author tells us that, in his day, only four Alpine passes were known, — those now called the Splügen and the Little St. Bernard, Mt. Genèvre, and one over the Maritime Alps. The first and last are manifestly excluded; we must choose between the other two. Hannibal, after crossing the Rhone, marched up the river, crossed the Isère and entered the Insula, as the territory between the Rhone, Isère and Mt. du Chat is called. Here he assisted one Brancus in gaining his disputed throne, and this chief conducted him to the entrance of the Alps, and furnished him with food and clothes and shoes. At the first pass, — the Chevelu, — Hannibal was attacked by the tribes living in the valley beyond; but by a clever night-attack, he gained possession of it, and descending into the valley, destroyed their chief city, modern Chambéry, and fully rationed the army. From this valley he marched up the Isère to modern Séez. Along this route we find that Polybius' account of the days' marches and his tables of distances accurately tally with the topography. On the way, some of the valley barbarians entered into alliance with him, but it was with a treacherous purpose, which Hannibal suspected, and which was soon revealed.

THE passage of the Alps by Hannibal, while one of the most wonderful operations in military history, was but a step in his gigantic conception of an invasion of Italy. Infinitely greater as a feat than Napoleon's passage of the Great St. Bernard in 1800, it was yet, like Napoleon's, but a part of one superb plan. As a wonderful thing to do, it is equaled only by Alexander's crossing the Hindu-Koosh.

Hannibal's passage of the Alps has a military value calling for no greater space than his victories at the Trebia or at
Cannæ.   But as it has been for two thousand years a shuttlecock of historic disputation, it will be treated at considerable length and somewhat controversially.   Some of the minor
points, having no special influence on the general result, — to
discuss all of which would demand an entire volume, — are
omitted.

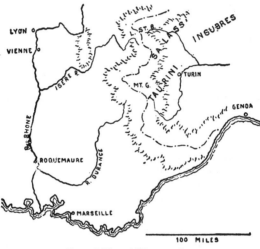

General Map of Rhone to Po.

The two ancient historians who have treated of the Second
Punic War at greatest length are Polybius and Livy.   Those
portions of the works of Polybius treating of the life of Hannibal, which have survived to us, show this historian to be
preferable to Livy as a guide in all matters military.   Especially is this so in the relation of the passage of the Alps.
The fact that Polybius was a soldier, trained under Philo-
pœmen, and that he lived and wrote but a generation after
Hannibal's extraordinary campaigns in Italy; that he had
talked with men who had lived through the terrors and sacri-

fices of the time, and that he personally visited the Alps and went over the route pursued by Hannibal, of which, at that time, there could have been no question, should alone suffice to place his narrative above that of Livy, who lived and wrote during the reign of Augustus, who copied largely and by no means always accurately from Polybius, and who wrote in a far less judicial spirit than the Greek. Livy quotes as one of his authorities " Fabius, a contemporary of this war; " but he may have copied from Fabius as inaccurately as he has from Polybius; and in any case, Polybius at first hand is better than any author at second.

Not to notice the fabulous in his writings, we cannot adopt Livy as a guide and get Hannibal across the Alps by any known route without constant contradictions and inconsistencies. Polybius, while not boasting the beautiful style of Livy, states his facts in a far more accurate manner. We can take Polybius in hand, and by crossing the Little St. Bernard, have but one or two of his phrases to construe otherwise than in their literal meaning. The distances he gives are accurate, the topographical features tally, and — most important factor of all — this route appears to have been the one which Hannibal would be apt to select; for it was the only one which would bring him into the country of his Gallic allies in Italy, the very thing he had set out from Spain to do.

In one matter only is Polybius wanting. He rarely uses the names of peoples, rivers, mountains or towns. As he was writing for his own countrymen rather than for Romans, it is not wonderful that he should have avoided the use of names which were not only unmeaning to the Greeks, but would militate against the clearness of his story. His geographical statements, however, are as accurate as those of any ancient author; his descriptions of the route are excellent. Had

Polybius used but one or two more names, there would be no room left for controversy. As between Polybius and Livy there is no question as to whom it is best to follow, — certainly in this part of Hannibal's history. You cannot reconcile their accounts nor construe Polybius in the light of Livy's statements, though in most of the known treatises on

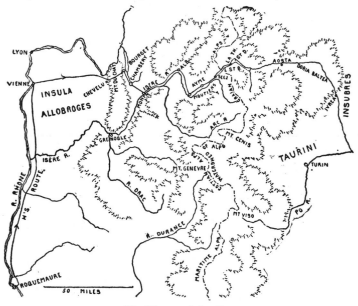

The Rhone and the Alps.

this subject, some three hundred and fifty in number, the feat is often attempted. Polybius' account is all but contemporary, is that of a soldier, and bears internal evidence of accuracy. So much cannot be said of Livy's, so far at least as the passage of the Alps is concerned. Livy sustains Polybius in most of what he narrates by copying him. Whenever he is lame or inconsistent it is apt to be when he departs from his Greek predecessor.

The Alps were not really well known to the Romans until

the time of Augustus. The only peoples to whom they were familiar were the Gauls. The earliest military road was probably made by Pompey, over Mt. Genèvre, when he had Iberia assigned to him as a province. Livy tells us of five migrations of the Gauls into Italy and the routes they pursued, — the earliest being almost six hundred years before Christ; but his account is naturally confused, for the facts are legendary. Each tribe in all probability made its way through the pass most convenient to its own territory. That the Alps had been far from insurmountable is clear, for Polybius also tells us that "the Gauls inhabiting the banks of the Rhone, many and many times before Hannibal, and very recently besides, have crossed the Alps with immense forces, to fight the Romans and assist their brothers of the plains of the Po." These passages of the mountains in no manner lessen the extraordinary character of that of Hannibal. The difference between a savage horde crossing the Alps in summer and among friends, and the passage of a regular army with all its trains, including elephants, after snow had fallen and among enemies, need not be insisted on. And, moreover, it was not the mere feat of the passage, however wonderful, but the gigantic conception of the whole plan of campaign, which elicits our wonder.

It is well to begin by reducing our problem down to its lowest denominations. Unless we do this, there is such a mass of plausible matter to be waded through that the reader's patience would fail him.

From Polybius comes our earliest information on the subject of the Alpine roads. Strabo tells us that Polybius, in some of his books now lost, mentions, as the only ones known to him, four passages of the Alpine range: first, one "through the Ligurians, close to the Tyrrhenian Sea," that is, over the Maritime Alps from Nice to Genoa; second, one "through

the country of the Taurini, which Hannibal traversed," that
is, the Cottian Alps, or over Mt. Genèvre; third, one " through

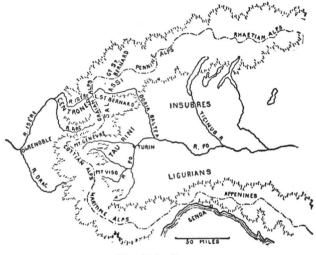

The Alpine Passes.

that of the Salassi," that is, the Graian Alps, or the Little
St. Bernard ; fourth, one over the Rhætian Alps, or the
Splügen.

With reference to the words " which Hannibal traversed,"
they are probably spurious, or a misunderstanding of Strabo's, for in his detailed account of Hannibal's passage of the
Alps, Polybius himself distinctly states that Hannibal
emerged into the land of the Insubrians, his allies; or, what
is the same thing, into the land of the Salassi, their clients. It
can scarcely be claimed that Hannibal would preferably essay
a passage which would lead him into the land of the Taurini,
the enemies of his allies, and therefore his own, and thus voluntarily add the expectation of armed conflict to the difficulties of the mountains.

If, then, Strabo is correct in quoting these four passes as

the only ones which Polybius knew, it is clear that among them we must choose our route. For where such specific information is at hand, given by so good an authority as Strabo, it seems unwise not to give it heed. Now the first and fourth passes are clearly excluded; the first on account of the presence of the Roman army at Massilia, the fourth as being much too far to the east. We are narrowed down to the two central passes, Mt. Genèvre or the Little St. Bernard. In lieu of the former, Mt. Cenis or Monte Viso might be selected. And it is between these passes that most of the critics make their choice.

It is the Little St. Bernard which appears best to satisfy the relation of Polybius, and that it is the one which Hannibal apparently took will now be explained at length. It is to be noted, moreover, that Cornelius Nepos, in his life of Hannibal, states that the Carthaginians crossed the Graian Alps, and Cælius Antipater, who wrote a hundred years after Hannibal, strongly suggests in his narrative the Little St. Bernard.

It will be permissible here to say that for many years the author has been the advocate of the Mt. Cenis route, in this following Napoleon's dictum; but a close study of the authorities, and a repeated crossing and careful comparison of the several passes, with Polybius and Livy in the hand, has convinced him that he was wrong.

Hannibal, we have seen, did not leave Cartagena in early June, 218 B. C., until he had received a deputation from the Boii and Insubres, dwelling on the Po, who had lately been at war with Rome, and who sought his assistance and promised aid in provisions and men. He was too good a soldier to march out on an unknown route over such a range as the Alps, and against such an enemy as Rome, with less. "He had," says Polybius, "made exact inquiries with respect to the fertility of the country at the foot of the Alps and near the Po, the number of its inhabitants and their courage in war," and the Carthaginians had long had Gauls in their service. The Insubres and the Boii who had come to Spain to see him could and did give him very fairly accurate details about the Alps and northern Italy, as well as assured him how warmly they would embrace his alliance. They " declared that the passage of the Alps was indeed very laborious and difficult, but not at all impossible." The fact that he was aiming to join the Insubres and Boii is one of those on which we must rely to show why Hannibal should have chosen the Little St. Bernard rather than the nearer passage over Mt. Cenis or Mt. Genèvre. He knew the Alps only by hearsay, and perhaps did not know that he must march a greater distance to gain his allies' territory; but no doubt had he been aware of the longer route his allies' guides would lead him, he would have taken it in order to reach a friendly country on which he could rely as a base. For Hannibal was an old campaigner, and had too long marched to and fro in the mountains of Spain not to know what the passage of the Alps might mean ; and he would scarcely elect to lead his army, which the march must under the most favorable conditions seriously fatigue and deplete, at once into the land of foes, not to speak of the danger of these foes blocking the passes through which he must descend from the watershed of the Alps upon the plains of Italy, and of their thus catching him in a cul-de-sac.

One of the chief elements of Polybius' account on which we rely to trace Hannibal's march are the tables of distances. These we must unquestionably accept. It will not do to brush these aside, as there is often a disposition to do by those advocating Livy as a guide. Polybius, it is universally agreed, is the most accurate and consistent of the authorities, especially in military matters. We cannot drop out of sight any part of his narrative; nor is this necessary, for the whole may be made to tally with great accuracy. Over the first part of the way — from Cartagena to the Rhone — the Romans had by Polybius' time made a road, and had so marked the route every eight stadia, that is, every Roman mile, that Polybius could give the distances *ex cathedra.* We may fairly assume that the rest of his distances are reasonably correct, as he had passed over the ground himself. At any rate, it is all we have to rely on. If any substantial portion of Polybius is brushed aside, nothing but guesswork remains. Polybius' uniform accuracy commends these distances to our undoubting acceptation.

The most important distances are, "from the Rhone, for those who are traveling along the river in the direction of its source," to the ascent of the Alps, fourteen hundred stadia; the Alps themselves, twelve hundred stadia. In addition to this, Polybius tells us that from Cartagena to the Ebro are twenty-six hundred stadia; and from the Ebro to Emporiæ, sixteen hundred stadia; and from thence to the passage of the Rhone, sixteen hundred stadia; so that we have Hannibal's entire march mapped out. For though the Roman road was built after Hannibal's day, such roads were apt to follow the old country routes which may have been in use for many centuries previous; and especially is this so in the Alps, where the watercourses or mountain-gaps mark out the natural roadways.

Thus we begin first by narrowing ourselves down to the choice of Polybius as our guide, on account of his universally accepted accuracy and of his being the only contemporary writer who gives us details, and whom we have at first-hand; and, secondly, by taking him without omission or alteration, supplementing by other authors when they do not disagree with him. Let us see how well this works.

Hannibal reached the Rhone at Roquemaure, and actually crossed the river a league above. This seems to be well proven by the description of the river and by its distance, as given by Polybius, from Emporiæ, the Insula Allobrogum (or Delta made by the Rhone, Isère and Mt. du Chat), and the sea. The distance from Emporiæ is given as sixteen hundred stadia, two hundred miles; and it is actually two hundred and four from Emporiæ to Roquemaure. The whole distance from crossing the Rhone to the foot of the Alps being given as fourteen hundred stadia, one hundred and seventy-five Roman miles, Polybius says that from the Insula to the Alps was eight hundred stadia, one hundred miles, leaving seventy-five miles from the crossing to the Insula. Roquemaure is just about seventy-five miles from the confluence of the Rhone and Isère, that is, the Insula. It is also sixty miles from the ancient seashore line, at say Foz; and Polybius states the sea to be about four days' march from the place of crossing, which, at fifteen miles a day, is accurate enough. Moreover, the Rhone here " flows in a single stream," which does not often occur, as the Rhone is generally full of islands; and it is improbable that Hannibal crossed below the river Durance (where there is a similar stretch without islands), as he would in that event have had that stream to cross as well. The island where Hanno passed the river is just above Pont St. Esprit, opposite La Palud.

The proof of our assumption that Hannibal crossed the Little St. Bernard lies largely in the accurate tally of days and distances from the crossing of the Rhone. These must be carefully computed, even at the risk of being somewhat tiresome.

As already narrated, the army was got over, excepting the elephants, on the fifth day after the arrival at the Rhone. On the sixth day, the five hundred Numidian horse was sent out towards Massilia, and came back with the Romans at their heels; and the army held the meeting at which the chiefs of the allies on the Po were presented. On the seventh day the infantry set off up the Rhone, and on this and the eighth day the elephants were got across. On the ninth, Hannibal, with the cavalry and the elephants, followed the column as rear-guard.

Three days after, Publius Scipio reached Roquemaure. This gave six days for his scouting-detachment to rejoin him and for him to march to Roquemaure. It being eight days' march (four down and four up), he evidently made it, as Polybius says, " with all possible haste."

Polybius describes the Rhone as flowing towards the setting sun of winter, that is, about from northeast to southwest. Here is clearly an inaccuracy, though, indeed, the Rhone, in a general line from its source to its mouth, does so run. But it first flows west and then south, making an angle at Lyons. In this, as in other matters, Polybius, writing for the Greeks, who knew nothing of this part of the world, no doubt meant to describe the general direction of the river and of Hannibal's march; and no doubt his own ideas of the direction were as limited as those of all ancients in respect to geography. He had no instruments, and spoke solely by the sun and stars.

After crossing, Hannibal reached the Insula in four days' march; but the infantry, — with baggage, presumably, — which formed the head and bulk of the column, had two days' start, and thus marched the seventy-five miles in six days, twelve and one half miles a day. As they had several rivers to cross on the route, bridging some of which would eat up time, this rate of speed was good. The rear-guard — elephants and cavalry — easily made the same distance in four days, nineteen miles a day, for it was unincumbered with baggage, and had the road prepared for it.

The Insula is well described by Polybius by likening it to
the Delta of the Nile, but having rugged mountains on one
side instead of the sea. It can be nothing but the triangular region between the Rhone and Isère, closed on the east
by the Mt. du Chat. The description tallies with Polybius'
statement that the course of the Rhone is southwest. That
his geography was no better than that of the day is small

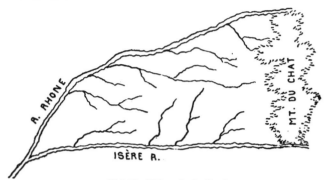

Polybius' Idea of the Insula.

wonder. He likens the mountains on the third side to the
position of the sea in the Nile Delta, and no doubt had in his
mind something like the accompanying chart. The fact that
this triangular territory is level and very abundantly watered
adds to the accuracy of the description. It is universally
accepted as the Insula of Polybius.

At the Insula, Hannibal found two brothers contending
for their kingdom, — probably a tribe of the Allobroges,
though perhaps a larger sovereignty. Embracing the cause
of the eldest, Brancus, who was also the one favored by the
majority of the tribe, Hannibal made a strong ally, from
whom he received much subsequent assistance in munitions,
corn, clothing, arms and shoes, the latter of greatest value
on the mountain roads, and in protection from the rest of the
Allobroges as far as the foot of the Alps.

Some modern authorities, relying on the difficulty of crossing the Isère at its confluence with the Rhone, of which Polybius does not speak, make Hannibal march up the left
bank of the Isère as far as the Drac or the Arc, and thence
turn towards the mountains up one or other of these streams.
But Polybius rarely mentions difficulty in crossing rivers;
Hannibal's men were expert pontonniers. The Allobroges
lived in the Insula, and, to aid Brancus, Hannibal must
have crossed the Isère in any event, having done which there
was no reason for him to recross it. Again, the left bank of

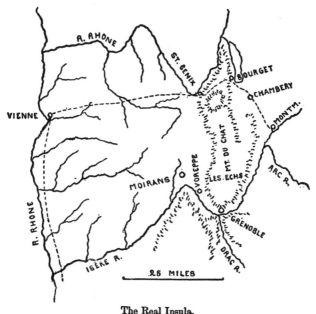

The Real Insula.

the Isère was in places almost impassable to an army, especially one with cavalry and elephants. Near Grenoble
the defiles were too narrow for troops to file through, and
the streams to be crossed were rapid torrents. The modern road is largely blasted in the rock. And as Polybius

says that Hannibal moved fourteen hundred stadia up "the river," meaning no doubt the Rhone, and not the Rhone *and* the Isère, and expressly states that Hannibal "crossed (the Alps) in the part where they touch upon the Rhone," it would seem that the Isère route, which makes him cross the range so far away from the Rhone, is inadmissible. The only places where the Rhone touches the Alps at a practicable gap are Martigny, near the Great St. Bernard, — then an unknown pass, and therefore not to be considered, — or St. Genix, where is the entrance to the Mt. du Chat, one of the foothills of the Alps. This latter is therefore clearly indicated, and it is the route we are now to follow him over.

There is but one difficulty in the distance of fourteen hundred stadia "along the river" from the crossing of the Rhone to the foot of the Alps. It obliges Hannibal to leave " the river " — that is, the Rhone — at some point, and move across country to another point, "on the river." But it is quite natural that his Gallic guide should have told him how many miles he could thus save, and equally natural that Polybius should not mention the cutting off of the angle at Lyons, for "along the river" would naturally cover such a deviation, if Hannibal regained "the river" at the end of his short-cut, while to leave the Rhone for the Isère would not. Hannibal probably left the Rhone at Vienne and rejoined it at St. Genix, marching along the then usual route via Bourgoin, afterwards made into a Roman road.

There are some lesser indications that Hannibal came this way, upon which, however, it will not do to lean too heavily. In 1714, a silver shield, with the common Carthaginian device of a lion and palm, and engraved in a manner unlike Roman work but much like Carthaginian medals, was found at the village of Passage, which lies on a hill where, on this route, you first get a view of the main chain of the Alps.

This shield, now in the Louvre, may have been, it is thought, a votive offering made by Hannibal on his approach to the greatest mountain chain of Europe, which he was about to cross. And indeed the name Passage is by an ancient tradition of the place said to come from the fact that Hannibal marched that way. Still, such traditions are unreliable. The Alps are full of them, and the modern are with difficulty to be distinguished from the ancient.

Near modern Aouste, Brancus, the chief of the Allobroges,

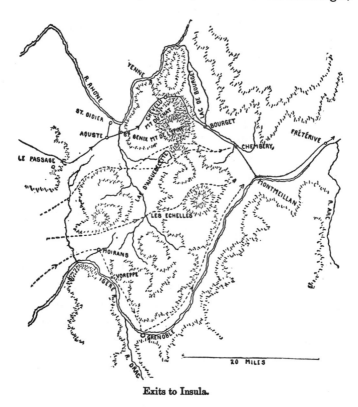

Exits to Insula.

left Hannibal. Here the flat country ends, and Polybius states that the chief " secured them from all attack till they

drew near the foot of the Alps." From the confluence of
the Rhone and Isère to Chevelu, at the foot of the Mt. du
Chat, is, by our route, just about one hundred miles, the eight
hundred stadia of Polybius. From St. Genix the Rhone
cannot be followed far upstream, owing to its precipitous
banks from La Balme to Yenne, and around the head of the
Mt. du Chat, where the present road has been blasted a considerable part of the way. Hannibal probably struck from
St. Genix over the hills by Chevelu, with only the guides
from his Padane allies as a compass.

There are now several passes from "the Island" over the
foothills of the Alps. The most southerly one, by Moirans
to Voreppe and Grenoble, can scarcely have been the one
selected by Hannibal; for he would not have come so far up
the Rhone, merely to go back on his steps. He would rather
have kept along the Isère to begin with, and we have shown
the difficulty of this route. The next northerly one is Les
Echelles, which was not opened until the seventeenth century, and up to that time had at many places stairs cut in the
rocks to aid in the ascent. To Hannibal's elephants and cavalry, not to mention pack-mules, this route was an impossibility. Hannibal probably did not even know of it. Next come
two routes to Chambéry, on either side of the lake of Aigue-
bellette, but they are only practicable for mules. The last
is the Mt. du Chat, the Chevelu Pass, so called from the village at its western outlet; and this alone fulfills the table of
distances, which are best taken from the later established
Augustan Itinerary, or which may be roughly reckoned
from the course of the roads to-day. This alone is "where
the Alps touch upon the Rhone." Moreover, it is vastly
easier than the others, and Polybius says that Hannibal
reached the Alps at a place "through which alone the army
could pass." This leads us to suppose that the others were

as yet unknown, and at his time it is altogether probable that only this one was practicable. All things considered, the Chevelu Pass comes nearest the description of Polybius ; and even to-day the people tell you that there is no road (by which they mean none over which they care to take you) across this range between the Chevelu Pass and the Grande Chartreuse, that is, the first one above cited.

When Hannibal reached the foot of the mountain he found that the Allobroges from beyond the Mt. du Chat, notified perhaps by those in the Insula who had sided against Brancus, had occupied the pass he intended to use. He camped, and sent out his Gallic guides as spies, to ascertain the exact

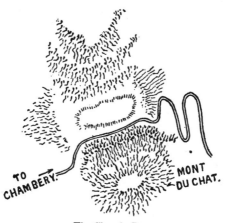

The Chevelu Pass.

situation. These came back with the information that the barbarians held the pass in force only in the daytime, but retired to their village, on the farther side of the pass, to spend the night. This was a common custom among the barbarians. Operations at night were looked on as impossible. But Hannibal was not of like mind. He ordered many campfires to be lighted, to fortify the barbarians in the impression that he would not stir till morning, — an old and worn-out ruse, which, despite its simplicity, is apt to succeed, — and then, heading his best troops in light order, he seized on the pass after nightfall, apparently unopposed.

At the summit of the pass, on the left going in the direction Hannibal took, the rocks are not high, — less than one hundred feet above the road. On the right rises to a considerable altitude the peak called the Mt. du Chat, which gives its name to the range of which it is the summit. The left hand rocks were probably then as now covered with a scrub growth, and are full of hiding-places, where for about a quarter of a mile archers could send down a murderous fire on a column passing the defile. This falls in well with what Polybius states the operations of the Allobroges and Hannibal to have been. They had probably taken up a position on this rock, from which it would be hard to dislodge a force, as well as on the heights opposite ; and on their decamping, after dark, Hannibal took advantage of the situation, and placed his own troops on the same height.

He now had possession of the defile, but he had a very steep and difficult descent before him. The mountain on the Chambéry side rises sharply from the valley, and the road to-day is cut into the hillside in zigzags. Still he had the enemy at a disadvantage. When daylight came, and the Allobroges returned to the pass, they found themselves checkmated ; but seeing with how great difficulty the Carthaginians were making their way beyond the defile (there was probably only an apology for a road, a mule-path, at best), they began several simultaneous attacks at different places on the marching column. The pack train especially suffered from this attack. There seems to have been a regular stampede, such as we sometimes see in our Indian wars, and many wounded and frightened animals rolled down the precipice, which at the outlet of the defile lies on the left of the road; for whatever path there was must have led downward, with the heights upon the right.

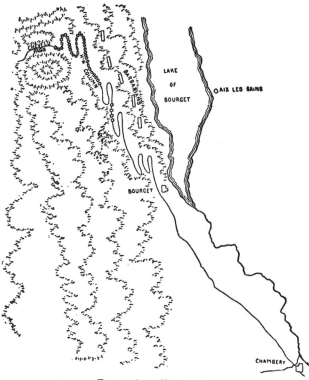

Descent from Chevelu Pass.

Seeing the danger to his baggage, the preservation of which was of the highest necessity in his mountain march, Hannibal advanced on the Allobroges, with the body which had seized the defile; and after some time, " as he made his attack from higher ground," was enabled to drive them back. Had the barbarians been able to attack the column from above, Hannibal would have been in soro strait, but his possession of the defile enabled but few to reach the ground above the road. They fought so stubbornly, however, that most of them were killed; for the lay of the land was such that they were compelled to fight up the steep mountain-side. This, in olden times, was a much more serious obstacle than since the invention of gunpowder, for it was hard to hurl darts effectively against an enemy standing on ground far above you. The train was then enabled to make its way out of the bad ground of the pass, and down the road, towards the plain beyond.

Some writers have placed at modern Chambéry the town to which the barbarians retired at night from the pass Hannibal had just forced. But the site of this town is too far from the pass to enable the barbarians to get to it each night and regain their posts by morning. Bourget would be a much more likely place, though Chambéry was apt to be the location of the chief place of the valley.

The road, from the pass down to the foot of the Mt. du Chat, overhangs the lake of Bourget, and the fact that Polybius does not mention this splendid sheet of water has been quoted against this route. But the lake had no military significance, and it was natural enough that Polybius should not mention it in connection with a military operation, any more than expend rhetoric on the magnificence of the Alps.

On reaching the level, Hannibal advanced on the city of the Allobroges, which he easily captured, as it was bared of defenders. Very likely this was on the site of modern Chambéry, about ten miles from the pass. Here he found many horses, beasts of burden and captives, and corn and cattle enough for three days' rations. These rich supplies coincide with the natural fertility of the Chambéry plain, to which the plains about modern Aix les Bains are tributary. In fact, the entire valley of the Isère is rich beyond any other which is the approach to a pass suggested as the one by which Hannibal crossed the Alps. It is perhaps the only one west of the main range able to sustain an army living, as Hannibal's was, on the country. The destruction of their town was a salutary lesson to all barbarians of the vicinity.

From Chambéry to Montmeillan, the valley is four to six miles wide, a rich level of alluvial land, which character it retains in all but its breadth to Albertville. Judging from the numbers sent against Hannibal at the defile, it was well populated, which is the equivalent of fertility. From Albertville the valley is for a dozen miles towards Moutiers somewhat narrower, and inclosed between steep hills; but a number of ruined feudal castles still show that its productiveness is not recent, and to-day a very expensive railroad is building up the Isère, for the trade of the valley alone. Except in one or two places, where it narrows almost to a gorge, it is

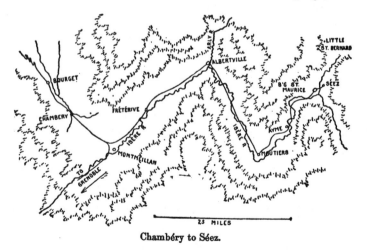

Chambéry to Séez.

wide and fertile, and the slopes are not only cultivated upwards for miles, but there are levels at the tops of the abutting hills which sustain large parishes. The entire valley is in marked contrast to any other route suggested; and it is certainly of all of them the one which was surely productive, and was apt to have a population of sufficient size to build roads, at the time of Hannibal's passage. To construct a road up the Isère from the Chambéry plain is nowhere of extreme difficulty; any of the other passes are in places impracticable, except for the modern military road built at an enormous cost. With the slender means at the command of the barbarians, therefore, the Isère route was apt to have by far the best road for an army to take.

Hannibal camped for one day at the captured village, no doubt to collect rations and forage, as well as to give his men a short rest after their perilous work, and to explain to them their further route. Like all great generals, he was apt to keep touch with the mood of his men; and often convoked them in assembly, which stood in lieu of a stirring order of the day. The army appreciated its perilous undertaking. On either hand were high knife-blade or saw-tooth ridges, at the north the lake of Bourget, on the south the white-topped outlying spurs of the Alps, on the summits of which fresh snow had already fallen. This outlook on the mountains they had yet to cross must have had a repellent effect on the Carthaginians. The Alps at times look remorseless. But Hannibal seems to have found no difficulty in cheering up his men. He had a persuasive tongue.

Assuming that as far as the Mt. du Chat our route has been correct, — and the distances, it will be observed, agree as closely as the necessary slight changes of route will allow, — there remained to be made, according to Polybius, from the "entrance to the Alps" to the "foot of the Alps" at the Italian plains a march, in fifteen days, of twelve hundred stadia, or one hundred and fifty Roman miles. The first day was the one taken up by fighting through the defile just passed, and the army lay encamped at its close on the

plains of Chambéry, where they spent the second day in rest
and making ready for the dangerous march before them.
Polybius tells us that on the fourth day after resuming the
march (the sixth from the "entrance to the Alps"), the
march being now along the Isère, envoys from the inhabitants (Centrones, into whose land he was just entering,
at modern Albertville) came out to meet the Carthaginians
with boughs and garlands, offering hostages and supplying
cattle to its troops, "desirous," they said, "of neither doing
nor suffering any injury." Hannibal was shrewdly suspicious
of their intentions, but deemed it wise to conceal his mood.
He saw that to openly antagonize them would place him in a
bad predicament. He "pretended to enter into an alliance
of amity with them," took some of their number as guides,
in addition to those he had received from his Insubrian allies,
and marched on two days farther, which brought him to "the
foot of the highest ridge of the Alps."

It is nowhere suggested that the army lost its way, and
indeed the Little St. Bernard is so plain a gap in the range
that guides were almost unnecessary, except to point out the
details of the route. This can scarcely be said of any other
pass. Having reached this spot on the eighth day from
Chevelu, Hannibal found his suspicions confirmed; the defile leading from the valley to the pass was occupied by the
barbarians, who attacked the head of his column at its entrance, which was "difficult of access and precipitous." This
was no doubt near Séez, at the foot of the Little St. Bernard.

There are grave objections to the proposition advocated
by many, in this following Napoleon, that Hannibal turned
from modern Montmeillan up the Arc and crossed the Mt.
Cenis, though indeed this might now be the better route for
an army to take. First and foremost, the route is not men-

tioned by Polybius as known to him, as it certainly would have been if Hannibal had passed over it. Nor does Strabo mention it. Again, the valley of the Arc is narrow and rocky and far from rich. It would be unable, indeed, to sustain an army at the present day. It could not feed a sufficient population to equip an army capable of holding head against Hannibal, as was done in the passage of the main ridge. The Mt. Cenis road would lead him into the land of the unfriendly Taurini. Even the authority of Napoleon cannot overcome these objections.

Napoleon attacks this question with his usual assertiveness, in a way to bear down all controversy. And in so doing he argues, unconsciously of course, from misstatements. He says that Polybius and Livy both allege that Hannibal first entered Italy in the land of the Taurini. But Polybius expressly says that Hannibal entered Italy in the land of the Insubrians; it is Strabo who says that Polybius states that he debouched into the Taurinian territory, — in other words second-hand evidence, and probably spurious at that; and were it not so, Polybius is surely more credible in his own words than by the hearsay of even Strabo. Were not Strabo expressly contradicted by Polybius, he would be entirely credible, but in this instance we cannot pay heed to what he says.

Putting aside the fact that only four passes are mentioned by Strabo, it is clear that Napoleon argues like a soldier of this century; not as Hannibal must have done in crossing the greatest of mountain ranges quite unknown to him, and with an equally unknown but gigantic problem beyond. It seems evident that Hannibal would make every possible sacrifice of distance, ease and even safety, in order to descend from the Alps among friends. Moreover, the Mt. Cenis valley is barely three fourths of a mile wide in any place, and narrows

down to a few hundred yards. It is a desolate, poverty-
stricken valley now, — what must it have been in Hannibal's
era? How could he have fed his men along this route?

Napoleon was apt to speak as well as to act from his intuitions. But even Napoleon's intuitions are not history,
though, indeed, they were so wonderful as often to make it.
And, curiously, in this matter of crossing the Alps, Napoleon did not seem to be positive about the Mt. Cenis route.
For one day on the passage of Monte Cervo, he is said to
have remarked: " Il [Annibal] n'a pu prendre qu'un des
cols du revers septentrionale du Viso," which leaves a considerable choice of passes.

And, after all said, the question is not what a military
man would do or ought to do, but what does Polybius say
Hannibal did?

It will not do to assume that Hannibal knew very much
about the Alps. This is where Napoleon errs. What
he knew he had learned from his allies, the Insubres, and
from his own officers who had been, not all through the
Alps, but only through such passes as would lead to the territory of the Insubres. It is scarcely probable that the Insubres knew much about any of the Alpine passes except
the one at their very doors; and it is still less probable
that they would have directed Hannibal or Hannibal's officers to a pass or passes which would lead him into the
domain of the Taurini, their enemies. The question for
Hannibal's topographical engineers, if any were with the
embassy which visited the Padane Gauls, to answer was, not
which was the easiest of the passes of the Alps, but was the
passage which would lead the army to the territory of their
allies a practicable one? Still, had they been called on to
answer the first question, they must have pointed out the
Little St. Bernard. For this is not only the easiest in the

Alps for an army, but it and the Mt. du Chat are those
which are the most readily followed, even without guides.

Now, if Hannibal did really cross the Mt. du Chat and
head up the Isère towards the Little St. Bernard, the distances of Polybius should agree with the miles to be covered
along this route. And we find that they do very closely
agree. The army would naturally follow the river, for this
was the only practicable way, and along its banks was subse-
quently built the Roman road. In three days from Bourget
or Chambéry, four from the western foot of the Mt. du Chat,
the army would reach the Arly, at modern Conflans or
Albertville, where they would be met by the envoys of the
Centrones, above mentioned, whose boundary this river was.
Almost to modern Moutiers on the sixth, and to modern
Ayme on the seventh, would be fair marches, and the middle
of the eighth would find the army at modern Bourg St.
Maurice or Séez. The march so far would be easy and along
a valley where the barbarians would not be apt to attack, for
it is several miles wide near Chambéry, and from one upwards near Albertville, which would enable Hannibal to forestall any attack with ease; and that there was no fighting
is what Polybius tells us. From Bourget to Séez is seventy-
five miles. To make this in six days is twelve and a half
miles a day, — a fair rate of speed for a long column, especially while gathering rations. So far, Polybius' account
coincides as well with this route as it is possible to expect.

XVI.

THE SUMMIT OF THE ALPS. OCTOBER, 218 B. C.

HANNIBAL'S suspicions were confirmed. At the defile at the foot of the Little St. Bernard, his pretended allies made an attack on his marching column; and it was with extreme difficulty that he beat them off and saved his army, and this with heavy loss. The mention of "a certain white rock," by Polybius, enables us to locate the battle-field. During the battle, the train was pushed on ahead up towards the summit of the pass, and when the army reached the spot it rested two days. Polybius describes a plain at the top of the pass crossed by Hannibal, which corresponds with that at the top of the Little St. Bernard. Here Hannibal cheered his army by showing them that they were on the watershed and that their course would now be downward, towards fertile Italy. Snow had fallen, there was no vegetation, and the loss of part of the train in the late battle made the prospect serious. On the way down, the men had difficulty in keeping to the road, or in maintaining their footing. Many slid down the precipices and were killed. Not far down they found the road carried away by a landslide. Starvation stared them in the face; but Hannibal managed to get the road repaired and thence descended to pasturage. The elephants were all but dead before they got forage. In three days from the break in the road they reached the level country and were among friends. Taking all these facts into consideration, there remains small doubt that it was the Little St. Bernard by which the Carthaginians crossed the Alps. The one fact suffices that they were led by Insubrian guides, and this pass alone, among those then known, would take them into friendly territory. Moreover, on this route, the days and distances accord better with those given by Polybius than they can be made to do over any other pass.

THE ground at Séez admirably coincides with what Polybius tells us of the attack made at the foot of the highest pass by the barbarians on the Carthaginian column. It was the end of October. Following is substantially his account.

Though Hannibal had seen fit to receive the advances of the barbarians who met him at the Arly, he had yet, with commendable prudence, taken his measures to be ready for a possible attack. He placed the baggage, elephants and cavalry in front, while with the heavy-armed troops he held the

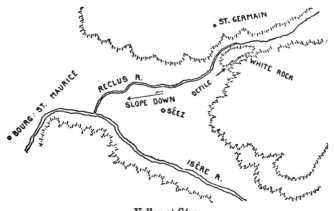

Valley at Séez.

rear. When the Carthaginians, in this order, "were passing through a ravine very difficult of access, and closed in by steep and rugged heights, . . . the barbarians, having, meanwhile, assembled together in great numbers, made a sudden attack." The column had apparently made some progress through the defile, but the barbarians, who had secretly lined the heights bordering upon it, " advancing along the sides of the mountain " as fast as the Carthaginians through the defile, rolled rocks and hurled stones upon them, and spread such confusion and disorder in the ranks as to cause the loss of a vast number of men, beasts of burden and horses. Though but few, and these the most active of the barbarians, could clamber up the steep sides of the ravine, it was difficult to cope with this attack ; but, as the bulk of the barbarians had apparently fallen on the rear-guard as it was moving up the Séez slope, they were more easily held in check.   Hannibal saw at once that if he was able to hold the mouth of the

defile, he could fend off pursuit, and by suitable flanking parties hold back the attacks on the column filing through. He,
therefore, with half the army, occupied "a certain white rock,
strong from its position," which commanded the approaches
to the defile, and, making his bivouac close to it for the night,
was able to drive off the enemy, and get his entire column
through by morning. For the enemy had difficulty in making his way along the precipices bordering the defile during
the day, and after nightfall could scarcely do so at all.

The train and cavalry and elephants had been kept in motion all night, and were well on ahead ("now separated from
him"), with part of the infantry column following on. These
suffered next day only from isolated attacks by smaller detachments, which may perhaps have advanced along the easier
slope above St. Germain, so as to head off the Carthaginian
army. The exhibition of the elephants, which the barbarians
had never seen, and upon which they looked as something
supernatural, always checked their advance. On the following, the ninth day, Hannibal made his way to the head of
column and reached the summit of the pass. Here he halted
to reorganize his column, and camped two days, during which
time many stragglers and animals came in, contrary to all expectation. The pack-animals had, however, mostly lost their
loads. This fight, and that at the Mt. du Chat, must have
been very severe, as much of the total loss is to be ascribed
to them. So far Polybius, interspersed with explanations.

Now let us look at our terrain. Just below Séez, the valley of the Isère, which here is wide and level, and to-day under fine cultivation, narrows, and makes a sharp bend to the
southeast; and it is here joined from the northeast by the
Reclus, a stream having its rise in the Little St. Bernard, and
fed by numberless brooks from the mountains on either hand.
The ground from the river slopes up, and finally, after a

rise of about six hundred feet in a slope of over a mile, narrows to a gorge. This slope has on either hand high mountains, and forms an excellent defensive battle-field for any one backing up against the defile.

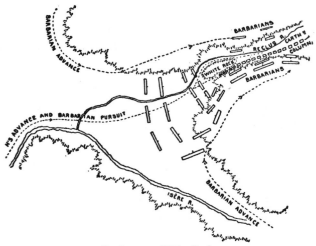

Battle at the White Rock.

Up a ravine on the left bank of the Reclus, probably went the old Roman road. It is also probable that whatever road the barbarians had then made ran up this bank. That they had made a road through the pass we are not only informed by the authorities, but we know that the pass is utterly impracticable without a road of some kind. The population on this route was quite equal to making fair roads for foot and packs, which the necessarily sparse population of the Mt. Cenis would not be apt to have done. Dominating this road, as well as the Reclus, between which it stands boldly out, is a high white rock of gypsum, whose face is naked, and which is here universally known as La Roche Blanche. To-day it is mined, and the rock ground into fine plaster. With reference to this rock, a tradition exists in the place that a great battle was fought at its foot. Huge bones are said to have been dug out of the river-bed ; and we know that fully half the elephants perished on the passage. Too much faith must not be placed on such notions, however, as the Alps are full of traditions, many of them of deliberate fabrication.

The Carthaginian advance was probably up the ravine road. The barbarians, anticipating this, had sent a detachment up the heights on either side, had occupied the defile some way from the entrance, and had waited in the woods for the column to get well engaged in the defile before they attacked it. The bulk of their force was on the plain in Hannibal's rear. Hannibal's task, then, was to defeat the attack on the marching column, as well as to prevent the main body of the barbarians from pursuing. For this latter purpose, he backed up against the Roche Blanche, in which position he could with a handful oppose a host. Possibly a column of light troops may have made its way up the rocky bed of the river, which corresponds well with the words used by Polybius, and have joined the main column nearer the source of Reclus.

The Roche Blanche is perhaps three hundred feet high and commands the whole vicinity, though we must not forget the short carriage of the arms of Hannibal. It is probable that Hannibal only backed up against the rock and did not use the top of it, though indeed he may have placed archers and slingers at the top to advantage. What he did was to form his line in front of the mouth of the defile, and there hold the enemy in check.

The road all the way up is very narrow and difficult, and the army could well spend all night getting through the defile ; but as we ascend towards the source of the Reclus the valley widens, and here Hannibal could make his way to the head of column, so as to " lead it to the summit," as Polybius says he did.

Within the present generation there has been built through the Little St. Bernard a military road which, by many and long windings along the left bank and far above the Reclus, reaches the summit. The old road on the right bank is now

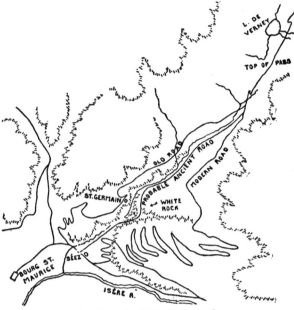

Roads up the Little St Bernard.

practicable only for mules. The Roman road, as well as the Gallic road, probably ran nearer the stream, — in places climbing up the slope to avoid a particularly bad spot.

Thus the army reached the summit of the pass, and here it rested two days.

There is here what Polybius calls, and what may, in the midst of the rugged splendor of the higher Alps, properly be called, a plain, perhaps a couple of miles long, well sheltered by the surrounding heights, and having not far from its centre a small lake, from which rises the Doria. This exactly corresponds to Polybius' description of the summit of the pass by which Hannibal crossed. The summit is full of rocky hills and vales, and gradually slopes towards the northeast. So good a camping-place for an army of thirty thousand men, at the very top of an Alpine gap, it would be hard to find elsewhere. And though the fact has no particular value, it may be mentioned that near by is a large inclosure of stones, somewhat similar to Druidical temples, universally known as Hannibal's circle, where he is supposed to have held a council. Were this so, however, it must be assumed

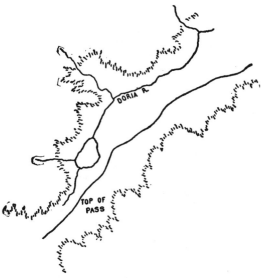

Plain at top of Little St. Bernard.

that he did not find time to stop to build a memorial of the event. These traditions go for nothing.

When we come to reckon distances, it is to be noted that from Chevelu to this plain is a trifle more than eighty miles. One might vary the distance by ten per cent., for mountain roads are long or short according to the grade sought to be kept. The distance tallies closely enough. The army had been eight days, not counting the rest-day, on the way. This is as well as mountain marches can be made. The battle did not seriously delay the column, which was kept in as rapid motion as possible. But Hannibal's anticipation of battle had obliged the van to wait until the trains, which usually marched in the rear, could gain the head of column.

We now approach what to some has appeared to be a difficulty.

" There was already snow collected on the summit of the mountains, as it was now near the setting of the Pleiades " (end of October). " Wherefore, seeing his troops in a state of great dejection from the hardships they had suffered and those that still awaited them, Hannibal sought, by drawing them together, to raise their drooping spirits. The sight of Italy was the readiest expedient he had for this purpose, for it is so close beneath the mountains that, when viewed together, the Alps appear as a citadel of Italy. Pointing out, therefore, to his soldiers the plains adjacent to the Po, and reminding them of the friendly disposition of their inhabitants, the Gauls, towards them, and showing them the place where Rome itself was situated, he in some degree renewed their courage. On the morrow they decamped and began the descent."

So far we have always taken Polybius literally; but if the above passage is to be so understood, the Little St. Bernard route must be abandoned, or Polybius classed with the romancers. And the advocates of other passes have laid great stress upon this paragraph. No actual view of the plains of the Po can be had from the summit of the Little St. Bernard Pass. Some claim that Polybius was speaking literally of the plains of the Po, as he was of course figuratively of the site of Rome, which is four hundred miles distant as the crow flies, and maintain that a view can be had of the plains of the Po from heights flanking some other passes. But there is less difficulty to be encountered in taking Polybius to mean that Hannibal pointed out the downward slope of the mountain and the downward flow of the watercourses, which begin right here, and told his men that at the foot of the heights where they then stood lay the lands of the friendly Gauls, and beyond it Rome, than there is in making the rest of Polybius agree with any route near which the plains below can actually be seen. There is no special violence done to Polybius in reading this whole passage figuratively; and though there are one or two crests from which, under very favorable conditions, a dim view of the plains below may be had, there is not a single pass in the Alps from which any one pretends that the Po can be seen. From the only other pass known to Polybius which comes at all near to fitting his relation, Mt. Genèvre, no view of the Padane valley can be had. The romantic account of Livy of itself fully proves the author's ignorance of the Alps. Indeed, Livy makes no pretense to have written his history anywhere except in his study; and while its value in other respects is undoubted, in military matters, it is, when in conflict with Polybius, certainly to be placed far below the latter, who spoke of things he had seen, if not been a part of.

It was close upon November. Hannibal had been a month too late in his crossing. The early snows had fallen, the surface of which, on the southerly exposures, thawed during the day and froze at night. The climate of the Alps was probably more severe two thousand years ago than to-day. These southern peoples in their half-naked condition must have suffered beyond telling. Nothing shows the wonderful power of this man, Hannibal, over men better than the patient endurance of their danger and toil by his soldiers.

The savages offered no more opposition to his advance, but the steeper and more rugged descent on the Italian side made the progress of the army difficult and slow.   The mountain paths — they could have been no more — were hidden by the

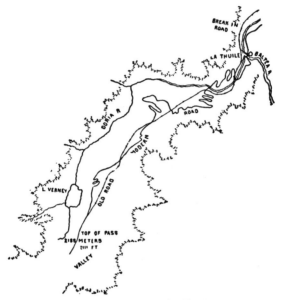

From top of Pass to La Thuile.

snows.   Whoever missed his footing slid hopelessly down the precipices.   Thousands were thus lost.   But the men were hardened to losses, looked forward to what awaited them at the foot of the mountains, and kept up their courage.   They needed it sorely.

Early on the first day of descent, the eleventh in the Alps, we are told that the army reached a place where the road had been carried away by a landslide for a stadium and a half, — about three hundred yards.   Such slides were usual in this place, but the present one was more extensive.   The men all but lost heart.   Hannibal tried to avoid the place

by a circuit, but a fresh fall of snow lying upon a body of
the last year's fall, yet unmelted, rendered the footing absolutely treacherous and prevented the men from making any
headway. The fresh snow on the sharp slope slipped upon
the old, or, being trodden through, the men and horses
slipped on the glassy surface underneath; the loaded mules
once down could not be got on their feet; many slid down
the sharp declivities; many were engulfed in the old drifts.
Hannibal abandoned the attempt as impracticable. The
army went into camp, and the men, sick and well, in relays,
were set at clearing, propping up and rebuilding the road, a
task of great risk and difficulty. Hannibal was everywhere
with cheering word and active help. During the twelfth day
of the passage, so many were the hands and so willing the
hearts, enough progress was made to get the horses and pack-
animals through, and these were at once sent down to the
pastures below the snow-line. It required much effort during the coming three days, on the part of the Numidians,
whom Hannibal put at the task, to repair the road sufficiently to get the elephants past the broken part. These
poor beasts were nearly famished, for they were yet above
the line of vegetation.

Thus Polybius. Now let us see how well our route chimes
in with our author. The old last century road down from
the summit of the Little St. Bernard runs from the lake
through a valley of slight width, beside the Doria, some six
miles to the first place which can be called a level. As the
crow flies, it is but three miles; by the modern military road,
which zigzags down at a fair grade, it is nine. The nature
of the ground corresponds well with Polybius' description of
precipices down which the men slid and fell, for the first part
of the way is rugged, and the last part exceedingly steep and
difficult; there is little beside a succession of precipices, and

with snow upon the ground there would be only the most
treacherous footing. From the lower end of the summit
plain one may see far below, at the foot of the sharply descending mountain side, the village of La Thuile (ancient

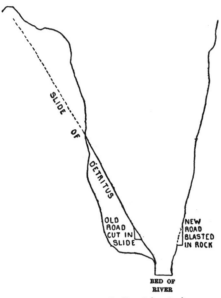

Artolica), in a small
but fertile valley,
where the Baltea,
from the glacier of
Mt. Ruitor, on the
right, joins the Do-
ria, and makes a
stream of goodly vol-
ume, which rushes
down at a sharp in-
cline in a torrent of
great power. Just
below this valley, the
Doria-Baltea, as it is
now called, enters a
ravine where it has
cut its bed deep into
the solid rock for a

The Break in the Road (section).

distance of some miles. On the right, the rocks rise from
the river-bank perpendicularly to a height of many hundred
feet to the mountain side behind. On the left, the hills are
slightly farther back and equally high, but they are of a very
friable sort of schist, the detritus of which has slid down from
time to time, and formed, for a height of over one thousand
feet, a mountain slope of sharp descent. On this left bank,
as you enter the gorge, is a place where for just about three
hundred yards the slides are at the worst; and the old road
used to be so constantly covered by avalanches and landslides
as to be eventually abandoned for the right bank, where it has

now been hewn in the rock. These slides and avalanches come down a funnel-shaped ravine which discharges itself in a narrow cleft, and from the rotten structure of the heights near by, these slides, as well as the avalanches, must have been usual from remote antiquity. So much snow comes down at times, so narrow is the river-gorge, and so overhanging are the rocks which shelter its bed from the sun, that in exceptional years the snow remains in huge banks throughout

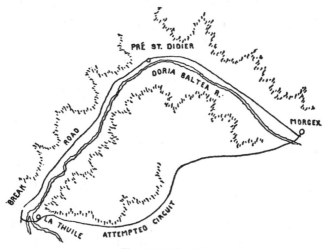

Hannibal's Circuit.

the summer, and sometimes even makes a natural bridge over the torrent for a long distance. Such a thing occurs nowhere else on this route, and it is quite unusual anywhere.

Now the La Thuile valley, by the ancient path, was less than six miles from the summit, and Hannibal reached the broken place in the road on his first day's march down early enough to try to turn the place by a circuit before camping. This distance would agree very well with what Polybius tells us. In attempting the circuit, Hannibal may have tried to cross the river on the snow, which would account for a part of his losses. Or these, indeed, may have occurred in following the road as far as the break, and in the first attempt to cross it. Or, more probably, he may have tried to pass the river above, at La Thuile, intending to skirt or march back of the heights on the right of the river, where there is a possible though difficult passage, very likely not then known to his guides, and at this season highly unpromising. The attempt, whatever it was, failed of success.

The camp at the entrance to the broken road was probably in the La Thuile plain, and was pitched at the end of the first day. The next day was taken up in repairing the road, and on the morrow the horses and pack-train were got through and sent to pasturage down the mountain. To-day, vegetation ceases about two miles from the summit of the pass. In Hannibal's day there appears to have been none in October on this plain. It is scarcely necessary to mention, certainly not worth while to confute, Livy's story about softening the rocks with vinegar. It may stand as a pleasant bit of fiction.

La Thuile to Pré St. Didier.

At the end of the gorge wherein was the broken way is another steep mountain side, and at its foot, in a lovely valley, modern Pré St. Didier, under the frowning glory of Mt. Blanc. Here the valley bends to the southeast on its way to Aosta below. In Hannibal's era, the valley was inhabited by the Salassi, clients of the Insubres. The lighter animals must have been sent down below St. Didier, because there is not enough pasturage at this point for so many animals for any length of time. And Hannibal must have wished to keep the nearest forage for the elephants, soon to follow. Here, in October, with fresh snow in the La Thuile valley, would be the highest pasturage.

Well out of this difficulty, says Polybius, Hannibal rejoined that part of the army which had gone down to pasturage, and in three days from the broken way "descended boldly into the plains which are near the Po and the territory of the Insubrians." He had left Cartagena five months before with ninety-two thousand men. He had crossed the Rhone with thirty-eight thousand foot and over eight thousand horse. He had now under the colors but twelve thousand African and eight thousand Spanish infantry, and six thousand horse; and these were so worn out with toil and suffering, with lack of provision and extremity of weather, that "both in appearance and condition they were brought to a state more resembling that of wild beasts than human beings."

Hannibal must have been singularly careful of his cavalry to have brought it through with so small a proportionate loss. This no doubt was the result of his having saved it as much as he could. He as well knew what its value would be to him on the plains of the Po as Alexander knew the value of his Companions; and he had done his best to keep it intact. But the condition of the army was pitiable. How many of the nine or ten thousand pack-animals which must have accompanied the army were left is not told.

"Hannibal's whole care was therefore directed to the best means of reviving the spirits of his troops and restoring the men and horses to their former vigor and condition."

Apart from Polybius' positive statement, the fact that Han-

nibal divided his army in the manner described, and spread
his animals over the country at pasture, goes a long way to
prove that he was in the land of friends, — the Insubrians,
— and not among the inimical Taurini.

It is not improbable that the horses and pack-animals were
headed by the infantry on the way down the mountain.   To
judge from Polybius' words, as well as military sense, they
were under command of Hannibal, who would certainly be
apt to be with the van, whether marching to meet friends or
foes ; and Polybius says the Numidians were ordered to pro-
ceed with the repairs of the road, which, after three days,
they made practicable for the elephants.

In three days from leaving the broken road Hannibal
reached the plain, where he " encamped at the foot of the
Alps " at a point which was one hundred and fifty miles
(twelve hundred stadia) from where he entered them.   This
point is clearly near modern Ivrea.   Now the distance from
Chevelu to Ivrea is just about one hundred and fifty miles by
the Augustan Itinerary, made but two hundred years later
than Hannibal's era, and it is less than one hundred and
seventy miles, measured by the much longer modern road.
This is near enough to an agreement, for mountain roads are
long or short, according to the grade they seek to make along
the steeper parts, and the extent of the zigzags they cover
upon the hillsides.   To compare the old with the modern road
over the Little St. Bernard, though this is an extreme instance, illustrates this point.   Indeed, it is not quite certain
to what part of the column Polybius might refer when he
says that the army reached a certain point on a certain day.
A column of thirty thousand men and baggage in these
mountains would be twenty miles long, at least.   Dates and
distances are wont to be measured by headquarters.   Exact
accuracy cannot be expected, as headquarters may one day

be with the van, and another day with the rear. But in this case it was probably with the van.

One is apt to find discussion in most works on the Passage of the Alps by Hannibal as to just what is the " entrance to the Alps," and what the " foot of the Alps," to which Polybius refers. Any one familiar with this mountain-range, who remembers the plain of the Po, from which the gigantic barrier rises, as it were a wall, directly from the plain, will have no difficulty in agreeing that, by the Little St. Bernard, the " foot of the Alps " is reached near Ivrea, which is but seven hundred and eighty feet above the sea, and where one immediately, and without the succession of minor heights usual in our mountains, sets foot on the alluvial levels of the great North Italian plain. The same thing applies in almost equal degree to Chevelu, for the Mt. du Chat rises sharply up from the rolling country on its west, and is the first barrier which does so rise. It is the first mountain which has to be crossed in the route from the Rhone to the Little St. Bernard, and it is in reality a mountain, rising to the height of two thousand feet or more from a merely rolling country. That Chevelu and Ivrea are the " entrance " and the " foot " of the Alps along this route seems certain.

Now as to the days. The army broke up from the summit on the eleventh day, having reached it early on the ninth, and camped there two days, the ninth and tenth. The broken road was reached early on the day of starting, the eleventh. The road was repaired on the twelfth, and "the beasts of burden and the horses were immediately led down to the plains." If Hannibal headed the van, leaving the Numidians to get the elephants through, as is altogether probable, he spent the thirteenth, fourteenth and fifteenth days in reaching " the foot of the Alps " with the van-guard. This is the number of days given by Polybius. If Hannibal stayed with the ele-

phants, we should have to reckon from the van-guard, or
else count three days more, or assume that Polybius meant
that it was fifteen days to the point where the chief obstacles of the Alps were overcome, which was fairly the case
at Pré St. Didier. For though there are several awkward
defiles from St. Didier to Ivrea, especially one halfway to
Aosta, and one at Fort du Bard, there are none to be com-

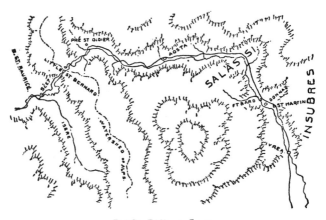

Pré St. Didier to Ivrea.

pared to the one below La Thuile, where the snow added its
list of complications to the treachery of the ground. It
seems more plausible to assume that Hannibal was with the
van when it reached Ivrea.

The distances and days come curiously close to Polybius'
estimate, who at the time had not the Augustan Itinerary to
go by. They are as follows: —

ITINERARY THROUGH THE ALPS.

1st day, passage of the Mt. du Chat and to Bourget.
2d day, halt on Chambéry Plain.
3d day, to near Montmeillan.
4th day, to Frétérive.

5th day, to Albertville.

6th day, to a point near Moutier.

7th day, to Ayme.

8th day, to Séez, and the fight at the Roche Blanche. The column marched all night, so that it reached the summit next morning.

9th day, at the summit, which was reached so early that this was really a day of rest.

10th day, rest.

11th day, start down the mountain, to the break in the road, and attempted circuit.

12th day, work on road, and horses got through.

13th day, Numidians work on road, and van marching down to foot of Alps.

14th day, Numidians work on road, and van marching down to foot of Alps.

15th day, Numidians work on road, and van reached Ivrea, at foot of Alps. At close of day the elephants were got through break in road.

One more tradition may perhaps be mentioned bearing upon the Little St. Bernard being the route pursued by Hannibal. At Donnaz, just above St. Martin, and opposite the Fort du Bard, the road is chiseled out of the rock, which comes down to the very edge of the river. Tradition assigns this work to Hannibal, and for many centuries this pass has been known as that of the Carthaginian army. It is not probable that Hannibal had anything to do with this work; but the tradition is interesting, if not reliable.

Appian is sometimes quoted as an authority on the War against Hannibal. But he is quite unsatisfactory. A fair sample of his work is his description of the passage of the Alps, which is as follows: " When Hannibal came to the Alpine range, he found not even a road which led upwards, let alone one which led across, for it is extraordinarily steep. Notwithstanding this, with great boldness he ascended the mountain, under all manner of difficulties. For as it was full of snow and ice he was forced to cut down the woods and to burn them, and then subdue the heat with water and vinegar, and break up the softened rock with iron hammers, and thus make himself a path, which is yet accessible, and is known as the pass of Hannibal." This, for a historian who wrote in the reign of Trajan, is rather lacking in equipoise.

To resume our narrative. " When, therefore," says Polybius, "Hannibal's troops were sufficiently recovered from their fatigues, he first of all invited the Taurini, who dwell at the foot of the Alps, to enter into an alliance with him, they being then at war with the Insubrians, and but ill-affected towards the Carthaginians. Upon their refusal, he surrounded their chief city, and took it after a siege of three days, putting to the sword all who had opposed him."

This passage follows immediately after the paragraph reciting the care Hannibal gave to reviving his army's spirits and restoring its vigor. It seems clearly to show, in addition to Polybius' explicit statement, that Hannibal emerged from the Alps among the Insubrians, his allies, and that after he had rested there, he attacked the Taurini. Apart from the absolute statement of Polybius, we cannot suppose that the Taurini, inimical to Hannibal, would neglect the chance of attacking him as he emerged, weary and demoralized, from his long passage of the mountains. In fact, one of the best reasons why Hannibal should steer for the Insubres, and not for the Taurini, was that he was by no means certain that the Romans might not be at the outlets of the Taurinian passes, waiting, in connection with their Gallic allies, to fall upon him in the naturally exhausted condition in which he must emerge from his arduous march.

The following table of dates, as given in the first column, has been compiled by Lavalette. They are as nearly accurate as ingenuity can make them. Some critics make the dates two months earlier, in which case they would be as in the second column. But Lavalette's dates accord with Polybius' reference to the setting of the Pleiades, as the others do not.

Left Cartagena	May 30.	March 30.
Crossed Ebro	July 15.	May 15.
At Elne	September 15.	July 15.
Crossed Rhone	September 27.	July 27.
At Vienne	October 12.	August 12.
At entrance of Alps	October 17.	August 17.
At summit of Alps	October 26.	August 26.
At foot of Alps	November 1.	September 1.

A month earlier, Hannibal would have had a much more easy time. Little snow was apt to be found late in September or early in October, and plenty of forage was on hand for the beasts, up to a considerable elevation. That, at the late season of his march, Hannibal's commissaries could have managed to get together provisions for thirty thousand men and eight thousand horses, without counting the sumpter-animals, which must have amounted to nearly ten thousand more, reflects great credit upon these officers. And that they did so tends to prove that the march was over the route indicated, the fertility of which is vastly greater than that of any other.

Nothing better shows the fearful exposures of this wonderful march than the fact that from the Rhone to the Po Hannibal had lost twenty thousand out of forty-six thousand men.

The distance covered in these five months was nearly twelve hundred Roman (say eleven hundred English) miles, but this period counted all the delays from the enemy in Catalonia, at the Rhone, and through the mountains. The loss had been slight from the Rhone to the first mountain pass, heavy from thence to the summit, almost as much so from the summit down. The truth of this numerical record is vouched for by the inscription cut upon a column, later erected by Hannibal

near the promontory of Lacinium, in Calabria, before referred to.

Hannibal had reached his goal. He had with him a force
of twenty-six thousand men, exhausted physically and morally
from their extraordinary toils and danger. What he had
gained is well put by Napoleon: " Cet Annibal . . . qui ne
descend en Italie qu'en payant de la moitié de son armée la
seule acquisition de son champ de bataille, le seul droit de
se combattre." Extraordinary man; wonderful army! Nothing but the tireless nerve tension of their ever-confident chief
prevented this small force from melting away like the snows
they had crossed when springtide brings its heat. And here
they were, with naught to help them but the promised alliance
of a few Gallic barbarians, while they had the present enmity
of at least an equal number to overcome. It may be doubted
whether Hannibal himself, at this moment, could consider his
military programme as successfully inaugurated.

What was the purpose of this reckless army? To attack
on its own soil a people capable of raising three quarters of
a million of men; a people which, in the last conflict, but a
generation since, had utterly overthrown — all but exterminated — the Carthaginian power and nationality. Truly, in
any other than an army led by such a man, an undertaking
like this would have been the wildest frenzy. It was like
Alexander setting forth with his handful of Macedonians to
overturn an empire whose armies were numbered by the
millions. But we cannot doubt that Hannibal had taken
even such a situation as this into his calculations; and relying on his own good arm and brain, had resolved to face it, —
to dare this and any other danger for the chance of bringing
to his feet the cruel, rapacious power of Rome, which had inflicted such injustice and degradation on his beloved country.
And in a Hannibal this was not frenzy. The man whose

courage cannot be daunted, whose mind and body are incapable of fatigue, whose soul burns with the divine spark of genius, may always confront the impossible. And Hannibal had faced all this with a full knowledge of what he was about to do. To him there was no impossible. To him, with his honest cause and unconquerable purpose, there must be a way. It is, indeed, when such a hero looks the all but impossible in the face that he is at his greatest. It is here that he shines forth, clad in all his virtue. Be it that the palm of the victor awaits him, be it that he is destined to sink beneath the weight of his herculean task, at such a time he is no longer man. He is a demigod!

Cornu Player.

XVII.

THE ARMY OF ITALY ON THE PO. NOVEMBER, 213 B. C.

THE valley of the Po was very rich. It was inhabited by the Gauls, a fine people living on the luxuriance of the land. The Po is the main obstacle to the invasion of Italy, and its main line of defense. It and its affluents form a barrier difficult to be overcome. The Romans were at Placentia, a city which can be attacked only by forcing a passage of the Po from the north side, or by the defile of Stradella on the south bank. The Army of Italy was ready for its work. It was admirably organized, and despite its losses a short rest put it in good heart. Hannibal learned with surprise that Scipio had come back to confront him on the Po, and was now at the head of the prætorian army which had been defeated by his allies, the Boians. He was preparing to move upon Placentia, when he heard that the consul had moved across the Po and was about to advance towards him. This simplified a difficult problem to the dimensions of an open-country battle. Hannibal, of course, was strategically bound by the topography of the Padane country, but not in the same way Napoleon was. He moved straight towards Scipio by crossing the Ticinus at its upper fords and marching down its eastern bank. Here, at the head of his cavalry, he ran across Scipio, who was out on a reconnoissance with his horse and light foot. A combat ensued, in which the Romans were defeated and Scipio badly wounded. The consular army retired across the Po. Hannibal had won the first innings.

THAT the peninsula of Italy was peopled by diverse nationalities was a fact in Hannibal's favor. In the northern zone, filling the valley of the Po, lived the Gauls; the Italian tribes occupied the centre; the Greek colonies monopolized the southern zone. As we have seen, Hannibal had based his calculations primarily upon the alliance of the Gauls; a second factor was possible aid from Macedon; a third, and the most important one, was the disaffection towards Rome which he might breed among her colonies and allies south of the Apennines by the victories he felt confident he could win.

Hannibal was looking down from the foothills of the great range he had crossed upon the valley of the Po, which, like a vast garden, walled in by the Alps and Apennines, lay smiling at his feet. Then, as now, it was wonderfully fertile, though more wooded in those days. Every species of grain and fruit, flax, wine and oil, was yielded to an easy culture. Herds of cattle and flocks of sheep and droves of pigs found abundant pasturage. Horses were bred in the Venetian country. All authors bear testimony to the fruitfulness of the region at that day; and Polybius tells us that a generation later the traveler was generously entertained at hostelries for one quarter of an obole, or about one cent, a day.

The Gauls who inhabited this region were a tall, straight, handsome race, living simply on the luxuriance of the land. Flocks, vines, and a few ingots of gold, easily hid or carried away, were their sole riches; raids across the Apennines were their recreation, from which they were wont to return with their carts laden down with booty. There were still many cities which, under the Etruscans, had been great and beautiful, and the Gauls themselves had made some slight progress in the arts.

Cutting this level valley from west to east ran the Po, taking its rise in Monte Viso, and, increased by many affluents, making its way through a course of three hundred miles to the Adriatic. The Po is but a dozen feet deep on the average, except in floods which cause its overflow, when it may be fifty. At Turin it is one hundred and seventy yards wide; at the confluence of the Ticinus five hundred; at Cremona one thousand. Its fall is moderate; on the plains it is a sluggish river.

The Po and its affluents form an obstacle which cannot be

avoided by whoso would invade Italy from the north. In the west, the Po is itself small, but its affluents are important; in the east the river itself is a boundary. On descending the Alps, one is met by the affluents of the left bank, which make respectable lines of defense. Behind these is

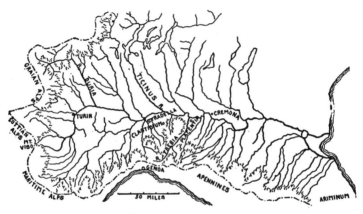

The Po and its Affluents.

the splendid line of the Ticino-Po-Trebia. The key of this line is at the defile of Stradella, at whose mouth then lay the fortress of Clastidium, modern Casteggio.

To an army descending from the Alps, the Po is the first object of attack. To an army seeking to forestall an attack from the Alpine region, the Po is the line of defense. The Maritime Alps sweep down in a semicircle from the Cottian, to join the Apennines on the Gulf of Genoa. The Apennines throw out an immense bulwark towards the Po, which, at Stradella, forms the defile above mentioned. This defile is the key of the country, the cross-roads, so to speak, of the entire section.

The strategic value of "the knot Pavia-Stradella-Piacenza" was fully recognized by Napoleon. It did not exist for Hannibal. But Hannibal was governed by the general topography as much as the First Consul. The Romans, in their contests with the Gauls before the Second Punic War, had in their way ascertained the relative importance of the various towns. Piacenza is nowadays the pivot of operations of the central Po. It cannot be escaped. "Un bon fort au defilé de la Stradella couvrirait l'Italie du côté de la France," said Napoleon. Placentia in Hannibal's time possessed the same importance.

The Romans had held Placentia for some time, and had made it strong. Their allies, the Ananes, could hold the defile of Stradella. Several of the new colonies had been fortified. Clastidium was an oppidum. The Romans thus held the Po at the knot. Farther down they held Ariminum and the passes of the Apennines. If Hannibal moved down the right bank of the Po, he would be stopped by the defile. If down the left bank, the Ticinus was a first barrier.

In regard to the military value of the Padane country as a whole, Napoleon once said: "Lorsqu'on tient l'Italie septentrionale, le reste de la peninsule tombe comme un fruit mûr." This was true a century ago, but it was not true in the days of Hannibal. His work lay beyond the Apennines. But he had as much to do on the Po as the great Corsican.

The Carthaginian army has been already described. Let us add a word about the Army of Italy. We know little about Hannibal's officers, except that they were presumably all Carthaginian aristocrats, and that they had been through a long and arduous training. Unlike Alexander's, few are ever mentioned by name.

There were Mago, his brother, young, full of vigor and élan, who commanded the Carthaginian legion, and was frequently sent on detached duty; Hanno, son of Bomilcar, a distinguished infantry general; Maharbal, son of Imilco, commanding the entire body of cavalry; Adherbal, chief of engineers; Hasdrubal, a cavalry general, peculiarly distinguished at Cannæ; Carthalo, commanding the light cavalry; Bostar, Bomilcar, Gisgo, aides. Numbers of young Carthaginians accompanied the army, and to them later was confided the command of allied contingents.

The subsistence department is clearly defined by Polybius. There were special officers who went out with the foraging parties and gathered corn and beef and wine, and had charge of the depots of victuals. We hear that in Italy the soldiers had regular issues of beef, grain and wine, with cheese, hams, vinegar to cut the water, oil for rubbing their bodies, and, curiously enough, perfumery for the hair. And the quartermaster's department must have been equally well organized. The elephants and horses never seemed to want for forage. Medical service we learn nothing about, but we hear of a celebrated African surgeon, Synhalus, who was with the army. Veterinary care is once or twice hinted at in the authorities. Paymasters were kept regularly at work, and Hannibal's own private wealth, as well as his share of the booty, was wont to flow into their coffers.

There were no doubt topographical engineers. Polybius, Livy, Silius Italicus, speak of some kind of maps. The Romans of this day had "itineraries," which were either written (annotata) or sketched (picta), and the Carthaginians were far in advance of the Romans in clever devices. However he may have used these officers, Hannibal always finished by making his own reconnoissances.

The ancients were clever at signaling, and if a signal-corps was not attached to the Army of Italy, we yet see repeated instances of the use of signals by smoke and flags.

It was while resting in Piedmont that Bostar, Hannibal's aide-de-camp, who had been dispatched to the temple of Jupiter Ammon in the Libyan desert, returned with a cheering oracle. This Hannibal used to advantage in encouraging his men. It is not probable that he had asked of the deity the foolish question Alexander is said to have put. Priestcraft was not so rampant in his camp as in the Romans'. Livy makes this a reproach, in fact.

To return to our narrative. We know practically nothing about the siege of Turin. The passage of Polybius above given, supplemented slightly by some of the other authorities, Livy, Nepos and Silius, is all there is. It is evident that Hannibal tried all reasonable means to persuade the Taurini to join his cause; but being unable to do so was compelled to take harsh measures against them. By making a sudden dash and unexpected assault, he captured this chief city of the tribe, later Augusta Taurinorum, and, deeming an example necessary to his own safety, he sacked it and put the inhabitants to the sword. This act so effectually spread terror among the Ligurians and Celts of the Upper Po, that they chose at once to join his alliance. Such a motive may not have won him very warm aid, but it was better than open opposition, and Hannibal knew just how to use his tools. He placed none too much reliance on them. With this vigorous measure he secured his rear from interference when he should advance, and no doubt Hannibal intended at the outset to show that he could be very generous to allies, very cruel to enemies.

Hannibal had learned through the Gauls and his own spies, whom he kept actively at work in every direction, — he even had spies in Rome for years, — that the senate was greatly disturbed by the news of his presence in Italy; but that, instead of rising to the occasion, they had remained of divided counsels. He learned, also, with the utmost surprise, that Scipio had returned from Massilia to confront him. This news must have largely modified his plans. Neither he nor Scipio had expected the other so soon.

To recapitulate. There were two principal Roman armies this year; one destined for Spain, and already there, while its commander, Scipio, as we have seen, had hurried back to the Po: one destined for Africa, which, under Tiberius Sempronius, had been wasting its time in Sicily, in pursuit of the Carthaginian fleet sent to ravage the Italian coast. The second Carthaginian raiding-fleet had been wrecked in a storm. Of the two consuls, Publius Scipio had just landed at Pisa, while Tiberius Sempronius, who of course still deemed Hannibal at Saguntum or somewhere south of the Pyrenees, was dividing his efforts between the Carthaginian fleet and preparations to cross over to Carthage, and thus — should he ever get there — oblige that city to call back Hannibal for its defense.

These several contingencies had been foreseen and ably provided for by Hannibal. Before leaving Spain, as we remember, he had brought over Carthaginian troops and placed them under his brother Hasdrubal; and had sent Spanish troops to Carthage. Thus the armies in each place were not apt to fail in their duty on account of any political upheaval. Their interests were merely mercenary, and they were wont blindly to follow their chief, who in each place was wedded to the Barca cause. Moreover, the Spanish troops sent to Carthage were personally devoted to Hannibal, and could be counted on to join willingly in any scheme which would prevent those of his fellow-citizens who were headed by Hanno and opposed to himself from overturning the present régime.

The only force to oppose the advance of Hannibal was the prætorian army under Manlius, amounting to twenty thousand men; and a further force at the recently planted colonies of Placentia and Cremona. This latter force was numerically considerable. Some twelve thousand colonists had come thither to oust the aborigines; but most of them were old and unfitted for war.

The Boians and Insubrians were already in active revolt, the former vexed beyond endurance by the founding of Mutina and Placentia and Cremona as Roman colonies, and the distribution of their lands to Roman citizens, and both encouraged by the news of Hannibal's approach. Manlius, while marching from Ariminum to relieve Mutina, which the Boians had attacked, had been cleverly ambushed and badly beaten by these Gauls as he was filing through a forest road. The relics of the Roman army and colonists, much more demoralized than their actual loss would warrant, had taken refuge on a hill, where the barbarians had held them in a state of blockade until reinforcements to the amount of a legion, under Atilius, had been sent to repair this disaster, when the Romans recovered their spirits and ground, and retired to Mutina. Scipio found, on reaching the scene, which he did on the day Turin was taken, a force of from twenty to twenty-five thousand men again in possession of Mutina, Cremona and Placentia. He assumed command of all.

His intention had been to attack Hannibal as he emerged from his perilous passage of the Alps, if indeed he ever got through, before he should have time to recover from its exhaustion. Had the Romans had a consular army at Turin, when Hannibal emerged from the Alps, it might have gone hard with the Punic captain. But the insurrection of the Gauls prevented Scipio's doing as he designed; and it was imperative to rest his troops after their late defeat, and find his own bearings in cisalpine Gaul. He must have been the more astonished of the two to hear that Hannibal had already established himself among good allies, captured Turin, and stood ready to try conclusions.

Scipio would have been wise to remain on the right bank

of the Padus, and dispute its passage at Stradella and Placentia, until he could be reinforced; for Hannibal had as yet
shown no disposition to cross the river at its upper fords. Instead, however, of doing this, and doubtless fearing a general
rising of the Gauls in favor of Hannibal, he crossed the
river somewhere between the Ticinus and the colony of Placentia, thinking to impose upon the natives, — the same idea
as later in making his new camp on the Trebia, — and took
up a position near the mouth of the Ticinus. Here the
ground was level and in the highest degree unfavorable to
him, for Scipio had but two thousand horse, while Hannibal
had thrice the number, not to count the Gauls; and the
plains about the vicinity were as if made for the evolutions
of cavalry. Moreover, the Ticinus, while a good line of defense, must be held in its entire length to be held at all; for
it can be crossed at many points. Scipio's advance savored
more of courage than discretion. He went into camp and
set to work to bring his men into good heart and discipline.
He had by no means gauged the opponent who was about to
move against him.

There is a tendency among some of the modern historians
of Hannibal to make this general manœuvre on the line of
the Po much as Napoleon, with a more perfect art, with the
history of centuries of warfare in this region before him, and
with a close knowledge of its minutest topographical details,
would be apt to have done. This does not appear to be warranted by the facts of the case. Hannibal was unquestionably one of the world's greatest soldiers. His strategic intuitions had as yet been equaled by no one but Alexander. It
was he who taught Rome the art of war, and this so crisply
that his teachings were perpetuated, and not, like Alexander's, lost to the world of that day. He knew and showed
the Romans that mere fighting is not all there is of war. He

may with propriety be called the father of strategy. And
there can be little doubt that Hannibal had fully studied all
the features of the country he was about to invade, and made
himself familiar with its geographical and topographical out-
lines, so far as he was able to learn them. But strategy,
which is still nothing but the highest military expression of
the art of deceit, was in that day, as a rule, mere stratagem,
and we can scarcely assume that the Carthaginian general
was called on to look as closely into the strategic mapping of
the country as Bonaparte was both compelled and able to
do; nor indeed that his topographical engineers had found
time to reduce the country to a map so detailed. Some of
the cleverest of military critics seem to work on the theory
that such and such a course was the proper one for a good
strategist to take, and that therefore Hannibal did so, for-

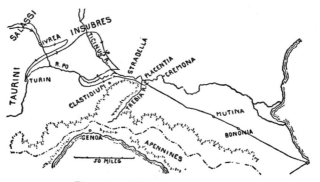

Placentia and Hannibal's Manœuvre.

getting that there was no strategy in Hannibal's era, except
that which came from his own intellectual conceptions, and
that what we call strategy to-day is the science which Alexander and he were, to be sure, the first to put into practice, but which has since been developed by such giants as
Cæsar, Gustavus, Prince Eugene, Marlborough, Frederick
and Napoleon; and forgetting also — and this is the main

point — that the old authorities give us facts which we may not overlook. No doubt Hannibal was largely governed by the salient features of the valley of the Po in the course he followed; but we must not assume more than this. Our true rule should be, first and always, to glean our facts clearly and crisply from the original sources; when statements conflict, to select the most reliable, or most probable, to base upon; and then from these to divine what may have been Hannibal's intuitive reasoning upon the conditions presented to him, which resulted in his taking the action history tells us of.

Now there is a dispute as to the movements of Hannibal and Scipio at this moment. Let us apply our theory. The two earliest of our authorities, Polybius and Cornelius Nepos, state the battle of the Ticinus to have been fought upon the banks of the Ticinus itself. Silius Italicus places it on the Eridanus, another name for the Po, — but as he is a poet we will not rely too much on him. Florus places it between the Po and Ticinus, that is, in one of their angles of confluence, which may be said to agree with Polybius and Nepos. Livy states that it took place five miles from Victumviæ, west of the Ticinus, after Scipio had crossed not only the Po, but the Ticinus as well. He does not say why in this he does not follow Polybius, whom he copies so continually.

Polybius gives not only the clearest but the earliest account of this first battle between the Romans and Carthaginians, as well as the one which appears to accord best with the probabilities. "Publius," he says, "had already advanced across the Po, and in order to pass the Ticinus had ordered that a bridge should be built over it. While waiting its completion," he assembled and harangued his soldiers. "On the morrow the two armies advanced, the one against the other, along the Ticinus, on the side which looks out upon

the Alps, the Romans having the river on their left, the Carthaginians on their right. The second day, the foragers of
each party having given notice that the enemy was near, each
one camped in the place where he stood. On the third, Publius with his cavalry, sustained by some light-armed troops,
and Hannibal with his cavalry only, marched each from his
side into the plain to reconnoitre the forces of the other.
When they saw, from the dust, that they were not far apart,
they put themselves into battle order."

This is a perfectly clean statement, such as Polybius always
makes, and Polybius had been on the ground when many
who saw the battle were still alive, — the only historian who
had this advantage. What he says places the battle-field on
the left or east bank of the Ticinus, the Romans facing substantially north, and the Carthaginians substantially south.

How does this accord with what Hannibal would be likely
to do? The Carthaginian general had just completed the
capture of the capital of the Taurini, and had probably returned to the Insubrians, where he was patching up fresh
alliances with the Gauls, and making ready to advance, when
news was brought in by some of the numerous scouting-par-
ties which he had sent out in all directions, both Gauls and
Numidians, that Scipio had already crossed the Po. Here
was an unexpected piece of good luck. Though well aware
of the Roman habit of forcing the fighting, Hannibal had
apprehended that Scipio would hold himself at Placentia,
and seek to defend the line of the Po there and at the defile
of Stradella. In order to attack him in the open field, which
was what he desired to do, Hannibal would have had to lure
him out of Placentia. This he might have accomplished either
by threatening Cremona, which was on the north bank of the
Po, or by a turning movement around Scipio's left across the
upper Po, and thence down the right bank, which would lead

him through the Stradella defile, and leave Scipio the advantage of choosing ground less good for the Carthaginian cavalry than the plains on the left bank. Under the circumstances Hannibal was probably on the point of trying the first plan, relying on the impetuosity of the Roman character and the national habit, when the welcome news reached him that Scipio was about to meet him half-way.

Hannibal calculated that Scipio would not cross the Ticinus, but would back up against Placentia, with Cremona on his right, and await developments. He therefore marched towards and passed the Ticinus, from which he was not far distant; and no doubt did so for greater certainty at one of the upper fords near Lake Maggiore, thence advancing south along the river.

Scipio, on the contrary, had already crossed the Po, and was making ready to cross the Ticinus and to advance towards the Vercellæ region, which he supposed Hannibal would be most apt to aim for after capturing Turin, when he heard that Hannibal had crossed the Ticinus; and instead of using his bridge, which was in all probability near the Po, moved at once up the Ticinus. On the second day of his march, — perhaps twenty-five miles from the Po up the east bank, — the two armies met. It was mid-November, 218 B. C.

It does not seem as if Scipio could have marched as far north as Somma, near the lake, where the scene of the battle has been placed by some historians, nor does the situation accord with the authorities.

This simple deduction from the facts stated by the earliest of our ancient authors, the one whom all agree in acknowledging as uniformly reliable, and who in this case is amply sustained by others, seems to be preferable to an argument founded on the strategic values as they are understood to-day.

These, however useful to Napoleon, were probably never appreciated by the Carthaginian.

Hannibal, meanwhile, had strongly impressed on his own troops the evident fact that they had but the single choice of conquering or being destroyed to a man. He felt convinced and assured them that success would at once bring all these Gallic peoples under his standard, and the army marched cheerfully to meet the Roman legions, which were at the same time advancing rapidly towards them, but, to credit Livy, in by no means as good morale.

A curious story is related as to the means Hannibal employed to impress this alternative of victory or slavery upon his soldiers. He had with the army a number of the hostile Gauls whom he had captured in the Alps. He had kept the young warriors in chains, had illy fed them, and had punished them with cruel stripes. He now brought these youths before the army, and exhibiting to them such weapons as Gallic kings are wont to use for single combat, and richly caparisoned steeds, he asked which of them would be willing to fight to the death with a comrade in order to earn freedom and such arms. One and all eagerly demanded the privilege of the duel, for victory would be liberty, and death a deliverance from their present evil state. Lots were drawn, and several pairs of combatants fought in the presence of the army. Those to whom the lucky numbers did not fall, and who must still languish in slavery, equally felicitated the living victor and the vanquished dead. This object-lesson had a marked effect upon the Carthaginian army.

The two detachments were approaching each other. Scipio had his two thousand Roman and allied cavalry, some Gallic cavalry, and his light troops; Hannibal had his body of six thousand horse. Inasmuch as Hannibal so greatly outnumbered the Roman general in cavalry, his line also extended far beyond the flanks of his opponent. The Romans advanced slowly, with the velites and Gallic horse in the first, and the Roman and allied cavalry in the second

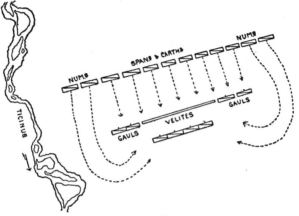

Battle of the Ticinus.

lines.   Hannibal, on the contrary, had but one line, with the Numidians on the flanks and the Spanish and Carthaginian heavy horse in the centre.

The velites, who, we remember, were young soldiers, opened the action, but, speedily demoralized by the appearance of their new foe, after throwing a few darts, fled through the cavalry intervals, and allowed Hannibal to charge down upon the Roman line.   The Roman opposition was stanch, and the battle wavered for a while, many Romans dismounting and fighting on foot; but the Carthaginian horse proved greatly superior, as they had years before in Sicily.   They not only exceeded the Romans in numbers, but in activity and discipline, and were already on the point of breaking the Roman front, when the Numidians, who had ridden around both of Scipio's exposed flanks, fell smartly upon his rear, and, dispersing the velites who had there taken refuge, fell to sabring the disconnected Roman horse right and left without mercy. The entire Roman formation was quickly broken up, only a small body remaining firm around the person of wounded Scipio, and retired in much confusion to the camp. The Carthaginian loss was heavier than the Roman, says Polybius, but does not give the figures.

This defeat was perhaps partly due to a severe wound received by Scipio early in the action. He was with difficulty rescued and borne from the fight by his seventeen-year-old son Scipio, — later so distinguished as Africanus, the victor of Zama. Hannibal deemed it wise not to follow up the Roman force, which he supposed would retire upon the infantry and to the protection of its camp. He expected nothing less than a general engagement on the morrow. He had now the moral effect of a first success upon his side, — a distinct and solid gain. He more clearly than ever grasped the idea of his superiority in horse, and saw what should be the selection of his future battle-fields whenever available.

The loss of this first combat — it scarcely rose to the dimensions of a battle — should not militate against the Roman general. The encounter of his own with Hannibal's cavalry on the Rhone had naturally misled him, and to his grievous loss. But Scipio was a good soldier; it was his feeling of Roman invincibility which had led him into rashly measuring arms with an older soldier. He too late recognized his error in meeting Hannibal without the support of his foot, and under such conditions that he must almost certainly leave the victory to his enemy.

The Romans, on the succeeding night, retired from their camp straight on the bridge they had built over the Po. On arrival at the river, Scipio decided to recross to the south side, which he did, skillfully and well, destroying behind him the bridge, which was of rafts, says Livy, and again took post at a camp near Placentia.

XVIII.

HANNIBAL did not follow up Scipio, but marched two days up the Po, crossed it, moved unopposed through the defile of Stradella, camped below Placentia, and offered Scipio battle. The wounded consul could not accept the gage. The Roman senate, appalled at this first defeat, ordered the consul Sempronius from Sicily to reinforce Scipio. Hannibal was in position to head him off, for he lay on the direct road between Placentia and Ariminum, by which Sempronius would have to march. Scipio was awkwardly placed, and was threatened by a general insurrection of the neighboring Gauls. He moved out of his Placentia camp, across and up the Trebia, and built a stationary camp on the borders of the river. His object is not very clear, as his manœuvre did not cut Hannibal's communications with the upper Po. For, having moved his camp nearer Scipio's, the Carthaginian general was able to capture Clastidium, beyond the Stradella Pass, and from it draw large supplies of rations. But this gain was coupled with a loss. Sempronius in some manner avoided Hannibal's watchfulness, slipped round his flank, and joined his colleague in his camp on the Trebia. Hannibal had now no alternative but to fight both consuls, and set about luring Sempronius, whose rashness he well knew, into a pitched battle on unequal terms, before Scipio should recover from his wound.

HANNIBAL, one of whose marked characteristics was to look coolly and prudently at a success accomplished, was wise enough not to follow too far the retreat of the Roman army, and perhaps have to force a passage across the Padus, in their teeth. He sent a force in pursuit, which captured the Roman garrison of six hundred men at the bridgehead at the Padus ; or, as we may infer from some of the authorities, the force holding the bridgehead at the Ticinus.

The bridge on the Po had been broken down on Scipio's retreat. Cœlius Antipater relates that Mago, with the cavalry and the Spanish infantry, at once swam the Po, while

Hannibal sought fords farther up the river. But Cœlius romances occasionally. Those who know the Po will hesitate before crediting the story, as indeed Livy does not.

It was not now worth Hannibal's while to remain on the north of the Po, in the vicinity of Placentia. He had accomplished a primary gain and won much credit among his new allies. He could scarcely force the river near Placentia without unnecessary loss, for Cremona was on his flank. Moreover, this route towards central Italy was not a promising one, for the Romans held the outlet of the lower Padane country by the possession of the road from Ariminum via Mutina to Placentia. And the Po became harder to cross the farther down he marched. He preferred to effect a passage of this great river without opposition or great effort, if he could. Still, if he wished to attack Scipio at Placentia, the most important thing for him to do was to cross speedily to the south of the Po, and seize the intervening pass of Stradella. He therefore filed his column to the right, crossed Scipio's bridge over the

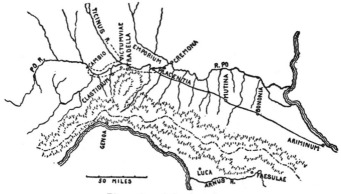

Placentia and the Apennines.

Ticinus, and marched two days upstream to a point in all probability not far from modern Cambio, here crossed the Padus with his van, on a bridge of boats of temporary construction, and went into camp to give time for building a stronger bridge so as to get his foot and trains across with more safety. He at once sent his brother Mago out with a sufficiency of horse to scour the country and make sure of Scipio's whereabouts. To his camp here — as there had to other camps — came embassies from many of the Gallic tribes of the north bank, hitherto allied to Rome, who offered him their aid with men and victuals. The Gauls were as good as their word. In addition to much in the way of breadstuffs, no less than sixty thousand men of foot,

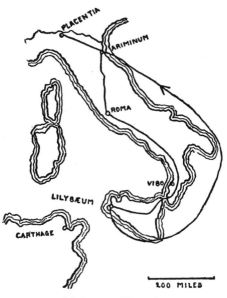

Lilybæum to Placentia.

and four thousand horse, at one time or other joined the Punic standard.

The Romans held Clastidium, at the mouth of the defile of Stradella, but this oppidum apparently offered no opposition to his free use of the pass, for, when he continued his advance, on the second day after putting his van across the Po, Hannibal, with a march of about fifty miles, reached the vicinity of Placentia, and in front of the town on the third he offered battle to Scipio. This being declined, — for Scipio was confined with his wound, — he camped some six miles from the city.

Scipio had no choice but to hold himself where he was, until he could be reinforced by the other consul, Sempronius; for he could not intrust the safety of his legions to a lieutenant. The presence of his colleague was imperative.

The Roman senate was both astounded and alarmed at the sudden appearance of Hannibal on the Padus, and the more so when news of the battle of the Ticinus was received. The consul Tiberius Sempronius was ordered speedily to reinforce Scipio. Sempronius was at the farther end of Sicily, at Lilybæum, but got under way as soon as possible. He left the prætor M. Æmilius in Sicily, with the fleet of fifty ships, sent Sextus Pomponius to the territory of Vibo in Bruttium, and, himself proceeding by sea, marched his army via Rome to Ariminum. This was done in forty days, being about sixteen miles a day; from Ariminum they came by forced marches to Scipio's aid. Livy says the entire army came by sea, but there are indications in other authors which seem to make him wrong in this particular.

The exact place near Placentia where Hannibal camped cannot be given, but it is thought to have been southeast of Placentia, on the Nura. He apparently had two objects in view; one, to prevent the junction of the two consuls, and the other, to accept the friendly overtures of the Boii, who dwelt in the northern foothills of the Apennines, were wavering in the balance, and needed his presence by way of encouragement. By this manœuvre he severed the communications of Scipio with Sempronius, and should have been able to prevent their junction, and beat Sempronius while on the march to join his colleague. His own communications, by this change of position, were laid open to attack by Scipio, and would have been seriously compromised were it not that he was in the land of friends, and had a vast superiority in horse. He ran the invariable risk of such a manœuvre. That

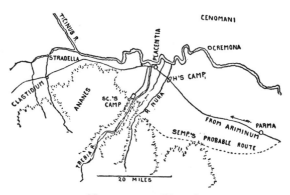

Manœuvres near Placentia.

he still kept his communications open, by what exact means we do not know, is well attested by the fact that, while encamped at this place, he was able to gain possession, by treachery, of the post of Clastidium.

Now here is one of the earliest and best instances of the taking up of a central position between two armies of the enemy. It was like Napoleon's manœuvre of 1796, and Napoleon himself recognized the fact. " J'étais," he says, "dans une situation plus favorable qu'Annibal. Les deux consuls avaient un intérêt commun : couvrir Rome ; les deux généraux que j'attaquais avaient chacun un intérêt particulier qui les dominait : Beaulieu celui de couvrir le Milanais ; Colli celui de couvrir le Piémont." There is no such crisp and masterly manœuvre in early history as this, and it shows, by his own unfeigned acknowledgment, whence Napoleon drew his inspiration for some of his masterly strokes of genius.

Scipio was awkwardly placed. The path to Genoa, by which he had personally come to Placentia, was in the hands of Hannibal's allies; Hannibal, astride the direct road from Ariminum, could stop Sempronius from joining him other than by a circuit. He was isolated. Moreover, he was troubled by a defection among the auxiliary Gauls in his own camp, of whom two thousand foot and two hundred horse deserted one night, after tumultuously killing a number of the Roman men on guard. This, Scipio feared, was the signal of a more general outbreak, and he wished to keep his hold on the Ananes, near by, which was nearly the only tribe of the vicinity which had remained faithful to Rome. This he thought he could do by camping in their midst. Only through the aid of his allies could he hope to regain and hold the pass of Stradella.

Scipio was an active soldier, whom even wounds could not quell. He determined to try on Hannibal a diversion which might make him quit his prey. He left in Placentia a suitable garrison, and moved out of his camp near the place with the bulk of his force, straight west and across the Trebia; whence, moving south, he took up and fortified a stationary camp on the left bank, in a position somewhat on a line with Hannibal's camp on the Nura. On the march he was interrupted by an attack of the Numidians, who were always on the alert; but his rear-guard alone suffered any loss, for these cavalrymen turned aside to pillage his abandoned camp near Placentia, and afforded him time to get the bulk of his forces across the Trebia. They were sometimes unreliable.

Scipio did not go far enough in his manœuvre. While to all appearances he had placed Hannibal where he must retire, and by means of a battle at that, he did not assure himself of the pass of Stradella, but left the Carthaginian line open, presumably by a circuit around his left to the mouth of the defile. Indeed, Hannibal's light cavalry, of which he had so great an excess over the Romans, seems to have been equal to holding all the surrounding country and of cooping Scipio up in his camp. Battle was what Hannibal wanted, and Scipio desired for the moment to avoid. Scipio's manœuvre was good ; his morale was not equal to it. He had not gone far enough. He was bound to wait for Sempronius.

Scipio had wisely established his new camp on ground which was rolling upland, not far from the foothills of the Apennines, and broken enough to be less fitted for cavalry than near Placentia. In a stationary camp he was safe enough from assault. Placentia, on which and up the Padus he expected to rely for rations, as well as on Clastidium, were neither far distant. He was apparently in a position from which he might retrieve the disaster at the Ticinus. The Cenomani, on the north of the river, had remained faithful, and threatened the Insubres, Hannibal's chief supporters. Properly used, unless he should prove to have too little cavalry, his army could cut Hannibal off from the upper Po and his allies there. The strength of the Roman camp prevented his isolation from being a substantial danger ; but while his move had been a handsome one for the purpose of compelling battle, it does not appear in what its advantages lay as a position in which to wait for Sempronius, or even compromise the Carthaginians. For he had secured neither the pass of Stradella, nor the road which might enable the reinforcements under Sempronius to reach him from Ariminum, which lay through a country largely in revolt, and actually in Hannibal's hands. To secure the fidelity of the Ananes may, after all, have been his main object.

Hannibal paid no heed to Scipio's manœuvre, except to

assure himself that his communications could be kept open at need. Scipio, safe in his stationary camp, did not pretend to control the road to Placentia, as he could ration himself from Clastidium if he so wished. Probably the light horse of both parties scoured the whole country. This was the usual habit, and common means of foraging.

Hannibal had ascertained at an early date that Sempronius was ordered to northern Italy, and it seems at first blush rather strange that he did not seek to engage Scipio's army before he should be thus reinforced. But battle could not be forced in those days of walled cities and intrenched camps; and Scipio was warily biding his time. He could not be attacked to advantage, and Hannibal always liked to see the chances on his own side. He had as marked a mixture of the bold and discreet in his composition as Gustavus Adolphus. The delay is further explainable by Hannibal's having so much to do to secure his footing among his new allies that he was unable to push forward. Just so much time had to be spent in councils and negotiations. It was wiser for him not to undertake the offensive until the entire territory of cisalpine Gaul was either in alliance with or in subjection to him.

Hannibal had manœuvred superbly in thus interposing between the two consuls. But he lost his game for all that. In some way Sempronius gave him the slip and joined his colleague. By what route or how, history does not tell us. It is not even made a matter of boast by Livy, and yet it must have been a very clever march. Colonel Hennebert, in his very learned work, suggests that he marched via Fæsulæ and Luca, and thus twice crossed the Apennines. But even if the Arnus marshes were dry at this season, it scarcely seems a probable thing for him to do. It is more likely that he moved south of the Carthaginians through the forest roads of the northern foothills, even though this was Boian territory, allied to Hannibal. It is possible that it was while Hannibal was engaged in his early efforts on Clastidium that Sempronius slipped through. But Clastidium was small game; Sempronius was big. It seems as if Hannibal should himself have watched Sempronius. We must lay a lapse at the door of even this captain.

Whatever the means, Sempronius did escape Hannibal and did effectuate his junction with Scipio. Both consuls were now encamped on the Trebia. They were in a position to make the Carthaginian fight for his communications. But battle was just what Hannibal wanted, provided always that he could choose the occasion and the field.

Hannibal had established a new camp on the right of a small affluent of the Padus, somewhat less than five miles east of the Trebia, probably what is to-day called the Trebiola. Here he also received proposals from the Ligurians to join his forces and furnish him provisions. There were plenty of Roman haters in northern Italy, when it was safe to play that rôle. Hannibal saw that he must not rely too much on his new allies for food. He needed a large magazine of supplies. He turned to Clastidium, where the Romans had large quantities of breadstuffs. That even the two consuls had not severed his communications with the upper Po is evident, for while they were discussing the situation with a view to active operations, Hannibal had been at work on this town. What measures he took to force the place we do not know, except that he prepared to assault it; but the governor was more open to the show of gold than to threats, and surrendered the place. It proved an excellent capture, of which Hannibal made good use and fully rationed his army, much to the disgust of the Roman consuls. And, as Livy says, " it served as a granary for the Carthaginians while

they lay at the Trebia," a further proof that Scipio's manœuvre had failed to cut Hannibal off from the upper Po.

The Ananian Gauls, among whom the Roman army lay,
were afraid or unwilling to join the new coalition, or else
they were waiting to see whether the Romans or Carthaginians would win in the battle soon to come. Making this a
pretext, but really because he desired to taunt Sempronius
to action before the recovery of Scipio from his wound, —
for Hannibal knew Sempronius to be hot-headed and lacking
in the discretion of his colleague, — the Carthaginian general sent out a force of two thousand foot and one thousand
horse, Numidians and Gauls, to ravage the Ananian territory
so as to prevent the Romans from procuring forage and corn.
The Ananes of course turned to the consuls for help. Scipio,
as yet unable to leave his quarters, strongly advised against
giving up the excellent position they held, preferring a policy
of caution. Sempronius was for battle. The consuls went
to the extent of indulging in all but acrimonious discussion
as to what it was wise to do. Sempronius would by no
means hearken to Scipio's advice. He sent out the bulk
of his horse and some thousand bowmen to drive the Carthaginians from their work of destruction. This force
crossed the Trebia, and won a cheap victory over a small Carthaginian detachment which was retiring to camp laden with
booty ; and which, reinforced in its turn, faced about and
drove in the Romans. Sempronius now moved out with a still
larger force, consisting of all his cavalry and light troops, and
beat off the reinforced Carthaginian column. Hannibal,
having accomplished his purpose, and not desiring a general
engagement under the existing conditions, contented himself
with steadying his troops and left the Romans to retire. Hannibal had whetted Sempronius' appetite for a pitched battle.
Livy, who, like a good ward-politician, is in the habit of

"claiming everything," in this instance calls the affair a draw.

Proud of his success, and desirous of coming to blows with Hannibal before Scipio could recover and assume command, — and particularly as the time for the election of new consuls was drawing nigh, — Sempronius took measures looking towards a general engagement, heedless of Scipio's caution to beware of the wily foe.

Hannibal was equally eager to engage, but proposed to get the chances in his favor; for the Roman army was now some forty thousand strong, and not counting barbarian allies on either side, considerably outnumbered his own. The Gauls also were noted for their inconstancy, and Hannibal desired to give them an opportunity to profit by the defeat of their enemy, rather than wear out his own welcome. To lie still doing nothing was the most dangerous policy, especially as winter was coming on, and to delay meant to weary his allies by taking up winter-quarters among them, which he did not want to do without some very marked success to retire upon. The new Roman levies had as yet had no hardening in war; his own troops were quite restored in strength, and their morale was of the highest; his opponent was a rash soldier; Hannibal well knew the situation of the Roman army; everything looked favorable.

There are not a few who read the authorities to mean that Hannibal had all this while remained on the west bank of the Trebia, while the Romans held the east, — in other words, that Hannibal had made no effort to cut Sempronius off from Scipio. But not only was it natural that Hannibal should move among his allies, the Boians, but the balance of evidence goes to support the statements above given. Polybius, Livy, Nepos, all state that Scipio on leaving Placentia crossed the Trebia to encamp, and moreover it was to quiet his allies, the Ananes, that he moved among them. If Hannibal had remained west of the Trebia, he would have been among the Ananes, and there would have been no special reason for Scipio's moving from Placentia. But when Hannibal cut Scipio off from his colleague, there was a definite reason for the consul's change of camp, particularly so if, as is possible, he so placed himself as to afford Sempronius a better chance of joining him. These facts, coupled to the positions of the armies in the coming battle, which are not disputed, appear to decide the matter to be as stated.

No field can be established with absolute certainty for the battle of the Trebia, but the following account and plan accord well with the authorities and with the topography they describe. The locality given is in fact the only one in the vicinity which will do so with accuracy.

We have seen that shortly after Scipio had gone into his camp on the Trebia, Hannibal had moved his Nura camp to the Trebiola, much nearer to the enemy. Here he had been ever since, facing the Romans on the other side of the Trebia.

Roman Helmet.

XIX.

THE BATTLE OF THE TREBIA. DECEMBER, 218 B. C.

To the left of Hannibal's camp was an overgrown ravine, a branch of the Trebiola. Here he hid a party of two thousand choice troops under Mago, and before daylight next morning sent his Numidians, who had eaten their morning meal earlier than usual, across the Trebia to attack the Roman camp, and by retreating induce the Romans to follow them back. This was well done. Sempronius ordered his entire army into line, and though his men had not broken fast, he pushed them across the river. The day was raw; snow was falling; by the time the legions had crossed the Trebia fords the men were chilled through. The Carthaginians had, on the contrary, eaten and rubbed themselves with oil before their camp-fires. Sempronius was already half beaten. The two lines formed, and despite their bad condition, the Romans fought stanchly. The Roman horse was, however, soon beaten by the Carthaginian, which then turned in on the flanks of the Roman infantry, and at the same time Mago emerged from ambush and fell on the Roman rear. The elephants had demoralized the Gallic allies in the consular army, and the whole Roman force was surrounded by the Carthaginians. Ten thousand of the centre legionaries, under Sempronius, cut their way through Hannibal's centre and marched to Placentia; the balance were either killed, or trodden down by the elephants, or drowned in the Trebia. Scipio decamped under cover of a storm on the succeeding night and made his way to Placentia. Sempronius went to Rome. Hannibal held the entire country. Both armies sought winter-quarters, after some further slight exchanges, Hannibal in Liguria, Scipio at Ariminum, Sempronius at Luca. Hannibal's base on the Po was secure. But in Spain, Cornelius Scipio had practically recovered Catalonia.

HANNIBAL was a master of stratagem. Having ascertained by the use of numerous Gallic spies — and they were good ones, having affiliations in both camps — all the facts relating to the enemy which he deemed essential to his purpose, he carefully scrutinized the ground between the two armies and east of the Trebia. It was an open plain, well suited for the evolutions of cavalry, and on its southerly limit lay an overgrown waterway — a branch of the Trebiola, in fact — whose high banks, covered with underbrush, were capable of concealing a considerable force. In this retreat he placed in ambush his brother Mago, with a chosen body of one thousand horse and an equal number of the best of the light troops, all men of known resolution; and on the following morning, the Carthaginian army having been ordered to take hearty nourishment before daylight, he sent the Numidian horse beyond the Trebia to annoy the enemy, and, if possible, lure him from his camp and across the river before the hour of the morning meal. The whole Carthaginian army he ordered to make itself ready for battle. This was not far from the end of the year B. C. 218.

The Trebia is, in its upper course, no more than a mountain torrent. On the plain near the Po it is at times full to overflowing; at times low and shallow — a mass of sandbanks. At this season it was full. It is the barrier which covers the eastern debouch of the defile of Stradella, and by its valley, moreover, lies the straight road from Placentia to Genoa. It is an important stream. History has lined its banks with blood.

No sooner had the Numidians shown up in the vicinity of the Roman camp, than Sempronius sent out his cavalry to drive them off, sustaining it with six thousand velites; and himself, in impatience to seize what was to him apparently an excellent opening, at the head of the entire army moved out as to battle. It is a constant rule of war to get all the chances, or as many as you can, on your own side; Sempronius was preparing to get them all, on this occasion, on Hannibal's.

The Numidians had their orders. They skirmished with the cavalry for a while, then, feigning defeat, which these

nomads could do with astonishing cleverness, recrossed the
river. Sempronius could not restrain his ardor. He had
beaten these wretches a few days since; why not again to-day?

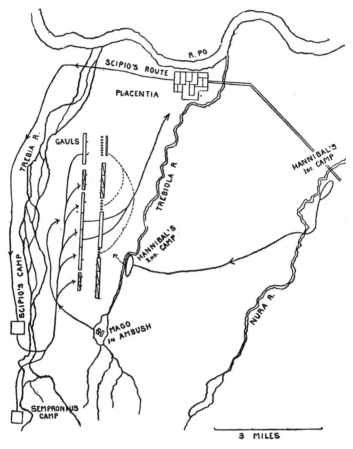

Battle of the Trebia.

The day was raw; snow was falling; the troops had not yet
eaten their morning meal; yet, though they had been under
arms for several hours, he pushed them across the fords of
the Trebia, with the water breast-high and icy-cold.   Arrived

on the farther side, the Roman soldiers were so chilled that they could scarcely hold their weapons.

Hannibal was ready to receive them. His men had eaten, rubbed themselves with oil before their camp-fires, and prepared their weapons. He might have attacked the Roman army when half of it was across, with even greater chances of success. But when he saw his ruse succeeding, he bethought him that he could produce a vastly greater moral effect on the new Gallic allies, as well as win a more decisive victory, by engaging the whole army on his own terms.

Sempronius was in the worst possible position. He had a river — fordable in places, to be sure, but still a serious obstacle — at his back, and an army to command, which was not only not in the best of heart, but physically weakened by lack of food and the morning's exposure. But he did not recognize this weakness; he only considered how he had, as it seemed to him, driven the Numidians back across the river. He cheerfully moved forward into line of battle, calling in his horse. He had sixteen thousand Roman and twenty thousand allied infantry, and four thousand Roman and allied cavalry. He drew up this army in the usual three lines, throwing out the velites to the front, and placing the cavalry on the flanks. The Gallic auxiliaries were on the left of the legions. He then advanced to the attack.

Hannibal opened the action by sending out eight thousand light troops and his one thousand Balacrean slingers as a skirmishing first line, to sustain the Numidian horse in its retreat. His main line of twenty thousand infantry, including Gauls, he disposed a mile in front of his camp, in phalangial order, the Gauls in the centre, the Africans on either side of them, the war-hardened Spaniards on the flanks. His cavalry was now, with the Gallic auxiliaries, fully ten thousand strong. This he posted opposite the cavalry on the Roman flanks, but as the Roman front was longer, there was left an interval on each flank between his foot and horse. This interval he filled with his elephants.

The Carthaginian skirmishers, much fresher and older at the business, soon drove in the Roman velites. Hannibal then called them back, and sent them to support the elephants, in the intervals spoken of. The velites fell back, and rallied behind the triarii, and the line advanced, the principes checkerwise behind the intervals of the hastati, and the triarii in reserve, with sure Roman steadiness.

So soon as the two lines met, for in those days of short-carriage weapons, lines did meet, the Roman centre forced the fighting, but the Roman wings of infantry, which met the elephants and light troops, were unable to make any headway, though, to the surprise of all, the Romans did not take alarm at the appearance or tactics of the elephants. Hannibal now ordered forward his cavalry of both wings, and after a sharp charge and tussle they broke the Roman horse, and drove it from the field. A part of the Carthaginian horse followed up this retreat, while another part, assisted by the light troops and the Balacreans, who did astonishing execution, turned inward upon the flanks of the Roman infantry. The elephants had been driven back by the legionaries, but Hannibal dispatched them to oppose the Gauls on the extreme Roman left, where they did the best of work.

Meanwhile, Sempronius' centre, composed of the Roman legions, with that wonderful tenacity of which even their green troops were capable, despite the wrecking of their horse and the fearful danger to the infantry wings, had pushed in the Carthaginian centre, where fought the Gauls and Africans ; and, elated with its success, and no doubt imagining that it was on the eve of victory, had advanced so far that it had become separated from its wings. The Numidian and

Carthaginian cavalry were now making fearful havoc among these wings, which contained the allied foot, and shortly surrounded and quite cut them off from the successful centre. At this moment, too, Mago emerged from hiding, rode around the Roman right, and, falling upon their rear, completed the destruction. The bulk of the line was cut to pieces on the spot. A hardy portion fought its way through to the river, but the men were here mostly either killed or drowned. What the horse did not cut down, the elephants trampled under foot, or the Trebia swallowed up. Very few were able to cross to camp.

The front of the centre, ten thousand strong, probably the principes and hastati of the Roman legions, which were not immediately reached by the attack of Mago, resolutely held together, formed circle in close order, and made their way to Placentia, under Sempronius, who, if not a discreet general, showed himself a doughty fighter. Hannibal was too busy destroying the wings to be able to prevent this escape of Sempronius with the central body. A few stragglers also made their way to Placentia. Scipio at once broke camp, and, crossing the Trebia by night, under cover of the cold and storm, which, added to the toils of the day, kept the Carthaginian army closely housed, marched in haste to the same place, with the few troops which had been left in the camps. In Placentia, Scipio took command. Sempronius returned to Rome, sending a courier ahead to announce that he had fought a battle, and that, except for the bad weather, he would have won it. A part of the troops were sent to Cremona, so as to divide the Roman force for winter-quarters.

This battle is the only one during Hannibal's Italian campaigns in which the phalanx encountered the legion, and again the balance was not even. But that the legion possessed manifest advantages over the phalanx is in nothing so powerfully shown as in the fact that before Cannæ Hannibal largely armed his phalangites Roman fashion; and though he did not adopt the manipular organization, we are led to believe that he made changes in his phalanx which altered its one-shock disposition to one in which there was mobility more nearly approaching the Roman line of cohorts. In Spain, legion and phalanx frequently met, with mixed success in the early years, but eventual superiority for the legion — or for Roman discipline — towards the end.

Hannibal did not follow beyond the Trebia. He had fought a masterly battle and won a decisive victory. But his losses had also been serious. They are, unfortunately, not given. The Gauls in the centre had especially suffered. He had lost nearly all his elephants, many by the cold. His brilliant success was more than compensation for any loss, and he now felt that he had a base perfectly secure in the alliance of the Gallic tribes. For these looked upon him as their savior from Roman tyranny. Had he not beaten the invincible Roman infantry man to man? No doubt remained with whom rested the credit of this first campaign. He followed up his success by numerous raids around Placentia and near-by Roman strongholds, thus keeping the legions in a state of constant uneasiness.

The Roman army was shut up in Placentia, with its communications cut with Ariminum and Etruria. Scipio made no show whatever of leaving the place, and Hannibal knew his cautious habit and did not attempt to lure him out to battle. He also knew that a fresh army would in early spring be sent to Scipio's relief; and recognized that though he was superior to the Roman general in horse, he was far behind him in foot, and might not have so easy a task as with Sempronius. Hannibal saw that he must be active in order to keep his advantage and to satisfy the demands of his Gallic allies. The very security of his position depended upon this fickle people remaining friendly, and he made every effort to satisfy them and procure additional allies.

Hannibal held the entire country. The Numidians or Gauls scouted undisturbed over the whole of it.

The means Scipio had of getting food was by ships up the Po, for Hannibal ate out and laid waste all the contributory territory which Scipio might have used, — sparing of course his own allies. A strongly fortified though small town, Emporium, on the right bank, aided in keeping navigation open. Hannibal made up his mind to surprise the place, and did indeed move against it one night with his cavalry. But by a system of preconcerted signals, or by the tumult, or by couriers, Scipio was called to its rescue. He came up with his cavalry at a rapid pace, followed by his legions in close order. A slight wound received by Hannibal in the cavalry action which followed was the cause of the defeat of his horse. This obliged the Carthaginians to retire. But Hannibal shortly repaired this disaster by the capture of Victumviæ, a citadel which might interrupt his communications with Liguria. The inhabitants of the vicinity, who had taken refuge in Victumviæ, made a gallant show of opposition, marching out to the number, says Livy, of thirty-five thousand men, to meet him in front of the town, but he gave them so summary a beating that the town decided to surrender. In order to terrify the garrisons of other towns, Hannibal, according to Livy, decided to put the Roman soldiers found here to the sword, and gave the place to his men to plunder.

The winter weather now detained him some time in quarters ; but in February (B. C. 217) a milder period set in, and Hannibal undertook a campaign up the Trebia into the Apennines, thinking to make an irruption into Etruria, and there create a diversion in his favor, and if possible detach the province from Rome. But he was met in the mountains with so severe a spell of weather that, after camping two days, he was fain to retire, losing a large number of men, animals and seven of his precious elephants. He went again into camp not far from Placentia. Livy's description of the storm reads like the one so graphically sketched by Curtius, in which Alexander's army suffered so severely in the Parapamisus.

Sempronius' defeat at the Trebia had not served to discourage or teach this officer caution. He had now returned from Rome. With his fiery impetuosity, for which to a certain degree he deserves credit, he determined, before retiring from Hannibal's front, again to cross swords with the Carthaginian. The opportunity was soon afforded him. Hannibal, after his mountain adventure, had returned to within ten miles of Placentia. One day, apparently while intent on making a reconnoissance in force, with twelve thousand foot and five thousand horse, Sempronius sallied forth to meet him, and to accept Livy's relation (Polybius does not mention the engagement), the consul's attack on Hannibal's line was so sharp that he forced him back to camp, and even went so far as to attack the camp intrenchments. Then, satisfied with the seeming advantage, he began to withdraw. This was Hannibal's opportunity. He debouched from camp with the bulk of his force, the foot from the front-gate, and the cavalry from the side-gates with instructions to fall on the Roman flanks. A hotly contested combat was the result, which only night arrested. Sempronius withdrew from the field with a loss of six hundred foot and three hundred horse, including five Roman war-tribunes, three allied præfects and many other officers. Hannibal's loss was about equal. Livy calls this a drawn battle, but the advantage had remained with Hannibal.

The Roman generals had determined to retire from Placentia before going into winter-quarters. They had become convinced that they could not longer hold the line of the Padus to advantage. Leaving garrisons in Placentia and Cremona, Scipio retired on Ariminum; Sempronius retired on Luca, across the Apennines into Etruria. By this division of forces, the two consular armies protected the two lines of operation from cisalpine Gaul to Rome, — the one east, the other west of the main range of the Apennines. At this period the danger of a division of forces never seemed to be understood. Hannibal was alone aware of its weakness; but he was not always able to take advantage of this error on the part of his opponents.

The method of the day of intrenching camps placed even a small army in comparative security, provided it did not accept battle when offered. Forcing battle, as it can now be done, was not then possible. But, by parity of reasoning, an army did not protect any given line as well as when it is at all times ready to fight for its object.

The consuls deemed the presence of at least one army in cisalpine Gaul imperative. Either of the consular armies could be speedily reinforced up to the strength of Hannibal's. And as winter-quarters were by both parties deemed a *sine quâ non*, — as they always had been, indeed, by every one but Alexander, — both contestants subsided into quiet until spring should bring forage for their animals on the march.

The question has been suggested why Hannibal should have allowed the Romans to retire from Placentia unopposed, or indeed to divide and retreat eccentrically, without falling upon and destroying one or the other of the consular armies. Perhaps his absence from the scene and his wound are the best explanation, though such operations were not so easy in the days of daily intrenched camps as they are now. Much

time was moreover consumed in negotiations with the Ligurians.   The relation of all the historians is more or less ob-
scure.   We constantly find gaps which can be filled only by
guess-work.   Such gaps, in the case of a master like Hannibal, are the more to be regretted, as we often have to pass
over some incident or lapse without a proper understanding
of the conditions, and thereby lose half the benefit of our
study.

The reason why Hannibal did not endeavor to take Placentia and Cremona, so as to deprive the Romans of their last
foothold in cisalpine Gaul, is probably that he had no material wherewith to conduct a siege.   In fact, he appears to
have had none during his entire campaign in Italy.   Mention of such is nowhere made.   Moreover, Hannibal seemed
always to feel, and it was probably true, as of Frederick,
that his proper strength was on the battle-field, or in strategic
combinations, and not in sieges.   He had no time to sit down
before strong places.   The only siege in which his ability was
ever brought strongly to the fore was that of Saguntum.
And the holding by the Romans of these places in no wise
militated against his general scheme.   He did his work with
as much liberty as if they had been in his own possession.
They were effectually masked by his alliances with the neighboring Gauls, and each contained but a small garrison.   They
were in fact soon evacuated.

The whole of cisalpine Gaul thus fell into the hands of
Hannibal.   He was now very eager to disembarrass his hosts,
the Gauls, from the burden of his army, and to make them
yet warmer allies by giving them a chance at the riches of
Italy.   But the severity of the season prevented his carrying
out the expedition he had planned into Etruria, and forced
him to winter in Gaul.   He took up his quarters in Liguria.
The Apennines separated him from Sempronius at Luca.

The Ligurians definitely joined Hannibal's standard, and furnished him as hostages a number of Roman officers, two quæstors (C. Fulvius and L. Lucretius), two military tribunes and five knights, most of them the sons of Roman senators.

Meanwhile in Spain, Cnæus Cornelius Scipio, who had sailed from Massilia, as above narrated, had won some success against the Carthaginians. He had landed near Emporiæ, had by clever management gained the coast-land between the Pyrenees and the Iberus, and after defeating and capturing Hanno, in a battle near Scissis, had got possession of a considerable part of the interior. His policy was pacific, and his occupation promised success. But Hasdrubal marched across the Iberus and surprised the crews of the Roman fleet, which had landed near by and carelessly dispersed, and killed a number of them. After these latter unimportant exchanges, Hasdrubal went into winter-quarters at New Carthage, Cnæus Scipio near Tarragona, where he divided much booty among his soldiers.

Hannibal's carefully prepared base in Spain had already received a damaging blow.

Soldier's Cloak.

XX.

THE ARNUS MARSHES. SPRING, 217 B. C.

THE Padane country was lost. The new consuls, Servilius and Flaminius, proposed to hold the approaches to Rome on the two main roads, at Arretium and Ariminum. Flaminius was a hot-headed man, though not lacking ability. He had the bulk of the consular forces at Arretium. What the consuls should have done was to join their armies and fight Hannibal; but they could not see the risk of divided forces. The Carthaginian determined to invade Etruria. He did not wish to move by the main Roman road, via Placentia and Mutina, because the consuls expected him that way. His only other route was across the mountains to Genoa, along the coast to the Arnus, and up the river. This led him through a section of land overflowed in spring, and peculiarly marshy this year. The obstacle was a dangerous one; but it was because he could debouch on Flaminius unexpectedly that he chose it. He broke up from winter-quarters, and after a difficult and costly march reached Fæsulæ, much to the surprise of the consuls. In central Italy, Hannibal expected not only to win victories, but to be able to seduce some of the Roman confederates from their allegiance. In doing this lay, in fact, his only hope. Alone, he could accomplish nothing, even with victories, and he knew it well. Rome was too strong in material resources. But if he could break up the Italian Confederacy, he could dictate a peace at the gates of Rome.

THE consuls elected for the ensuing year — B. C. 217 — were Cnæus Servilius and Caius Flaminius. It was intended that the former should protect against the approach of Hannibal the line of the Via Flaminia through Umbria to Ariminum, while the latter should cover the road which was later the Via Cassia, leading through Etruria via Arretiv Florentia and Luca. These roads were not yet the great highways of a later age, but they were good of their kind.

No unusual preparations were made by Rome. The four legions were reinforced up to their normal strength, and the

cavalry was somewhat increased. Rome had no idea that she
would be called on for undue exertions. The forces from Placentia and other fortresses on the Po were drawn in to reinforce the consular armies. They could readily drop down the

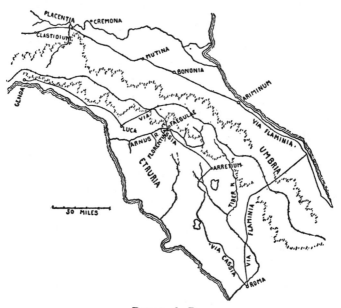

Rome to the Po.

Po and along the coast to Ariminum. The two consuls expected later to concentrate north of the Apennines and again
rescue the line of the Po.

Flaminius was of an aristocratic family, but though he had
espoused the cause of the people, his quarrelsome character
lost him many friends and clients. The nobility hated him,
and he is generally represented as a demagogue. He was
really a man of progress, with an honest and vigorous nature,
but had made more foes than friends by proposing an agra-
rian law when he was tribune. He was of an impetuous,
over-confident nature, but had shown some years before,

against the Gauls, that he did not entirely lack military capacity, as he certainly possessed some civic virtues. But
these were overclouded by his peculiarities. He now began
in his usual wrong-headed way, and quarreled even with the
senate before leaving Rome for the north, which fact enables
Livy to explain the coming disasters by portents and omens.
Flaminius had reason to fear that he might be again recalled
by this sometimes arrogant body before he could join the
army, as it had formerly tried to recall him from Gaul by
appealing to the superstition of the people. Taking at Ariminum the two legions which properly belonged to Servilius,
in addition to the two he had got by lot from Sempronius,
who, we remember, had retired on Luca before winter, he
concentrated at Arretium. Here he purposed to wait quietly
until the roads became passable, when he supposed it would
be time enough to block them against Hannibal. But he
found that the Phœnician did not wait for practicable roads.

Servilius remained in Rome to raise additional forces
and to make arrangements for victualing both armies. In
March he moved to Ariminum with two new legions, to hold
head against the Gauls, who with coming spring would be
apt to move. Scipio was ordered to Spain, his province of
last year, with two legions; and there were, besides, one in
Sicily, one in Sardinia and one at Tarentum. The six legions ran the force of the consuls up to over fifty thousand
men.

Servilius would have been better with Flaminius. There
was no immediate peril from the Gauls. Alone, the Gauls
were not dangerous. Under Hannibal they were much to be
feared; but once beat Hannibal, and they would leave him
without delay. Hannibal was the enemy whom it was essential to crush. This could only be done by numbers, if at all.
But the consuls did not yet know their man.

Hannibal had no idea of wasting his time defending the valley of the Po against Roman assaults. His work lay among the confederates in southern and central Italy. His scheme was a constant offensive, and we shall see that so long as he had strength to do so, he kept even the Romans, the very essence of whose policy was push, strictly to a defensive rôle. He well knew that should he defeat one consular army after another, this would not be defeating Rome. He must weaken the Italian Confederacy in order to strike at the root of her power. Victory was necessary, but it was only a first step. Unless victory affected in his favor the Roman allies, it could do him no eventual good. Hannibal was too old a soldier not to know that the Roman military organization was better in the long run than his own, even if the legion was not at this time better than his own phalanx. He saw that Rome could prolong the contest indefinitely, and would keep on improving, while he could not expect to do so. He by no means underrated his foe. His plan must be unremitting activity by which he could undermine the morale of the Roman senate, and a succession of victories which should incline to his cause the Roman allies. Rome had absolute material preponderance. All Hannibal had to oppose to this was his burning genius. And in his greatest successes he never forgot this limitation to his power; nor did his divine fury ever mislead him.

Hannibal made strenuous efforts, even at this time, to induce some of the allied cities to come over to his standard. He gave them to understand that his attitude towards Rome tended directly to their benefit, and that they could all gain their independence if he succeeded. The allied prisoners whom he had captured he treated generously and sent back without ransom. That he massacred the Roman prisoners is altogether doubtful, but he probably he drew a crisp distinction between them and their confederate brothers in adversity. He managed to produce a good impression, but it was as yet too dangerous a thing for any of the socii to break openly with Rome. On the other hand, the Gallic allies of Hannibal were getting restless, from having to sustain the war on their territory instead of gathering plunder on the enemy's. Hannibal was often put to severe straits to allay this feeling, which is described as being at times so strong that his assassination was planned. And it is related by Polybius that Hannibal was obliged to resort to all manner of subterfuges and personal disguises of costume to escape this constantly threatening danger; especially so, as he was always active in personally reconnoitring the country, and in judging what he ought to do with his own eyes.

Flaminius had an army of four legions; at the normal strength with allies about thirty-six thousand men. Servi-

The Arnus Marshes.

lius had half the number. While the senate had not waked up to the full danger of the situation, Rome had this year over one hundred thousand men in the field. She needed more before the year was out.

When spring opened, Hannibal determined to move to Etruria as a first step towards an invasion of central Italy. There were two directions from Liguria by which he might do this. The main route, over which the Romans marched their army to the Padane country, was excellent. From Liguria, however, it ran by a long circuit through Clastidium, Placentia, Mutina and Bononia, to Ariminum, before it crossed the mountains, though there were several gaps in the Apennines, with country roads turning southerly off this route — later the Via Æmilia. The only other road then practicable was one which the Ligurians had not infrequently used in their raids into Etruria, but which was little known to the Romans. It lay across the mountains to Genoa, and then along the coast to the mouth of the Arnus, whence a march up the right bank would bring Hannibal to the left of the Roman position at Arretium, on the southern foothills of the Apennines.

If Hannibal attempted the highway or any of the roads leading off it, the consul Flaminius could make his progress all but impossible by besetting the mountain passes, and the country was such that he would be unable to make valid use of his cavalry. Moreover, the other consul, Servilius, would soon reach Ariminum with two legions, — as Hannibal well knew, for these things were reported to him by spies whom he never neglected to keep in motion, — and could readily harass his rear should he attempt to force the mountain passes. On the other road, the territory at the mouth of the Arnus was at this season one huge marsh, which took days to traverse, and happened this year to be deeper overflowed than usual, a state of things which would last many weeks, and might subject him to as much toil as the passage of the Alps. This seemed to the bold Carthaginian, however, the lesser evil, and he chose it. The route he knew to be full of difficulties, but as it was the

surest and quickest to the heart of Italy, as it turned the
Roman position, and as it was the one on which he would not
be looked for, it was the road which best suited his ideas.
Obstacles he knew not, when they lay between him and
Rome.

The Romans gauged Hannibal's manœuvres in the light
of their own. They had always dictated the method of
war, and could look at it only thus. So far, Hannibal had
sought battle, and they supposed he would still do so by the
simple means of moving directly up to their position. They
were watching the valley of the Padus and the passes of the
Apennines leading upwards from the lower part of the river.

Hannibal had been camping in a level country of vast extent. He was now to enter upon the mountain country, near
whose foothills he had won his first pitched battle. Most
generals excel either in upland or lowland war; Hannibal
had been trained, and was equally at home in both.

The backbone of the Apennines runs down the length of
the peninsula of Italy, at times rising to an altitude of ten
thousand feet, at times merely a rolling country with occasional mountains accentuating the range. Throughout their
length the Apennines are now cut by numerous excellent
roads; the population is large, and the cultivation abundant.
In Hannibal's time, many communities lived in these hilly
fastnesses; and the valleys smiled with grain and oil and wine.
But the roads, excepting those which always followed hard
upon Roman occupation, were probably mostly such as peoples
can produce whose transportation is done by pack-animals
alone. The Gauls of the Po had carts, but they lived in the
plain; the mountaineers of Italy used no vehicles at that day;
they own few now.

At intervals, rather rare, in this mountain chain, there were
alluvial plains, and frequently the shore extended well out to

sea from the foothills. But the general character of the whole peninsula was upland, and there were in central and southern Italy but three plains of marked extent; those along the Arnus, the happy fields of Campania, and the prairies of

The Plains of Italy.

Apulia on the opposite coast. Still, almost all portions of central Italy, on either side of the chain, made good campaigning ground, and the mountains could at intervals be readily crossed.

We do not know as much about the roads as we could wish. But where the great turnpikes with which the Romans invariably followed up their conquests did not yet exist, there were no doubt excellent substitutes in the country roads, either native or Roman. The neighbors of Rome were all but as active in internal improvements as herself. Neither the consuls nor Hannibal appear usually to have been hampered by lack of practicable roads, though in such a country

certain positions and gaps have a constant and peculiar strategic value, and are used by preference. The Roman roads
were so apt to follow the paths indicated by the roads of the
populations which preceded their occupation, that we may
fairly consider that intercommunication between all parts of
Italy was excellent, certainly better than that we Americans
were fain to content ourselves with in our Civil War. Hannibal had only infantry, cavalry and pack-trains ; he could
practically go anywhere where there were mountain-gaps.

Hannibal broke up in early spring, probably March, 217
B. C. He had wintered in the vicinity of modern Alexandria.
The first part of the march towards Etruria was not over-
burdened with difficulties. The range from the Ligurian
country to Genoa is rugged ; but his troops had campaigned
in Spain, and the Gauls knew the land tolerably well. From
Genoa to modern Spezzia, he kept along the cliff-roads.
Nearing the Luca country, he also neared the Arnus
marshes. Just what the extent of this submerged section
was, we only know from the ancient authors. It does not
now exist. It is called a marsh. It probably was alluvial
land covered by the usual spring overflow, this year excessive. At first blush, especially to judge from the fact that
Luca was a Roman colony, one would suppose that there must
have been a practicable road around the north of the flat land
of the Arnus. But that there was none must not only be assumed from the authorities, but is evident from the structure
of these foothills. Roads in plenty there may have been, up
into the valleys of this southern slope of the Apennines, and
some across the range ; but to attempt to march along the
length of the slope would have been to encounter a never-
ending succession of precipices and torrents, as well as a zigzag path as long in miles as the entire peninsula. Hannibal
was obliged to essay the passage of the marsh. Through this

there was a road, fairly good during the dry weather, but at this time considered impassable.

But the Carthaginian knew not the meaning of the word. There was no road he could not utilize. He set out confidently on his perilous march. In the van he sent the Spanish and African troops, with the most necessary and valuable of the baggage, so that these, his best troops, should not suffer, and that the treasure and essentials should be got across the marsh before the road was too much trodden down by the column. It is not probable that a large quantity of baggage was taken. Hannibal was well aware that if he lost the game, he would need none; if he won, he would have food and treasure in superabundance. He probably kept his treasure in small bulk. Next came the Gallic allies — the least reliable of his army — followed by Mago with the horse, whose duty it was to persuade these troops to diligence, if possible; but, if necessary, to push them on by the use of force.

The van with the baggage got through without all too great loss. They were old and hardened troops, and found the road, such as it was, still unbroken by recent travel. But the Gallic column, unused to and impatient under such exposure, lost heavily from fatigue and deprivation. The whole army was four days and three nights marching through water, where only the dead horses, dead beasts of burden or abandoned packs afforded any chance to rest. Many horses and mules cast their hoofs. Hannibal personally made the march on the last remaining elephant, — the rest having all perished at the Trebia or in the Apennines, — and during this season of exposure lost an eye from an inflammation which he was unable to attend to, and which was seriously aggravated by overwork. Cornelius Nepos states that he had to be carried in a litter from this time until after the battle of Trasimene.

The army finally reached firm land and went into camp, on

the north bank of the Arnus, on the heights of Fæsulæ (Fie-
sole), overlooking the plains of modern Florence, where it
found store of good provisions, the province being one of the
most fertile in Italy.

Unlike Alexander, Hannibal did not do brilliant things for
their own sake; but that he was always ready to face the
most perilous and harassing undertakings in order to place
himself nearer the accomplishment of his object, this march
proves almost as well as the passage of the Alps. He had
completely turned his adversary's position and had again won
his choice of a theatre of operations.

Roman Corselet.

XXI.

A FLANKING MANŒUVRE. SPRING, 217 B. C.

ARRIVED in Etruria, Hannibal began manœuvring to lure Flaminius out to battle. This he did largely by devastating under his very eyes the country the consul had come to protect. Finally, unable to draw Flaminius out of his camp at Arretium, Hannibal moved around his left flank and cut him off from Rome; and this without losing his own line of operations. The manœuvre was as neat as any of Napoleon's. Still Flaminius remained in camp, and Hannibal determined to move towards Apulia, where he could better negotiate with the confederates, and whither he felt sure the consuls would follow him; which, if they did, would afford him a chance of drawing them into a pitched battle. As Hannibal passed Lake Trasimene, he came to a place very suitable for an ambuscade; and hearing that Flaminius had broken camp and was following him up, he stopped and camped on the road to Perusia.

HANNIBAL found that the Etrurians were well inclined to rise against Rome, and needed but the encouragement of success to determine them. He made careful study of the whole region, as well as the condition of the Roman army, which lay southeast of his at Arretium. "The plans and temper of the consul, the situation of the country, the roads, the sources from which provisions might be obtained, and whatever else it was useful to know; all these things he ascertained by the most diligent inquiry," says Livy. This well illustrates Hannibal's constant habit.

Etruria was rich in victuals and could furnish the Carthaginians material assistance, and the Roman general was, thought Hannibal, hot-headed enough to be betrayed into a battle on as disadvantageous terms as had been Sempronius. Having studied out his problem, — and particularly the methods of Flaminius, for "it is to be ignorant and blind in

the science of commanding armies to think that a general has
anything more important to do than to apply himself to learning the inclinations and character of his opponent," aptly says
Polybius, — Hannibal crossed the Arnus to the south bank.

Flaminius lay intrenched in a stationary camp at Arretium. His intention, very likely, was to move forward to
Luca, when the conditions of the road should allow, in order
to close up the passes debouching at that point, while his colleague should move from Ariminum to replace him where he
now stood. The two consuls would thus close up the avenues
of the Apennines. Padane Gaul was lost to them.

Flaminius had a certain repute, acquired partly in the field,
more largely in the forum, but he was in no sense fitted to
cope with Hannibal. So sure was he of victory that his camp
is said to have been thronged with non-combatants who had
assembled for spoil. But this has been the case in the camps
of better soldiers, — Pompey's at Pharsalus, as an instance.

Arretium lies at the northern outlet of a long and level
valley, some ten miles wide, of which Lake Trasimene forms
the southern boundary, and in a species of gap, which debouches into the valley of the Arnus. The entire surrounding country is hilly, but fertile and accessible. Flaminius
was as much astonished at Hannibal's sudden appearance on
his left, as Scipio must have been to find that Hannibal had
crossed the Alps. He at once sent word to Servilius of Hannibal's near presence.

Hannibal's march from the Arnus was deliberate, at every
step seeking for indications of the consul's purpose. He was
living on the country, but in addition to what he took for
victual, he thoroughly plundered the land, partly to gather
booty, by the distribution of which he hoped to gain new adherents to his cause, but mainly to work Flaminius up to a
proper pitch of fury. For seeing the land he had come to

protect reduced to a desert under his very eyes, the consul
was the more apt to lose his head. But though the smoke of
burning villages and the outcries of pillaged inhabitants rose

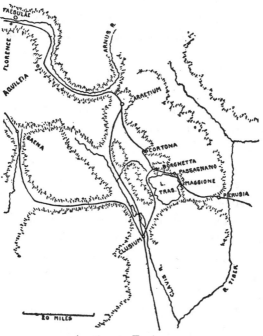

Arretium to Trasimene.

like a spectre to appall the consul, he showed no sign of moving from his stationary camp at Arretium. He was held
there by the advice of his colleague and lieutenants.

It was then that Hannibal conceived another of his brilliant
manœuvres. We are told nothing about it by the ancient
authors, whose knowledge of war confined them solely to the
description of battles. But it is apparent enough to us. He
was still in the Aquileia region, north and west of Arretium.
Marking his progress with fire and sword, he headed southerly, and marching boldly around the consul's left flank, he

made for the Clavis above Clusium. By this handsome
march Hannibal cut Flaminius off from Rome. It is probable that he sent his heavy train by way of Sæna (modern
Siena), and made his march in order of battle, as he was
apt to move by the flank past the Roman camp, the more
bitterly to taunt the Roman general. The operation did not,
however, partake of the danger which would beset it to-day.

Here again is shown — as by Alexander on two several occasions — the clear conception of the enemy's strategic flank,
with all its advantages, having, of course, reference to the
difference of arms and war-methods. Nor by his manœuvre
had Hannibal recklessly cut himself loose from his base,
though he was living on the country and independent of it, as
it were; the fact is, that the complete integrity of his line of
communications with the Luca country, and beyond to Liguria, was preserved by the valley of the modern Elsa, near
whose sources lay the town of Sæna, which was a route much
shorter than that of the consul from Arretium. While this
line of retreat was unquestionably difficult, it was far less
so than Napoleon's, after he had entered Italy by the Great
St. Bernard. Every week tended to reduce the overflow of
the Arnus. A more perfect case of cutting the enemy from
his communications can scarcely be conceived.

It goes without saying, that the consequences of losing their
line of communications was not fraught with the danger for
the ancients which it is to-day. Flaminius had no long trains
of food and ammunition to be cut off and captured. He did
not depend for his daily bread, nor for his ability to fight a
battle, on what could reach him from Rome. But he was
none the less cut off from the capital. If he fought, it must
be under morally and materially worse conditions than if his
line was open; and the effect on his men of having the enemy
between them and Rome, as well as of their being held back

from a battle, could not but be disastrous. While Hannibal's manœuvre could not accomplish the result against Flaminius which Napoleon's did against Melas or Mack, it was none the less the work of a master-hand, and affords the intelligent soldier a lesson in strategy, if it cannot be used as an illustration to the young student of the modern art of war.

Hannibal continued to tempt Flaminius to battle by all the arts he knew how to practice. He relied upon the consul's well-known vehemence for this result, and doubted not that it yet would come. It was in fact only the joint entreaties of all Flaminius' lieutenants which had constrained him so long to hold the defensive rôle.

It would seem as if Flaminius, when he found that Hannibal had got between him and Rome, would have sent for Servilius to come immediately to his assistance. Nothing but concentration and action could overcome the Carthaginian general. Flaminius could well have prevented the success of Hannibal's manœuvre by a timely occupation in force of Clusium, or some point near it. But to learn to play such a strategic game was no part of a Roman's military education. Up to this time, strategy had been a closed book to the Romans. They understood how to fight. Manœuvring was an unknown art. Perhaps the two consuls could not act amicably together in one body; and Servilius was deemed to be necessary in Ariminum to hold the Gauls in check. It is altogether likely that it never entered Flaminius' head that Hannibal could by any possibility reach his rear.

Hannibal continued to waste the country after collecting what material he needed, and finally, when he saw that Flaminius showed no inclination to accept his gage of battle, he moved down the Clavis to Clusium, devastating as he went, thence across the river due east to Lake Trasimene, and around its north side to the road leading by that bank to Perusia.

Hannibal has been criticised for thus moving so that a force of thirty thousand men should be on his rear. But Hannibal at this moment may be said to have had no rear. He was living on the country in every sense, and all his actions were based on what he had ascertained about the character, position and force of his antagonist, and what he felt sure he would do ; and Hannibal was rarely deceived in such matters. No doubt the most essential factor in calculating a campaign is the weight of the opposing commander. This Hannibal had surely gauged. He had moreover retained his line of operations until he saw that he must run a further risk, and under the circumstances he was wise to run it. He was seeking for the proper field of battle, and felt sure that Flaminius would by and by follow him to it. It must be remembered that Hannibal did not look upon these strategic manœuvres of his in the same light that he would have done had he lived and fought to-day. Then, as now, battle was the purpose of all manœuvres, but then more than now. The consuls were safe in their camp. Rome was safe within its walls. The moral or political effect which Hannibal could produce by marching even up to the walls of Rome was not what to-day would be produced by such an act. Nothing would suit Hannibal's purpose or extend his influence in Italy except to beat the Romans in battle ; and in his march around Flaminius' left, he was aiming first and foremost at battle on a suitable battle-field, and in a secondary sense at a change of base. He had tried his best to bring Flaminius out to fight, and this was a new resort to accomplish the same end. As Flaminius was not disastrously affected by Hannibal's cutting him off from Rome, so Hannibal did nothing unwarranted in cutting himself loose from his own communications.

The other and perhaps stronger consideration for Hanni-

bal's march was the fact that it had been from the inception
a part of his programme at the proper time to throw up his
base on the Padus, and make a new one for himself in central
or southern Italy, where he could readily communicate with
Carthage by sea, as well as be closer to his prospective allies,
those cities of the Roman confederacy which he might succeed
in detaching from their allegiance. It was doubtless at this
moment that he determined to give up his old line of operations, and acted accordingly. His march accomplished both
his aims.

Flaminius was wrought up to a high pitch of wrath by
this march and devastation of Hannibal's. He again called
a council of war, though he had determined in any event on
his own responsibility to follow and chastise the insolent
invader. The council advised caution, to wait for Servilius
and merely to send out his horse to hamper Hannibal's movements and prevent his laying waste any more of the country.
But vexed still more at being crossed, Flaminius at once
ordered the troops under arms and moved on Cortona, a
strongly situated town on a high hill jutting from the eastern
range of the valley south of Arretium, and half-way on the
road to Trasimenus. According to Livy there were many
signs and portents of approaching disaster. The keener-
witted officers shook their heads, but the army was of the
mood of its commander. The march was made without any
particular order or precaution, — a fact well known to the
Carthaginian general.

Flaminius is taken to task by both Polybius and Livy,
as well as by many modern writers, for thus moving on Hannibal. They appear to judge him solely by the event, and
by his naturally quarrelsome disposition. This criticism
does not seem to be well earned. It would have been less
than soldierly, with Hannibal moving around him with daily

taunts, ravaging with fire and sword the land of the people
he was supposed to defend, and having actually got between
him and Rome, to do less than seek to attack him. Flaminius is blamable for not having forestalled Hannibal in
reaching the road to Rome, and is blamable in the highest
degree, in the presence of a captain who within a few months
had in two encounters shown the Romans the necessity of
the greatest caution, for not moving with such precaution
as to prevent his being surprised, even though such was
not the habit of Roman marches; or, if you like, blamable
for not waiting for the other consul, on the ground that you
cannot do better than get together your very utmost force
on the eve of battle; but clearly he was not wrong in following up, with a view to attack, or at least with a view to
harass, the enemy which his chief duty as consul it was to
destroy. He was not wrong in moving out to face Hannibal.
He was blamable for his methods only. He might readily,
while waiting for Servilius, have taken up a position to observe his enemy and seek to place him at a disadvantage
before bringing him to battle. He could have seriously hampered the Carthaginians without risking his own safety. He
was not bound to plunge into an open snare.

It was in the manœuvring that one general showed his skill,
and the other his want of it. Flaminius could in no wise
cope with Hannibal, who had from the instant he appeared
in Italy shown the highest conceptions of the art of war.
His operations had been bold as well as wise. His battles
had been skillfully conducted; his march into Etruria had
been stolen on Flaminius and made by a path the latter had
never conceived that an army could tread, — like Alexander's
march around Mt. Ossa in Thessaly, or his march by the
Pamphylian Ladders, and with similar results. He had
crossed, without a battle, the Apennines, the obstacle at

which the consuls had felt sure they could arrest his progress. He had skillfully gauged the ability of each of his
opponents, and had acted accordingly. He now stood ready
for the final arbitrament of battle, so soon as it could be had
on even terms, and was doing all that in him lay to force the
consular army into it. And it must be added that Hannibal's political good sense was equal to his military skill. No
captain has ever succeeded whose policy did not march
abreast with his manœuvres. That Hannibal eventually failed
was not from lack of intelligent policy, but because he had
no aid from home, and because the Latin confederacy had
been builded with a cement altogether too strong.

Legionary with Scale Armor.

XXII.

THE BATTLE OF LAKE TRASIMENE. APRIL, 217 B. C.

ON the east bank of the lake, Hannibal put his whole army in ambush to trap the Roman consul. The locality is south of modern Passignano, where the mountains come down to the lake and make a narrow plain, closed in at both ends by a defile. Through this plain and defile ran the road. On the heights bordering the plain, Hannibal placed his light troops; at the end of the plain, near the entrance defile, the Gauls and Numidians; at the south end his heavy troops. Flaminius was intent on following up and chastising the invader. He left Cortona, marched to the lake and camped. Next morning, at daylight, he entered the defile, at the end of which he could see Hannibal's camp on the hill over which ran the road to Perusia. A morning mist aided to conceal the ambushed Carthaginians. So soon as the entire Roman army had entered the plain, the defile was closed by the Numidians. Flaminius was advancing without order or care, when suddenly his van was attacked by Hannibal's heavy troops, and the signal was given for a general attack. The entire Carthaginian force fell on one flank of the Romans, who were in order of march, and had the lake on the other flank. There arose at once a *sauve qui peut*, and in a brief space the whole army, except six thousand men, who cut their way through to Perusia, were killed or captured. The six thousand were taken next day. Flaminius did not outlive his shame. Within a day or two, Maharbal defeated a reinforcement of four thousand Roman horse, killing half and capturing the rest. This was the worst of Roman defeats. After the battle, though the road to Rome was open, Hannibal was wise enough not to try to march on the capital. He saw the impossibility of the undertaking, and moved down to Apulia instead, from whence he could communicate with Carthage. Rome showed her wonderful capacity for resisting disaster as never before. Fabius Maximus was chosen dictator, and he made Minucius his master of the horse.

JUST how far away from the consuls Hannibal might have marched, or what was his original motive in moving towards Perusia, can only be guessed, though it is evident he first of all desired battle. But while on the march he took notice of the topography of Lake Trasimene, and its singular fitness for an ambuscade. If his plans were at once to move farther south, he altered them at this place. He no doubt studied his scheme with care. He may have remembered his father's able trapping of the Libyan rebels in the Tunisian defile. He learned at the moment that Flaminius had left Cortona to follow him up. Divining from the impetuosity of his character that his pursuit would be conducted in a headlong manner, Hannibal, instead of keeping on towards Perusia, bethought him again to attempt an ambuscade, not with a small force, but with his entire army, in these same defiles of the Lake of Trasimene. The idea was no sooner conceived than acted on. It is the only instance in history of lying in ambush with the whole of a large army.

The exact location of the battle is not stated by Polybius or Livy, but on carefully comparing these authors with the locality itself, it appears altogether probable that it took place between the defile at modern Passignano and the hill over which the road ascends on the way to modern Perugia. The topography here not only admirably fits the statements of these authors, but is exactly the place Hannibal would have chosen for the work in hand. This is not the spot selected by all modern critics, many of whom make the locality of the battle between Borghetto and Passignano.

The plain at whose apex lay Arretium (Arezzo), and on the eastern flank of which Cortona juts boldly out on a mighty hillside commanding the valley, ends at Lake Trasimene, the ranges on either hand spreading out and continuing on around the lake. On the northeast shore, at modern Borghetto, the range descends to the water side in a gently sloping hill; then recedes so as to form a wide plain between hills and lake; and again, at modern Passignano, it impinges on the lake in a huge, bold headland, terminating in a precipice of sheer rock, which overhangs the water. From the hills across the plain, which is entirely a flat, alluvial deposit, run a number of small brooks of no size or volume, except in spring. The lake has a depth of thirty or forty feet; the mountains to the east rise gradually to an average height of fifteen hundred feet above its surface; the plain is about five miles long, and at its widest some mile and a half.

Southeast of the exit of this first plain, at modern Passignano, is another and less wide plain, some four miles long, which is terminated at Torricella by the hills again impinging on the lake, and over these hills the road now runs, some three hundred feet up and down, by way of Maggione to Perugia. It appears probable that this is the scene of the battle. In Livy's day, tradition would have still been reliable. Polybius could certainly identify the spot. From both of their descriptions of ground and ambush, the author inclines to the belief that the battle was not fought on the first plain reached by Flaminius, though this is the one now pointed out to tourists as the battle-field. There is no difficulty in understanding the battle, after visiting the locality itself.

The changes in the lake during the last two thousand years have not altered the features named by both Polybius and Livy, namely, a narrow entrance-defile, a narrow plain, which, indeed, Livy also calls a defile, and a hill closing the farther exit. And the second plain was much better fitted for ambuscade, as the mountains at places came down close to the shore, and at no place is the plain, even to-day, more than half a mile in width. In Hannibal's day it was probably narrower yet. Small brooks also cross this plain.

On the hill at the southern exit of the plain he had chosen, Hannibal camped where he was in full view of any one entering at the northern defile, and spent the night in placing his troops. Below the camp, he posted his heavy infantry — Spanish and African — upon a slight elevation, from which

they could rush down with effect upon the Roman head of
column when it should reach the position. His heavy cavalry
was on the right of this infantry force, where it had ample
charging ground, prepared to take the Roman head of column

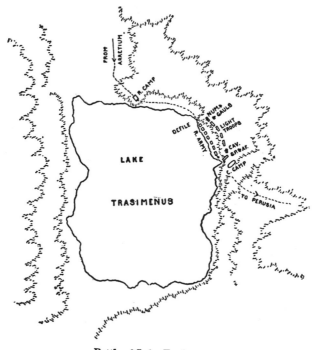

Battle of Lake Trasimene.

on the left flank. For an army passing this way had but a
narrow path to follow. His light troops, bowmen and slingers, were posted at intervals all along the heights overlooking
the plain, with orders to keep well hidden in the woods, and
to debouch sharply when the order for attack should be given;
his Numidian and Gallic cavalry and the Gallic infantry was
hidden in the hills well back in the depths of a wooded valley
at that end of the defile which the Romans would first enter,

but so placed that the cavalry could quickly sally out and close the entrance when the game was trapped.

It was April. Flaminius, marching from Cortona, camped at sunset at a place conveniently situated on the road before it reaches the ominous defile, not unlikely on the hillside of modern Borghetto. He was so overcome with indignation at his predecessors, and at the circumstances which had enabled Hannibal to ravage one of the most fruitful regions of Italy, that he was incapable of harboring any idea except determination summarily and severely to chastise the barbarian. For, much as Hannibal exceeded, in all that was intellectual and cultured, any Roman general of the day, he still remained, as we to the followers of Confucius, an outer barbarian. Flaminius easily ascribed the defeat on the Ticinus and at the Trebia to causes other than lack of caution. The invariable victories of the past had made every Roman feel himself invincible. With his enthusiastic and angry legions the consul might well feel able to overthrow any foe. Little he thought that he was to be one of those who, for Rome's eventual good, was by succumbing to Hannibal's abler method to teach a lesson in the art of war. For Rome, in order to make complete her splendid equipment, system and discipline, needed to learn that war is an intellectual game and not merely a contest of giants.

In the usual Roman fashion, Flaminius made no attempt to reconnoitre the ground in his advance, or to send out parties who should ascertain the whereabouts of the enemy. Hannibal, we must believe, took every precaution against his ambuscades being made known to Flaminius. The best disposed of the inhabitants of this section were but half-inclined to favor Hannibal's presence, and there must have been many arch-Romans among them, who, unless such precautions had been taken with exceptional skill, would be apt voluntarily to report to the Roman general the situation of the Carthaginian army. It is surprising indeed that Hannibal's plan succeeded.

Flaminius was eager to come up with Hannibal. He broke camp very early the next morning, — considerably before daylight, — and began his march in the midst of a morning fog, common in the vicinity of any large sheet of water, and which on this day lasted well into the forenoon. He hoped soon to reach the rear of his enemy, whom he no doubt imagined to be evading him for the purpose of continuing his ravages unmolested. To these the consul determined to put a stop.

One must call his imagination into play for the horrors of this memorable battle. A general description and the result alone are given in history. The Roman army, in slender column, skirted the precipice which formed the entrance to the fatal plain. As the head of column reached the open ground, the army spread itself out for convenience of marching. From the entrance, and above the fog which covered the surface to no great height, Flaminius had seen, on the hills at the southern end of the plain, the tents of Hannibal's camp, some four miles off. He imagined the Carthaginian army to be collected at that spot. Eager to come to blows with his enemy, he pushed rapidly on, and hurried up the column in the rear. The entire Roman army passed into the open space without discovering any sign of an ambush. The morning fog was all in Hannibal's favor.

As the head of column reached the vicinity of the southerly exit, and began to halt to close up ranks, for they were now near where Flaminius had seen the Carthaginian camp, the Roman right was suddenly saluted with a loud blare of trumpets, — the signal for a general attack by all parts of the ambushed Carthaginian line, — which signal they again heard repeated and repeated along the hillside on their front and towards their left as far as the gap they had just filed through; and immediately thereupon they saw, advancing upon them through the rolling clouds of mist, the serried ranks of the Carthaginian phalanx. To add to the consternation of the moment, the thundering tread of charging horse, and the terrible shout of horsemen galloping to certain victory, came rushing down upon the head of column from the left.

The first idea of the Roman officers was that they had merely thrust their van into an ambuscade, and must at once withdraw it. The head of column was compromised. But they were soon undeceived. As far down the marching line as they could hear, for see they could not, the enemy's light troops on the heights, with exulting shouts, debouched from hiding, and rushing down the hills towards the carelessly spread-out Roman column, discharged their hail of leaden bullets and fired their darts and arrows upon the Romans, who were utterly unprepared for resistance and in nothing resembling order of battle; while from several of the heights, which in this plain came down close to the water, fell a constant rain of arrows and sling stones. Nor could the surprise and terror of the head of column exceed that of the rear, when, rushing from their wooded screen in the upper valley, the Numidians and Gallic horse and foot fell furiously upon the disordered troops.

It must be remembered that there was at that day no regular order of march in a Roman army, and Flaminius' eagerness to get up with Hannibal had probably made speed rather than care the order of the day. There was no front, no flank, no rear. There was no way of retreat. On one side was the lake; on the other the hills from which debouched bodies of unseen but active foes; on right and left the attack of well-prepared and carefully arrayed battalions, instinct with the ardor of victory already won. Never was army worse compromised, never was army more certain of destruction. The Gauls had as yet had no chance to wreak their ill-will for many acts of cruelty done upon them by their Roman conquerors, and they now glutted their vengeance to the full. The Carthaginians saw that to-day they might wipe out the defeat and shame of the war in which their fathers had been so terribly punished, so deeply humiliated. The butchery was savage.

The Roman soldier, unconquerable when fighting within the lines of disciplined combat, appeared here to be no better than a brute beast led to the shambles. In the brief space of three hours, before the morning mists had lifted, there was no semblance of an army left, and still the butchery went on. Legions, cohorts, velites, triarii, all were mixed in one confused mass. Even the small bodies which hung together to defend themselves seemed incapable of wielding their arms; thousands threw themselves into the lake to seek a fate to them less cruel; other thousands put an end to their own existence. Livy states that so horrible was the tumult that neither party was aware of the occurrence of an earthquake, which at the very moment of the battle " overthrew large portions of many of the cities of Italy, turned rivers from their rapid course, carried the tides up into the rivers, and leveled mountains with an awful crash." A body of six thousand men cut its way through towards Perusia, no doubt under cover of the fog. Not exceeding ten thousand men all told escaped this fatal day. Of the remaining thirty thousand, half were killed in their tracks, half captured. Hannibal's loss did not exceed fifteen hundred men, mostly Gauls.

Hannibal at once sent Maharbal with the Spanish foot,

some archers and the heavy cavalry in pursuit of the body which had escaped through the lines to Perusia. They were surrounded next day on a hill they had occupied, and obliged to surrender to save their bare lives. On their surrendering, the Romans were made prisoners of war, the allied soldiers were all sent home without ransom. " I come not," said Hannibal, " to place a yoke on Italy, but to free her from the yoke of Rome." Some authorities have stated that of the whole force but six hundred cut their way through; that but nine hundred were captured; and that the rest, including Flaminius, were cut to pieces. Flaminius indeed fell with the rest. Well for him that he did! The first quoted figures are probably more nearly correct than the latter, which seem to go beyond probability. Certainly, however, Rome had never as yet seen so sad a day.

Plutarch relates that Hannibal sought long for the body of Flaminius, to give it burial, but was unable to find it.

The Roman soldier must not be underrated. The ten thousand legionaries of the centre at the Trebia cut their way through the Carthaginian army in good order, despite the utter demoralization of the rest of the army. The six thousand leading troops at Trasimene did the like. The Carthaginian was an older, not a better soldier. In material and basis of organization, and in the natural discipline and character of the race, the Romans were by far the stronger. The advantage of the Carthaginian soldier was the training which comes of long service and a strong leader; and the whole body profited by the expertness of its cavalry; but any superiority of the Carthaginians as an army lay solely in Hannibal's genius.

The Roman army here showed a decided capacity for panic. No wonder, perhaps, for the column was not in hand. But the instinct for panic has always existed among troops in greater or less degree. No soldier has ever, on the whole, been so free from it as the American volunteer, — or, rather, no soldier has ever so quickly recovered from the effect of panic and returned to duty. Lines were driven back during our civil war in apparent great confusion; but a few hundred yards to the rear these same lines would of their own motion rally, apparently ashamed of having broken, and advance to renew the fight with no semblance of panic left.

Tacitus tells us that the Romans were accustomed to demand their rights of their enemies with weapons in hand, and not dumbly and by stratagem, and Ælian says that it was a virtue peculiar to the Romans to employ neither ruse nor artifice to overcome their enemies. Livy and Valerius Maximus cry out against Hannibal's ruses as instances of deceit. But the Romans were not so free from stratagems as they pretend; the difference between theirs and Hannibal's was but in the degree of ability displayed. And war cannot be conducted on a basis of frankness. It is strictly a game of wits, of deceit. Rob the able general of all which comes within the ken of stratagem and you paralyze his right arm.

After the battle Hannibal went into camp to give his men their well-earned rest. But hearing that a force of four thousand horse had been sent, under the pro-prætor Cnæus Centenius, from the consular army of Sempronius at Ariminum, to reinforce Flaminius, and to give the latter a somewhat nearer mounted equality to the Carthaginians, Hannibal sent Maharbal out to meet it with a part of his own cavalry and some light troops. In a battle shortly fought, Maharbal defeated Centenius with a loss of half his number. The rest took refuge on an adjoining hill, where, next day, Maharbal made the balance prisoners. Again humiliation to the proud Roman name.

The road to Rome was open to Hannibal, and he has been

often criticised, as after Cannæ, for not at once marching upon it. But Hannibal was more far-sighted than Pyrrhus. He knew it would be impossible to take the city by a *coup de main*. It was over a hundred miles distant. It was always well garrisoned and in two days could raise a large force. He knew the Roman character for stanchness all too well. So long as the Latin confederacy remained without a breach, there were still many times as many men to defend Rome as he himself could put in front of the capital; and to attack the capital might, until some of the allies were clearly weaned from their allegiance, be but the cause of a new birth of good-will towards Rome. The allies as yet knew Hannibal and his intentions little. He was still to them a barbarian invader, and despite his victories an unknown quantity, and Hannibal recognized the fact that these allies could only be detached from the Roman alliance by a continued series of victories, added to a much longer diplomatic suasion than he had yet found time to use.

It was evident to Hannibal that he could make no progress without appealing to the interest of the allies. This indeed was his universal rule. He had thus won the Gauls to his side, and he must thus influence the Italians. By a system of generosity backed by victories on the one hand, and by living on their land and occasional devastation on the other, he thought he might eventually rely on self-interest to bring about their defection from Rome. Success alone would not do. His three victories had, while strictly due to his own able generalship, been won under circumstances which might not again occur. And he would have shown a weakness which was no part of his character had he failed to appreciate the fact that Rome had within its walls many men abler than those he had yet encountered. He was strong in the field, owing largely to his cavalry; but of what use was his cavalry when coping with walled cities? He had no siege-machinery; he knew that Rome was heavily fortified, and he was not insane enough to expect the senate to open her gates to him as the servile satraps of Babylon and Susa had done to Alexander. Perhaps as good a proof of Hannibal's remarkable generalship as any during his whole life is his refraining from marching on Rome at this moment and after Cannæ. No one has ever doubted this man's remarkable courage or exceptional spirit of enterprise, — has he not abundantly proved them? But greater than these was that wonderful balance of judgment which always overrode every other quality, and was perhaps never wrong.

It has been sometimes said that Alexander captured cities in his campaigns as well as won battles; that Cæsar did the like; why, then, if he was an equal soldier, should not Hannibal have marched on and captured Rome? But it must be remembered that Alexander and Cæsar commanded each the very best army of his day, an army drilled, disciplined, armed and equipped in a manner so far beyond that of any he encountered, that the odds were entirely on his side so far as actual fighting or any feat of engineering was concerned. Alexander and Cæsar had siege - material which was the best of its day, and, with few exceptions, the cities they captured had much cruder means of defense, excepting walls. And each had under his command a trained corps of engineer officers, the most expert of their day. Despite which, we have seen how Alexander, when he matched himself against the science and strength of Tyre, came as near failure as he ever did; and we shall see Cæsar recoil from the walls of Gergovia.

In Hannibal's case the circumstances were exactly reversed. He had no siege-enginery in Italy, or at least the authorities so lead us to infer from their silence on the sub-

ject, and, if any, but a small equipment of missile-throwers.
The art of using engines had perhaps degenerated since the
days of Alexander. Those famous field and mountain bat-
teries of his had been forgotten. Nor, indeed, had Hannibal
anticipated their use. He had expected to win pitched battles to weaken Rome, and use diplomacy to detach her allies.
A plan which contemplated long sieges of the numberless
strong places of Italy would have been from its inception
doomed. We shall see what a mistake of this kind Hasdrubal made when later he followed his brother to Italy. Siege-
material was not an essential in a campaign in Italy. Cities
could be won by bargaining better than by force. Cavalry
was the arm of most importance. And while Hannibal's
army was veteran, so far as work and the hardiness of the
field was concerned, it never had come near the wonderful natural subordination inherent in the Roman and allied legions.
His recent allies, the Gauls, furnished him only a wild and
unreliable contingent; and the numerical strength of his
stanch troops was pitifully small compared to the enormous
forces of men, trained to arms from their youth up, which
Rome could within a few days — almost hours — oppose to
him at the gates of her capital. And to the Roman soldier
"actual war was but a bloody repetition of his daily drill, as
his daily drill was but a bloodless campaign." The balance
in the matter of army ran decidedly against Hannibal instead
of in his favor. Nothing, perhaps, shows how well Hannibal
recognized the better arms and equipment of the Roman legion than the fact that he shortly reorganized his Libyan
foot on a Roman basis. Just what the details of the changes
may have been we are not informed, but he armed them
with the Roman weapons taken at Trasimene, and Livy observes that one could at a distance scarcely tell the difference between Carthaginians and Romans.

Again, the walls of Rome were strong and defended by skillful officers and large bodies of good, if new, troops, who would be fighting for their homes and precious Rome, their gods and household fires. And in a few days after Hannibal had sat down before Rome, an army of relief vastly larger than his own would have come to besiege himself. Imagine Alexander before Tyre, with an enormous Persian army in his rear to shut him in, and without a fleet; what would have been his chances? Imagine Cæsar opposed at Alesia with an army of relief of disciplined legions. Hannibal would have been in still worse case. With yet only a few of the confederates wavering in their allegiance to Rome, and barely looking upon Hannibal as a possible recourse in case of future unquestioned success, he would have been wanting indeed in good judgment had he undertaken such an operation. And as to marching on Rome for the mere sake of so doing, and without a definite object, this was not Hannibal's understanding of the art of war. We shall recur to this subject after the battle of Cannæ.

Turning, then, from a prize he saw he could not yet win, he ravaged the fertile plains of Umbria, attacked the fortress Spoletum, but was repulsed from before its walls, — clearly from lack of siege-material, — marched eastward across the range to Ancona, thence south along the Adriatic, and, spreading devastation right and left upon his road, levied contributions all over Picenum, which was covered with Roman farms. His men could not be kept from retaliating even upon innocent yeomen the horrors suffered by their fathers in the First Punic War. In the southern part of this province he gave his troops a few days' rest among its plethoric granaries, well earned by a year's hard campaigning, and sadly needed. For the men were in bad condition, suffering from scurvy and other camp diseases caused by deprivations, and

the horses were much reduced. The men are said to have
bathed the horses in old wine to cure them of an irruptive
disease. Hannibal then proceeded towards the south, apparently marching along the eastern foothills of the Apennines,

From Trasimene to Luceria.

so as to cross the streams at their narrowest, through the land
of the Pretutii, Hadria, the Marsi, the Marucini and Peligni,
and stopped in Apulia, in the neighborhood of Arpi and Luceria. He hoped to open communication by sea with Carthage, and thus make for himself a new base of operations in
this province. From here he sent dispatches home by sea to
announce his successes to the Carthaginian senate, and we
may readily imagine the rejoicing caused by the welcome
news.

Luceria was one of those locations which have always been
selected by able generals to command the adjoining country.

The place has long been known as the key of Apulia. The town lies on lofty but level ground, sloping easily to south and east, but sharply to north and west. On the west the plateau projects into a site now crowned by the ruins of a

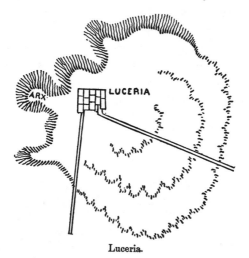

Luceria.

mediæval castle. Here stood the arx of the Romans, who had held it from 314 B. C. Hannibal made this place a coign of vantage from which to dominate Apulia.

The stanchness of the Roman character, that supreme virtue which deserved to conquer the world, as it did, was never more fully shown than now. The gathering rumors of disaster, so new to Roman ears, and which grew the more the news came in, the cumulative effect of a third and infinitely worse defeat — slaughter — than those of the Ticinus and Trebia, were all but paralyzing. The common people were instinct with terror; even the senate was dismayed beyond immediate power to act. But what made Rome great was the presence of men — of a class, indeed — which was always able to rise superior to disaster. And it was so now. This class took the matter into its own hand, and the plebs followed its lead. No word of peace was heard; no idea of aught but stubborn defense of the Roman soil. There was but one thing to do. A dictator must be appointed. Under the law of the land the dictator must be nominated by the consuls, — and one was dead, the other distant. The necessity was pressing, but the love of law reigned supreme. The senate allowed the people to elect, not a dictator but a pro-dictator. The choice fell upon Q. Fabius Maximus, and he, as was the rule, chose as master of the horse — his most important lieutenant — M. Minucius Rufus.

Carthaginian Coin.

XXIII.

FABIUS CUNCTATOR. SUMMER, 217 B. C.

ROME was put in a state of defense, and Fabius Maximus, who had been made dictator, at once went to work to repair the disaster. Servilius had transferred his army to Rome, and Fabius, after raising some fresh troops, marched out to meet Hannibal, who, when he reached Luceria, found the dictator's army at Æcæ. The Romans were well supplied; Hannibal had to forage. Fabius was cautious in all his movements; kept in the hills where the enemy's cavalry could not attack him, and harassed the Carthaginians with small-war. This was just what gave Hannibal the greatest trouble. It deprived him of the possibility of winning victories. There was a great deal of opposition to Fabius' policy, but he in no wise altered it. Finally, Hannibal was driven from Apulia by sheer lack of an enemy to fight, and made his way to Campania, one of the richest parts of Italy, hoping that dread lest he should devastate the province would bring Fabius to battle. The dictator slowly followed, still keeping on the defensive. Minucius and the army were anxious for battle; but despite Hannibal's devastation Fabius refused to undertake the offensive.

FABIUS was a scion of one of the old aristocratic families. He himself was of a moderate, wise and reasonable character, and had already rendered excellent service in Roman wars. His intelligence was broad. He is said to have conformed to all the religious and formal rites of the state, less because he believed in the Roman gods than because he deemed religious faith a necessary anchor of good government. And knowing how powerfully superstition rules the masses, he did not leave Rome until the Sibylline Books had been consulted. He was then ready to set out to face the great Carthaginian.

Rome was quickly put in a state of defense, and sundry weak places in the walls were repaired. Minucius, master of

the horse, was instructed to raise two additional legions,
which was speedily done.   Orders had already been given to
forestall the expected march of Hannibal on Rome (so soon
as it should be known that he was advancing) by devastating
the country, burning the crops and houses, removing the
breadstuffs, destroying the bridges and retiring the population into the towns and strong places, so that nothing should
be left for Hannibal to subsist upon.   If he marched on
Rome, it should be through a howling waste.   As matters
turned, these orders were not carried out.

Meanwhile, Fabius took command of the army of Servilius, which this general, after a few slight exchanges with
the Gauls, had promptly and sensibly transferred from the
valley of the Po to Ocriculum, near Rome, so soon as news
had reached him of the defeat at Lake Trasimene, and which,
increased by the two supplemental legions, amounted to an

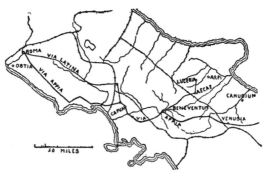

Via Appia.

effective of fifty thousand men.   To Servilius was given the
duty of raising a fleet to protect the coast of Italy from probable Carthaginian invasions, for the Carthaginians had just
intercepted a Roman fleet sailing from Ostia for Spain with
provisions.

Though the allies showed no sign of defection, but each

city in turn closed its gates on Hannibal, Rome did not deem it wise to allow Hannibal in their midst without the presence of a Roman army as counterweight. Fabius took this matter in hand, and, advancing along the Via Appia, which led him towards and through Campania and thence through the mountains of Samnium, via Beneventum, into northern Apulia, he advanced to Ææ, within half a dozen miles of his adversary, intending to prevent his ravages, but not proposing to accept battle on disadvantageous terms. When Hannibal passed Luceria toward Arpi, he found the dictator on his flank at Ææ.

The Romans exceeded the Carthaginians in number, but were weaker in cavalry. They were well provisioned, and so placed that they could constantly receive supplies by way of the Beneventum country, and needed to forage but little for their rations. This was a manifest advantage, as the campaigns of all ages have shown; for to supply an army in an enemy's country, and sometimes in a friendly one, always means large detachments of troops and a great tax on the intelligence and time of the commander. Napoleon has said that the general who cannot provide for his troops is ignorant of his business. This is doubtless true, but it does not make the difficulties any the less. And in that age, half or two thirds of an army was habitually obliged to be absent on foraging duty, — a vast danger.

Fabius, who had no doubt been selected in a spirit of revulsion at the military demagoguism of Flaminius, acted on this knowledge. He moved with the utmost caution, and with his troops well in hand. He kept at a safe distance and in the hilly country bordering the vast Apulian plain, where cavalry could not so easily operate. He harassed Hannibal by picking up his foraging parties, which had grown overbold and reckless, and making a small-war wherever he could. He

never lost Hannibal from sight. He never got so near him
as to give him an advantage. He insisted on the strictest
performance of all their duties by the soldiers, protected his
few foragers by proper detachments of cavalry, kept the men

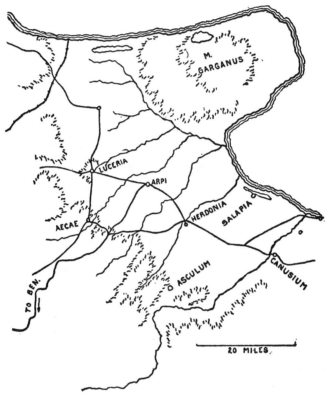

Luceria and Vicinity.

close in camp, permitted no straggling, and when he marched,
it was in so cautious a manner and with such van- and rear-
guards and flankers, that none of Hannibal's manœuvres,
marches or countermarches, none of his offers of battle, none
of his wiles, were of any avail. Hannibal tried every stratagem, every taunt, to impress Fabius with a willingness to

fight. He shifted camp constantly, moving round the Romans from place to place and ravaging under their very eyes. He disappeared for a day or two, and again came back to the vicinity of Fabius. He marched away, and laid ambushes, into which he hoped Fabius, by following, might fall. But all proved useless. Fabius was of a different mould from his predecessors in command. He kept either close to camp, or moved with a caution proof to all that Hannibal could do.

There was little in Rome or in the Roman camp which was concealed to the Carthaginian. His activity in procuring information was abnormal. Even the secrets of the capital or of the headquarters of the consular armies were delivered to him. And though he was in the enemy's country, the Romans knew nothing of his. To organize and use such a service well is a wonderful proof of ability, and throughout his entire career, Hannibal showed that he was equal master of the grand operations, and of the minutiæ of war.

This singular change of policy from the universal rule of the Romans — which was summary, unquestioning attack under all circumstances, relying solely on the fighting quality of the legions — has excited the admiration of all historians and soldiers. Fabius' troops were excellent, but new ; Hannibal's less good in material, but old and experienced. The Romans could reinforce their army ; Hannibal could look for little help. Fabius had not much cavalry ; in this Hannibal was rich. Every motive pointed to just this policy ; and yet it was, as it were, an absolutely new invention of this level-headed soldier, a positive departure from Roman precedent. He was teaching himself and the Romans a new system of war. And it was exactly what Hannibal the least desired, — the one thing he saw that he could not long stand up against. Still, wise as this policy was, — it was in fact the only one which was not under the circumstances fatally weak, — Minucius

was much dissatisfied with it, and, like Sempronius and Flaminius, he also desired a battle. But the proof of Fabius'
wisdom lay in the fact that Hannibal was of like mind with
Minucius.

Eventually this clever manœuvring worried the Carthaginian into leaving Apulia, where he had not met with the
hoped-for support of the population, and into marching
through the land of the Hirpini across the Apennines and
into Samnium, which he did by moving around Fabius' flank
and through the same valleys by which the latter had advanced. This must have been an operation of great delicacy
and beautifully conducted. We have no details of it.

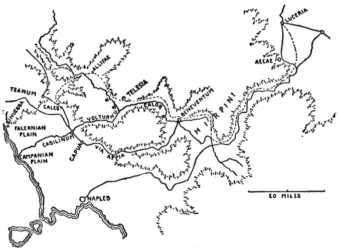

Hannibal's Route to Campania.

At this point the Apennines are not high. A few of the
peaks rise to an altitude of from three thousand to four thousand five hundred feet; but between the ranges, which branch
out in every direction, are valleys and plains of more or less
extent, and much beautiful rolling upland, susceptible of excellent cultivation. The streams are not large in summer;

in spring they are torrents. Some of the hillsides are of naked limestone, and at the highest part of the range the surface is stony and sterile, and there are now few trees. The country was presumably well wooded in those days.

At Beneventum, which lay strongly fortified on the Via Appia, on an eminence high on north and east, but sloping down on south and west, in the midst of a pleasant, rolling, fertile country, whose hills vary from one hundred to five hundred feet above the valleys, he found the gates closed and the town unassailable. He ravaged the vicinity, and proceeding down the Calor, captured Telesia, where a vast store of booty rewarded his efforts. It had been made a depot for the grain raised in the fertile valleys near at hand.

Hannibal now heard from spies in Capua that he might expect to capture that wealthy city. It was the most important of the cities dependent on Rome, and felt itself grievously oppressed by the arrogant capital. Hannibal had formed connections there and hoped for its alliance; and turning from Telesia, he kept on through the mountains between Samnium and Campania, crossed the Vulturnus, near Allifæ, headed through the passes in Mons Eribanus, and, descending by way of Cales into the Falernian plain, selected a camp on the north of the river, near Casilinum, and strongly fortified it. He then sent out Maharbal to ravage the vicinity, which was done with his accustomed thoroughness as far as Sinuessa.

This plain, Campania Felix (even to-day called Campania Felice), consisting of the Falernian to the north of the Vulturnus, and the Campanian to the south of it, was perhaps the most beautiful and fruitful part of Italy, fed by nature, as well as by the commerce of the adjoining sea-towns. Its fertility was wonderful. Then as now the land was capable of raising two crops of grain and one of hay each year, not

to speak of vines and olive-orchards and abundant cattle.
No land except the Nile-washed fields of Egypt rivaled its
productiveness.   In no place could Hannibal have more seriously attacked the dignity or the sentiment or the welfare of
Rome.   Livy states that Hannibal blundered into it by an
error of his guide, who mistook Casinum, whither Hannibal
desired to go, for Casilinum.   But this scarcely seems probable.   We know too much of Hannibal's careful topographical
studies to believe that he had any other plan than to move
into Campania Felix.   Hannibal had hoped that fear lest he
should ravage this most fruitful region of Italy, where immense booty could be gathered, would compel Fabius to
come to battle; or, in the event he did not do so, that some
of the towns of Campania — particularly Capua — would join
the Carthaginian standard in order to save their property, in
case the Romans should be unable to protect them from the
invader.   For to allow Hannibal to destroy the crops of these
lovely plains would be to acknowledge that they dared not
dispute with him the possession of the open country.

Fabius followed at an interval of one or two days, won-
dering greatly at the daring of Hannibal, but content to
observe him from a safe distance by marching along the foothills, and never descending to the plain where he might be
forced to accept a battle.   The Numidian cavalry continued
to scout the country, leaving the mark of the torch on every
acre, while the Roman legionaries gazed on this destruction
with gnashing of teeth from helpless wrath, and a growing
desire to finish the campaign by one desperate and instant
blow.   From this, however, Fabius resolutely refrained.

Of the soldiers' opinion Minucius warmly partook; he could
not understand Fabius' policy, and it was not long before a
considerable faction arose in the camp against the dilatory
management — the sloth and cowardice, as they called it —

of the dictator in command. Nor were the Roman people and senate far from joining the cabal. But all this had no manner of effect on the constant mind of Fabius, who, while listening to his colleague, pursued his own plans, unruffled by opposition nor disheartened by the present humiliation. He now camped athwart the roads to Rome on the

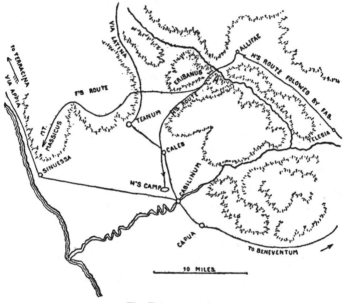

The Falernian Plain.

foothills of Mt. Massicus, at a place near Falernus Ager, where he could not be successfully assaulted, and from where he could extend his lines to hold the pass by which Hannibal had entered Campania.

We cannot but wonder why Hannibal, who was so anxious to gain over the allies, and whose policy had been one of generosity towards them, should have resorted to devastating their lands, thereby not only irritating them, but destroying his own means of foraging. Upon many of these questions we have barely the stated fact, with no explanation given by the contemporary historian, and are left to draw our own conclusions. We must not lose sight of the fact that the historians of Hannibal were for the most part his bitter enemies; and that even their facts must sometimes be taken with a grain of allowance.

Hannibal accumulated an immense quantity of victuals and booty, which he destined for the approaching winter, — but this was only one motive. Perhaps he despaired of attaining any success with the Roman allies in Campania, and concluded that he might as well make them an example for the purpose of being able to approach the others with both a record for abundant generosity and relentless cruelty. With regard to the latter quality, we can say nothing except that war has always been cruel; that two thousand years ago it was worse than cruel; and reflect that, until within a few generations, civilization has been unable to rob war of its element of utter savagery. Nor was Hannibal in any respect worse than the Romans. Be it as it may, Fabius certainly understood that his enemy was in his every act sapping the possibility of success for his cause, and all the more clung to his cunctatory policy. The pertinacity with which Fabius stuck to this manifestly proper line of conduct, against the most grievous opposition, redounds vastly to his reputation for strength of character, despite the fact that one of his cognomens was Ovicula, or the Lamb. The comparison between Fabius and Washington, however old, clings constantly to one's mind.

XXIV.

A CURIOUS STRATAGEM. FALL, 217 B. C.

THOUGH Fabius would not fight, he made an excellent plan for trapping Hannibal in the Falernian plain. He closed the southern exit at Casilinum on the Vulturnus, held the Via Appia and Via Latina in force, and put a corps in the defile by which Hannibal had entered. The Romans were abundantly supplied; the Carthaginians had only the small valley to depend on. Fabius' plan was to wait until Hannibal sought to escape, and then to attack him in flank or rear. Hannibal was really in bad case. But he hit on a happy stratagem. Having fruitlessly offered battle to Fabius, he took two thousand beeves, and tying torches to their horns, drove them at night up the slopes of the mountains inclosing the defile he had come in and proposed to leave by. The Roman force holding the defile, imagining the Carthaginians to be escaping through the woods, left the defile to attack them; Hannibal promptly occupied it, and his column and trains speedily made their way through. After this stratagem he made a raid towards Rome, and finally went to Geronium to winter. Fabius merely followed him up, with his old caution. All parties now began to lose faith in Fabius and his policy.

THOUGH cautious, Fabius lacked not alertness. He devised a plan for surrounding Hannibal, and took his measures accordingly. The northern half of the plain, — the Falernian, — where the Carthaginian army had been committing its ravages, had the unfordable Vulturnus on the south, with but a single bridge, at Casilinum, held by the Roman garrison at that town; it had on the east a line of difficult hills whose only debouch was the pass by which Hannibal had entered, for the main road to Beneventum was south of the river; on the west was the sea; on the north Fabius and the Latin colony at Teanum blocked the road and closed the Latin Way. The Appian Way, also leading northward, had several fortified places along its course, and passed through the defile of Terracina as well. Thus the exits of the Falernian plain were all closed. Polybius says that the mountains on the north and east of the plain had but three outlets. By this he unquestionably means the Via Appia or main road via Beneventum, the more difficult pass near Allifæ, by which Hannibal had entered, and the Via Latina through Teanum. The plan thus organized by Fabius was excellent.

Hannibal had finished his work, but without meeting with the political success he had anticipated; he now proposed to gather together his booty and march to the other coast or to southern Italy, where he could spend the winter in greater comfort and security. Fabius had foreseen all this and acted accordingly. He had sent Minucius to put in a state of defense the defile of Terracina, where the mountains come down to the sea, so as to hold the Appian Way to Rome; another force of four thousand men he had sent to hold the pass of Mons Eribanus (or Callicula), as the defile to Allifæ was named; he had strengthened the garrison of Casilinum, and with the main Roman army now moved from Mt. Massicus eastward, along the hills towards the road which Hannibal must use, to a point where he could readily observe the Carthaginian movements. Fabius proposed to wait till Hannibal, after destroying or consuming the provisions of the valley, should try to make his way out. He would then have him at an utter disadvantage. In his rear Fabius had all Latium and Samnium to victual his main army; his force at Casilinum had the Campanian plain for supplies; Minucius was on the Via Appia, and his four thousand men in the defile could depend on Beneventum. The dictator was in a position to wait for battle on his own terms.

Hannibal fully understood the difficulties of his situation, and having carefully gathered his booty, sought to study the means of leaving the valley. It was early fall. It was essential that he should pass the next winter in some region not yet devastated by the war. His immense train of booty was a very serious factor in his calculations. And it may be well here to point out that in weighing the operations of Hannibal, such factors must not be lost sight of. Nearly always in Roman or allied territory, he was forced to move with large trains, which the Romans, having victual on every hand, could dispense with. What Hannibal accomplished was with every element in favor of his enemies, and scarcely a single tactical or strategic value on his own side.

It is probable that at this time Hannibal had a very large train of wagons, which he had taken from the farmers of the Falernian plains. As a rule, his trains consisted only of sumpter-animals. He had to pay his men, and give them much booty; he desired to provide for the winter; he must keep on hand treasure for the subvention of towns he hoped to induce to join his cause. For the moment, he was unusually loaded with trains.

Hannibal could not debouch by either the Appian Way or the Latin Way leading to Rome, as these roads were not only held in force, but a movement along them would bring Fabius at once down on his flank while he was cutting his way out. It was, moreover, not the direction he desired to take. He could not well cross the Vulturnus, because Fabius could fall upon his rear during the serious operation of forcing the river. The mountain pass on the east by which he had entered was held by Fabius' detachment of four thousand men, and Hannibal reckoned that this was the direction from which he would be for that very reason least expected, especially as he had acquired the reputation of not pursuing the same road twice, and it was by no means an easy pass. This exit was the one Hannibal chose for his passage. But it was

an operation of some delicacy, for if his way was stoutly disputed, it was altogether likely that he would be attacked by
Fabius from the rear during his movement. Having chosen
his route, as a first step, he must drive the Romans out of the
pass by force or stratagem, and he set about it in a curious
manner. He had come in that way, and he knew the lay of
the land very accurately.

Operations were opened by a cavalry demonstration on
Minucius, to divert Fabius from the idea that he would seek
to leave the valley in which he was — a very trap to any but
a Hannibal — by way of the mountains. Minucius sent
Hostilius Mancinus out to meet the Numidians, and this
officer drove them back to camp. Following them up too
hastily, Hostilius was met by Carthalo with the whole body
of horse, badly cut up, and himself slain. The relics of the
Roman cavalry took refuge in Fabius' camp. Hither, too,
Minucius had returned, after securing the defile of Terracina.
Even this defeat in no wise changed the Roman ardor for a
general battle, though it showed Fabius that he was right in
clinging to his own scheme of defense.

Next day Hannibal drew up in battle order in the plain
below Fabius' camp, and endeavored to bring him out to
fight. He would have been glad to measure swords in
earnest with Fabius, and did his best to bring about this end.
Fabius also drew up his army in front of his camp, but refused to move down to the plain, contenting himself with
beating back a skirmishing attack of horse, which must have
been severe, as Livy acknowledges a Roman loss of two hundred men killed, and with his very natural habit of exaggerat-
ing the enemy's, states the Carthaginian loss at eight hundred.
Finding this last resort to engage battle on at least even
terms a failure, Hannibal was driven to ruse. Fabius had
made up his mind not to fight till Hannibal tried to escape,
when he would take him in flank or rear.

The Carthaginians had collected several thousand beef-cattle. Hasdrubal at this time had charge of the engineering detail of the army, and to him Hannibal gave his orders. Selecting two thousand of the most vigorous of these creatures, pitch-pine or other dry branches tied in fagots were

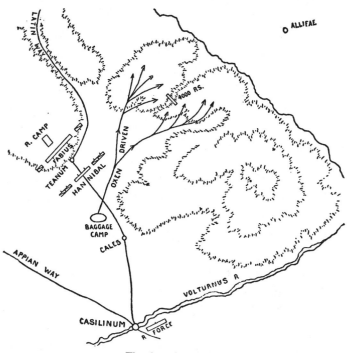

The Oxen Stratagem.

fastened to their horns, and towards the middle of the night, — in the third watch, — having lighted these strange torches, Hasdrubal's pioneers, aided by the light infantry, drove the cattle up the slopes inclosing the defile of Mons Eribanus, which was held by the enemy. Maddened with fear and pain, the bullocks rushed in all directions up the hill and into the woods, giving to the Romans the impression that the Carthaginian army was trying to escalade the heights with torches. The defenders of the defile imagined from the noises on the heights that Hannibal's troops were escaping through the woods over the mountains, thus turning the defile they felt unable to force, and, leaving their position, at once set out to oppose them or cut off their retreat. When they reached the heights they were equally puzzled and dismayed by meeting an array of mad bulls in lieu of Carthaginian phalangites, and not only made no pretense to fight, but forgot all about the defile they had been ordered to hold. The beeves rushing hither and yon prevented any serious engagement on the heights. Having aided the pioneers to drive the beeves as far as necessary, the light infantry attacked the defile through which Hannibal proposed to march. They found it almost unprotected, and at once possessed themselves of it. Fabius, fearing to fall into some new ambuscade of Hannibal's, remained close to his camp, though he drew up his army in order of battle.

Having thus opened the defile, Hannibal lost no time in setting out on the march, for which his entire column stood in readiness. The African infantry was in the van. The cavalry followed. The baggage-train and booty came next. The Spaniards and then the Gauls closed the column. From this defile his head of column soon emerged upon the valley of the upper Vulturnus near Allifæ, whence his road was clear. For by hurrying a detachment down the Vulturnus to the junction of the Calor to hold this point, the road via Beneventum was open to him and closed to Fabius. The marching was forced, and before morning the whole army and baggage-train had passed beyond the reach of Roman interference.

As the morning mists were dissipated, Fabius discovered his four thousand men who had been stationed to hold the defile and the heights, still skirmishing all along the line with the Carthaginian light infantry, who were now sustained by the Spanish and Gallic rear-guard of Hannibal's column. Under cover of this combat, the Carthaginian column had been enabled to retire in perfect safety, after throwing the Romans back into the valley they had just left, with a loss of not far from one thousand men.

Hannibal now went into camp at Allifæ, well satisfied with the success of his very remarkable and ingenious stratagem. Before thinking of winter-quarters, however, he determined to impose still further on Fabius by leading him to believe

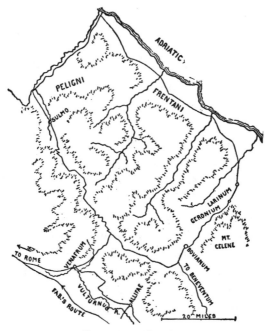

Campania to Geronium.

that he would move to the vicinity of Rome, through eastern Latium. He could continue his ravages and collect booty for a while longer, owing to his enemy's utter discomfiture at his escape. He marched up the valley of the Vulturnus to Venafrum ; but instead of making towards Rome, he kept within Samnium, crossed the Apennines and descended by Sulmo to the plains of the Peligni, where he gathered additional rich stores.

To read the ancient historians' account of Hannibal's method of foraging with his Numidian cavalry, calls vividly to mind the forays of Sherman's bummers. Barring the cruelties practiced by the barbarian horse, one might imagine one's self to be reading of Georgia instead of Italy.

Fabius followed up Hannibal's march along the hills, showing no little skill, and keeping always between him and Rome. Hannibal had found his diversion a failure ; he could not lure Fabius to battle. Learning that in Geronium, near Larinum, there was abundance of booty and much wheat, he soon altered his course towards the land of the Frentani. Unable to seduce the inhabitants of Geronium by promises or threats, Hannibal attacked and took the place by storm, razed it to the ground, leaving the walls and a few buildings for magazines, and put the inhabitants to the sword. He then strongly fortified a camp near by, and began amassing victual for the winter, sending each day two thirds of his force out foraging, each party being charged to bring in a given quantity of wheat, and deliver the same to the commissaries. Having secured none of the Italian allies, he must take up winter-quarters *al fresco*. Fabius slowly followed the Carthaginians, and finally went into an equally strong camp at the foot of Mt. Calene in the territory of Larinum.

XXV.

MINUCIUS. FALL, 217 B. C.

HANNIBAL had had wonderful military success, but the fidelity of the Roman allies had prevented his making any substantial gain. The Romans had suffered grievous defeats, but they had not lost ground; for the integrity of the Latin confederacy held good. The dissatisfaction of senate and people at Fabius' policy grew apace. Fabius was called to Rome, and left Minucius in command, with orders to pursue the same course. For a while Minucius obeyed orders, but soon he descended to the plain, intent on trying conclusions with Hannibal. The latter was forced daily to send out two thirds of his men as foragers, for he was accumulating victual for the winter. On one of these occasions Minucius attacked his camp and came near winning a success; but some of the foragers returned and Hannibal drove the Romans off. This action, reported at Rome, gave Minucius a great repute, and he was made equal in power with the dictator. When Fabius arrived, Minucius took half the troops and moved to a new camp. Here Hannibal managed to lure him into an ambuscade, and would have utterly destroyed his army, had not Fabius opportunely appeared on the scene. Minucius, after this check, was satisfied to work under Fabius' orders; and Fabius recovered his standing with senate and people. Both armies went into winter-quarters.

THE allies were in a pitiable condition. The vaunted power of Rome had failed to be of any protection to them. The barbarians had for months ravaged their lands, and no one had dared lift a hand against them in aggressive defense. The feeling against Fabius and his policy grew apace and waxed bitter. The summer of 217 B. C. was gone. Hannibal had marched throughout the length and breadth of Italy. He had won brilliant victories. He had shown that the Romans were unable to cope with him in open battle. This was a sad military record for Rome. On the other hand, not one of the Italian confederates had proven traitor; not one of their cities had voluntarily opened its gates to the invader, — a wonderful political record.

This fidelity was far from what Hannibal had counted on. He had had reason to believe that the Roman allies would yield him their support so soon as he proved his ability to help them ; but it was not so. Hannibal had too well-balanced a mind not to know that this strong fealty foreboded evil; that he and his army alone could not accomplish all he must, if he would not fail ; and though his character was such as to lead him to wait patiently for results, he must have comprehended that he was no whit further advanced than when he descended from the Alps upon the Po. Still he was not discouraged. He knew that time works wonders, and he hoped that the successes which he felt certain that he could win when the next year's campaign should come, might still change the current of opinion. He had taken up his winter-quarters for B. C. 217–216 in the richest part of Apulia ; had accumulated stores enough for a number of months, and immense booty, and had established his magazines and hospitals and quartered his troops in a position which he could afford for a while to hold, till he could again try to disaffect the allies. With this he was fain to be content.

Fabius, on the other hand, not cast down despite his humiliating want of success and apparent lack of stomach, — his playing the part of " Hannibal's lackey," as it were, — never wavered in his belief that his policy was the only one by which to cope with this subtlest of adversaries. He too could be patient and wily, even if not on a par with his great opponent. But being shortly after called to Rome on public business, — to make certain annual sacrifices, and probably to satisfy the senate as to what he had done, as well as to still complaints, — he was compelled to leave the command in the hands of Minucius, which he did with orders to continue his system, and by no means to risk a general engagement.

As is almost invariable in such cases, there was a show of reason in the dissatisfaction with Fabius' non-fighting strategy. The Romans called him Hannibal's pedagogue, since he did nothing but follow him up and down, and wait upon him, says Plutarch. Still more, there were several circumstances which told against him. Hannibal, no doubt with a sincere admiration of his opponent (for what soldier has not generous impulses?), had ordered that certain estates belonging to Fabius should be excepted from the general devastation. This gave immediate rise to a cry of treason among the citizens of Rome. Livy charges Hannibal with deceit in this matter; but the Carthaginian showed repeatedly, by scrupulously observing the funeral rites of his fallen adversaries and by other acts of good feeling, that he possessed the soldier's warm heart, and Livy is unsupported in his slur. Again, Fabius had concluded a convention with Hannibal for the exchange of prisoners, in which any excess of men was to be paid for by either side, at a certain rate in money. For such a treaty Fabius had a clear precedent in the First Punic War. Fabius had received two hundred and forty-seven extra men. For these the senate refused to pay, declaring his convention void. Hereupon, Fabius sold the estates saved harmless by Hannibal and paid the ransom himself. But even so public-spirited an act as this could find those to misrepresent it. Fabius' stay in Rome was prolonged for many days.

Minucius had for a while ridden to orders, but, urged on by his own ambitious courage, as well as by the advice of his friends, he finally determined to cross swords with his antagonist, and Hannibal discovered the indications of this purpose with evident satisfaction.

Left to his own devices, Minucius had lost no time in approaching the Carthaginian army, and after keeping to the hills for a few days, had descended to the plain and camped

within five miles (A) of it.   Hannibal had been in the daily
habit of sending out two thirds of his force into the surrounding country as foragers, keeping the small balance on hand

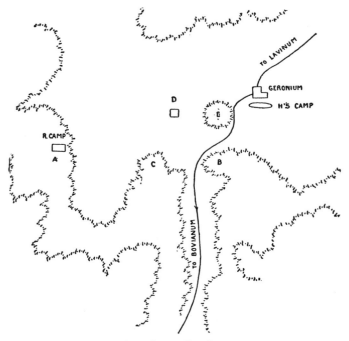

Operations at Geronium.

to protect the camp.   When the Roman army came nearer,
these foraging parties for a while were cut down to a much
smaller limit, in the expectation that Minucius would show
signs of fighting; but as Hannibal was busy accumulating
winter stores, which, having so much cavalry, he must make
very ample if he would keep his horse in good condition, he
was soon again compelled to resume foraging on the old
scale.

The country about Geronium was rolling but open.   Aware
of Fabius' departure, Hannibal doubted not that Minucius,

whose excessive ardor he well knew, would before long essay to attack him. Nothing loath, and with the purpose of fostering such an attack, he left Geronium and moved his camp to an eminence (B) some two miles from his camp at the town, and somewhat nearer the Romans, where he could better observe their movements and keep them from attacking his foragers. Then throwing forward by night a force of two thousand Numidians, he occupied a hill (C) between the two camps, as an outpost which should be a direct threat to the Roman camp. This small detachment, which had not intrenched itself, Minucius next morning early attacked with a superior force and drove away, establishing his own camp in the place it had been holding. This brought the two camps into close proximity.

Hannibal expected and hoped for a general engagement; but Minucius was wary and could not be drawn out. For several days Hannibal had kept all but his whole force in camp, anticipating that he could taunt Minucius into risking a battle, but when he saw that he could not bring it about, he was constrained himself to resort to Fabian tactics, and again to send out the bulk of his men as foragers day by day; for he had a goodly number of herds to graze, and must not consume the vast stores accumulated for the winter, if he expected to keep his men in good stomach for the spring campaign.

Minucius was not slow to profit by Hannibal's thus weakening the force in camp. He sent out his cavalry to cut off the foragers and herdsmen, ordering them to take no prisoners. A very large number of these men were intercepted and killed. He himself led his infantry in order of battle against the Carthaginian camp. Hannibal, thus taken at a disadvantage, — for he had but a third of his force in camp, — was neither strong enough to leave his intrenchments nor yet to afford aid to his foragers; the Roman infantry was eager to wrest a present advantage from the enemy, and advanced so gallantly that the legionaries had begun to pull out the palisades of which the stockade at the top of the Carthaginian wall was made; and it was with great personal exertions that Hannibal was able to hold his own till a body of four thousand foragers, who had sought refuge from Minucius' horse in the camp at Geronium, was collected and brought to his assistance by Hasdrubal. He then drove away the assailants and drew up in order of battle before his camp, ready to chance the day upon an equal fight, but the Roman general deemed it prudent to retire. The Carthaginian losses had, however, been large, both at camp and among foragers. Livy says they were reported to be five thousand Romans and six thousand Carthaginians, and Minucius might congratulate himself on a successful diversion. If he had made his best attack on the supply-camp at Geronium, and a lighter one on the military camp occupied by Hannibal, he would very likely have been able to capture the former and to destroy a large part of Hannibal's winter rations; for it was held in but small force, — an evident lapse on the part of the usually very careful Carthaginian, who perhaps took too many chances on Minucius' lack of enterprise. Livy sums up the affair by saying that Minucius conducted an enterprise " rather joyful than successful," so that we may assume that the Roman gain was not great, nor Hannibal's check severe.

Hannibal appreciated the danger he had run, and feared that Minucius, who had shown himself both bold and able, might some day attempt to interpose a force to cut him off from his camp at Geronium, or to surprise the town, which was but illy fortified, while his foraging forces were absent. He decided to return to his former camp. Minucius at once occupied the hill he had yielded, and camped in the very spot he had just left (B).

The test of military skill is, unfortunately, often made to consist only of success. While this is, within its bounds, an excellent rule, it must be remembered that temporary success may not mean eventual gain. The Romans were tired of Fabius' prudence, which, in their very natural and characteristic manner, they termed mere timidity. Minucius' slight gain, to which Hannibal probably gave little thought as a matter of success, was magnified into a wonderful performance, particularly as Hannibal foraged thereafter with more caution, and the Roman soldiers began to breathe more freely. Minucius not only became the hero of the hour, but as magister equitum he was made by the senate the equal in rank of Fabius the dictator, a thing never before known in Rome, and now only brought about by an excited condition of the public mind. It had been almost impossible for Fabius to justify his conduct in the eyes of the senate ; and the fickle populace — through the tribune of the people, Metillius — took open sides against him. Fabius, however, maintained his equipoise, and set out to rejoin the army. Few characters in history have exhibited so great continence under trying circumstances.

It will not do to elevate Fabius into one of the great generals of the world. He has not earned that rank. Able to a degree and possessing noble qualities, he was, perhaps, more the creation of circumstances than the creator of a new method. He was brought to the front as a foil to the idiotic foolhardiness of such men as Sempronius and Flaminius, and naturally of a hypercautious nature, he was, for the moment, the very man for the place. But it was Roman grit and political soundness, not Fabius, that saved the republic. An indefinite course of such a policy as his would have ruined the cause. The Roman generals of the Second Punic War were Marcellus and Nero and Scipio. It is honor enough for Fabius to rank beside them.

In order to enjoy the authority his elevation gave him, Minucius proposed to Fabius (or, as Polybius has it, Fabius proposed to Minucius, when he saw that Minucius was bound

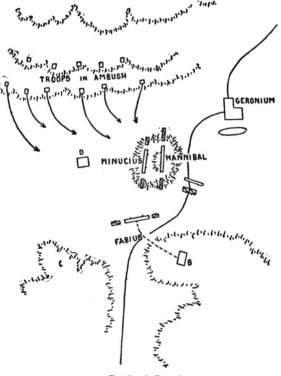

Battle of Geronium.

to be rash) to command on alternate days, or to divide the army, each taking two legions and a fair proportion of other troops. Fabius saw less danger in the latter proposal, as Minucius could in that case jeopardize but half the army in case he should undertake a dangerous offensive, and accepted this arrangement. Minucius at once withdrew his two legions from the old quarters, and camped, a mile and a half away,

well forward in the plain (D), so that the three camps stood
not far from equidistant from each other.

Hannibal was entirely satisfied with this change, which he
soon perceived from the division of the camp, from his scouts
and from deserters who, Livy says, went over to him, and at
once based a plan of action upon it. Between the two camps
stood a hill (E), commanding either. Hannibal determined
to take advantage of Minucius' evident desire to fight to lure
him if possible into an ambuscade. He accordingly, one
morning just at daybreak, sent a small force to occupy the
hill, with orders to demonstrate sufficiently to draw on the
Romans to an attack, and to hold the hill only for a short
time when the Romans should have advanced. Meanwhile,
in some ravines and behind some accidents in the ground,
which Minucius had not perceived because the ground was to
all appearances devoid of obstacles, Hannibal had concealed
during the night about five thousand infantry and a body of
five hundred Numidian horse, in such detachments of two
hundred and three hundred each, and such positions that
they would fall upon the Romans' flanks and rear when the
latter should move against the force on the hill. And that
their presence might not be discovered by the Roman scouts,
he kept the Roman line busy by the activity of the skirmishing detachment.

Nothing is easier, with proper precautions, than to hide
behind even slight undulations of ground a considerable force
of men. Any one familiar with our prairie country is well
aware of this.

No sooner did day open than Minucius, perceiving that
Hannibal had occupied the hill, sent some light troops, followed by a column of cavalry, to dislodge the Carthaginians
and take possession of it. Hannibal kept on supporting his
men on the hill by small reinforcements, so as to induce

Minucius to bring his entire force into action. After a while, irritated at the opposition of the enemy, and too much annoyed to perceive any other thing, Minucius ranged his legions in order of battle and advanced in full force against the height. Hannibal on his side threw in his own heavy troops. The velites, thus overmatched, were hustled back on the Roman line, and threw it into considerable confusion; but this was soon corrected, and the legions advanced in tolerable order. By the time the sun was up the combat had become general. At the proper moment, on a given signal, the hidden bands emerged from ambush upon the flank and rear of the Romans. Instant and perilous panic was the result. The Roman legions turned to flee, and the Carthaginians began pursuit. The rout of the Trebia seemed imminent, when Fabius, who had held his troops well in hand and ready for battle, anticipating that he might be needed to come to Minucius' rescue, appeared upon the scene, moved sharply forward to sustain Minucius' broken ranks, and reëstablished the failing fortunes of his colleague.

Fabius at this moment stood ready to offer Hannibal battle in earnest with his whole force, and made bold front; but the latter, satisfied with what he had gained, and never caring for action unless he could have it on his own terms, his men being, moreover, somewhat dispersed with the pursuit, deemed it wiser to decline, and retired to his camp. "Did I not tell you," said Hannibal jestingly, "that this cloud, which always hovered upon the mountains, would, at some time or other, come down with a storm upon us?"

The Roman losses were very heavy, especially in the bravest of the legionaries, and the velites were all cut up. Minucius, humbled at his ill-success, was sensible enough to see, and man enough to acknowledge, his own folly and the wisdom of Fabius. He openly declared to the troops that the fault was solely his, laid down his equality in command, and offered thereafter to act strictly under Fabius' orders. From this time he abode by the discreet advice of the dictator.

These incidents at once turned the current again in Fabius' favor, and every voice in Rome and the army was raised to yield him thanks for his skillful and magnanimous conduct.

Hannibal fortified the hill where the battle had taken place, occupied it with a strong force, drew a line of intrenchments from the hill to his camp and went into winter-quarters.

The term of Fabius as dictator was about to expire, and the command of the army devolved on the consuls Servilius and Atilius, who had succeeded Flaminius, until new consuls should be elected and take command. The Roman army retired to its old location on the slopes of Mt. Calene, near by, to winter.

Servilius, at sea, had not had much good fortune. He had made a descent on the African coast, but had been beaten off. On the other hand, the Spanish fleet under Hasdrubal had also suffered a complete defeat at the hands of Cnæus Scipio, near the mouth of the Iberus; and the latter had driven back to Carthage a fleet which was to land reinforcements for Hannibal at Pisa. The Romans had made a decided gain at sea. We have seen what Cnæus Scipio's success had been in 218 B. C. on the Spanish mainland, and that P. Cornelius Scipio, his brother, had joined him with eight thousand reinforcements in 217 B. C. Thus encouraged by substantial aid, as well as the moral effect of the naval victories, the two made bold to advance, and soon reached Saguntum and strongly established themselves near that city. By their military skill and judicious policy, they made large conquests among the allies of Hasdrubal, thus weakening the Carthaginian cause in Spain. Hannibal was not happy in the lieutenants he had left behind him.

XXVI.

ÆMILIUS PAULUS AND VARRO. SPRING, 216 B. C.

In 216 b. c., Æmilius Paulus and Terentius Varro were consuls, and Rome had nearly one hundred thousand men in the field. Æmilius was a man of the highest character; Varro was of low birth and without those qualities we most esteem. Hannibal and the Roman army lay facing each other at Geronium until May. He had tried to lure the consuls into an ambuscade, or to battle, without success. The Romans were gaining in ability; and the number of veterans in their ranks was now considerable. The vicinity of Geronium had been eaten out; Hannibal must move to new quarters, for he had not the aid of the population to bring him supplies. There was a great depot of bread-stuffs at Cannæ, south of him, on the Aufidus, which the Romans were care-lessly guarding. By a secret and clever march, Hannibal seized on Cannæ. The consuls were at a loss what to do. Cannæ was in the Apulian plain, where Hannibal could make efficient use of his cavalry. But the senate ad-vised another battle, if it could be had on equal terms; and the consuls marched to Canusium, south of the Aufidus, and camped six miles from the Carthaginian. Here, a few days after, Varro crossed swords with Hannibal, and won a certain advantage. This whetted his appetite for a pitched battle, much to Hannibal's delight. The Romans had eighty thousand foot and seven thousand horse to Hannibal's forty thousand foot and ten thousand horse. They had also established a small camp on the north bank, to protect their foragers. Both sides prepared for battle.

NEXT year, b. c. 216, C. Terentius Varro and L. Æmilius Paulus were consuls. Varro was the popular, Æmilius the senate's candidate. As prætors, Pomponius Matho, Publius Furius, M. Claudius Marcellus and L. Postumius were chosen; and the two latter were respectively assigned to Sicily and Gaul. The senate made unusual exertions to raise troops, and put nine Roman and nine allied legions, each of five thousand foot, into the field, making with the horse ninety-eight thousand men, a much larger force than Rome had so far reached in the Second Punic War. Still the cavalry was less than Hannibal's and vastly inferior to it, and cavalry was the winning arm. The Scipios in Spain were continued in command, and an expedition against Africa from Syracuse was planned. One of the new legions was assigned to the prætor L. Postumius, whose orders on leaving for Gaul were to create such a diversion as might result in the Gallic auxiliaries in Hannibal's command being recalled to the defense of their own country. The proconsul Servilius was ordered by Æmilius to undertake no operations in force against Hannibal, but to exercise his men in slight skirmishes and exchanges with the Carthaginians, so as to lend them confidence and aplomb, — a duty which Servilius apparently performed with skill and success. The troops this year all took a new oath " never to fly from the enemy, never to leave the ranks except to get weapons or palisades, to kill an enemy or save a fellow-citizen." Rome was now in earnest if ever.

The new consuls were the antipodes of each other. Æmilius was an aristocrat, a man of noble character and fine bearing, and a good soldier, courageous but discreet, who, as consul three years before, had commanded with credit in Illyria, and brought that war to a successful issue. He had intelligence enough to approve the Fabian policy. Varro was a plebeian, son of a butcher, and is generally represented as a brutal and common demagogue. Polybius calls him base and worthless. But the historians are apt to be partial to the patricians, and Varro had given, and later on gave again, signs of ability, though no doubt he was open to the gravest criticism and, according to some, to the charge of lacking stomach to fight to the bitter end.

Hannibal remained in his camp at Geronium until May, the Roman army still encamped where it had been all winter in his front, backing on the foothills for protection from the

Numidian cavalry. The recklessness bred of Minucius' success had been quite dissipated by Minucius' later failure. But under Servilius the condition of the Roman soldiery had constantly improved.

Why Hannibal remained at this point so long, as well as many other interesting circumstances, are left without explanation by the historians, who only speak of waiting for the crops to yield forage and rations. Contrasting the Carthaginian's long period of rest in winter-quarters with Alexander's abnormal activity, which knew no seasons, no obstacles, no difficulties, these apparent delays appear strange in a man whom we know to possess no less real energy than the great Macedonian, and to whom at first blush we assume time to have been of the essence of success. His army had now enjoyed a long respite from work, and he must himself have been anxious for action. During the winter and spring there had been frequent outpost combats, but nothing of which the historians make more than casual mention. But in these combats the Roman legionaries gradually acquired experience and hardihood. They were transforming themselves from raw levies to seasoned troops, and the number of men who had seen service was fast increasing. We can only guess that Hannibal's time had been taken up in negotiating with the Roman allies of southern Italy, and that he was waiting developments. Nothing shows the extraordinary force of character of the man better than the fact that, with such heterogeneous elements as those of which his army was composed, he experienced no difficulty in keeping his troops in heart and health during the winter, — a season which is always prejudicial to discipline, owing to the enforced idleness, to the impossibility of finding work for the men to do.

While in this vicinity, Hannibal tried one or two more stratagems to gain an advantage over the Romans. After a certain affair of the outposts, in the spring of 216 B. C., in which he may have suffered somewhat more loss than the enemy, though probably not seventeen hundred killed to the Romans one hundred, as Livy states, Hannibal withdrew from camp during the night, the men bearing naught but their weapons, and leaving the tents and equipage in disorder, as if the Carthaginians had suddenly retired in a panic. Moving off to a distance, he concealed his infantry in the cover of some hills, his cavalry near by and his baggage-train beyond. He hoped that the Romans would plunder his camp, and that he might take advantage of the disorder thus engendered. He had left the camp-fires burning, in order to lead the Romans to believe that he had intended to persuade them that he was still in camp, so that he might retreat to a greater distance before they caught up with him. The Roman generals came dangerously close to falling into the trap. The army had been ordered into line; but the consuls were restrained partly by fear of a ruse, partly by the bad appearance of the sacrificial victims. For once these annoying omens proved of use. As a rule, unless in the hands of a man like Alexander, who could turn the priests to good account and lead the oracles by his own better judgment, they were an unmitigated nuisance, a hindrance to all military operations. In this instance, before the legions actually advanced, news was brought in from the front that the Carthaginians were lying in ambush beyond the hills.

Such a stratagem appears to us trivial indeed; but ancient history is full of such, — both successes and failures. And when we consider, for example, how Hannibal escaped from the Falernian plain by his stratagem of the oxen, and what the conditions of ancient warfare were, the originality of such proceedings, and their not infrequent singular success, excites our admiration. Even in modern war, less good ruses have lain at the foundation of great victories.

One word about Livy, whose statements with regard to Hannibal are often manifestly inexact, like the one above quoted, namely, that the Carthaginians, in a combat having no serious consequences for them, lost seventeen hundred men to the Roman one hundred. Much of what Livy says it is impossible to accept without reading between the lines for explanation. That what this arch-enemy of Hannibal's tells us about him makes him out one of the greatest of men, in spite of all his slurs and charges, should be praise enough. Cornelius Nepos all but overdraws the picture when he says that " as long as he continued in Italy, none made a stand against him in a regular engagement, none, after the battle of Cannæ, pitched a camp against him in the field ; " but he is far more near the truth than Livy in his attempts to underrate his work. And yet it is on Livy, after Cannæ, that we must rely for our facts. Polybius' history exists only in fragments after 216 B. C. We shall construe Livy as we go along, usually by his own statement.

Advancing spring had brought to a low ebb the stores which Hannibal had accumulated for the winter ; and the neighborhood had been completely drained by the presence of both the armies. The Roman senate, moreover, had ordered all farmers to bring their grain into the fortified cities. The Carthaginians found that they must make a change of location for mere subsistence ; and it had also become certain that Hannibal must win some signal success to encourage his own and intimidate the enemy's troops. He was in a position which demanded constant success. A single bad failure meant destruction. The Romans had the whole population at their service for victualing, as well as many large depots of provisions and munitions of war, which enabled them to remain wherever they chose ; while Hannibal, regardless of strategic reasons, was compelled to move from place to place for the mere purpose of feeding his army. For the inhabitants were still generally hostile. He was compelled to detach considerable forces of foragers, thus at all times weakening his own main body, and affording the Romans the additional chance of falling upon these detached parties. It was essential for him to lay hold of some large town for a storehouse for the approaching campaign, and this in a region as yet unexhausted by the presence of an army.

The Romans had created a magazine of stores at Cannæ, in Apulia, on the Aufidus, from which they were rationing the army in Hannibal's front. The northern portion of Apulia is an immense plain, — the largest south of the valley of the Po. It is not far from fifty miles from northwest to southeast, and half as wide. Small parts of this prairie land are to-day bare and unproductive ; for the most part it is rich, and produces largely all kinds of grain and much good wine. Cannæ occupied a position on the southerly boundary of the region, and, as Polybius says, commanded the whole country, — probably meaning as a town which was fairly well fortified, and was the principal grain mart of the section. By very gross mismanagement, this depot, though garrisoned, had not been so well provided with defenses as to be placed in security against capture out of hand by a large force. These facts Hannibal had fully ascertained by the use of constant spies. The time of the early harvest had arrived, and there was plenty of forage for the beasts and grain for the men, — everywhere except in the region which had been eaten out during the winter by both the armies. The vicinity of Cannæ, a big plain, afforded the Carthaginian chances for manœuvring which he had not in his position near Geronium. Everything spoke in favor of a change of location.

To reach the Aufidus, Hannibal must turn the Roman position unobserved. This, by skillful and well-concealed movements and forced marches, he managed to do, reached Cannæ and seized it, with its abundant supplies. To judge by the topography and the roads then probably existing, he

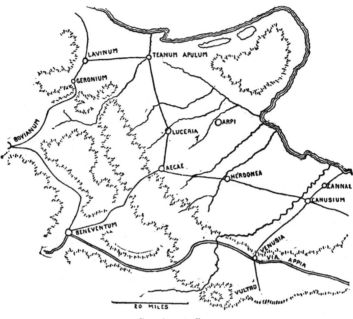

Geronium to Cannæ.

left his camp-fires burning at his camp near Geronium, and retired rapidly on Larinum, whence by Teanum Apulum, Luceria, his old stronghold, Æcæ and Herdonia, he reached Canusium and Cannæ. It is probable that there was a road along the coast, but this required the building of too many bridges for a rapid march. The Romans must pass by Bovianum and Beneventum to reach Æcæ; or from Beneventum the Via Appia would take them to Venusia, whence there was a road to Canusium. Once on the march, Hannibal's cavalry could easily have prevented the Romans from interfering with his progress, even if they had tried. And after they discovered his departure, they did not guess his objective.

Not only had Hannibal provided himself with a storehouse full of victuals, but he had robbed the Romans of a fine town and magazine, in a section of country of great importance to whomever held it; and he had also placed himself between the Romans and much of the grain-giving section of Apulia, where the wheat earliest came to maturity. This afforded him every hope of compelling the enemy to give him battle.

The proconsuls, who appear to have still been in command until the new consuls should join, had been negligent indeed. They could readily have kept a sufficient garrison in the citadel of Cannæ, but this, little anticipating Hannibal's turning march, they had not done. They could have kept watch on Hannibal, but so illy did they do this that they were scarcely aware of his breaking camp, and knew absolutely nothing of his direction, until they heard of the fall of Cannæ. No Roman could keep track of Hannibal. His marches were too rapid and secret. Thus suddenly deprived of their largest magazine, the proconsuls sent helplessly to the senate for orders, saying that they could not avoid battle if they followed up Hannibal, for he was in a level country, where they would be at the mercy of his cavalry.

It was Hannibal's cavalry which so far had been his right arm in battle, his means of gathering rations. Without his cavalry he would have starved. Like Alexander, the Punic captain understood and utilized this arm as it deserved. It must not be forgotten that the dangerous zone of the weapons of the heavy foot was not over twenty yards from its front, and that cavalry could thus charge close up to a line of battle; while the farther carrying missiles of the velites were far from deadly to well-armed men. Small wonder that the enemy's cavalry was the dread of the Romans, who had nothing wherewith to match it.

The proconsuls were instructed by the senate to await the arrival of the new consuls, for special reliance was placed on Æmilius Paulus, who had orders to try conclusions with Hannibal in another general engagement, if it could be done on even terms. The consuls, arrived on the ground in early summer, themselves readily saw that they must either leave Hannibal in possession of Apulia, or follow him up and harass him as Fabius had done, or settle the matter by fighting; and that the latter should be done soon was the evident sentiment of the conscript fathers. They had eight Roman legions and the accompanying allies. The Roman legions had been purposely raised from four thousand foot and two hundred horse to five thousand foot and three hundred horse, and the allied legions had the same number of foot and twice the horse per legion. The whole consular army was thus eighty thousand infantry and seven thousand two hundred cavalry, against Hannibal's forty thousand infantry and ten thousand cavalry.

The assembling of this enormous army for one duty showed the anxiety Rome was beginning to feel as to her ability to cope in any way with the Carthaginian. The Roman numerical superiority was vast. It brings Frederick to mind, whose battles were all but invariably fought against odds as great or greater.

But there were other factors in the problem. A leaven of Hannibal's troops were his old and tried soldiers, accustomed to victory and not liable to panic; the Romans were many of them young and inexperienced in actual war; and though there was, perhaps, as large a percentage of veteran material, that is, soldiers of several campaigns, in the Roman army, it was not beyond the chance of losing heart in any unforeseen contingency. Even the raw Roman legionary was capable of dying where he stood, with face undaunted towards the foe. He had shown this valor many times. But demoralization is an element impossible to foresee, difficult to arrest. And the Roman, brave as he was, must have looked with some dread at the coming conflict, though eager to punish this ruthless destroyer of his farms, his hearth-stones and his household gods. Punic craft was an uncertain danger which he could not forecast or provide against. It was really a question of leaders more than armies. In this the invaders had the distinct advantage. Again, divided authority reigned in the Roman camp; there was but one will in the Punic forces. One of the consuls was a headstrong leader; we know what Hannibal was. In these last factors lay the chief advantage of the Carthaginians as against the Roman vast numerical superiority.

It was highly dangerous for the Romans to leave Hannibal in Apulia. One more campaign such as the last might detach the Apulian confederates from the Roman alliance. A Fabian policy on these broad plains was far from an easy problem, and perhaps had long enough obtained. The consuls had received instructions from Rome to bring Hannibal to battle. They broke camp and marched to Canusium, which they reached in two days, and took up a position between five and six miles from Hannibal's, who had established himself in a strongly intrenched camp near the town of Cannæ. The camps backed respectively on Canusium and Cannæ, which were about seven miles apart.

The country is a huge prairie. From his quarters at Cannæ, Hannibal could look northwest forty odd miles to the long range which divided Samnium from Apulia; on his right lay the sea; on his left rose the distant peak of Vultro; at his back the ranges of southern Apulia. In his immediate

front were the sinuous windings of the Aufidus, emerging from
the hills on the west and flowing a bare half mile from both
Canusium and Cannæ. Between him and the mountains on

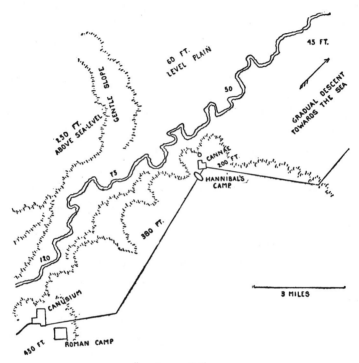

Canusium and Cannæ.

the northwest lay a flat alluvial plain of great extent, hemmed
in between these mountains and the sea; behind him was a
rolling country. The ground towards Canusium and beyond
was clear, with a gradual rise and slightly accentuated surface.

The Aufidus is the only river of Italy which breaks through
the Apennines. Its general course is northeast. Just before
reaching Cannæ, it emerges into the perfectly flat plain of
which we have just spoken.

The consuls, it will be remembered, commanded on alternate

days. Varro desired at once to attack. Æmilius feared lest a battle on a plain, where Hannibal could use his confessedly superior cavalry, might again be fatal, and desired to lead the Carthaginians to a spot where the infantry would have the most of the fighting. Varro characterized Æmilius' policy as Fabian; Æmilius reminded Varro of the fate of Sempronius and Flaminius. Such dissension foreboded no good.

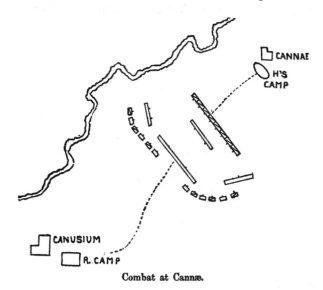

Combat at Cannæ.

The next day after the arrival of the army at Canusium, being one on which Varro's turn to command came, he marched out from camp and offered battle on the ground between the two camps. Hannibal accepted the gage, and at once attacked the Roman van of heavy troops with eight thousand light in-fantry and all his cavalry, and threw the Romans into some confusion. But Varro had cleverly supported his line with cavalry, among whose turmæ he had interspersed some velites and a few legionary cohorts, says Polybius; and, moreover, he had a considerable preponderance of force in line. He fought his men well, and though Hannibal kept up the action till evening, using apparently every effort to overcome the Roman legions, the Carthaginians had decidedly the worst of this first encounter. The Romans kept the battle-field. Losses are not given.

Hannibal retired to his camp at Cannæ. If these are all the facts, he had made a mistake in not ordering up some of his heavy foot, and Varro had shown more discretion in his

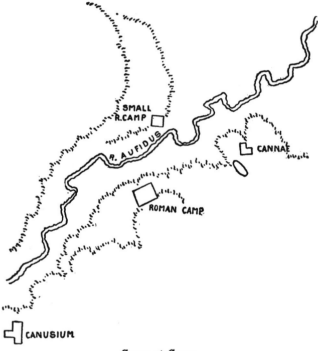

Camps at Cannæ.

management. But Hannibal was probably the gainer in that Varro's appetite had been whetted for further action, a thing most earnestly desired by the Carthaginian.   It seems to be a question whether Hannibal did not purposely allow Varro this success. He did not put in his whole force, as he would have done had he desired a battle *à outrance.* When he fought, he wanted different conditions. The Roman camp was advanced to the location of the battle-field.

On the evening of this day, after their successful combat, the Romans lay encamped on the south side of the Aufidus, three miles only from the town of Cannæ. Next morning, Æmilius took command. He was badly placed in the open field, where, despite his numerical superiority, he could not well resist the tactics of Hannibal's cavalry. Neither wishing to remain where he was, nor to try to follow up Varro's success of yesterday, nor to withdraw to better ground, lest this movement to the rear should dishearten his men, he took an aimless course, for that reason a weak one. His foragers and watering parties were being harassed by the Carthaginian scouting detachments on the other side. He sent one third of his force across to the northern bank of the Aufidus, which at this season is everywhere fordable, to a place a trifle down-stream, where he had a number of foragers, partly to sustain these and partly to form a secondary camp, from which he might annoy the enemy's parties which were roaming all over the plain in quest of corn. This smaller camp was nearly a mile from the main camp and a trifle farther from Hannibal's.

Hannibal saw this uncertainty in manœuvres with satisfaction. He divined that the moment had arrived for which he had longed for months; that it was about to come once more to the arbitrament of battle, this time, perhaps, a final one. He had probably heard that the Romans had decided on a more vigorous policy, and he knew that Varro was precipitate, and that Æmilius would be necessarily drawn into active measures. Both commanders made stirring addresses to their armies, Hannibal promising certain victory, and

Æmilius showing the Roman soldiers, by the experience of yesterday's success, that the Carthaginians were not invincible.

Polybius and Livy both give the harangue of Æmilius to the consular, and that of Hannibal to his own army. The latter bears the true ring of the great captain. Whether fanciful, or preserved by tradition, or otherwise recorded, it is what we can well imagine this soldier to have said to his soldiers. Thus ended his glowing words: " Tell me, warriors, could you have asked of the gods more than to bring the enemy to action on such a ground, where our cavalry is sure to overwhelm him? Thank ye the gods for bringing us certain victory! Thank me, your general, for bringing the enemy where he cannot decline to fight! By your former combats ye have gained the open country of the Roman! By to-day's victory ye shall have his cities, his treasures, his power! Let us hasten into action! I promise you victory, and, the gods willing, I will make my promise good!"

Hannibal bade his troops prepare their weapons and strengthen themselves with rest and food; and, on the second day after, he left the camp and formed his army in line of battle with the right leaning on the Aufidus, and invited Æmilius to join battle, having probably made his tactical calculations with care; but the latter, not liking the flat terrain, and knowing that lack of forage for his enormous number of beasts would sooner or later constrain Hannibal to move his quarters, contented himself with strengthening both his camps, reinforcing his outposts and the communications between the camps, and hoping that Hannibal might attack him in this position. Not caring to run so great a risk, Hannibal, after standing in line all day, was compelled to forfeit whatever dispositions he had made. He returned to camp, but sent out his Numidians to the other side of the river to attack the Roman foragers, and to prevent their seizing the banks so as to cut off a proper water supply, or if possible to prevent their watering their own horses. This latter the Numidians did to good effect, marching up even to the gates of the Roman camp.

Knowing that on the next day Varro would be in command, and that he would be burning to avenge the taunt of battle offered and declined, Hannibal made up his mind to again seek battle; and he made arrangements to do so with his entire forces, leaving eight thousand men to guard his camp.

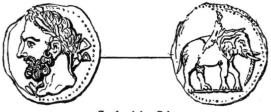

Carthaginian Coin.

XXVII.

THE BATTLE OF CANNÆ. JUNE, 216 B. C.

HANNIBAL had sent his Numidians across the river to attack the smaller camp. Varro next day crossed to protect it, and Hannibal also crossed and offered battle. The Romans faced southerly, the Carthaginians northerly. Varro had sixty-six thousand foot and seven thousand two hundred horse in line to Hannibal's thirty-two thousand foot and ten thousand horse. Hannibal backed on the river to prevent his flanks from being overlapped. Varro crowded his maniples together so as to strengthen his line and be more certain to crush his opponent; but he was really losing his mobility and giving his men a feeling of uncertainty in this new formation. Hannibal put his Spaniards and Gauls in the centre, and his Africans on the flanks of this infantry; eight thousand horse on the left and two thousand Numidians on the right. He advanced his centre in a salient, so as to take the first shock of the Roman onset, purposing to withdraw it gradually, and then if the Romans followed it to have his Africans wheel in upon their flanks. So it happened. The Carthaginian horse defeated the Roman and allied horse and drove it from the field, pursued by the Numidians. The Roman foot broke in the central salient of Hannibal, but when they followed it up, crowding in their eagerness out of all formation, the Africans wheeled in on their flanks, and the cavalry rode down on their rear. The entire Roman army was destroyed; Hannibal lost but six thousand men. The defeat was due to Varro's blundering tactics and Hannibal's superb manœuvring. There is no victory in history which was more fairly won.

THERE has been much discussion as to which bank of the Aufidus the battle of Cannæ was fought on. There has been still more discussion as to just how the armies faced, whether at right angles to the river, or parallel to it. An intimate knowledge of the field makes both matters plain. Polybius clearly states that Varro crossed the river from the main camp, that is, to the north bank, and, reinforcing his legions from the little camp, drew up in line in such a way as to face south. This statement is fully confirmed by Livy, who evidently copied from Polybius, as he uses substantially the same words. He had no evidence to conflict with the Greek historian. Moreover, both state (Livy again copying) that the sun, *when it had risen*, was inconvenient to neither, facing, as they did, northerly and southerly. The hour of opening the engagement was probably sunrise, and in June the sun rises in the northeast. Hannibal is also said by these authors, and by Appian and Plutarch, to have had his back to the wind Vulturnus, or southeast wind, which blows now, as it did then, in the June harvest-time. Both authors state that the Roman cavalry on the right leaned on the river ; but they do not state that this remained so throughout the battle. Such a position, according to one theory of the battle, would conflict with the other statements and the topography, and if we were to throw out anything, the assumption that the Romans fought with their right on the river is the one which we can best dispense with. But this does not seem necessary to be done, as will be seen. The tactical manœuvres are all clearly ascertained, and these form the chief interest of the battle.

Reading these positive statements in connection with a knowledge of the topography of the region, derived from personal examination, makes it seem incontestable that both commanders crossed to the north bank. There was reason for it. Hannibal did so not only because the ground was there quite level and better suited to his cavalry, but also because he felt sure that the danger to their new camp would make the Romans anxious to accept battle. Varro did so to protect the new camp, and because he thought he could back up against a slight rise in the ground just above this camp, — at that day considered a decided advantage. So when he crossed, left in front, he first began to form line, facing east, "placing his cavalry in the right wing, which was next the river," where it stood with its rear to the small camp which

Hannibal's men had attacked the day before, and might attack again. But when Varro saw Hannibal's formation backing on the river, his natural ardor, and the fact that he so

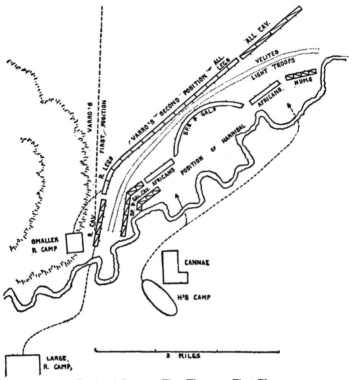

Battle of Cannæ.   First Theory — First Phase.

largely outnumbered the Carthaginians, induced him to accept
Hannibal's offer of battle, and either to pivot on his right-
centre and swing round his centre and left opposite to Hannibal, or to move his whole army into one straight line, " facing
southerly," actually southeast. The former theory satisfies
all the statements of Polybius and Livy, and no other does.
The second one satisfies all these statements, except the one
that the Roman right was on the river.

Arnold has read the histories to mean that the Carthaginians were on the south side and had their left flank on the river, while the Romans had their back to the sea, in other words, that their positions were reversed. It is scarcely probable that the Romans would purposely cut themselves off from Canusium and Venusia. The habit of fighting with the camp in the rear of an army was all but universal at that day, and particularly the rule among the Romans; that they would manœuvre so as to back up against the enemy's camp before engaging battle seems inadmissible.

Swinburne tells us that the Aufidus, after having flowed straight east for some time, makes a sharp elbow towards the south, and thus describes a very wide semicircle, precisely opposite the position where was the Carthaginian camp, and that it was in this part of the plain that the principal effort of the battle occurred. Niebuhr has adopted this theory of the terrain and position of the rival armies, and Colonel McDougall, in his admirable volume on Hannibal, has followed their statements. The theory of the left bank and the northerly and southerly facing of the armies is without doubt the best. It accords with the historians' record, and satisfactorily elucidates the manœuvres. But there are some topographical errors in Swinburne, Niebuhr, and McDougall, which are apparent to any one who has studied the battle on the field itself.

The general course of the Aufidus between Canusium and Cannæ is exactly northeast. The river is full of windings; but there is not now, nor is there any appearance of there ever having been, a southerly bend of the river two or three miles wide. Standing to-day on the slight elevation, crowned by several hillocks which hide the relics of the ancient town of Cannæ, perhaps one hundred and fifty feet above the plain, and looking out towards the Aufidus, one's eye is at once caught by a marked southerly sweep of the river. To any one who has not seen·an army of fifty thousand men in line, this sweep would appear large. This is probably what Swinburne saw and described. But it is in reality less than one half mile wide; and to locate the battle of Cannæ within this sweep is to seek to fit the foot of Gargantua into the slipper of Cinderella. The length of the Roman and Carthaginian lines must have been at least three miles.

Historical as well as topographical errors are easily propagated; the author fell into this one before studying the battle on the field. The mistake is now rectified. The accompanying charts give the correct topography of the region, and it is thought the true location of the troops. They certainly fit both the authorities and the terrain; and no other plan will do so. The only statement to be rejected, and this only if we accept the second theory, is that Varro leaned his right — the Roman cavalry — on the river; and this is met by the probability that he did so on first crossing, and afterward changed his mind. It is much more probable that, with his great superabundance of forces, he threw his cavalry around in a crotchet or circle to reach the river or to lean on the small camp, which being itself near the·river, would amount to the same thing. This first theory is to be preferred. It accords entirely with the authorities and best with their clearly described course of the battle.

The disposition of the troops adopted by many historians, including Mommsen, to the effect that the armies crossed to the north bank, and that the Carthaginian left and Roman right leaned on the river, each backing in the direction of his own camp on the other side, disregards the positive statements that the Romans faced southerly, and the Carthaginians northerly and with their backs to the wind Vulturnus. In such a position, if they stood at right angles to the river, the

Carthaginians would be facing all but south, and the Romans all but north, the very reverse of what both Polybius and Livy tell us; and, moreover, Hannibal would be unapt to attack uphill, as this position, in addition to leaving his right flank in the air, would make him do. Had his right flank been thus misplaced, he would have been apt to make it stronger than he did by merely posting his two thousand Numidians there. If we intend to be governed by what Polybius and Livy tell us, we must accept the positions as laid down.

Varro had made up his mind to fight. He could not stomach the insult put upon the Roman army. Before daylight on the morning succeeding the attack of the Numidians on the lesser camp, all his preparations had been completed, and without consulting his colleague, he put his troops under arms, and, leaving eleven thousand men — perhaps two legions, perhaps extraordinarii and other supernumeraries — in the larger camp, with orders to attack Hannibal's camp during the battle, he crossed the river, left in front, and joining the bulk of the forces of the lesser camp to his own, prepared to offer battle. Polybius and Livy both state that Varro crossed first; but it is probable that Hannibal had either left some skirmishers on the farther side, or had shown him some other indication that he would give battle on that bank.

Hannibal on his side forded the stream in two columns and drew up his army so that it backed on the river. His front he had previously covered with archers and slingers in such a manner as to hide his tactical formation from the Roman generals as well as to shield his crossing. The Roman line, by its greater extent and number, could readily overlap his own, and thus endanger his flanks. But by backing on the river, he could, if desirable, so manœuvre his cavalry, which was on the flanks, as to throw it back at a slight angle to the river bank, and thus save his infantry from being taken in reverse.

Seeing Hannibal's general position, the Roman consul, already over, concluded to draw up in the plain opposite the Carthaginians. He was burning to have it out with this arch-enemy of Rome. No doubt every soldier in the ranks was equally ardent. But Varro held fast to the smaller camp and the river.

This theory of the battle may be thought to be weak in that it makes Hannibal fight with a river at his back. But at this distance from the sea the Aufidus is everywhere fordable at the early harvest-season, so that the river was practically not a danger; or at least a lesser one than being overlapped, and in any event a decisive defeat now would be the end of Hannibal's career. This he well knew, and he proposed to make his men fight out the battle to the bitter end. The river helped to do this.

Varro also threw out his light troops in advance. He saw that it would not avail him to extend his line beyond that of Hannibal, as the troops on the flanks would, owing to the Carthaginian position, have nothing in their front and be unable to take part in the battle; but in order to make his line the heavier he changed the formation of his legions, so that, as Polybius tells us, "the maniples were nearer each other, or the intervals were decreased more than usual, and the maniples showed more depth than front." This is construed by some modern authorities to mean that Varro made his maniples sixteen deep and ten front, instead of ten deep and sixteen front as usual. Such a change would decrease his front to near that of Hannibal's. There is nothing to show just what the change was.

Whatever the change, it was a great error. The men were unused to the formation, and the mass was so dense that it could not act. Varro had sixty-six thousand infantry in line, that is, out of his eighty thousand men he had left eleven

thousand in the larger and three thousand in the lesser camp.
Had he left the formation as it was, and put twenty thousand
of this infantry in reserve, this body might have changed the
entire result — called on at the proper moment to act. They
could have fallen on the flanks of the Africans when these
troops wheeled in to encompass the packed masses of the
Roman legionaries.

The infantry was in the usual three lines, — fourteen legions in all, if two were left in camp. Varro seemed intent
on as many changes as could be made. Instead of giving
the Roman legions the centre, as usual, he placed them on
the right, the allied on the left. The Roman cavalry, twenty-
four hundred strong, was on the right flank. The allied cavalry, forty-eight hundred strong, was on the left. It would
have been better to place all the cavalry on one wing and
make its use a decisive one. If all the horse in one body on
the left could have succeeded in breaking Hannibal's right
when the centre fell back, it would have gone far to produce
a victory. But the one adopted was the only formation
known at that day, and was almost uniformly adhered to.
Æmilius commanded the right, Varro the left wing, — the
proconsuls, Atilius and Servilius, the centre.

Hannibal had placed on his left, opposite the Roman cavalry, his heavy Spanish and Gallic horse, eight thousand
strong, leaning on the river, two thirds in a first and one
third in a second line, all under command of Hasdrubal;
and on his right, facing the allied horse, his two thousand
Numidians, also leaning on the river. The cavalry on the
left could not only probably crush the opposing cavalry, but
could cut off the retreat of the infantry to its camps, if he
beat it. No doubt this heavy body was placed here with this
in view, another instance of Hannibal's appreciation of what
the enemy's strategic flank means. Of the infantry, the

Spaniards, in their purple-bordered white tunics, and the Gauls, naked from the waist up, were in the centre, in alternate bodies. His best troops, the Africans, which he had armed Roman fashion from the weapons captured at the Trebia and Trasimene, he placed in the usual order, on either flank of the Spanish and Gallic foot. The cavalry and the

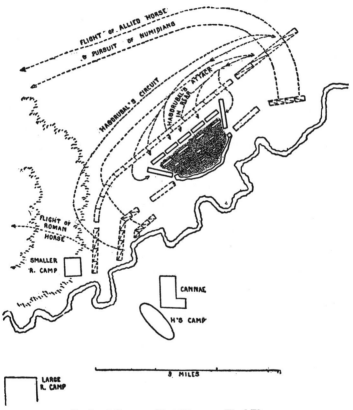

Battle of Cannæ. First Theory — Final Phase.

Africans he hoped might leaven the whole lump. His infantry we suppose to have been drawn up in the Greek manner, in phalangial taxes, each of one thousand and twenty-

four men.   The African infantry was in sixteen ranks, as
usual; the Spaniards and Gauls were reduced to ten ranks.
He had in all some thirty-two thousand infantry in line, that
is, his total foot was forty thousand, and he had left eight
thousand in camp.

Hannibal had been obliged to make his centre thin to
cover the ground he was to occupy, but he had seething in
his brain a manœuvre from which he proposed to snatch
an advantage from this very weakness, even though the Romans had made their own centre heavier.   He had no difficulty in predicating the general position of the Roman
troops in line, and he had no doubt matured his manœuvre,
and impressed it on his lieutenants.   Hannibal commanded
the centre in person, with dashing Mago to help him; Hanno
had charge of the right; and, as we have seen, Hasdrubal
commanded the cavalry on the left.   It could not be in better hands.   Maharbal is stated by Livy to have been on the
right.   Likely enough the difficult problem of the Numidians was committed to his charge.

In making his left-wing cavalry strong, Hannibal had in
mind the fear that Varro might again mix foot with his
horse upon the right and that he might need a solid body to
defeat this mixed array.   He had no doubt that Hasdrubal
with his eight thousand men would beat the Roman horse,
however sustained, and if necessary be able to go to the aid
of his own right, where but two thousand Numidians were
placed.   These were to play a skirmishing game, to which
their temperament and tactics were peculiarly suited.   The
cavalry problem settled, came the question of infantry.
Hannibal was as familiar with the tactics of Marathon as
any man alive; and he had at the Trebia seen how the Roman centre had pierced his own and escaped the general
slaughter.   Acting on both ideas, Hannibal proposed to ad-

vance his centre and then gradually allow it to withdraw, under the weight of the heavy Roman legions, to such a distance as should enable his wings to wheel in upon them and take the advancing centre in flank. But it was a dangerous evolution, unless carried out with the greatest exactitude, and unless the advance of the Roman centre was checked at the proper time. This checking would be aided by the knowledge of the men that the river was in their rear; but particularly by the fact that the centre had been fully prepared for the proposed manœuvre, and that Hannibal himself was to be the ruling spirit of the work.

The Carthaginians, remember, faced northerly, the Romans southerly. The rising sun was on the flank of either. The wind was southerly, — Florus says from the east, in reality southeasterly, — and blew the sand and dust into the faces of the Romans. The light troops of both sides opened the action, which lasted with alternate success for some time and was very fiercely contested by each line. Hannibal had rehearsed the details of this new manœuvre with all his subordinates, hoping that the Romans would be lured into aiding its execution. He had a way of making his purpose clear to his lieutenants, and himself proposed to see personally to its being properly done. During the preliminary fighting of the light troops he advanced his centre — the Spanish and Gallic infantry — in a salient or convex order from the general line, the phalanxes of alternate Spaniards and Gauls on the right and left of the central one, probably advancing *en échelon* thereto; but when the fighting began the whole assumed one huge convex line of more or less regularity. The space occupied by these troops must have made a crescent of nearly a mile and a half. The wings where the African infantry was posted kept their position on the original line.

While this was being done, Hannibal ordered Hasdrubal,

with the eight thousand heavy cavalry on his left flank, to charge down upon the twenty-four hundred Roman horse opposed to them. This they did with their accustomed gal-

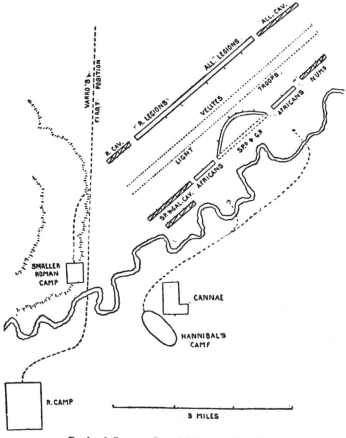

Battle of Cannæ.　Second Theory — First Phase.

lantry. The shock was tremendous, but handsomely maintained by the Roman knights, who contested every inch with the greatest obstinacy, and, when dismounted, fought on foot to the last. Many purposely dismounted in order not to be

driven from the place by sheer momentum of horses. When
word was brought to Hannibal by a staff officer that the Roman cavalry had largely dismounted, " This pleases me better than if they had been delivered to me bound hand and
foot," said he.   The combat was not carried on by successive
shocks, as usual in cavalry engagements; but by stubborn
hand-to-hand fighting with the white weapon, like that of
Alexander at the crossing of the Granicus.   But the weight
and experience of the well-trained Carthaginians was far too
great.   They rode down the whole body of Roman horse, and
soon had crushed it beyond reorganization.   Æmilius himself
was wounded, but he escaped the ensuing massacre and joined
the infantry of the centre, hoping yet to turn the tide of victory.   It is probable that the infantry of the Roman right
was placed *hors de combat* by this victory of Hannibal's
heavy squadrons, and thrust back in disorder, or else pushed
in on the centre.   It could not have maintained itself against
the weight of eight thousand heavy cavalry on its flank.

The Numidians, opposed to the allied cavalry on the Roman left, had orders to skirmish with it, but not to bring
about serious work for the time being.   Livy relates that a
party of five hundred Numidians, hiding their swords under
their cloaks, pretended to desert to the Romans, and being
received and placed in the rear, later fell upon the Romans
from behind.   Appian places this incident in the infantry,
and narrates remarkable feats which the five hundred men
were able to perform.   All this we may relegate to the domain of pleasant fable.   The Numidians as a body skillfully
accomplished their purpose by riding in squadrons round and
round the Roman left flank, and by their peculiar tactics
held their foes from serious attack until the Carthaginian
heavy horse, having utterly destroyed the Roman cavalry and
swept it from the field (a bare handful escaping up river),

made, under the inspired leadership of Hasdrubal, a circuit by the rear of the Roman army, and rode down upon the allied cavalry from behind. Then the Numidians, seeing their opportunity, attacked sharply in front, and, between these two bodies of veteran horse, there was speedily left not a single Roman or allied horseman on the field, except the dead and wounded. The Numidians were then put in pursuit of all who fled, while Hasdrubal, with the heavy cavalry, turned to sustain the African foot.

During the cavalry fight, but long before the Carthaginian horse had finished its first work on the Roman right, the light

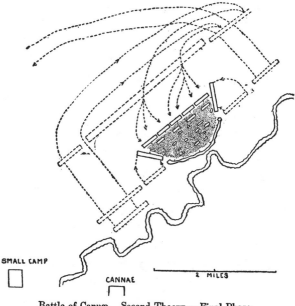

SMALL CAMP

CANNAE

2 MILES

Battle of Cannæ.   Second Theory — Final Phase.

troops of both sides had been withdrawn through the intervals, and had taken place in second line behind the Carthaginian army, and in rear of or in line with the Roman triarii.

Each had been ordered to form where they could act as reserve, to fill gaps in the lines of heavy infantry, or to furnish fresh weapons.

Varro had committed error upon error. In endeavoring to make his line so strong as to be, apparently, irresistible, he had ordered the maniples of principes to advance into the intervals between the maniples of hastati, instead of remaining in second line, as usual; or else he had drawn the maniples of each line together, so as almost to obliterate the intervals, thus preventing the principes from advancing through the hastati to sustain the combat when needed. The relations are not entirely clear; but the words of Polybius, above quoted, show the principle of his changes. This novel formation not only gave the troops a feeling of uncertainty as being irregular, — and this especially to the new troops, — but crowded the whole line out of its accustomed mobility. Still, with its never failing spirit, the heavy Roman line sharply advanced to the charge. Striking the apex of Hannibal's salient, the fighting at once became as fierce as the fury which filled the breasts of each; and Varro, eager to follow up what he felt sure was an approaching victory, ordered the triarii, sustained by the velites, to move up to support the already overcrowded first and second lines, and to drive back the obstinate Carthaginian centre, which Hannibal now reinforced by his light troops, to keep up the spirits of the men and better carry through his tactical manœuvre.

The legionaries fought stoutly and soon accomplished their purpose; they drove back the Spaniards and Gauls, but to the perdition of the Roman army. Varro saw sure signs of victory by breaking Hannibal's salient, and now depleted his wings to strengthen the already overcrowded centre. His every act was playing into Hannibal's hands. For as the Roman line, three in one, pressed on, the ranks became crowded out of all shape, and the one feature of the legion, its great elasticity of movement, was cast to the winds. Still the Roman soldiers, individually and in groups, though fast losing their maniple formation, fought their way into the enemy's line, step by step. The Carthaginian salient was steadily thrust back, and back, and farther back, until from a salient it straightened to a line of battle, and then, yet farther yielding, it began to assume the form of a reëntering angle. Into this breach the Roman infantry now poured, shouting their cry of victory.

They were met, not by a flying foe, but by the fatal consequence of overaudacity. So closely had their lines been formed and so sharply had they become pressed in that the soldiers had no room left to wield their weapons. The five feet square of the Roman legionary had been crowded down by more than half. Still the mere weight of the mass of men with their knobbed shields kept pushing back the Carthaginian centre, which Hannibal in person was handling in the thickest of the fray, and which, by his skillful dispositions, he kept in astonishingly good order and without a symptom of demoralization. Wherever he appeared, was cheerful confidence and courage. The Carthaginian infantry wings, as the Roman centre pushed forward, also advanced steadily and in admirable order, thus all the more crowding the Roman line, which itself had now assumed the form of a wedge and had begun to lose all semblance of its maniple structure. Plutarch and Appian state that the southeast wind blew with such violence as to all but blind the Romans with the sand which flew in their faces, and seriously to hamper their movements.

The decisive moment had come. Hannibal, seizing it with the instinct of the born commander, gave the anticipated order to his African infantry on the wings. These, pre-

viously prepared, wheeled round in perfect order to the right
and left and closed in upon the flanks of the Roman masses,
whose ardor had now huddled them together in shapeless
masses and quite destroyed their ability to manœuvre as well
as fight. Not until this moment had Varro's legionaries seen
that their hoped-for victory was ruin. But soldiers quickly
seize the meaning of what transpires around them. The Romans grasped their peril, but were Romans still. They fought
as bravely as for a triumph, but soon the last ray of hope
was gone. The consul in command had already fled with the
allied cavalry, while his brave colleague, Æmilius Paulus, had
been manfully struggling to rehabilitate the disorder of the
maniples, exposing his person with the utmost recklessness,
but in vain.

At this moment the heavy cavalry under Hasdrubal, having destroyed the Roman and allied horse, returned to the
field and rode down upon the Roman rear like a thunder-
cloud. Breaking into small detachments, it rode into their
midst and sabred the legionaries right and left. Parts of the
cavalry made their way through the intervals of the African
foot-phalanxes, and aided in the butchery of the Roman
soldiery on the flanks. The battle was ended, but not the
massacre. No quarter was asked or given. The legionaries
died with their faces to the foe, as so many Romans had done
before them. The bloody work continued till but a small
group of prisoners was left alive.

Livy and Polybius variously put the killed at from forty
thousand to seventy thousand men. Mommsen credits the
larger figures. Varro, who early escaped from the fray with
the cavalry of the Roman left, managed to turn up with a
squad of seventy men at Venusia; Æmilius Paulus fell in the
midst of his legions covered with wounds, in the vain effort to
retrieve the disaster. Servilius, Atilius, Minucius, two quæs-

tors, twenty-one military tribunes, a number of ex-consuls, prætors and ædiles and eighty senators perished with the army. In all certainly over forty thousand foot and four thousand horse remained upon the field.

During the battle, the eleven thousand men who had been left behind by Varro to attack Hannibal's camp carried out their orders; but Hannibal had been wise enough to leave the camp well provided against them. The Romans were driven back with a loss of two thousand men. Some seven thousand Roman infantry cut their way out from the battlefield and reached the small camp on the north side. Another body of ten thousand crossed the river and rejoined the large camp. Some six or eight thousand prisoners were made; ten thousand to twelve thousand men escaped into the country; and a body of four thousand men — no doubt the bravest — left the camp at night, eluded the Carthaginian scouting parties and marched to Canusium. Next day those who remained in the camps surrendered at discretion. They were allowed to purchase their freedom at the rate of three hundred denarii for a Roman, two hundred for an ally, one hundred for a slave, and to depart with one garment.

The splendid Roman army of eighty-seven thousand men had vanished as if swallowed up in an earthquake. Among the men who reached Canusium were Sempronius, four military tribunes, Scipio (later Africanus Senior) Appius Claudius and Fabius, son of the dictator. These officers found a small force of forty-three hundred men, and at once organized means of holding the place. Shortly after they learned that Varro had reached Venusia, a score of miles westerly from Canusium, with four thousand men. Sending to him for orders and reporting their condition, Varro shortly joined the forces at Canusium, and out of the fourteen thousand men who gradually assembled there began the nucleus of a new army.

Hannibal's loss had been barely six thousand men, of whom two thirds were Celts. Few were merely wounded. A wounded man had no chance in that fight. Hasdrubal, in command of the cavalry, had shown himself a *beau sabreur* of the highest order by the vigor of his charges and by returning to the battle-field in lieu of pursuing to a distance. His feat was like Cœnus' ride by the rear of Porus' army at the Hydaspes. It was the fine handling of the cavalry which permitted the infantry to carry out its programme.

This victory, it is seen, was largely due not only to the handling but to the excellence of the Carthaginian horse. It is hard to explain why the Romans should have been so persistently careless in improving this arm. There is no question that Hannibal owed his marching and foraging capacity, and certainly his success on the battle-field, more to his skill in using this arm than to any other one thing. At this period, when projectiles were cast to no great distance, cavalry could hover in the immediate vicinity of infantry, ready to fall upon it at any moment. The march of infantry on a plain in the presence of cavalry was difficult and dangerous. There was no reason whatsoever why the Romans should not have raised and disciplined a large force, as able to cope with Hannibal's as the infantry. They did so later, but it took them several years to discover the secret. In 1861 and 1862 our cavalry stood in the same position; but it took a short time for us to improve it into the gorgeous body of ten thousand horse commanded by Sheridan.

Few battles of ancient times are more marked by ability on the one side and crude management on the other than the battle of Cannæ. The position was such as to place every advantage on Hannibal's side. The manner in which the far from perfect Spanish and Gallic foot was advanced in a wedge in echelon and under the most vehement of attacks by the

Roman legions, was first held there and then withdrawn step by step, until it had reached the converse position of a re-entering angle, and was then held in place by ordering up the light troops, — all being done under the eye of Hannibal himself, — is a simple masterpiece of battle tactics. The advance at the proper moment of the African infantry, and its wheel right and left upon the flanks of the disordered and crowded Roman legionaries, is far beyond praise. The whole battle, from the Carthaginian standpoint, is a consummate piece of art, having no superior, few equal, examples in the history of war.

In direct contrast to this was the bad management of Varro. The errors he committed have already been pointed out. He robbed his army of all its mobility, — the one quality in which the legion was supreme, — first by deepening ranks, and then by crowding in more men where were already more than the space would allow. He undertook with new troops to make alterations to which they were unaccustomed. He left the command of his legions to subordinates, nor when his centre began to show signs of confusion was he on hand to correct it. Æmilius Paulus, wounded, essayed to do the work which Varro should himself have done. Varro intended, to judge from his assuming command of the left, to undertake some decided manœuvre with the cavalry of that wing; but he failed to make any marked demonstration against the Numidians, and fled from the battle-field — as is claimed — before the battle was absolutely lost. He failed to steady the cavalry of the right wing with foot, an advantage which he had learned by the success of but a day or two before. Altogether his conduct is checkered by errors, and stamped by the ugly seal of having survived the disaster due to his blunders. Æmilius Paulus is the Roman hero of Cannæ. And Hannibal, after the action, recognized this fact by a persistent search for his body and by paying the highest honors to his remains in the burial of the slain.

The news of the disaster of Cannæ, unequaled in Roman annals, was not to be the end of the disasters for this year. It was later followed by the intelligence that the prætorian army on the Po had been destroyed by the Gauls. It is hard to say whether political or social distress was uppermost in Rome. Few things show how drained of its better element the country already was more than the fact that the normal number of the senate — three hundred — had dwindled to one hundred and twenty-three. No less than one hundred and seventy-seven new senators had to be elected to fill the body.

It is here that we are compelled to take leave of Polybius as a constant companion. His work exists only in fragments after this battle. We cannot be so sure of our facts, or of doing as ample justice to the great Carthaginian as he deserves.

The relations of these campaigns by the ancient historians are so full of gaps, and often so contradictory, that it is impossible to always explain the movements or delays. Why Hannibal, after the battle of Cannæ, did not at once seize Canusium, which had but ten thousand defenders, is one of the questions we must ask and leave unanswered. He doubtless had some prevailing reason; we cannot allege one, but we may assume the existence of a convincing one to him. Again, shortly after the battle, Marcellus was able to reinforce this garrison with another legion. How Hannibal, alive to all his chances as he was, could have allowed Marcellus to do this is inexplicable. It would seem that some of the facts essential to a correct judgment must have been omitted in the narration, or have perished with the missing volumes of Polybius.

XXVIII.

AFTER CANNÆ. SUMMER, 216 B. C.

HISTORIANS often blame Hannibal for not marching on Rome immediately after Cannæ. That he did not, is one of the most decided proofs of his ability. A Pyrrhus could do so reckless a thing; but not a Hannibal. Rome was twelve days' march away. She had over forty thousand men to defend her strong walls. How could Hannibal, with his less than forty thousand men and no siege machinery, expect to take Rome, when allied forces, numbering hundreds of thousands, would certainly assemble in his rear? Hannibal was bold beyond any one in history in invading Italy, but he was not rash. He would have been insanely rash to march on Rome. He had two things to count upon, — help from home, and the disaffection of the socii. Without the first he must soon succumb. Without the last he could never conquer Rome. What he now did was to seek to influence the socii to join his cause. As a soldier alone, with his limited forces, he could not win the peace he aimed at. A great part of his time must be devoted to the political side of his problem. He now lay on his arms, with a military record unequaled in Roman annals, and sought to win his end by a persuasive policy. He looked farther into his problem than those who would have him do a foolhardy thing because it was brilliant. Rome rose to the occasion as never before. Not for an instant did she dream of peace, compromise, or anything but resistance to the last man. If Hannibal had marched on Rome, he would have ended the war, perhaps, but by the destruction of his own army.

IT is related by Livy that after the battle of Cannæ Maharbal asked permission to follow up the advantage gained with the horse and light troops, promising Hannibal that in four days he should sup in the Capitol; and that on Hannibal's declining this proposal, Maharbal exclaimed: " Thou knowest indeed, Hannibal, how to win a victory, but thou knowest not how to use one ! "

It is not unusual for historians to blame Hannibal for not

at once marching on Rome. Let us see what his chances were. We have no hint of what he himself thought, of what his reasons were for not so doing; we must content ourselves with collecting a few guess-work facts and endeavoring to argue as he did.

Two facts are peculiarly prominent in Hannibal's campaign in Italy. First, he had opposed to him the troops of the strongest and most intelligent military power of the world, — some of which were, to be sure, comparatively raw in active duty, but yet trained to war from their youth, mixed with legionaries of many campaigns, and instinct with the courage of fighting for their own soil. It will not do to claim that Hannibal's troops were veterans, — the Romans levies of a day. During the first three years this was partly true, and defeat, no doubt, somewhat drew the temper of the Roman blade, but during the rest of Hannibal's campaigns the Roman army was much superior to his own in all but one quality, — that strange influence which a great general exercises over the soldier. It will be noticed, that whenever the fighting was on equal terms, from the beginning the Roman soldier gave a good account of himself. But Hannibal's victories were won by tactical genius and his skillful use of his cavalry arm, not by mere fighting. In the latter, the legionary was always equal, if not superior, to the phalangite. So that one cannot compare the task of any other great captain to Hannibal's, with any show of fairness.

Secondly, Hannibal had calculated absolutely upon being able to detach some of the allies and colonies from their fealty to Rome, to break up the Italian confederacy. We cannot imagine him to have set out on his marvelous expedition without having made this the prime factor in his calculations. Hannibal was no madman, as some authorities have tried to make Alexander out to be; he was a keen, close calculator.

But he would have been insane indeed if he had ventured into Italy without a reasonable basis for this expectation. He was well justified in calculating on such defection. There had always been a good deal of opposition to high-handed Rome among all her allies and colonies, and it was a fair assumption that many, if not most of them, would be glad to free themselves and humble their conqueror and mistress. In this expectation Hannibal had been entirely disappointed. He had gone as far towards breaking up the confederacy as it was possible to go. If Cannæ would not weaken the allegiance of the allies, only force would do it, for success and terror had reached the highest notch. Despite which, none of the allies — the socii who had made equal alliances with Rome — had shown any disposition to meet him other than with the sword; none of the colonies, except in distant Gaul, had met him even half-way. He had captured towns and territory, and had garrisoned citadels. But the aid he received was not that aid which enables a conqueror to hold what he takes, except with the strong hand. And without just such aid Hannibal could not only not win ; he could not be otherwise than defeated in his contest with mighty Rome. To assume that Hannibal did not see all this, and that he was not fighting against hope almost from the second year, is to underrate this man's intellectual ability. No one probably knew all Hannibal's thoughts. He was so singularly reticent that Roman historians called him treacherous, because no one could from his face or conduct gauge either his thought or intention, or calculate upon his acts. He had no Hephæstion, as had Alexander. We learn nothing of his inner thoughts or motives. But no doubt he was keenly alive to the failure, so far, of his calculation on the disaffection of the allies.

And now, after the overwhelming victory of Cannæ, he had to weigh, not only the strategic and tactical difficulties, but the still more serious political ones. Indeed, Livy hints that he was busy about just this. If the allies — or a good part of them — could be induced to join his cause, Rome would fall sooner or later. If not, he could never take Rome, or permanently injure the Roman cause.

Hannibal was fighting, not to conquer Italy, but to win such a peace as should insure to Carthage the possession of Sicily, Spain, Sardinia, Corsica, and put Rome on her good behavior. To capture Rome was but a means towards an end. The chances were, in a military sense, all against his seizing Rome by a *coup de main.* If he failed, the game was lost. It was far wiser for him to still seek to influence the allies, which he could now do with a record of wonderful victories, such as the Roman world had not yet seen. Hannibal was not a military gambler. He never risked his all on a bare chance, as some other soldiers have done. He sifted and analyzed his facts with scrupulous care. And every reason prompted him not to risk the loss of his all on the chances of a brilliant march on the enemy's capital, twelve days' distant, which had only its boldness to commend it, and every military reason, as well as the stanch Roman heart, to promise failure as its result. For there was no obsequious satrap to open its gates and welcome the conquering hero. If Hannibal marched on Rome, he must be prepared to besiege the city, and we have already shown how impossible this was. "Modern campaigns are decided on the battle-field. Of old, a fortress might neutralize the greatest victory. After the landing of Regulus, Carthage was in vastly greater danger than Rome ever was; and yet the weak and vacillating senate of Carthage made a stand and won."

Hannibal probably at this time harbored the hope that after this fourth and overwhelming defeat of the Romans, the allies would finally see that their interests lay with him, and

the time which he now spent in the vicinity of his late battle-
field was no doubt devoted to political questions, the favorable
solution of which could be better brought about by not for
the moment risking his present unquestioned military supremacy. He was negotiating with the larger cities, and it was
but a short time before Capua, the second city of Italy, cast
in her lot with him. Such a triumph had much more value
than the destruction of another consular army. Hannibal
knew the fact and worked hard for this very end.

Hannibal had two things to hope for: reinforcements from
Spain and the disaffection of the allies. The first had been
rendered largely nugatory by the successes of the Scipios, and
the other seemed unattainable. Carthage had done something
to aid Hannibal, but he was not to expect much. This he
had known from the beginning, though he had placed entire
reliance on aid from Spain. Carthaginian fleets were busy
threatening the Italian coast and keeping Roman fleets away
from Africa. There was as yet no port of disembarkation
for Carthage in Italy. For many years the Barcine generals
had made war in Spain self-supporting, and Carthage would
expect the same now in Italy. Hannibal's resources, though
well husbanded, had begun to dwindle, his veterans grew
fewer, his men failed to get their pay. But Cannæ stirred
up the Carthaginian senate, which resolved to aid the war
both in Spain and Italy.

A treaty was made with Macedon to land an army in
Italy, Philip hoping by such means to regain Epirus; and
Hiero of Syracuse being dead, the new king joined the
Carthaginian cause.

Now was the chance for Carthage if ever. If she could
have looked at the matter broadly, and not through the eyes
of political envy; if she could have concentrated in southern
Italy the easily raised thousands of good African foot and

horse; if she could have forgotten Spain for a bare year, and aided Hannibal instead; if she could have utilized Macedonia and the promised resources of Sicily, there is no doubt that such a peace could have been dictated to Rome as would have given the Punic power the upper hand in the western Mediterranean for many generations. But Carthage was blind and indolent, and the splendid work done by Hannibal with the Army of Italy was wasted.

The institutions and laws which gave Rome strength never demonstrated her greatness so well as now. The people which had created these institutions, which had made these laws, never rose superior to disaster, never exhibited the strength of character of which the whole world bears the impress, so well as now. The horrible disaster to both state and society — for there was not a house in which there was not one dead — by no means changed the determination of the Roman people, however horrified the cool-headed, however frightened the many. Not that among the ignorant there was not fear and trembling, but it was not the ignorant who made up Rome. The more intelligent and courageous element spoke with a single voice. The prætors at once called the senate together to devise ways and means. Fabius advised first to send out a portion of the cavalry to ascertain the situation of Varro and Hannibal, which was done. The senate remained in constant session. All Rome was in affliction, but this must not interfere with the necessity of saving the commonwealth — and courage must be outward as well as in the heart. The word " peace " was forbidden to be pronounced in the city. Mourning was limited to thirty days. Tears were prohibited to women in public. New energies were at once put at work. In view of the alarming circumstances and the impossibility of carrying out the requirements of the law, the senate itself made M. Junius Pera dictator, who

chose Tiberius Sempronius Gracchus as master of cavalry.
The entire male population above seventeen years of age was
enrolled. Four new legions and one thousand horse were
thus added to the city's garrison. All mechanics were set to
work to make and repair weapons. Old spoils hung in the
temples were taken down for use. The walls were already in
a state of excellent defense. The senate purchased and
armed eight thousand slaves and four thousand debtors or
criminals, with promise of freedom or pardon. This is the
first such instance in Roman history. Naught but stubborn
resistance to the last man was thought of.

Rome could count on for the immediate defense of the
city : —

Two urban legions	10,600 men.
At least among the old soldiers over age . .	10,000 men.
Slaves and freedmen	12,000 men.
With Marcellus at Ostia, two legions . . .	10,600 men.
Total	43,200 men.

This was a larger force than Hannibal commanded.

Finally, Varro was heard from. He announced that he
had rallied the wreck of the army at Canusium, and that
Hannibal showed no intention of marching on Rome. A
moment's breathing spell was had. But the list of disasters
was not yet filled. The rumor of two Carthaginian descents
upon Sicily at the same moment came to the ears of the senate. That part of the coast which was the territory of
Hiero, king of Syracuse, a Roman ally, who had recently
supplied arms and men to the army at Cannæ, was being
ravaged, and another fleet was threatening Lilybæum and a
portion of the island subject to Rome. Speedy help must be
had if the Sicilian possessions were not to be forfeited. But
much help could not be afforded. All the men who could be
spared from the fleet at Ostia were of necessity called to

Rome, and the commander, Marcellus, was ordered to Canusium with a legion to add to the troops to oppose Hannibal, while Varro was recalled to Rome to give in his report. Thus depleted, the fleet was sent to Sicily.

When one considers the immense resources of Rome and the comparatively small number of men commanded or procurable by Hannibal, when one looks at the dauntless front presented by the freedom-nurtured republic, it is all the more apparent that there could be but one end to the conflict. Rome still numbered her possible levies by the hundreds of thousands. Hannibal's force was only that with which he had so far made his conquests, plus a number of local recruits, and he looked forward with uncertainty to any further outside help. The anxiety of the most stout-hearted, the terror of the weak in Rome, was justified, but Hannibal himself saw the outcome as it must be, — unless the allies could be persuaded to join him, — and bent all his resources to this end, neglecting, perhaps, his military scheme for the greater political necessity.

That there was grave demoralization among all but the strongest hearts, even in the army at Canusium (and at the front demoralization is always less marked than at the rear), nothing demonstrates more than the fact that a number of young nobles, headed by Lucius Cæcilius Metellus, who were at this place, seriously proposed to leave the Roman army and seek to establish a colony in some other part of the world, or to offer their services to some king, as Livy says, deeming the days of the supremacy of Rome to be numbered. A defection like this would have been fatal, for from such an origin it would have spread like wildfire on all sides. It is related that Appius Claudius and Publius Scipio, when informed of this conspiracy, at once visited the chief projectors, and sword in hand forced them to swear never to desert the republic while in danger. Thus was this most threatening of all the clouds dissipated.

Some allege that Varro put down the outbreak. But after this had been done and he had brought the army to a state of decent discipline, on the arrival of Marcellus, who was placed in command, Varro returned to Rome, to submit himself to the mercies of the people and senate, bearing with him the responsibility for the most grievous disaster Rome had ever suffered. If it was really Varro who restrained the defection above mentioned, and calmed the panic of his troops to the extent of again making them reliable, this would show him to have been a man of uncommon character, however faulty as a soldier or unworthy in a social aspect. And his returning to Rome to bow to the will of the people, acknowledging the entire blame to be his own, shows a certain nobility of character which we cannot but weigh highly in estimating him. He was employed in one or other military capacity till the end of the war.

The dignity of the senate maintained itself in receiving Varro. Though full of his bitter political enemies, though he had been the cause of the death of the nearest relatives of each and all, though he had brought about the gravest danger Rome had ever seen, this noble body, in lieu of punishing Varro for his defeat, thanked him publicly "for that he had not despaired of the republic." Much has been said in denunciation of Varro. But that the Roman senate, in this hour of peril and grief, should have so acted seems to show that there still was a good side to this man, which history does not bring to the fore, as of necessity it must his weakness and want of skill. How much of the condonation by this public body was due to the chastening influence of such an overshadowing disaster as Cannæ cannot be said. But the fact does not remain without significance.

XXIX.

MARCELLUS. FALL, 216 B. C.

HANNIBAL gave all his Italian prisoners their freedom, and placed a ransom on the Romans; but the senate refused to allow their families to enrich the Carthaginian by paying this ransom. A large number of cities in southern Italy joined Hannibal, but the socii clove to Rome. The confederacy was like a Cyclopæan wall. Hannibal moved to Campania. He aimed to get a seaport in this province as a base for further operations, but he was unable to lay hold of one. Capua, the second city of Italy, joined him, and he won several smaller towns, among them Casilinum; but at Nola, Marcellus, who was the coming Roman general, checked him in an attempt on the place, with heavy loss. The Hanno party in Carthage was voted down, and reinforcements were ordered from Spain to Italy; but the Scipios defeated Hasdrubal Barca, and prevented their leaving the peninsula. Cannæ had been a great gain for Hannibal, but it had not brought him that support which would enable him to win. The cities which joined him did so because they looked on him as a new master, and not from approval of his course; in many instances from hatred of Rome. The structure which Rome had erected in Italy was sound enough to stand every test. Hannibal went into winter-quarters in Capua.

THOUGH in need of money, Hannibal, after the battle of Cannæ, sent his Italian prisoners home without ransom, as a bid for the support of the confederates against Rome. Having fixed a ransom upon the Roman prisoners, he sent a deputation of these prisoners, accompanied by Carthalo, a noble Carthaginian and commander of the light horse, to Rome, with authority to treat with the senate or else with the families of each. The deputation made a good showing to the senate, but this body, with the wonderful self - confidence which always characterized its actions, refused to allow Hannibal to be enriched in this manner, either from the state or from private funds, declined to treat with Carthalo, and

ordered him forthwith to leave Roman territory. Pliny
states that Hannibal avenged this insult in a terrible manner
upon his Roman prisoners. Livy and Polybius do not mention the fact, as the former would assuredly have done had
there been any truth in the report; and unnecessary cruelty
was foreign to Hannibal's character or intent. Such an
act would have made his future battles harder to win, for no

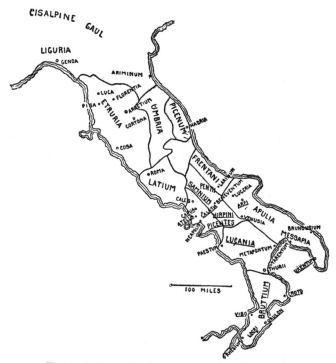

Hannibal's Allies after Cannæ.   (His allies underscored.)

Roman soldier would thenceforth have surrendered. History
shows only too well what fighting capacity such a spirit in an
army breeds. Policy was Hannibal's strongest characteristic,
and reprisals upon the persons of his prisoners would have
been in the highest degree impolitic. He would scarcely
have invoked such a weapon against himself.

These last wonderful successes of Hannibal, coupled to his generosity to the Italian prisoners, proved too much for the fidelity of some of the Roman dependencies. Livy tells us that there joined Hannibal: Arpi in Apulia, and Uxentum in Messapia; all the Bruttian towns, — of which, however, some few had to be besieged; most of the Lucanians; the Salernian Picentes; the Hirpini; the Samnites except the Pentii; and Capua, which, it is said, could raise thirty thousand foot and four thousand horse, with the neighboring towns of Atella and Calatia. The aristocrats in all the cities unwillingly joined or openly opposed Hannibal. The South-Italians held to Rome, having many Roman garrisons, and because Rome had been gentle to the Greeks in Italy. Neapolis, Rhegium, Thurii, Metapontum, Tarentum resisted Hannibal. Croton and Locri were stormed. Brundisium, Venusia, Pæstum, Cosa and Cales, Latin colonies, that is, Roman fortresses, remained faithful. If Hannibal restored Italian liberties they would suffer. "Not one Roman citizen nor one Latin community had joined Hannibal." "This groundwork of the Roman power could only be broken up, like the Cyclopæan walls, stone by stone," says Mommsen.

Still Hannibal may have seen in what had occurred the beginning of real success, and have devoted himself to following up this political gain. It must be noted that the Roman colonies which joined Hannibal scarcely did so of their own free will. They felt that they were conquered, and were but accepting a new master for an old one. Beside this fact, a chain of Roman fortresses still covered the land and kept these new allies restless. What Hannibal had gained was not hearty support, but uncertain submission.

Hannibal, after plundering and destroying the two Roman camps near Cannæ, marched up the Aufidus and into Samnium to the land of the Hirpinians, and here he possessed himself of Compsa by the treachery of a strong party which had embraced his cause. This place he made a depot of stores and booty, leaving his brother Mago to seduce other towns in the district. Later he sent him into Bruttium with a strong division to help forward the cause, and Hanno to Lucania on a similar mission; while he himself, with the bulk of his army, moved into Campania. Reaching Neapolis, he tried to seize an entrance into the city by ruse, and came very close to succeeding, but failed at the last moment; and as the Romans had thrown a garrison into the place, and it was very well fortified, he could not undertake a siege. In fact, he scarcely had time, in view of all the conditions surrounding him, to sit down in front of any strong place, unless of the greatest importance.

In addition to Neapolis, Nuceria and Cumæ, the latter on the coast, from which he might have had easy communication with Carthage by sea, — and Hannibal much needed a seaport, — proved too strong for him to gain; but Capua, which for some time had looked on Hannibal as the eventual conqueror of Rome, and therefore deemed it politic to be among the first to play into his hands, — though the Romans had endeavored to cajole her by the offer of a leading share in the struggle, — concluded an alliance with him and received his army. This was a first and most distinct triumph, though Capua made some marked reservations in her compact with Hannibal, such as that he should have no right to compulsory service of the population of Campania, nor to interfere with the city laws. Atella and Calatia, near by, followed the lead of Capua.

Cannæ, says Mommsen, was the direct result of the mutual suspicions and jealousies of the senate and the citizens of Rome. The first consequence of this was the appointment of such men as Flaminius and Varro. Demagogism had seized the reins. What the Scipios in Spain had done was due to their being good men beyond interference. Even Fabius was not above acting on political prejudices in what he did. His cunctatory policy was in part a protest to the insane combativeness of Flaminius and Varro. It was the present reconcilement of senate and people which gave back to Rome her strength. She had been taught by bitter experience that she could not successfully conduct war with political quarrels at home. She put her best men in command, and kept them on the duty they showed they could perform.

Marcellus, who was the coming man, had received his training, and a good one, against Hamilcar in Spain, and had conducted the late wars against the Celts, in which he slew

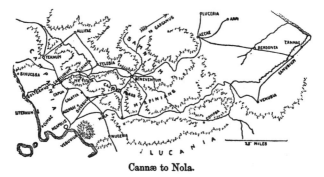

Cannæ to Nola.

with his own hand Britomartus, the king of the enemy, and took his spoils. He was noted for strong military common-sense as well as personal prowess. He had erected a temple in Rome to Honor and Valor, of which he himself was the embodiment. No man deserved better of the republic. Still, splendid a character as Marcellus was, it was not he who rescued Rome. It was the Roman citizen. Marcellus was but the most useful of the citizens, and the most brilliant. He was the first Roman who combined boldness with caution.

His method in dealing with Hannibal was far beyond that of Fabius. He was the father of the system which eventually drove the Carthaginians out of Italy.

While Hannibal was endeavoring to add to his list of allies, Marcellus had been withdrawn from Canusium, and had marched by way of Beneventum and Allifæ with two legions, the wreck of Cannæ, to Teanum Sidicinum, where reinforcements from Rome and Ostia reached him, and thence to Casilinum to cover the line of the Vulturnus. The dictator, M. Junius, had been able, out of the two legions raised in Rome and the slaves and debtors, to leave a suitable garrison in the capital and to advance with twenty-five thousand men to the same locality. Here were armies exceeding in numerical strength those under command of Hannibal.

Mago, after his work in Bruttium, embarked for Carthage to make his chief's report and ask for reinforcements. Neither Carthage nor Rome was at this moment undisputed mistress of the sea ; for Carthage had made some strides in her naval growth, and troops could at any time be debarked in Bruttium without all too grave risk. It was the salvation of Rome that Hannibal's worst enemies were in Carthage, among the supporters of Hanno, and that the reinforcements which ill-success made it essential to send to Spain constantly proved the excuse for denying triumphant Hannibal that which might have enabled him to conquer a glorious peace in Italy.

As showing what the rock was on which Hannibal's success was wrecked, the answer of Hanno in the Carthaginian senate to the message of Mago may well be quoted from Livy. "This, then," said he, "is what you say: 'I have slain the armies of the enemy; send me soldiers.' What else would you ask if you were conquered ? 'I have captured two of the enemy's camps, full of booty and provisions; supply

me with corn and money.' What else would you ask if
plundered or stripped of your own camp? Since, as you say,"
he continued, "the battle of Cannæ annihilated the Roman
power and it is a fact that all Italy is in a state of revolt, in
the first place, has any one people of the Latin confederacy
come over to us? In the next place, has any individual of the
five and thirty tribes deserted to Hannibal?" When Mago
had answered both these questions in the negative, he continued : "There remains, then, still too large a body of the
enemy. But I should be glad to know what degree of spirit
and hope that body possesses." Mago declaring that he did
not know, " Nothing," said he, " is easier to be known. Have
the Romans sent any ambassadors to Hannibal to treat of
peace? Have you, in short, ever heard that any mention has
been made of peace at Rome?" On his answering these
questions also in the negative, " We have upon our hands,
then," said he, " a war as entire as we had on the day on
which Hannibal crossed over into Italy." And on this theme,
whose basis was clear truth, he opposed all sending of aid to
Hannibal. His premises were correct, — but only literally
correct, actually wanting in breadth of view ; his conclusion
was therefore absolutely wrong, — in a military sense, at
least. The man who showed he could command success
should have been sustained, even if all Iberia fell under Roman sway. Conquer a peace at the gates of Rome, and the
evacuation of Spain could be demanded as a condition. This
simple fact Carthage never could comprehend. She aided
Hannibal, but in a stingy manner.

The Carthaginian senate, unwilling to listen to Hanno,
voted that four thousand Numidians, four hundred elephants
and much money should be sent to Hannibal, and that twenty
thousand foot and four thousand horse should go to him from
Spain. But all this was done with the sloth bred of success
and of lack of common purpose.

The integrity of Rome and the opposition of Hanno wrecked Hannibal's wonderful work.

The surrender by Capua of her Roman fealty was followed by the similar action of a number of other Italian cities. Excepting that some cities with Roman garrisons could not be reduced, Hannibal had gained all southern Italy below a line extending from the mouth of the Vulturnus to the promontory of Mons Garganus.

Nola, east from Neapolis, had a Roman garrison, but the popular party offered to open the gates to Hannibal. Marcellus, who was near Casilinum, was warned by the Roman party in Nola in season, and, anticipating Hannibal's seizure of the town, marched up the Vulturnus to Caiatia, crossed and, passing along the east slope of the mountains back of Suessula, threw himself into the town and prevented the Carthaginian from taking advantage of this offer. Hannibal then made another attempt to take Neapolis, but this too failed, on account of recent reinforcements under Silanus, sent to the city by the Romans. Nuceria, however, he took in a short siege by starvation, and, giving the inhabitants their lives, plundered the town and razed it to the ground. He then marched back to Nola.

It is extremely difficult in many cases to ascertain the roads by which Hannibal or the Roman generals marched. The authorities are not always in accord, nor do we know just where there were practicable roads. But careful comparison of authors and topography usually results in coming close to the truth. In this case, we know that Marcellus marched back of Suessula; and as there is but one valley through which he could march, except by a very extensive circuit, it is assumed that a country road led along this valley in his age, as there does to-day.

Marcellus was himself in a difficult position in Nola, having only the senate of the town in his favor. He began by winning over to his side the leader of the Hannibal faction, Bantius, a young man whom, wounded at Cannæ, Hannibal had generously cared for and sent back to his native town loaded with favors, and who had headed the scheme for going over to the enemy. Deprived of Bantius, the popular party was more easily controlled. Still danger from this quarter was not put aside, for it was reported to Marcellus that other leaders of this party had agreed with Hannibal, that when Marcellus should make a sortie from the town or draw up for battle outside, they would plunder the baggage and close the gates upon him.

Hannibal was encamped before the town, and there were daily skirmishes between the contending outposts and light troops.

Not feeling that he could long hold on under such conditions, Marcellus made up his mind to risk an attack on Hannibal, and thus cut the knot of the difficulty. It was a bold step. His plans were matured with masterly skill. He quietly drew up his line inside the walls, opposite three gates on the side where Hannibal was observing the town. He armed the walls with invalids and noncombatants, and parked his baggage-train in one place, with a sufficient guard of extraordinarii to prevent plunder, if attempted. Opposite the middle gate he drew up the Roman cavalry and old legions; at the other gates the allied legions and cavalry, and the light foot under Valerius Flaccus and C. Aurelius. He forbade any of the inhabitants to approach the walls, under threat of summary penalties.

Hannibal had been drawn up all this day in battle order, in front of his own camp, anticipating an attack by Marcellus or the usual skirmishes. He wondered that the Roman army did not emerge from the gates, and, seeing no garrison on the walls, naturally concluded that Marcellus had discovered his connection with the popular party, and did not dare to come out, lest he should be betrayed. He imagined that if he attacked he would be able to take advantage of the commotion

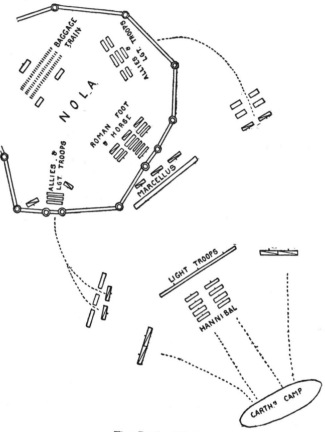

First Battle of Nola.

and indecision which would ensue. Arguing thus, he fell into Marcellus' trap, — he, the master of stratagem, — and though the day was far spent, at once made arrangements to attack the town. Sending the light troops forward, he ordered the

phalangites to provide themselves with ladders and whatever
machines, useful in an assault, happened to be at hand, and
to advance in column on the town.　The horse followed after.

The head of column had scarcely reached the wall, — it was
not in the strictest order, laden as it was with all manner of
tools, in addition to arms, and far from anticipating an attack, — when the gates were thrown open and, with a tremendous onslaught, Marcellus rushed forth, personally leading the centre, formed of the survivors of Cannæ, in two lines
of cohorts, and followed by the cavalry.　The Carthaginian
light troops were at once hustled back, and a formidable assault immediately made on Hannibal's phalanx.　Every man,
including noncombatants in the rear, had been ordered to
join in the battle-cry, to simulate numbers.　The allied horse
at the same time charged out of the side gates, hoping to take
the phalanx in flank ; but Hannibal, though surprised, was
far from losing his head, and had at the opening of the attack ordered up his own mounted troops on his either wing.
The suddenness and stoutness of the onset made a distinct
impression on the Carthaginians, and inflicted much loss.
But these veterans were not to be easily demoralized.　In a
short period, Hannibal, by his personal efforts among his
men, reëstablished the battle, and was about to turn the tide
of action, when the second line of the Roman wings charged
out of the side gates, and again took the Carthaginians on
both flanks.　The whole affair had been so admirably managed by Marcellus that Hannibal gave up trying to rescue
the day, and retired, in entire good order, but having suffered heavily in casualties.

Just now, such a success was a hearty encouragement to
the Romans.　They had fairly beaten Hannibal at his own
game — ruse.　As Livy says, " not to be vanquished by Hannibal then was a more difficult task to the victorious troops

than to conquer him afterwards." To Marcellus belonged
the entire credit. He had shown himself worthy to lead Roman soldiers.

Marcellus punished the ringleaders of the popular party
in Nola with death, garrisoned the town so as to put it beyond capture out of hand, and moved to a position above
Suessula, where he intrenched himself.

Hannibal gave up hope of capturing Nola, and retired to a
camp near Acerræ, not far from Suessula. He attempted to
take the town by siege; but the inhabitants managed by a
sortie to break through the line of circumvallation before it
was finished, and escaped. Hannibal then destroyed the
town.

Marcellus was both brave and discreet. Though he had
once checked Hannibal under favorable conditions, he by no
means flattered himself that he could cope with his great
antagonist. He could play a Fabian game when it was useful; he would risk nothing needlessly; and he now held his
fortified heights, whence he could watch Nola and Neapolis,
and at the same time keep open his road of communication
along the hills with the dictator, who was at Teanum.

The dictator, M. Junius, with his twenty-five thousand
men, was reaching out towards Casilinum. Hannibal learned
the fact. He was anxious to capture this place, — an important strategic centre, built, as it was, astride of the Vulturnus. He had had reason to hope that Casilinum might
yield itself, as so many of the Italian cities had done. But
when he marched against the town, he found that he was mistaken. It had a garrison of about fifteen hundred men, of
whom some Prænestians appear to have been the controlling
spirit. They had extinguished the pro-Hannibal party by
executing many of them for treason, and had retired into that
part of the city which lay on the north bank, where they made

a most stubborn defense in the citadel.   It seems as if Hannibal was compelled to operate against the town within a very limited space where he could use but few troops.   As at Saguntum, numbers were not of much avail.   The bend in the river obliged the garrison to defend but a very small part of their wall.   The first Punic assault was headed by Isalca, a

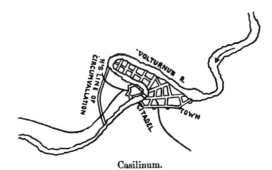

Casilinum.

Gætulian, and being partial only, and met by a sharp sortie, had no chance of success.   Then a general assault, under Maharbal, was ordered, but, though this officer was wont to do good work, he too was repulsed by the plucky garrison in a sudden rush from the gates.   Hannibal had underrated his enemy.   Even reproaches addressed to the conquerors of Saguntum, says Livy, and the promise of a mural crown, did not provoke a stout enough assault to capture the citadel. He was driven to besiege it.   He employed vineæ and mines ; but both were met by bulwarks and counter-mines by the garrison.   Every effort he could make seemed to be set at naught by the excellent situation of the place.   Leaving a portion of his troops to hold the lines of circumvallation he had made so as to keep it blockaded, he withdrew with the others to Capua, where he prepared to go into winter-quarters for the winter of B. C., 216–215.   From Capua he controlled the south side of the river.

On finding that the Carthaginians had surrounded Casilinum with works, and that the blockade was not readily to be broken, M. Junius returned to Teanum. Marcellus appears to have remained in his camp on the hills back of Suessula.

During the year B. C. 216 the two Scipios made still further progress in Spain. They badly defeated Hanno and Hasdrubal Barca, and drove them back of the Ebro. This not only seriously cooled the ardor of the Spanish allies of Carthage, but the situation in Iberia was made a pretext by the Hanno party in Carthage to prevent the sending of reinforcements to Hannibal. In the effervescence produced by Cannæ, Hasdrubal had received orders to march to Italy to join Hannibal, and Himilco had been sent to Spain to succeed him; but the defeat of his army by the Scipios, which occurred in the attempt to carry out his orders, and the consequent desertion of his Spanish allied troops, so entirely crippled him in strength that the programme could not be carried out. The Scipios commanded the sea, the Pyrenees and the Ebro, and through the Massiliots, Gaul. Spain was severed from Italy. Thus Hannibal was left to his own resources.

All this was fatal to success in Italy. Sicily was kept under Roman alliance or control; but Sardinia revolted. And we have seen that the prætor and consul-elect, Posthumius, in the course of this year, was ambushed and killed, and his army utterly destroyed by the Boii in cisalpine Gaul. Under these conditions all northern Italy was ripe for a fresh rebellion. Even small forces under experienced Carthaginian officers might have not only seized Sardinia and Corsica, but again raised all Gaul into active hostility, a condition which would have been of vast assistance to Hannibal, and might have eventuated in inducing the Etruscans and Umbrians to join the coalition against Rome. Such a situation would have been a brilliant one for the Carthaginians. But the management of armies by politicians is as old as the world, and fraught with failure. While the soldier must always be the servant of the statesman, it behooves the statesman to study well into the requirements of the military problem. Spain was no doubt important; but it could not weigh in the balance against the campaign in Italy. Success here secured Spain; success in Spain might not affect the general result.

Towards the end of the winter, Casilinum was beginning to be much reduced by famine. Many men cast themselves from the walls, and others courted death by exposing themselves on the walls to escape the pangs of hunger. M. Junius had been called to Rome. His magister equitum, Sempronius, at Teanum, whom he had forbidden to engage in battle with Hannibal, was afraid to bring the garrison relief. But holding the upper river, he was able to send down by night casks filled with provisions, which the garrison intercepted. This continued until the Carthaginians discovered the trick. Then he floated down the stream huge quantities of nuts, which were caught by screens. At the other end of the line Marcellus kept close in his camp commanding Nola, its inhabitants fearing an attack by Capua, in case his army should leave, nor took any steps to act in concert with the army of the dictator. Under these circumstances, and being reduced down to eating the leather thongs from off their shields and equipments, mice and such roots as they could dig, the garrison of Casilinum was obliged to treat with Hannibal, who finally saw fit to accept its capitulation at a ransom of seven ounces of gold per man, and allowed it to depart to Cumæ on payment of the sum. This brought to an end a difficult operation and put into Hannibal's hands a valuable town, for Casilinum, situated astride of the Vulturnus, controlled the most essential bridge of the vicinity, over which passed the Appian Way. After its capture, Hannibal turned it over to the Capuans, but placed a Carthaginian garrison of seven hundred men in it, and made it an outpost to Capua, on the road to Rome.

Soldier's Cloak.

XXX.

CAMPANIA. 215 B. C.

" THE debauch of Capua " is purely hypothetical. It is true that up to the winter of 216–215 B. C. Hannibal won great victories, that afterwards he won fewer; but it had nothing to do with Capua. That Hannibal's army lost fighting capacity was due to two causes: the disappearance of his veterans, who were replaced by a poor element, and the fact that the Roman gain in skill and quality reduced Hannibal's status proportionately. That he assumed a defensive rôle was due to the political conditions and to his numerical weakness; to the fact, moreover, that the Romans now refrained from accepting battle, conscious of Hannibal's ability, and worked on the theory of tiring him out by a systematic small-war, — in other words, of starving him out of Italy. The Carthaginian army was between forty and fifty thousand strong. The Romans had this year one hundred and forty thousand men under the colors, of whom eighty thousand faced Hannibal, not counting garrisons. Capua induced Hannibal to remain in Campania, where, too, he still desired to make a base by securing a good seaport. The Capuans endeavored to aid in the scheme, but their efforts were weak. Meanwhile Hanno, in Lucania, was badly defeated; and Marcellus raided into Samnium among the new Punic allies. On the other hand, a small reinforcement from Carthage reached Hannibal. Making a second attempt on Nola, he was again thrust back, much as before, but the ensuing battle was drawn. Finally Hannibal retired to Apulia to winter. In Spain the Scipios once more beat Hasdrubal, and prevented his bringing aid to Italy; and the home senate gave Hannibal no further support.

THAT history repeats itself is true in more than one sense. A statement made by one historian is apt to get carried down the course of ages by mere repetition, without examination of its truth or falsity. It was said by Livy that the laxity of discipline in winter-quarters at Capua in B. C. 216–215 was the means of so entirely weakening the morale of Hannibal's army that thenceforth it was no longer able to win the great victories of yore. But this is not true.

"The debauch of Capua" is purely hypothetical. Hannibal's army, for a dozen years more, on Livy's own showing, continued to be the terror of Rome, all of whose generals and armies were in the highest degree shy of attacking it. The pride of the Romans had been so lowered by the Carthaginian successes that one can scarcely blame Livy for the hard things he has said of Hannibal. The winter-quarters at Capua may have been characterized by conduct very natural as a relief from the severity of the three years' strain of incessant campaigning, which had entailed trial, fatigue, hunger, exposure, danger and deprivation such as few armies ever undergo. It would have been strange if such had not been the case. But the army was not essentially weakened by its Capuan winter. So good a disciplinarian as Hannibal must have guarded against this. We have abundant proof of his exceptional ability in organization, and the facts prove that the army, after this winter in Capua, was practically in as good condition as before. It would be astonishing if winter-quarters in a gay city like Capua should not in some measure affect the discipline of an army which for several years had camped in the open field; but the injury was not permanent.

Hannibal had doubtless lost in fighting ability, but it was in one sense a proportionate loss only, for the Romans were growing in ability to manœuvre as well as fight; and so far as actual loss of fighting ability is concerned, it came from the disappearance of his veteran element, — of the larger part of the men who had come with him across the Alps, and from the necessity under which he stood of placing in their stead any and all sorts of material ready to his hand, no part of which could in any manner compare with even the raw levies of Rome.

That Hannibal's star from this year on seemed to pale;

that he seemed henceforth to resist defeat rather than win another succession of victories like the Trebia, Trasimene and Cannæ, is due more to the fact that other men than Sempronius, Flaminius and Varro were put into the field to lead the Roman troops; that the Romans were gradually learning the trade of war, and that Hannibal was outnumbered much more than he had previously been; in other words, that the Romans themselves had been taught a series of lessons from which they were beginning to profit.

And it must not be forgotten that Hannibal's problem, after Cannæ, was completely changed. We shall see how and why he shifted from the sharp offensive to a purely defensive rôle. It was not because his army had been debauched by Capuan orgies.

The defeat at Cannæ had borne the best of fruit to the Romans. Such a lesson, hard as it was, had been necessary to rouse that in the nation which always came out in times of grave political peril and rehabilitated the fortunes of the city. They had learned not only that they must put aside their internal quarrels and join hands in the common effort, but they saw that in pure, open warfare they had no one who could match Hannibal. They had learned that in the long run, with a mixture of Fabian and aggressive policy, they would certainly exhaust his resources and beat him. They had seen the folly of Varro, the wisdom of Fabius, the boldness of Marcellus'; to this they added the ever-present Roman courage, discipline and fidelity; and they knew that the Roman organization was more durable than any which Hannibal could maintain on Italian soil.

The war had begun as an offensive one on the part of Hannibal, and had been met with a defensive — into which they had been forced against their normal habit — by the Romans. From now on, each party waged the war on what is called an offensive-defensive plan. Great battles in the open field gave way to camps strongly fortified in naturally good strategic centres, to manœuvring on the communications or about the flanks of the enemy, to an intelligent effort to seize upon important points. And when combats and battles came about, they were not called forth by a mere desire to win victories or to destroy armies, but by the desire to obtain a better defined advantage in a strategic sense. All this makes the last twelve years of the war of much greater interest to the student, though to the casual reader less brilliant, than the first few years. Hannibal's genius shines forth in threefold effulgence from this time on.

The loss of the army sent in 216 B. C. to cisalpine Gaul, already referred to, occurred after this fashion. Posthumius was marching through a wood, where the Gauls had laid an ambush for him. They had sawed a large number of trees nearly through, so that by a slight shock they would go down like a row of dominoes. Entering the wood, Posthumius and his twenty-five thousand men were caught in this snare, and either crushed to death or killed by the ambushed Gauls. The stratagem was ably conceived and executed, and the barbarians had relied on the well-known carelessness of the Roman armies on the march.

After the news of this defeat had been received, it was resolved by the Roman senate to give up any attempt for this year to carry on war in cisalpine Gaul, but merely to keep an observation army there.

Rome had her full share of troubles. The pro-prætors, Otacilius from Sicily, and Cornelius Mammula from Sardinia, complained of want of funds to pay and corn to feed their troops. But opportune succor was forthcoming. Fortune aided Rome as she aided herself. Hiero of Syracuse helped Otacilius, and the population of Sardinia put Cornelius Mammula out of his difficulties.

One of the consuls of the succeeding year, B. C. 215, was Posthumius. On his death he was succeeded by Marcellus, who declined on account of omens, and then by Fabius, the old dictator. His colleague was Tiberius Sempronius Gracchus. Rome made an extraordinary effort to place a force and generals a-field able in some sense to cope with Hannibal. Defeat and disaster had been harsh, but admirable teachers. Varro and Cannæ was the last bad error of Rome. Wisdom and strength now came to the fore, showing up doubly marked against the querulous and weak conduct of the Carthaginian senate. And fortune after Cannæ leaned towards her. The three army-commanders who opposed Hannibal were tried men: Marcellus, proconsul, and Fabius and Sempronius, consuls.

After some preliminary changes, followed by the casting of lots for the legions, to Fabius was given the command of the army, now at Cales, which had been under the late dictator at Teanum, and which consisted of two Roman legions with the usual complement of other troops; to Gracchus' lot fell that of the levies of volunteer slaves, and twenty-five thousand allies, says Livy. He assembled at Sinuessa, from which place he advanced to Liternum to protect Cumæ and Neapolis. Marcellus, as proconsul, retained the command of two legions at his eyrie back of Suessula, overlooking and protecting Nola. All the Cannæ fugitives were sent to Sicily for service, as a punishment for breaking their oath in that battle; these were joined by the less good material from Junius' army; and the two legions which had been in Sicily were brought back to Rome. Otacilius commanded the fleet in Sicily.

The Roman senate thus made good its threat to punish those who at Cannæ had failed to do their duty. The knights were dismounted and sent as foot to serve in various parts of Italy, and other degradations, including loss of pay, followed.

Varro was the sole and only exception. One is fain to feel that Varro was the most guilty of all the soldiers who escaped from this disastrous field. But the manifest fact that the senate honored him on his return, for that he had not despaired of the republic, and that they now exempted him from penalties, — and the Roman senate, despite the bitterness of politics, was a body of men whose superior has rarely been seen in history, — seems to indicate that there were excuses for his conduct which we do not now understand, and which the historians do not give us.

Marcus Valerius, the prætor, was ordered to the command of Varro's late legions in Apulia, and with the legions which returned from Sicily and twenty-five ships, was to protect the lower coast about Tarentum and Brundisium. There were also given the prætor Fulvius twenty-five ships to protect the coast near Rome. There were two legions in Sicily, — the Cannæ survivors, — one in Sardinia, one in Tarentum and two in Spain. This made a force of eight legions to oppose Hannibal, and six on outside operations, a total, including the excess of Gracchus, of over one hundred and fifty thousand men. Though the army destroyed in cisalpine Gaul was not replaced, Varro was sent to Picenum to head off any reinforcements which might come thence to Hannibal by way of the coast, Picenum being Varro's native province.

Imports and taxes were doubled to pay for these troops and material. A small-war by the Italian cities which remained faithful to Rome was organized against their deserting brethren. In Apulia, Brundisium, Luceria and Venusia; in Lucania, Pæstum; in Samnium, Beneventum, were Roman strongholds in the midst of these revolted provinces; and Cumæ and Neapolis remained true.

The plan of the Roman senate was to surround and watch Hannibal on all sides. It would not again stake its all on one cast. The defeat of a single army should not again bring the republic to the verge of ruin. A policy of counteracting what Hannibal had accomplished in acquiring control of so many Italian cities, it was thought would still further weaken him. This system was certainly not in accord with what might be called brilliant grand-strategy; for once Rome had found more than her match; but it was well adapted to the singular conditions under which Rome was struggling against her dangerous opponent, and worked well in the long run.

The force which Hannibal could command can only be estimated. The substantial Carthaginian reinforcements intended for him were diverted to other purposes. Mago was sent to Spain and Hasdrubal to Sardinia with what had been originally voted, and should certainly have been sent to Hannibal. After Cannæ there remained some thirty-four thousand infantry and nine thousand horse. Of this force, two divisions — how strong we do not know — were detached to Bruttium and Lucania, and these had much pains in holding head against the three Roman legions of Apulia and the partisans of the Italian cities. The meagre reinforcements which eventually reached him were only in cavalry and elephants. Hannibal, to offset this, had recruited a goodly number of men in Samnium and the Capuan territory. This had given him a considerable numerical force, but not of the quality of his daily dwindling veterans. It is not improbable that the detachments he had to make were offset by these levies, and that he had immediately under him thirty-five thousand foot and ten thousand cavalry, or perhaps as much as fifty thousand effective. For a man like Hannibal this was still a respectable army. But he had a vast work to do with this limited force.

From abroad he received some encouragement. Philip,

King of Macedon, under an arrangement with Carthage, sent him ambassadors, who, on the plea of a mission to Rome, managed to reach his headquarters, and concluded with the Carthaginians an alliance offensive and defensive, which was to include the landing of a Macedonian army in Italy. Hannibal had reason to hope that Tarentum, where he had many friends, would finally fall into his hands and thus give him the much desired important seaport, by which relations with Carthage and Macedon could be maintained. Carthage had likewise made an alliance with Hieronymus, the new king of Syracuse, from which Hannibal hoped for some advantageous results.

Forces in Campania, 215 B. C.

So soon as the season opened, Hannibal took up a position and intrenched on Mt. Tifata, a height commanding Capua. Over seventy-five thousand men at Cales, Sinuessa and Liternum, and Nola surrounded him. But his position was strong and central, and controlled the entrance to valleys where he could pasture his herds, and which furnished excellent and healthful camps for his men. He decided not to undertake the offensive, but awaited events, ready to act in whatever direction he might be called, preferring to lie in wait for some error on the part of the Roman generals of which he could take advantage, than to initiate operations. He was counting on Macedon, help from home, and additional allies in Italy. He could not force the fighting; he had not men enough; he must wait for openings, not create them. The Roman armies were all strongly intrenched. He had been compelled to turn over a new leaf.

Neither party moved. Hannibal busied himself with negotiations. Fabius clung to his old tactics of harassing the enemy, and interfering with his foraging, but without risking anything which might bring on a decisive conflict. The other generals bided their time. No attack on Hannibal was attempted. Nothing is more interesting than the manner in which this extraordinary man's personality imposed upon his adversaries. Even those who least lacked ability and aggressiveness were unwilling to meet him on equal terms. The scrupulous care they constantly exercised to keep well away from a battle in the open is a wonderful tribute to the skill and fighting capacity of this captain. And this wariness lasted till the end.

The Roman senate, among its other laws passed for this occasion, and in order to prevent Hannibal from victualing his troops, decreed that the inhabitants of the district where the rival armies were manœuvring should harvest the early crops, and carry the grain to the fortified towns before summer opened, under pain of having their homes devastated and being themselves sold into slavery. Everything was done to hamper Hannibal's movements, to neutralize his capacity for assuming the offensive. But no step was taken towards driving him from the land by force of arms. This was too big a task.

One of the early events of the new campaign was an attempt by the Capuans to seize upon Cumæ, whose citizens they had vainly sought to engage in revolt against Rome. Unable to make headway by such means, they resorted to the stratagem of inviting the leading nobles and officials to a conference at Hamæ, where there was a solemn sacrifice at this time, intending to seize upon the city during the solemnities. The Cumæans suspected something of this kind, and informed Gracchus of the facts. This officer had recently moved from Sinuessa to Liternum, on the coast above Cumæ. The Capuans had put fourteen thousand men in hiding near Hamæ, which was about three miles from Cumæ, with orders, after midnight, when the celebration should be at its height, to fall upon and seize Cumæ. But the scheme did not prosper. Gracchus arrived at the camp of the Capuan detachment before they set out, and falling unawares upon the force, cut out and killed some two thousand men of them, with a loss to himself of but one hundred; plundered their camp, and himself quickly occupied Cumæ, lest Hannibal, who was near by, on Mt. Tifata, should move out against him at Hamæ, which was an open place. In fact, Hannibal sought to do this very thing, hoping to catch Gracchus unawares; but reached Hamæ to find the Romans gone.

On the following day, Hannibal appeared again before Cumæ, and blockaded the place. As he had been unable to get Neapolis, he would have much liked Cumæ as a seaport. Both parties prepared for vigorous work. A tower was erected by Hannibal from which to mount the wall, and a corresponding one by Gracchus to defend it. Gracchus was fortunate enough to succeed in setting fire to the Carthaginian tower, and, in the flurry connected with this incident, made so sharp a sortie as to inflict, says Livy, a loss of thirteen hundred men killed and fifty-nine prisoners on the besiegers. Hannibal next day essayed to draw Gracchus out to fight in the open, but the wily Roman was not to be taken at a disadvantage, and the Carthaginian was fain to retire to his mountain stronghold, neither he nor his allies, the Capuans, having accomplished their purpose. Hannibal's poor success with nearly all his sieges in Italy shows that he was illy equipped for this work, and, like Frederick, he had perhaps not the patience, nor the aptitude for engineering which he possessed for every other branch of the military art. Fabius at Cales was detained by bad omens from helping Gracchus. " Nor," says Livy, " dared the other consul, Fabius, who was encamped at Cales, lead his troops across the Vulturnus, being employed in taking new auspices." This was Fabian tactics with a vengeance, when he had the chance of falling on Hannibal's flank at Cumæ.

This was not the only disappointment of these times. Hannibal was henceforth destined to possess his soul in patience under many a hard blow of fortune. His lieutenant, Hanno, met Sempronius Longus, a legate of Marcellus, at Grumentum in Lucania, and suffered a galling defeat and a loss of two thousand men, beating a hasty retreat to Bruttium. And Valerius made an inroad from Luceria into the Hirpinian domain about Beneventum, took three cities and one thousand prisoners, punished with death some of Hannibal's chief allies, and made good his retreat. This year was a sad one for Carthaginian luck.

Fabius finally got his auspices fixed, and was ready to advance beyond Cales with the purpose of joining hands with Marcellus and Gracchus, in the vicinity of Suessula. As Hannibal held Casilinum, he followed the same route as Marcellus, passed the Vulturnus near Caiatia, and under cover of the hills, well back of Mt. Tifata, marched towards the proconsul unopposed. In coöperation with Gracchus, he took several towns (Compulteria, Trebula, and Saticula) which had admitted Carthaginian garrisons, made many prisoners, and punished the leaders of the Hannibal party. Nola having still a very considerable popular party which favored Hannibal, Fabius sent Marcellus back to that city, of which he had some fears, while he himself took possession of Marcellus' camp on the heights. It is not, however, probable that cautious Fabius was guilty of such an act of foolhardiness as to march his army between Capua and Mt. Tifata, where Hannibal lay encamped, as Livy relates, especially when there was nothing to be gained by it.

Gracchus, from his camp at Cumæ, at the same time made an advance towards Capua, which brought the three Roman armies near enough to mutually sustain each other. Hannibal was practically hemmed in and robbed of his ability to act in Campania, by this large Roman force so systematically distributed. There was no army between him and Rome, but the reasons for his not marching on the capital we already know. Each Roman army lay in its intrenched camp or walled city, showing no inclination to fight; and it must be borne in mind that a battle could not be forced against a camp any more than against a fortress. Very exceptional circumstances only brought about the attack of a camp. Hannibal could not afford to assault either without a special gain in so doing. In the open country he would not have hesitated a moment to attack the total forces if he had room to manœuvre. But the Fabian tactics were bearing fruit. The Romans preferred to wear Hannibal out by safer operations than fighting. They were holding the bulk of the Campanian plain against him. The three armies knew that sooner or later hunger would drive him away, and leave

Capua to their mercy. They were covering the country on which he must rely for bread.

Hannibal's position had many difficulties. He could not desert Capua. This important ally must not be left to the mercy of Rome. But he had watched over the city until it had been able to harvest the crops ; it was strongly fortified, and he hoped would be able to hold its own, — at least for a while. He desired to aid his friends in Nola by advancing towards that town. Certain Carthaginian reinforcements of cavalry and elephants, under Bomilcar, had reached Locri in Bruttium, and Hannibal feared they might be intercepted by Fabius, as Appius Claudius, from Sicily, had vainly attempted to do. A multitude of cares called for his attention. He was in demand everywhere. The enemy could afford a policy of inaction, albeit with abundant means to carry on a vigorous campaign ; not so he, though he had but a fraction of what was essential to do his work. He must constantly keep in action. For want of success was starvation to this bold intruder on the territory of Rome.

Marcellus, from Nola, in connection with the prætorian army under M. Valerius, at Luceria, had made some raids into the land of the Hirpinians, Lucanians, and Caudine Samnites, and had played Hannibal's own game at devastation by fire and sword. These poor peoples, between the upper and nether millstone, cried for help to their new ally. Hannibal, to withdraw Marcellus from his quarry, left his fastness on Mt. Tifata well garrisoned, and marched on Nola, hoping to take by escalade this to him important town. But Marcellus, who was both intrepid and vigilant, had already returned and was ready to meet him. Marcellus was as cautious as Fabius, while not afraid of a sharp offensive. In the raids he had made we are told that he systematically reconnoitred his ground and carefully secured his retreat. He had acted in Hannibal's absence as if his enemy were near at hand. He had profited by the misfortunes of his predecessors in command.

Near Nola, Hanno joined his chief with a part of the four thousand recruits and elephants from Carthage, — a much needed reinforcement, and one which, however small, sensibly cheered the veterans of the harassed Punic army.

Hannibal first tried to gain Nola by treachery, but failed. This town seemed to be a stumbling-block to him. As on the first occasion, when he advanced to the assault, expecting nothing less than the repetition of the counter-attack of some months previous, Marcellus, watching the opportune moment, rushed from the gates with such vehemence that he drove in the head of Hannibal's column at the first shock. Hannibal got the men, however, speedily in hand. The fight was sharp but undecided. A heavy thunder-storm put an end to it this day, and Hannibal sat down before the town.

Three days after, when a strong party of foragers — a considerable part of the whole army — had gone out from the

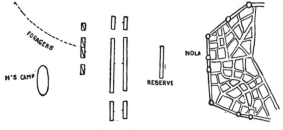

Second Battle of Nola.

Carthaginian camp, Marcellus seized this opportunity of depletion to the enemy's ranks to draw up in battle array outside the town and offered battle. Nothing loath, though not

in force, Hannibal accepted the gage. The distance between
the town and Hannibal's camp was about a mile. In this
space the forces met. Marcellus had armed the citizens of
Nola, and held them in reserve, — a novel thing with a Roman general, for the triarii and extraordinarii were as a rule
the only reserve to the legion; the Carthaginian foragers, attracted by the tumult, returned in season to act as reserve to
Hannibal. The Romans opened the battle by their usual attack, made with great vigor, under Marcellus' inspiring conduct. Equally stanch was Hannibal's defense. The battle
hung in the balance many hours; the fighting was stubborn
and bloody, but apparently without any manœuvring. Finally
Roman discipline asserted itself. That the Roman soldier was
much better than any but the few veterans of Hannibal is
well shown by the victories he won so soon as he got good
generals. The flat ground was not such as to enable Hannibal to take any advantage of stratagem. He was driven
back to his camp — according to Livy — with a loss of five
thousand men killed, six hundred prisoners, six elephants,
and nineteen standards. Marcellus withdrew into Nola,
claiming a loss of but one thousand men. The looseness of
Livy's entire narrative makes one the more regret the loss of
Polybius' books which treated of this subject. Great credit
is due Marcellus for this day's operations. Next day, under
a tacit truce, each party buried its dead.

Thus Livy. But his account, properly summed up, looks
more like a drawn battle than the doubtless overstated Carthaginian casualties warrant. If Hannibal retired to his
camp, so did Marcellus to Nola. If Marcellus had won so
marked a victory, how did Hannibal save his army in a perfectly flat plain? Why should there have been a " tacit
truce " to bury the dead, when Marcellus had control of the
field of battle? That Hannibal did not win a victory seems

certain, for the proconsul held Nola. That Marcellus won one is, to say the least, doubtful. All the statements of Livy, weighed together, point clearly to a drawn battle. None the less credit is due to the Roman soldier; none the less had Marcellus shown that so far he was the best Roman general of this war. But his retirement to Nola, where he remained and did not interfere with Hannibal's further movements, militates absolutely against Livy's would-be claim of a great Roman victory. Hannibal returned to Mt. Tifata.

Three days after, a body of twelve hundred and seventy-two of his new troops — Spanish and Numidian horse — deserted to the Romans, in whose service they remained throughout the war. This was indeed a hard blow. Happily they were not his veteran troopers. This is the only instance of any but isolated desertion from his ranks.

Fearing that this second failure at Nola might have a bad effect upon his army, Hannibal abandoned his camp on Mt. Tifata and marched for Apulia, where he took up winter-quarters in the vicinity of Arpi. He had been probably accumulating provisions with this object in view, since the call upon him by the Hirpini and Samnites.

Hanno was sent back to Bruttium with the troops he had brought.

It is entirely natural that during the period of Hannibal's success the Romans should have been reluctant to attack him on the march. It was too uncertain a problem. Now that they had found that even he was not invulnerable, it is a curious tribute to Hannibal's ability that, despite their numbers, they never sought to disturb his movements. They limited themselves strictly to following him up and seeking to prevent, so far as in them lay, his securing too large a territory to plunder. They never dared assume the offensive against him in the open field. And now when Gracchus fol-

lowed Hannibal to Luceria with his army, he contented himself with watching him. Fabius remained at Suessula, which
he was able to revictual fully, and strengthening the intrenchments and leaving a large body there, advanced
towards Capua and began to ravage its territory. The
Capuans could oppose him only by partisan warfare, having
no regular troops, but their irregular horse stood them in
good stead. They fortified a camp outside the town and
placed in it six thousand of their foot. Fabius allowed the
Capuans to sow their late crop of grain, in fact retiring to
allow them to do so, and when it ripened reaped and con-
veyed it to Suessula, returning to which place, he went into
winter-quarters. Marcellus, leaving only the necessary garrison at Nola, was instructed by Fabius to send the rest of his
troops to Rome, where it was easier to winter them. Fabius
fortified and garrisoned Puteoli, near Neapolis, which was the
centre of a great wheat traffic.

During this winter there was a constant exchange of combats between Romans and Carthaginians in Apulia. When
Hannibal was not personally present, the Romans generally
had the advantage. These wonderful soldiers were gradually
learning the ways of their foes and regaining confidence in
themselves.

In Bruttium, Petelia resisted eight months all the efforts of
Himilco. When it fell, it carried with it Consentia, Locri,
and, after a fierce resistance, Crotona. Rhegium remained
faithful to Rome. The Bruttians were strongly wedded to
the cause of Hannibal, but individual cities still held out.

The Scipios in Spain, despite lack of money, clothing and
corn, had followed up their successes during the year B. C.
215, had been well sustained by the Roman senate, had advanced from the Ebro to the Guadalquivir and had beaten
the Carthaginians in two pitched battles, with a loss of thirty

thousand killed, six thousand prisoners, ten elephants and one hundred and one standards.

In Sardinia, the Roman arms were crowned with success. Mago, Hannibal's brother, had just got ready to put to sea from Carthage with fifty ships to join the Carthaginians in Bruttium. He had twelve thousand foot, fifteen hundred horse, twenty elephants, and one thousand talents of silver. But at the last moment Sardinia begged assistance from the Carthaginian senate. Mago was therefore sent to Spain, and some Spanish forces under Hasdrubal to Sardinia, which it was thought would be an intermediate point between Spain and Italy, valuable to the cause in every sense. This was true, but the Carthaginian senate was none the less frittering away its resources. The Carthaginians had no success in Sardinia. Manlius Torquatus, with twenty-three thousand men, was too much of a match for them. In two battles he utterly overthrew them, with five thousand men killed and captured, and again subjugated the island. The Carthaginians retired to Iberia. Their men and means were wasted.

Otacilius had won a naval victory over a Carthaginian squadron, but had not succeeded in heading off Bomilcar, who managed to land his troops and money at Locri, and report to Hanno. This petty reinforcement, while of value as far as it went, was of a piece with the shortsightedness of the Punic government.

As a last ounce, the Macedonian ambassadors, returning home from making their treaty with Hannibal, had been taken prisoners by a Roman ship and sent to Rome. The information thus seized enabled the senate to provide for the possible danger from this source. A fleet was sent to Brundisium under the prætor Valerius, who from that port was to raise among the Greeks, if possible, a coalition against Macedonia.

Thus unsupported by his home resources and unable to lure the Romans into battle in the field, Hannibal was gradually but surely losing ground. The fortunes of the war seemed to be going over to the Romans. This was naturally the result of their improved management, and was the due reward of the manfulness of their conduct during the disasters of the first years. The improvement in the fortunes of Rome was, however, less marked in its campaigns against Hannibal than in Spain and Sardinia and at sea.

More strongly in favor of Roman success than anything which the Romans themselves could do, was the despicable policy of the Carthaginian senate. Hannibal had begun his Italian campaign by establishing a base on the Po, where he could receive, and had a right to expect, support from Spain on his right and from Macedon on his left. The chances and demands of the war had led him to a series of brilliant marches and strategic manœuvres, which had carried him to the south of Italy. Here he had established a new base, and he had still more right to expect that his Macedonian allies would now sustain his right, as they could more readily do, and the home government his left. What he had accomplished had been in absolute accord with his original plans. He had been disappointed only in the lack of Italian support and in affairs in Spain.

If we can imagine concord sufficient in the Carthaginian senate to send Hannibal reinforcements to southern Italy, where they might readily land at Locri or Crotona, — for Syracuse was now open to the Carthaginians, and the Roman fleet at Brundisium was held in check by the Macedonians; if we can imagine a descent in force on the Italian coast by Philip; these might, if anything could, have turned the scales of disaster against Rome. These things could have been better done immediately after Cannæ than at any later period.

Hannibal was then at the height of his repute. Only his weakness in men encouraged his opponents to measure swords with him. With such reinforcements as he had counted on, as he was entitled, from his brilliant successes, to expect and demand, Hannibal's campaign could scarcely have been a failure. But while Hannibal was a consummate statesman, he was no politician. He had been brought up in camps. He had no popular leader at home to represent him. The Hanno, or peace party, was uppermost in Carthage, and Hannibal was left to his own resources, and to such fortune as his own unaided genius might compel.

The general scheme of Rome was a defensive one. She must hold the Pyrenees, which her excellent generals in Spain enabled her to do. This forestalled any new descent on the Padane region. She must head off the Macedonian army and prevent its reaching Italy. This danger was ably provided against by Valerius. She must keep up communications with Sicily, for which purpose Messana was the key-point. She must, by constant activity and courage, prevent Hannibal from gaining any more headway. In all these things, aided by the fatuity of the Carthaginian senate, she was measurably successful. The position of Hasdrubal after the defeat on the Ebro was critical. Carthage looked at Spain, not as a means, but as an end, forgetful that unless Rome was defeated at home, Spain would always be held on an uncertain tenure, and diverted the promised help from the Italian to the Iberian peninsula. The Macedonian alliance proved useless; and Rome held Brundisium by land and sea. The Cannæ legions, banished to Sicily, held head against the Syracusans and Carthaginians in the north and east of the island. The considerable forces raised by Carthage in the happy effervescence of Cannæ were frittered away. Hannibal was left alone.

If there was in Rome at the end of this year any one of sufficient foresight and coolness to properly gauge the situation, he could well call the crisis past. Rome was saved. A little more perseverance and the end would come. But Hannibal yet sorely tried their patience.

Signum.

XXXI.

MAKING A NEW BASE. 214 B. C.

THIS year Rome had two hundred thousand men afield. Of this force, four armies, of over twenty thousand men each, were to oppose Hannibal. The Roman plan was the same as last year, but the capture of Capua was projected. Hannibal was obliged to resort to a pure defensive, a rôle which he carried through with wonderful aptness, in marked contrast to his former bold offensive. He was narrowed to the South Italian provinces, but here he held full sway, excepting only Roman fortresses. Capua saw that the consuls were threatening her. She called on Hannibal for help, who left Arpi and marching around the armies in his front, made for Campania. The consuls remained quiet. Hannibal tried to seize on Cumæ, Puteoli or Neapolis as a seaport, but failed. He might have captured either by a siege ; but siege-operations were not his forte. He tried once more to get hold of Nola, but once more Marcellus checked him. Hanno, seeking to join his chief, was stopped at Beneventum and defeated by Gracchus with total loss of his army. Hannibal left Campania, having helped the Capuans to harvest their crops. He had hope of capturing Tarentum, from which city he had received advances, but he reached it three days after its garrison had been reinforced by the Romans from Brundisium. So soon as he left Campania the consuls laid siege to and captured Casilinum, as a first step to attacking Capua, and later ravaged Samnium, and punished all Hannibal's adherents in the cities they could capture. The Romans had made a marked gain this year.

FABIUS for the fourth time, and Marcellus for the third time, were elected the consuls of B. C. 214, the fifth year of the war, and as prætors Fulvius, Otacilius, Fabius, son of the consul, and Lentulus. Rome made still greater exertions than in the preceding year, and placed no less than twenty legions, (that is, twenty Roman and twenty allied), or over two hundred thousand men in all, in the field. They began to see that patience under reverses, and a careful study into the causes of their failures, could accomplish better results than mere brute force. But they kept an abundant force afoot.

In Sicily, the Carthaginians were wasting material which might be of unbounded use to Hannibal. The senate could not see that a peace dictated at the gates of Rome was the only comprehensive or lasting one. The Romans had in the island two legions under Lentulus, and the same force under Q. Mucius in Sardinia, and under Manius Pomponius in cis-alpine Gaul, which, added to the army of Spain, made eighty thousand men in all. When spring opened, the troops left winter-quarters. Fabius had two legions of new levies which had rendezvoused at Cales. Marcellus took command at Suessula with two. Gracchus at Luceria, opposite Hannibal, had two volunteer-slave legions, and backed on Beneventum. The prætor Fabius, in Apulia, had two. Two were in garrison in Rome. Varro, in Picenum, had one, which lay, as it were, in reserve to the two in Gaul. Valerius at Brundisium had one. Otacilius commanded the fleet, and one hundred new ships were built, — making one hundred and fifty in all. The fleet was manned by a direct tax on the wealthy of so many sailors each for so many thousand asses of property.

Of the above twenty legions, fourteen were old; six new ones were raised. This enormous force, of which about one third were new men and one half were Roman citizens, was, directly and indirectly, what Hannibal had to contend with. Nor did it comprise the garrisons in the Roman oppida. The theory of the war continued the same, — to surround the Carthaginian with several armies, to harass and tire him out with small-war, but never, except when the chances were all in their favor, to fight a general battle. Four Roman armies were arrayed in the field immediately against Hannibal: Fabius at Cales, Marcellus at Suessula, Gracchus at Luceria, young Fabius in Apulia. This drew a line which held him to southern Italy, but within this line, excepting only the Roman oppida, he had full sway. While two or more of these armies should watch his movements, the other forces would

Armies opposite Hannibal, B. C. 214.

attack his lieutenants or allied cities. Was ever invader so overmatched?

Hannibal was at Arpi, where he had wintered. Hanno lay in Bruttium, whose ports, except Rhegium, which was protected by Messana, were in Carthaginian hands. No army faced him.

In Campania, the Roman objective was the capture of Capua, the most important of Hannibal's allied cities, as it was the second city of the peninsula. The intention of the consuls was obvious.

The Capuans, alarmed at these extraordinary preparations in Campania, clearly aimed at them, sent word to Hannibal that he must at once come to their aid. Hannibal was in grave difficulty. He was called on to play a waiting game. Nothing but an army from Macedon, or Hasdrubal with troops from Spain, or heavy reinforcements from Carthage, could now enable him to do more than hold his own. Meanwhile, he must seek to keep his allies from getting disheart-

ened at the defensive rôle which was forced on him. He en-
acted his part with consummate ability. No one fathomed in
Hannibal any distrust in the future. "We hardly recognize,
in the obstinate defensive system which he now began, the
same general who had carried on the offensive with almost
unequaled impetuosity and boldness; it is marvelous in a psy-
chological as well as a military point of view, that the same
man should have accomplished the two tasks prescribed to
him — tasks so diametrically opposed in their character —
with equal completeness," says Mommsen. He had no less
than ninety thousand men directly opposed to him, whose special duty it was to hamper his movements. The Carthaginian
senate deemed it more essential to hold Spain and play with
Sardinia than to reinforce Hannibal, who was thus left to his
own resources of courage and patience to work out the problem he had undertaken. He had long been compelled to
narrow his field of operations to the provinces lying south
of the Vulturnus-Garganus line. While he was thus near
enough Carthage to be able to communicate with her, as well
as keep a constant pressure on Rome, he had lost his hold
on his original allies of the Po.

Capua's appeal was irresistible. In response to her cry
for help, Hannibal left Arpi at once, and moving boldly
around Gracchus' flank at Luceria, he gained the road to
Beneventum, and by forced marches, no doubt via Telesia
and Caiatia, reoccupied his old position on Mt. Tifata. That
none of the Roman armies deemed it prudent to interfere
with this march seems odd enough. It certainly shows that
Gracchus was wary of approaching him; and it shows either
that the two consuls were equally prudent, or that Hannibal
marched so rapidly as to keep ahead of the Roman messengers who were undoubtedly dispatched by Gracchus to his
chiefs. The latter is improbable. No army can march so
fast.

Arrived on the spot, Hannibal saw that there was no immediate preparation to besiege Capua. But once there, he
bethought him to try a diversion to unsettle the intention of

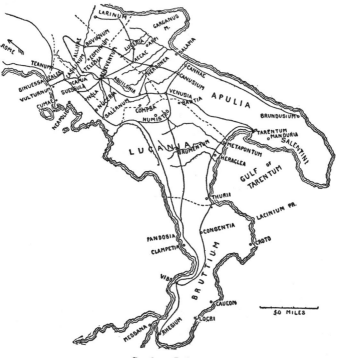

Southern Italy.

the consuls, and if possible seize on a seaport on the Campanian coast. Such a port all his efforts so far had failed to
get. Leaving his Spanish and Numidian forces in the camp
on Mt. Tifata, he marched straight across the country to the
Cumæ region, and established a secondary camp at Lake
Avernus, near this city. His purpose was to capture Puteoli,
near by. But Puteoli was too strongly garrisoned for a *coup
de main,* — it had stout walls and six thousand men, — so that
he was fain to content himself with devastating the adjacent

territory as far as Misenum promontory, and moved towards
Neapolis. Fabius, the consul, hearing that Hannibal was in
Campania, joined his army near Cales, to observe Casilinum
and Capua, and ordered Gracchus from Luceria to Beneventum, to be replaced by the army of the prætor Fabius.

Neapolis and Vicinity.

About this time Hannibal received a deputation from some
of the young nobles of Tarentum, offering to open the gates of
this town if he would come to that region. The offer was
tempting to the last degree, as Tarentum would furnish him
with a harbor of great value, either looking towards Carthage or Macedonia, and he determined to take advantage of
the proposal so soon as he could absent himself from Campania.

It was of the highest importance to Hannibal to make for
himself a solid base in Campania, where not only was his
most important ally, Capua, but which lay singularly well for
his purposes, with both the Via Appia and Via Latina leading direct to Rome. But Capua and Mt. Tifata alone could
not enable him to operate against Rome, when, as he still

anticipated, he should receive reinforcements from home or Macedonia, and should secure more of the Italian allies. For he had no near-by port of disembarkation. He must have either Neapolis or Cumæ, or both if possible, for this purpose. He moved to and fro over the vicinity, seeking an opportunity of gaining the one or other.

Just why Hannibal was so much opposed to sieges, it is hard to say; but to judge by the event, he distrusted his own powers in such efforts. Though part of his army was on Mt. Tifata, he could at this time have sat down before Cumæ, Puteoli or Naples with a fair show of success, and without running any graver risk than his general situation compelled, even if the Romans had attempted to raise the siege. There is something we are not told which is needed to explain this odd aversion to siege-work. That the towns were well walled and garrisoned by Roman soldiers is not a sufficient explanation. Still we must not forget the overwhelming forces surrounding him.

Hannibal's near approach to Nola, when he had reached the vicinity of Neapolis, induced his old friends, the commons, to invite him to renew an attempt on the city, assuring him of the present certainty of assistance from within. But Marcellus, who was Hannibal's black-bogy whenever Nola was the question, opportunely learned of this message from the Roman adherents in the city. He was at Cales in consultation with his colleague. The legions which had fallen to his lot had been wintering in the Claudian camp above Suessula. He hurried from Cales by the roads back of Mt. Tifata, and collecting a picked force of sixty-three hundred men, anticipated Hannibal in reaching Nola and checkmated the scheme. Hannibal had been slow, for he had little cause to place confidence in the Nolan people.

In order to further his project of making a good base of

operations in Campania, Hannibal ordered Hanno, who had
recruited his army up to seventeen thousand infantry and
twelve hundred Numidian horse, to leave Bruttium and join
him in the former province. Nola being on the direct road
and held by Marcellus, Hannibal advised his lieutenant to
march by way of Beneventum. As matters eventuated, it
would have been better for Hanno to march due north to
Nuceria, towards which point Hannibal could have moved
by his right to join him.

As we have seen, when Hannibal left Apulia, Fabius had
ordered Gracchus from Luceria on Beneventum, while Fabius
junior should take his place in his absence. This would have
been, if intended, a very neat strategic manœuvre by Fabius,
— and it has been so ascribed to him by more than one
critic, — for as Nola barred one of the roads to Hanno, so the
possession of Beneventum closed the other. But Fabius had
no idea of Hanno's projected advance. He had occupied
Beneventum as a strategic centre, and probably with the hope
of cooping Hannibal up in Campania, as on the last occasion
he had failed to do. He may have incidentally had in mind
the closing of the roads to reinforcements. But there is no
evidence of other foresight.

Hanno and Gracchus appear to have reached Beneventum
about the same time, but the proconsul got possession of the
city by the aid of its Roman garrison, and barred the way.
Hanno was unable to join his chief without a battle. The
Roman generals were ready enough to fight Hannibal's lieutenants ; but not so the great captain in person, who repeatedly marched past Beneventum in the teeth of Roman armies, without meeting an attack.

Hanno camped on the left bank of the Calor, some three
miles from the town. Gracchus moved up and camped within a mile of him. He had four legions, two of which were

composed entirely of those debtors and slaves to whom freedom had been promised if they won their first fight. Up
to this moment all had been waiting for the time to come

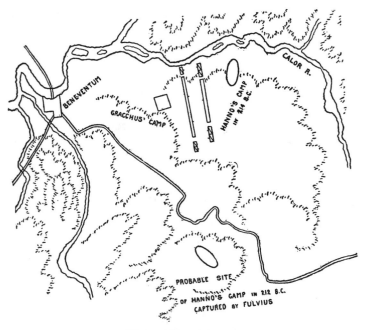

Hanno at Beneventum.

when the redeeming of the promise might be claimed; with
the consent of the senate and Marcellus the consul, Gracchus now definitely promised them immediate freedom if
they did their duty as they should in the approaching battle,
and "each brought him the head of an enemy." The legions, in great joy, assured him that their freedom would
surely be won.

Next day, Gracchus drew up his army in order of battle.
Hanno did the like. His seventeen thousand foot were
mostly recruited in Bruttium and Lucania. The bulk of his

twelve hundred horse was African. Both armies went into action confident of victory. The first shock was remarkably severe, and for several hours the event was doubtful. The slaves were so eager in cutting the heads off the killed and so hampered by many holding on to a head thus got, that they were jeopardizing the battle. Gracchus was obliged to send them word to fight instead of gathering the ghastly trophies, as they had already fairly earned their freedom. At the same time he ordered in his cavalry, until now held in reserve, on Hanno's flanks; but the Numidians fought with so much energy and skill that the fate of the battle seemed to hang on accident. Gracchus again sent round word through the legions that the freedom would not be granted, unless the enemy was speedily beaten. Thus encouraged, the legions made one supreme and desperate effort and drove the Carthaginians back to their camp, entering with them. A number of Roman prisoners in the Carthaginian camp having procured weapons and fallen upon the rear of Hanno's army, the Roman triumph became complete. Barely two thousand men and Hanno himself survived. The Roman loss was some two thousand men; thirty-eight standards were taken.

The well-earned freedom was given to the entire legions, as had been promised. But some four thousand of the men who had not proven themselves as brave as the majority, and had not penetrated the Carthaginian camp, though freed, were punished by being sentenced to eat their evening meal standing during the rest of their term of service. The morning meal, it will be remembered, was always eaten standing; the evening, and heartier one, sitting or reclining.

Gracchus was received at Beneventum, after the victory, with open arms, and his entire army feasted by the citizens. He then marched into Lucania, to prevent Hanno from raising another army there, and after some passages of arms, gradually forced him back to Bruttium.

Livy speaks of Fabius as being the moving spirit of this campaign, though he had but equal authority with his colleague. If he was, he deserves due credit for his intelligent action in bringing Gracchus to Beneventum. To Gracchus must be awarded equal credit for his bold attack on Hanno, for his good management of the battle, and for following him up as he did, to secure the full fruit of his victory.

This unhappy defeat robbed Hannibal of the assistance of his reinforcements, and put an end to any hope of present success in Campania. No such untoward event had as yet befallen him. He was unwilling to leave this province without one more essay on Nola, which, if he could take it, would offset almost any other loss. While Gracchus was campaigning in Lucania against Hanno, Hannibal, having eaten out the Neapolis territory, had broken camp and moved near Nola, camping on its west. Marcellus reinforced himself by bringing Pomponius, the pro-prætor, with the bulk of his forces from the Claudian camp above Suessula, and planned to give battle to Hannibal. He sent his legate, Claudius Nero, with a chosen body of horse, by a long circuit from the east gate, to attempt to fall on Hannibal's rear during the battle which he himself would provoke by attacking in front. On the next morning, he drew up his legions and attacked the Carthaginian army. For some hours the combat raged fiercely, but as Nero was not heard from, Marcellus deemed it wise to withdraw. He had lost four hundred men, and had inflicted a loss of two thousand men on Hannibal. Nero turned up later, alleging that he had lost his way and had not been able to find the enemy. Such are the facts stated by Livy.

It is well to examine these facts. Livy, construed by Livy, often yields light. He says that "the Romans had unquestionably the advantage, but as the cavalry did not come up in

time, the plan of the battle which had been agreed upon was
disconcerted, and Marcellus, not daring to follow the retiring
enemy, gave the signal for retreat when his soldiers were conquering."

From this language one would scarcely assume a marked
victory on Marcellus' part; nor can one credit the casualties
given.   Marcellus had great energy; why should he retreat
" when his soldiers were conquering "?   The probability is
that it was an even thing.   Everything points that way.

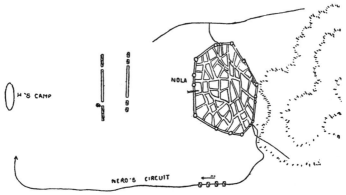

Third Battle of Nola.

Livy goes on to say that Marcellus reproached Nero with
having prevented him from inflicting on the Carthaginians a
second Cannæ.   But Nero was a splendid marcher.   His part
in the Metaurus campaign is the finest strategic feat of the
Romans during the entire war, as well as one of the exceptional marches of history.   It is probable that the route cut
out for him was too long for the time given, or at least that
the fault did not lie entirely with him.

After all said, the third battle of Nola must be set down
as drawn.   Yet it was a feather in Marcellus' cap, for Hannibal had failed of his purpose.   Both the Roman generals and
legions were now of far better stuff.

Next day, Marcellus again offered battle. But Hannibal, apparently despairing of ever winning a fight at Nola, declined it, turned face from the town which had thrice repulsed him and marched out of Campania. He had been unable to make a new base in this province, and purposed to turn his attention to the more promising field of Tarentum. He had stayed with the•Capuans long enough to forestall the Roman siege for this year and to enable them to get in their harvest. This was all the service he could render them under the present awkward conditions.

The consuls made no attempt to interfere with his leaving Campania. They no doubt breathed the more freely, the further he was from Rome. If Hannibal had been seriously defeated at Nola, this conduct lacked every element of enterprise.

Though his genius never shone so brightly as now and from this time forward, Hannibal's star was paling so far as concerned material success. He arrived at Tarentum three days late. Marcus Livius, an officer sent by Valerius from Brundisium, had anticipated him in entering the city, and had so effectually rallied the Roman sympathizers that no rising could be made in Hannibal's favor when he reached the place. Hannibal acted with sensible moderation in sparing the region, where he still had many friends ; and, gathering his store of wheat from Metapontum and Heraclea when the season was over, he left for the north to take up winter-quarters at Salapia. His horse he sent to better foraging grounds among the Salentinians and in the mountains.

It will be observed that Hannibal never lost his hold on the country near Luceria, the key of Apulia. While he was obliged by his failure in Campania to resort to a base in extreme southern Italy, he purposed to hold the avenue by which any possible reinforcements might reach him overland from Spain. This avenue he kept open until the fatal day of the Metaurus wrecked the possibility of help from this direction.

So soon as Hannibal left Campania, Fabius undertook the long desired siege of Casilinum, which he had been prudent enough not to begin in earnest with the Carthaginian army

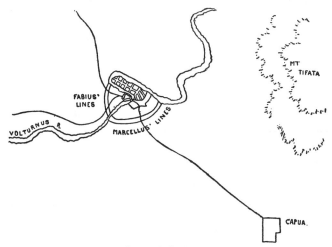

Siege of Casilinum.

near at hand, though he had made a slight attempt on the town while Hannibal was near Neapolis. To make his work tell to the best advantage, he invited Marcellus to move up from Nola to help him on the south bank, where he could at the same time observe Capua in order to prevent its interference with the siege-operations. Nola was strengthened by Marcellus with two thousand men and could take care of herself in the absence of Hannibal.

Casilinum was garrisoned by seven hundred of Hannibal's veterans and two thousand Capuans under Status Metius. Marcellus moved to Casilinum, where he undertook work from the left bank, while Fabius pushed the siege from the right.

Owing to the situation of the town astride the river, their camps were not connected. Marcellus' position was held in sufficient strength to keep the Capuans within walls. The besieged defended themselves with so much intelligence and obstinacy that Fabius was inclined to withdraw; but Marcellus persuaded him to persevere. Finally, hard pressed to the last degree, the garrison capitulated to Fabius, with the understanding that the men should be allowed to retire to Capua. But Marcellus, alleging that he knew nothing of the terms made with Fabius, — at all events without the latter's knowledge or consent, — and being on the side from which the garrison must emerge to go to Capua, took possession of the gates and fell upon the unsuspecting column, killing or taking prisoners all but fifty of the entire number. The prisoners were sent to Rome, except these fifty, who reached Capua in sad plight.

While this unhandsome act by Marcellus was by no means an unusual one, it is one of those which go far to give to the Roman cry of Punic Faith a ridiculous aspect. During this, as well as all their wars, the Romans were so far from immaculate that they can bring no accusation against the Carthaginians, and least of all against Hannibal, whose character emerges unsullied from all their attacks.

The immediate results of Gracchus' victory over Hanno had thus been the forced retirement of Hannibal from Campania and the capture of Casilinum, two brilliant successes which now gave the consuls free scope to lay siege to Capua whenever the occasion should be favorable.

Marcellus again returned to Nola and Suessula. Fabius moved into Samnium, to join hands with Fabius junior in Apulia, and with Gracchus in Lucania, and, in coöperation with them, regain some of the revolted cities. Hanno having retired to Bruttium, the three Roman armies had everything their own way, and took occasion to ravage all the region allied to Hannibal. The Samnites of Caudium especially suffered. Some twenty-five thousand people are said to have perished in this retribution. A number of Roman deserters were captured and sent to Rome for execution. The armies took by storm Compulteria, Telesia and Compsa, Melæ, Fulfulæ and Orbitanium in Samnium; by siege Blanda in Lucania and Æcæ in Apulia, and dealt out severity in abundant measure to all Hannibal's adherents. They then retired to winter-quarters, — Fabius at Suessula, Marcellus at Nola, Gracchus in Lucania, and Fabius, Jr., in Apulia, not far from Hannibal at Salapia. The only ray of light was a severe slap given by Hanno to a lieutenant of Gracchus, "not much less disastrous than he himself had received at Beneventum," says Livy, about the time of the capture of Casilinum.

During this year Hieronymus, king of Syracuse, who had abandoned the Roman alliance, was assassinated by a cabal, and a new treaty with Rome was made by the conspirators. It was, however, of short duration, for the Carthaginian influence again gained ground, and Syracuse declared war on Rome. Many cities of Sicily followed her example. Marcellus was sent with his two legions to calm the storm. Hannibal had never desired the war to extend to Sicily. He was soldier enough to understand the value of concentration, the danger of frittering away one's forces in outside operations. But just because he opposed a Sicilian campaign the Punic senate was glad to foster it, as it had fostered the unnecessary war in the Iberian peninsula. At the same time Philip of Macedon had assembled an army and a fleet with which to invade Italy. But Valerius left Brundisium, sailed to Apollonia, where the Macedonian fleet lay, defeated the army and burned the fleet. Thus ended the Macedonian alliance with Hannibal.

This year and the coming ones were fruitful in instances of Roman patriotism. Private wealth was cheerfully poured into the coffers of the state and the heaviest taxes were honestly paid. Many citizens served in the armies without pay.

The results of the year were entirely in favor of the Romans. The tide had set in their favor. Every element was on their side. The legionaries were not only equal, they were superior to the troops opposed to them, among whom were but few of the Carthaginian veterans. Numbers grew with the Romans as they decreased with Hannibal. Their generals had been trained in a good school, and were doing justice to their master's instruction. To oppose all this there was but one element on the other side, — the burning genius of Hannibal.

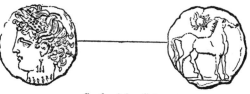

Carthaginian Coin.

XXXII.

TARENTUM WON. 213 B. C.

In 213 B. C. the Romans again raised over two hundred and twenty thousand men. The year had few marked occurrences. Hannibal remained near Tarentum, watching his chance. Marcellus was sent to besiege Syracuse, where Archimedes kept him at bay for eight months with his remarkable mechanical devices. The succeeding year the legions were raised to twenty-three. The Romans found difficulty in recruiting men; Hannibal much more. The Carthaginians had the good fortune to capture Tarentum by treachery; but the Roman garrison kept the citadel, in which they were besieged by land and sea. The Tarentine fleet was in the inner harbor. Hannibal moved it to the outer bay, where alone it could be of use, by carrying the ships through the town on wagons and sledges. The consuls undertook the siege of Capua. This city called on Hannibal for aid, as they had been unable to harvest their crops. Hannibal sent Hanno to Beneventum to accumulate victual and deliver it to the trains which he notified the Capuans to send there. Hanno's part was well done, but owing to Capuan dilatoriness his army was caught by the consul Fulvius, during his absence foraging, and cut to pieces. Hanno escaped.

THE consuls for the year B. C. 213 were Tiberius Sempronius Gracchus and the younger Fabius. As prætors were chosen M. Atilius Regulus, Sempronius Tuditanus, Cnæus Fulvius, and Æmilius Lepidus. The Roman armies lay as follows: Gracchus, in Lucania, had two legions with which to continue the war in that province. Fabius remained in Apulia with two legions, his father, late dictator, accompanying him as legate. Æmilius, prætor, was at Luceria with two legions. Fulvius, prætor, succeeded the late consul Fabius at Suessula, where were two legions. Varro remained in Picenum with one. In Sicily were Marcellus and Cornelius Lentulus, — the latter in the western part of the island, known as the Roman province, — each with two legions.

The prætor Sempronius was in cisalpine Gaul with two legions, and the pro-prætor Mucius in Sardinia with two. The Scipios in Spain had two legions. In garrison in Rome

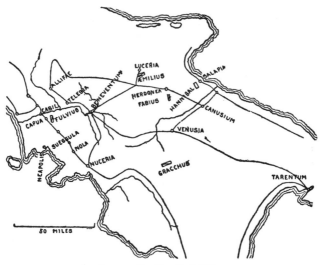

Armies opposite Hannibal, 213 B. C.

were two; while Valerius carried to Greece one legion. Of this enormous array of twenty-two legions, thirteen were in Italy, of which eight were intended especially to confront Hannibal, namely, Æmilius' two at Luceria, Fabius' two at Herdonia, Fulvius' two near Capua, and Gracchus' two between Hanno and Hannibal. It is well to recite this list of legions to show what Hannibal had to contend with. This enormous force of two hundred and twenty thousand men seemed certain to overwhelm his cause. The eighty thousand men who specially surrounded him should be enough, it appears, to put a speedy end to the war.

It is hard to describe the operations of this year. The records are very inexplicit, and like the later years of the Seven Years' War, there was apparently little done by either

side. And yet it was a year of intense anxiety to Hannibal,
who was hoping against hope ; he recognized that the stars
in their courses were fighting against him.

The earliest operation of importance in this campaign was
the capture of Arpi by Fabius, who attacked the place at
night in a thunder-storm, when least expected. The garrison
consisted of five thousand of Hannibal's men and three thousand citizen-troops ; but a thousand Spaniards went over to
the Romans at the critical moment. The Carthaginians
made so respectable a show of resistance that they were able
to capitulate with right to move to Salapia. The town of
Arpi thenceforth remained under Roman control.

Signs of yielding to the pressure, even in Capua, began also
to be noticed. A number of the noblemen of this city sent
word to Fulvius, the prætor, that they would surrender themselves to the Romans on condition that their possessions might
be restored to them in case Capua was taken. Hannibal's
structure in Italy seemed ready to go to pieces.

Hannibal's position at Salapia became perilous. His win-
ter-supplies were exhausted, and there was nothing in the
vicinity to forage on. Two Roman armies in his immediate
front, — one at Luceria, one at Herdonia, — and still another
in Lucania, seemed to shut him in beyond possibility of moving. He was not strong enough to undertake an offensive.
He was holding himself in Italy in the hope that further reinforcements might reach him. So long as this hope lasted, he
would not abandon the peninsula. But Salapia became un-
tenable. He determined to move to Tarentum. His one reliance was in his small remaining force of cavalry, the arm
that never failed him ; and under cover of a curtain of Numidians, he set out to march along the coast. The Romans
deemed it unwise to interfere with his march, and not far
from Tarentum he spent the summer, hoping that he might

be able to capture it, or that his friends within would induce it to open its gates. Meanwhile, he made a small-war upon some of the towns of the Salentinians. Capua he was compelled to leave to its own resources, but happily it was not molested. Gracchus indulged in a partisan war in Lucania, of no importance. Bruttium began to show awkward signs of a new leaning towards Rome, and some of her cities surrendered themselves to the authorities. Others would probably have followed this example, had not an officer of the allied legions heedlessly begun devastating a part of the province. This general was thereupon attacked by Hanno and badly defeated. Such impolitic cruelty on the part of the allies gave a decided set - back to the sentiment which had begun to run in favor of Rome.

In Spain, too, little was done. The peninsula was then, as later, peculiarly fitted for partisan warfare. The population cared not whether Rome or Carthage won. They were restless, unreliable, and unstable. Such tribes as were within the districts conquered by either party accepted its rule without difficulty. The main utility of this work of the Scipios was to keep the Pyrenees barred, and thus prevent reinforcements from marching to Italy. At Tarraco they made a new Rome, as the Carthaginians had made a new Carthage. They had carried the war almost to southern Spain. Syphax, king of part of Numidia, was induced by the Scipios to join the Roman alliance, and placed his troops under the eagles. This seriously weakened the Spanish cause of Carthage, for Syphax kept Libya in a ferment, and Hasdrubal Barca was called to Africa with the flower of the Spanish troops. Hasdrubal induced Masinissa, prince of the Massylians, to join Carthage. This prince defeated Syphax in a bloody battle, and Hasdrubal was able to return to Spain with reinforcements and an army under Masinissa.

The one occurrence of this year which rises above mediocrity is the siege of Syracuse by Marcellus. In the preceding year, as already noted, owing to the death of the old king, Hiero, and the turbulence of the short reign of his young and weak grandson, Hieronymus, Syracuse had joined the Carthaginian cause, under two of Hannibal's emissaries, Epicydes and Hippocrates, and Marcellus had been sent there to besiege it.

The siege is made principally of interest by the ingenious mechanical devices of Archimedes to resist the approaches of the Romans. The siege of the city by the Athenians in B. C. 415–413 has, in other respects, more interest.

Marcellus began by capturing Leontini, inland eighteen miles to the northwest, and then set to work to shut the city in by sea and land.

Alexander and his engineers had given the first real impetus to the art of fortification and sieges which was to any extent lasting. The Greeks in every part of the world took up the subject, and applied to it all the art and science then known. The siege of Rhodes by Demetrius Poliorcetes, in B. C. 305, exemplified the progress made, and proved the value of the purely scientific man in furthering the commercial interests of every nation, by devising better ships and by constructing better harbors, as well as in fostering their political security by a better system of fortification. This latter gave rise to more scientific means of attacking fortified places.

The centre of learning at that day was Alexandria in Egypt. Pure learning, as well as the allied mechanical arts, throve singularly there. All branches of literary and scientific work emanated chiefly from this great city. Distinguished mathematicians and mechanical engineers of all kinds here had their headquarters. Syracuse, being an important seaport, desired to benefit by all this, and Hiero, the late king, had sent Archimedes, a native Syracusan, to Alexandria, to learn all about the new inventions which had begun to evoke so much interest.

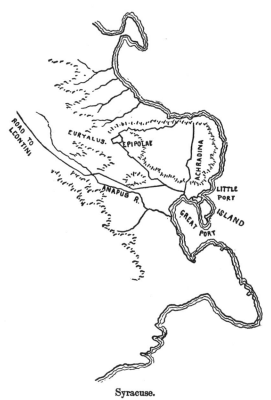

Syracuse.

Archimedes not only learned all that was taught by the Alexandrian savants, but improved upon what he had learned, and put it all into practice in the siege of Syracuse. Without doubt, much is true in all the relations concerning his wonderful mechanical devices and engines. But there is also — probably because the old historians did not fully understand the various mechanisms — some exaggeration in

the description of them. It is said by Plutarch that his artillery was capable of wonderful aim and distance, throwing
enormous stones with never failing accuracy, and projecting
showers of darts into the Roman camps in such a manner as
to render siege-operations all but impossible by the land or
sea forces. From huge derricks he dropped heavy stones
upon the ships which approached the walls, or else chains
bearing grappling devices, with which he seized them, and
either overturned them or dragged them upon the rocks. It
is asserted that by means of burning-glasses he set the Roman
fleet afire. This is perhaps not credible, but no doubt exists
that Archimedes did, by his fertility in devising means of resisting the approaches of Marcellus, and by his wonderful
enginery, render. futile all the efforts of the Romans to lay
regular siege to the town for eight long months, and converted
the siege into a mere blockade. Nor was it on account of the
want of skill on the part of Marcellus. This excellent soldier
erected all the known machinery of siege and proceeded with
his usual energy. He built a huge sambuca, a tower on eight
large vessels lashed together, so high that it overtopped the
walls. But before this unwieldy structure could be approached to the wall, Archimedes destroyed it by his ballista-
fire, and in like manner destroyed the pent-houses and tortoises by which the Romans endeavored to approach the walls
to undermine them. When Marcellus, in the idea that Archimedes' engines were so huge that they could only operate at a
distance, moved up near to the walls, Archimedes, who had
perforated the walls for this very purpose, showered upon the
Roman troops such clouds of rocks, darts, and beams, that
a hasty retreat had to be beaten. So demoralized did the
Romans become that the sight of any new thing on the city
walls gave rise to all but a panic.

Finally it was decided that Appius Claudius should remain

with the fleet and part of the troops at Syracuse, while Marcellus should move with the rest into the interior to punish the towns which had revolted from Rome.

Next year, B. C. 212, owing to the absence of the consuls, there was first appointed a dictator, C. Claudius Centho, who chose Q. Fulvius Flaccus his magister equitum. Thereafter were elected as consuls Q. Fulvius Flaccus for the third time, and Appius Claudius, the officer who was engaged in the siege of Syracuse. The prætors chosen were Cnæus Fulvius Flaccus, C. Claudius Nero, M. Junius Silanus and Pub. Cornelius Sulla. Centho then retired as dictator.

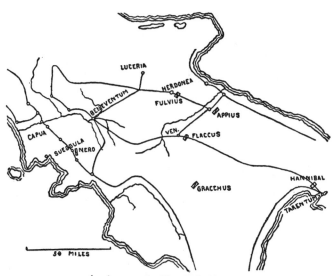

Armies opposite Hannibal, 212 B. C.

Hannibal was opposed by the two consuls, each with two legions; Nero took post at Suessula with two legions, and to prætor Fulvius, with two, fell Apulia. Junius Silanus was sent to Etruria, which threatened trouble. Sulla held Rome. The usual interchanges of legions took place by lot. Gracchus, proconsul, was in Lucania; the pro-prætor of the same name was at Ariminum; Marcellus, proconsul, continued the siege of Syracuse. The two Scipios were still in Spain. Otacilius kept the fleet, Valerius Greece and Mucius Sardinia.

All these forces, twenty-three legions, would be at their full strength over two hundred and thirty thousand men. It is asserted by some that the legions were not filled to the legal strength, and that these twenty-three legions amounted only to about one hundred and forty thousand foot and twenty-five thousand horse, — in all one hundred and sixty-five thousand men. It is true that the population had been exhausted. Hannibal had overrun many provinces which had been wont to contribute recruits, and had pressed many available men into his own service. There were no longer so many men of given age to be raised in the territory held by Rome. Hannibal had weakened the resources of the city by a good half. Moreover, every Roman was not a patriot. Contractors, then as in other eras, were ready to thrive on dishonesty and the sufferings of their countrymen.

Yet the balance of authority is to the effect that these legions were of the legal standard; in other words, that over two hundred and thirty thousand men were under the colors. A new method which placed in the ranks all men of any age capable of bearing arms was adopted to recruit the legions. And those lacking in years or strength could do garrison duty and leave field-work to the able-bodied. When all this was finished the Romans had put five armies, or ten legions, — one hundred thousand men, — into the field against Hannibal. This captain could number in all about forty thousand effective for the field. He had under arms about double this number, but most of his troops were Italians and largely employed in garrisoning the towns in their respective provinces. He could scarcely put in line the force stated, and these fell far below the quality of his old troops, which formed scarcely a leaven, indeed, to the lump, — far below that of the Roman legions. None the less throughout the year Hannibal marched to and fro through southern Italy, in and out among the surrounding armies, and none but kept a respectful distance. No Roman general ventured to meet him in the open field. This testimony to the ability of the Carthaginian is beyond any words. Weak in numbers and resources, with an army composed of poor material, he was yet the dread of the noblest Roman of them all, — and there were able men in command.

This course of the Romans was sensible. It would have been folly for the senate to assume that their generals were able to beat Hannibal on equal terms, and again order an immediate advance on the enemy. They had learned wisdom by the failure of this aggressiveness in the first three years of the war, and they were profiting by it. They were wise, even though their legions had the advantage of experience and their generals grew more expert under Hannibal's tuition. The Roman cause was gaining while Hannibal's was declining. It was becoming hard for the Romans to raise men, but it was doubly so for Hannibal. The senate saw that the policy of starvation was the one to pursue.

This year's campaign was opened by a felicitous event for the Carthaginians. The Tarentines had become much enraged by the execution of their hostages in Rome, on account of an attempt to escape, fostered by Punic emissaries, and a strong party sprang up in Hannibal's favor. The Carthaginian camp was about fifty miles from Tarentum. Communication was opened with Hannibal and a treaty made, under which the city was to be surrendered. Measures were taken to put the Roman garrison in the citadel off its guard.

Hannibal moved up nearer the city at the appointed time, marching in such a way that his approach would seem to be nothing more than a raid of light troops, such as were constantly occurring. He had ten thousand chosen troops under his command, and had covered his advance with Numidians who should seize or kill all peasants or others who could

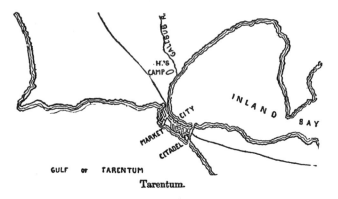

Tarentum.

convey the news of his coming. The Roman garrison-commander sent out a small body of horse to meet the Numidians, who were taken for mere foragers, and received word from prisoners captured that Hannibal was still in his camp.

At night Hannibal moved up to the gate called Temenis (now Porta di Napoli), which faced northwest towards the mainland ; this was opened by his friends, who killed the Roman sentinels on duty, while another small party did the like at another gate. Leaving two thousand horse outside, Hannibal marched into the market-place, and dividing two thousand Gauls of his force into three parts, sent each of these under conduct of a friendly Tarentine into a different part of the city, with orders to cut down all Roman soldiers, but to treat the citizens with honor. Aroused by the noise, the Roman garrison assembled, and ascertaining that the city had been captured, hastily withdrew in squads to the citadel,

each one getting there as best it might. Hannibal, not knowing the lay of the land, did not reach it in time to head them
off. But the Romans did not get to the citadel without considerable loss in the darkness.

This capture is a good sample of the manner in which Hannibal became possessed of many towns. It speaks poorly for
the performance of guard-duty by Roman garrisons, despite
the remarkably stringent regulations drawn up for them. The
fall of Tarentum was followed by that of Heraclea, Thurii
and Metapontum, whose garrisons were successively withdrawn by the Romans to save the citadel of Tarentum.

After taking Tarentum, Hannibal armed its citizens and
put it in condition to hold for his cause. But he saw that
unless he had a fleet, he would probably be unable to drive the
Roman garrison from the citadel, which was situated on a
point of land, the sea sides of which were protected by inac-
cessible rocks, and the city side defended by a wall and a
wide and deep ditch. And as the citadel commanded the
harbor, so as to exclude Hannibal from its use, the greater
part of the value of Tarentum had not been gained. For the
citadel stood at a point from which the Romans with their
ships could even aid in besieging the town, and at all events
could harass him in its possession so as to oblige him to hold
it with a large force. The channel from the sea to the inland
bay was cut by a bridge in the hands of the Romans. The
garrison of the citadel was speedily reinforced up to five thousand men with plenty of material of war, but nothing more
was for the moment done.

The citadel was too strong to be taken by assault. Hannibal contented himself with drawing lines of circumvallation
against it and suitably manning them. During the construction of these, he cleverly led on the Romans to make an energetic sortie. His men had orders, in case this happened, to

simulate defeat and retire, some to the rear, in order to lure
on the enemy to a greater distance, some to the side-streets,
where they could fall upon the Romans when they should retreat. This was done. The garrison detachment pursued the
apparently broken Carthaginians, and these, turning upon

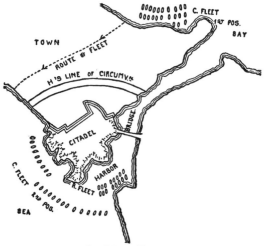

Citadel of Tarentum.

them at a given signal, took them in flank and rear, killed
a large number, and drove the rest into the ditch. But the
citadel had meanwhile been firmly held and Hannibal profited
little by his stratagem.

The lines finished, Hannibal withdrew to a camp outside
the town, near the river Galesus. But, restless under the
menace of the presence of the Romans in the citadel, he soon
returned and attempted siege-operations. These proved unsuccessful, as the garrison had been made too strong by a
reinforcement from Metapontum. While he was getting his
siege-machinery into place, the Romans made a determined
sortie upon the works, and managed to burn his towers, vineæ
and artillery. It would seem that the citadel could not have

been impregnable, for while it was hard to approach from the sea on account of the rocky coast, it was not on an elevated site, but rather on a level, having but its wall and ditch to protect it from the town. Sieges in olden times were apt to be prolonged ; and Roman soldiers made a garrison hard to oust.

In order to starve out the garrison, the harbor, now held by the Romans, must be blockaded as well. Indeed, to victual the city, it was essential to have control of the sea; for provisions came in too slowly by land, and the Carthaginian army required rations as well as the inhabitants. The Roman fleet held the narrow channel from the open sea to the inland bay, where lay the Tarentine fleet. Hannibal devised a means of dragging their vessels on wagons and sledges across the town from the inner harbor into the roadway, and oversaw the operations himself. In a short time the Tarentine fleet cast anchor before the citadel, much to the surprise of the garrison. Having given Tarentum control of the sea, and thus blockaded the Roman garrison, Hannibal withdrew to his old camp, fifty miles distant.

The consuls undertook the siege of Capua, an operation which had long been in contemplation. Including Nero's, they had six legions, nominally sixty thousand men, and this left four legions, or nearly forty thousand men, in Apulia and Lucania. Campania was quite at the mercy of the Romans. The consuls first united their forces at Bovianum in Samnium as a diversion to withdraw Hannibal's attention from their real objective, hoping to invest Capua undisturbed. This succeeded admirably. The Capuans had been closely watched for many months and unable to sow their crops. Famine was staring them in the face. They appealed to Hannibal for aid, and their messengers safely made their way to his headquarters.

Being unwilling to leave matters in Tarentum for the moment, Hannibal ordered Hanno from Bruttium to Beneventum, to make an effort to revictual this devoted city. Gracchus in Lucania was in Hanno's front and Nero at Suessula would, during his march, be on his flank, but so lax was the matter of scouting and reconnoissances, or of procuring information by spies, that Hanno eluded both, safely reached Beneventum and fortified a camp near the place, before his enemies knew of his intention of leaving Bruttium. He had probably marched via Nuceria, from which place country roads led northward over the mountains to Beneventum. Notifying the Capuans to send in haste all their carts, beasts of burden and other means of transport, he amassed in his camp all the grain of the surrounding country. The heedless Capuans were all too slow. " They executed this business with their usual indolence and carelessness." They sent only a small train of four hundred wagons. Hanno, vexed enough at this lax response to his dangerous undertaking, told them that he would not be responsible for the results, and sent them back for more. Before the Capuans got to Beneventum with a second train, this time of two thousand wagons, the Roman consuls in camp at Bovianum, though Hanno had advanced his cavalry as a curtain to his operations, learned from the people of Beneventum what was going on. Fulvius at once made for that city to interrupt the proceeding, and entered it.

Arrived at Beneventum, Fulvius found that Hanno was out with a large force on a foraging expedition, believing himself to be sufficiently protected by his outposts of horse. The rest of the army was in camp, which was admirably chosen in a strong and steep location, and well fortified. But the immense train of wagons and the collection of Campanian drivers and local rustics made it impossible to preserve good discipline.

Fulvius moved at once upon this camp by night, and at sunrise made a sharp assault upon it, despite its difficulties. The attack and defense were both admirable. The first on-sets of the Romans were driven back with slaughter. But the Roman troops no longer feared the Carthaginian phalangites. They had recovered their ancient feeling of invincibility when Hannibal was not there. After repeated efforts they reached the ditch of the camp. Here again a bitter struggle ensued, the Carthaginians from above having so nearly the upper hand that Fulvius was about to sound the recall, when Vibius Acculalus, the leader of an allied cohort, and Titus Pedanius, a centurion of the principes, threw their standards over the wall into the camp. This was done without concert between them, and roused the zeal of the legionaries to the highest pitch. They made so desperate a charge at the wall that a number of cohorts surmounted it. Seizing this advan-tage, Fulvius, instead of the recall, sounded a new charge all along the line, and the entire body of Romans poured as one man into the camp. The Carthaginians were slaughtered wholesale, — six thousand being killed; while seven thousand others, including the Capuans and their wagons, were cap-tured. The camp was destroyed, and Fulvius retired to Ben-eventum, where shortly he was joined by his colleague, Ap-pius Claudius. Hanno learned of this disaster at Cominium, and escaped to Bruttium with the foraging party he was com-manding. Gracchus was as much lacking to allow·Hanno to return without molestation as he was to have allowed him to pass up to Beneventum without challenge. On either march he should at least have followed and annoyed him.

This operation was well begun by Hanno, who eluded the Roman armies on his either hand, and made his way to Ben-eventum with consummate cleverness, and but for the in-explicable sluggishness of the Capuans, might have been entirely successful. The event does credit to the Roman consuls. The determined attack of Fulvius on Hanno's camp, in view of the importance of Beneventum, as well as the conduct of his army, deserves due praise. All this in nowise detracts from Hannibal's intelligent plan in sending Hanno to the succor of Capua. Its failure lay solely in Capuan dilatoriness. The combinations of Hannibal deserved a better fate.

The general manœuvring of the Romans had gained in effectiveness. It cannot be said to have been characterized by any special ability; but in its care and intent, it was in marked contrast to the manœuvring of earlier years. All the Roman generals showed a dread of Hannibal which has no parallel in history except in the case of Frederick; and, as with Gracchus in the march just narrated, they were often lacking in the performance of the evident duty of commanders. But the gain was marked.

Carthaginian Coin.

XXXIII.

A WONDERFUL MARCH. 212 B. C.

THE consuls now turned to the siege of Capua, which again appealed to Hannibal for help. Four armies, numbering over eighty thousand men, barred the way from Tarentum to Capua; it seemed impossible for Hannibal to make his way to his hard-pressed ally. But he started, and by wonderful marching, of which we have unfortunately no details, and by the dread all Roman generals had of his approach, he reached Mt. Tifata, and next day entered Capua. A battle was shortly fought, in which the Romans appear to have been getting worsted, when some cavalry from Beneventum appeared on Hannibal's flank and obliged him to withdraw. The consuls, in order to draw him from Capua, retired from the siege, one of them towards Lucania. Hannibal felt compelled to follow, lest his holding on the south coast should be lost. Having thus lured him away, both consuls returned and resumed the siege. This work had been ably done. On Hannibal's way back to Tarentum, a Roman army barred his path. This he destroyed, and turning aside to Herdonia, likewise destroyed the army of the prætor Fulvius. Not seeing how he could benefit Capua without further reinforcements, Hannibal returned to Metapontum. He had got possession of nearly all the south coast of Italy, but the Tarentine citadel held out. In Sicily, Marcellus took Syracuse; but the Scipios in Spain were defeated and killed. Despite his destruction of two Roman armies, Hannibal had made a less gain during this than during the former year.

THE siege of Capua now monopolized the attention of the consuls. There was grave fear that Hannibal might again appear to succor the town which had been so devoted to his cause. Large supplies were accumulated on the Vulturnus, in Vulturnum, at its mouth, and at Casilinum, to be used in the proposed siege. Had Hannibal been in Campania, the consuls could not have accomplished this without interruption. But Nero, at the Claudian camp above Suessula, the two consuls surrounding the city with their double army, and

the prætor Fulvius, presumably in the Venusian country,
watching the Appian Way, closed every avenue and made a
network of armies, through which even Hannibal, it would
seem, could not penetrate. While they held Beneventum,
and there was always a good force here, they were able to
prevent Hannibal from thrusting himself in between their

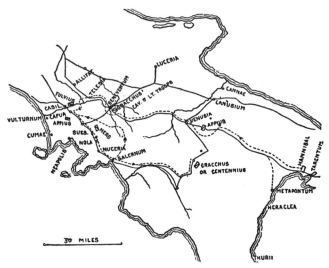

Armies between Hannibal and Capua, 212 B. C.

armies in Lucania and Campania, and thus making their
efforts futile by turning on one or other.

The Capuans, foreseeing what was sure to come, again appealed to Hannibal for succor. Though the season was already spent and he had lost heavily in his former efforts in
their favor, Hannibal felt that he must again attempt whatever was possible. He sent them as a preliminary two
thousand of his matchless Numidian cavalry, which he could
himself illy spare, to keep the enemy away from their
fields. These admirable light troops succeeded in passing
through the Roman cordon of armies and in reaching the

city. Mago (not the Barca) appears to have been the commander of this body of horse. He must have been an able partisan.

Hannibal could not well afford to leave the south coast. Some of the adjacent towns of Lucania were falling into his hands. Heraclea and Metapontum had been taken by himself, and Thurii by Hanno. This work was all important to him, as it promised him the entire coast from the Adriatic to the straits of Messana, Rhegium and the citadel of Tarentum alone excepted. The Roman fleet had just broken through the Tarentine navy and revictualed the latter, and Hannibal all the more needed the other harbors from which to communicate with Carthage, and in which to receive succor, if it should be sent. But though loath to interrupt his labors here, he none the less lent an ear to the appeal of Capua, and set out to march towards that city through Apulia. Though well aware of the difficulties besetting his path, he felt that Punic craft outweighed Roman watchfulness.

The battle of Beneventum having disposed of Hanno, for some time at least, Gracchus was enabled to bear a hand in the siege of Capua. He was ordered to leave his heavy infantry, under suitable command, where it could safely watch Lucania, and move to Beneventum with his light infantry and cavalry. The consuls wished to utilize their cavalry for the outlying armies, for they could not but appreciate how inefficiently their outpost duty was performed. The addition of Gracchus' force would concentrate between Hannibal and Capua some seven thousand cavalry, a larger body than usual with the Romans. And the value of Beneventum as a strategic centre was fully appreciated by the consuls.

Unhappily for the Romans, Gracchus was killed in an ambuscade, which, Livy says, was treacherously laid for him by one of Hanno's lieutenants. He was an excellent soldier,

brave, generous, intelligent. After Marcellus, he first obtained successes over Hannibal. His legionaries, largely
slaves manumitted after the battle of Beneventum, feigning
to consider themselves bound personally to him, and therefore released from service by his death, dispersed. Lucania

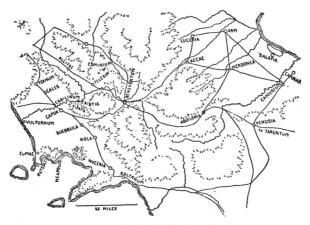

Scene of Hannibal's March to Capua.

was for the moment disgarnished of troops, and the road to
Capua made more easy to Hannibal, when M. Centenius, a
sort of soldier of fortune, of great personal strength and
courage, but of no capacity whatever, was given command,
and raised sixteen thousand men for the defense of the province.

It seems to be commonly accepted by the historians from
whom Livy quotes that the body of Gracchus, on being sent
to Hannibal, received distinguished burial rites. Livy leans
to belief in this fact, and frankly admits the honors paid by
Hannibal to his other fallen foes.

The consuls approached Capua. They entered the plains
and sent out small parties to harvest the half-ripe wheat.
The Capuans sallied out and waylaid these parties, in con-

nection with the Numidian cavalry, under command of Mago, and inflicted a loss of fifteen hundred men on them. This was but a temporary check to the consuls. They camped in front of Capua, intent on making some headway with the siege so long deferred. The Capuans saw the Roman lines of circumvallation growing about them, and felt that their hour had come, when to their extreme joy, and the no less surprise of the Romans, Hannibal suddenly appeared in his old position on the slope of Mt. Tifata, from which place he descended and entered the town.

It is extraordinary that the Roman generals should have so carelessly manœuvred as to allow Hannibal thus again to retake his old position. It should have long ago been seized by the Romans and fortified for their own uses against Capua. Not only would this have kept Hannibal from occupying the place, but it would have furnished a key-point from which a descent on his flank or rear could be made in case he occupied the plain before Capua.

That Hannibal marched from the south coast by way of Beneventum, and no doubt Venusia, we are informed by Livy. By what road he reached Campania from Beneventum is uncertain,— not unlikely by Telesia and the Caiatian country. Or he may have passed by the Caudine Forks, northeast of Suessula. Once past Beneventum, he could march that way without interference save from Nero. The former route is the more probable.

It is incredible almost that Hannibal should have evaded the prætor Fulvius, who was in the Venusian region, such troops as held Beneventum, and who, at least, must have had abundant opportunity to send word ahead of his presence there, and the armies of the consuls near Capua and of Nero at the Claudian camp, and reach Tifata. That he should have been able to march from Tifata into Capua, with the consuls' four legions preparing to besiege the city, and already engaged on their lines of circumvallation, almost passes belief. Still such is the statement of Livy and the other historians.

It is such feats of marching, such inexplicable and unexplained exploits of daring and skill, which place Hannibal so far above other generals. It cannot be supposed that for a forced march like this Hannibal would head a large army; and that he should dare force his way into the very midst of enemies outnumbering him many-fold, through roads which he must expect to find beset in his front and closed behind him, and with every reasonable expectation of battle, shows the Carthaginian to be, in his power of manœuvring, marching and deceiving his enemies, without a peer. It shows, as nothing else can, what the dread of the very name of Hannibal meant. That the common people, or the common soldier, or the centurion, should partake it, is no wonder. But this dread equally possessed the consul, the prætor, the legate, the tribune. We know that the camp and battle discipline of the Romans was good; we know that their system of outposts, reconnoissances and scouting was in quite inverse ratio to it. But nothing except the rarest ability, and the power of making the enemy dread his very approach, can explain such a march as this last one of the Punic leader.

After two days, during which the Capuans were intoxicated with his presence, and felt that they were now safe from their persecutors, Hannibal emerged from the city and offered battle to the consuls. It was accepted. The first shock was handsomely given and taken, but the numerous cavalry of Hannibal, including Mago's and the Capuan, was beginning to make an unfavorable impression on the Roman formation, when a body of horse made its distant appearance on the flank of both armies. It was the cavalry of Gracchus'

army which was being brought from Beneventum towards
Capua by the quæstor Cornelius. It " excited alarm in both
parties equally, lest those who were approaching should be
fresh enemies, and, as if by concert, both sounded a retreat,"
says Livy. But Hannibal of course knew that they could not
be his troops; they must be enemies; and a large body of
Roman cavalry on his flank could not but jeopardize the day.
He was wise in retiring. The Romans, on the other hand,
had every reason to believe that they were friends; and it is

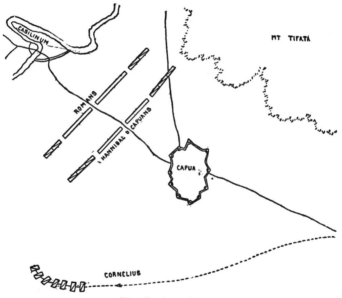

First Battle of Capua.

probable that they had been so roughly handled, as to be on
the point of losing the day, when the appearance of this *deus
ex machina* obliged Hannibal to withdraw. Livy for once
acknowledges a heavier Roman than Carthaginian loss.

It is not desired to convey the impression that Livy is in-
tentionally unfair. How could he write about Hannibal with-

out prejudice? But in order to arrive at the truth, we must often dissect his statements and compare his facts to discover their fair meaning.

It was evident that Hannibal must in some way be induced to leave Capua, or the best efforts of the two Roman armies would be thwarted. To bring this about, the consuls separated and did a really able piece of work. They knew that Hannibal would ask for nothing better than to have them stay about Capua and enable him to lure them into some stratagem, — a thing they had even a more hearty dread of than an open battle with him. So the consuls tried Hannibal's own game. They decamped from in front of Capua. Fulvius moved towards Cumæ, while Appius took up the march towards Lucania.

Hannibal, who saw his foothold in southern Italy threatened, for his force there was very small, decided to follow Appius. He could not allow the results of so much effort on the southern coast to be prejudiced. He marched out of Capua and in the wake of Appius. The sudden raising of the siege by the Romans was of short duration; for while the Capuans were still rejoicing at their supposed deliverance by Hannibal from their foes, Fulvius so suddenly reappeared from Cumæ that he all but forced an entrance into the town; failing in which, however, he again sat down before it.

Hannibal pursued Appius, but the latter, who had a good start, by a series of excellent forced marches eluded him, not unlikely by filing to the left at Salernum, and marching by way of Abelinum to Abella, and down to the plain near Suessula, from whence he returned to Capua and rejoined his colleague. However careless the consuls had been in allowing Hannibal to enter Capua, they had ably retrieved their error. Their stratagem was thought out and carried through with decided cleverness. Capua had benefited naught.

Hannibal saw no good to be attained by a new attempt to aid the city, and concluded to return to Tarentum, where he was greatly needed, when he found that M. Centenius Penula with his new levies barred his passage, intent on battle. Just where this was is not known, but probably in the northwest part of Lucania.

This Centenius had been in several campaigns in subordinate positions, and behaved with courage and intelligence. He was past the age of duty, but had asked and obtained from the senate leave to raise volunteers, promising to deal heavy blows at Hannibal in his own fashion, and to trap him with his own devices; a boast which was credulously heeded by the conscript fathers. The senate foolishly gave him eight thousand men, and in Lucania he doubled this number by recruitment, and now stood athwart Hannibal's path.

No sooner did Hannibal appear than Centenius offered him battle. Hannibal was not loath to accept it. The men led by Centenius made an exceptionally good fight, and for two hours Hannibal was unable to make any impression upon them. But Centenius, overanxious to win a victory, or at best determined not to survive a defeat, put himself at the head of his soldiers. Here he fell, more bravely than discreetly. His men soon lost their confidence, and surrounded by Hannibal's horse, were all cut down except about a thousand of their number who escaped and dispersed.

This victory was in a measure compensation for the failure of Hannibal's pursuit of Appius, but better was to come. Another easy triumph was at hand in the presence of the prætor Fulvius, who had but eighteen thousand men at Herdonia, which he was besieging.

From northwest Lucania, a road led to Venusia, — perhaps more than one. Heading in this direction, Hannibal shortly reached the vicinity of Herdonia, — probably via Aquilonia.

Here he heard that Fulvius was laden with booty and had, from easy successes, become careless in his discipline. Knowing the impatient character of Fulvius, and hearing also that the troops were overeager for a fight and probably in a poor condition for battle, Hannibal chose his camp where a good battle-field lay before him, and preparing during the night an ambuscade of three thousand light foot in some farm yards and woodlands near by, he sent Mago and some two thousand Numidians to occupy all the roads in the rear of the enemy. Fulvius, who had promised his impatient men to fight the next day, accepted the gage of battle so soon as Hannibal had drawn up in front of his camp, and moved to the attack.

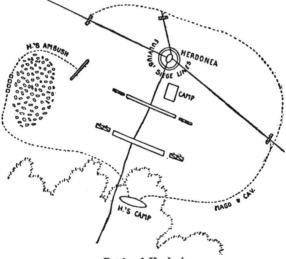

Battle of Herdonia.

Hannibal was superior in numbers as well as skill. Fulvius, in order to make his front equal Hannibal's, decreased his depth against the protests of the tribunes and, mixing the cohorts of the Roman and allied legions in one line, drew up with his horse on either flank, and covered by his light troops.

Hannibal formed as usual in phalangial order, sixteen deep, cavalry on the wings, skirmishers in front. The Roman line scarcely stood the first shock. Fulvius, less daring in deed than in threat, fled from the field at the earliest sign of disaster. His legions, taken in front and flank and rear by Hannibal's phalangites and Numidian horse, were absolutely destroyed. Scarce two thousand men were able to make their escape from the sword of the Carthaginians.

Thus, in a few weeks, the Romans had lost three armies as well as any standing they had gained in southern Italy. Hannibal, despite his success, felt constrained to return again to Tarentum, and here he remained during the rest of the year. He made a fresh effort to capture the citadel, but with renewed failure. He then attempted Brundisium, but this likewise proved too strong for him, as he had no adherents within its walls.

That Hannibal should have moved down to southern Apulia at a time when he had dispersed three Roman armies and when the siege of Capua had reached a culminating point has by many critics been looked upon as a mistake. We can only guess at his motives. His army was probably difficult to manage. Of material absolutely lacking homogeneity, he may often have been unable to allow himself to do what he so easily did in the first three years of his Italian campaigns. That he would have difficulty in maintaining himself at Mt. Tifata was clear. Three armies of over fifty thousand men surrounded Capua, and had so fortified their position that he would have been unable to effectuate anything towards raising the siege, while he would fatigue and worry his troops, and scarcely be able to victual them. He knew that Capua could stand a long siege, and he had reason to expect reinforcements from Carthage. It was these which he was preparing to receive by his efforts to control the southern coast. If they came soon, he would be in position to go to the relief of Capua with a better chance than if he returned there now. Had Hasdrubal come to southern Italy at this time instead of later by way of cisalpine Gaul, Hannibal might still have won a great measure of success. It seems that he was wiser to reserve his efforts in favor of Capua until he could act efficiently, than to fritter away his forces on work to which he knew by his late experience he could not succeed in doing justice.

The Roman senate was much disappointed at these reverses, which had been entirely unlooked for. But the promise of a Capuan success came in to compensate for this, and the siege was vigorously pushed. The consuls began to surround the town with a siege wall. They had abundant supplies in their great magazines of wheat at Casilinum and those made at Puteoli and at the fort at the mouth of the Vulturnus, to which corn came from Sardinia, Sicily and Etruria. The men of Gracchus' army who had dispersed were gradually captured and once again assembled under the colors and added to the others; the bulk of the army of Claudius Nero was called from the Claudian camp above Suessula, and the siege was pushed by the three armies from three sides. Two lines of walls as usual, with ditch and rampart, and towers at intervals, were made to resist the Capuans from within and Hannibal from without. These works took all winter, and the Capuans, despite many efforts and one rather severe engagement, in which they appear to have lost by dividing their forces, were unable to break through. Only on one or two occasions and before the line was complete could they even get a messenger to Hannibal to implore his instant help. These messengers found Hannibal at Brundisium, which he was seeking to capture, the citadel of Tarentum having so far resisted all his efforts. He promised, as early the next year as he could move, to go to their aid and to raise the siege, adding with proud consciousness of power (though it must have been with the secret feeling that his was the waning cause) that he had once raised the siege of Capua, and that the consuls would not sustain his approach again.

Some time before, a deputation of Capuans, who were somewhat faint-hearted, had made advances for amnesty to one of the consuls. The Roman senate now gave notice through these officers that to all Capuans who would surrender before the ides of March a free pardon would be granted; but this offer was indignantly rejected by the more courageous citizens, who browbeat the weaklings into silence.

The Roman strategy of the past three years had consisted in constantly opposing two or more armies to Hannibal, and never, unless under the most exceptional conditions, giving him a chance to fight them in the open field. These armies sought to tire him out by fatiguing marches, constant skirmishes and famine. This general military policy they followed from this time on. The consuls always had from eighty thousand men upwards to oppose to Hannibal, whose army was gradually deteriorating in quality and rarely more than half reached those of the Romans in effective strength. It was by his remarkable power of adapting his means to the end to be accomplished that Hannibal maintained himself; until he was recalled to Africa he moved all over Italy, and uniformly marked his progress by defeat of his foes or their retreat from the open.

The constancy of the consuls to their one object of besieging Capua deserves credit. On several occasions they met with disaster which interrupted their prosecution of this work, but they always returned to it with undiminished energy. When their dispositions to protect themselves against Hannibal's approach by occupying Beneventum and Suessula had been nullified by the death of Gracchus and Hannibal's bold march, they might very naturally have raised the siege. They, however, did nothing of the kind, but returned to their work as soon as they had lured Hannibal away, and this they continued with equal heart after the folly of Centenius and the cowardice of Fulvius had lost them a second and a third army. We shall see them hold to their quarry under yet more trying circumstances.

Hannibal's year had been less successful than the last. To be sure he had destroyed three of the Roman armies. But Rome could bear this loss. His gain at Tarentum, after his entire year's work, had been next to nothing, owing to the persistent holding of the citadel by the Roman garrison. He had been lured away from Capua by Appius, and it was no equivalent that the Romans had lost two armies as well as their footing in Apulia and Lucania. On the whole, the Romans again had the best of it in Italy.

We left Marcellus blockading the land side and the port of Syracuse, and raiding in the interior. After Appius Claudius had been elected consul, Marcellus single-handed continued the siege, which for many months resisted all efforts. The Carthaginians sent an army to Sicily, and the Syracusans sent one out of the city to join it. Marcellus' position threatened to become difficult. But during a certain festival which had lured some of the garrison from their posts, the Romans escaladed the walls and got into the city proper. From their position they managed to isolate the Euryalus, or fort on the western extremity of the walls. The allied armies now approached, and, in connection with a sortie of the garrison, tried to raise the siege. But Marcellus held his own; nor was the Punic fleet more fortunate. A pestilence attacked the allies, who were camped on low ground along the Anapus, while Marcellus in the suburbs was well placed. Finally the

Roman general, by tampering with the garrison, got into the " island," and shortly after the gates were opened to him. Marcellus allowed the city to be given over to his army to plunder, and in the confusion Archimedes, its celebrated defender, lost his life. Soon the whole island of Sicily was brought under Roman sway, and so remained. In addition to the success in all-important Sicily, the Roman admiral Otacilius captured one hundred and thirty vessels of wheat in the port of Utica.

The Roman gain in Sicily was offset by an unfortunate campaign in Spain. The Carthaginians had three armies on foot, under Hasdrubal Barca, Hasdrubal, son of Gisgo, and Mago. The Scipios had, after their marked successes of the past few years, been unwise enough this year to divide their forces. Cnæus Scipio, who confronted Hasdrubal Barca, lost the bulk of his army by defection (for his opponent was clever enough to pay his Spanish troops to desert), and was forced into retreat. Publius Scipio faced Hasdrubal Gisgo and Mago, to whom Masinissa, of Numidia, was allied. In a great battle, shortly occurring, the Roman army was all but destroyed and Publius Scipio lost his life. After this the allies turned on Cnæus Scipio and handled his army equally severely. The fate of Cnæus is not known. The wreck of the Roman armies retired north of the Ebro. The Roman cause seemed desperate, but the Carthaginians were again defeated and forced beyond the Ebro by the signal ability of a young Roman noble, L. Marcius, who succeeded to the command, and by several stout blows did much to reëstablish the Roman foothold in the peninsula.

XXXIV.

CAPUA. 211 B. C.

THE Roman plan for B. C. 211 was to capture Capua while acting defensively against Hannibal. The Capuan cavalry had held head against the Romans, until the latter mounted the best velites behind their cavalrymen, — an old device in the East. This recovered their ascendency by making the Roman horse steadier, and confined the Capuans within walls. Again these allies appealed to Hannibal, and again, leaving his south-coast business, the Carthaginian marched to their aid. Reaching Tifata, he sent them word to make a sortie on a given day and hour, and he would attack at the same time. This plan was carried out, but unsuccessfully. The superior force and intrenched lines of the Romans could not be broken. The Capuans were driven back into the city, and Hannibal sounded the recall. Seeing that direct means could not raise the siege of Capua, Hannibal tried an indirect one. He marched straight on Rome. At an earlier stage of the war, fear for the capital would at once have induced the Roman generals to follow; but they had been well taught; they did not budge. Hannibal knew he could not take Rome. He had barely twenty-five thousand men, and Rome had forty thousand. Fulvius, with a picked force of sixteen thousand men, marched to Rome; but this left fifty thousand men at Capua. Arrived at the capital, Hannibal ravaged the land up to the very gates, and then retired. He had failed in his object. Capua was soon after captured, and the citizens executed or sold into slavery. The Carthaginians were now confined to Apulia, Lucania and Bruttium.

THE consuls of B. C. 211 were Publius Sulpicius Galba and Cnæus Fulvius Centumalus, — not the one defeated at Herdonia. These officers entered on their duty as usual on the ides of March. As prætors there were chosen L. Cornelius Lentulus, to whose lot fell Sardinia, M. Cornelius Cethegus for Apulia, Caius Sulpicius, who, with Marcellus, went to Sicily, and C. Calpurnius Piso for the Roman garrison. While Appius Claudius and Fulvius Flaccus continued to conduct the siege at Capua as proconsuls, Sulpicius and

Fulvius, the new consuls, were supposed to hold head against Hannibal. For this purpose they had the two legions of slaves enfranchised by Gracchus, which after his death had dispersed but been again collected, and two legions which had been doing garrison duty in Rome. Their legions were very likely not up to the limit. There is some obscurity as to just what the consuls were doing during the exciting scenes of this campaign. The proconsuls bore the leading part, not they. Claudius Nero assisted the proconsuls before Capua, with his two legions, making six legions besieging the town. C. Sulpicius was ordered to recruit his two legions for Sicily up to the proper standard from the troops defeated under Fulvius in Apulia. These men, like the survivors of Cannæ, were punished by constant service out of Italy throughout the whole course of the war, and were forbidden to take up winter-quarters within ten miles of any town. Their commander, Fulvius, had been exiled, and gone to Tarquinii. The same forces as last year — two legions — were in Etruria, under the pro-prætor M. Junius ; two legions were in cisalpine Gaul under the pro-prætor P. Sempronius ; two legions each were in Spain, Sicily and Sardinia, the latter under C. Cornelius. Otacilius, with one hundred ships and two legions, and Valerius with fifty ships and one legion, had assigned to them the coast of Sicily and Greece respectively. In all there were twenty-three legions afoot, making a grand total of two hundred and thirty thousand men.

The two consular armies intended to confront Hannibal were supposed to confine him to southern Italy, but not to act offensively. It was deemed of more importance to keep troops in Etruria and cisalpine Gaul than to come to blows with Hannibal, and now that Syracuse had fallen it was in the highest degree essential to complete the conquest of Sicily. The citadel of Tarentum was well-provisioned and safe for the nonce. The sixty thousand men before Capua sufficed to hold the lines inclosing that fated city, which had been made as strong as Roman art could make them, while Hannibal was to be treated to a strict defensive. Until Capua was reduced, no active steps were to be taken against him. No special siege - proceedings were undertaken. The city was blockaded rather than besieged. Hunger was invoked instead of force.

The Capuans were looking constantly for the arrival of Hannibal, and made frequent sorties. In these their cavalry, the basis of which was the Numidian horse sent them by Hannibal, always proved superior to the Romans, but the infantry was so far inferior that the sorties were generally driven back with loss.

Despite this fact, the Romans found that they must do something to offset the superior quality of the Capuan cavalry, which caused them no little trouble. The Roman light infantry contained, among much less good material, the most active and vigorous youth of the nation. The velites had always been thoroughly exercised in rapid movements, and many of them could act with cavalry in almost all its manœuvres. A new formation was now made. The velites, who were armed with seven darts, four feet long and steel pointed, and with short bucklers, mounted and rode behind the cavalrymen in the swifter manœuvres, and even in the charges; and when the shock came, they leaped to the ground and attacked the dismounted enemy with their darts. This was a very ancient device, and long in use among the Carthaginians; but it was a novel one among the Romans; and a line of infantry suddenly appearing from the midst of a line of cavalry so entirely upset the calculations of the Capuans that their ascendant was lost, both in the cavalry and light troops. This new body of men proved so useful that it was

added to the legions at Capua, in maniples. Its use did not
spread far nor last long.

The Capuans, reduced to the last extremity, and foreseeing
speedy surrender unless Hannibal intervened, managed to get
a messenger to him (a Numidian, as on the last occasion),
imploring him to come at once to their aid. Hannibal was
undecided which he must do first, again attack the citadel of
Tarentum, or move to Capua, — the possession of the first
being of the greatest importance to him, and the loss of the
last a calamity he dared not contemplate. He finally decided
to go to the assistance of his faithful ally. Leaving his heavy
train and sick behind, he started from Tarentum by quick
marches and with his best troops, some thirty thousand
strong, and the thirty-three elephants brought by Hanno.
His direct road lay along the Via Appia, through Venusia
and the Beneventum country. He passed unchallenged the
walls of Beneventum, and marching rapidly along the familiar
roads, reached the confluence of the Calor and Vulturnus,
seized by assault on the oppidum of Caiatia, and filing to the
left, camped in a valley in the rear of Mt. Tifata. There
seems to be no proof that his presence was unknown to the
Romans, as is often alleged. It would be practically impossible for thirty thousand men in an enemy's country to appear
within five miles of a blockading force of sixty thousand
without discovery. As usual, the Romans preferred not to
attack Hannibal, but prepared to fight for their lines around
Capua. Just what the consuls were doing while Hannibal
marched from the south coast to Capua does not appear.
Shortly after they were in Rome.

Sending several couriers to penetrate into Capua (of whom
one managed to do so) Hannibal gave his friends within the
walls instructions to make a sortie at a given hour on the
next day, while he would assault the lines from the outside at

the same time.   He proposed to debouch from the northern
slope of Mt. Tifata, and attack the Roman lines on the north
of Capua.

Hannibal appeared at the time stated in front of the Roman intrenchments.   The Capuan army made a sortie *en
masse* from the city - gate on the Vulturnus side, aided by the
Carthaginian garrison under Hanno and Bostar, while the

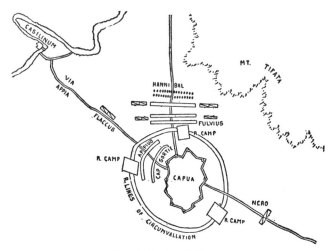

Second Battle of Capua.

citizens on the walls made a horrible din with brass vessels,
"similar to that which is usually made in the dead of night
when the moon is eclipsed," says Livy.   At first this joint
attack — which was made suddenly — came near to overcom-
ing even the perfect defenses of the Roman lines, for the Romans were not certain, until they saw Hannibal's approach,
from what quarter to look for the attack.   But recovering
themselves, Appius undertook to hold head against the
Capuans, while Fulvius, with the bulk of the army, turned on
Hannibal.   The triarii, extraordinarii and velites were left to
man the walls of the camps, as well as the lines of circumval-

lation. Nero was holding the lines towards Suessula and personally occupied the Via Appia with the cavalry of the sixth legion; and the legate C. Fulvius Flaccus, brother of the consul, commanded a body of twenty-four hundred allied horse out towards the river to secure communications with Casilinum.

The task of Fulvius was far from being an easy one. When he saw Hannibal descending the road from Mt. Tifata he seems to have taken the hastati and principes of the three consular armies, nearly forty thousand men, to have sallied from the intrenchments and drawn up in two lines, with his cavalry on the wings. Hannibal had drawn up his whole force in one phalangial line, the elephants behind, and the heavy horse, four thousand strong, manœuvring on the flanks.

Hannibal took the initiative. The shock was delivered with his usual sudden impetus and received with equal stoutness. So bold, however, were Hannibal's men that a simple phalanx of the old Spanish infantry, followed by its quota of elephants, forced its way through the sixth legion in the centre. If Hannibal could have had enough men to form a second line or a reserve, he might have pierced through Fulvius' defense and have penetrated the lines. But the Roman maniples closed up again after the Spanish troops had broken through, and, under the splendid exertions of Quintus Navius, a centurion of gigantic stature, who seized a standard and led on the men, and of Marcus Atilius, the legate, they shut out the brave Spaniards from retreat, while the reserves of the camp, under the legates Licinus and Popilius, stanchly defended the intrenchments against them. The elephants fell into the ditch and were killed; and after a desperate struggle, the Spaniards were surrounded, and died to a man, arms in hand. The Romans, in fighting of this kind, had no superiors. There was no room for manœuvring.

Hannibal, seeing that his task was not to be accomplished, for the rest of his line had not succeeded in making a distinct impression, sounded the recall. He withdrew in perfect order, the horse from the flanks closing in behind the troops to cover their retreat. The Romans did not follow him up. He had undertaken the impossible, out of fidelity to his Capuan allies. Against intrenchments, with fewer men and those of less good material, he had had no chance whatever of success.

In none of his battles, won or lost, was Hannibal so placed that he could not hold his troops in hand. A defeat with him never went beyond lack of success. No one, until the fatal day of Zama, inflicted anything like a crushing blow upon him.

Meanwhile the Capuans, though making an equally brave effort, had been driven in by Appius, who, except for the ballistas and scorpions on the wall, would have entered the city with them. The joint attack had failed, as some authors say, with a loss of eight thousand of Hannibal's army, three thousand Capuans, and thirty-two standards. The Roman loss is not given. Others speak of the attack on Capua as of much less importance.

Hannibal saw that he could not protect Capua by direct means. He resolved to attempt to do so by indirect ones. It was evident that the consuls could not be successfully handled by any force he could bring against them. They had beaten back both the Capuans and himself, and this without seriously depleting their siege lines. He could not remain idle near Capua. Hannibal possessed a keen sense of honor ; he felt that he must make still another effort for this gallant ally. He appreciated her fidelity and present strait. As he could not raise the siege by driving the Romans from their work, might he perhaps not lure them away ? He gathered at the Caiatian fort all the boats which could be found on the river above the Roman lines, and furnished his men with ten days' rations. He sent out a Numidian messenger who should pass for a deserter. This man managed to penetrate into Capua with Hannibal's notice to his friends not to be alarmed at his disappearance, but to await news of a great success. He lighted his camp-fires at evening, to mislead the Romans into believing him still present, marched his men down to the river after night-fall, crossed before morning to the north bank and burned the boats. Next day, when Appius and Fulvius expected a fresh attack, these officers were astonished to see the Carthaginian camp vacated. Hannibal had marched straight on Rome.

This is the first instance of which we have any record in which a thrust at the enemy's capital has been used as a feint to withdraw him from a compromising position.

It is not probable that Hannibal had any idea that he could capture Rome by a *coup de main.* If after Cannæ he came to the conclusion that it was not a wise step to take, all the more must he have so determined now. But he did expect that his march would induce one or both the Roman proconsuls to leave Capua and follow him, and thus not only raise the siege of Capua, but give him a chance of one more open-field fight with a Roman army. At all events it was an admirable stratagem, and one in which he has had many imitators, but had no predecessor.

Livy states that Hannibal marched along the Latin Way, and also says that Cælius is doubtful whether he did not march through Samnium; and, though there is some disagreement as to what the authorities show, Mommsen leading him " through Samnium and along the Valerian Way past Tibur to the bridge over the Anio," it would seem that his manifest intention of a march on Rome, for the purpose of luring the proconsuls away from Capua, would induce him to

take the direct road. Either the Latin or the Appian Way
was the nearest route, and the Appian Way was best left to
the Romans to follow him up on. There was no necessity of
his going so far out of his way as Samnium, and to retire

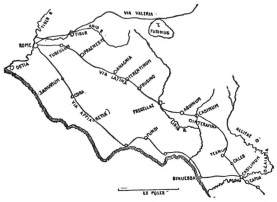

Hannibal's March on Rome.

into that province would not convey to his opponents the
very impression he was anxious to produce, namely, that
Rome was in immediate and grave danger.

Hannibal did not march fast, — another sign that the capture of Rome was not his objective. He was delayed in
places by bridges which the Latins had broken down. But
he proceeded at a leisurely gait when he could have forced
the marching, ravaging as he went, and looking for signs of
the following of the consular legions. But these came not,
and, choking down his disappointment as best he might, he
followed on his course through Cales, which he reached on
the second day after crossing the Vulturnus; Casinum, where
he spent two days foraging, — Livy calls it ravaging; then,
by Interamna and Aquinum to Fregellæ, where he was delayed at the Liris River by a bridge broken down by the
inhabitants; and so along the Latin Way by Frusino, Feren-

tinum, Anagnia, Præneste, to Tusculum, which he could not
enter; until he reached the Anio, on whose left bank he
camped, some six miles from Rome. His Numidian horse at
once began to devastate the region. The poor countrymen
fled from their homes only to be cut down by the wayside.

Fulvius had quickly guessed the design of Hannibal, and
had notified the senate, which moreover had been already informed by the inhabitants of Fregellæ, who had broken the
bridge on the Liris. The consternation in Rome was great.
The scenes after Cannæ threatened to be repeated. Fabius
and a few senators kept almost the only cool heads. The
majority were for at once raising the siege of Capua and
bringing the proconsular armies to the capital. Fabius, who
fully understood Hannibal's manœuvre, pointed out the folly
of doing just that thing which Hannibal most desired and
was aiming to bring about. The garrison of Rome was sufficient. Hannibal had just been repulsed from before the
mere siege-intrenchments of Capua; how should he take
Rome with its lofty, substantial walls, manned by over twenty-five thousand soldiers, new to be sure, but still Roman
soldiers? Finally, a middle course was agreed to. The proconsuls were to be notified of what the garrison of Rome
actually was, and left to decide what should be done.

Fulvius did not for a moment lose his head. He sent a
courier to inform the senate of what he deemed it wise to do.
He knew that Hannibal would probably produce a great
commotion at Rome, but he had no fears that the Carthaginian general could capture or would even attempt to capture
the city. If after the victory of Cannæ he had not made
the attempt, how should he now, after a defeat before Capua?
The Roman generals were beginning to feel that they could
better cope with Hannibal than of yore. The demoralization of the first three years had disappeared. Fulvius had

decided on what was wise, and he was speedily on the march to Rome with fifteen thousand chosen infantry and one thousand cavalry, leaving nearly fifty thousand men at Capua under wounded Appius. Knowing that Hannibal had marched by the Via Latina, Fulvius moved north by the Appian Way, sending ahead messengers to have rations provided by the population on the way, at Setia, Cora, Lanuvium.

Fulvius, says Livy, was detained at the Vulturnus by Hannibal's burning the boats, which obliged him to make rafts in order to cross. This looks as if the bridge at Casilinum had been broken down. But owing to Hannibal's purposely slow marches, he arrived in Rome the day Hannibal neared its walls. Rome thus had, in addition to Fulvius' army, its own garrison, a part at least of the two consular armies, and all the troops of Alba, which came to Rome at once. It is difficult to say what the total force was. The consuls were in Rome, but we are not told which of their legions were with them. There were certainly over forty thousand men in the city. It stood in no danger whatever. Troops were disposed in the citadel, along the walls, at the Alban Mountain and at Fort Æsula. This force would have made an assault by Hannibal mere folly, with his much less than thirty thousand men, even if he had harbored any intention of so doing. He contented himself with advancing along the left bank of the Anio to within the short distance of three miles of the walls and making a reconnoissance as far as the temple of Hercules near the Colline gate. After a slight skirmish, in which his own Numidians crossed swords with the Numidians who had deserted him, he retired to the camp which he had established near by.

The populace in Rome was in such a state of excitement and terror that the senate passed a law that all former dictators and consuls should again resume their functions until the enemy had left the vicinity of Rome. This was necessary to suppress acts of positive madness. Nothing shows the popular scare so well as the fact that the appearance of the Numidian deserters, as they marched through the city to go out to encounter Hannibal, so affrighted many that there arose a cry that the city was taken, and multitudes retired to

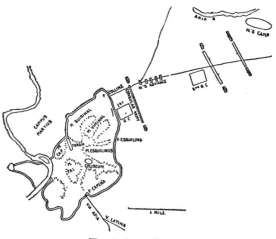

Hannibal near Rome.

their housetops and cast stones down upon their own legions. The other side to this picture is the statement that the very ground on which stood Hannibal's camp was sold in Rome, at the moment of its occupation, for its usual market value. The intelligent Roman was a level-headed man.

Fulvius had entered Rome by the Capuan gate, had at once marched through the city, and now, with the consuls, occupied a position outside the walls between the Esquiline and Colline gates, reinforced with the bulk of the Roman garrison. The consuls did not propose to be provoked into risking a general engagement, unless they themselves invited it at their own time. Hannibal, who was anxious to fight on anything like even terms, though not ready to shatter his phalanx against the walls of Rome, resented this inaction by pillaging the region, while waiting news from Capua. This soon came in, and much to his chagrin he learned that the blockade was in no sense relieved; but that fifty thousand men still held the lines. He recognized that he had failed in his object. His disappointment must indeed have been keen. He saw at a glance that Capua, that faithful city, must be left to her fate. He could do naught which might avail her. He could not raise the siege by assault. Stratagem had failed him. Even if he had nothing else to call upon his time and exertions, he saw no way of helping Capua. It was useless to try to oppose the fifty thousand troops intrenched before that town. If he marched back by the Latin road, Fulvius and the consuls would have been down upon his rear; if by a circuit through Samnium, they would have reached Capua before he could do so, and his chances would have been still less. To return thither, even, would place him between two Roman armies, each nearly twice his strength, and for no advantage. Moreover he was obliged by the importance of the affairs in the south, on holding his position in which his entire salvation depended, to regain Apulia.

Fulvius and the consuls now moved their camp nearer to Hannibal's, and on the next day drew up in line on their own ground to invite an attack. Livy says the battle was prevented by a heavy storm of rain and hail; and that the same thing occurred on the succeeding day, which the Carthaginians interpreted as a divine command not to attack the city. The cause rather lay in the fact that Hannibal saw no eventual good to be derived from an assault on the Roman position, and deemed it wise to withdraw. He retired along the Valerian Way through the Alban territory and that of

the Peligni, whence striking southerly by Æsernia, Bovianum
and Herdonia, he reached northern Apulia, and continued
his march towards Tarentum.

The consuls harassed his rear, and Fulvius returned to
take command at Capua. At the Anio, near Tibur, whose
bridge had been broken while Hannibal was occupied in
front of the capital, the Romans attacked him, captured a

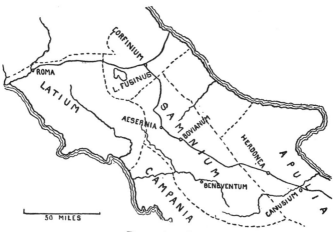

Retreat from Rome.

large part of his booty, and gave him a serious check. But
he shortly paid them off. Turning in his tracks a few days
later, he made on their camp a night attack which was so entirely a surprise that it demoralized and nearly broke up their
army. The consuls beat a hasty retreat in far from good
order, nor stopped till they reached a position well into the
mountains. Livy tells us little about it.

Reaching Apulia, Hannibal continued his march through
Lucania, and from here made a rapid diversion into Bruttium, against Rhegium, hoping to surprise this town, so important to him. But disappointed in so doing, he returned
to Tarentum. Here he learned the surrender of Capua from
hunger.

So soon as the devoted town got news of what had happened, the citizens gave way to despair. Though the Roman senate offered his life to whomsoever would come over before a stated day, no faith was put in the promise, and no one accepted it. Many of Hannibal's adherents took their own lives by poison. Hanno and Bostar remained in control, as every one else lost his head. After some days the senate nominally, though the commanders in reality, were compelled to surrender unconditionally. The Romans put to death those who had been the chief supporters of Hannibal, and expatriated others. The citizens were generally sold into slavery, and all property was confiscated to the uses of the Roman people. Most of the artisans and poorer inhabitants were left undisturbed, and a prætor was sent to govern the city.

The fall of Capua obliged Hannibal to change his tactics. Masters of Campania, the Romans could debouch upon Apulia or Lucania at will. He was no longer able to retain the numberless small cities in these provinces, which he had hitherto garrisoned and made of use, not only as a moral force, but to control the territory adjoining them for foraging. He saw that his campaigns must be narrowed to a small section of southern Italy. The number of his enemies, and want of reinforcements, were tightening the toils around him, — though indeed no opponent had yet dared to come too near his reach.

In the past ten years Hannibal had taught the Romans how to make war. This march on Rome, one of his best pieces of strategy, which abundantly deserved success, if undertaken at the opening of his campaigns, would certainly have accomplished its object of luring away the Roman generals from their quarry. Now it had accomplished nothing. His pupils were graduating in the school of war, and commanded means which their master lacked more than ever. We, who owe so much to Roman civilization, recognize the fact that Hannibal could not succeed, ought not to have succeeded. Our military regrets are easily swallowed up in our historical satisfaction. But one thing we may be proud to owe to Hannibal. He was the earliest teacher of the Romans in the broader lessons of war. From him they learned what strategy can accomplish against force; and this knowledge, improved by them as the Romans improved everything they touched, has descended, among their other great legacies, to civilized mankind.

The Romans, though in a certain sense successful, and though Fulvius' cool calculations, under the trying ordeal of Hannibal's march on the capital, deserves the highest encomium, could scarcely congratulate themselves upon what had been accomplished this year. Hannibal, with a tithe of their force, had once again marched throughout Italy, and not only defied the capital, but devastated its territory to the very gates. For one hundred and fifty years this had not been done. He had marched in and out and between the Roman armies, had beaten them whenever the odds were not all against him, and had retired unharmed from before forces thrice his own in number. He still had a solid foothold in the south.

Altogether, this year, while favorable to the Roman cause, and while showing great advance in self-reliance and ability on the part of the Roman generals, must be considered as vastly more brilliant, in a military sense, for the great Carthaginian. The darker his cause, the brighter the effulgence of his genius. There are things to which words can do no justice. It is well to read and reread, to trace upon the map, the operations of the years of Hannibal's decline in Italy, as we would sit and gaze at the canvas or marble of a great

master. To those who know what war in its intellectual
sense can be, such lecture will best show what manner of
man this giant was.

Etruria this year showed decided signs of discontent; the
Latin colonies were weary of the burden of the war, and
grew more restless; in Spain the death of the two Scipios
gave Hasdrubal abundant opportunity to join his brother in
Italy. Had he done this, — had he landed in Bruttium, as
he could well have done, — the fate of the world might have
been changed.

To repair the disasters in the peninsula, Claudius Nero
was sent to Spain, with some thirteen thousand men. His
early manœuvres were excellent. He succeeded in shutting
Hasdrubal up in his mountain fastnesses, where he could
compel a surrender. But Hasdrubal managed to outwit him
by perfidy, as the Romans phrased it, and escaped. Nero,
"harsh, irritable and unpopular," was an excellent general,
but lacked the political wit to keep the Spaniards in subjection. The Roman senate, far from content with the result
accomplished by Nero, dispatched thither Publius Cornelius
Scipio — now twenty-four years old — to take command.
But it was too late in the year to do aught but go into winter-quarters.

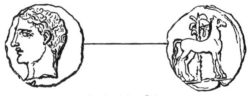

Carthaginian Coin.

XXXV.

ANOTHER ROMAN ARMY DESTROYED. 210 B. C.

THE plan of 210 B. C. was to take from Hannibal as many of the towns he had captured as possible. There were two hundred thousand men under arms. Hannibal was unable to hold as much territory as before, and evacuating a number of his strongholds in order to utilize the garrisons, he destroyed them. The consul Fulvius, with twenty-two thousand men, was corresponding with Herdonia, which was ready to betray its Carthaginian allies. Hannibal was in Bruttium. He gathered a force of thirty thousand men, and rapidly marching on Herdonia, drew up in line of battle, before Fulvius heard of his arrival. In the succeeding conflict Fulvius was killed, and his army cut to pieces. Hannibal destroyed the town, and sent the inhabitants to Bruttium. He then retired to Numistro. Here Marcellus followed him up. A battle ensued, with indecisive results. Both the Romans and Hannibal had begun to marshal their armies in two lines, as they found that one line was not sufficiently solid. In both these late battles such was the formation. Hannibal retired from Numistro, followed by Marcellus, who exhibited marked ability in his manœuvres. Sicily was entirely reduced this year. In Spain, Scipio (later Africanus) captured Cartagena by a bold and able *coup de main.* Hannibal wintered at Tarentum; Marcellus at Venusia.

MARCELLUS and M. Valerius Lævinus, who had done so well in Greece, were consuls of the year 210 B. C. The prætors were Publius Manlius Vulso, L. Manlius Acidinus, C. Lætorius and L. Cincius Alimentus. The plan of the year was to conduct a small outpost-war against Hannibal, and endeavor to rescue from his holding as many towns as possible; to leave the citadel of Tarentum to take care of itself; and to reduce the forces somewhat by consolidation of legions, discharging the highest paid soldiers from motives of economy. Twenty-one legions remained on foot, — the reduction still left over two hundred thousand men under arms.

Valerius had been fighting Philip of Macedon. Before leaving Greece to enter upon his consular duties, he concluded an alliance, offensive and defensive, with Ætolia, which gave Philip enough to do to keep his own territory from invasion for him to seek to invade Italy.

The taxes rendered necessary by the war were weighing very heavily on all the citizens and colonists of Rome. The constant sacrifices increased. General discontent was rampant. Lævinus, on the assembling of the senate, protested against the severity and inequality of these imposts, and urged that the upper classes should give an example of their patriotism. He moved that each senator should present to the coffers of the state all the gold, silver and jewels he possessed, except only what was suitable and proper for the uses of his wife, daughters and table. This proposition was hailed with acclamation. At the closing of the senate on that day, the Forum swarmed with the rich, accompanied by their slaves bearing burdens, each vying with the other in laying his offering at the feet of the fatherland. The example was followed by every class; and the treasury was filled more easily and to better effect than it could have been by any species of taxation. And this with abundant satisfaction to all.

Marcellus, first assigned by lot to Sicily, exchanged with his colleague for the war against Hannibal. A soldier of exceptional capacity, Marcellus was of a harsh, uncompromising disposition, and had made numberless enemies in Sicily. He took command of two legions in Samnium; Cnæus Fulvius, proconsul, headed a force of two legions in Apulia; Q. Fulvius remained at Capua with two; Valerius took charge of Sicily, where he had four legions and the fleet, — for, fully to reduce this island was imperative. The other armies remained much the same.

Hannibal's entire scheme was now changed. He still looked forward to receiving reinforcements from home, or to Hasdrubal's joining him from Spain, though heartsick at the hope deferred, and foreseeing failure in the end from the ill-concentrated effort. But with or without aid, he would not leave Italy until driven from it or recalled by the Carthaginian senate.

He could no longer afford to hold so much territory in Samnium, Lucania and Apulia. He needed the garrisons of the many towns now under his sway for service in the field. His army was dwindling, and he must concentrate his forces in lieu of dispersing them throughout the friendly colonies. The fate of Capua had produced a disastrous effect on these allies, who began to see that the Carthaginian was the losing side, and Hannibal feared that his garrisons might many of them be attacked by the citizens of the towns as present enemies, even if late friends. He therefore evacuated a number of the least important places, and lest they should fall into the Roman hands he razed most of them to the ground. This proceeding, however essential as an act of war, of necessity operated much in his disfavor with the colonies.

In Apulia, Salapia was the first town to fall by defection to the Romans, and its garrison of five hundred Numidians, after a very desperate resistance, was massacred. In Samnium, Marcellus captured Narronea and Meles, and about three thousand Carthaginians in garrison.

The proconsul Cnæus Fulvius Centumalus lay encamped before Herdonia. This was one of the first cities which had joined Hannibal after Cannæ. Hannibal learned that Fulvius was corresponding with the people of Herdonia, and fearing lest relaxed discipline might enable Fulvius to capture the town, he left his baggage in a safe place in Bruttium, where he had been camping, and taking a force stated at thirty thousand men, of which six thousand was horse, he advanced in light order and by rapid marches to Herdonia, where he at once went into camp near Fulvius. Under cover

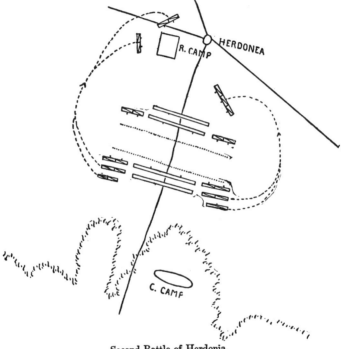

Second Battle of Herdonia.

of the hills, before the latter heard of his arrival, Hannibal drew up in line and offered battle. Fulvius had but twenty thousand infantry and less than two thousand horse; but he was unwilling to decline the combat. He hastily formed his men in two lines of cohorts, one Roman and one allied legion in each line, the velites in the front, the horse on the flanks. Hannibal likewise had two lines, both of foot and heavy horse, the latter having the light-mounted men in their rear.

It will be noticed that the habit of making two lines of cohorts was growing. In battles against the nations so far encountered, the Romans had found the one line of cohorts, that is, one line having the principes, hastati and triarii, sufficient. But against the violent onslaughts of Hannibal, the Roman generals had begun to double their lines. The Carthaginians had found the same device serviceable against the wonderful tenacity of the Roman legionary, and used two lines in many cases, beginning with this period. As about this time there was a transition in Hannibal's organization, so that his phalanx was gradually adopting some of the features of the legion, it is hard to say how heavy a line this made.

The battle opened by an advance of infantry on both sides, the horse remaining *in situ*. Noting that the attention of the Roman general was exclusively devoted to his line of cohorts, Hannibal thrust out his second and third lines of cavalry to fall on the Roman flanks. By a rapid circuit the Numidians on the right attacked the second Roman line in the rear; the horse of the left charged down on the extraordinarii in the camp. While this was going on, Hannibal moved his second line up to strengthen his first, and made another forward movement. The Roman legions fought stanchly and without losing ground or formation, until one of the legions of the second line, — the sixth, — attacked by the Numidians, fell into disorder and communicated this disorder to its leading legion, — the fifth. Perceiving this, Hannibal redoubled his efforts, and the Roman army, thus compromised, speedily showed signs of demoralization. The defeat at once turned to massacre. Fulvius, eleven tribunes, and a vast number of soldiers were killed. The rest, except some three thousand men who escaped to Marcellus in Samnium, were captured. From seven thousand to thirteen thousand men are said to have been slain.

Herdonia, which Hannibal no longer trusted, was destroyed, and its inhabitants sent to Metapontum and Thurii.
The traitors who had corresponded with Fulvius, he executed.
He then returned to northern Lucania and camped on an
eminence west of and near Numistro, proposing either to capture the place or make a bid for Marcellus to attack him.
Marcellus, who was essentially a fighter, seemed anxious to
wipe out the defeat of his colleague, and moved from
Samnium on Numistro and camped. The day after his arrival he drew up in the plain opposite Hannibal, with his left
not far from the town. He likewise marshaled his legions
in two lines of cohorts, in each line two legions, and as usual
the velites out as skirmishers and the cavalry on the flanks.

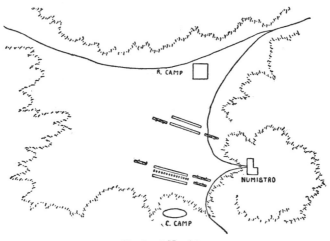

Battle of Numistro.

Hannibal did the like, his right leaning on the hills near the
town, his heavy infantry in two lines, the Spaniards in the
first, the Africans and Gauls in the second, with the elephants
between the lines and the light troops and Balacrean slingers
in front.

When the light troops of both sides had opened the fight, the elephants were driven forward, but apparently met with no success. The two first lines maintained the struggle with alternate success from the third hour till towards night. They were then relieved by the second lines, on which darkness fell before either had produced any impression on the other. This battle is so entirely unlike Hannibal's usual tactics, that one is fain to doubt the accuracy of the narration. As a rule, he showed originality of conception and execution. Here, neither was the common parallel order varied from, nor the fighting forced, nor anything like grand-tactics put to use. Frontinus says the victory remained with Hannibal.

Next day Marcellus again offered battle, standing in line from sunrise till late in the day, but Hannibal declined it. He was beginning to distrust the stanchness of his troops, and he had gained a distinct admiration for the steadiness of the Roman legions when well led. Marcellus, says Livy, spent the day under cover of his line of battle, gathering spoils and burning his dead. During the coming night Hannibal stole a march on the consul and moved away, intending to make for Tarentum. Marcellus followed hard upon his heels and reached him at Venusia. Hannibal made halt and about-face. Here for several days, Marcellus kept close to him, and annoyed him by frequent small outpost-attacks, not coming again to open conflict. Hannibal then retired in a zigzag route through Apulia, making many night-marches and taking refuge in numberless stratagems to lure Marcellus into a fight under disadvantageous conditions. But Marcellus could not be so trapped. He would neither march at night nor come to battle, unless he himself dictated the terms; but he followed and watched his opponent for many weeks, harassing him with small-war in true Fabian style, cautiously feeling every step. For this reason he marched only by day and after careful scouting. He exhibited in this pursuit uncommon ability. But the fact always remains marked that, however able his opponent, when Hannibal failed, his army was never seriously damaged ; when he won, the enemy was apt to be destroyed. The fact itself so constantly recurred, that frequent reference to it can scarcely be avoided.

Hannibal returned to Tarentum to winter, and Marcellus took up his winter-quarters at Venusia. The citadel of Tarentum was suffering for want of provisions, but still held out. An attempt to victual it was made from Rhegium, but was beaten off by the Tarentine fleet. The tenacity of the Roman garrison was remarkable.

In Sicily, Valerius succeeded in mastering the whole country. He was greatly aided by Mutines, a distinguished Numidian officer whom Hanno, by unjust treatment, had disaffected, and who had surrendered Agrigentum to the Romans and embraced their cause. Some of Mutines' campaigning is among the best samples of the use of cavalry in large bodies to be met with in history. The bulk of the Sicilian troops could now be used for the *coup de grâce* against Hannibal. Syphax, a Numidian king, concluded an alliance with Rome, and ambassadors were sent to Africa to stir up further ill-feeling against Carthage.

Publius Cornelius Scipio, son and nephew of the Scipios lately killed, had succeeded Nero in Spain, at the early age of twenty-four. During the first part of this year, he captured New Carthage, dealing a serious blow to the Punic supremacy in that country.

This was a fine example of the seizure of a strong place out of hand. Scipio was not at the head of the Roman soldiers of the Second Punic War, as his victory at Zama over Hannibal and the favoritism of Livy are wont, in the minds of most readers, to place him. But he was an able general, and he

was now exceptionally fortunate in his lieutenants, Lælius
and Silanus.

This capture of New Carthage was unquestionably a fine
bit of work. It was early spring. Scipio was aware that
Hasdrubal Barca was expecting to force his way across the
Ebro in the effort to reach Italy to join his brother. He had
some thirty thousand men, a force none too big to hold head
against Hasdrubal. He determined to make a dash on
Cartagena, the Carthaginian-Spanish capital, not only for the
sake of the place, but to draw the spirit from the enemy by

Forces in Iberia, B. C. 210.

doing them a damage. If he left any force behind to defend
the Ebro, he would not have enough men for his enterprise.
He decided to run the risk. Breaking up from Tarraco
early in the spring of 209 B. C., he led his whole force south-
ward, before the Carthaginians were afoot. Hasdrubal Barca
lay with his army at the head-waters of the Tagus ; his name-
sake, son of Gisgo, was at its mouth ; Mago was at the Pillars of Hercules. No Carthaginian army was within twelve
days' march of Cartagena.

Scipio marched fast. Herein lay the success of the plan.
The fleet under Lælius accompanied him. In seven forced
marches he reached the place, and the fleet sailed into the
harbor on the same day. The city had a garrison of one
thousand men.

The city of Cartagena lay on a high and rocky tongue of
land running out into the harbor, with a salt-water lake on
the west, whose mouth discharges into it close by the town.

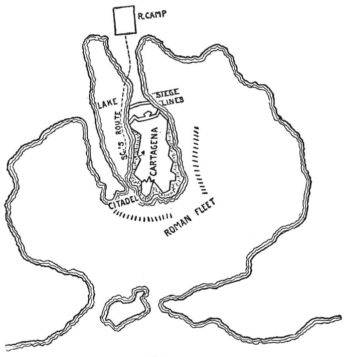

Cartagena.

The garrison woke up suddenly to the fact that they were
surrounded on three sides by the fleet, and on the fourth by
the Roman army. They had not even a chance to send to
their distant friends for succor. But the commander, Mago,

behaved gallantly. He had sufficient arms, and he made the citizens man the walls. He attempted a sortie, but it was driven back with loss. Scipio immediately began siege-advances along the narrow neck of land, and worked his men hard to tire out the garrison. This he succeeded in doing by constant relays of fresh troops.

Scipio did not expect to capture the city from this point. He had learned that there was a weak spot in the wall on the lake side, approachable when the sea was at ebb tide and the lake less full; and here he calculated to make an assault. None but isolated fishermen had ever used this path, which was probably unknown to the Cartagenian garrison. Re-doubling his efforts on the land side and ordering the fleet to make a feint to draw the attention of the besieged, at midday when the tide was out and a strong north wind blew the water towards the harbor, he headed a party of five hundred escaladers with ladders, and led them along the beach to the spot, the men wading to the middle in some places. As he had expected, and indeed had been able to observe from an eminence outside the city, the wall here was found undefended. The Romans made their way into the city and easily took it. Mago, who had thrown himself with five hundred men into the citadel, surrendered.

Immense booty, great supplies of military stores, prisoners and hostages of high rank, and the best harbor in Spain, rewarded Scipio's bold enterprise. Having accomplished this *coup de main* within a week after his arrival before the city, Scipio held a review and manœuvre of his army and navy.

" On the first day the legions under arms performed evolutions through a space of four miles; on the second day he ordered them to repair and clean their arms before their tents; on the third day they engaged in imitation of a regular battle with wooden swords, throwing javelins with the points covered with balls; on the fourth day they rested; on the fifth they again performed evolutions under arms. This succession of exercise and rest they kept up as long as they stayed at Carthage. The rowers and mariners, pushing out to sea when the weather was calm, made trial of the manageableness of their ships by mock sea-fights. Such exercises, both by sea and land, without the city, prepared their minds and bodies for war." — Livy.

This describes the exercises constantly indulged in by the Roman army and navy, both in peace and war, and is interesting on this account.

Having put the town in a proper state of defense and suitably garrisoned it, Scipio marched rapidly back to Tarraco, which he reached before Hasdrubal had got ready for the spring campaign. He deserves great credit for his intelligence and courage in this matter.

The fatal grip of Roman numbers was gradually tightening around Hannibal. Alone, with but himself to rely upon, he was obliged not only to resist this mighty people, but to contend with bitter political enemies at home. He was well aware that everything was on the wane for him; that nothing could enable him to make headway in Italy but speedy and large reinforcements. These had been so often promised and so often delayed that Hannibal must have lost faith in their ever coming. We cannot suppose that Hannibal was not keen-eyed enough to see that failure was but a question of time. With full appreciation of what he had done, with full confidence in what he might have done if properly sustained, he must have felt that his ground was slipping from under him, that he could not at the same time fight Rome and Carthage.

XXXVI.

TARENTUM LOST. 209 B. C.

THE senate in 209 B. C. decided to besiege Tarentum. Fabius was one of the consuls, and undertook this duty, while the other consul, Fulvius, was to engage Hannibal's attention in Samnium and Lucania, and Marcellus do the like in Apulia. The force on foot was much the same. The financial condition of Rome was distressing; famine was threatened, and some of the Latin allies refused their quotas of men. But the republic held on. Marcellus began operations by moving on Hannibal. The latter felt like saving his men rather than fighting, as his plan now was to wait for reinforcements from Carthage or his brother, Hasdrubal, from Spain. He moved from place to place, Marcellus cleverly following. Finally it came to battle near Asculum. On the first day Hannibal beat Marcellus badly; on the second, Marcellus won, according to Livy, a victory. But he shut himself up in Venusia for the rest of the campaign, while Hannibal marched throughout the country. This did not look much like a Roman victory. The Romans this year recaptured many of Hannibal's allied cities, and besieged Caulon. While Hannibal sought to raise the siege, Fabius managed to get possession of Tarentum by the treachery of a part of its garrison. The loss of this city was a grievous blow to the Carthaginian.

IN B. C. 209 there were elected, as consuls, Q. Fulvius Flaccus, the hero of Capua, and Fabius Maximus. The former was chosen for the fourth, the latter for the fifth time. The prætors were Veturius Philo, Quintus Crispinus, Hostilius Tubulus, and C. Arunculeius.

The plan of campaign made by the senate was as follows: Fabius, with two legions, was to besiege the city of Tarentum, still held by the Carthaginians and their allies, so as to deprive Hannibal of this storehouse and convenient point of communication with Macedonia and Carthage. This was perhaps now the most important objective of the Roman arms.

Once driven from Tarentum, Hannibal would be near to being driven from Italy for want of a base. The Romans still held the citadel, but its capture by Hannibal had on several occasions been imminent, and the Roman efforts to revictual it had not always been successful.

To Fabius fell this important duty, mainly because he was a patrician, and received the support of the controlling class. Fulvius had gained reputation by capturing Capua ; Marcellus, by taking Syracuse. Both had fought Hannibal in the open field with credit. But despite these facts, and the additional one that Fabius had not proved himself a fighter, — and to fight was still the Roman's chief boast and characteristic, — he enjoyed not only the confidence of the patricians, but all classes saw that he first had grasped the theory of the war which must be waged against Hannibal, unless Rome was to succumb. The Roman theory of government was that men should not be elected too often to the highest office, nor continued too long in any one command. It was felt that there was less danger to the republic in changing frequently — even if the right man was taken from work well done — than in leaving any one man too long in a position which might lead to abuses. Despite this, Fabius was again honored with the consulate. There was a general feeling that there could be no danger to the republic from him.

Two armies were to aid the siege of Tarentum by indirect manœuvres. Fulvius, with two legions which had returned from Sicily, was to lay siege to other towns in southern Samnium and Lucania, which were still held by Hannibal, but were wavering in their fealty to him ; while Marcellus near Venusia, with the two legions he had commanded before, was to amuse Hannibal by constant diversions, so as to keep him in northern Apulia, and thus aid these several siege-operations. Crispinus, prætor, had two legions in Campania, with headquarters at Capua. C. Hostilius commanded in Rome; Veturius went to Gaul; Arunculeius to Sardinia; Sulpicius remained in Macedonia.

Valerius Lævinus was again sent to Sicily as proconsul with L. Cincius, and in command of four legions. Here he organized additional troops from the Numidians of Mutines and the Syracusans, for the defense of the island. From Sicily he was to victual Fabius at Tarentum, and assist him with vessels. A force was dispatched by him to operate near Rhegium, and another one to attack Caulon. The fleet assisted in these movements, protected Sicily, and made descents upon Africa to annoy the Carthaginians and spy out their plans. Scipio remained in Spain, his command being indefinitely continued. The total force in the field was twenty-one legions, in addition to the Sicilian levies. The whole plan of the year's operations was skillfully devised.

The financial straits of Rome were serious. The currency was debased, but this afforded no permanent relief. Soldiers were not paid. Contractors furnished supplies on credit, and cheated the republic because they had made themselves necessary. The farms were not cultivated for lack of labor; the price of wheat was thrice the usual figure. A famine would have occurred but for supplies from Egypt and the fact that Sicily was no longer a battle-field, but again bore abundant crops. On the other hand, evidences of patriotism were many. Officers and many soldiers served without pay. The owners of the manumitted slaves waited for their purchase-money. The wealthy, who relatively were the worst sufferers, aided the state with great alacrity.

The Romans now learned that Hasdrubal had made large levies in Spain, intending to join his brother in Italy. This news was made more bitter by the refusal of twelve out of the thirty Latin socii to furnish their yearly contingent of men or money, alleging that they had been drained to the bottom and had no more. There was, moreover, much dissatisfaction among many of the allied cities, about the treatment of the Cannæ soldiers. If the example thus set should spread, Rome was beyond question lost. Why had not Hannibal at this moment reinforcements from home? Here was the chance which even Cannæ had not brought about. The temper of these twelve confederate cities conclusively show what Hannibal had been able to do with his bare handful of men and his scanty means. Without a great victory for seven years, his own tireless patience, his marvelous manœuvring, and his skillful policy had brought twelve out of thirty of the socii to the point of refusing to go on with the war.

The crisis was alarming. But the consuls were equal to the emergency. Their influence on the deputies of the eighteen still faithful allies was such that these responded not only to the demands of Rome, but held themselves ready to do all that Rome might ask. The twelve recalcitrant allies were simply ignored. No present punishment was attempted.

Money was still harder to get this year than last. Supplies, arms and clothing for the large armies in the field were often pitifully wanting. But if Rome thus suffered, what may we imagine Hannibal without any resources whatsoever, to have undergone? Instead of a patriotic people at his back, he had a jealous, abusive opposition, or at best a silent, stingy lack of support at home. Instead of allies who — with small exception — generously gave their all to the cause, his adherents were gradually falling away. And yet this year his genius stood him in stead of weapons, clothing, rations, friends.

The news of Hasdrubal's probable march to Italy was indeed a terrible one for Rome. It was plain that Hannibal must be beaten before the arrival of his brother. The Car-

thaginian captain had marched from winter-quarters in
Tarentum to Canusium, with intent to capture the town.
Most of his allied cities had been rent from or had deserted
him, but he felt that he must hold the high road through
Apulia. Only by keeping this open could he hope to join
hands with his brother. He had no idea of being penned in,
be it by one or by a score of Roman armies. He did not
want to fight, but was ready to do so to secure his end. And
the question of rationing his army was dependent upon having elbow-room.

Acting under the general plan agreed upon between the
consuls, Marcellus decided to move upon Hannibal. The
Roman generals, from Hannibal's being so often obliged to
decline battle, had begun to assume that he had lost his ability
to fight, — that, in other words, they had formerly overrated
him. Marcellus held the same opinion. He broke up from
Venusia as soon as there was forage and marched against
Hannibal, thinking to harass him by smaller operations, and
perchance engage him in battle; at all events do what would
enable Fabius the more easily to progress with his siege-
operations against Tarentum. Hannibal was worse beset
than ever. Fulvius had marched into Lucania. Caulon was
being besieged by the Sicilian fleet and some land forces.
All the towns the Carthaginians had held in Samnium had
surrendered. While Marcellus was planning to keep Hannibal in northern Apulia, his footing on the southern coast was
threatened to be cut away from him. If ever a captain had
a desperate game to play, to this great soldier's lot it had
now fallen. It had become a mere question of existence
until he received help to continue the war.

Hannibal's genius and energy rose to the occasion. Marcellus approached Canusium. Hannibal, with his wonted
determination not to strike until his blow should tell, retired

from the open plains to the uplands on the right bank of the
Aufidus, west of Canusium.   The ground here was much cut
up and wooded.   Marcellus followed him day by day, camp-

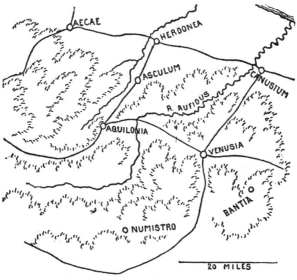

Canusium-Numistro-Herdonia Region.

ing near by and constantly offering battle.   Hannibal had
no men to lose, even for the honor of a fruitless victory, and
avoided everything but the daily skirmishing of light troops
and horse.   The Romans could replace their men lost in action ; not so Hannibal.

It soon appeared that if Hannibal continued upstream too
far he ran the danger of getting entangled in the mountain-
region and of being shut in between Fulvius, who was in
Lucania, and Marcellus.   He therefore chose to cross to
the north side and moved to the plains between Asculum
and Herdonia.   Marcellus followed him sharply up and
came upon him just at the moment when he was busy fortifying his camp.   The Romans, elated with the pursuit of

what they already deemed a beaten enemy, fell upon the working parties with such suddenness and energy that Hannibal found himself compelled to turn and offer battle in pure self-defense. The action lasted till night without material gain on either side, and each army retired to its fortified camp, — the two being on either side of the Asculum valley.

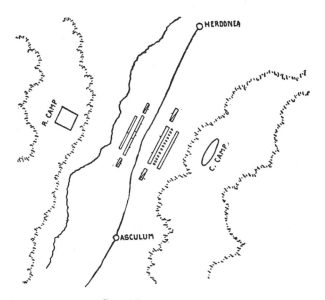

Second Battle of Asculum.

By daylight next morning both armies drew up in order of battle for a renewal of the conflict. Hannibal was tired of the pursuit of Marcellus, and though he could not afford to fight — men were so scarce with him that he must accomplish his ends by manœuvring rather than by attrition — he saw that nothing less would rid him of his enemy. His line was twofold, with the elephants between them. Marcellus' army stood likewise in two lines. In the first was the right allied legion, then the extraordinarii, then the twentieth Roman legion; in the second, the eighteenth Roman and the left allied legions.

The battle was fiercely contested from the outset. After some two hours of desperate fighting, the right allied legion and the extraordinarii were driven in, and though Marcellus quickly ordered up the eighteenth to their support, the entire line gave way in considerable confusion and fell back on its camp with a loss of two thousand seven hundred men, two tribunes, four centurions and six ensigns. Marcellus deserves credit for saving his army from a massacre.

Marcellus punished the runaways, but determined to fight again next day, to wipe out the stigma of defeat. This he proceeded at daylight to do, placing the left allied and eighteenth Roman legion in the first line, and the cohorts which had lost their ensigns between them. In the second line were the twentieth Roman, the extraordinarii and the remaining six cohorts of the right allied legion. Marcellus personally commanded the centre, his legates Cornelius Lentulus and Claudius Nero the wings. Hannibal wondered at Marcellus' determination to face a second defeat, and regretted the necessity of another battle, but as nothing else would suffice, he also drew up in two lines, in the first his Spanish veterans, — few indeed now left, — and the elephants, as on yesterday, between the lines.

Again came the shock of battle, sharp, severe. The strain was long maintained, but without result until Hannibal ordered forward the elephants. These unwieldy animals, equally dangerous to friend and foe, at first brought the front Roman line into some disorder, — so much in fact that had not the tribune Decimus Flavius seized the ensign of the first maniple of hastati of the eighteenth legion, and rallied the Roman legionaries about the spot where the elephants were committing havoc, the confusion would have spread

beyond repair. But under this leadership the Roman soldiers regained heart and the wounded elephants were driven
back through the Carthaginian ranks, where they bred more
mischief than they had done in the Roman cohorts. The
Roman generals utilized this moment for a general advance,
and attacked the Carthaginians with such fury that they
were driven back to their camp in some disorder. The gates
of the camp being obstructed by dead elephants, the phalangites, in seeking refuge, were obliged to climb over the walls,
and a great number of them perished in the ditch and at the
stockade. The Carthaginian loss (perhaps for both days)
is stated by Livy at eight thousand men and five elephants,
the Romans at three thousand. No mention is made of the
cavalry of either side. Though it is probable that Hannibal's cavalry had been much reduced in number, it must
have borne some part in the fight.

Such is the account given us by our only original source,
the Roman historians. But mark the result. Hannibal next
day retired unopposed to Bruttium, where the siege of Caulon by the Romans demanded his attention. Tarentum he
felt that he could rely on to hold out. Marcellus, whose
great number of wounded, says Livy, prevented him from
following Hannibal, — though Marcellus was a man of exceptional energy and would scarcely have allowed this to
stand in his way if there was not a more serious reason, —
withdrew into Venusia, which place he did not leave the rest
of the year, though Hannibal confessedly marched through
the length and breadth of the land. Marcellus " was kept
from pursuing by the number of his wounded men, and re-
moved by gentle marches into Campania, and spent the summer at Sinuessa, engaged in restoring them," says Plutarch,
while "Hannibal ranged with his army round about the
country, and wasted Italy free from all fear." Plutarch

mistakes the locality, but agrees in the main fact with the
other authorities.   This looks less like a defeat of Hannibal
on the second day than the result of a brilliant victory.   And
it is fair to read this victory between the lines of Livy.
Certainly, Marcellus' task had been to keep Hannibal in
northern Apulia; he had failed to perform it; and under
Livy's statement, in view of what he himself further records,
Marcellus can scarcely be credited with a day won.

Moreover, at the close of the year in Rome, at the time of
canvassing for new consuls, there was a vast deal of criticism
of Marcellus' conduct at this time, and he was openly accused
before the Roman public in the Flaminian circus by the plebeian tribune Publicius of losing both these battles.   " Marcellus was under an ill report, not only because he had failed
in his first battle, but further, because while Hannibal was
going wherever he pleased throughout Italy, he had led his
troops to Venusia in the midst of summer to lodge in houses,"
says Livy.   It will not do to underrate Marcellus.   He was
a brave and excellent soldier, whose ability stands out in
cheering relief above the average of Roman generalship in
these years, but too many victories must not be ascribed to
him.   There is no doubt that Hannibal had been undesirous
of fighting, and now retired into Bruttium, partly because he
must recruit his battle-torn ranks, partly to relieve Caulon,
but he does not appear to have been driven away by a bad
defeat.   The Romans continued to occupy upper Apulia,
Marcellus in Venusia being the centre-point.

Fulvius, having nothing in his front, now made a raid
into the Hirpinian, Lucanian and Volcentian domain in lower
Samnium.   Left without support or hope of it, these peoples,
hitherto strong adherents of Hannibal's, surrendered their
towns and the Carthaginian garrisons, without attempt at
opposition.   Fulvius was politic enough to treat the towns

with moderation, and, as a result, a number of others in Lucania followed suit. Even some in northern Bruttium began negotiations with the Romans.

Fabius opened operations among the Salentini. Here he first captured Manduria, with a four-thousand garrison of Carthaginians. He thus cleared from his rear a stronghold of the enemy which might be awkward for him while he attacked Tarentum. Reaching this latter place, he camped on the south side of it, hard by the mouth of the harbor. The Carthaginian fleet had just sailed away to Corcyra to aid in the Macedo-Ætolian war. Fabius utilized this opportune occurrence to collect ships from all sides and build artillery and towers both for land and ship use, prepare for a vigorous siege of the city, and to act in common with the Roman garrison in the citadel.

Meanwhile Hannibal had marched to Caulon. Here the besiegers, who consisted largely of freedmen and slaves, raised the siege, and withdrew to an adjoining eminence. The position was strong, but Hannibal soon managed to surround the force, shut it in, and after the lapse of a few days compelled its surrender. While relieving Caulon, Hannibal had fully counted on Tarentum being able to hold its own, as without treachery it would have done. No sooner had he put aside the danger, than he started with forced marches for this city, intent on disturbing Fabius at his task. But he was just too late. He had nearly reached Tarentum, when the news of its surrender came to him. His chief port was thus in the hands of the enemy.

Fabius had expected a long and tedious operation in front of Tarentum, though he held the harbor and the citadel. But luck was on his side. He had managed, by fostering a *liaison,* to treat with one Philomenus, the commanding officer of a Bruttian detachment of the city garrison, who agreed to give up to him a certain portion of the wall where he commanded. To carry out his scheme, Fabius moved with a portion of his fleet from his position on the south round to the east side of the town near the spot agreed upon. On the next day, before daybreak, at a given signal, demonstrations were made all along the line, with trumpets blaring and as much noise as could well be made. Nico and Democrates, in command, scarcely knew to which side to turn, and under cover of the confusion, the Roman legionaries landed from the vessels, mounted that part of the wall which had been selected and which was found deserted, and speedily opened the gates. At daybreak all Fabius' troops forced their way into the town. Nico and Democrates made a stout resistance in the market place, but were overpowered and both slain. The slaughter was immense. The city was given over to plunder, thirty thousand inhabitants were sold as slaves and much treasure was taken.

Hannibal, on reaching the vicinity, camped three miles distant from Tarentum. But as he could now accomplish nothing, in a day or two he withdrew to Metapontum. From this place he tried one more stratagem on Fabius. He caused letters to be sent by the authorities of the town to this general, proposing surrender on given terms on a certain day, while he, with his army, marched out and lay in ambush on the road he hoped Fabius might take. The cautious Roman came close to falling into the trap, but, held back by inauspicious sacrifices, he finally remained in Tarentum. Seeing his scheme thwarted, Hannibal definitely took up his quarters in Metapontum, where he was watched at a distance by the three Roman armies. Despite the serious reverse in the capture of Tarentum, it appears that Hannibal remained practically master of the entire region within the boundaries of the Roman forces. He marched to and fro on his foraging excur-

sions and gathered victual. He burned and destroyed or captured whatever seemed good to him. None of the Roman
generals, nor indeed all of them together, saw fit again this
year to try conclusions with him. Well indeed was he characterized as dirus Hannibal.

In Spain, Scipio had proceeded in a politic as well as energetic manner, and had largely brought over the Spanish tribes
to the Roman idea. Those along the Iberus had almost uniformly joined his cause, and Indibilis and Mandonius, two of
the highest chiefs of Spain, came over to him. There being
no more danger at sea, he beached his vessels near Tarraco,

Iberia.

and broke up his navy to increase his land forces, so as to be
able to guard northern and invade southern Iberia at the
same time.

Early in the spring, he crossed the Iberus and moved south
to Cartagena, from whence he undertook a campaign against
Hasdrubal. The latter was still in southern Spain, but was
intending to advance north, hoping to cross the Pyrenees.
It came to battle at Bæcula, near the river Bætis. Hasdru-

bal fought defensively, in a strong position on an eminence difficult of access. Scipio attacked him stoutly in front, and created a lively diversion on both his flanks. Despite his position, Hasdrubal's army was badly beaten, as the Romans claimed, with a loss of eight thousand killed and twelve thousand captured. With the remnants of his force, army-chest, elephants and best troops, Hasdrubal withdrew behind the Tagus. This retreat was well-managed, if his defeat was as serious as claimed by Livy. As there seemed small prospect of holding Spain, Hasdrubal now concluded to march to Italy.

It was arranged that on his leaving, Hasdrubal, son of Gisgo, should retire into Lusitania, and avoid all conflict with Scipio; that Masinissa should patrol southern Iberia with three thousand horse, and that Mago should go to the Balearic Islands to recruit and from there endeavor to ship his forces to Italy, should this prove advisable. Hasdrubal himself, after filling up the gaps in his ranks as well as he might with such men as the few remaining Spanish allies could furnish him, finally made his arrangements to move through Gaul. It was several years too late.

The Romans might properly be disappointed with the result of this year's campaign. They had, to be sure, recovered Tarentum, but they had by no means accomplished results commensurate with the force they had in the field. Marcellus, against whom the largest amount of criticism was launched, defended himself by claiming that no Roman general had yet defeated Hannibal in the open field, and he at least had more than once been bold enough to fight him. He did not in his defense assert that he had beaten Hannibal, though Marcellus was not noted for modesty. He claimed that he had fought him on many occasions and had come out of the fray without losing his army. This indeed was, in view of the Roman experience in this war, a sufficient plea.

But it adds weight to the assumption that Hannibal was the victor at Asculum. Perhaps there are no statements more apt to be unreliable than those concerning campaigns or battles, emanating from the parties concerned. We have seen this demonstrated to the fullest extent in our own civil war. And as we are following in this case the Roman historians, we may be sure that we are giving Hannibal in no event too much credit.

Legionary's Pack.   (Antonine Column.)

XXXVII.

MARCELLUS' DEATH. 208 B. C.

MARCELLUS and Crispinus, consuls of 208 B. C., faced Hannibal in Lucania and Apulia. The Carthaginian was growing weaker year by year, but he still held to his work, he was still the terror of Roman generals. From Metapontum he advanced to Venusia as a mere attack in self-defense. Here both consuls joined forces. Marcellus was anxious to bring Hannibal to battle; but before he completed his plans he fell into an ambuscade and was killed. He was, with Scipio and Nero and Fabius, the stay of Rome. His career had been an enviable one. Hannibal gave his body honorable sepulture. Having taken Marcellus' seal-ring, Hannibal tried to use it to capture Salapia, but was foiled. Crispinus, wounded in the same ambuscade, shortly died. The Carthaginians remained masters of southern Italy. Scipio in Spain won victories, but he did not prevent Hasdrubal from escaping him and marching towards Italy. In this far he failed of his object. Scipio had shown himself brilliant rather than solid. Rome looked forward to fighting two of the lion's brood instead of one.

MARCELLUS had hosts of friends. His defense to the attacks brought against him was voted to suffice, and in the eleventh year of the war, B. C. 208, he was elected consul for the fifth time, with Titus Quinctius Crispinus as his colleague. The prætors were Licinius Crassus, Licinius Varus, Sextus Julius Cæsar, and Claudius Flaminius.

Nearly all the Spanish tribes having left the Carthaginian alliance, there was no danger to be anticipated in the affairs of the peninsula. But though Hasdrubal had been beaten by Scipio, it was a question whether this had not led to a still more dangerous condition of affairs. For, having finally learned by bitter experience that Spain could not best be held for the Carthaginian cause by fighting in Spain, Hasdrubal was about to seek his fortune in Italy, as Hannibal had done before him, and as he himself should much sooner have done, and to leave the wreck in Spain for future attention. The Romans had little to fear from Hannibal's army. This had been so weakened that it had naught left but the strong will of its commander. The body was hectic, wasted, exhausted by long marches, desperate fighting and constant privation; but as the heart of the man will surmount the weakness of the body, — as you may read in the flashing eye the un-altered devotion to the cause, the unflagging courage and the unchanged ability to do great deeds, so was Hannibal the soul and impulse of this army. And one may read in his every act that heart and head are to the army what they are to the man, — that an army crawls on its belly but in one sense.

So far from Hannibal being an actual threat to the Romans, it was he who was in narrow straits. But the news that Hasdrubal was about to join his brother was naturally alarming beyond its actual danger. In anticipation of this invasion, the Roman colonies in Etruria were on the eve of rebellion, and the senate was obliged anew to take hostages, — from Aretium alone, one hundred and twenty senators' children, — and cisalpine Gaul had already revolted. In Carthage there were great preparations evident for some purpose, but for what purpose was not known. Rome had gained so hearty a dread of Carthaginian generals in the past dozen years that it was difficult for her to calmly survey her position. One had brought her to the verge of ruin. What might two do ?

The forces of the Romans were divided as follows : Mar-cellus and Crispinus, each with his army of two legions, faced Hannibal in Lucania and Apulia. Claudius occupied Taren-tum and vicinity with the old army of Fabius, two legions strong. Fulvius was in Capua with a legion. The army was again reduced by two legions, twenty-one only being in active service. Etruria, cisalpine Gaul, Sardinia, Sicily and Spain were still held as heretofore, and two legions garrisoned Rome. The fleet was much increased, so as to provide for a proposed descent upon the African coast and to protect the southern shores of Italy.

Crispinus had been engaged in besieging Locri, on the southern coast of Bruttium, and had accumulated a vast amount of siege-material and supplies. To counter this menace Hannibal marched to Lacinium, and by his threatening presence effectuated a raising of the siege without a fight. Crispinus was fearful of being bottled up in the toe of the boot. It had been determined that the consuls should act together, and finding that he could accomplish nothing at Locri, Crispinus joined Marcellus, who had been some time at Venusia. The consular camps were some three miles apart east of this city between Venusia and Bantia. Hannibal, who had wintered in Metapontum, on learning of Crispinus' junction with Marcellus, had deemed it wise to follow up the movement, — a mere attack in self-defense, but with no intention of forcing battle, and now lay an equal distance south of them. His own force we do not know; but he had forty thousand men in his front; twenty thousand men were in rear of his right wing at Tarentum, whence they could debouch at any moment to coöperate with the consular armies. This was in any event more than double his effective, not to speak of the superior quality of the Roman troops. He was in a dangerous situation, for in case of disaster his only retreat was on Metapontum or Heraclea, his last two strongholds on the coast, and to retire might be a difficult operation, with active enemies ready to fall upon his rear and flank. But he was used to such positions. Bruttium was his natural base, and most of the towns he still held. He must do his best to keep this one province free from invasion, and a simple defensive would encourage the Romans too much. His advance accomplished thus much, but he limited his touch of the consuls at Bantia to mere feinting.

Hannibal was always in motion. This was partly necessary for subsistence; it was partly his method. He was always an unknown quantity to the Romans; and the fact that they never could guess where he would be next day, or what his aim might be, explains to a certain extent their constant dread of him. This dread too, which is frankly acknowledged by Livy, and lasted till Hannibal left the country, goes far to show that the so-called victories of the Romans were questionable. If they had found that they could beat Hannibal in open fight they would have been far less liable to the panic they exhibited whenever they came within his reach.

While lying here, Hannibal learned from Thurii that a force from Sicily had been ordered by the consuls to take Crispinus' place at Locri, and that a legion from Tarentum had been instructed to join them. He at once sent a body of two thousand cavalry and three thousand infantry from his best troops to intercept this last detachment. These forces placed themselves under cover of the hill of Petelia so as to ambuscade the Roman legion, which, not suspecting the presence of an enemy, was marching from Tarentum in careless order. The stratagem was well-planned and fully successful. Falling upon the Roman flank, the Carthaginians killed two thousand men, captured twelve hundred, and sent the rest terror-stricken back towards Tarentum, having accomplished which brilliant feat, they returned to camp.

Marcellus, whose courage was always of the best, was anxious again to bring Hannibal to battle. He was not foolhardy enough, however, to do this without an effort to get the conditions on his side. Marcellus deserves abundant credit for

his courage; but it was coupled with a sensible appreciation
of his own limitations. Hannibal was this year still less able
to indulge in the costliness of general engagements, and saw
that he must avoid crossing swords unless to gain a signal advantage. He was the more driven to stratagem, as he had
both consuls to engage.

There was between the two camps a little wooded eminence
not held by either army. The Romans were unacquainted
with the slope towards the Carthaginian side, and Hannibal
had not considered the hill as well fitted for a camp as for an
ambuscade. In the woods, well out of sight, he had placed a
Numidian post with this object.

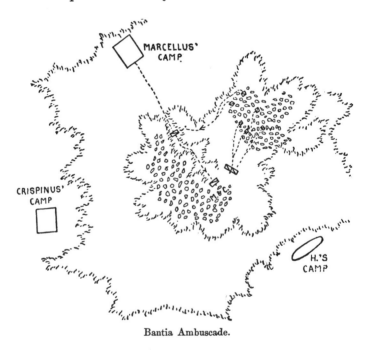

Bantia Ambuscade.

The consuls thought the hill an excellent place for an out-
post-camp, or indeed for a camp for the entire army, which,

well-intrenched, might be of value in bringing about an active encounter. "There was a general murmur in the Roman camp," says Livy, "that this eminence ought to be occupied and secured by a fort, lest if it should be seized by Hannibal they should have the enemy, as it were, immediately over their heads." It seems that under even the best leaders the legionaries gave expression to their opinions. Leaving orders for the troops to be ready to change camp, in case they should decide upon occupying the hill, the two consuls set out to reconnoitre the ground for this purpose. They were accompanied by the tribunes Marcellus, who was the consul's son, and Manlius, two præfects and but a small body of two hundred horse. The approach to the hill was through a short ravine, opening on the plain where lay the Roman camps. The Numidians posted in the wood had videttes out, but in concealment. These saw the approach of the party, and, recognizing the consuls, gave notice to the commander of the outpost, who hurried a few horsemen around to occupy the ravine behind the consular party, and as they approached the height fell upon them with great suddenness and fury. The Roman cavalry escort were partly Etruscans. Of these some of doubtful loyalty turned and fled. The rest of the escort were Fregellans, about forty men. They surrounded the consuls and fought for their own and their leaders' lives. But there was no chance of safety. Marcellus soon fell with his death wound, and Manlius and one of the præfects were killed. Among the severely wounded were Crispinus and Marcellus the younger. The latter both managed to escape with the handful of uninjured, but Marcellus' body remained in Hannibal's hands, who buried it with all honor. It is well to note the fact, stated by the Roman historians, that Hannibal uniformly paid this tribute to his dead foemen, It makes all the more prominent the horror of the treatment of

the body of Hasdrubal, after the Metaurus, and aptly illustrates the weakness of the Romans in their slur against Hannibal for what they call his savage cruelty. The cry of Punic
Faith and the accusation that Hannibal was barbarous are
about on a par.

After this, for the Romans, lamentable event, Hannibal
moved forward and occupied the hill as a camp, perhaps
thinking he might see an opportunity of benefiting by the
temporary dismay of the Roman legions. Crispinus retired
to the protection of the hills and guarded himself carefully
against Hannibal's approach.

Marcellus was sixty years old. His military career had
been an enviable one. He had conquered the Gauls; he had
captured Syracuse, he had several times fought Hannibal
and only on one occasion been decisively defeated. This
last, despite the disparity of numbers in his favor, is praise
enough. He ought not to have conducted a simple reconnoitring party which a subaltern might have headed; or, if he
did so, it should have been with more care or a larger force;
but this is small criticism. His death was a severe blow to
the Roman cause, and a large gain to Hannibal. While the
Carthaginian was unable to fight battles during this campaign,
he was skillful enough to strike smaller blows whose effect
was almost equal to a victory over a consular army. We
can scarcely sustain Livy in characterizing the ambuscade
at Bantia as " Carthaginian treachery."

The seal ring of Marcellus had fallen into Hannibal's possession. Crispinus was afraid that he would use it for some
stratagem, and sent word to all the principal towns to be on
their guard against all things smelling of ruse. Hannibal
did in fact endeavor by its use to again secure possession of
Salapia. He needed to hold northern Apulia so as to retain
a means of joining hands with his brother Hasdrubal when he

should arrive. He wrote the city word under Marcellus' seal to be ready on a given day in case he should want the garrison for any service. At the appointed time he approached the town, the van headed by some Roman deserters. But Salapia had received warning and had her chosen warriors at the gates. On the arrival of the Carthaginians the portcullis was raised as if to receive the troops, and some six hundred were admitted, when suddenly it was dropped; those who had marched in being at once cut down, while the walls, previously manned, showered arrows, darts and stones upon Hannibal's army. The stratagem thus failed. Hannibal was not with the van. He had a way of mixing caution with boldness, as no one else.

After the affair at Bantia, with some intermediate and unimportant manœuvres, the army of Marcellus, under his son, took refuge in Venusia, and Crispinus in Capua, where the consul died of his wounds. Hannibal, foiled in his hope of worsting the Roman army, turned back and marched on Locri, besieged by Cincius, who had brought his force and material from Sicily. Mago was in command of the town, and at Hannibal's approach made a sortie in force with great suddenness and vigor. The resistance was sharp, but short and vain. Taken in front and rear, the besiegers fled to their ships, leaving on the field all their camp equipage, victuals and siege-material.

Thus Hannibal remained master of southern Italy. No army disputed him its possession. The situation was one of armed and warlike quiet. Hannibal was able to forage at will. He held the entire province. Interest now centred in Africa and the north, to which Hannibal must look for valuable succor as the Roman senate for danger. The Carthaginian winter-quarters were in Metapontum.

It was evident, though Scipio claimed the victory at

Bæcula, that Hasdrubal had not been prevented from accomplishing his object. Scipio had shown energy and skill, but his youth had outrun his discretion. The Spanish programme was clearly to keep reinforcements from coming to Italy. The elder Scipios (this one's father and uncle), and even C. Marcius, with very inferior forces, had accomplished this end. But Scipio was young and ambitious; unwilling to content himself with a defensive attitude, he had launched out into activity greater than demanded by the circumstances, and had allowed Hasdrubal to escape him. Of what consequence was Spain to Rome, if Rome should find Hannibal, with Hasdrubal to back him, too much for her resources and skill in Italy? A judicious offensive was no doubt Scipio's best method: but he lost sight of the fact that his main object was defensive, that is, to protect Rome from another Barcine invasion. This Scipio had not done. He had so manœuvred as to place Rome in greater peril perhaps than at any other time. But fortune was always on Scipio's side. Nero came to the rescue and at the Metaurus rectified Scipio's error. Rome forgot the peril he had caused her, and Scipio still remained the hero of the day. While not denying Scipio the praise he justly earned, it is clear that the larger part of his success came from the favor of the fickle goddess.

During the autumn news came from Massilia that Hasdrubal had crossed the Tagus, had turned the sources of the Ebro and entered Gaul, where he had enlisted numberless recruits. He had made his way to the northern coast of Spain, had marched along its shore and passed the Pyrenees by the western gaps. He had followed the line which Wellington later took after the battle of Victoria. He passed the winter of 208–207 B. C. in Gaul, and was waiting for spring to cross the Alps on the same route Hannibal had pursued. It was a woful pity for the Carthaginians that he had waited or been delayed so long. Had he even been able to join his brother during the campaign just conducted, the chance of success for the Carthaginian arms would have been many fold what it was after another winter. Hasdrubal's arrival after the death of the two consuls would have been a thunder-clap.

Rome thus could expect next year to have two of the lion's brood to fight. If one had been so hard to combat, what could she do with two, when Marcellus was dead, Fabius beginning to be enfeebled by old age, and none of her generals able to engage Hannibal even with a vast preponderance of power? Rome did not yet know Caius Claudius Nero.

Boar. — Gallic Ensign.

XXXVIII.

HASDRUBAL AND NERO. 207 B. C.

NERO and Livius, consuls of 207 B. C., had Hasdrubal to face in the north, Hannibal in the south. The latter undertook the northern problem, with three armies of twenty thousand men each. Nero had an equal number. Hasdrubal left Spain too late to cross the Alps the same year. He crossed early in the spring, but did not push to a junction with his brother, engaging in the useless siege of Placentia instead. The Romans knew his movements well; not so Hannibal, to whom news could only come through two sets of armies and a hostile country. Hannibal twice advanced to northern Apulia, hoping for news, but both times was pushed back from lack of men, losing heavily in affairs forced on him against his will. At Grumentum Nero and Hannibal crossed swords, to Hannibal's loss, if we can credit Livy. Certainly his army was now of very poor material, and Nero, save only Marcellus, the stoutest opponent the Romans had yet sent against him. Despite defeat, Hannibal again advanced to Canusium, where he awaited news from his brother. Nero closely watched him. Hasdrubal's messengers fell into the hands of the Romans, who found out his plans and were able to take means for meeting them, while Hannibal was ignorant of the projects of both.

THE thirteenth year of the war, the twelfth campaign in Italy, B. C. 207, was opened by appointing to the consulate the most competent of the Roman generals, Caius Claudius Nero. For several years he had held important commands, and had done them justice. To him was joined M. Livius Salinator, an old man, who twelve years before had been consul, and had then given proof of capacity. He had been accused of peculation, but on trial been acquitted. The accusation had embittered him ; he desired to keep out of public life, and at first refused to serve. He had for some reason a particular prejudice against Nero. But the entreaties of the senate prevailed. Livius accepted the consulate, and was publicly reconciled to his colleague. The prætors were Lucius Porcius Licinius, Caius Mamilius, Aulus Hostilius Cato and Caius Hostilius Cato. In view of the approach of Hasdrubal, two additional legions were put into the field. Scipio sent reinforcements from Spain, and Mamilius from Sicily, more than fifteeen thousand men, all told.

To Livius was given the task of holding head against Hasdrubal in the north. His own two legions were supplemented by two others under Porcius, already in cisalpine Gaul. A third army of two legions, under Varro, was in Etruria. Thus Hasdrubal was to be welcomed by three armies of twenty thousand men each.

In the south, Hannibal had likewise to face three armies:

Armies between Hannibal and Hasdrubal.

that of Nero, which had been Marcellus', that of the proconsul Fulvius, lately Crispinus', in Bruttium, and the two legions in the territory of Tarentum and the Salentinians, under the pro-prætor Q. Claudius. These three armies, like those of the northern country, were later consolidated into two, by the consul taking the Tarentine legions to double up his army, which being done, the army of Bruttium moved to the Tarentine territory. One legion, under C. Hostilius, stayed in Capua; two defended Rome. Aulus Hostilius was in Sardinia, and C. Mamilius in Sicily. There were in Italy but fifteen legions this year; but under the eagles there were nine armies, in all twenty-three legions. These were supplemented by three fleets, in Spain, Sicily and Greece.

Hasdrubal was without question a good soldier, but he appears to have been of a careless habit. He is considered by some to have shown himself Hannibal's equal; but the pattern of Hannibal has been paralleled but a few times in the world's history. Hasdrubal's campaigns in Spain were not characterized by much success accomplished. His campaign against the Scipios was brilliant, but the rest of his operations bore uniformly no fruit, and this generally from want of good management rather than want of ability. His movement from Spain was delayed beyond reason. Had he joined Hannibal after beating the Scipios in 212 B. C., while Hannibal was still near the zenith of his success, and held Capua and Tarentum, had destroyed one consular army at Herdonia, and had dispersed another, the Barcas would have come nearer the fulfillment of their purpose. It was well for Rome that Hasdrubal did not do so. The intervening four years were the ruin of the Carthaginian cause in Italy.

It would have been wiser for Hasdrubal to seek to join Hannibal in southern Italy. To force a junction with him over the wreck of all the enormous intervening armies, if he entered northern Italy, was a task to overtax even his brother. It was a far greater risk than to face the Roman fleet in transporting a lesser army across the sea. He no doubt counted on Gallic aid ; but when he reached the Po, he made no efficient use of his Gallic allies, and they were in no sense of the same value to him, with Hannibal already in Italy, as they had been to Hannibal when he had to fight Rome single-handed. When Hasdrubal set out to march overland, though he had Hannibal's experience to guide him, he left Spain so late that he had to winter west of the Alps, and thus gave his enemies abundant time to make preparations to meet him. That they did not do so even more efficiently was due to the Gallic insurrections and to Roman laxness, not to Hasdrubal's activity.

Hannibal was the first who ever led a regular army, with its baggage, not to speak of elephants, across the Alps. Hasdrubal's crossing can in no sense be compared to his. The only mountain passage recorded in history which does compare to it is Alexander's crossing the Parapamisus. Hannibal's passage was made against serious opposition, and with none but unreliable information about the ground he had to cover. Yet, from his entrance to his exit from the Alps was a bare two weeks. Hasdrubal encountered only friendly greetings and assistance from the transalpine Gauls, receiving guides, food, and even troops. The past dozen years had made the intercourse by this route over the Alps much more frequent, and the roads were correspondingly better. The tribes had learned that the Carthaginians were not enemies they themselves had to fear, but that they were aiming at the equally dreaded and hated power of Rome, which all the Gauls now were eager to see humbled.

Hasdrubal took a much longer time than Hannibal in his entire passage ; but he finally descended to the valley of the Padus. Once there, his first efforts should have been to push as straight and as fast to a junction with Hannibal as properly reconnoitred but forced marching could carry him. But

Hasdrubal had not the keen military insight of a great soldier. His first effort was a mistake. Under the impression that he would by its capture inflict grievous damage on the Romans, he sat down before Placentia, and unable to take it by a first assault he began to besiege it. His project was a dismal failure, and its consequences fatal. Here, too, he deemed it wise to wait for reinforcements which were on the way from Liguria and Gaul, — another foolish step, — and not until then did he march on Ariminum. He did not grasp the fact that for every thousand men he could gain, the enemy would find time to concentrate five against him; nor, indeed, that Hannibal would count on him to push through at once, and would act accordingly. Hasdrubal's tardiness might not have worked against him years before. But the Romans had received a dozen years' good schooling, and they better knew how to take advantage of mistakes.

The consternation at Rome, on the news of Hasdrubal's arrival being spread, was only equaled by the dismay which followed Hannibal's early victories. It was not now one son of Hamilcar over whom success must be won, but two, and Hasdrubal's ability was overrated. Should both the brothers win in the coming battles, what would become of Rome?

The Romans were quickly and fully advised of Hasdrubal's arrival and movements. But not so Hannibal. News could come to him only through the enemy's double lines, those facing himself and those facing his brother. Spies were of small use. Porcius, who was in Hasdrubal's front, had retired on his approach, retarding him as much as possible, while Livius marched towards his lieutenant, who had already fallen back to the line of the Metaurus, and from this point still farther back to the little river Sena. Here the consular army sat down in its camp to await the new-comer.

As in a number of cases, so here the location of the battle-

field is uncertain. On the whole, it is safest to follow the
account of Livy, who states that Livius' camp was near Sena.
It is rather hard to explain why the consul should pitch his
camp at this place. The direct road from Ariminum to Rome
— one branch of the Via Flaminia — turned from the coast
at Fanum Fortunæ, north of the Metaurus, and ran southwest towards the capital; and as, at Sena Gallica, or on the
line of the Sena, the consul could not hold this road, it would
seem as if he would take up the only position which commanded both branches of the Via Flaminia, the one which
ran inland and the one which followed down the coast. The

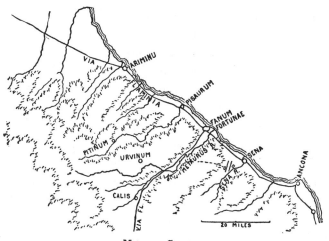

Metaurus Country.

consul's task was to protect the road to Rome as well as the
coast road, by which Hasdrubal could join his brother. At
Fanum Fortunæ, at the mouth of the Metaurus, he protected
both; at Sena, but one. Fanum was the key-point; Sena
had no importance whatever.

The movements of Hannibal are not clearly set down by
the ancient historian. It appears that he left his winter-

quarters at Metapontum before the new consuls were afoot, moved through Lucania to Apulia, where he went as far up as Larinum, near the Tifernus. This was unquestionably in the hope that Hasdrubal would very early seek to push south to join him; or in the expectation that if he did not find Hasdrubal's army he would procure news of it on which he could himself act to advantage. He did hear news, but to his great disappointment it was that Hasdrubal was besieging Placentia, instead of marching immediately south to a junction with him. And as he foresaw the danger he was running of being hemmed in away from his base by the numerous Roman armies then changing stations to correspond with the lots drawn by the consuls; as he desired to understand Hasdrubal's plans before undertaking any serious march; and as the south coast was a necessary future base for both armies, which he must protect at all hazards, he moved back to southern Lucania. If Hannibal had any understanding with Hasdrubal, it could be but a very partial one; and to advance towards him without definite knowledge of his whereabouts was to risk the loss of the campaign as well as of his base. He had but one army. The Romans understood and acted on this fact. Hannibal's evident programme was to keep quiet and preserve his forces from injury until he could communicate with Hasdrubal, and then, in coöperation with him, deliver one hearty blow.

It was on his march back, just as he was leaving the territory of Larinum, that, according to Livy, C. Hostilius, who, before the consul Nero had joined the army, was marching northward from Tarentum to meet his chief, ran across Hannibal on the march, and cut out from his column four thousand men and nine ensigns. This is another of the actions which are so imperfectly described that nothing can be stated but the bald fact, and this subject to doubt. If it is as stated, it goes to show that the quality of Hannibal's present forces was very low. Unless he had a great deal of ragged material under his colors, his column was not apt to march in straggling order, as Livy says he was doing when attacked by Hostilius. We know indeed that his veterans had practically disappeared, and that most of his men had been forced into the service; but the few words devoted by Livy to the subject are not convincing.

All this may look like unwillingness to credit Livy, who, in many respects, is the most valuable of the Roman historians. But during the past thirty years, we Americans have seen so many utterly unreliable statements with regard to our civil war put before the public in good faith by well-equipped witnesses of the event, that it appears wise to distrust the statements of one of Hannibal's worst enemies, unless we find them well vouched for by the attendant circumstances. Many of Livy's facts are contradicted by what he tells us himself in some other place.

Nero now joined his forces to those brought by Hostilius, which made an army of forty thousand foot and twenty-five hundred horse. His headquarters he established at Venusia, and his main object was to prevent Hannibal from marching north to join the new army, which after weary waiting had come to his relief. Hannibal found it necessary to retire to Bruttium. His recent losses were directly traceable to Hasdrubal's delay.

In Bruttium, Hannibal reinforced himself with all the garrisons he could spare, and moved along the great road from Rhegium on Grumentum in Lucania, intending once more to reach out towards Hasdrubal, and hoping on the way to capture Grumentum, which had been one of those towns which through fear had surrendered to the Romans. He camped near the city. He was anxious to avoid the attrition of bat-

tle by every means in his power, until he could strike in connection with Hasdrubal. At the same time, Nero, with much
precaution, moved from Venusia on Grumentum, and occupied a camp about a mile from Hannibal's. He was soldier
enough to know that Hannibal did not want to fight, and to
be anxious to force a battle on him if it could be done on
advantageous terms.

The Carthaginian rampart was only five hundred paces
from the city walls. Between the camps the ground was
level. Hannibal lay with the town in his rear, the Aciris on
his right, Nero facing him, the Aciris on his left. On Hannibal's left were several naked hills, not at all fitted, apparently, for an ambuscade and unsuspected by either party.
Hannibal had probably grown to believe that ambuscades
were of no further use, and that the consul would be on his
guard against them ; but if the account of Livy is accurate,
he paid no heed to the operations on his own flanks. On the
open plain were daily skirmishes between the outposts and
light troops. Nero kept close in camp, as if intent only on
barring Hannibal from a march northward to join Hasdrubal.
Hannibal, however anxious to get away, fearing that he could
not well advance or retire without a battle, drew daily up in
order and awaited Nero's attack. He understood the character of his opponent well, but thought that if he could get
Nero to make a direct attack he could beat him.

Nero was unwilling to run the risk, but concluded to try
upon Hannibal one of his own stratagems. He managed to
send, under command of Tiberius Claudius Asellus, a tribune, and P. Claudius, a præfect of the allies, by night and
unperceived, five cohorts and five maniples, to the rear of the
hills on Hannibal's left, with orders to debouch from cover
at a set time.

Next morning both parties made ready for battle, Hanni-

bal giving the earlier orders, and the armies filed out from
camp and deployed into line. Hannibal's hastily raised
levies had not yet been subjected to careful discipline, and
the deployment was irregularly made on the Carthaginian
side, with considerable confusion in the lines. Nero at once

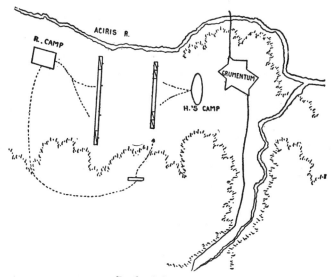

Battle of Grumentum.

took advantage of this confusion to make a sharp and unexpected attack on Hannibal's light troops with his cavalry.
Hannibal's presence, however, began to restore order; the
Roman right wing was coming steadily into action, and the
battle was fully engaged before any regular formation had
been completed on either hand. The Romans were under
better discipline and had the advantage of the initiative.
The Carthaginians showed no demoralization, and resisted
the spirited Roman assaults with great determination. "Hannibal among the terror and confusion would have drawn up
his troops while fighting, which would not have been an easy

task unless to a veteran general with veteran troops," says Livy, and the Carthaginian lines were pretty well holding their own, as fresh detachments were hurried up to fill the gaps. Hannibal was busily occupied in restoring order and with considerable success, when the Roman detachment, which had been sent round back of the hills, debouched with its war-cry on the Carthaginian left flank. Hannibal's men were at once seized with fear lest they should be cut off from camp, and made a speedy and confused retreat to its protection. Nero pushed his cavalry upon their rear. Had not the camp been near at hand a second Cannæ might have occurred, claims the Roman historian. The retreat was not without eight thousand killed, seven hundred captured, and the loss of nine ensigns and six elephants. The consul limited his casualties to five hundred men, Romans and allies. The event proved the result of this so-called victory to be more like that of a drawn battle.

These lost battles of Hannibal's, if we were to give them entire credit, would as fully show the wretched material he now had in his ranks as they would prove the great advance in steadiness of the Roman troops. The evidence of Livy, who makes constant efforts to rehabilitate the Roman reputation for fighting, is clearly to the effect that it was the poor quality of Hannibal's army to which so frequent defeat was due. This in no wise robs Nero of the full credit of conducting a brilliant stratagem under the eyes of the very father of stratagem. While we cannot accord to Nero a victory on this field, it is nevertheless true that Marcellus and he were the fighting men of Rome as Fabius was the originator of its better policy. Nero in some respects stands at the head of all the Roman generals of the Second Punic War, though the Romans had a habit of calling Marcellus their sword and Fabius their buckler.

Next day Nero again offered battle, but Hannibal was not strong enough to engage. Nero, according to Livy, buried the dead, — a token of victory, — and harassed Hannibal as much as he could with his cavalry, and by daily advancing to the very ramparts of Hannibal's camp, " so near to the gates that he almost appeared to be carrying in his standards."

Hannibal felt compelled to withdraw. This he did in the third watch of the night, by leaving his camp-fires lighted, and the foremost rows of tents standing, with a few Numidian sentries left behind to make an appearance of occupation, which they did, and afterwards joined the column. He marched straight for Apulia. Nero did not find out his absence till late next day, having been singularly cautious about approaching the Punic camp ; and after he found it out he lost much time in plundering. Hannibal had evidently not lost his ability to march. But when Nero started, he pursued the Carthaginians vigorously, and coming upon them near Venusia, by a sudden and unlooked-for attack, cut out some two thousand men from the column. Hannibal, who had moved on Apulia, in renewed fruitless search of news from Hasdrubal, was too much weakened by these losses to make it safe to try to hold his own, without still further reinforcements, in the midst of so many Roman armies. He turned back to Metapontum, " marching by night and over mountain roads to avoid a battle," in search of new levies, which he sent out Hanno to pick up. On their arrival he again advanced by the same route to Venusia and thence to Canusium. Nero had constantly dogged his footsteps, even as far as Metapontum, leaving Q. Fulvius in Lucania during his absence. Hannibal's persistency as well as his skill in eluding Nero and his better army, which, consisting of a selection from the two consular armies of the past year, were old and seasoned troops, over forty thousand in number, was marked.

Thus, despite the defeat described by Livy, Hannibal had won his point. He aimed at gaining a position in Apulia, where he could await messengers from Hasdrubal. That he had not been defeated must be assumed from this fact alone. No doubt he suffered severely in the drawn battle at Grumentum, but Nero was unable to prevent him from gaining Apulia and, after he had gathered recruits to replace those he had lost, from holding himself there. All the facts here narrated are taken from Livy, without addition or detraction. But that Livy's facts are not beyond question it is well to point out. If we had a history of Napoleon from only the English standpoint, or a history of our civil war from only southern or northern writers, we should come far short of accuracy. Indeed, a meeting of the veterans of the Third Corps of the Army of the Potomac, under distinguished leaders, in 1886, deliberately voted that the opening days of Chancellorsville were "one of the most noted tactical victories of modern times" for the Union arms!

But were the relation of these constant victories of the Roman armies over Hannibal true, it would in no wise militate against his skill. It can be readily understood that Hannibal, whose Spanish and African veterans had all but disappeared, and whose means of recruiting, arming and equipping his men — let alone disciplining his heterogeneous mass of half-hearted Bruttian allies — were very limited, was often able to offer but a poor resistance in open combat to the enormous odds of excellent troops under the best generals Rome afforded, his own pupils of a dozen years' standing, and all instinct with the one set purpose of crushing the hated invader. But it becomes difficult to understand, if we accept as accurate the number and extent of his defeats and losses, how Hannibal could still maintain his footing as he did. If these victories were won by the Romans, how came

it that Hannibal was never so badly defeated as to have his
retreat cut off, or be totally disabled? The fact remains, on
Roman testimony, that Hannibal was able to move about at
pleasure, and that, when he retired from before great numbers
or because his own weak condition did not allow him to fight,
he none the less, by some flank manœuvre or night march, accomplished substantially what he sought to do. That he was
apt to be beaten in open fight, after the Romans had learned
to be cautious about stratagems, is natural; that he was able,
even when beaten or when he failed of victory, still to compass his ends is the wonderful feature of his work. His
later campaigns are an everlasting pattern of defensive manœuvring, as his early ones are of offensive strategy. On
the Roman side it seems curious that no attempt was made
to operate on Hannibal's communications while he was at the
front. His base was depleted of troops, and the evident objective of one of the Roman armies was Hannibal's rear.
But as none of the consuls and prætors liked the task of
meeting the Carthaginian in the open field, so most of them
even fought shy of his lieutenants in his allied cities.

Nero had been closely following up Hannibal. Why he
did not again attack him at Canusium, — just where indeed
Nero was, — we do not know. But he had evidently made his
way to a position north of Hannibal, to head him off from
marching farther towards Hasdrubal.

Hannibal had forty thousand men in his front, twenty
thousand behind him at Tarentum, ten thousand on his left
at Capua and twenty thousand in Rome. His own force we
do not know. It was probably not over thirty thousand men,
of whom two thirds were Bruttians of recent levies. He was
not strong enough to force his way on either side of the
Apennines through this barrier to join his brother. Every
main route was held by the enemy in force. He had prob-

ably hoped, by advancing into Apulia, to oblige the Roman generals to concentrate their troops, and thus enable Hasdrubal's messengers to penetrate to him.   He had no doubt of their being on the road.   He had twice been driven back to Bruttium to recruit his forces, which battles fought against his will had depleted.   He had again advanced.   His marches at this time seem erratic; but they are explained by the weakness of his army, the necessity he was under of saving it all he could, and his desire to communicate with Hasdrubal.   He was ready to march forward to join hands with him, or even to fight his way through, so soon as he knew what direction Hasdrubal would take, who, from the Padus, might pass either by way of Etruria or Umbria.   Now less than ever, while looking forward to what he had awaited for many years, could Hannibal afford general engagements for any other than the one purpose of forcing a junction with Hasdrubal.

It was in the hope of receiving some message from Hasdrubal that Hannibal now remained at Canusium.   It was a dangerous position to occupy, surrounded by Roman armies and with such an able general as Nero on his heels wherever he turned.   Nothing in the Roman annals excites our admiration more than Nero's excellent manœuvring, within its limitations, against the great Carthaginian.   But Canusium was as good a position as Hannibal could well occupy until he knew how to coöperate with the newly arrived army of invasion. Until he heard from it, he could undertake nothing.

As might have been expected, Hasdrubal had failed in his siege of Placentia, and then had finally turned towards Ariminum to join his brother.   He had sent messengers from Placentia, telling Hannibal of his throwing up the siege and proposing to meet and join in Umbria.   Hasdrubal was to follow the Flaminian road along the coast and then at Fanum, at the mouth of the Metaurus, turn across the Apennines to

Narnia, hoping to meet Hannibal on the way. The messengers, four Gallic and two Numidian horsemen, had, curiously
enough, traversed all Italy in safety, at the time Hannibal
was retiring towards Metapontum, but had got off their track,
turning towards Tarentum and not Metapontum, and had
been made prisoners near Tarentum. They were bearers of
Hasdrubal's entire plan of operations written in Carthaginian
vernacular. This was not a clever device. Hasdrubal might
better have dispatched one man or two every day for some
time with false plans to deceive the enemy, and with the real
plan confided to the messenger's memory. Hasdrubal risked
the outcome of the entire campaign by risking the loss of the
knowledge of it. The messengers were captured by some
Roman foragers and taken to Caius Claudius, pro-prætor at
Tarentum, who, after some delay and the exhibition of instruments of torture, ascertained who the men were. He at once
sent them with an escort of cavalry and Hasdrubal's un-
opened letter to the consul Nero.

When Nero had got this plan, he had already half beaten
the enemy. Had Hannibal received Hasdrubal's message, it
is certain beyond a peradventure that he would at once have
attacked Nero, and thus have forestalled all which this wide-
awake and enterprising general did; or else would have stolen
a march around his flank and made his way north.

This mishap of the messengers is but one more fact which
forces on our attention Hannibal's crass bad luck. If Alexander was born under a lucky star, so, assuredly, was Hannibal born under a luckless one. It seems as if Fortune de-
lighted to betray him and to thwart his best-laid plans.
While fortune is largely of a man's own making, it cannot
be admitted that there is not in war, as there is in all human
events, such an element as simple luck.

XXXIX.

THE METAURUS CAMPAIGN. SUMMER, 207 B. C.

POSSESSED of Hasdrubal's plans, Nero had a splendid opportunity, and he used it in a manner to show the stuff that was in him. He notified the senate of his purpose, but waited for nothing. Secretly taking seven thousand men, the pick of his army, and leaving the legions under a legate in front of Hannibal, who, owing to Nero's careful method, knew nothing of his departure, the consul started north to join his colleague. With the aid of wagons for the infantry, he marched two hundred and fifty miles in seven days, and reached Sena, where lay Livius. This march of Nero's, his conduct at the Metaurus and his return to Hannibal's front, are a fine example of the use of interior lines. They form the most brilliant page of Roman achievement in the Second Punic War. Hannibal had no idea that the Roman consul had left his army, which to all appearances was still intact. Hasdrubal had advanced to the Sena but had not manœuvred ably. He had lost a chance to evade Livius and march towards Hannibal, and when he found that Nero had arrived, he seemed to lose moral force. He retired from the enemy's front, and back to the river Metaurus. The consuls followed him up, and forced battle on him. Hasdrubal drew up his men ably, and fought stoutly. But his army was demoralized, and a flank attack by Nero decided the day. Hasdrubal was killed and his army destroyed, in a second Cannæ. Nero then hastened back to his army. In two weeks he had marched five hundred miles and won the great Roman victory of this war.

NERO, then, became possessed of the messengers who bore the plans of Hasdrubal. These were translated by an African deserter. Here was one of those opportunities which show a man in his true colors. There was an extraordinary danger. It must be met by an extraordinary means. Nero at once advised the senate — as he was bound to do — of what he had learned, and of the plan he had devised to check the Carthaginian brothers in their proposed junction in Umbria. This the senate promptly confirmed. They believed in Nero and acted up to their belief. The Capuan legion was called to Rome; new troops were enlisted in the city garrison and the two city legions were sent up to Narnia.

Nero did not wait. He proceeded with his plans. Mounted messengers were dispatched along the road through Picenum to Larinum, Marrucia, Frentana and Prætutia, ordering the farmers to collect all the victuals, wagons, beasts of burden and fresh horses at convenient places, to help forward the march of an army. Nero made preparations for leaving the bulk of his army in front of Hannibal, while he himself should march at high speed, with a small but chosen band of his best troops, on whose devotion he could rely, to join Livius. Acting with Livius he hoped to destroy Hasdrubal, and then be able to turn upon Hannibal before the latter could accomplish anything against his lieutenant. What he left in Hannibal's front sufficed, if properly handled, to hold him there, or else to follow him north if he should break through, so as to reinforce the Roman army wherever Hannibal should attempt to strike it.

To prevent Hannibal from knowing what he was about to do, he gave out, even in his own camp, that he was preparing an expedition to Lucania to attack some of Hannibal's cities. He made the most careful arrangements to prevent a knowledge of his real direction from reaching Hannibal. It is to be regretted that the details of what he did are not known. Not one of his soldiers had any conception what the objective was, till they had marched a good many miles north. He had with him but six thousand foot and one thousand horse, but these were of irreproachable quality. Sufficiently far on his way, he explained his plan to his men, showed them how much depended on their strength and courage, and called on them for the one exertion of their lives. He explained the situation fully to them; convinced them that what was apparently rash was really the safest, surest road to victory; that Livius' army was the largest and best of all the Roman forces, and that with their aid the enemy must be defeated. His men were wrought up to the highest state of enthusiasm and confidence.

Scarcely a soul in Rome but was frightened at the bold scheme of Nero's. He had left his army in charge of a lieutenant whose capacity in large commands was not yet proven. He had withdrawn from Hannibal's front the very flower of his troops. He was marching to meet the man who had overcome him by deceit in Spain. What if Hannibal should attack his army, thus left behind under a legate, and contrive another Cannæ ? What if he should escape the legate, follow Nero and destroy his small force on the way ? What if Hasdrubal should again defeat him by ruse, as he had once defeated the Scipios in Spain? To the Romans, Hasdrubal was as dreadful a foe, for the moment, as Hannibal. Again was the excitement and dread of defeat at its highest pitch in Rome.

The progress north of Nero's small army was a triumphal march. The tired infantry was carried in wagons. The entire population was devoted to speeding them on their way, and lined the roadside in crowds to welcome them, encourage them, and pray the gods for their success. They marched night and day ; they eat their rations without stopping. Nothing was allowed to arrest the constant motion of the column.

This manœuvre of Nero will always remain, not only a wonderful instance of marching, but a sample of the finest strategy, — the first of its kind. It is one of the best examples of the proper use to be made of interior lines in either ancient or modern times. There was of course danger that Hannibal would follow him. But this was remote, for Hannibal must take fifteen days to do what Nero was able to accomplish in seven, aided as he was by every soul in the population. The main danger lay in Hannibal's discovering his absence and attacking his army, which he had left under the legate Quintus Catius, while he himself was away. But war is a game of risk. Nero could not eliminate this element. It is he who limits the risk best who wins. This Nero did by keeping his own counsel and acting with extreme speed.

Nero made the extraordinary distance of two hundred and seventy Roman miles — say two hundred and fifty English — in seven days. And a considerable number of old soldiers and youths under age, met on the way, catching the infection, voluntarily joined the ranks of the consular army for the campaign. He arrived with a larger and better force than that with which he had started.

Nero, while on the march, sent forward messages to Livius to ask how he would prefer to have him join his army, — by night or by day, — and whether as a separate body or a reinforcement, suggesting that it was best to conceal his own arrival from Hasdrubal. Livius opened his camp to the new-comers, some of the men crowding into tents in double numbers, each tribune receiving a tribune and each centurion a centurion, so as not to increase its size. Having no baggage and being few in number, this was not difficult; and as Nero hid himself in the valleys until he could make his junction at night and in the protection of some hills, Hasdrubal knew as little of the arrival of Nero as Hannibal knew of his leaving. No more camp-fires were lighted than before, and the utmost secrecy was kept.

A council of war was immediately held, the prætor Porcius being present. The majority were for giving the newly-arrived troops a day's rest, but Nero strenuously opposed such a suggestion, lest a day lost should bring Hannibal upon them or upon Nero's own army, which lay in Hannibal's front; and it was agreed by all to force a battle on the morrow. According to Livy, the council was held on the morning after Nero's arrival, and the troops drawn up for battle immediately after. If this is so, Hasdrubal must that day have managed to decline the engagement.

The two consuls were, according to Livy, in their intrenched camp near Sena, and Hasdrubal was camped less than half a mile distant.

Why Hasdrubal, when he found that the road to Rome was left open, by the consuls taking position at Sena instead of Fanum, did not steal a march on them and advance towards Narnia, as he had notified Hannibal that he would do, sending other daily messengers to Hannibal to give him notice of his movements, cannot be said. He may, before Nero's arrival, have ascertained that he had but one consul before him, and have believed that it would be wiser to seek to beat him, than run the risk of moving farther on into the bowels of the land, and by such advance enable the consuls to join forces and thus incur the risk of having two to fight. At all events, he chose battle as a first step.

At point of day after the council, the Roman legions deployed in battle order in front of their camp. Hasdrubal was prepared to accept the gage, and backed up against his intrenchments. Before attacking he rode forward with a small escort to reconnoitre. There was an apparent increase of the Roman forces. He noticed that many of the shields looked rusty, instead of bright, as a Roman legionary's shield always was on the day of battle. Many of the horses he saw looked thin, as if they had recently made a long march. These and other indications raised his suspicions. He drew back, and sent out some scouts to examine the matter further, and make some prisoners if possible. He told them to observe the men going to the river for water, if any were more sunburned than usual; and sent another party to ride around the camp and see whether it had been increased, or the signals were sounded more than once.

The scouts reported that they heard only one in Porcius', but two signals blown in Livius' camp. Nero had been anxious to conceal his arrival until he could force battle on the enemy. When he came face to face with him, and Hasdrubal could no longer avoid the combat, Nero proclaimed the fact that he had two consuls to meet instead of one. He believed this would impair Hasdrubal's morale, as indeed it did.

The report of the scouts, and his own observation, convinced Hasdrubal that he had both consuls before him as well as the prætor Porcius. He feared that some great disaster had befallen Hannibal; that the second consul had eluded him by a stratagem he could not credit. Or had his own messengers to Hannibal been captured? Without knowledge of this plan how should Nero be there? Troubled by these thoughts, Hasdrubal held his own all day, evacuated his camp after nightfall, and retired towards the Metaurus, purposing to cross so soon as he could do so.

What Hasdrubal's eventual purpose may have been in retiring, we cannot guess. If he did not care to engage both consuls, now was his time to show himself able to manœuvre. If, instead of retiring on the Metaurus, Hasdrubal had left a strong rear-guard in camp, and had moved by his right towards the Flaminian Way, he would have found his road open, and, assured that the consuls were both at Sena, could have escaped them, and made some distance towards his brother before they followed. But it looks as if Hasdrubal was acting from demoralization. The task which Hannibal had performed unruffled for a dozen years, and under vastly more difficult conditions, seems to have overtaxed Hasdrubal at the outset. Hannibal had been alone; Hasdrubal was marching towards a friendly army. Hannibal and he were, to be sure, operating on exterior lines and were seriously hampered by the forces interposed between them, which prevented their manœuvring with common purpose. But this does not explain Hasdrubal's sudden retreat. The loss of moral force following such withdrawal was alone enough to forfeit the battle which must ensue. It is unlike the man; Hasdrubal was more apt to err on the side of boldness than discretion. He was no longer himself. Having advanced to the vicinity of the enemy, he should by all means have fought him. His object was to join Hannibal rather than to beat a Roman army; but this was a matter to have considered beforehand; he could not afford to retreat when in presence of the enemy, particularly with his heterogeneous and unreliable forces, with which prestige was everything. An advance along the Flaminian Way towards Rome would have encouraged his army; a retreat to the Metaurus must inevitably draw their temper. Hasdrubal's conduct looks like that of a man who is not abreast of his work. One finds instances like this in every great war; in our own civil war notably that of Hooker at Chancellorsville.

It is related that Hasdrubal was deceived by his guides; he may not have been careful in watching them. They escaped, one by hiding, and one by swimming the river, and Hasdrubal lost his way. In the darkness, the troops straggled, broke ranks and mixed up organizations, so as to place the army in the worst possible condition for meeting the enemy. Having reached the Metaurus, Hasdrubal, to preserve order, instructed the ensigns to march along the banks, so that each taxis and syntagma might keep its proper place. But in the dark these ensigns could not be seen, and the rolling ground, wooded for the most part, without guides, was a

very labyrinth, while the increasing steepness of the river-
banks along which Hasdrubal was seeking a ford for the
army, broke up all semblance of formation. It seems curious
that he could not find his way back over the route he had
advanced on. The march of an army leaves a wide track.
Finally, after the march had been continued all night and
most of the succeeding day, and many of the men — especially
the Gauls — were almost dropping from fatigue and inanition, they were reached by the Roman van-guard of cavalry
under Nero, shortly followed by the light troops under Porcius. These attacked his rear of column smartly, and brought
Hasdrubal to bay.

The Romans were eager for battle. Hasdrubal was badly
dispersed. He was not much more than ten miles west from
Fanum in a direct line. No ford was at hand. He saw that
he could not cross the river with the Romans at his heels; he
must stop and fight for it. His troops were discouraged and
the effect of this retreat on the Gauls had been fairly disastrous: they had no rations; they had lost their rest; they
were in sorry condition for battle. Livius soon arrived on
the ground with the heavy foot, ready to engage, and there
was no more chance of avoiding the conflict.

It is hard to decipher from Livy — Polybius' account is
very short — whether the battle was fought the same evening
or the next morning. It is probable that both parties camped
and drew up their forces for battle the succeeding day.

Hasdrubal deserves credit for marshaling his forces so
well under such trying circumstances. He spent the night
collecting his men, and drew up his phalanx in good order to
resist the Roman attack. His line lay along a slight rise in
the ground. His left flank was covered, probably by a small
brook or low piece of ground, at least an obstacle difficult
to pass. The African and Spanish foot was on the right,

with which Hasdrubal personally proposed to make his strongest effort; the Ligurians in the centre; the Gauls, always unreliable on his left, covered by the obstacle. His ten

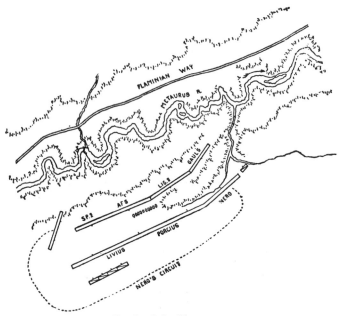

Battle of the Metaurus.

elephants were in front of his centre. Cavalry is not mentioned. If Hasdrubal had any amount of this arm, it was probably in the rear. His "line was rather long than deep," says Livy, "rather deep than long," says Polybius.

We do not know the size of Hasdrubal's army. It has been thought by some authorities to have been far superior to the Roman army. As Livius and Porcius had been unwilling to attack it before Nero's arrival, it may have been numerically equal to the forty thousand men now in the Roman line. But in quality it was far less good.

In the Roman line Nero with his seven thousand chosen

men stood facing the Gauls; Porcius was opposite the Ligurians. Livius had the Spanish and African infantry to contend with. The Romans were in the usual formation by cohorts. The Roman horse, there being no Carthaginian horse for it to cope with, was in rear of the triarii.

Hasdrubal saw that he must win this battle, or forfeit every hope for which he had crossed the Alps. His Gallic allies were protected by the obstacle in their front; his Ligurian allies were stanch; he hoped to win an advantage with the Spanish and African foot on his right, as the Romans would probably attack this wing, the left being under cover. This prompted him to open the battle by a hearty attack on Livius. Soon the fighting became general all along such parts of the line as could be reached. Livius and Porcius, though their legions fought with true Roman grit, could make no impression on Hasdrubal's Spanish and African phalanx. The elephants were as usual equally dangerous to both sides. At first they were sent against the Roman line and created grave confusion in the Roman ranks, but being driven back made similar havoc among their own friends, and " ranged to and fro between the two lines . . . like ships floating about without rudders." Nero did his level best on the Roman right, but without results. He could not cross the ground in face of the Gauls, who, despite their weariness and hunger, which drove many to desert, held the lines in good style. Finally, having convinced himself by repeated efforts that the same obstacle which prevented his own success would in the same way prevent theirs, should the Gallic troops attempt a serious attack, Nero left the front line of maniples to hold head against this wing, and moved those of the principes and triarii by the rear of the Roman army over to their left. This manœuvre showed the same *coup d'œil* and was similar to that which won Marlborough such renown in the battle of Ramillies.

It was a complete surprise to both Carthaginians and Romans, when Nero, debouching from behind the rolling ground, appeared in line on the Carthaginian right flank and sharply attacked the Spaniards in the rear. The front attack of Livius was at once doubled in vigor and effectiveness. This timely manœuvre decided the victory. The Spaniards and Ligurians, surrounded and crushed, fell to the last man facing the foe. The Gauls were cut down with scarce a show of resistance. Many in fact were found asleep in the fields and woods. They lacked that courage which can stand a long drain upon the physical powers.

Hasdrubal had in the combat acted with courage and good sense. He " called back the flying and restored the battle in many places where it had been given up." Finally, after heroic efforts to redeem the day, " sharing equally in every danger," seeing the battle irretrievably lost, he rode into the midst of a Roman cohort sword in hand and died " as was worthy the son of Hamilcar and the brother of Hannibal."

No such defeat had taken place since Cannæ. Livy sets the slain at fifty-six thousand men, with fifty-four hundred taken. Except some six thousand prisoners, and such as escaped the Roman sword, the whole Carthaginian army perished. The Roman loss was eight thousand killed. Polybius gives a much less number, — ten thousand Carthaginians killed in battle, and two thousand Romans; but he says that, excepting a few distinguished prisoners, the whole army of Hasdrubal was put to the sword. Whatever is the truth, Cannæ had been avenged, and Nero had bitterly repaid Hasdrubal for the deception practiced on him in Spain. The Punic phalanxes were destroyed, and Hannibal's last chance of conquering Italy disappeared with them.

" So completely were even the victors satiated with blood and slaughter that the next day when Livius, the consul, received intelligence that the cisalpine Gauls and Ligurians, who had either not been present at the battle or had made their escape from the carnage, were marching off in one body without a certain leader, without standards, without any discipline or subordination; that if one squadron of horse were sent against them they might be all destroyed, he replied, ' Let some survive to bear the news of the enemy's losses and of our valor.' " — Livy.

This whole campaign reflects the greatest credit on Nero, and is far from creditable to Hasdrubal. Every step in the undertaking was carefully studied by the Roman, and he never failed to get time — in such operations the one needful element — on his side. In this instance, it was all the more essential to the safety of the army he had left behind. Speed is one of the greatest values in war. . Nero had marched to better effect than any Roman before him. The march from and back to Hannibal's front is a lesson to all military students. Not one among the Roman generals had profited as had Nero from the lessons of his great antagonist. The manner in which he utilized the moral effect of his junction with his brother consul, away beyond the numerical reinforcements he brought him, was masterly; we have seen its effect on Hasdrubal.

Hasdrubal's fault was essentially lack of speed and decision. The delay in moving out of Spain, the siege of Placentia, were fatal errors. As to join Hannibal was his one object, so soon as he met Porcius and Livius, if he did not propose to give them battle, he should have withdrawn with the precautions Hannibal was wont to use, and have sought touch with his brother by the Flaminian Way. It was his delays, coupled to his unwise method of communicating with his brother, which defeated him.

Just what Hannibal was doing during the full two weeks

of the enactment of this to him fatal drama, history does not reveal. That portion of Polybius which should deal with this question is lost. Livy is silent on the subject. His remaining thus quiet makes Nero decidedly the hero of the act. The character of Hannibal shows so much both of energy and precaution, and he was as a rule so extremely careful as well as skillful in procuring information of the enemy's whereabouts, that we are at a loss to explain how he could in this instance have been so blinded, even by the excellent precautions of Nero, as to have remained quietly in camp while Hasdrubal was being destroyed. There are facts connected with the matter which we do not know. While his rôle was necessarily to preserve his army intact and wait for news of Hasdrubal, the fact that Nero was able to deceive him as he did gives this consul a credit beyond all his fellow-generals of the Second Punic War. Still we must remember that the consular army itself remained in Hannibal's front. Nero had only taken a small part of it with him. Hannibal was in the enemy's country, where information was not easy to get, and his Numidians, his eyes, had all but disappeared.

Nero hastened back to Apulia, bearing the head of Hasdrubal. He returned by the same route and means, and this time made the march in six days. He had thus put behind him considerably over five hundred miles, and had fought perhaps the most important battle of this eighteen years' war, in the short space of two weeks. Scipio's victory at Zama ended the war, but Nero's skill at the Metaurus alone made Zama possible. Reaching the vicinity of Hannibal's camp, Nero stuck the gruesome symbol of his victory on a pike in front of the Carthaginian outposts, or else threw it in among them, "repaying in this way his great antagonist, who scorned to war with the dead, for the honorable burial which he had given to Paulus, Gracchus, and Marcellus."

It was found by the outposts and carried to Hannibal. The Carthaginian prisoners were also exhibited at a distance, and and two were sent into the camp to tell the story.

Hannibal thus learned of the death of his brother and the destruction of his own plans at the same moment. He gave utterance to one of the few expressions of his of which we have any record, that in this sad spectacle he recognized the impending doom of Carthage. He withdrew to Bruttium, and with him took all his auxiliaries of Metapontum and other towns in Lucania. Good as the occasion was for Nero to pursue Hannibal, he made no attempt to do so. Probably Hannibal could have foiled him, but the advantage of following up a victory was rarely understood in ancient times.

The danger had been as great as after Cannæ; the defeat of Hasdrubal made it certain that Rome was saved. The capital was in a delirium of joy. The effect of the victory of the Metaurus was enormous on both citizens and allies. For the first time in twelve years Rome breathed freely, and saw the triumph of a victorious general. For to Livius, as commander in the province and of the bulk of the forces at the Metaurus, was granted the greater triumph; to Nero the lesser, though they were associated in the same procession. History, however, recognizes better than the Romans to whose skill, courage and clear conception the victory was really due. And it is said that this too was understood by the senate and people, as well as by Livius' army, which had been recalled and took part in the triumph; for "it was observed that the men wrote more verses in their jocular style upon C. Claudius Nero than upon their own general," says Livy. Nero, though an unpopular aristocrat, was the hero of the day.

Remotely, it was Scipio's successes in Spain which won this victory, as it was Scipio's carelessness which had allowed Hasdrubal to march to Italy. The one offsets the other.

Had Hasdrubal kept his Spanish resources and his fleet on the coast, he might have joined Hannibal in southern Italy, instead of crossing the Alps, and we can readily conceive how differently the Italian campaigns might have eventuated. But Scipio had robbed him of the power to do this. If not in the small galaxy of stars of the first magnitude, Scipio may fairly claim rank among stars of the second. Men are — indeed must be — judged by success. Scipio was beholden to Fortune far more than to his own ability ; but he honestly won his way, and is entitled to the laurels won by ending the war both in Spain and Africa. For to him — under good fortune, and aided by the unwise administration and intestine broils in Carthage — Rome owed her eventual salvation.

This year in Spain, Hanno, with a third army of reinforcements from Carthage, had supplanted Hasdrubal, son of Gisgo, who had been filling the vacant place of Hasdrubal Barca. Mago had returned from the Balearic Islands. Both these generals moved into Andalusia, but were defeated by Silanus, Scipio's legate, and Hanno was captured. The relics of their armies retired to the province of Hasdrubal, son of Gisgo. This officer, placing garrisons in such Andalusian cities as he still controlled, shut himself up in Gades. Masinissa, with his light horse, scoured southern Spain. The work of this cavalry-general affords one of the most interesting examples of the proper use of cavalry on a large scale in the history of war. He and Mutines were born commanders of horse. Gades was too strong to attempt, but having captured Oringes (near modern Seville), and garrisoned it, Scipio retired into winter-quarters at Tarraco. Spain was all but cleared of Carthaginian forces.

The fleets, meanwhile, had had fairly good fortune on the coast of Africa and against Philip.

XL.

SCIPIO. 206–205 B. C.

THERE were still nineteen legions in service the next year. Rome was well armed, but her conduct was lax. The farmers could begin to return to their devastated homes. Hannibal was confined to Bruttium; but the Romans could not drive him from Italy. The fear which even the best Roman generals exhibited of Hannibal speaks volumes; and this fear is acknowledged by even Livy. In Spain, Scipio fought a battle at Bæcula, in which the tactical manœuvre was handsomely devised and executed. Hasdrubal, son of Gisgo, was defeated and his army dispersed; and Scipio reduced the entire peninsula. Scipio was a brilliant rather than a great general. He had many qualities which command popular suffrage; his personality was in his favor. But had he been placed where Marcellus or Nero was placed, he would have failed. In 205 B. C. he was made consul, and to his lot fell Sicily, from which island every one believed he would soon carry the war into Africa. Scipio was apt to take the bit in his teeth, and there was a strong element against him in the senate, because he was thought to be unwilling to serve the republic with perfect subordination. Still, much power was left to him. Mago, Hannibal's brother, landed at Genoa, and began to collect an army of allies, in addition to over twenty thousand men he brought. But the Roman armies in his front neutralized his efforts. The war in Bruttium had become a mere raiding war, and the sole event of the year was the loss of Locri by Hannibal. In 204 B. C. Scipio as proconsul was permitted to continue his long-delayed preparations for a descent on Africa. Epidemics ravaged the armies in Bruttium. Little was done on this account.

Q. CÆCILIUS and L. Veturius Philo came into the consulate in the thirteenth year of the war, B. C. 206. They had particularly distinguished themselves as legates at the Metaurus. The prætors were C. Servilius for Sicily, Cæcilius Metellus in the city, Tiberius Claudius Asellus in Sardinia, and Q. Mamilius Turinus on foreign duty. The situation of affairs had undergone an entire change. The disaster at the

Metaurus had put Hannibal upon the strict defensive in Bruttium and Lucania, and the senate saw its way to decreasing the number of legions to nineteen, of which only four — the two consular armies — were placed in Hannibal's front. Capua and Tarentum were held each by a legion; and Rome and Etruria, Sicily and Sardinia, were defended as before, the usual shifting of stations taking place. The naval force underwent no particular change.

It was quite natural, though unwise, that, upon the severe moral strain and depletion of resources which Rome had undergone, there should follow a laxity of purpose in the prosecution of the war. Every intelligent citizen of Rome could see that the war had definitely turned in her favor, and that it was but a question of time when Hannibal would be driven from Italy. But, though nearly two hundred thousand men were under arms, there was little energy put into ridding the republic of its harassed but still redoubtable enemy.

Up to this moment, for some years past, all the country people had, by instructions from the senate, taken refuge in the towns. They were now ordered back to their farms and to tillage. This order was carried out so far as possible in the provinces not too near the seat of war, as well as in the vicinity of Rome. But there was little left to be done by those farmers who were poor. Their lands had been devastated, had got choked up with weeds and scrub growth, and they had almost no means of restoring them to productiveness.

When lots were drawn, Cæcilius took Nero's army, Veturius that of Q. Claudius, the pro-prætor. The consuls chose for opening the campaign to make a raid on the district of Consentia, in upper Bruttium, which they began to ravage; but they were cleverly entrapped in a defile by some partisan bodies of Bruttians and Numidian archers, and escaped with difficulty. They then retired to Lucania, which they readily brought into subjection.

Hannibal could not move out of Bruttium. His forces were quite unequal to fighting or even campaigning with any promise of success. He was hoping against hope for some further recognition from home, some aid in men and material. He could undertake nothing, but clung to his work with a despairing grasp. Weak as he was, however, neither of the consuls chose to come within reach of his arm. His patience and constancy under these trials, and the dread his name still inspired, show him up in a far greater measure than any of his triumphs. Even Livy, who is full of depreciation of Hannibal's abilities, says: "The Romans did not provoke him while he remained quiet, such power did they consider that single general possessed, though everything else around him was falling into ruin;" and is compelled to follow up this statement with a panegyric.

For thirteen years Hannibal had held more or less territory within the bounds of the Roman confederacy, far from home and his natural base. His old army had quite disappeared, and a motley array of hybrid material had taken its place. For three or four years he had had nothing which he could oppose to the Roman legions without danger of, — without actual defeat. His troops had often neither pay, clothing nor rations; their arms were far from good; they may have foreseen eventual disaster as did Hannibal. And yet the tie between leader and soldier never ceased to hold; the men he had were all devotion to his cause. Driven into a corner, where he must subsist his army on a limited area, which he could only do by forcing under his standard every man possibly fit for service; among a people whose greed for gold and plunder was their chief characteristic, he was yet able not only to keep his phalanxes together, but to subject them to excellent discipline, — not such of course as that which was the legitimate pride of the Romans, but under the conditions remarkable. The Carthaginians had only dreamed of keeping Spain; their one great captain, with all his possibilities, they had blindly neglected. He was left absolutely to his own resources. And yet, — it is so wonderful that one cannot but repeat it again and again, — though there were around him several armies of Roman veteran legions, for nearly all Romans were veterans now, such was the majesty which hedged his name, that neither one of the opposing commanders, nor all together, dared to come to the final conflict with him. Even after the Metaurus, when the Romans knew what the effect of this defeat must be on the morale of Hannibal's army, if not on himself, this dread of the very name of Hannibal, even by the best of the Roman commanders, was unparalleled. They must have each and all recognized that it needed but one joint effort to crush out his weakened and depleted semblance of an army, and yet none of them was apparently willing to undertake the task. Whatever the Roman historians may tell us about these years, is not here really a great and stubborn fact which testifies to more than a thousand written pages?

When we look at the condition of Carthage, its political imbroglios and the bitterness of its factions, it ceases to be a matter of curiosity that so little was done to aid Hannibal. Spain had been a mine to Carthage, not merely self-supporting, but yielding vast revenues. The peace-party had not the foresight to comprehend that every nation which had to do with Rome must eventually be neutralized if not swallowed up by her, and it was natural that they should prefer to hold Spain to winning in Italy. They believed that they could do the first, they doubted the other. They were lavish of their means to Spain for this reason; and the victories of Hannibal seemed to them, described by the oily tongue of Hanno, no greater than those of Hasdrubal. That a durable peace could not be conquered in Iberia did not appear to be understood.

Hannibal, on the contrary, could see, as his father had seen before him, that there was no *modus vivendi* with Rome until she had been taught such a lesson that she would act a defensive rôle and not again venture to attack Carthage. Like Napoleon, Hannibal saw that a peace, to be a peace, must be conquered at the doors of the enemy's capital. This was his policy. It was the proper one; but it failed because he could not control the resources of Carthage.

Yet it is passing strange that the jealousies of the Carthaginian ring should have been such that it could not see that wherever Hannibal was not, there was failure; that Hannibal was the man for their opportunity; that not Spain but Italy was the battle-field on which they could win. Spain had been constantly, steadily reinforced, while within her own borders there had been everything to draw from; the Roman forces against Carthage there had never had overwhelming odds; yet Spain was falling away from her grasp.

Scipio this year fought a decisive battle in Spain, the tactics of which were original and crowned with success. Hasdrubal, son of Gisgo, and Mago had lain in front of Gades. They had collected at various places in Bætica, an army stated as high as seventy thousand foot, forty-five hundred horse, and thirty-two elephants, of which force, however, less than half were Africans and Numidians, the balance being made up of hastily-raised Spanish militia. With part of this numerically respectable, but intrinsically weak, body — what might not the half of it have accomplished under Hannibal's discipline in Italy? — the two Carthaginian generals moved up the left bank of the Bætis and crossed to Ilipa

(or Silpia), a place above modern Seville, on the right bank
of the river, where, by adding reinforcements, they reached
the number stated, and proceeded to Bæcula. The Carthaginian camp was on the slope of a hill facing a valley, with
a similar slope running up from the other side, and with
the right flank of the camp towards a small affluent of the
Bætis.

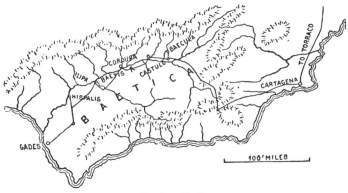

Southern Spain.

Scipio had four Roman legions and an equal number of
Spanish levies. Remembering the fate of his father and
uncle through the treachery of their Spanish allies, he had
been wise not to overbalance his force. He had been in
winter-quarters in Tarraco, from which place he advanced to
Cartagena, whence west to Castulo on the Bætis, intending
to give battle to the enemy. After leaving garrisons along
the route, he had left some forty-five thousand foot and three
thousand horse — of which number twenty-four thousand
were the Roman and allied legions. His movement against
Hasdrubal and Mago was on such a line as would cut them
off from the nearest road to Gades, which lay along the south
bank. If he beat them, he could the more certainly compromise the whole army. This was another instance of attack-

ing the enemy's strategic flank. He went into a camp on the opposite slope from the Carthaginians, with his left towards the stream mentioned.

Mago and Masinissa sharply attacked the Romans with their cavalry while they were going into camp, but Scipio had anticipated a possible attack, and had kept a body of Roman horse in hiding, while, as usual, protecting the building of the camp with his light troops and some cohorts. The foot held the Carthaginians in front, and the Roman cavalry took them in flank, and drove them off with loss. Both armies lay facing each other across the valley. For several days nothing but outpost-skirmishing occurred, in which the new levies on either hand were sizing up each other, and each army was marshaled before its camp. But neither offered battle. It must be remembered that no army attacked up-hill if it could be avoided, because the enemy's spears, darts, arrows and stones had so much more effect from a height. An army in line in front of its camp was rarely attacked.

The usual habit with the Carthaginians was to place the African foot in the centre and the Spaniards on the flanks. During these days of waiting, Scipio placed his Romans in the centre and his Spanish allies on the flanks. It grew to be understood in both camps that such was to be the formation for the approaching battle. Acting on this knowledge, Scipio formed his line. He proposed not to pit Spaniard against Spaniard, but to oppose the Spanish infantry in the Carthaginian army with his Roman legions, and to use his own Spaniards against the African centre. Like Wellington in a later age, he preferred not to put too great dependence on his Spaniards in battle. Scipio would naturally force the fighting with his Roman legionaries, and this would bring the brunt of the attack upon the flanks.

The day on which Scipio designed to offer battle, he had

his men eat their morning meal at a very early hour and filed out of camp with so much commotion as to induce Hasdrubal to leave his quarters before his men had broken fast. The battle was opened by the light troops and horse of both sides, and the formation of the line went on behind them. The Carthaginians had as usual placed the African foot in the

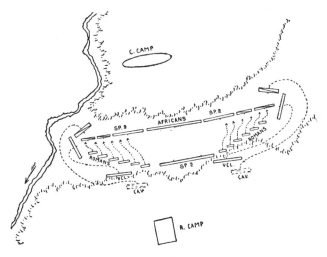

Battle of Bæcula.

centre, the Spaniards in the wings, the elephants in front. When the Carthaginian cavalry was withdrawn, it was placed, the heavy in rear of the flanks, the Numidians outside the heavy. The Carthaginian army, without its morning meal, was not in good condition. The Romans were well prepared. Scipio had retorted on Hasdrubal the ruse of Hannibal at the Trebia. He could profit by others' experience.

Scipio had prepared his troops for an exact and difficult tactical manœuvre. His Roman and allied legions were on the flanks and were pretty sure to beat the Spaniards in the Carthaginian army; but the Spaniards who were in his centre, opposed to the excellent African infantry in Hasdru-

bal's, were apt to fail at a critical moment. For this possibility he sought to provide.

Some five hundred yards from the enemy, Scipio brought
his heavy foot into line, still covered by his skirmishers. The
Spanish legions, as well as the Roman and allied, all stood in
the usual checkerwise order by maniples. On the withdrawal
of the skirmish line, the men fell back through the intervals
and formed, the velites in rear of the flanks of the legions,
the cavalry again in their rear. This done, the cohorts moved
forward. It was too late for the Carthaginians to change
their dispositions if they so desired. Scipio had purposely
prolonged the contest of the light troops so as to keep the
enemy busy without allowing him to change formation, and
tire him out from lack of food.

The Carthaginian line extended some distance beyond the
Romans' either flank. When within two hundred paces,
Scipio gave the order to the centre to continue its movement
straight forward, but at a slow and regular step; to the wings
to oblique at a rapid gait, the right wing to the right, the left
wing to the left by cohorts so as to strike the Carthaginian
line at its extremities, while the light foot and horse, by a
turning movement at a *pas de charge*, surrounded the right
and left flanks of the enemy respectively. Scipio commanded
the right cohort, to give the direction; Marcius and Silanus the
left. Within striking distance, the oblique movement ceased,
the legionaries moved to the front and struck the enemy a
staggering blow, while the light foot and horse fell upon their
flanks. As intended by Scipio, the centre had not yet got up
to engaging distance, and was held back so as to continue to
threaten the Carthaginian centre and prevent the African infantry from coming into action, but without risking its blow.

Scipio thus had a concave line of battle, or rather a double
oblique line with centre refused. Whether the wings ad-

vanced in echelon or not cannot be said; no doubt they advanced in some similar oblique order. The entire manœuvre appears to have been executed with the utmost skill and precision, just as planned. The Carthaginian horse, nonplussed at the novelty of the dispositions, was late in charging, and thus lost its first momentum. The elephants, wounded by many spears, rushed back towards the Carthaginian line, inflicting upon it the damage intended for Scipio. In a short but sharp and decisive struggle, the Carthaginian cavalry and the Spanish phalanx proved entirely inadequate to resist the onset of the Roman wings, and were dispersed and largely cut down. The African centre, however, which Scipio's Spaniards had kept in place, could not be demoralized. It withdrew in good order, and enabled the wreck of the wings to rally upon it.

The whole battle is a pattern of excellent tactics, as skillfully designed as brilliantly executed. The strategic soundness of Scipio's dispositions is shown in the fact that the Carthaginians were, as he intended they should be, thrown back off the line of retreat on Gades, which was across the river and ran down the left bank; the army was compelled to retreat down the right bank. Nearly all the Spanish allies of the Carthaginians forsook them. Scipio followed up Hasdrubal's retreat. On reaching the mouth of the Bætis, Hasdrubal was about to go into a fortified camp, but Scipio again attacked him, and but six thousand men saved themselves in the camp out of the fifty thousand who fought at Bæcula. Most of these six thousand deserted in a few days to the Romans. Hasdrubal fled by sea and reached Gades. Leaving a force of eleven thousand men under Silanus to watch the camp, which not long after surrendered, Scipio retired to Tarraco.

During the balance of the year Scipio captured Gades, and

subdued the rest of the peninsula. Spain became a Roman province; but it was subject to constant insurrections, and there was always danger that it would rise in favor of Carthage.

Much of his success Scipio owed to his lieutenants. Lælius and Silanus were of an ability to command higher rank than they enjoyed. They did much for which brilliant Scipio managed to reap the credit. Still there is much which is admirable in Scipio's work.

Hasdrubal sailed to Carthage. Mago, Hannibal's brother, with large treasure, sailed for Minorca, where he wintered, with authority from the Carthaginian senate to go to cisalpine Gaul and raise troops to join his brother, Hannibal.

Thus Scipio's marked good fortune and fine abilities had enabled him to end the war in Spain. The cause of Carthage had all but reached its ebb tide. But Scipio had once again allowed a lion's whelp to escape him. What Mago might accomplish remained to be seen.

Marcellus had ended the war in Sicily; Publius Sulpicius that in Greece; Scipio that in Spain. But the war still went on in Italy, though the best generals and troops were at hand in the peninsula.

Scipio was a brilliant rather than a great general. He had early begun his career, as we have seen, by saving his father's life at the Trebia. When, as it is related, he was chosen by the people for the Spanish army because he was the only candidate who presented himself to undertake this difficult mission, he became at a single leap the favorite of the people, and always so remained despite his errors, which were many and serious. Scipio was handsome and manly, enthusiastic and courageous, intelligent and full of self-confidence. He was not the man to constrain fortune, but he was born under a lucky star, which was better. When he failed from the result of his own errors, Fortune always came to the rescue. She did as much for him as for Alexander, while Scipio did but a tithe as much for himself as the son of Philip. Scipio believed in his own star and was adroit in acting up to his belief. He was honorable, envied no man, treated all with consideration. He was highly educated and refined, and a general favorite. But he considered himself above criticism, and often acted in what was really a high-handed manner. He was never called to account for many acts which in others would have been insubordination. He did no more for Italy than Marcellus, less than Nero, but he has descended into history as a greater character than either. Less able in many respects, his work was supplemented by opportunities not awarded them, and what he did bore fruit which all men could see. Scipio never hid his light under a bushel. Had Scipio faced Hannibal when Marcellus or Nero was called on to do so, he would probably have failed. Fortune saved him for Zama, when Hannibal had no longer an army and he himself had inherited the best of its size Rome had put into the field.

It was just that Scipio should be rewarded with the consulate the next year, B. C. 205. P. Licinius Crassus was his colleague. There were still nineteen legions under arms. The prætors were Cn. Servilius for the city, Spurius Lucretius for Ariminum, L. Æmilius for Sicily, and Cnæus Octavius for Sardinia. Q. Cæcilius remained in Bruttium as proconsul. To Crassus the care of the situation in Bruttium was confided.

To Scipio's lot fell Sicily, but it was understood by him, and by all who wisely scanned the situation, that the war should now be carried over to Africa. Though he was not the only good soldier in the service of the republic, he was the one whose personality captured the suffrages of the average citizen, and all Rome looked to Scipio as the man to give the finishing touch to the struggle. There seems to have been much the same glamour about Scipio as there was in 1861 and 1862 about McClellan. But Scipio met the tests he was put to after a better fashion. In the senate, however, and among the most thoughtful, was a division on the question of moving into Africa. A considerable faction distrusted Scipio, not on account of his military conduct, but because he showed a disposition not to ride to orders, but to look at things *de haut en bas*. Fabius Maximus was among those who opposed Scipio's being sent to Africa. Livy asserts that Scipio had openly declared that he would transport an army into Africa through the medium of the people if the senate opposed him; and on being publicly asked in the senate whether he would submit to the conscript fathers and abide by their determination in the matter, replied that he would act as he thought was for the interest of the state, facts which accord well with Scipio's character, but are more consistent in a politician than in the military servant of a republic. The result was that supplies were withheld from Scipio. But as he had permission to accept volunteers, an appeal to the allies soon enabled the new consul to create a fleet, and later the senate gave him fuller support. Nor was Scipio idle. That twenty quinquiremes and ten quadriremes could be built and launched in forty-five days, as was done, shows diligence on his part and experience in shipbuilding among the allies.

Mago had raised twelve thousand foot and two thousand horse. He set sail towards summer from Minorca, landed at Genua and took the place. Soon large numbers of the native tribes joined his standard. Carthage sent him some seven thousand men, seven elephants and money. But M. Livius from Etruria, and Lævinus with the city legions, four in all, by moving, the one to the Ariminum country, and the other to Arretium and its territory, not only arrested Mago's expected supplies of Gallic troops, but cut off his advance into the interior as well.

The war in Bruttium had taken the form of forays. Hannibal's Numidians had set the example in the business, and they were quickly followed by the Bruttians, with whose character a raiding war well comported. The Romans were not slow to follow suit. But the campaign had practically been nullified by violent epidemics in both the Roman camp and Hannibal's. The sole incident of the year was the loss to Hannibal of Locri. He had previously abandoned Thurii. While Scipio was completing his preparations to go to Africa, he was led by certain rich exiles from Locri to make an attempt to seize on this town, and thus still further hem in Hannibal. He managed through these exiles, who were in Rhegium, and some Locrian prisoners taken by the Roman raiding parties and ransomed for the purpose by the exiles, to get into communication with the garrison of one of the citadels of Locri, and, by the aid of a conspiracy excited among some of them, who then helped the Roman forces from within, to seize upon it. The operating force was three thousand troops from Rhegium under two military tribunes, Sergius and Matienus, and the pro-prætor Q. Pleminius. Hamilcar, commander of the Carthaginian garrison of Locri, appears to have been careless, and the Carthaginian soldiers under bad discipline. A panic seized the garrison upon the first attempt of the Romans to scale the walls, which was done by but a small party, and the first citadel was lost. Hamilcar hereupon withdrew into the second citadel. The townsmen held the city between the two citadels, which were not far apart, awaiting events. Pleminius held one and Hamilcar the other.

Hearing of the threatened capture of Locri, Hannibal at once moved thither, and sent orders ahead from the river Butrotus for Hamilcar to make a vigorous sortie when he

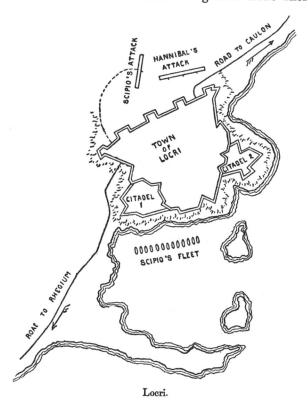

Locri.

himself should attack the town and the citadel held by the Romans. Scipio at Messana heard of Hannibal's movement on Locri, and, setting sail with the next tide, arrived in the port a few hours later on the same day that Hannibal put in an appearance. During the night he landed his men and hid them in the town, whose population leaned towards the Romans. When Hannibal next day advanced to the attack of the town, Hamilcar having begun the battle, and was placing his ladders in position, Scipio led out his troops from one of the town gates and attacked him in flank and rear. Quite unexpected, this attack demoralized Hannibal's raw levies, and, completely upsetting his plans, forced him to retire to camp; when hearing that Scipio was in command, and that the Locrians were favorable to him, he left Locri, and ordered Hamilcar to evacuate the second citadel and follow him. Scipio left a garrison in Locri under Pleminius, and returned to Sicily. Hannibal's Bruttian levies were now of such poor material that he was often unable to get them to face the Roman veteran legions. He had to acknowledge defeat on more than one occasion from this cause.

The Carthaginian rule had been severe, but Roman cruelty and rapacity surpassed everything the Locrians had so far endured, and they had good cause to regret the change. The account of the conduct of the Roman troops and their commanders shows that even Roman discipline could be lax, and Roman laws disregarded, among themselves as well as towards outsiders.

During this year the Macedonian imbroglio was brought to an end by a treaty of peace with Rome. The Carthaginian senate, too late aware that its failure to sustain Hannibal had brought about the danger of a new descent upon Africa, now sent to Philip to urge a fresh invasion of Italy. It was in vain. A small Macedonian corps sent to Carthage was the only response. When Carthage could be saved, the senate would not; now that the senate was willing, Carthage was beyond saving.

Scipio was not elected consul the succeeding year, B. C. 204, but was allowed, as proconsul, to continue his preparations for a descent on Africa. He does not seem to have been very expeditious about the business. In this he resembled McClellan, as well as in his popularity. All thinking men

saw that the best manner of ridding the country of Hannibal, who, like the Old Man of the Sea, had bestridden Italy
for so many years, was to force his recall from the peninsula
by attacking Carthage on her own soil. Scipio could see this
fact, and he appeared anxious to cross the strait; but his
tardiness looks as if he too may have been wary of too close
a contact with the giant, however weakened, unless he could
have things his own way.

The consuls were M. Cornelius Cethegus and P. Sempronius Tuditanus. To the latter was confided the task of
watching Bruttium with freshly levied legions; to Cornelius' lot fell Etruria, with the old army. Two additional
legions were continued in Bruttium, under Licinius. The
total force under arms was again nineteen legions. The prætors were Claudius Nero in Sardinia, Marcius Ralla in the
city, Scribonius Libo in Gaul, Pomponius Matho in Sicily.

The twelve Latin confederates which had in B. C. 209 refused to furnish their contingents were punished now that
Rome had recovered her equipoise. They were Nepete, Su-
trium, Ardea, Cales, Alba, Carseoli, Sora, Suessa, Setia,
Circeii, Narnia, Interamna. They were compelled to furnish
double the number of men which were properly their quota;
and these were not only drafted from the wealthy classes,
but were sent out of Italy on the hardest service. A heavy
tax was imposed upon these socii.

Epidemics still raged in the camps of the Romans and
Carthaginians in Bruttium, which prevented Hannibal, if inclined even, to undertake any special operations. As he had
waited, year after year, for the advent of Hasdrubal, conducting practically but a defensive system of warfare in a country
he had invaded, so now, again hoping that his brother Mago
might have better fortune, he based his hopes on what Mago
should accomplish in Liguria, and patiently held his ground

on the enemy's soil, eager to seize any opportunity which good fortune might present of joining forces and once more becoming an active menace to Rome. His army, weak years ago, was still more so now. His inability to relieve Locri shows the poor quality of the force he headed. He was hand-tied. As servant of the Carthaginian senate, he could do nothing but await orders where he stood. As adviser of the Carthaginian senate, he had found in his days of prosperity that he was not hearkened to, — how should he be heeded now? And yet he knew full well that the war was drawing to a close; that the term of his usefulness as a soldier had expired.

Among Scipio's political successes while in Spain had been the detaching of Masinissa, a king of Numidia, and Syphax, king of Massæsylia, from the Carthaginian alliance. Hasdrubal, son of Gisgo, on his return from Spain, had however managed, by giving him his daughter in marriage, to reclaim the latter to the Carthaginian cause. It became essential that Scipio should hurry his preparations for the African campaign, lest his men should catch alarm by hearing of the defection before sailing; lest, indeed, the defection should spread. For the alliance of the native kings was one of the conditions to which Scipio and his army attached a peculiar value.

Gallic Swordsman. (Antonine Column.)

XLI.

ON TO CARTHAGE. 204-203 B. C.

SCIPIO sailed from Lilybæum in the spring of B. C. 204. He had over thirty thousand of the best troops, mostly Cannæ survivors, hardened by many years' service in Sicily. He landed near Utica. Carthage was terror-stricken. She had small means with which to resist a good army. But Hasdrubal and Syphax raised a respectable force, though it was of poor material, for the defense of the capital. Hanno was pushed out with a cavalry division to reconnoitre, but was defeated and cut up. Scipio was but a day's march from Carthage, which was practically undefended. If it be held that Hannibal, after Cannæ, should have marched on Rome, twelve days distant, well defended and with allies by the hundreds of thousands, what shall be said of Scipio for not seizing this opportunity ? Yet, by some critics, Scipio is ranked with Hannibal as a soldier. Scipio besieged Utica, while Hasdrubal was raising an army. When this appeared, Scipio was in bad case. He retired to winter in an intrenched camp. Opposite Hannibal in Italy there was little doing. In a battle near Crotona he won the first day, and lost the next ; but he still held on. This quiet continued through the winter. Hannibal hoped that Mago might win some success. In Africa, Scipio, in the early spring, beat Syphax and Hasdrubal, and destroyed their armies. These generals got together another only to have that also destroyed. Mago, in northern Italy, was defeated by the Romans, and died of his wounds. Hannibal was ordered back to Carthage. No hope left, the great captain embarked his army and landed at Hadrumetum, where he wintered. Rome was finally freed of the worst enemy she had ever encountered.

HAVING completed his arrangements, by the permission of the senate to take with him whatever troops from Sicily he chose, Scipio set sail from the port of Lilybæum, and, after some danger on the passage, landed not far from Utica, at the " Fair Promontory," in the spring of B. C. 204. His fleet anchored in the roadway of the town. He had two (perhaps three) strong legions, Roman and allied, — between thirty and thirty-five thousand foot and horse. Fifty war-galleys protected four hundred transports, on which the army was embarked. He had chosen those legions numbered five and six, which had been formed of the survivors of Cannæ, and had been on duty in Sicily as punishment for what had been deemed breach of their oaths in flying from that awful field. These troops were, in Scipio's eyes, guiltless of the charge, and they were veterans hardened by many years' campaigning in Sicily, and burning to wipe out the stigma attached to their names, and to regain the favor which they, as representatives of the defeated soldier, had under the austere Roman law been condemned to forfeit. Other Roman legionaries had survived defeats; Varro, the head and front of the disaster, had been pardoned, and had since been constantly in command; these men were merely the scape-goats, no worse than the others, but selected to be sent out into the wilderness. Scipio could not have better chosen. These legions were bound to him, body and soul, not only for this act of generosity, but from a soldier's appreciation of Scipio's brilliant and winning qualities. They, as well as the other legions, were strengthened up to sixty-five hundred men, of which three hundred were horse. The places of those who were no longer fitted for hard campaiging had been filled by volunteers. He carried with him none but the best material. It was probably the stanchest Roman army of the war.

Some generals would have declared these means insufficient; but Scipio possessed an abundance of self-confidence which supplemented material strength in all but severe tests. He was eager to command the expedition to Africa; he feared that some one might supplant him, and he sacrificed everything to this end. The number of his army has been stated from ten thousand to thirty-five thousand and upwards; Cælius inclines towards a still greater number. He says that

" birds fell to the ground for the shout of the soldiers, and that so great a multitude went on board the fleet that it seemed as if there was not a man left in Italy or Sicily." Paying small heed to such a highly-colored statement, the number was probably not far from thirty-five thousand men. This was a third more than Hannibal commanded when he attacked Rome in her strength; and in Carthage Scipio had an opponent ground down to extreme weakness by the attrition of the war, and lacking every quality and resource which made Rome powerful. There was embarked on the fleet forty-five days' rations, of which fifteen were cooked, and water for an equal period.

Scipio first proposed to besiege Utica. He deemed it wise to secure a foothold in some city. He moved his forces up from the fleet to a camp about five miles from the place, with this purpose in view.

Carthage was now as terror-stricken as Rome had been. There was at the moment no army, no general. She had

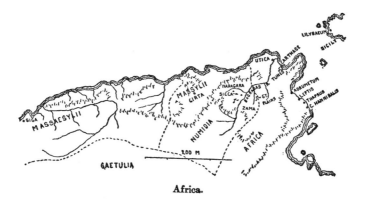

Africa.

known that a descent would be made on her coast, but with her usual improvidence she had failed to prepare for the event. She had for years frittered away her resources in short-sighted schemes instead of supporting her one captain on the true battle-ground for her cause, — Italy. We can imagine that she sadly deplored her neglect of Hannibal now that it was too late.

Mention has already been made of the two rival African kings who had already figured in the Spanish campaigns, Masinissa, the ruler of the Massylians, whose capital was Cirta, and Syphax, ruler of the Massæsylians, whose capital was Siga. Of these, the Carthaginians had succeeded in attaching to their cause the latter, by treaty and a marriage with the daughter of Hasdrubal. Masinissa, an old rival of Syphax for the hand of Sophronisbe, had succumbed to the new alliance, and was wandering in the desert with a few horsemen. In addition to what Syphax could bring, Carthage, by summary efforts, managed to raise twenty thousand foot, six thousand cavalry, and one hundred and forty elephants, — all of questionable quality. Hasdrubal, son of Gisgo, who was the general most fit for command, was for the moment on a mission to Syphax. A fair fleet lay in the harbor. A Macedonian corps was awaited, and some Celtiberian mercenaries. This force was in marked contrast to the nearly eight hundred thousand men Rome had been in a position to raise, when the Carthaginians descended from the Alps upon the Po, — to the two hundred thousand men she could have put in line at a week's notice. It well marks the difference in the task of Scipio and Hannibal.

As a first step, a small party of five hundred Numidians had been sent out. These had crossed swords with the Romans and been defeated. Then Hanno, whom Livy calls the son of Hamilcar, was dispatched with a body of four thousand horse to observe the Roman army. This general set out on his reconnoissance and camped some eight miles distant from Utica, in a town named Salera. Scipio, not liking the

threat of this corps, sent out Masinissa, who had joined him
with a Numidian body of horse, two thousand strong, to
skirmish with Hanno, and draw him back to a place where he
had stationed the bulk of his Roman cavalry in hiding behind

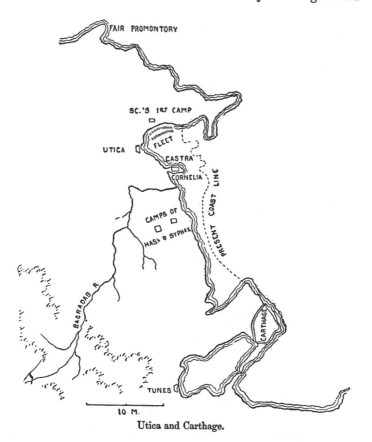

Utica and Carthage.

some hills. Masinissa accomplished his duty well. Hanno's
courage quite outran his discretion. He rightly gauged the
size of Masinissa's column as much smaller than his own, and
considering nothing more broke hastily out of camp, and fell
in careless order upon the Numidians, his ancient allies, now

all the more bitter enemies. Masinissa simulated retreat.
Hanno followed, eager for a first success. His expected triumph was short. Reaching the plain near which the Roman
horse lay in ambush, Masinissa turned again upon Hanno,
whose ranks were much broken by his overeager pursuit,
while the Romans debouched from their hiding and charged
in upon his flanks. The defeat was overwhelming. Hanno
fell at the head of some three thousand men, among them two
hundred of the most prominent sons of Carthage.

Now was Scipio's chance, if ever. Carthage was practically defenseless. She had all but no army to man her walls,
and while these were strong, they could not be readily held
against serious attack. Scipio had thirty - seven thousand
men. A small body could watch the fleet and observe Utica.
A strong day's march would bring him to the gates of Carthage. If he could not enter them at the first rush, he could
without effort shut the city in by land and by sea. And it
was at the gates of Carthage that Scipio could soonest end
the war. But he let his opportunity slip and returned to the
siege of Utica.

It is a common habit to place Scipio on a par with Hannibal, because he was victor in the battle of Zama. That the
best general is not always the winner in a battle, or at the
end of a long war, is abundantly proven by history, ancient
and modern. We Americans need not go beyond our own
recent history to prove this fact.

If it be assumed — as it often is — that Hannibal, after
Cannæ, was lacking in energy for not undertaking a two-
hundred-mile march upon Rome, well defended, and with
ample garrison, under the adverse conditions already pointed
out, what criticism shall be passed upon Scipio for neglecting
this exceptional chance of taking defenseless Carthage close
at hand? If Hannibal had failed in an attempt on Rome, the

consequences might have been disastrous, fatal to his entire scheme. But Scipio ran no danger whatsoever. He could retire from before Carthage to his base at Utica, if his anticipations should not be realized on reaching that city. Instead, then, of a vigorous course of action, he contented himself with foraging and collecting booty, which he sent by his fleet to Sicily and Rome, as if to show what he could do was more important than to accomplish results. It was safer and more like Scipio to content himself with the lesser problem. But this action helps to place him where he fairly belongs in the rank of generals.

But if Scipio lost time, not so Hasdrubal. During the forty days Scipio was wasting in siege-preparations before Utica, this officer and his ally Syphax had been able to muster an overwhelming army, — stated by Livy at not less than eighty thousand foot and thirteen thousand horse, — and suddenly appeared in Scipio's front. It is probable that the bulk of this army was a mere rabble, all but worthless in pitched battle against Roman legions. But it put an end to any chance Scipio had of capturing Carthage out of hand. The vicinity of this force, indeed, obliged the Roman general to desist from the siege and go into defensive winter-quarters. He was, in other words, driven back to his ships. He took up a strong position north of the Bagradas, near the coast, on a peninsula jutting out into the Gulf of Carthage, where he could take advantage of and protect his fleet, and wintered there, strongly fortifying his camp, at a place since known as Castra Cornelia. The contrast of Hannibal's early work on reaching Italy, and that of Scipio on reaching Africa, is answer enough to those who place Scipio on Hannibal's level.

The war in Italy had practically died out from sheer inanition. Hannibal was entirely shut in by surrounding armies — at least forty thousand men — to the neighborhood of Crotona, without a possibility of undertaking anything, and relying solely upon the slender chance of Mago's accomplishing some lucky stroke in Liguria. He was no longer able to force his way towards the north; his army was of a quality quite unequal to active operations. If he showed any military activity beyond the few recorded instances, we can only guess at what it may have been in the light of the terror which undeniably still hung about his presence. A very few Roman generals, not to count the foolhardy ones, had dared to attack Hannibal, — Marcellus, Fulvius, Nero, — when conditions were well on their side. None of them, however, had been able to inflict such a defeat on him as to compromise his safety, — such a defeat as the Roman arms had often suffered at his hands. The average Roman general was scrupulously careful not to burn his fingers. In Hannibal's case the vaunted Roman fighting qualities were kept in the background.

The consul Sempronius was ambitious to see what impression he could make on Hannibal, whom he apparently encountered on the march not far from Crotona, his present base, — probably foraging. We have no details of the combat, nor any but Livy's account. It appears that Sempronius' attack was a failure. He was beaten with a loss of twelve hundred men. But what he could not do with twenty thousand men, the consul thought he might accomplish with forty thousand. Annoyed at his defeat, he retired and called on Licinius to join him. This made four Roman and four allied legions. Hannibal could have had no more than half the number. The Romans camped near Crotona and again offered Hannibal battle. Feeling constrained to accept it, for he must keep open his way for foraging, Hannibal emerged from the gates. But the weight and quality of the Roman troops were too great for him to win another victory. He was obliged to retire into Crotona with a loss, as claimed by Livy, of four thousand men. The Roman loss is not given. The consul had won a questionable victory; but Hannibal was still on Italian soil. Nor does it appear that this Livian defeat in any wise hampered his movements. The Roman army retired, and Hannibal, except for his loss in men, was uninjured. He was still free to move throughout Bruttium. Clampetia was taken by storm, and Consentia and Pandosia voluntarily submitted, but nothing else was accomplished by the Romans this year in Bruttium.

The consuls for B. C. 203, the sixteenth year of the war, were Cnæus Servilius Cæpio and C. Servilius Geminus. The former took Bruttium in charge, the latter Etruria. The prætors were P. Cornelius Lentulus in Sardinia, P. Quinctius Varus at Ariminum, P. Ælius Pætus in the city, and P. Villius Tappulus in Sicily. Scipio was confirmed in his office as proconsul till the ending of the war. There were this year twenty legions, somewhat over two hundred thousand men, and one hundred and sixty ships for duty.

Publius Sempronius was continued in command for a year and succeeded P. Licinius. Cæpio got Bruttium by lot, and commanded the army of Sempronius; Servilius Geminus got Etruria and took that of M. Cornelius. Lucretius was continued in command in order to rebuild Genoa, destroyed by Mago. Three thousand men were levied for Sicily, which had been depleted of troops by Scipio, and forty ships were on the Sicilian coast. The fleet was divided. Lentulus and Manlius retained command in Spain. Success in Africa was felt to be the great object in view, and everything bent to this one thing. Clothing and corn went thither from Sicily and Sardinia, and arms and all kinds of material from Sicily.

We left Scipio in his winter-camp at Castra Cornelia, near Utica, and his enemy, powerful in numbers if not of soldierly material, in his front, camped some six miles away. The

Carthaginians had utilized their fleet in raids on Scipio's supplies. Scipio, during all his period of delay, was endeavoring
to gain Syphax to his cause; perhaps the Carthaginians were
seeking to delay Scipio's operations by having Syphax keep
up negotiations with Scipio looking towards peace, in the hope
that either Mago might succeed in Italy, or that Hannibal
might return to take command at Carthage. Nothing came
of these negotiations, as it was scarcely expected there would;
but Scipio was able to learn about the movements of the
enemy, by means of his Roman emissaries who went to and
fro between the camps. He sent with his negotiators centurions of ability and clad them as servants, whom, as not
apparently soldiers, the enemy allowed to wander through the
camp, where they could see and report all its details. On the
whole, if the Carthaginians profited by delay, Scipio gained
more than they could profit. The information thus derived,
with " more artifice than honor," says Mommsen, for Scipio
had not only no intention, but no right to negotiate for peace,
enabled him to form a project for defeating the Carthaginian
plans. His negotiators and their " servants," of whom he
chose different ones on each occasion, so as to have as many
points of view as possible, had reported that the discipline
within the Punic lines was lax — the more so for the negotiations, very naturally — and the camps badly guarded.

When he had learned all he desired, Scipio broke off the
negotiation. "Thus," says Livy, " he put an end to the truce,
in order that he might be free to execute his designs without
breaking his faith," — a wonderful instance of literal hon-
esty. During the entire war there is no sample of " Punic
Faith " which approaches Scipio's trickery in this matter,
unless it be Hasdrubal's negotiations in Spain with Nero.
Hannibal misled the Romans by every device, known and unknown; but he never violated a truce, nor is there an instance

of his deceit on record which the conditions do not fully justify. Scipio was perhaps warranted in playing what he understood to be the Carthaginian game; but the Romans
could not afford to throw stones.

Early in the year B. C. 203, Scipio dispatched a corps of
two thousand men to take up the same position near Utica
which he had previously occupied, and shipped engines and
siege-material to the place, in order to lead the enemy to believe that he was about to resume the siege, and at the same
time to forestall a sally while he should be absent. This ruse
succeeded absolutely. Hasdrubal and Syphax kept only this
movement in view, while Scipio had made his plans to attack
and burn their camps. Under cover of the diversion on
Utica, Scipio broke up one night, shortly after dark, he commanding one half his army, and his efficient legate the other.
To Lælius and Masinissa was assigned the task of setting
fire to the camp of Syphax, the huts in which were woven of
reeds and covered with mats; he himself undertook the Carthaginian matter, where the huts were of wood, equally in-
flammable. By the knowledge acquired of the enemy's can-
tonments, both parties so moved as to close all the debouches
to their camps by suitable bodies of troops; and from the fact
that there was no out-post service, nor any regularity in the
shape of the camps, the surprise was easy. Lælius and Masinissa first reached the camp of Syphax and set it on fire.
The frightened Africans, supposing the fire to be accidental,
rushed out unarmed, only to be met by another form of death.
The Carthaginian army, equally terrified at the fire, and
quite unaware of its origin, lest their own should fall also
a prey to the flames, deserted the camp in herds. They fell
in like manner upon Scipio's legions, which cut them down
without mercy. Having thus destroyed the bulk of the Carthaginian army and dispersed the rest, the camp of Hasdrubal

was also set on fire. Only twenty-five hundred men and the two generals are said to have escaped. No less than forty thousand men were killed and five thousand taken, with endless Carthaginian nobles, eleven senators, one hundred and seventy-four ensigns, twenty-seven hundred horses and six elephants. Scipio then actually set about resuming the siege of Utica, as well as moved out into the adjoining country, and captured several towns.

The Carthaginian senate behaved with courage and prudence; it " breathed the spirit of Roman constancy," says Livy. Hasdrubal and Syphax managed to collect new troops in a comparatively short time. These, with the fugitives who reassembled, amounted to thirty-five thousand men, including Celtiberians, of whom a fine body was enlisted in a town named Abba, and a few Macedonians who had come from Philip. This force they again brought to confront Scipio on the " Great Plains," five days' march from Utica.

But they accomplished nothing by their energy and diligence. Scipio again moved against them and took up a position on a hill five miles from the king's camp. For three days constant skirmishing occurred between the lines : on the fourth the lines met in battle. The Carthaginian line consisted of a miserable lot of rustics and vagabonds, whom nothing could constrain to face the Roman charge. Only the Celtiberians in the centre fought with any show of valor. These men fell where they stood; the rest decamped, but were largely overtaken and cut down. The slaughter ended, Scipio detailed Lælius and Masinissa, with a chosen body of horse sustained by some light infantry, to follow up the fugitives and to prevent their reassembling. Both leaders again escaped. Hasdrubal took refuge in Carthage and Syphax fled towards Cirta.

Scipio, who was bringing up his engines to the walls, then

left to the fleet the duty of blockading the port of Utica; and marched with the bulk of his army against Carthage, ravaging the country on the way, and capturing several towns which were necessary to holding his position. Their names are not given us.

Syphax was not readily abashed. His newly-wedded wife, the daughter of Hasdrubal, exerted great influence over him and prevailed on him to remain true to his alliance. He retired to Numidia, whither he was followed by Lælius and Masinissa, a march of fifteen days. He tempted fortune in still a third battle against Lælius and Masinissa, but was wounded and this time himself captured. On this occasion his then capital, Cirta, which he had taken from Masinissa, fell into the hands of the Romans. Scipio could congratulate himself on having able lieutenants.

The Carthaginians showed a worthy spirit of resistance; everything was done to fortify and victual the city for a siege. No mention was made of peace.

Advancing to Tunes, Scipio found this town abandoned by its garrison. He occupied it, in the hope that his near presence might oblige Carthage to surrender. The Carthaginians sent orders to Hannibal and Mago to return to Carthage. They then essayed to destroy the Roman fleet and relieve the blockade of Utica, but unsuccessfully: and the news of Syphax's defeat robbed them of any hope of continuing the war to any advantage. The peace party prevailed; Hasdrubal was condemned to death, though the sentence was afterwards revoked; overtures of peace were made in earnest. Later, when the patriot party again won the upperhand, the senate made a veil of continuing negotiations for peace, hoping that time might aid their cause. They begged for an armistice, made a show of agreeing to all the terms Scipio proposed, including the evacuation of Italy and Gaul; the cession of

Spain and all Mediterranean islands ; giving up all their war-
vessels except twenty ; and the payment of a heavy indemnity in wheat and money.   A truce was agreed to while the
treaty was sent to Rome for ratification.   Meanwhile the
Carthaginians were aiming to get Hannibal and Mago back
in season to forestall further disaster.

Mago had advanced into cisalpine Gaul as far as the territory of the Insubrians.   The proconsul M. Cornelius and the
prætor Quinctilius, with four legions, moved up to oppose
him.   It would have perhaps been wiser of Mago to avoid
battle, and make a push southwards to join fortunes with his
brother.   But he chose to fight and displayed all the family
skill and courage.   The Roman cavalry was defeated by
Mago's elephants, and the legions thrown into confusion.   Victory appeared certain for Mago.   But a Roman troop bravely
attacked the elephants, which, as usual, wheeled around on
their friends and turned the tide.   Serious wounds prevented
Mago's personal efforts to retrieve the disaster.   The loss of
the Carthaginians was five thousand ; of the Romans, twenty-
three hundred killed, figures which show heavy fighting.
Among the Romans were three military tribunes, twenty-
two distinguished knights, and several centurions.   The relics
of the Carthaginian army retired to the coast.   But a small
portion of his forces reached Africa, for which place they
sailed on receiving the senate's orders to return.   Mago died
on his voyage home.

Thus was extinguished the sole remaining hope of Hannibal.   He was now in every sense alone, for Mago was his last
brother.   Hanno had fallen the year before when Scipio first
landed in Africa.   Towards the end of the summer he too
received the orders of the senate to return to Carthage.   The
Fates were inexorable !   For years the smiles of Fortune had
ceased for him.   They now beamed warmly upon the young

Roman chieftain who was laying siege to the capital of his own dear land, as he had hoped, but despite heroic efforts had been unable, to lay siege to Rome. For years he had acted the manly part; he had sought in vain to win back the favor of the capricious nymph. Now the last hope had fled. He must return home to conquer the invader at his own doors, or see his country once more humbled to a greater degradation than before.

Hannibal accomplished a difficult military feat in saving his army in Bruttium. Curiously enough, he was not seriously interfered with during his operation, despite that the senate had ordered the Roman army in his front to attack him. If it did so, we have no record of it. Perchance Hannibal's measures were too well taken to warrant interference. Valerius Anteas states that the Romans fought a battle with Hannibal in which five thousand Carthaginians were slain. But there are no other records of such an action, and Livy doubts it. Hannibal embarked at Crotona and brought his army safely to Africa. He left a few small garrisons behind to protect his movement, which the consul later reduced; and on his own ships, for Carthage sent him no fleet, and not covered by the truce existing between Scipio and Carthage, but by his own skill and rapidity, he embarked for Castra Hannibalis.

Hannibal had been obliged to kill his horses for lack of transportation. That he killed those Italians in his army who refused to accompany him to Africa is not to be credited. He could persuade many and force the rest aboard, and did in fact do so. That many went against their will is an additional reason for his having such poor material in his ranks at Zama. Hannibal reached the African continent in safety, with some twenty-four thousand men, disembarked at Leptis towards the end of the year B. C. 203, and wintered at Hadrumetum.

Hannibal had set out from Carthage as a mere boy. He had victoriously fought his way all around the Western Sea; he now returned as an old man to seek to save a lost cause. Emboldened by his return, the Carthaginians broke the truce, made but for a purpose, by seizing some Roman vessels bearing victuals for Scipio, which had been driven into the port of Carthage by a storm, and by attacking Scipio's messengers, who came to Carthage to demand satisfaction. Scipio, perhaps expecting nothing less, began preparations to resume hostilities.

"Meanwhile, hope and anxiety daily and simultaneously increased; nor could the minds of men be brought to any fixed conclusion, whether it was a fit subject for rejoicing, that Hannibal had now at length, after the sixteenth year, departed from Italy, and left the Romans in the unmolested possession of it, or whether they had not greater cause to fear, from his having transported his army in safety into Africa. They said that the scene of action certainly was changed, but not the danger. That Quintus Fabius, lately deceased, who had foretold how arduous the contest would be, was used to predict, not without good reason, that Hannibal would prove a more formidable enemy in his own country than he had been in a foreign one; and that Scipio would have to encounter not Syphax, a king of undisciplined barbarians, whose armies Statorius, a man little better than a soldier's drudge, was used to lead; nor his father-in-law, Hasdrubal, that most fugacious general; nor tumultuary armies hastily collected out of a crowd of half-armed rustics, but Hannibal, born in a manner in the pavilion of his father, that bravest of generals; nurtured and educated in the midst of arms; who served as a soldier formerly, when a boy, and became a general when he had scarcely attained the age of manhood; who, having grown old in victory, had filled Spain, Gaul and Italy, from

the Alps to the Strait, with monuments of his vast achievements; who commanded troops who had served as long as he
had himself; troops hardened by the endurance of every species of suffering, such as it is scarcely credible that men could
have supported; stained a thousand times with Roman blood,
and bearing with them the spoils not only of soldiers but of
generals.   That many would meet the eyes of Scipio in battle
who had with their own hands slain Roman prætors, generals,
and consuls; many decorated with crowns in reward for having scaled walls and crossed ramparts; many who had traversed the captured camps and cities of the Romans.   That the
magistrates of the Roman people had not then so many fasces
as Hannibal could have carried before him, having taken them
from generals whom he had slain." — Livy.

While this is not quite true, it reflects the probable sentiment at Rome.   So far as Hannibal's veterans were concerned, any old soldier can estimate for himself how many
would be apt to be left out of twenty-six thousand men after
sixteen years of constant campaigning without substantial
reinforcements in an enemy's country, where, not to refer to
the losses incurred in battle, every month's victual had to be
gathered at the point of the sword.   There are no historical
data from which to figure; but Hannibal's " veterans " could
have been but a handful.

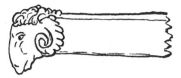

Head of Ram.

XLII.

ZAMA. SPRING 202 B. C.

THE last year of the war, B. C. 202, had no important incident but the battle of Zama. Carthage had made a truce with Scipio, but broke it. Hannibal essayed to negotiate a peace, but failed. Both generals drew up at Zama for a last struggle. Scipio had twenty thousand heavy foot and fourteen thousand light, twenty-seven hundred Roman and six thousand Numidian horse. All of this was of the best. Hannibal was very weak in cavalry. He had a small number of Carthaginian horse and two thousand Numidians. His total infantry was under fifty thousand, and he had eighty elephants. The quality of his army was low. Scipio drew up his cohorts as usual, and with cavalry on the flanks, but the maniples did not stand checkerwise. They were back of each other, making long lanes through which the elephants could be driven to the rear. The elephants were in Hannibal's front line. Then came the Gauls and Ligurians of Mago, unreliable to the last degree. The second infantry line was of Carthaginians, Africans and Macedonians, fairly good. The third had the Italians Hannibal had brought over with him from Bruttium, mostly against their will, with a very small leaven of his old soldiers. In the battle the elephants proved useless. Scipio's cavalry drove Hannibal's from the field, as Hannibal's had Varro's at Cannæ. The Carthaginian first and second lines made poor resistance to Scipio's hastati and principes. In the struggle of Hannibal's third line against Scipio's fresh formation, it seems that Hannibal came very close to victory; but the Roman and Numidian horse returned from pursuit, and fell upon his flanks and rear. The battle was lost, and Rome imposed her own terms on Carthage. Hannibal lived nineteen years after Zama, partly in the service of his country, partly as a fugitive from Roman hate.

THE coming year, B. C. 202, the consuls were M. Servilius Geminus and Tiberius Claudius. Each desired Africa as his sole province, but neither received it; Scipio was retained, but Claudius was allowed to go to Africa with equal authority. There were sixteen legions in service, including the three on duty in Africa. Scipio was continued in his command.

Hannibal had joined to his own army of twenty-four thousand men the remains of Mago's forces, twelve thousand strong, which had returned from Liguria, and some new levies, —forty-eight thousand men in all. He had with much effort procured some two thousand Numidian cavalry from king Tychaos, but had not had time to discipline the body. His army numerically was strong enough. He had carried through his most successful campaigns, had won his most brilliant victories, with less. But he lacked now that famous cavalry which had always been his strongest arm, and the infantry was far from being reliable or such as he had in his palmy days been able to command. In this respect Scipio was vastly his superior. It may fairly be claimed that the legions about to face Hannibal were the best which had ever fought for the cause of Rome.

Scipio had taken his revenge for the Carthaginian breach of the truce by passing from Tunes into the rich valley of the Bagradas, devastating right and left and selling the inhabitants as slaves. He had got up the valley to the region of Sicca. His purpose was not only retaliation, but to isolate Carthage, cut it off from supplies from the interior, and strengthen his own position. His work was thorough, if not ·bold. The result of this work Hannibal foresaw must soon prove fatal. Urged by the Carthaginian senate and by this manifest fact, he left Hadrumetum and advanced to Zama, not far from Sicca, about five days' march southwest of Carthage, near which place the Roman army already lay.

The exact location of Zama is not known. It was probably on the west bank of the Bagradas. Hannibal was intent on either concluding a satisfactory peace, which he himself now saw was the wisest thing to do; or, if this was impossible, of appealing for the last time to the arbitrament of arms. Some of his spies, sent out to ascertain the position of Scipio, were captured. Instead of being given the treatment usual to spies, these men were by Scipio's orders conducted through the Roman camp, shown everything, and sent back to report what they had seen to Hannibal. Scipio was satisfied with his army, and what he could do with it.

Hannibal sought and obtained an interview with the Roman general. This took place near Naraggara, towards which place both armies moved, and camped four miles apart. The interview was held between the two camps on a hill in sight of all. The generals dismissed their suites, retaining each only an interpreter. There is not a more interesting picture in history than the encounter of these two men, who had never personally met, yet knew each other's character and ability so well. The greater was the representative of the losing cause; the servant of a senate and people which had ruined his country by their folly; the one man who had been right when his government had been wrong. The other was the servant of a republic whose stanchness and wisdom no disasters could defeat, whose cause was bound to win, not because it had greater generals, but because of the strength of its organization and the soundness of its body politic. The interview led to no results. Scipio insisted on the unconditional surrender of Carthage. This Hannibal would not grant. There remained but an appeal to battle.

It is altogether probable that Hannibal was acting under positive instructions from the Carthaginian senate. That body was unteachable and not apt to forego its right of dictation. Aware of his lack of strength, it would have been more like Hannibal, had he been unhampered, to manoeuvre for a better chance for battle than in an open plain with the superiority in cavalry on the enemy's side. However this may be, the two armies next day drew up before each other in the open plain near Zama, for a last and bitter struggle. The

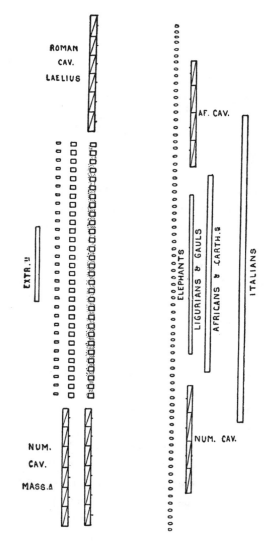

Troops in line at Zama.

date of October 19, fixed by a certain solar eclipse, is not correct. The time was probably the spring of 202 B. C.

Scipio had lately received reinforcements, brought by Masinissa, of six thousand infantry and six thousand Numidian cavalry. The cavalry was of the best; the foot would fight well in company with the Roman legions. He had his two Roman and two allied legions. That he had three, as stated by some authorities, is doubtful. His two counted eight thousand hastati, eight thousand principes and four thousand triarii, twenty thousand heavy foot. His light troops, including Masinissa's, were at least fourteen thousand strong, and he had twenty-seven hundred Roman and allied cavalry, and Masinissa's six thousand Numidian horse. His total force was thus nearly forty-three thousand men.

Hannibal had hitherto been superior in cavalry. This time it was the reverse, though the exact number Hannibal could dispose of is not known. There was some Carthaginian cavalry, but it was green, and there were only two thousand Numidians, usually Hannibal's chief reliance. He had been unable to bring his horses from Italy, so that his old cavalry, if any of it was left, was newly mounted and mixed with the Carthaginian. His infantry force, including twelve to eighteen thousand light troops, was somewhat short of fifty thousand men, and he had eighty elephants. Numerically he was stronger, in material far weaker, than his opponent.

Scipio's legions were formed in the usual three lines, but the maniples, instead of standing checkerwise, were placed behind each other, the intervals making long lanes right through the army from front to rear. In the first line the light troops filled the intervals, with orders to attack the elephants and drive them back on Hannibal's line, or failing this, to vacate the intervals by stepping behind the hastati or principes, and allow them to tramp through these lanes to the rear of the army, wounding them on the way. This arrangement, in view of Hannibal's large number of elephants, was admirable. Masinissa, with his Numidian cavalry, stood on the right flank; Lælius, now quæstor, with the Roman and allied cavalry, on the left.

Hannibal placed his elephants in front and his infantry in three lines. In the first were the mercenary light troops, — Ligurians and Gauls, whom Mago had enlisted in Italy, Balearians and Moors, twelve thousand strong. On these Hannibal was far from placing reliance. He posted them in front, hoping to tire the Roman hastati and blunt their weapons. In the second line, at the usual distance in rear of the first, were Africans, Carthaginians and Macedonians, also about twelve thousand in number. These were the troops which had been raised by Carthage after Hasdrubal's last defeat. They were of fairly good material, but fresh levies, not yet used to campaigning and unaccustomed to their surroundings. They were placed between the two lines, says Polybius, so that each one should be forced, according to the maxim of Homer, to show his bravery in spite of himself.

In the third line were the troops he had brought from Italy, commanded by Hannibal in person, about twenty-four thousand in number. We already know the composition of these troops. There was a small nucleus of old stock in them, in which the instinct of victory was still strong. But the bulk was made up of Bruttians enlisted in the past few years, most of whom would have preferred to remain behind in Italy to crossing to Africa to fight the battles of Carthage, — men pressed into the service, in fact. The whole body was the same which had, during the past few campaigns, barely held its own against the Roman legions in action, and this only by the ability of its chief. The one element in its favor was the personal devotion of the men to

Hannibal, despite the fact that he had thus forced them away from home.

The front of this third line was about equal to Scipio's, which being the case, the first and second lines must have been very thin or of much less front, probably the latter. The third line was, as it were, held in reserve farther back, over a stadium from the second line, so that, if beaten or called in, the two first lines could retire about its flanks without confusion. The infantry was all in phalangial order. The African cavalry was opposed to Lælius; the Numidians were on the left, opposite to Masinissa.

This formation was well conceived. Hannibal not only hoped that his cavalry would be able to prevent the Roman line from encompassing the flanks of his first and second lines, but that these lines would break, or at least seriously unsettle, the steadiness of the Roman centre, whereupon he might, with his reserves, complete their defeat before the triarii could reëstablish the fight. This patchwork body was appealed to by as many different motives as there were nationalities. The Gauls fought from native hatred of Rome; the Bruttians from fear of Roman vengeance, love of pay and hope of spoil; the Ligurians in the hope that they would return to the fertile plains of northern Italy; the Africans from fear of the tyranny of Masinissa, if they should not conquer; the Carthaginians alone from love of country. This was material in great contrast to Scipio's. There was defeat lurking in it, unless, perchance, Hannibal's personality should exert an exceptional influence, and things worked well.

There appears to have been no preliminary fighting of light troops between the lines. As the engagement opened, after the Numidians had indulged in some skirmishing, Hannibal's elephants were pushed sharply forward. But the Romans received them with the blast of many trumpets, usual at the beginning of a battle, and now employed for a double purpose, and with their battle-cry and a violent clashing of spear and sword on shield. This attempt to frighten these ill-trained monsters produced such good effect that, in lieu of trampling down the legionaries, they rushed wildly to right and left or through the Roman lanes, while many of them stampeded towards the Roman right wing, whence they were driven against the Numidian cavalry on the Carthaginian left, throwing it into great confusion.

This disorder was at once taken advantage of by Masinissa, who was a cavalry leader of no mean order. He dashed down with his own Numidian horse upon the Numidian allies of Hannibal to so good effect, that these squadrons were speedily broken and driven in utter disarray from off the field. Other elephants, wounded and chased by the velites, of whom, however, they had crushed many, fell back upon the Carthaginian cavalry and produced marked confusion in its ranks. Lælius, equally sharp-eyed as Masinissa, launched his own horse upon the Carthaginians at this instant, broke their ranks and sent them whirling backward, beyond usefulness for the day. The Roman and Numidian cavalry followed in pursuit. The elephants, as has so often been the case in war, had proved allies of the enemy. Thus at the outset Hannibal was deprived of his entire body of horse. His flanks were naked.

The same cavalry manœuvre threatened to lose Zama which had won Cannæ.

The elephants and cavalry thus disposed of, the infantry alone remained to contend for mastery. Scipio noticed that, while of less front, Hannibal's first two lines were heavier than his own. He remembered that the Gauls, more than once, with their fierce gallantry, had broken through the intervals and attacked the flanks of the Roman maniples, and

he feared that his centre might be broken. Instead of filling
the intervals of the hastati-maniples with the principes, he
gave orders quickly to close the intervals of the maniples of
the first line on the centre, while the second and third lines
should keep their distances so as to overlap and protect its
flanks, and be ready to move up to sustain the first line.
He thereupon sounded the charge.

The Gauls and Ligurians of the first Carthaginian line
fought with consummate bravery, but proved no match for
the tremendous shock of the veteran Roman legions.

"In addition to this there was one circumstance, trifling
in itself, but at the same time producing important consequences in the action. On the part of the Romans the shout
was uniform, and on that account louder and more ter-
rific; while the voices of the enemy, consisting as they did
of many nations of different languages, were dissonant. The
Romans used the stationary kind of fight, pressing upon the
enemy with their own weight and that of their arms; but on
the other side there was more of skirmishing and rapid movement than force. Accordingly, in the first charge, the Romans immediately drove back the line of their opponents;
then pushing them with their elbows and the bosses of their
shields, and pressing forward into the places from which they
had pushed them, they advanced a considerable space, as
though there had been no one to resist them, those who
formed the rear urging forward those in front, when they
perceived the line of the enemy giving way, which circumstance itself gave great additional force in repelling them."
— Livy.

Hannibal's second line, consisting of Carthaginian and
African new levies, unlike their Roman antagonists failed to
second the efforts of the first line, but moved up to its support in so undecided and sluggish a manner that the first-line

allies conceived the impression that the Carthaginians were
about to desert them.   Maddened with fury at this idea, and
at the same time borne back by the Roman hastati, they
turned upon and attacked the Carthaginian second line, thus
for the moment emulating the elephants in giving succor to
the foe.   The second line resisted the onset, however, better
than they had sustained the fighting of the first.   In a brief
space the relics of the first line had disappeared around the
flanks of the second and practically dispersed, like the elephants and cavalry.   Order was reëstablished by Hannibal,
and a temporary resistance to the onset of the hastati, who
were weary with fighting, was enough to throw the latter into
considerable confusion.   Even the principes were somewhat
unnerved, which speaks well for the fighting done by the
Africans and Carthaginians.   But the principes recovered
themselves and came up at the opportune moment to sustain
the flanks of the hastati, and, with a joint effort, Hannibal's
second line was definitely broken and hustled back.   Its first
disorder was multiplied sevenfold.   So wild was its flight
that only the protended lances of Hannibal's third line prevented its rushing upon and disorganizing this also.

The ground between the rival armies was littered with
dead and wounded, and with the weapons of those who had
lost them bravely, and those who had cast them away in flight.
Scipio sounded the recall to his hastati, and sent out his velites to collect the Roman wounded.

Hannibal still had his twenty-four thousand Italian troops.
Among these were the few remaining veterans of his Old
Guard, whose intense devotion to their chief made them all
but invincible.   But they were a bare handful, which could
not leaven the lump.   Scipio's velites and hastati had already
suffered great loss and were disorganized by the effects of the
struggle, but his principes had lost but few men, and his

triarii were fresh. The Romans had more and better men. There was not apt to be manœuvring; the battle was to be decided by the shock and by hand-to-hand fighting.

The Roman and Masinissa's cavalry had pursued the Carthaginians too far from the field, but Scipio was confident that it would return in time to turn the tide in his favor. He could afford to wait. Hannibal, on the contrary, proposed to seize the period of their absence to advance upon the Roman line, hoping to crush it before the horse could return to its aid.

Some historians read Polybius and Livy to say that Scipio took time to re-form his troops, and then attacked Hannibal; but the time must have been short, — one of those half-hour lulls which frequently occur in action. It was unlike Hannibal to await an attack, or allow a loss of time under such conditions. He must positively beat his enemy before the return of the cavalry, or lose the battle and his country's cause.

Scipio, in order to deliver a final effective blow, found it necessary to rearrange his troops. This looks like changeableness, but shows his troops to have been well in hand. Hannibal's reserve line was equal in front to Scipio's, and there was always, with this crafty general, the danger of a flank movement. This Scipio desired to guard against, and if possible overlap Hannibal's flanks. Believing that the enemy's first and second lines had been so thoroughly beaten as not to be available again for the day, and that he had only the reserve to contend with, he determined to put in the triarii, leaving the extraordinarii and velites in reserve. In the short lull, while Hannibal was disposing of the scattered troops so as to be able to advance his fresh line in perfect order, the Roman principes were ordered quickly to close their intervals from the centre towards each flank and move up on either flank of the hastati; the triarii performed the same manœuvre, and moving right and left took place on the extreme flanks of the legion. Scipio can have had barely time thus to extend his main line when the Carthaginian reserves were seen advancing. Hannibal's front had been equal to Scipio's front of principes, with regular intervals. It was thus equal to

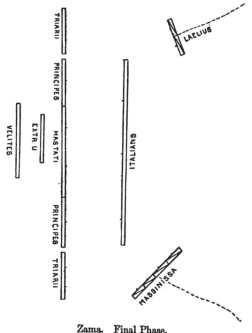

Zama.   Final Phase.

Scipio's present line of hastati and principes without intervals, and therefore the triarii extended beyond Hannibal's flanks.

The depth of Hannibal's phalanx cannot be stated with accuracy. He had long ago assimilated his formation somewhat to the Roman, but the details we do not know. It is probable that it was ten deep, the same as the file of a legionary maniple. It had not been the old Greek phalanx for some years; it had been extended and the depth decreased to correspond more nearly to the Roman standard.

Scipio, by his last change, had now practically formed the Roman legions into phalangial order, though the space occupied by each man was somewhat greater with the Romans. Hannibal's troops, all through the Italian campaigns, had gradually taken to the Roman weapons, so that each was what might be called a phalanx of legionaries. Scipio had not lost many men; and though his hastati had been fighting hard, the rest and the ordering up of the principes and triarii on their flanks, and the presence of the reserves immediately behind them, would encourage them to one more effort. He still had twenty-eight thousand men in line, and the velites and extraordinarii in their rear. Hannibal had twenty-four thousand, with no reserves.

The shock was tremendous. The contention at once became desperate. Hannibal's veterans were fighting for their firesides as well as victory, and gave the example to the rest. The struggle was uncertain. Every manly effort was put forth. The battle, on the Roman side, was for the mastery of the world; on the Carthaginian, for the possession of Africa. Hannibal and Scipio each put his last ounce of moral strength into inciting the ardor of his troops. Each was omnipresent. To each this was the crowning act of the great drama. The lines met in hand-to-hand contest and held desperately to their ground. The event seemed to hang upon a hair.

It is said that Scipio was about to be overwhelmed. But Fortune, once the friend of Hannibal, but now on the side of his younger rival, turned from him in a pitched battle for the first time. Lælius and Masinissa, with such of their victorious squadrons as were not cutting down fugitives, returned from pursuit of the Carthaginian horse at just this instant. Square against cavalry was of no avail in the days when deadly weapons carried a bare fifty feet; and Hannibal's line was struggling to overcome the Roman legion. Lælius and Masinissa fell with the white weapon upon Hannibal's line in flank and rear. There was not a single mounted man to oppose their deadly onslaught. This was the *coup de grâce.* No courage, no genius, on an open plain, could turn the tide of victory. Surrounded and crushed, Hannibal's phalanx, with the historic body which had won at the Trebia, Trasimene, Cannæ, now but a small group, sustained nobly its reputation. It held aloft its ensigns, and faced the foe till it was cut to pieces where it stood. The vanquished of Cannæ were the victors of Zama.

The soldiers of the first and second Carthaginian lines had most of them taken to flight; but in a flat country the cavalry allowed few to escape. Some twenty thousand of Hannibal's army remained on this bloody field; other twenty thousand were made prisoners; one hundred and thirty-three standards and eleven elephants were lost. The Romans had, it is stated by Livy, but two thousand killed. Polybius gives fifteen hundred. Both are manifestly in error. The loss must have been greater.

Appian is frequently quoted as an authority on the Second Punic War. But he is unreliable. Most prominent in his account of the battle of Zama, which he treats at considerable length, is a duel between Scipio and Hannibal, and another one between Masinissa and Hannibal, much in the Homeric strain. Out of his picturesque and interesting narrative we can doubtless glean a stray fact or two; but Appian can scarcely be used when in conflict with Polybius, Livy, or even Plutarch.

When Hannibal saw that the battle was irretrievably lost, knowing that his country now needed his counsel more than ever, he displayed a greater moral courage than his brother Hasdrubal, and left the field with a small escort to return to Hadrumetum. Scipio plundered Hannibal's camp and then returned to Utica, proposing to lay siege to Carthage so soon as he had recuperated from the efforts of the battle.

The loss of the battle of Zama left the Carthaginians no means of further resisting Rome. They at once tendered submission, and were obliged to accept the terms offered by Scipio, namely : —

1. To make reparation for breaking the truce. 2. To deliver up all their war-ships but ten, and all their elephants. 3. To deliver up all Roman prisoners and deserters. 4. To undertake no war outside of Africa, nor in Africa without consent of Rome. 5. To restore Masinissa to the throne they had taken from him. 6. To provide for the Roman army three months. 7. To make an annual payment of two hundred talents for fifty years. 8. To deliver up one hundred hostages to be chosen by the Romans. Had Hannibal not been beyond reach at the moment, his surrender would have been demanded ; and, as in the case of other brave soldiers who had fought against Rome, his life would have paid the forfeit. Generosity to a beaten enemy was not one of the Roman virtues.

This humiliation, at the end of a war of eighteen years, was but a prelude to the Third Punic War, which resulted in razing Carthage to the ground.

The constancy of Rome during the Second Punic War is best measured by the casualties. These have been stated at three hundred thousand men. They must have largely exceeded this amount. Although Livy's figures manifestly underrate the Roman and overrate the Punic losses, we find from this historian's figures, supplemented by an occasional estimate, that the Army of Italy (by which is meant the force which crossed the Alps, kept up by recruitment among Hannibal's Italian allies, and reinforced by the paltry squads which reached him from Carthage) lost in pitched battles in Italy and at Zama, about ninety thousand men. This includes no losses from the constant small-war, nor deaths from wounds or disease ; nor does it count any part of the enormous losses of the other armies in Italy or by Hannibal's allied cities, or by the operations in Spain or elsewhere. It is fair to assume that for every man killed in action two die in camp. This would make the losses of the Army of Italy during its sixteen years' campaigns, some two hundred and seventy thousand men, or nearly seven times its average strength of say forty thousand men.

Now, the Roman casualties in these same battles were over one hundred and fifty thousand men, taking the smaller figures given by the ancient authorities when a massacre ensued — *i. e.*, estimating lower losses than those given by Livy. The Romans may not have lost so large a percentage in camp, for the sum of their battle losses is high on account of these same massacres. But assuming their camp losses to be one hundred thousand men in the armies which fought Hannibal, the total would rise to a quarter of a million men. The armies on outside operations must have lost at least an equal number ; making a sum of half a million men during the sixteen years. This seems to be a low estimate, but it was a terrible drain on the population of Rome.

Hannibal was later enabled to return to his native city. He lived nineteen years after the battle of Zama ; he devoted himself to the service of Carthage, and was elected chief magistrate ; but, in endeavoring to check abuses, he raised against himself enemies in the government ; and when, in B. C. 195, he was suspected by Rome of fostering an alliance against her with Syria, and his delivery as a hostage for the good behavior of Carthage was demanded, Hannibal was forced into flight.   He took refuge with Antiochus, king of Syria, who not long after was at war with Rome.   Had Antiochus been wise enough to follow Hannibal's advice, he might not have been beaten at Magnesia.   In the treaty of peace which ensued, he was ordered to deliver up Hannibal to the Romans, but, learning of this clause, Hannibal again fled, this time to the court of Prusias, king of Bithynia.   Rome never felt secure until his death.   This occurred, some say by suicide, at the age of sixty-four, fearing that Prusias might be induced to deliver him up.

Outpost Blockhouse on River.   (Antonine Column.)

XLIII.

THE MAN AND SOLDIER.

THE Barcas traced their lineage back to Dido. They were at this period the most distinguished of the noble families of Carthage. Hamilcar had four sons, Hannibal, Hasdrubal, Hanno and Mago. Three died in defense of their country. The greatest lived to aid Carthage in her sorest need. Hannibal's education was of the best. All that Carthage could teach, and Greece withal, was assimilated by him. He wrote several books in Greek. His military education he received from his father, and practically in Spain under his brother-in-law, Hasdrubal. When his father died, Hannibal became the head of the Barcas. The Phœnicians were no taller than the Romans, but the beauty of their women is often spoken of. Hannibal was tall for his race, strong, and of commanding presence. His features were noble, and his smile as friendly as his anger was terrible. He was peculiarly endeared to his army by his sharing all their dangers, as well as by his skill and strength in martial exploits. His character was pure and noble. All that his enemies have been able to say cannot besmirch it. What we know of him has been written by his enemies; he is the sole great captain of whom we must thus judge. The Roman historians credit him with exemplary virtues; they charge him with cruelty, perfidy, impiety, avarice. As regards cruelty, war was, at that era, cruel beyond anything we can imagine. That Hannibal was less cruel personally than the Romans appears conclusively from their own testimony. His perfidy consisted in the employment of stratagems in war, which even to-day are allowable, but which the Romans could not understand. His impiety lay largely in his believing in other gods than the Romans. He was wealthy, perhaps avaricious; but he used his money, not for his own personal gratification, but to maintain his army and the war against Rome. Hannibal was deep, original, bold, secretive and self-reliant, persuasive as an orator and as a statesman. His power over men was extraordinary. No one ever held an army of such heterogeneous materials together under such trials as he. His career tells its own story best. No captain has so brilliant a record as he in the first three years in Italy, — but what he did in the dozen years after Cannæ is still more wonderful. He had taught the Romans how to wage war, and they waged it against him with ability. Abandoned by Carthage, he maintained himself in Italy by a series of bold and skillful campaigns against vast odds, which have no equal in history. He taught the Romans their trade, and is worthily named "The Father of Strategy."

In the galaxy of great captains the stars are equal. Many claim for Hannibal a lustre beyond the others. Measuring his task and resources by those of any soldier of history, he may be not untruthfully said to be *primus inter pares.* His character has already been drawn in his wonderful campaigns; but, at the risk of repetition, it is worth while to sum up the man and soldier.

The Barcas were an old race, on whose family-tree the names of Belus and Dido were written in letters of gold. Its pride was inborn; it held up its head from no upstart arrogance. Genius and patriotism stood at the service of every earnest project of the state, and ennobled the race more than its ancient lineage. While Hamilcar and his sons lived, the Barcas were distinctly the first family in Carthage.

Hamilcar had four sons and two daughters. Of the latter, one married a Massylian prince, the other Hasdrubal the Handsome; the sons were Hannibal, Hasdrubal, Hanno and Mago. Some authors exclude Hanno; but Livy mentions him as the son of Hamilcar when, in 204 B. C., he rode out at the head of his four thousand horse from the gates of Carthage never to return, and Valerius Maximus makes Hamilcar speak of "four lion's whelps which I have raised to exterminate the Roman name."

The earliest recollection of Hannibal was the sight of his father clad in mail; the first stories to which he listened were those of his father's wonderful defense of Ercte and Eryx against the Romans. His childhood's pleasures were in the camp; the keenest impulse on which he acted was hatred of the name of Rome. The Phœnicians were good haters. Hannibal proved no exception.

The most familiar story about the lad Hannibal is that of the oath taken by him at the instance of his father, before accompanying him to Spain. Silius Italicus places the scene in the sanctuary of Dido: " So soon as age will permit," the oath ran, " I will follow the Romans both at sea and on land. I will use fire and steel to arrest the destiny of Rome. Neither the gods, nor the treaty which forbids us war, — nothing shall stop me. I will triumph over the Alps as over the Tarpeian Rock. I swear it by the god Mars who protects me! I swear it, great Queen, by thy august manes! "

The education given to Hannibal, and already referred to, was — though Hannibal was his father's favorite — no doubt equally partaken by the others, and took root according to the character of each lad. The sons, like the father, were all soldiers ; each died a soldier's death, except Hannibal, who acted the part of a true patriot and lived to rehabilitate the fortunes of his native land.

Speaking of Hannibal's abilities, Dion Cassius observes that " he owed these advantages not only to nature, which had endowed him with her gifts, but also to a broad instruction. Initiated according to the custom of his country to the knowledge spread among the Carthaginians, he added to them the light of the Greeks." And referring to his mental gifts, " This great man," says Cornelius Nepos, " though occupied in such vast military operations, devoted a portion of his time to literature, for there are some books of his written in the Greek language, and among them one addressed to the Rhodians on the acts of Cnæus Manlius Vulso in Asia." Hannibal's teacher in Greek was a Macedonian named Sosyles, who, with one Philenus, was much in the Punic camp and in Hannibal's company ; and these two men contributed to the knowledge of Cornelius Nepos about the great Punic leader.

These facts, from Roman sources, abundantly prove Hannibal's mental equipment and culture. He was a "barbarian" among the Romans much in the same sense that we are barbarians to many of the peoples of the Orient.

On the death of his father, Hannibal formally succeeded him as the head of the Barca family. He perpetuated the teachings of Hamilcar.

The Carthaginians were not a tall race. Their average height did not probably exceed the Italian. But they were a handsome people. Many ancient authors refer to the beauty of the Phœnician women. Plautus tells us that they were straight as Grecian columns, of noble shape, and that they possessed the rare type of light hair with black lustrous eyes. The Carthaginian coins of the period show a distinguished cast of feature.

Hannibal was tall for a Phœnician. His figure indicated strength and agility; he carried his head high, and his face, which showed breadth and intelligence, was lighted up by an eye which beamed kindly on the friend, but which no one dared encounter when kindled by anger. His suit of hair was full, and he was wont to be much without head-gear.

It is immaterial for us to know whether Hannibal possessed beauty of feature; he certainly had stamped on his face that which is better. The only portrait of him which has any claim to authenticity, and this only because probably copied from some portrait existing at the time, — the Capuan bust given in the Frontispiece, — shows noble. lineaments; but these are marred by the Roman idea of the man, — by an attempt to express cruelty and passion.

The ideal Hannibal has been often described by Latin poets and authors, but in truth we know little of the man's person, except what we can judge from his life and his wonderful control over all who approached him. Nothing can

improve upon Livy's pen-picture of the young general when
he first joined Hasdrubal in Spain, which has been already
quoted. It was his strength, vigor and courage which most
strongly appealed to his soldiers. He excelled in all manly
sports; he was untiring in his performance of duty. He was
skillful and daring beyond any officer or soldier in his command. He once swam alone a river which cut off his cavalry
column, and from the other bank beckoned his men across.
He was the comrade of the common soldier as he was the
master of the whole army. He — as well as Alexander and
Cæsar — was noted for horsemanship, and his chief pride lay
in the beauty of his arms and steeds.

There are a few anecdotes which show us the human side of
Hannibal. He seems to have had his love for a jest. When
before the battle of Cannæ, Varro had hung out his purple
cloak as a signal for battle, "this boldness of the consul,"
says Plutarch, "and the numerousness of his army, double
theirs, startled the Carthaginians; but Hannibal commanded
them to their arms, and with a small train rode out to take a
full prospect of the enemy as they were now forming in their
ranks, from a rising ground not far distant. One of his followers, called Gisgo, a Carthaginian of equal rank with himself, told him that the numbers of the enemy were astonishing; to which Hannibal replied with a serious countenance,
'There is one thing, Gisgo, yet more astonishing, which you
take no notice of;' and when Gisgo inquired what, answered,
that 'in all those great numbers before us, there is not one
man called Gisgo.' This unexpected jest of their general
made all the company laugh, and as they came down from the
hill they told it to those whom they met, which caused a general laughter amongst them all, from which they were hardly
able to recover themselves. The army, seeing Hannibal's at-
tendants come back from viewing the enemy in such a laugh-

ing condition, concluded that it must be profound contempt
of the enemy that made their general at this moment indulge
in such hilarity."

Cicero tells us that when at Ephesus in exile, Hannibal at-
tended a lecture by a philosopher named Phormio. Among
other things, the lecturer expatiated upon the duties of a
commander-in-chief, much to the admiration of the audience.
Hannibal being asked his opinion, "I have seen," said he,
"during my life many an old fool; but this one beats them
all."

When Antiochus, proudly reviewing his enormous army,
and quite ignorant of Roman courage and skill in war, pointed
out his preponderance in force to Hannibal, and asked if
these were not enough for the Romans, — "Yes," said Hannibal, "enough for the Romans, however greedy they may be."

We seize on these paltry stories with eagerness because of
their scarcity. The personality of this great man is made up
of mere shreds and patches from the Roman authors.

Hannibal's character was pure and elevated. His habits
were simple. He drank little wine, and when chief magistrate of Carthage did not recline at his meals. He sometimes ate but once a day, rose at daybreak and retired late,
says Frontinus. He faced the cold of the Alps and the
scorching sun of Africa with equal unconcern. "Only a
woman needs shade," quoth he. Scarcely a fault can be
traced to him. Scipio's continence is a never-ending theme
of praise; but no word is said of Hannibal's fidelity to Imilcea, his Spanish bride, from whom he was, almost in the
honeymoon, separated for sixteen long years. "He is said to
have exhibited so much pudicity among so many female captives that one would scarcely credit his having been born in
Africa," testifies Justinus.

These facts are what his enemies tell us, and there is such

singular unanimity in their testimony, that we may well accept them as conclusive. Only by acknowledging Hannibal's great qualities could they mitigate the stigma of their inability to cope with him. Of all the great captains Hannibal stands alone in having not one word spoken of him by a friendly pen. This thing we must constantly bear in mind. Alexander had Ptolemy and Aristobulus beside him to record his glorious deeds; Cæsar wrote his own commentaries; but Hannibal's picture is drawn solely by his enemies. Polybius is the only even-handed historian he has; and as he was in the service of the Roman state, and gathered his materials from Roman sources, however fair he may have been, he could not but lean towards the bitter Roman prejudice. The few personal traits vouchsafed us, added to the earnest consistency of Hannibal's whole life, make up a character unsurpassed in its nobleness, which not all the venom of his foes has been able to besmirch.

Let us look at what these same enemies charge him with. Livy, after the pen-picture already quoted on page 150, adds: "Excessive vices counterbalanced these high virtues of the hero; inhuman cruelty, more than Punic perfidy, no truth, no reverence for things sacred, no fear of the gods, no respect for oaths, no sense of religion."

The impeachment may be summed up as cruelty, perfidy, impiety. To these is to be added avarice, of which it is stated by Roman and Greek authors that his own people accused him. "It is difficult," says Polybius, in summing up what ill may be said of him, "to decipher what was in truth the character of Hannibal, but one may say that with the Carthaginians he passed for avaricious, and as a cruel man among the Romans." Here, then, are four vices which it is well to examine. But this is the sum of all which is laid to Hannibal's charge, and we must judge him by the age in which he lived.

With regard to cruelty. It is only the cruelty exhibited in war to which the Romans referred. War has always been and is still cruel. It was peculiarly cruel in that era. Hannibal was herein no exception to his age. He punished for rebellion provinces which had once joined his standard. So did the Romans; what cruelty can exceed their treatment of Capua on its capture, or of Bruttium after Hannibal left the peninsula? Hannibal devastated provinces as a war measure or for subsistence; and no doubt his Numidians were guilty of much rapacity and many inhuman acts. But wherein were the Romans better? Did not Marcellus devastate the territory of Hannibal's Samnite and Lucanian allies with fire and sword, in revenge for their having given up the alliance of Rome when she failed to protect them from the Punic sword? Hannibal punished mutineers, deserters, faithless guides. There are fourfold as many cases on record during this war of the Romans doing the same thing.

In this connection the Romans speak with horror of the human sacrifices supposed to obtain in Carthage. These are not denied, but let us read Livy as to what was done in Rome, to propitiate the gods after the terrible disaster of Cannæ. "Meanwhile certain extraordinary sacrifices were performed, according to the directions of the books of the fates; among which a Gallic man and woman, and a Greek man and woman, were let down alive, in the cattle market, into a place fenced round with stone, which had been already polluted with human victims, a rite by no means Roman. The gods being, as they supposed, sufficiently appeased," etc. With what justice can the Romans denounce sacrifices to Baal? That it was only in the first century before the Christian era that Rome renounced publicly the habit of immolating prisoners to the gods, Pliny tells us. And that the Roman officers could be more brutal to conquered towns and provinces than the Carthaginians, is testified by Livy in his narration of what happened at Locri, and of the appeal of the Sicilians against Marcellus.

Cruelty was habitual with the Romans. " When Scipio," says Polybius, " believed that there had entered enough soldiers into Cartagena, he sent the most part against the inhabitants, as the Romans are accustomed to do when they capture a town by assault, with order to kill all they met, to give no quarter, . . . and thus to inspire terror of the Roman name." Scipio Æmilius cut off the hands of his captives — a common Roman punishment. Crassus hanged on crosses, erected on the road from Rome to Capua, six thousand gladiators. Cæsar exterminated in one day a tribe four hundred and thirty thousand in number, men, women and children, for fighting for their independence, — and by treachery at that. He cut the hands off thousands of Gallic prisoners, to cow their fellow-countrymen. All this is not palliative of Hannibal's cruelty, but it shows that the Romans cannot rightfully charge Hannibal with inhumanity, and that cruelty in war was not a personal vice.

Perhaps the most marked instance in which the Roman and Punic characters were contrasted was in the case of Nero. Hannibal, after the battle of Lake Trasimene, had scrupulously sought for the body of Flaminius, in the hope to give it honorable burial; he had paid the most devout rites to the bodies of Gracchus, Æmilius Paulus, Marcellus, all of whom had fallen in lawful warfare or in battle. How was he rewarded for this soldierly piety? When Nero had defeated Hasdrubal at the Metaurus, where this brave soldier had perished sword in hand, the consul cut off his head, and, transporting it a six days' journey, cast it, like the carcass of a dog, into the outposts of his brother's army. This incident is narrated by the Roman authors with the utmost unconcern.

Had Hannibal been guilty of such brutish conduct should we not have heard even more of his cruelty?

No instance of outrage or treachery alleged by the Romans against Hannibal but is more than matched by even gallant Marcellus' cutting down in cold blood the garrison of Casilinum, which had received from his colleague, Fabius, a promise of free exit to Capua; or by mild-mannered Fabius' punishment of Tarentum, or by cultured Scipio's devastation of the Bagradas Valley — or by scores of other instances. The Romans forgot their beam in gazing at Hannibal's mote. The Phœnician's cruelty was to Roman citizens. This the Romans could not forget. But when they punished Capua they forgot that the Capuans were men. So much for cruelty.

The matter of perfidy has been already spoken of in various places when Punic Faith has been the question. It is only in instances of this kind that Hannibal's perfidy is supposed to have been prominent. That ruses of war, allowable in all ages, but unknown to the Romans, should have been cleverly employed by the Phœnicians to entrap the Roman armies, sufficed to class all Hannibal's stratagems as instances of perfidy. The Romans learned the trick, and then " ce ne fût que la victoire qui décida s'il fallait dire *la foi punique* ou *la foi romaine*." Craftiness was a Punic instinct. It was as natural for Hannibal to resort to rapid and secret marches, to employ strange ruses, to make use of unexpected schemes, to lie in ambush, as for the Romans to push straight for their objective and secure their end by stout fighting. However distasteful to the Romans, this habit was fully appreciated by the clear-sighted. "Hannibal appears to me a great captain under very many conditions," says Polybius, " but what especially makes his superiority is that, during the many years he made war and under all the caprices of fortune, he had the cleverness to mislead the enemy's generals, without his enemies ever being able to deceive him." And the Romans were not slow to pattern by his skill.

Impiety. Wherein this consisted it is hard to say, unless in the fact that the Punic gods and worship were not in all respects those sacred to the Romans. We are told by the Latin authors that Hannibal paid a vow at the temple of Hercules in Gades, in the presence of his entire army, and called on the gods to approve his march on Rome; that he sent Bostar to the temple of Jupiter Ammon to ask the oracle to pronounce on his Italian expedition; that he told his army of the dreams sent to him by Jupiter; that he took Jupiter to witness his promises to his soldiers on the Padus, — with numberless other instances of his reposing trust in his own peculiar deities. The caption of his treaty with Macedon shows that he observed the formalities of religion. " In presence of Jupiter, of Juno and of Apollo; in presence of the goddess of the Carthaginians, of Hercules and of Iolaus; in presence of Mars, of Triton, of Neptune; in presence of all the gods who protect our expedition, of the Sun, the Moon, and the Earth; in the presence of the rivers, the fields, the waters; in presence of all the gods honored in Macedonia and the rest of Greece, in presence of all the gods who preside over war, . . . Hannibal and his soldiers have said," etc., etc. That temples were sometimes profaned by his soldiers is a fact common to all warfare, — but very rarely alleged against them. The Romans were not above desecrating temples, and in all ages down to the present generation, heathen and Christian temples alike have been used for defensive purposes in war.

When Hannibal gave up a town because he feared that the inhabitants would massacre his garrison, this was a " violation of his treaties " with them which showed that he had " no respect for oaths." When he razed a town to the ground because it had massacred his garrison, this was "worse than inhuman cruelty." Half of what we hear told of Hannibal's vices comes not from historians, but from Roman poets and playwrights, who were writing to cater to the taste of the Roman plebs, and, oblivious of fact, were prolific of their gibes to raise a laugh or sneer.

Hannibal used his hatred to advantage. But he was scarcely behind the Romans in this quality. It seems to strike Livy as indefensible that Hannibal should exhibit "hatred of the Roman name." This he certainly did from boyhood to old age, consistently and heartily. He hated Rome, root and branch, and with good reason. But his hatred was manifest solely in acts warranted by the international law of that day; and that he was less barbarous than the Romans is abundantly shown by their own testimony. The Roman authors persistently misrepresent every large-hearted act of the Punic chieftain; but Hannibal's conduct towards Fabius, in sparing his farm from devastation; the respect paid to the remains of Gracchus, Marcellus, Æmilius, and many other facts, show a chivalrous spirit, which, when we remember the hatred ingrained in his very fibre, speaks the generous impulses of the true soldier. Can as much be said of Nero, bearing brave Hasdrubal's head, to cast it, brutally dishonored, at the feet of his brother? And yet history does not reproach Nero with the act, and Nero was one of the best of soldiers, who, with Marcellus, and perhaps Scipio and Fabius, stood at the head of the Roman generals. "Les reproches de l'historien" (Livy) "sont donc des louanges," says Thiers.

Avarice. The Barcas were wealthy. Their possessions in Africa were vast. When Hamilcar conquered Spain, he added largely to the family property. One mine in the neighborhood of Cartagena, Pliny tells us, is reported to have yielded them revenues amounting to nearly five thousand dollars a day, then a much larger sum than now. It is not unlikely that Hannibal hoarded his means with covetous care. But he was not miserly. He neither locked up his gold, nor did he use it for his own personal gratification. Every coin went to buy or equip or feed one more soldier. Every grain of gold dust sharpened the point of a missile which should slay a Roman legionary. If this was avarice, then Hannibal must be found guilty of the charge.

Hatred, malice and all uncharitableness have painted the picture of Hannibal. But, if we thrust aside such manifest fabrications as best furnish their own refutation, there remain but a few things which are claimed to have been done in Hannibal's name by one Monomachus and by Mago the Samnite, which can be laid at the door of this great man. This Monomachus advised Hannibal to teach the men to eat human food, as a means of rationing them on their way to Italy. " It is this Monomachus, they say, who is the author of whatever cruelty was practiced in Italy with which they charge Hannibal," says Polybius.

For generations, the naughty Roman child was frightened by " Hannibal at the gates," as the little Briton was by " Boney," and the hatred of the Punic race as exemplified in Hannibal was mixed with a sentiment of dread which Horace best sums up as " dirus Hannibal." But putting aside Roman hate and fear, there is not in history a figure more noble in its purity, more radiant in its patriotism, more heroic in its genius, more pathetic in its misfortunes, than that of Hannibal. " Ce que la posterité a dit, ce que les générations les plus reculées repéteront, c'est qu'il offrit le plus noble spectacle que puissent donner les hommes, celui du génie exempt de tout egoïsme, et n'ayant qu'une passion, le patriotisme, dont il est le glorieux martyr." — Thiers.

The depth and fecundity of Hannibal's conceptions, the originality of his system, were what made him so difficult to match. His strength of character was invincible, his will was adamant, his heart free from disturbing passions. He was intrepid, mentally and physically, and his presence of mind never forsook him. His penetration, his ability to read the enemy's purpose, to gauge his opponent's character, enabled him to lead him astray and save himself from deception. He was singularly fertile in expedients. We do not know just how he eluded his enemies on his wonderful marches through territory held by their armies, but he did so constantly during his fifteen years in Italy.

Hannibal was equal as a statesman to what he was as a soldier. This is well shown by his conduct in Italy, and especially by what he did for Carthage after Zama. No man ever united more varied qualities in their highest expression than he.

Hannibal's control over men was singular. He had the genuine orator's power of convincing his audience, of charming his hearers. He was a true leader of peoples. His soldiers followed him blindly from equal affection for and confidence in him. He never saw a mutiny in his camp, which, when we consider the piece-meal construction of his army, is remarkable. " It is," says Polybius, " a singular thing that this Carthaginian general should have been seventeen years at war at the head of an army composed of different nations, countries and languages, that he should have conducted astonishing expeditions, and such that one could scarcely hope for success in them, without one of his soldiers even undertaking to betray him."

Hannibal's organizing ability was unmatched. Out of the most ragged material he could speedily produce a disciplined army. This power was bred of his knowledge of men, his steadfast purpose, his never-ending capacity for labor. He outweighed all men who came under his sway. Dion Cassius says he governed people by their interests; that he saw the real value of things and cared naught for the looks; that he was arrogant, but could bend to those he wished to honor or seduce; that those who were not devoted to him feared him. " He could lower the superb, elevate the humble, inspire here terror, there confidence; all this in a moment whenever he chose."

" Gifted," continues the same author, " with the liveliest power of conception, Hannibal could aim at his end by wise caution; and yet his sudden resolutions required a prompt spirit because they were instantaneous. . . . He profited by the present without making mistakes and strongly dominated the future. Of a consummate prudence in ordinary conjunctions, he divined with sagacity what was the best part to take in unseen cases. Thus he drew himself with fortune and at once from the difficulties of the moment, at the same time that his reason showed him the necessities of the morrow. Appreciating with equal justice what was and was apt to be, he always adapted his speech and actions with ability to the existing circumstances."

His power over men accomplished remarkable results. Reaching cisalpine Gaul, it was but a few weeks before the tribes of the whole province became his sworn allies. They remained faithful to his cause, and bore their heavy burden with cheerful alacrity, though notably the most unstable of peoples. Hannibal possessed a keen insight into human nature, as well as boundless personal magnetism. However little we are told of his appearance, we know that he carried that in his face and manner which lent wonderful force to what he said or did.

Hannibal's victories were as brilliant as any ever won; but

on these does not rest his chief glory. When he wrested
from the arrogant Romans the victories of the Trebia, Lake
Trasimene, Cannæ, he had opposed to him generals ignorant
of the art of war, which art his own genius, the instruction he
had received from his father, and his experience in many
hard-fought campaigns enabled him to use after a fashion beyond what the Romans had ever dreamed of. But Hannibal
instructed these same Romans in this very art of his, and his
later opponents fought him on his own system, and with the
wonderful Roman aptness at learning what he taught them at
so high a cost. These scholars of his, however, strong as they
became, in no sense grew to their master's stature. They
surrounded him on all sides, they cut off his reinforcements
and victuals, they harassed his outposts and foragers, they
embarrassed his marches, — all in the style he had shown
them how to use. For all that, though outnumbering him
many times, not one or many of them could ever prevent his
coming or going at his own good time or pleasure whitherso-
ever he listed, and never was a decisive advantage gained
over him in a pitched battle till the fatal day of Zama. Even
after Hasdrubal's death, his aggressors dared not attack him.
Like a pack of bloodhounds around the lion at bay, none
cared to close with him in a death-struggle. When, depleted
by the toils and losses of half a generation, he embarked for
Carthage, — the most dangerous of proceedings possible for
an army, — though the Roman generals had been ordered by
the senate to attack him, they did not attempt to embarass his
operation. The Carthaginian had laid his plans with too
much skill. Even Scipio, the most self-confident of the
Roman generals, seemed by no means anxious to encounter
him, except at a disadvantage.

Like all great captains, Hannibal not infrequently violated
the maxims of war. It is doubted by some able writers

whether there are such maxims. "It would be difficult to say what these rules are or in what code they are embodied," says a distinguished soldier, the author of one of the best of existing books on military science. The answer is, that these maxims are found in this very author's work, and in the history of every captain whose campaigns or battles he uses as illustrations. "Don't manœuvre so as to be obliged to form front to a flank," might stand for a good maxim of this author's. "It is dangerous to turn an equal adversary with one wing, unless you refuse or protect the other," is a crisp re-wording by him of a maxim we owe to Epaminondas. "Never do what the enemy wishes you to do," which is given as one of Napoleon's maxims, but which is as old as Xenophon, probably older, may stand as another. Referring to phrases similar to the one which stands at the head of this paragraph, "Such criticisms have only very vague ideas for their foundation," says this author. Too many soldiers of repute, from Napoleon down, whose ideas are usually credited with being far from vague, have used the phrase "maxims of war" to make it worth while to discard it. It has a settled meaning, like many aphorisms of the Common Law. It or any other axiom or proverb may be vaguely used. But if to employ the phrase "to violate the maxims of war" argues opacity of thought, we must condemn many admirable critics, beginning with Jomini. We may call these rules or maxims by any other name, or hide them in the ablest or clearest exposition, such guiding principles there are and always must be. Napoleon enunciated a few which are not inapt. Frederick did the like. Alexander and Hannibal and Cæsar showed what they were in their wars. The "Commentaries" give us as many excellent maxims as the "Anabasis," and Onosander fairly bristles with maxims. War has been likened to a game of chance; strategy to the thimble-rigger's skill in deceit.

Both similes are apt ; but there is more in war than chance ; strategy is broader than the ablest gambling. So long as military schools teach, so long as text-books treat of a science of war, so long will there be maxims. A change in nomenclature will neither expunge them from existence, nor destroy their usefulness.

Hannibal, like Alexander, was educated under certain rules, well known to the Greeks. These in later life he observed or disregarded, as the circumstances warranted, when a lesser captain would have been uniformly bound by them. The reason why he defeated the Romans so constantly in the first three years, and thereafter marched so boldly through and through their lines and in and out among their armies, was primarily owing to the fact that they were hide-bound in their principles and theories, and he was not. Whenever they expected him to do or refrain from a certain thing, he was sure to act as they least expected. When Hannibal disregarded what were at that day accepted as the rules of war, he did so with that admirable calculation of the power or weakness of the men and force opposed to him, which of itself is the excuse for the act by him who is able to take advantage of as well as to make circumstances. All great captains are cousins-german in this respect.

Napoleon aptly says : " The principles of Cæsar were the same as those of Alexander and Hannibal : to hold his forces in hand ; to be vulnerable on several points only where it is unavoidable ; to march rapidly upon the important points ; to make use to a great extent of all moral means, such as the reputation of his arms, the fear he inspires, the political measures calculated to preserve the attachment of allies and the submission of conquered provinces."

Great captains use the maxims of war only so far as they fit into their plans and aid their combinations. Success justifies them. The failure of the lesser lights who infringe these maxims, or who are blindly subservient to them, only proves them to be maxims indeed.

To some modern writers, the *dicta* of Frederick and Napoleon, the charts and diagrams of Jomini, are pedantic, antiquated, useless. No doubt there is a material advance in military criticism, which keeps pace with the growing comprehension of the art of war; but is it time to discard what these masters have said within not much more than a century? While "maxims" alone will not equip the general or make a well-read military critic, they are none the less a handy note-book, to remind him of what, with its kaleidoscopic modifications, he has more deeply studied. And, adding materially to our vocabulary, they subserve the purposes of clearness.

A familiar American instance will illustrate the matter. It is an ancient and well-accepted rule or "maxim" not to divide your army on the eve of battle, especially when in the presence of superior forces. Yet Lee did this thing at Chancellorsville, was justified by the circumstances in doing it, and won, considering the great disparity of forces, perhaps the most brilliant victory of the war. Another man, had he decided on such action, or perhaps Lee under other conditions, might have failed. It is a convenient expression to say that Lee "violated a maxim of war," and won when another would have lost. Lee knew Hooker's character, and risked his all on Hooker's keeping quiet during the second of May. At the same time, it was in defiance of a well-known rule of modern, as well as ancient, war, that he acted. If for no other reason than convenience and meaning settled by long usage, the phrase is acceptable until some one produces a more apt one which can be equally well and generally understood. If not satisfactory to English-speaking critics, it is yet in constant use among the Continental nations, who, it must be allowed, have carried war and its nomenclature to a higher degree than has been done in England or America.

When Hannibal reached Italy he began his campaigns with a bold offensive. Rome had been used to no system other than taking the offensive herself. To be driven to the defensive was so much of a novelty to her that it required the lesson of three or four bitter defeats to teach her that there was something greater than even her military audacity in the genius of Hannibal. These defeats, however, did teach Rome the necessary lesson. She went diligently to school to Hannibal, and first under Fabius, but more intelligently under Marcellus, began a system of what is called offensive-defensive, which was her only safety. From the time she did this, and put her ablest men to the front, the scale began to turn in her favor, because her body-politic was sound and her system right, and because the system of Carthage was blind in not sustaining Hannibal, and her political structure feeble from the corner-stone up. While Rome was acting the patriotic part, and with military sense, Carthage was intent on nothing but the holding of Spain as a mere mart for trade.

Apart from the fact that for the future of the world it was essential that Rome should be the winner in the struggle against Punic institutions, it was a predetermined fact that Rome must succeed, owing to her military soundness as against the military rottenness of Carthage. If Rome did not succeed in this war, she would in the next. It is all the more wonderful that Hannibal held himself for fifteen years in the Italian peninsula. It has already been pointed out how, after Cannæ, there were opposed to Carthage at all times twenty to twenty-five legions, of which four to twelve were in Hannibal's immediate front. The Roman armies always outnumbered him, as the allies did Frederick; at any time forces could be concentrated against him which to all appearance could not fail to overwhelm him. And yet, though under favorable conditions the bolder of the Roman generals were able to snatch minor successes from Hannibal, none ever had the hardihood to risk a battle to the bitter end, however great the odds. Nor was it the Roman army which finally drove Hannibal out of Italy. It was the military necessity and the call of Carthage to resist Scipio at her gates which rid Rome of this incubus of half a generation.

What makes Hannibal's military accomplishment so noteworthy is his skill as a strategist. As the Romans learned their trade from him, and what they learned has been perpetuated, Hannibal has been well called the Father of Strategy. Excepting in the case of Alexander, and some few isolated instances, all wars up to the Second Punic War had been decided largely, if not entirely, by battle-tactics. Strategic ability had been comprehended only on a minor scale. Armies had marched towards each other, had fought in parallel order, and the conqueror had imposed terms on his opponent. Any variation from this rule consisted in ambuscades or other stratagems. That war could be waged by avoiding in lieu of seeking battle; that the results of a victory could be earned by attacks upon the enemy's communications, by flank manœuvres, by seizing positions from which safely to threaten him in case he moved, and by other devices of strategy, was not understood. This came into play after Cannæ, when Rome adopted her new policy and Hannibal was compelled by poverty of resources to pursue the same course. For the first time in the history of war, we see two contending generals avoiding each other, occupying impregnable camps on heights, marching about each other's flanks to seize cities or supplies in their rear, harassing each other with small-war, and rarely venturing on a battle which might prove a fatal disaster, — all with a well-conceived and definite purpose of placing the opponent at a disadvantage. During this period, for the first time, the brain on both sides did better work than the sword. That it did so was due to the teaching of Hannibal.

The Romans, after Cannæ, waged war on a systematic plan and with their best men. Fabius was abler in the closet ; Marcellus and Nero were stronger at the front. Each year the Romans devised a general scheme with special details, and carried these out with firm but elastic measures. They always covered Rome and the most important provinces ; they kept Hannibal in view, and cut down his power of doing harm as fast as circumstances warranted. Each army had a definite and well-considered duty to perform, and was based on a province or city which enabled it to do this duty well. It was no longer a mere march to seek and fight the enemy : there was a far greater degree of intelligence and skill in what the Romans did. Though we cannot admire the hyper-caution, to call it by a mild term, which the Romans exhibited in their unwillingness to fight Hannibal *à outrance*, we must recognize the sound practical methods they pursued in other respects. They imitated Hannibal in his stratagems. They sought to divine his purpose and to conceal their own. They would fight only when everything was in their favor. They endeavored to starve him out rather than destroy him in battle. The finest piece of Roman strategy of the war, the march of Nero to the Metaurus and back, would never have been thought of by a Roman general, but for the study of Hannibal's methods.

The season of operations began as a rule so soon as there was forage growing for the beasts, and ceased with the crops. Compared with Hannibal, Rome had abundance of men, money, material. These were often hard to raise, but they were raised. The twenty-three legions which for several years were put afoot contained between two hundred thousand and two hundred and thirty thousand men, a remarkable number for the population sustaining the army. Nothing better illustrates the elasticity of the Roman military system. The methods pursued in collecting victuals, storing them, protecting the magazines and convoys, and generally in conducting the quartermaster's and commissary departments, were faulty at the start, but grew in excellence as the necessity grew. The same observation applies to the marching of troops with suitable van- and rear-guards and flankers.

The narration of their campaigns has demonstrated how much the Romans profited in their battle-tactics. By this is not meant the mere matter of fighting; this was always admirable; but the several battles of Marcellus, Nero and Scipio show a material advance in breadth of management. This would not have come about had not the intelligence of the Roman commanders been taxed to the utmost to meet Hannibal's remarkable dispositions; had they not been willing to imitate what he did. The fighting traditions of Rome, as well as the method of ranking troops for battle, militated against such mobility on the field as is common to-day. The Romans only knew the battle-order in the three lines of maniples of hastati, principes, triarii, with cavalry on the flanks and skirmish line in front. This was excellently adapted to the requirements of the majority of cases. The successive acts of the battle-drama — the opening by the velites and their withdrawal through the intervals; the advance of the hastati, sustained, when needed, by the principes; the holding back of the triarii and extraordinarii until called on to decide the conflict; and the endeavor of the cavalry to rout its opposing cavalry and surround the enemy's flanks and rear — were apt to be much the same. Variations in these successive acts were called out by coping with or imitating the originality of the Punic methods; and each variation was a gain.

Hannibal, though he copied the legionary system to a certain extent, retained the phalangial formation as a basis; but his dispositions varied as the circumstances varied. No doubt the legion — as it afterwards proved itself — was even then superior to the phalanx, except in the hands of a Hannibal; but for his raw levies, interspersed with his older troops, the phalanx was the steadier formation. That Hannibal should so long have kept his elephants, which Alexander discarded as more dangerous to friend than foe, is curious. We do not hear much about these creatures in most of the battles. They were generally kept well in hand, but were of doubtful value after the Romans became used to them.

Whatever the gain in battle-tactics, it cannot be compared to the growth of what among the Romans was the new science of strategy; for though the soundest strategy was exhibited by Alexander and by one or two other generals previous to this time, the Romans at the beginning of the Second Punic War had no conception of what such a science could teach them. After this struggle they proved themselves to be consummate masters of war.

In pursuit after battles neither party showed the abnormal energy and persistency of Alexander, whose sleuth-hound sticking to the heels of his beaten foe will ever remain the pattern of patterns. A battle won was not always put to use in the way the Macedonian did it. The conditions under which Hannibal fought made it impossible for him to produce the gigantic results which other captains have shown. He alone of all the leaders of history fought against a power and against armies which were unequivocally his superiors in intelligence, breadth, discipline, military training,—in every quality except only his individual genius.

In sieges and fortification the Second Punic War shows limited skill; but the Romans were superior to Hannibal. As with Frederick, siege-work was Hannibal's weak side, and he probably recognized the fact. The sieges of Capua and Syracuse show what Roman engineering methods were. They blockaded rather than besieged. The remarkable defense of Syracuse by Archimedes exhibits in a high grade the art of the time. As in most celebrated sieges the work was that of an individual.

Among the Roman generals, first in time came Fabius, great in his conceptions of the necessities of the moment, great in persistent execution of his conception, but often weak in active war. He was the father of the Roman system of defensive war, which turned the tide of fortune in favor of the republic. Next came Marcellus, who first put a period to Hannibal's successes and won so great credit in the capture of Syracuse. Marcellus combined the caution of Fabius with boldness equal to any task. It was he who best learned what Hannibal had to teach, and from him his brother generals caught their inspiration. " Hannibal himself confessed that he feared Fabius as a schoolmaster, Marcellus as an adversary ; the former lest he should be hindered from doing mischief; the latter lest he should himself receive harm," says Plutarch. Then came Nero, with equal boldness and intelligence, whose Metaurus campaign is the finest Roman feat of arms in the Second Punic War. Last, and by many considered the greatest, Scipio. But to rank Scipio beside Marcellus and Nero is praise enough. He was more brilliant than either, less solid; and had not Nero come to his rescue and at the Metaurus rectified his error in allowing Hasdrubal to escape him in Spain, he would scarcely have earned the reputation history has given him.

Excepting Hannibal, the Carthaginians were far inferior in armies and army commanders to the Romans. Even Hasdrubal, who came next to Hannibal, — with a long interval, — was not beyond Marcellus or Nero in ability. He occasionally showed a touch of the family genius, but not often. In junior officers and in rank and file, the Romans were far superior to Hannibal from the third year on.

As the Second Punic War furnishes one of the most interesting of military studies, so the origin and progression of all which makes this interest centre in Hannibal, with but a reflected light upon some of his antagonists. From beginning to end Hannibal is the pivot about which all else revolves. Every manœuvre in these seventeen years is traceable directly to what Hannibal willed or did. He was not only pivot but main-spring of the whole movement; to study him is to study the Second Punic War. The Romans properly called it The War against Hannibal.

The project of crossing the Alps, as we have already seen, was not Hannibal's, but his father's. It was Hannibal, however, who executed in all its details what was with Hamilcar a bare conception, even if a great one. He prepared his base by completing the conquest of Spain, and left in the hands of Hasdrubal and Hanno a territory which he calculated on their holding, and which they ought to have held. He had, with the utmost care, made himself familiar with the route he must follow, its peoples, its climate, its topography, and had won friends along his proposed path. The energy, skill, intelligence and determination with which he carried out his plan would have made him one of the greatest of leaders if he had never advanced beyond the Po.

But this was only a first step in Hannibal's military career. He had only begun to tax his resources. The self-reliant courage which prompted him, after he reached the Po, to

undertake the conquest of Italy at the head of twenty thousand foot and six thousand horse, with only the promised support of fickle barbarian allies to base upon, is marvelous. It
is the mark which stamps the genius — or the fool. Without
the iron will and intellectual grasp to do just such a thing,
no great captain ever accomplished his aim. Upon such a
rock have been shattered many reputations.

That Hannibal should begin with a distinctly offensive
campaign was in accordance with his enterprising nature, his
youthful ardor, his active temperament, his plan and his existing resources. Four brilliant victories rewarded this enterprise, which, joined to the bold flank-march through the
morasses of the Arnus, and preceded by the march from
Spain and the crossing of the Alps, illustrate a page which has
not its equal in the history of war.

However brilliant his success, we must remember that Hannibal depended on diplomatic rather than military gain. His
political aspirations centred in the hope that some members
of the Italian confederacy would forsake Rome. When,
after Cannæ, these aspirations began to pale, so also did his
military fortunes. Without the resources such seceders could
contribute, or constant reinforcements from Carthage, Hannibal could not expect to gain further ground or even hold his
own. While in history the first three years lend greater lustre
to the name of Hannibal, to one familiar with war the period
which follows far outshines it. From now on, the Romans
opposed Hannibal with their best men and arms, and, as in
those days they could do, declined to fight him while he was
still equipped for fighting. His own government forsook
him. He became the play of the winds of fortune. Daily
growing weak beyond the point where he was a match for the
able enemy who was daily growing stronger in numbers and
experience, he carried on a series of campaigns the like of

which the world has never seen. They are only approached in defensive skill and grit by those of Frederick. The ability so shown is beyond all praise. Unable to compass victory, Hannibal still remained master of the field. Never yielding an inch which he could occupy, he kept his enemy at arms' length by sheer command of intellect. Too weak to attack, he remained too terrible to his adversaries to be attacked. His utmost means sufficed to hold important points or keep the enemy from seizing them; to tire him by unexpected marches or surprise him so as to avoid attack; to strike a series of partial blows when he could not strike a heavy one; to avoid every blow intended for him or prevent its being decisive, — all this in the hope that Carthage would lay aside her quarrels and support him. With what consummate skill was all this done! Before Hannibal grew so weak as to be driven back to Bruttium, his work was full of brilliant resources, prolific in instances of clever management, a pattern of the highest art.

Hannibal has been the subject of close study by every great general; he has been the admiration of the soldiers of every age. Even the great Condé paid him a curiously Gallic compliment. "Messieurs," said he one day to a group of his officers, "si Annibal pouvait revenir, il battrait tous les généraux de Louis XIV.!"

That the campaigns of Hannibal cannot be so readily used to illustrate the operations of modern war as those of Napoleon is due to the difference in armament, the conditions of battle and the system of supplies. As a study in strategy, and in some instances in tactics, nothing exceeds in value the Second Punic War.

It is almost beyond a peradventure certain that had Carthage sustained Hannibal instead of wasting her resources on doubtful ventures in Spain, he would have dictated a peace on the Capitoline Hill.

Carthage was lost long before Zama. When Hannibal was ordered back to Africa, every chance of saving Carthage or of redeeming the fortunes of the war had already been forfeited. Had he won Zama, he must speedily have gone down in another battle fraught with the same results. Carthage had lost the game years before. It was but the genius of Hannibal which prolonged the struggle.

Caltrop.

XLIV.

HANNIBAL AND ALEXANDER.

HANNIBAL, as a young general, showed the same bodily strength, enthusiasm and gallantry as Alexander. Later in life, while never lacking boldness of conception and execution, he was not reckless. His moral bearing was higher; his passions well under control. Each had abundant will-power; each had remarkable intellectual qualities. Hannibal was probably a man of greater culture. Alexander, as king, commanded the fealty of his army, as well as won its love as leader. Hannibal had but his character to rely on; but he held the affection and duty of his men as no general in history has done. Both were keen and longheaded in diplomacy. Alexander always had success to aid him; Hannibal did his greatest diplomatic work under difficulties. The king was a prime favorite of Fortune. She smiled on Hannibal until after Cannæ; thereafter no man ever faced luck so contrary. Each conducted war with method, and a wise weighing of resources and work to be done. Hannibal was crafty, Alexander open and bold, in conducting a campaign; but both kept with equal clearness their object in view. Each was a master of logistics; each was careful in rationing, arming and equipping his army. As tacticians it is hard to choose between them. Arbela and Cannæ stand on the same level. Each inherited an army; each used it with extraordinary ability, and kept it in the best condition. Alexander got larger results from his victories; but this was owing to the conditions under which he wrought. Hannibal could not make his battles decisive; the Roman Republic was like a cyclopean wall. In pursuit and in sieges, the Macedonian was the bolder and greater. Gauged by the work he had to do, the resistance he encountered, and the means at his command, Hannibal outranks any general of history.

IT may not be amiss to draw a comparison between Alexander and Hannibal, or rather to point out certain salient and contrasting features in the life of either. Both were alike in the quality of their gifts and powers, but the factors governing the work of each varied widely.

We know so little about Hannibal's personal appearance that

we cannot assert that he possessed the charm of beauty which exercised so marked a sway in the person of Alexander. But in his other bodily qualities, endurance, strength, activity, as well as in his mental equipment, Hannibal was fully the peer of the monarch; in moral bearing by far his superior. His appetites were always curbed; they never overrode him as they did the conqueror of the Great King. His life was simple, abstemious, full of active employment, never given to indulgence. So far as character is concerned, — judged exclusively by his enemies, — there is shown to us by history no more perfect man, among those who have wrought on so gigantic a scale, than Hannibal.

Alexander was of a different temperament. Kindly by nature, he was hot-headed where Hannibal was measured. Both were tireless in activity of mind and body. Both had noble impulses. Both were guilty of cruelty, according to our standard; but the laws of war of their era called this forth rather than their individual character, and Hannibal's hatred of Rome was inspired by more grievous cruelties inflicted upon his own country by Rome. Hannibal was never guilty of an act of ruffianism, as was Alexander in the case of Clitus or of Batis, or of cruel injustice as in the case of Parmenio. Neither Hannibal nor Alexander permitted contradiction, but Hannibal was far beyond Alexander in self-restraint. It is said that from his face it could not be guessed what was passing within his soul. This self-control was possessed by Hannibal in so marvelous a degree that Livy accuses him of being naturally perfidious. Hannibal had no confidant or adviser. Alexander had Hephæstion, Parmenio, Craterus.

Will-power in each was strongly developed. But Hannibal at all times had his will under control. Alexander's fiery impulses not infrequently ran away with his discretion. The difference was primarily one of character; partly one of years.

Hannibal's great work was done in the thirties and forties; Alexander's in the twenties.

Hannibal's mind was as broad, delicate and clear as Alexander's, and he was less tainted with what may be called Macedonian roughness. His Greek training made him intellectually the superior of any of his opponents, for Greek learning and culture had not yet made their way among the naturally self-sufficient Romans. This training showed in the intelligent conception and execution of his projects and in the nicety of his discrimination. It was no doubt apparent in his personal bearing; but of this we have no record. The charge of cruelty against Hannibal is more than met by his chivalrous conduct to his fallen enemies, which distinctly proves that he had a gentle trait which was stronger than even his hatred. So much cannot be said of Alexander.

Hannibal's natural courage was great. The execution of his projects was not only bold but obstinate. In his youth he gave his men the same example of individual bravery as the king. His personal conduct is testified to by his bitterest enemies, but he did not, like Alexander, in his bursts of enthusiasm forget that the life of the general is necessary to his army and his country.

Hannibal's influence over his men was perhaps his most remarkable quality. He managed to preserve the strictest discipline without the cruel measures which were often, in ancient times, resorted to as a means of compelling subordination. He won the love and confidence of his men to an extraordinary degree. He was able to hold their affection in adversity as markedly as in prosperity. He could win from his soldiers the greatest efforts with cheerfulness. This control was obtained by the same means Alexander used, — never-ceasing personal care for the comfort and well-being of his army, his friendly bearing, his own example, and perfect justice in awarding punishments and rewards.

Hannibal, like the Macedonian, was gifted with the truest eloquence — not that eloquence of which mere grace is the chief ornament, but the power of saying those things which stir men's souls and shape their deeds. But few of his words are preserved by tradition.

Hannibal and Alexander won their standing among their men under different conditions. Equal in the personality which attracts the soldier, Hannibal kept his influence, not because he was king as well as general, not because he had in his army a leaven of men bound to him by allegiance as well as affection, but among a patchwork crowd of all nationalities, from African to Gallic and Bruttian, each with his own fealty, sentiments, habits and methods. And yet, during the fifteen years he campaigned in Italy, as is testified by all the Roman authors, but especially by Polybius and Nepos, there was never a mutiny in Hannibal's camp; nor (excepting what was shown in the desertion of the twelve hundred Spanish and Numidian horse and of a few isolated individuals) was there even dissension. We remember how much, on more than one occasion, Alexander had to contend against.

Hannibal was ambitious, as was Alexander. But the personal element was less prominent in Hannibal. His intense hatred of Rome was really at the bottom of his ambition to abate the arrogance of Rome. Nothing in Hannibal's life shows that he labored to create a name. Probably Gustavus, Frederick and he were more unselfish patriots than either Alexander, Cæsar or Napoleon. The latter were kings in their ambitions; not so Hannibal.

In his political management Hannibal was, as all soldiers who enact so great a part must be, sagacious and clear-headed, able and successful. No one could have gone so far to unsettle the very foundations of the power of Rome, the fealty of the confederates, unless he had been a very master of diplomacy. The manner in which he held the allegiance of the Gallic peoples, the most like weather-vanes of any of the tribes on Italian soil, was a *chef d'œuvre*. He knew just when to mix force with persuasion, just how far he could rely on what was told him, just how much he could get from any given alliance. He distributed gifts with a liberal hand; he used threats; he remorselessly punished those cities which deserted him. The result was that more than half the area of the peninsula was at one time or other subject to his will, and contributory to his arms. But the structure of the Latin confederacy remained sound, despite Hannibal's successes in war and diplomacy. When we consider how readily the Eastern peoples accepted the yoke of the new and conquering lord, and how strong the hold of Rome on her allies uniformly was throughout her history, we are tempted to believe that what Hannibal accomplished was beyond even Alexander's gigantic performance.

The marvel in the life of Hannibal is the amount he effected with the small means at his command against the vast resources of his opponents, and the length of time he maintained the struggle. Starting from New Carthage with one hundred thousand men, he had but twenty-six thousand left when he reached Italy. This force rarely grew beyond forty to fifty thousand men for field duty, while the Romans had from sixty to ninety thousand men immediately arrayed against him, not to count huge armies elsewhere. Without fleet or home support, relying solely on his own exertions, he was forced to resort to every diplomatic means to keep his allies in heart and induce them to furnish him with troops. This part of his work was difficult beyond anything which Alexander had to contend with.

Alexander always had luck running in his favor. This was a marked feature of his life. Hannibal's luck ran but a brief career, and after Cannæ no man ever had fortune's back more persistently turned upon him. Alexander was always victorious, and he and his men had the cheering effect of success to encourage them; Hannibal was rarely so, in the last dozen years, and was forced to hold his men up to their work against constantly blackening prospects. Alexander, after Arbela, commanded unlimited resources; loss of men was easily reparable. Hannibal's supplies of men and means came by the hardest, were in fact generally self-created; he could not fill the gaps rent in his line by battle. Alexander's campaigns were against a huge but unwieldy and rotten empire. Hannibal's were against the most compact and able nation of the world, at its sturdiest period, a nation which was the best type of a fighting machine. Alexander had no brilliant general, excepting Memnon, to contend against, and Memnon was so hampered by the jealousy of his Persian colleagues that his opinion could not prevail. Hannibal, during all but the first three years, had strong generals opposed to him. Alexander's enemies fought on a senseless method; Hannibal's on the method they learned from him. All this does not prove Hannibal greater than Alexander. Such giants override comparison. Alexander was the most brilliant in fortune; Hannibal was undeniably the most stanch and uncompromising and admirable in misfortune of all captains of whom we have any record.

Hannibal's art was based on the same appreciation of intellectual war as Alexander's. Each, as Napoleon expresses it, carried on war by a method, that is, by a well-conceived and intelligent plan, suited to the conditions and to the obstacles to be overcome. Hannibal always had a well-defined base, and never forsook it, unless for another which at the time was a better one for his purposes. He never so manœuvred as that he could not return to his base to victual or recruit. His communications were never compromised. This base was successively Spain, cisalpine Gaul, Apulia, Campania, Lucania, Calabria, Bruttium. Hannibal was bold in cutting away from his communications when necessary, but he always kept the road open, and always got back.

Up to Cannæ, Hannibal acted in a single body well concentrated. After Cannæ, he was compelled to divide his forces; but he was wont to concentrate and divide again as circumstances demanded. This, and the selection of the important points on which to concentrate, is a marked feature in his conduct. His movements were generally quick and decided, but prudent, secret and craftily thought out. He not only kept the enemy from a knowledge of what he was about to do, but led him to expect some other thing. His self-reliance and natural secretiveness and craft, as much as his want of material strength, led him naturally to resort to night-marches, surprises, ambushes, stratagems of all kinds. Such victories as the Trebia and Lake Trasimene, such a retreat as that over Mt. Callicula, are distinctly in Hannibal's vein. In this particular he is unlike Alexander, who not only did not as a rule do such things, but is said to have looked upon them as unworthy. But though Alexander declined to "steal a victory" at Arbela, he was more than once, as at the Persian Gates or among the Uxians, driven to stratagem to save himself.

Hannibal took none into his confidence. He knew his own plans and how he proposed to execute them, but he sought no advice. If his schemes failed it was solely for reasons within his own knowledge or circumstances beyond his own control. He had, like Alexander, the peculiar capacity of reading his opponent's character, of guessing his weaknesses, and of acting promptly and energetically on this knowledge.

After Cannæ, Hannibal was obliged to confine his natural

activity within narrower boundaries, was often compelled to periods of long inaction. His habit was to campaign only in summer, but if anything was to be gained no season was too hard, no obstacle too great, no difficulty such as to daunt him. Witness his passage of the Alps and the Arnus marshes. Alexander was more restless, and allowed no season to arrest or delay his movements. This is well shown by the extraordinary campaigns beyond the Parapamisus.

Hannibal's victualing of his men was ably done. He foraged in summer and collected rations in strong camps or towns for the winter season. That he never saw the time when his men lacked bread is a remarkable fact; for he had not Alexander's unlimited resources. His own personal means went to feed his army. This was miserliness to be highly commended, if indeed it be true that Hannibal was a miser.

Of Hannibal's tactical dispositions much has already been said. In logistics he was especially strong. His marches were always carefully made, with proper van-, rear-guard and flankers, at a time when such precautions were unknown. This art he taught the Romans by bitter experience. He suited the order of march of his troops to the existing conditions with great ability. Witness the columns up the Little St. Bernard and through the Arnus marshes. The Macedonian habit was equally ahead of its age, except in such cases as Xenophon.

In battle Hannibal adhered to the phalangial order to which he had been habituated. Alexander maintained his army on the footing Philip had given it. He could make no changes to advantage. Hannibal was not slow to see the superiority of the Roman organization and armament, and in the second year in Italy had already armed some of his troops with Roman weapons. He altered the Greek phalan-

gial disposition to a certain extent, leaning towards the legionary in what he did ; but we do not know the details of
his changes.   They are only referred to in general terms by
the ancient authors.   The effort was apparently to make the
phalanx cover more ground.

As was the habit with Alexander, Hannibal was apt to
choose open flat ground for battles, as best suited for his
evolutions, but he utilized every kind of accident in the
ground for stratagem.   Both were able mountain fighters.
Hannibal was not unapt to invite attack and meet it half-
way.   Alexander always attacked.   Both personally manœuvred as well as commanded their armies.   Their troops
fought well in hand and sustained each other admirably.
Both got the best work of which their men were capable.
Hannibal was singularly apt at making raw levies available.
Cavalry was the particular arm of each.   Both gave it the
best of care and demanded great things of it.

Some historians, by dint of repeating the words supposed
to have been uttered by Maharbal, after Cannæ, have convinced themselves that Hannibal did not follow up or get
results from his victories.   This is an error.   Few generals
have ever got better results, so far as they could be had.
The circumstances under which Alexander fought enabled
him to secure enormous remuneration from his victories.
This was not possible to Hannibal.   But to count his allies
after Cannæ shows that he made the best of use of his gain.
Alexander pursued the broken enemy with a ferocity and
determination never equaled.   Hannibal did not allow himself, in the ardor of victory, to be led in pursuit beyond what
the circumstances warranted.   He was equally cautious after
a victory as after a defeat.   He had a different enemy in his
front.

As a besieger Hannibal was not the equal of Alexander or

of some other generals. This was not his forte. The siege
of Saguntum is his only noteworthy success, and this does not
compare to the siege of Tyre. In Italy he was not accompanied by siege-material. He felt that sieges did not fall in
with his plans. They were costly in time, men and material,
and he often got hold of cities more easily by stratagem or
by storm. Even at Saguntum, after a long and exhaustive
siege, he lost patience and took the place by storm; and as he
assaulted it too soon, so the storming operations lasted five
days and cost heavily in men.

It is a common thing to compare Hannibal and Scipio.
This has already been commented upon. Scipio was a brilliant general, a fine diplomat. He was equipped with some
of the best qualities of man and soldier. His character was
blameless except that he lacked the sense of subordination.
He was a fine tactician. His influence over men was considerable. But he was fortunate in never, till Zama, having an
opponent who was his equal, in never meeting a force which
in any sense matched his own, taking all qualities into consideration. Except Hasdrubal, Scipio met no great general
in Spain or Italy. At Zama it was the Roman army and its
excess in cavalry which won; not Scipio. His capacity as a
captain should not be underrated, but he can in no wise be
placed beside Hannibal. The similes and anecdotes of the
Roman historians cannot be accepted for more than they are
worth. We must remember the violence of their prejudices,
which of necessity warped their judgment. Here is one of
Livy's stories.

" Claudius," says Livy, " following the history written in
Greek by Acilius, says that Publius Africanus was employed
in this embassy, and that it was he who conversed with Hannibal at Ephesus. He even relates one of their conversations
in which Scipio asked Hannibal ' whom he thought the

greatest captain?' and that he answered, 'Alexander, king of Macedonia; because with a small band he defeated armies whose numbers were beyond reckoning; and because he had overrun the remotest regions, the merely visiting of which was a thing above human aspiration.' Scipio then asked 'to whom he gave the second place?' and he replied, 'To Pyrrhus; for he first taught the method of encamping; and, besides, no one ever showed more exquisite judgment in choosing his ground and disposing his posts; while he also possessed the art of conciliating mankind to himself to such a degree, that the nations of Italy wished him, though a foreign prince, to hold the sovereignty among them, rather than the Roman people, who had so long possessed the dominion of that part of the world.' On his proceeding to ask 'whom he esteemed the third?' Hannibal replied, 'Myself, beyond doubt.' On this Scipio laughed, and added, 'What would you have said if you had conquered me?' 'Then,' replied the other, 'I would have placed Hannibal, not only before Alexander and Pyrrhus, but before all other commanders.' This answer, turned with Punic dexterity, and conveying an unexpected kind of flattery, was highly grateful to Scipio, as it set him apart from the crowd of commanders, as one of incomparable eminence." Whether true or not of Hannibal, this anecdote is characteristic of Scipio.

Hannibal excelled as a tactician. No battle in history is a finer sample of tactics than Cannæ. But he was yet greater in logistics and strategy. No captain ever marched to and fro among so many armies of troops superior to his in numbers and material as fearlessly and skillfully as he. No man ever held his own so long or so ably against such odds. Constantly overmatched by better soldiers led by generals always respectable, often of great ability, he yet defied all their efforts to drive him from Italy for half a generation. Not even Frederick was outweighed as was Hannibal, for though Frederick's army was smaller, it was better than that of any of the allies.

As a soldier, in the countenance he presented to the stoutest of foes and in the constancy he exhibited under the bitterest adversity, Hannibal stands alone and unequaled. As a man, no character in history exhibits a purer life or nobler patriotism.

Cap of Velite.

XLV.

LEGION VERSUS PHALANX. 197–168 B. C.

ROME soon stretched her arms abroad and grasped at foreign conquest. In so doing, legion was again pitted against phalanx. The first conflict was at Cynocephalæ. Here, on ground which was hilly and rough, the legionary proved easily superior to the phalangite with his long sarissa; and the Roman consul, though coming close to defeat, by tactical boldness and prompt action, aided by an able lieutenant, won a handsome victory. In the war against Antiochus, at the battle of Magnesia, the phalanx was sustained on right and left by other troops. In the course of the battle these were driven away, and the legionary cohorts, attacking the phalanx in flank and rear, easily cut it to pieces. The Macedonian phalanx could no longer manœuvre like Philip's and Alexander's. In a third test at Pydna, the Romans were at first driven in; but the pursuit of the phalanx opened gaps in its formation. Rallying his men, Æmilius pushed small groups into these gaps. The legionary with his gladius, when he got at his man, was easily superior to the unwieldy phalangite. The Macedonian formation was broken, and the phalanx annihilated. In all these battles, however, the best phalanx never met the best legion, under equal leaders and conditions. The value of the legion lay more largely in the character of the Roman citizen of that era than in its tactical formation. A hundred years later, when the Roman army consisted of material less good, the quincuncial formation disappeared, and the legion again became a phalanx, as it had originally been. But, for intelligent rank and file, the legion was indisputably better than the phalanx.

ROME was no lónger satisfied with her dominion in Italy. She had got a taste of foreign conquest, and the appetite grew with what it fed on. The senate, throughout the Second Punic War, had displayed rare wisdom, and entire ability to manage the affairs of Rome on a larger basis; and the aristocracy had, by its services, not only earned a title to recognition, but had imbibed an ambition which threatened to lead it beyond its purely patriotic impulses. The Romans showed

a marked gain in military boldness and skill. They played
the rôle of conquerors well. The army habit of nightly fortifying the camp, the limited baggage, and the fact that the
men carried ten or fifteen days' rations, made them independent and adventurous in their campaigns. Among the Greeks
and in Asia Minor, these advantages gave to the Romans a
strength beyond their numbers. They had Hannibal's instruction to profit by, and did not have Hannibal for an opponent. Their operations exhibited a much higher grade of
skill; and while they resumed the old habit of initiative which
Hannibal had compelled them to lay one side, they used this
in so discreet a manner that the victories they won were apt
to be followed by marked gain, and as a rule to give them
control of the enemy's cities. In fact, sieges became uncommon events, and assault, treachery or ruse were resorted to
for their capture, when the cities did not surrender. The
Romans had recovered all their ancient offensive instincts,
and the feeling of superiority which for half a generation
Hannibal had checked.

In narrating the campaigns of Pyrrhus in Italy, the relative value of legion and phalanx as military formations was
enlarged on. The Roman campaigns in Greece brought the
two methods once more into conflict.

Rome could not forgive Philip for the aid which he had
yielded to Hannibal during the Second Punic War, nor was
it long before the turn of Macedon came for retribution.
The Second Macedonian War lasted from 200 to 197 B. C.
It was terminated by the battle of Cynocephalæ.

Quinctius Flaminius, the Roman consul, and Philip, king
of Macedon, were near Pheræ in Thessaly. Each had moved
his army into close proximity to the other without intimate
knowledge of his enemy's whereabouts, though there had
been some outpost combats between the two. The Pheræ

territory, being much cut up by trees, hedges and garden-walls, did not afford a suitable battle-ground, and both generals concluded to make for the grain-fields of Scotussa, which lay across a range of hills from Pheræ. Two days' marches were made. On the third, rainy, lowering weather kept the Romans in camp; the king set out, but, owing to the difficulty in keeping his column from straggling in the fog, soon camped. He took the precaution to send a detachment to occupy the hills known as Cynocephalæ, somewhere on the farther side of which he divined the Roman army to be located.

The consul from his camp likewise sent out a detachment of one thousand light foot and ten turmæ of horse to beat the country and discover the location of the Macedonian army, warning the leaders against ambuscades, particularly dangerous under the curtain of fog, even in an open country, and ordering them to ravage the land by the way. This party happened to ascend the Cynocephalæ hills, and struck the Macedonians posted there by Philip. Each party, somewhat abashed by the sudden encounter, sent back word for succor, but indulged meanwhile in active skirmishing. The Romans were considerably outnumbered, but Flaminius sent up two thousand Ætolian foot and five hundred horse, which restored a fight already failing, and began to crowd back the Macedonians, whose heavy armor and weapons made them poor skirmishers, and gradually to drive them up to the summit of the hill.

Expecting nothing less than a general engagement, Philip had sent out a large part of his troops to forage. The fog had fallen from the summit of the hills so as to allow him to see that his troops had been pushed back, and the messengers from the front were urgent. Philip determined to sustain his advanced body at the risk of a battle. He dispatched the bulk of his mercenary troops and the Macedonian and Thessalian cavalry to the support of his hard-pressed men, and recalled his foragers. The reinforcement was opportune, and by its aid the tide was turned and the Romans hustled down nearly to the level plain, where lay their camp. Only the Ætolian horse, then ranking as the best in Greece, by its able resistance, kept the Romans from a *sauve qui peut.*

This slight success, the urging of his lieutenants and the general desire of the army to continue the fight, prevailed upon Philip, against his better judgment, to order up from the camp the entire Macedonian army with a view to battle.

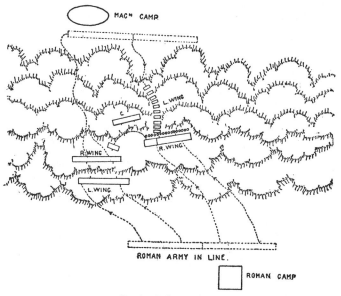

Battle of Cynocephalæ.

The ground was peculiarly unsuited to the manœuvres of a phalanx. The Cynocephalæ hills are rough and broken with sharp and ragged slopes. It was only a place for light troops. The Macedonian phalanx was no longer that of Alexander, which could fight on any ground. The conditions were much better suited to the legion, for the legionary was a skirmisher by no means to be despised. Flaminius ordered the Roman army into line, lest his men should be discouraged by the loss of even a partial engagement.

The king had a grand phalanx of sixteen thousand hoplites; two thousand peltasts; of allies and mercenaries, each two thousand, and two thousand horse, somewhat over twenty-four thousand men in all. The Roman force was about the same, and the consul had a superiority in cavalry, numerically and in quality.

The Roman detachment had fallen back to the valley not far from their camp, where the men had rallied. The arrival of the consul and reinforcements gave back their vigor to the troops. Flaminius ordered the Roman right to remain in place, and covered it with some elephants, and then advanced the left to sustain the skirmishers who had been driven back. With a stanch onset they once again began to force the Macedonians up the slope. This driving of the enemy uphill demonstrates excellent work on the Roman side. With the ancient weapons, to fight downhill was a distinct advantage. Missiles carried farther, and the men had a better footing, not to count the moral advantage of looking at your opponent literally *de haut en bas.*

Philip, with the right wing of the phalanx and the peltasts, was soonest on the field; the left, under Nicanor, was delayed by the difficulty of the ascent from the Macedonian camp. The king had got his right in line before the Macedonian mercenaries again began to fall back; he speedily rallied the flying men, and placed them on the right of the peltasts and phalanx.

Livy states that Philip ordered the phalangites to lay aside their sarissas, as less serviceable on the rough field than their swords. This would have made the contest, not one between legion and phalanx, but between Macedonians armed with a weapon they were not peculiarly skillful in wielding, and a poor one at that, and Romans armed with their terrible gladius. Polybius does not mention the fact, and the rest of Livy's account disagrees with this statement. But Philip did commit an almost equal blunder. He ployed his sixteen-deep phalanx into files thirty-two men deep, and directed it to take close order on the right, that is, with the men occupying each but one and one half feet space. On the rough ground, the king should have sought to give his line mobility rather than stability; but he transformed it into a body quite unwieldy on any but a plain, and if deprived of the sarissa, its chief weapon for close order, it would be helpless. The sword was the weapon of open order, when used at all.

Polybius states that the king advanced on the Romans with sarissas couched. Flaminius had again to advance uphill. But his men were in good spirits, and raised their battle-cry, on the signal for advance being given by the trumpet, with uncommon good-will, which augured good results for the outcome of the affair. The king had got his line well in hand on his own right, and the favorable ground, the heavy arms of the men, and his own personal exertions enabled him to check, and then to thrust back, the Roman left in marked confusion.

The Macedonian centre, which had already reached the field, did not join in the advance, but stood in place as mere lookers-on. Of what forces it was composed is not stated; probably part of the phalanx. Nicanor, whose men had been much disordered by the bad ascent from the camp, was leading the Macedonian left on the field in decidedly poor order for battle.

Philip's work had been sharp and decisive. The consul's

left wing, though under his own conduct, had been badly broken and was gone beyond rescue. But Flaminius had the eye of a soldier. He saw at a glance that he could best retrieve the battle by prompt action with his right, and he acted with the courage of his convictions. Leaving the left to hold its own as best it might, he immediately joined the right wing, threw it sharply forward, reached the summit of the hill and formed in good order before Nicanor's phalanx emerged upon the open slopes where the battle was engaged. Giving Nicanor no time to deploy, Flaminius struck his head of column a mighty blow. He drove his elephants at the half-formed phalanx, and followed these up with the sword. The result was not a minute doubtful. The Macedonian left, not ready for battle, was at once demoralized by the onset of the Romans and dissolved in confusion before it had fairly begun to form. The Macedonian centre appears to have been carried away at the same time. The Roman right followed in pursuit.

At this moment, a military tribune of the Roman right, whose name is not disclosed to us, seeing that his wing was victorious and that he could no longer be of use at this point, took quickly in hand his small detachment of twenty centuries of the legion and hurried by a circuit over to the rear of the Macedonian right, whose success had advanced it far beyond the general alignment and thus rendered it liable to just this manœuvre. Here he fell lustily upon the rear ranks of the unwieldy thirty-two-deep body of the phalanx. Unable to face about to meet this new assault, the phalanx began to waver. The Romans who fronted this body, encouraged by the diversion, plucked up a new heart and fell to again with reviving courage. It is a pity that the name of the intelligent Roman tribune has been lost. He deserves honorable mention.

The Roman right had won a complete victory; the left was

on the point of doing the same. Philip, startled beyond
measure at the new turn of affairs when he had supposed he
was winning the fight, galloped to an adjoining eminence to
overlook the battle as a whole, and seeing from thence the
irretrievable loss of the field, made haste to leave it. His
army was wiped out. No less than eight thousand men were
killed ; five thousand were taken. The Roman loss was but
seven hundred killed.

The result of the battle was to obliterate the power of
Macedon. But the relative value of legion and phalanx was
as little determined as ever. Extrinsic circumstances had
decided the battle.

Another instance of legion versus phalanx occurred in the
war against Antiochus, king of Syria. Antiochus had got
mixed up in Grecian affairs and had landed in Greece to free
it from Roman influence ; but by injudicious proceedings and
for lack of native support had been driven back to Asia
Minor. In 190 B. C. the Romans, under the consul Lucius
Cornelius Scipio, for the first time crossed the Hellespont and
trod the soil of another continent. Lucius had taken with
him as legate his brother Publius, victor of Zama. It was he
who really directed the campaign. The Romans gave battle
to Antiochus at Magnesia, on the Hermus, near the Sipylus
mountains. Livy gives a full and clear account of the battle.

The Romans were confident and strong, though fewer in
numbers. They "never despised any enemy so much."
After a thorough reconnoissance, Scipio advanced his camp
to the immediate vicinity of Antiochus, and on the third day
battle was offered. Antiochus, relying on numbers, did not
decline it. Scipio had two Roman and two allied legions each
of fifty-four hundred men. The former were in the centre.
The army stood as usual in three lines, hastati, principes and
triarii. The left of the line was not far from the river and

had but four turmæ of cavalry to protect it. On the right of
the Roman army stood Eumenes' foot, and the Achæans, three
thousand in number, and on their right the rest of the cavalry
of the legions, which, with about eight hundred of Eumenes',
made nearly three thousand men. On the extreme flank were

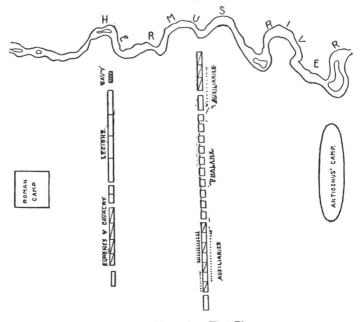

Battle of Magnesia. First Phase.

one thousand light troops. Scipio's total force was thus nearly
thirty thousand men, of excellent material throughout, well
disposed and in good heart.

The king's line presented a splendid but motley aspect
when compared to the consul's, which exhibited little of the
pomp and circumstance of war. In the centre was a grand
phalanx of sixteen thousand men, armed with the sarissa and
standing thirty-two deep. This gave it too little front and
such depth as to make it unwieldy rather than able. This

trick of doubling the depth of the phalanx, which seems to
have crept into use about this time, was a step backward
to the ponderous but useless masses of the Orientals. The
phalanx of Antiochus was placed in ten divisions each of
fifty men front, and between each two was an interval held
by two Indian war elephants of great size and courage, their
towers holding each four men, with a large supply of javelins
and other missiles. On the right of the phalanx was a body
of nine thousand horse, among them the agema, with sixteen
elephants in reserve. Next the horse were the Argyraspides,
or silver shield-bearers, the agema of foot; then twelve hundred Daän horse-bowmen and fifty-five hundred light troops,
with four thousand archers and slingers to cover the wing.
On the left of the phalanx were alternate bodies of horse and
foot, with elephants in reserve, much like and equal in numbers to those on the right. But the cavalry was covered by
a number of scythed chariots and war-dromedaries. The
king commanded the right, his son the left wing.

The morning was wet and foggy. The king's line was
longer than the Roman, and could not well be seen from end
to end. The moisture unstrung the archers' bows and made
unserviceable the slings and javelin thongs. The Roman soldiers, mostly heavy-armed, did not suffer this inconvenience.
The scythed chariots were opposite Eumenes, a general who
had learned how to deal with this arm. Before the battle
opened, he sent out the archers, darters and slingers to skirmish in their front, and by shouts and wounds to frighten
the chariot-horses and the dromedaries. This they readily
accomplished, and not only drove the chariots away from
their post, but these, wheeling, some to the rear, others to
right and left, so unsteadied the auxiliaries of the enemy's
left wing that they mostly took to flight before even coming
into action. The Roman cavalry was then sharply pushed

forward, and, owing to the confusion made by the flying chariots, dromedaries, elephants and auxiliaries, it made short work of the mailed horse which protected the flank of the phalanx. With scarcely any loss to the Romans, Antiochus' whole left wing had been dispersed.

The legions now advanced on the front and swung round on the flank of the phalanx, while the horse rode round to its rear. The elephants gave them no trouble, for they had long

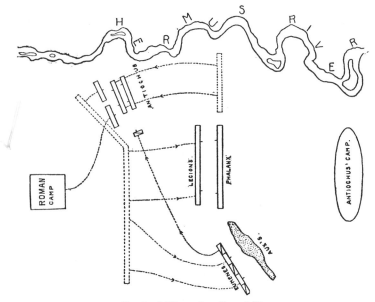

Battle of Magnesia. Second Phase.

ago learned how to avoid the danger of these monsters by wounding them in the sides and cutting their hamstrings. The flight of the left wing had already unstrung the phalanx, which needed to have its flanks protected, and the sudden onset of the Romans had allowed them to use their sarissas to but poor advantage. This was not the quick manœuvring phalanx of Philip and Alexander, which could face

Recovering themselves, and encouraged by the first show of success, the Romans, used to open-order fighting, quickly rallied to a man, fell upon the dissolving phalanx in front, flank and rear, and cut it to pieces. Plutarch says the battle lasted but an hour. This scarcely agrees with what is told about the course of the action. Both Polybius and Livy give the Macedonian loss as twenty-five thousand men killed, twelve thousand captured; the Roman as only one hundred, illy as the figures accord. Either this or the initial defeat of the Romans would appear to be an error, — unless, indeed, the Romans ran before they fairly got into action.

The legion had clearly won the superiority. No doubt its mobility, its reliance on the individuality of each man, the subordination of the soldier, and its suitability to the character of the Roman people, made the formation better than any phalanx of that day. But in reading the struggle of the two methods, it becomes plain that the best phalanx never met the best legion under equal circumstances and leadership. Pyrrhus was the only great general who ever led the phalanx against the Romans. Though his phalanx was not of good material, being largely Tarentines unused to the long spear, he nevertheless came close to success in a merely military sense. It was Roman discipline and character which won, rather than the Roman formation, though the legion had unquestionably a higher tactical value. The legion succeeded as the Romans succeeded. In the conflict between legion and phalanx the latter was never organized, drilled, manœuvred or led as it was under Philip or Alexander.

We shall see, in the succeeding century, when the material of the legion degenerated from the citizen whose service was a privilege rather than a burden, to the proletariat who enlisted as a means of a better livelihood, and the individuality of the soldier could no longer be depended on, that the mobility of the legion disappeared. The men were no more to be relied upon unless held close in hand by the general commanding, and unless they were massed for mutual support. The intervals between maniples became dangerous; they were gradually decreased and finally given up; the legion reverted to a body resembling the old Dorian phalanx from which it had sprung. The period of its elastic structure was coincident with the service privilege of the Roman citizen. So long as the terms citizen and soldier were equivalents, so long lasted the best period of the legion. The great victories it later won, the splendid work of which it was capable, were no longer due to the rank and file, to the Roman burgess, that perfect type of the citizen-soldier, but distinctly to the skill of the leader, to the talent of such men as Marius, Sulla, Pompey, to the genius of Cæsar.

Casting Javelin with a Twist.

APPENDIX A.

CASUALTIES IN SOME ANCIENT BATTLES.

Battle of	Date. B. C.	Number Engaged.	Nationality.	Number Killed.	Percentage.	Usual %.†	Loss of Enemy.	Remarks.
Marathon.	490	11,000	Greeks.	192	1¾	5	6,400	
Platæa.	479	38,700*	"	1,360	3½	4	257,000	*Hoplites, who alone fought.
Chæronæa.	338	50,000	"	2,000	4	4		
Thebes.	335	33,000	Macedonians.	500	1¾	4	6,000	
Granicus.	334	3,000	" Cavalry.	85	3	2	19,000*	*Mostly massacre of Greek Phalanx — 1,000 Persian horsemen fell.
Issus.	333	30,000	Macedonians.	450	1½	4½	100,000*	*The usual massacre.
Arbela.	331	47,000	"	500	1	4	40,000	*The usual massacre. Diodorus says 90,000, Arrian says 300,000.
Megalopolis.	330	40,000	"	3,500	8¾	4½		
"	"	20,000	Spartans.	5,300	26½	5		
Jaxartes.	329	6,000	Macedonians.	160	2¾	7	1,000	
Hydaspes.	326	14,000	"	930	6¾	5	12,000*	*Arrian says 23,000.
Heraclea.	280	25,000	Epirots.	4,000*	16	5		*Dionysius says 13,000 loss.
"	"	20,000	Romans.	7,000*	35	5		* " " 15,000 "
Asculum.	279	70,000	Greeks and Italians.	3,550*	5	4		* " " " "
"	"	70,000	Romans and Ital'ns.	6,000*	8½	4		* " " " "
At Rhone.	218	500	Numidian Cavalry.	200	40	2		
"	"	300	Roman Cavalry.	140	46½	2		
Geronium.	217	50,000	Carthaginians.	6,000	12	4		
"	"	50,000	Romans.	5,000	10	4		
Cannæ.	216	42,000	Carth. and Gauls.	6,000	14¼	4½	40,000*	*Some authors say 70,000.
" (Camp).	"	11,000	Romans.	2,000	18	5		
Nola, 2d.	215	20,000	"	1,000	5	5	5,000	
Beneventum.	214	20,000	"	2,000	10	5	15,000	
Nola, 3d.	214	20,000	"	400	2	5	2,000	
Asculum, 2d.		20,000	"	2,700	13½	5		
" 2d day.		17,000	"	3,000	17½	5	8,000	
Grumentum.		40,000	"	500	1¼	4½	8,000	
Metaurus.		40,000	"	8,000	20	4½	35,000	
Crotona.	204	20,000	"	1,200	6	5		
Mago's Battle.	203	20,000	Carthaginians.	5,000	25	5		
"	"	40,000	Romans.	2,300	5¾	4½		
Zama.	202	43,000	"	2,000*	4½	4½	20,000	*Clearly understated.

† For armies of this size in a very stubbornly contested battle.

From the difficulty of determining the wounded, only the killed are given in the above table. The discrepancies are no greater than can be found in histories of our own civil war. The figures are given without comment. A discussion on losses in ancient battles will be appended to the table in the volume on Cæsar.

APPENDIX B.

SOME ROMAN MARCHES.

THE Romans marched about 15 miles a day. The Consul Sempronius, in 218 B. C., marched his army of 20,000 men from Lilybæum to Ariminum, about 650 miles, in 40 days, or 16 miles a day. The only march worth adding to the table in Appendix A, of Alexander, is that of the Consul Nero, who, in 207 B. C., with 7,000 men, marched from the vicinity of Canusium to the Sena, 250 miles, in seven days, and back again in six, meanwhile, with the Consul Livius, winning the victory of the Metaurus. Wagons were furnished for the tired infantrymen by the country people along the route. This was 38½ miles a day, counting the battleday as the full equivalent of a march. It is one of the most noteworthy marches in history. Mention of rapid marches is not often made by Polybius or Livy.

INDEX.

broken road, 227; repairs road, 228;
reaches ": foot of Alps," 229; careful
of cavalry, 229; rests his army, 234;
attacks the Taurini, 234; his commissaries, 235; his determination, 237;
his plans on Po, 238, 239; bound by topography like Napoleon, 241; captures
Turin, 243; his spies, 243; his strategic
intuitions and limitations, 246, 247;
his movements after taking Turin,
249; his chances against Scipio, 249;
his calculations, 250; encourages his
troops by object lesson, 251; does not
follow Scipio, 253; captures bridgehead garrison, 254; his projects after
Ticinus, 255; crosses Po, 255; his
negotiations with Gauls, 256; marches
to Placentia, 257; his camp near Placentia, 257; his dangerous position,
258; his able manœuvre, 258; between the consuls, 259; his manœuvres, 261; his lapse, 262; moves
nearer Trebia, 262; seizes Clastidium, 262; eggs Sempronius on to battle, 264; must keep moving, 264;
plans battle on Trebia, 267; his skillful preparations for battle, 267 <i>et seq.;</i>
his dispositions at Trebia, 269; does
not pursue, 272; wounded, 273; captures Victumviæ, 273; moves up Trebia, 273; driven back, 274; his second
fight with Sempronius, 274; busy with
negotiations, 275, 276; had no siege
material, 276; his offensive policy,
281; his work to break up confederacy, 281; his chances, 281; sends
back allied prisoners without ransom,
281, 306; his personal disguises, 282;
moves to Etruria, 283; his choice of
roads, 283; good in upland and lowland wars, 284; his march into Etruria, 286; crosses Arnus marshes,
286 <i>et seq.;</i> order of march, 287;
his success, 288; studies problem, 289;
his manœuvres at Arretium, 289 <i>et
seq.;</i> cuts Flaminius off from Rome,
292; taunts Flaminius, 293; the ability of his manœuvre, 293, 297; lets
go his base, 294; could not attack
consuls, 294; his plans, 295; plans to
trap Flaminius, 300; a "barbarian,"
302, 606; his secrecy, 302; seeks Flaminius' body, 316; his reasons for not
marching on Rome, 308; his reliance
on allies, 308; compared to Alexander
and Cæsar, 309; recognizes Roman
superiority, 310; arms soldiers with
Roman weapons, 310; wiser than
Pyrrhus, 311; his march after Trasimene, 311; sends messengers to Carthage, 312; finds Fabius at Æcæ, 317;
unable to bring Fabius to battle, 318;
moves to Campania, 320; devastates
Falernian plain, 323; accumulates
immense booty, 327; his difficult position, 327; makes cavalry demonstra-

tion, 328; offers Fabius battle, 328;
his oxen stratagem, 329, 330; his foraging like Sherman's, 332; feints on
Rome, 332; takes Geronium, 332;
allies fail to join, 334; labors with
confederates, 334; spares Fabius'
farms, 335; method of foraging, 337;
manœuvres at Geronium, 337; taken
at a disadvantage, 338; works stratagem on Minucius, 341; remains long
at Geronium, 346; contrasted with
Alexander, 346; his powers of discipline, 346; his stratagem fails, 347;
necessity of success, 348; forced to
change location, 349; seizes Cannæ,
350; profits by loss of combat at
Cannæ, 356; his speech to his army,
358; taunts Varro, 358, 359; crosses
river, 365; marshals his troops, 367;
in phalangial order, 368; his force
in line, 369; in camp, 369; his theory
of the coming battle, 369; careful
preparation of manœuvre, 370; personally conducts manœuvre, 375; his
ability won Cannæ, 378, 379; what he
did after Cannæ, 380; why he did
not march on Rome, 382; diplomatic
instead of military work to be done,
382 <i>et seq.;</i> relies on disaffecting
allies, 383; failed of support of allies,
383; what he was fighting for, 384;
not a gambler, 384; negotiating with
cities, 385; frees Italian prisoners,
390; his allies after Cannæ, 392; had
not gained hearty support, 392; moves
to Campania, 393; his worst enemies
in Carthage, 395; gains all southern
Italy, 397; outwitted by Marcellus,
399; his operations in Campania, 401;
attacks Casilinum, 402; captures Casilinum, 404; his loss in fighting ability, 407; not due to Capua, 407, 408;
his plans changed, 408; assumes offensive-defensive, 408; his genius after
Cannæ more marked, 409; his forces
after Cannæ, 412; busy with negotiations, 414; his attempts on Cumæ,
415; hemmed in in Campania, 417;
his difficulties in Campania, 418;
could not afford inaction, 418; fails
against Nola, 418; receives 4,000 recruits from Carthage, 419; his defeat
at Nola, 419; questionable, 421; loses
cavalry by desertion, 421; marches
for Apulia, 421; takes up winter-
quarters at Arpi, 421; gradually
losing ground, 424; his plans and
difficulties, 429; his bold march to
Capua, 430; his campaign in Cumæ
region, 431; cannot capture seaport,
431, 432; renewed failure before Nola,
433; his reinforcements lost by battle
of Beneventum, 437; makes one more
effort on Nola, 437; loses third battle
of Nola, 438; leaves Campania, 439;
anticipated at Tarentum, 439; holds

LIST OF DATES.

LIST OF DATES.

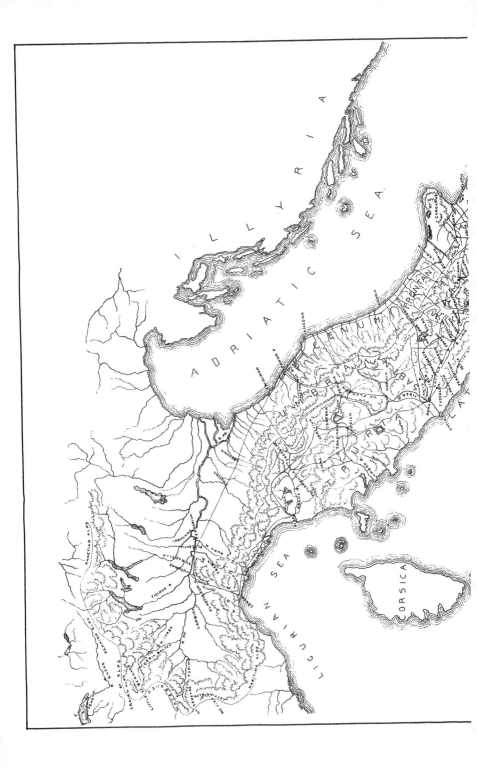

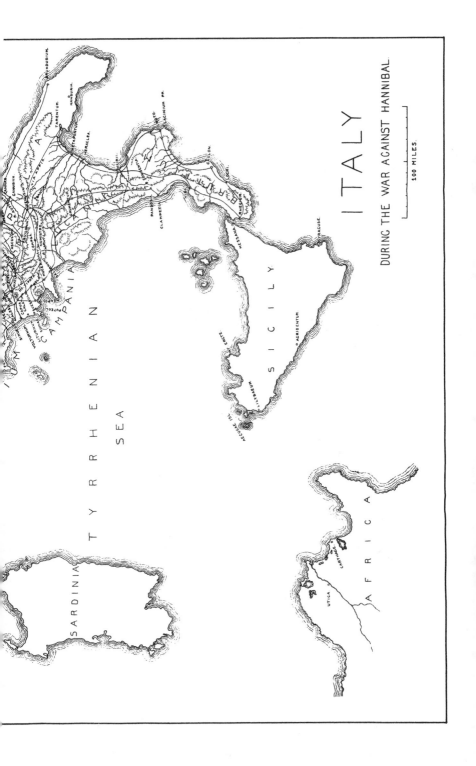

ITALY

DURING THE WAR AGAINST HANNIBAL.

100 MILES.

Other titles of interest

ALEXANDER
Theodore Ayrault Dodge
723 pp., 234 illus., maps, and
charts
80690-8 $19.95

THE ART OF WAR
Niccolò Machiavelli
Translated by Ellis Farneworth
Revised and with an introduction
by Neal Wood
336 pp.
80412-3 $12.95

**THE DISCOVERY AND
CONQUEST OF MEXICO**
Bernal Díaz del Castillo
Translated by A. P. Maudslay
New introduction by
Hugh Thomas
512 pp., 33 illus., 2 maps
80697-5 $16.95

**FIFTEEN DECISIVE
BATTLES OF THE WORLD
From Marathon to Waterloo**
Sir Edward S. Creasy
420 pp., 2 illus.
80559-6 $15.95

**THE GENERALSHIP OF
ALEXANDER THE GREAT**
J.F.C. Fuller
336 pp., 35 illus.,
80371-2 $14.95

GREAT CAPTAINS UNVEILED
B. H. Liddell Hart
New introduction by
Russell F. Weigley
289 pp., 1 illus., 5 maps
80686-X $13.95

**HANNIBAL
Enemy of Rome**
Leonard Cottrell
287 pp., 27 illus., 10 maps
80498-0 $13.95

INVINCIBLE GENERALS
Philip J. Haythornthwaite
240 pp., 160 illus.,
29 maps and plans
80577-4 $16.95

**JULIUS CAESAR
Man, Soldier, and Tyrant**
J.F.C. Fuller
336 pp., 17 illus.
80422-0 $14.95

LAWRENCE OF ARABIA
B. H. Liddell Hart
458 pp., 17 photos, 10 maps
80354-2 $14.95

**THE MILITARY MAXIMS OF
NAPOLEON**
Edited by William E. Cairnes
Introd. and commentary by
David G. Chandler
253 pp., 10 illus.
80618-5 $13.95

**SCIPIO AFRICANUS
Greater than Napoleon**
B. H. Liddell Hart
New foreword by Michael Grant
304 pp., 3 illus., 7 maps
80583-9 $13.95

**SLAVERY
A World History
Updated Edition**
Milton Meltzer
584 pp., 251 illus. 3 maps
80536-7 $22.50

**THERMOPYLAE
The Battle for the West**
Ernle Bradford
255 pp., 6 maps
80531-6 $13.95

Available at your bookstore

OR ORDER DIRECTLY FROM

DA CAPO PRESS, INC.

1-800-321-0050